Perennials

THE BUYER'S GUIDE

for PROFESSIONALS,
COLLECTORS & GARDENERS

HOLE'S DICTIONARY
of Hardy
Perennials

THE BUYER'S GUIDE
for PROFESSIONALS, COLLECTORS & GARDENERS

General Editor
JIM HOLE

Editors
Jan Goodall, Stephen Raven and Bob Stadnyk

HOLE'S

Published by Hole's
101 Bellerose Drive
St. Albert, Alberta, Canada
T8N 8N8
www.enjoygardening.com

Library and Archives Canada Cataloguing in Publication

Hole's dictionary of hardy perennials : the buyer's guide for professionals, collectors & gardeners / general editor, Jim Hole ; editors, Jan Goodall, Stephen Raven, Bob Stadnyk.

Includes bibliographical references and index.
ISBN 1-894728-01-7

1. Perennials--Dictionaries. 2. Perennials. I. Hole, Jim, 1956- II. Goodall, Jan, 1949- III. Raven, Stephen, 1953- IV. Stadnyk, Bob, 1958-

SB434.H65 2006   635.9'32'03   C2006-900906-6

Photography Credits

All photographs by **Akemi Matsubuchi** with additional photographs by:
Acadia University, Morton Centre Digital Herbarium Collection, page 412; **Anne van Acker,** page 424; **Larry Allain,** pages 406, 410 & 413; **Bailey Nurseries,** page 425; **Thomas G. Barnes, Ph.D,** pages 408 & 426; **Carla Beltgens,** pages 407, 418 & 422; **CFG Photo,** pages 418 & 421; **Joseph Dougherty,** page 423; **Neil Harper,** page 413; **Steffen Hauser/Botanikfoto,** page 409; **Louis-M. Landry,** page 423; **Glen Lee,** pages 411 & 424; **Richard May,** page 422; **Laura Militzer,** page 406; **Gary A. Monroe,** page 414; **Scott Peterson @ USDA-NRCS PLANTS Database,** pages 405, 409, 416, 419, 423 & 426; **James L. Reveal,** page 418; **Peter Schoenfelder, Pentling Germany,** page 416; **Gideon Singer,** page 414; **Bob Skowron & Rebecca Day-Skowron,** pages 408, 409, 410, 411, 412, 413, 414, 418, 419, 420, 421, 422, 423, 425, 426 & 427; **Kurt Stueber/www.BioLib.de,** page 409; **Mark Turner,** page 424; **Ian Young/www.srgc.org.uk,** page 427

Table of Contents

Genera

Acknowledgements

We would like to thank the Devonian Botanical Gardens and staff, particularly Barry Grieg and Linda Hewlitt, for use of their plant records and facilities; Bob Skowron and Rebecca Day-Skowron of RMRP (Rocky Mountain Rare Plants) for their help in sourcing and providing images and the staff and customers of Hole's Greenhouses & Gardens.

Preface

This dictionary contains the very latest information about thousands of perennials available on the market today. It also represents years of labour from the Hole's perennials staff, who have used their long, hands-on experience with thousands of perennial species and varieties to create the extensive Hole's perennials database that is the foundation of this book.

Hole's Greenhouses and Gardens started selling perennials in the mid-1980s. I'm pretty sure it was my sister-in-law Valerie who simply said one day, "Hey, we should have some perennials."

Valerie asked Dorothy Jedrasik, one of the bedding plant staff members, to order a few varieties. Well, Dorothy ordered about 30 or 40 plants and they did quite well—it seems that the more we offered, the more people wanted to try new things. Keeping track of all the information quickly became almost overwhelming. Dorothy put together a rudimentary perennial manual, a guidebook for the staff that included care tips for all of the perennials that Hole's was carrying. It wasn't fancy, but it did the job, and, like all good information, it saved the staff and customers a lot of time and headaches.

Eventually the demand for perennials grew so much that Dorothy recommended that Hole's create an official perennials department and devote some space and personnel to it. After some discussion, we appointed Bob Stadnyk to the job of developing the new department. Already a perennial enthusiast, he had the experience and the drive that was needed to take on the job.

Even as a kid Bob had spent a lot of time reading about perennials, visiting garden centres and searching, often in vain, for the exotic plants he read about in old library books. The hunt was part of the fun for him—he says there's nothing like the rush he gets when he manages to find a rare perennial that hardly anyone else knows about. Other collectors will know exactly what he means.

A unique culture exists among perennial growers, one that sometimes makes getting the perennials we want a challenge. There's a big difference between ordering bedding plants and ordering perennials: annuals are typically grown in huge crops by a small number of large suppliers; when Bob orders perennials, he has to deal with hundreds of individuals and small companies. For many of the rare plants, there are only a few specialty growers, not all of them willing to share their favourites.

It took some time to establish relationships with these growers. In a sense, Hole's had to prove itself to each supplier, sometimes by bartering for some rare plants with other special varieties we cajoled from still another grower. When Bob placed his first order of perennials, he brought in about 400 different varieties. Over the years, though, Hole's has managed to build up connections with perennial experts all over the world. Now we're ordering thousands of varieties a year.

Like an easygoing double fernleaf peony, the perennials department has grown over the years, slowly but surely. The depth and breadth of plants we carry have increased every season, and our collective appreciation of perennials has been enriched a hundred-fold as our exposure to their astounding diversity has risen. The primitive perennial manual—started by Dorothy and updated by Bob back in the beginning—evolved into the best-selling book *Perennial Favorites* by my mother Lois Hole, followed by *Perennial Questions and Answers* that she and I worked on together. This wealth of knowledge and experience leads us finally to the comprehensive dictionary you hold in your hands today. We believe it will be an invaluable reference to gardeners, collectors and professional growers for years to come.

— *Jim Hole,*
Hole's Greenhouses and Gardens

Introduction

This book is for anyone who loves perennials, whether they are retailers, professional growers or breeders, collectors of rare perennials, or novice or veteran home gardeners. Of course, there's a lot of cross-over between these groups, and perennial enthusiasts of every profession and skill level should discover something new to love in this book.

Different people have different priorities when choosing perennials:

- Professionals want reliable performers that are easy to raise and market and that will keep their customers happy with year after year of excellent garden performance.

- Collectors, who prize unusual colours, growth habits or simply rarity, will want to keep a close eye on each plant's availability rating.

- Hobbyist gardeners place a high value on ease of growth, flower and foliage colour and durability.

Years of experience in sourcing, growing and selling perennials have made one important fact abundantly clear to the staff at Hole's—to professionals, collectors and casual gardeners alike, gardening with perennials is about enjoying success.

For Professionals...

Many greenhouse industry professionals spend hundreds of hours and thousands of dollars trying to design the right product mix for their customers. Very few greenhouses have the infrastructure to track and research the thousands of perennials that are available on the market every year. This dictionary is designed to provide basic information to help today's professionals make buying decisions and then market their product effectively.

For Collectors...

One of the unique features of this book is its utility for collectors and enthusiasts. Hole's fields hundreds of inquiries each year from alpine enthusiasts, daylily collectors and other perennial fans of every stripe. It is always a thrill when a new plant is released or a rare species finally becomes commercially available, but there are few references for people looking for the latest and most exciting developments. This book is one such source, with listings of hundreds of unique and rare perennials.

For Gardeners...

If you are a gardener, *Hole's Dictionary of Hardy Perennials* can be your market guide. If you are looking for something different, something easy or even something that presents a challenge, this book has thousands of suggestions that, with a little bit of effort, you should be able to find on the market.

Perennials at Hole's

Hole's Greenhouses and Gardens is an accredited testing site for six international seed and plant breeding companies. Every year, Hole's uses its 1.5-acre trial garden and extensive growing ranges to test hundreds of new varieties of bedding plants, roses, vegetables, poinsettias and, of course, perennials. These trials help prove which new plant varieties show significant improvement over earlier varieties. This collaboration between the greenhouse and our suppliers helps bring only the very best plants to the market.

Hole's also enjoys a symbiotic relationship with the University of Alberta's Devonian Gardens. Every year, we exchange our trial data with the Devonian, doubling the knowledge of both organizations and discovering hundreds of new perennial facts every season.

Hole's employees are perhaps the company's greatest resources. Our full time staff are professional growers and the perennial staff in particular are avid, very accomplished gardeners, and each of their gardens provides unique challenges and opportunities, from wide-open acreages to small balconies. Collectively, these people have many decades of experience with perennials, and those experiences have informed every page in this book.

About This Dictionary

The information in this book comes from a number of sources. First and foremost among them is the exhaustive Hole's database, a massive collection of photos and information compiled by Hole's staff during the past several years. Most of the growing information is based on the hands-on experience of Hole's perennial growers; where such experience was not available, we turned to our most trusted suppliers, colleagues in the world of academia, gardening organizations and knowledgeable customers with many years of gardening under their belts.

While creating this book, we had to make several assumptions about perennials, our readers and the current state of the perennial marketplace. While these assumptions are not universally true, we think they are broad enough to cover most situations.

All of the perennials listed in this dictionary have recently been on the market, but some will be harder to find than others. Perennials listed as "rare," for example, may take some persistence to track down, and even common perennials are often limited in numbers every year. New varieties in particular may suffer limited supply, especially for the first two or three years after their introduction. And as you might expect, availability is usually higher in major urban centres than it is in smaller, more isolated communities, where mail-order services are an excellent resource.

Your experience as a gardener, collector or professional will influence how you view perennials. This dictionary assumes that casual gardeners understand basic concepts, such as the difference between clay soils and sandy soils, cuttings and seeds, division and other common attributes of the garden. Similarly, it is assumed that professionals know what it means to say that a perennial is "occasionally available from specialty growers," that it has "low ornamental appeal" or that it "rapidly overgrows its pot."

Sometimes, the "Buying Considerations" section will include a warning, such as "prone to powdery mildew," that appears in the advice for professionals, collectors and gardeners, but such a warning has a different impact for each group. To the professional grower, a vulnerability to powdery mildew not only affects a plant's potential performance on the sales floor, it makes it more difficult to grow successfully within the greenhouse, and thus lowers profit margins. To the collector, the flaw may be of little importance if the perennial is of sufficient beauty or rarity. A collector may even prize the flaw, seeing the vulnerability as just another aspect of the plant's personality. Casual gardeners, on the other hand, will see vulnerability to powdery mildew as a serious flaw because it makes the plant tougher to care for, and they may want to consider another plant.

Knowing which plants will suit your needs is the first step towards finding those plants. You might consider using this dictionary to compile a list of plants that catch your interest. Use scientific names for that list to ensure that the retailer you go to will know exactly which plants you need. One plant can have many common names, and one common name can be used by different people to refer to different plants; using scientific names avoids ambiguity.

Most gardeners turn to local greenhouses first when shopping for perennials. If you live in a medium- to large-sized metropolitan centre, there's a good chance you'll have a large variety of plants to choose from. However, there's always a chance you won't find the perennial you're looking for locally, especially if the plant in question is one the dictionary classifies as rare. In these cases, there are many mail order companies (including Hole's) that offer delivery of live plants across Canada. Failing that, many specialty perennial growers offer mail-order service of rare plants, but prices for this service are often justifiably higher.

Understanding Plant Names

When you're reading a catalogue, examining a plant tag or even looking up entries in this dictionary, the scientific names of perennials are included in italic type. Scientific names are binomial (have two parts): the first indicates a plant's genus, while the second describes its species (or more accurately, its specific epithet; a true species name consists of genus and specific epithet). All of the scientific names in this dictionary follow the standards established by the Royal Horticultural Society of the United Kingdom.

Flower colour is often incorporated into the scientific name of many plants. If, for example, a scientific name contains *rubrum,* you can be fairly certain that this plant will have quite a bit of red colour, because ruber is Latin for "red." *Epimedium* x *rubrum* (bishop's hat) is a good example. A plant that has *lutescens* in its name will likely have yellow flowers or foliage because *lute* means "yellow." Other colour cues come from words like *purpurea* (purple), *alba* (white) and *nigra* (black).

Some scientific names describe the type of soil in which the plants grow best. *Gypsophila paniculata* (baby's breath) is a good example: *gypso-* refers to gypsum or lime, and *phila* is Greek for love; true to its name, baby's breath prefers a "chalky" or alkaline soil with a fair bit of lime.

Sometimes common and scientific names work together to emphasize a point. The common name for the plant daylily, for example, offers a clue that its flowers last only a day, but the scientific name, *Hemerocallis,* is the clincher. *Hemero-* is Greek for day and *callis* for beauty; beauty that lasts only a day.

If a plant has *giganticum* in its name, the possibility exists that it may outgrow its allotted space in the garden. Or it can simply mean that it is the largest species in the genus or at the very least one of the biggest. Even with a rudimentary grasp of Latin, the "gigantic" in *giganticum* should be an easy clue. Other scientific names that include *maxi-* and *mega-* are giveaways that the plant in question is probably going to be big for its kind.

On the other end of the scale, the Latin prefixes *micro-*, *minut-* and *minim-* are certain to indicate that a particular plant may have some features that are smaller than typical for the genus or species. One can't say with certainty that a particular plant will be small because it has *micro-* in its name, but it does hint that distinctly small features are likely. The entire plant could be a dwarf variety, or perhaps just the leaves or petals are undersized in comparison to other plants of the same genus.

Understanding some Latin is extremely important if you are the adventurous type when it comes to consuming plants. A plant with the word *toxi-* (poison) in its name is definitely one to investigate more extensively.

People sometimes balk at the suggestion to learn a little Latin, but it's really not that difficult. In fact, you would probably be surprised at just how much Latin you already know. If you continue to upgrade your Latin, you may experience a greater degree of success in your garden.

Cultivars, Varieties and Breeding

As gardeners with even a little experience know, many perennial species are also available as named varieties or cultivars (cultivated varieties). Such varieties are the result of intensive breeding efforts by professional (and sometimes amateur) growers; specific cultivars often offer superior garden performance, or more vibrant colours, among other attributes.

Understanding the Dictionary Listings

The perennials in this dictionary are listed alphabetically by their genus name. Each genus gets a general description, followed by short descriptions of the perennials within that genus. ■-indicates that an image can be found in the Genus Picture Key.

Genus Information

Origin: the geographic region from where the plant originated (before it became a garden plant).

Selected Common Names: some, not all, of the names given to plants of that genus.

Nomenclature: the origin of the scientific or common names of the genus.

General Features: the height and spread, growth habit, flower and foliage characteristics and hardiness of the genus. The height and spread measurements are for plants at maturity grown in proper soil, with adequate care and in Zone 3 conditions.

Hardiness—Because zone ratings are often arbitrary or based on very limited data, we have substituted our own hardiness ratings, which describe a plant's ability to overwinter successfully given a relatively cold climate. Each plant is given a hardiness rating from A to D. Plants with an A rating can withstand very bitter winters, such as you might find in climate Zone 2 (see chart on next page). Each step down the scale, from B to D, indicates that the plant is less hardy. These ratings are given based on both research and our experiences with the plant in question, grown in the Edmonton, Alberta, region (Zone 3A).

Growing Requirements: the light, soil, location and propagation requirements of the genus. Over the years, Hole's has developed a long list of specific terms to define these attributes. If you're unfamiliar with any of our terms, you can find our definitions in the glossary (p. 402). Note that planting location recommendations are aimed at achieving the best performance from the perennial in question. Some plants recommended for "sun" may survive and even look decent in "sun to p.m. sun," but it is unlikely they will reach their full potential.

Buying Considerations

Professionals: the popularity of the genus with customers (based on our experience of sales volumes, requests and popular opinions), the availability of the plant from suppliers, its salability and the amount of shrinkage a retailer or grower can expect.

Collectors: highlights genera, species or varieties that are worth consideration by perennial enthusiasts, as determined by a scale based first on rarity, then on performance and lastly by cost.

Gardeners: the genus's ease of growth, how many plants to start with and any warnings about care of the plant.

What to Try First: the best species or varieties of the genus in question, as selected by Hole's.

On the Market

The species, subspecies, varieties and cultivars available within a genus are listed alphabetically. Each entry includes a short description of the plant's flowers, foliage or other distinctive features and its height and spread measurements.

This Book

The original intent of this book was to try and capture as much of the valuable experience gained by our staff over the years as we could and then share it with our readers. This has been a a project that spans many years even as the world of perennials continues to grow and evolve; thus *The Hole's Dictionary of Hardy Perennials* remains a work-in-progress and a project that will also continue to grow and evolve as each season passes. We welcome comments and suggestions from our industry peers and the gardening community to help us continue to improve this resource.

Light in this Book

Light requirements for the plants are based on a set of standard categories.

Sun ⚛ Plants need full sun all day long for best performance.

Sun to p.m. sun ⚛ Plants in this category will bloom and look fine if they receive afternoon sun, from noon until evening.

Shade ⚛ Shade plants prefer shade all day.

Shade to a.m. sun ⚛ These plants require cooler, less intense light. They can tolerate sun from morning until noon, but can't stand hot afternoon sunlight. They will also thrive in dappled light, as through a tree canopy.

Sun or shade ⚛ These plants adapt equally well to sun or shade.

Hardiness in this Book

The hardiness ratings in the Genus section are based on a scale of A to D and attempt to factor in such things as microclimates and year-to-year variations.

A ⚛ Plants grow readily Zone 2 or higher.

B ⚛ Plants have been grown in Zones 2 or 3.

C ⚛ Plants grow readily in Zone 3.

D ⚛ Plants have been grown in Zone 3.

THE GENERA A–Z

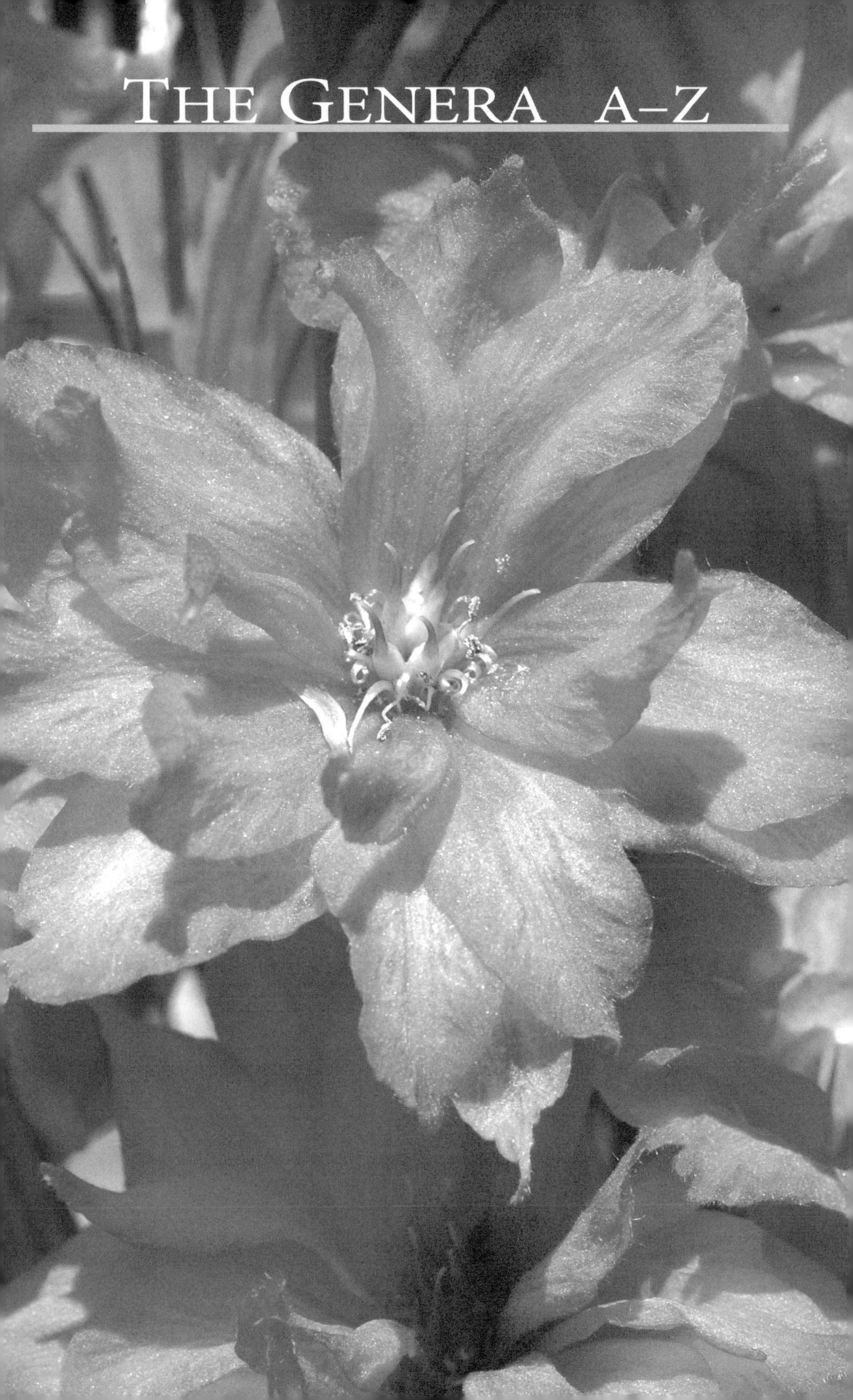

Acaena   p. 405 📷

Genus Information

Origin: New Zealand
Selected Common Names: sheepburr
Nomenclature: From the Greek *akaina* (thorn), referring to prickly fruit or spiny calyx.

General Features

Height: 2–10 cm high
Spread: 30–60 cm wide
Habit: groundcover, alpine perennial
Flowers: insignificant; summer
Hardiness: D
Warnings: invasive in warmer climates (keep contained to prevent spread)
Expert Advice: Produces colourful burrs after flowering that may stick to clothing or pet fur. Plant with sedum, cactus and other xeriscape plants.

Growing Requirements

Light: sun
Soil: fertile, well-drained soil
Location: sunny, hot, dry areas; xeriscaping; retaining walls; between paving stones; cascading over walls
Propagation: seed; division; cuttings
Expert Advice: Divide in spring. Plant on south side of house.

Buying Considerations

Professionals

Popularity: relatively unknown foliage plant
Availability: generally available from specialty growers; occasionally available as finished product
Size to Sell: sells best in smaller sizes as it matures fast
Miscellaneous: plants with "thistle" look have limited salability

Collectors

Popularity: of interest to alpine collectors; *A. microphylla* is unique

Gardeners

Ease of Growth: very easy to grow
Start with: one small plant and several for mass plantings

What to Try First ...

Acaena microphylla

On the Market

Acaena buchanani
Yellow-brown burrs in summer • Blue-green foliage • 8 cm high, 45+ cm wide

Acaena magellanica
Brown burrs in summer • Aqua-blue foliage • 5–8 cm high, 30–40 cm wide

Acaena microphylla
Bright-red burrs in summer • Bronze-green foliage • 2–10 cm high, 45–60+ cm wide

Acantholimon   p. 405 📷

Genus Information

Origin: Greece, Turkey, Syria, Armenia and Crete
Selected Common Names: prickly thrift
Nomenclature: From the Greek *akantha* (thorn) and *leimon* from *Limonium*, a related species.

General Features

Height: 5–20 cm high
Spread: 8–60 cm wide
Habit: slow-growing, cushion-forming perennial
Flowers: showy pink (occasionally red); late spring to summer; showy, papery bracts
Foliage: sharply pointed, rigid, needle-like, prickly; evergreen
Hardiness: C
Warnings: painful to handle
Expert Advice: Plant with sedum, cactus and other xeriscape plants.

Growing Requirements

Light: sun
Soil: sandy, well-drained soil
Location: sunny, hot, dry areas; xeriscaping
Propagation: seed; cuttings
Expert Advice: Take cuttings in summer. Resents being disturbed.

Buying Considerations

Professionals

Popularity: relatively unknown perennial
Availability: generally available from specialty growers
Size to Sell: sells best in mature sizes as it matures slowly
On the Shelf: high ornamental appeal when in bloom
Shrinkage: high; sensitive to overwatering

Collectors

Popularity: of interest to collectors; *A. hohenakeri* is unique, rare, has high visual impact in bloom

Gardeners

Ease of Growth: mostly difficult to grow as it needs close attention to growing conditions (*A. glumaceum*—best for gardeners)
Start with: one mature plant for feature plant

What to Try First ...

Acantholimon araxanum, Acantholimon bracteatum capitatum, Acantholimon glumaceum, Acantholimon hohenakeri, Acantholimon lycopodioides

On the Market

Acantholimon acerosum
  Pink flowers in early summer • Blue-grey foliage • 5–15 cm high, 20–30 cm wide

Acantholimon acerosum var. brachystachyum
  Red or pink flowers in early summer • 10–15 cm high, 10–20 cm wide

Acantholimon araxanum
  Rose flowers in summer • Silvery foliage • 10–15 cm high, 20–30 cm wide

Acantholimon avenaceum
  Pink flowers in early summer • 10 cm high, 20 cm wide

Acantholimon bracteatum
  Pink flowers in summer • 10–15 cm high, 10–15 cm wide

Acantholimon bracteatum ssp. bracteatum
  Pink flowers in summer • Blue-green foliage • 10–15 cm high, 10–15 cm wide

Acantholimon bracteatum ssp. capitatum
  Bright-pink flowers in summer • 10–15 cm high, 10–15 cm wide

Acantholimon caryophyllaceum
  Bright-pink flowers in summer • 2–5 cm high, 20–30 cm wide

Acantholimon caryophyllaceum ssp. caryophyllaceum
  Pink flowers in summer • Silvery foliage • 2–5 cm high, 20–30 cm wide

Acantholimon confertiflorum
  Pink flowers in summer • Silvery-blue foliage • Shrubby habit • 5–10 cm high, 15–20 cm wide

Acantholimon diapensoides
  Pink flowers in early summer • 5 cm high, 10–20 cm wide

Acantholimon ercias
  Pink flowers in early summer • 10–15 cm high, 25–30 cm wide

Acantholimon glumaceum
  Rose-pink flowers in early summer • 10–15 cm high, 45–60 cm wide

Acantholimon hedinii
  Pink flowers in early summer • 10 cm high, 20 cm wide

Acantholimon hohenakeri
  Rose-purple flowers in summer • 10–15 cm high, 15–25 cm wide

Acantholimon kotschyi ssp. laxispicatum
  Pink flowers in summer • Blue-grey foliage • 4 cm high, 10 cm wide

Acantholimon litvinowii
  Pink flowers in late spring • Blue-grey foliage • 5 cm high, 20 cm wide

Acantholimon lycopodioides
  Soft-pink flowers in summer • 2–5 cm high, 20–30 cm wide

Acantholimon reflexifolium
  Dark-pink flowers in summer • Grey foliage • 10–15 cm high, 25–30 cm wide

Acantholimon trojanum
  Pink flowers in summer • Blue-grey foliage • 2 cm high, 10 cm wide

Acantholimon ulicinum (syn. A. androsaceum)
  Pink flowers in summer • Grey-green foliage • 10 cm high, 20–30 cm wide

Acantholimon ulicinum ssp. purpurescens
  Bright-rose flowers in summer • Blue-grey foliage • 2–5 cm high, 20–30 cm wide

Acantholimon ulicinum ssp. ulicinum
  Pink flowers in summer • 10 cm high, 8–20 cm wide

Acantholimon venustum
  Rose-purple flowers in summer • Sea-green foliage • 15–25 cm high, 30–45 cm wide

Acantholimon aff. venustum
  Pink flowers in summer • Blue-grey foliage • Shrubby habit • 5–8 cm high, 15–20 cm wide

Achillea

p. 405

Genus Information

Origin: northern temperate regions
Selected Common Names: common yarrow, fernleaf yarrow, sneezewort, woolly yarrow, yarrow
Nomenclature: From the Greek hero Achilles who is said to have discovered its medicinal uses.
Other Uses: Used by herbalists since ancient Greek times to stop bleeding and fever.

General Features

Height: 15–100+ cm high
Spread: 20–90 cm wide
Habit: upright and groundcover types; long-lived perennial
Flowers: in clusters; June to September; (some) good for cutflowers
Foliage: ferny
Hardiness: A–C
Warnings: contact with foliage may irritate skin; A. millefolium is invasive (contain and deadhead to prevent spread)
Expert Advice: Newer varieties are being developed for the cutflower trade and to increase colour purity and intensity.

Growing Requirements

Light: sun
Soil: lean soil keeps plants compact and long blooming; tolerant of wide range of soils
Location: alpine gardens; banks; grasslands; damp meadows
Propagation: seed; division; cuttings

Buying Considerations

Professionals

Popularity: old-fashioned, garden standard
Availability: readily available as finished product
Size to Sell: sells best in smaller sizes as it matures quickly
On the Shelf: keep stock rotated; rapidly overgrows pot

Collectors

Popularity: not generally of interest to collectors

Gardeners

Ease of Growth: very easy to grow
Start with: one small plant

What to Try First ...

Achillea 'Cloth of Gold', *Achillea ageratifolia*, *Achillea filipendulina*, *Achillea millefolium* 'Cassis', *Achillea millefolium* 'Cerise Queen', *Achillea millefolium* 'Paprika', *Achillea millefolium* 'Sawa Sawa', *Achillea millefolium* 'Terra Cotta', *Achillea millefolium* 'Walter Funcke', *Achillea ptarmica* 'The Pearl'

On the Market

Achillea

'Anthea' • Primrose-yellow flowers in summer • 45–60 cm high, 30–45 cm wide

'Apple Blossom' • Light-pink flowers in early summer to fall • 60–90 cm high, 45–60 cm wide

'Cloth of Gold' • Intense yellow flowers continuously in summer • 45 cm high, 60–90 cm wide

'Coronation Gold' • Large clusters of golden-yellow flowers continuously in summer • 60–90 cm high, 60–90 cm wide

'Feuerland' • Yellow-centred, red flowers in summer • 90+ cm high, 45–60 cm wide

'Moonshine' • Sulphur-yellow flowers continuously in summer • 45–60 cm high, 45–60 cm wide

Achillea ageratifolia

White flowers in summer • Spreading habit • 15–20 cm high, 20–30 cm wide

Achillea clavennae

Silvery, silk-like flowers in late spring to early summer • Clump-forming • 20–25 cm high, 45 cm wide

Achillea filipendulina

Golden-yellow flowers continuously in summer • 90–100+ cm high, 60–90 cm wide

Achillea x *kellereri*

White flowers in summer • Silvery foliage • 15–20 cm high, 20–30 cm wide

Achillea millefolium

Blooms in late spring to fall • 30–60 cm high, 40–60+ cm wide

'Cassis' • Cherry-red in late spring to fall • 45–60 cm high, 40–60+ cm wide

'Cerise Queen' • Large-clustered, cherry-red flowers in late spring to fall • 45–75 cm high, 40–60+ cm wide

'Coral Beauty' • Coral flowers in late spring to fall • Fern-like foliage • 60–75 cm high, 45–60+ cm wide

'Debutante' • Orange, pink, yellow or red flowers continuously in late spring to fall • 45–60 cm high, 45–60+ cm wide

'Lavender Lady' • Clustered, lavender flowers in late spring to fall • 45–60 cm high, 45–60+ cm wide

'Madelein' • Soft lavender-pink flowers in late spring to fall • 45–60 cm high, 45–60+ cm wide

'Paprika' • Cherry-red flowers with yellow centres in late spring to fall • 30–60 cm high, 45–60+ cm wide

'Red Beauty' • Clustered, magenta-red flowers in late spring to fall • 45–60 cm high, 30–60+ cm wide

'Red Nathalie' • Red flowers in late spring to fall • Fern-like foliage • 60–75 cm high, 45–60 cm wide

'Sawa Sawa' • Deep-purple flowers in late spring to fall • Fern-like foliage • 60–75 cm high, 45–60 cm wide

'Summer Pastels' • Pastel-coloured flowers in late spring to fall • 50–60 cm high, 40–50 cm wide

'Terra Cotta' • Orange flowers fade to golden-yellow and bloom in late spring to fall • 75–90 cm high, 45–60 cm wide

'Walter Funcke' • Fiery-orange flowers in late spring to fall • 60 cm high, 45–60 cm wide

'Weser River Sandstone' • Deep-rose flowers in late spring to fall • 45–60 cm high, 30–45 cm wide

Achillea nana
White flowers in late summer • Tuft-forming • 5–8 cm high, 15–25 cm wide

Achillea ptarmica
'Ballerina' • Double, ball-shaped, white flowers in summer • 30–60 cm high, 15–30 cm wide

'Stephanie Cohen' • Clustered, light-pink flowers in late spring to fall • 45–50 cm high, 60–90 cm wide

'The Pearl' • Double, white flowers in early summer to fall • Moist, fertile, well-drained soil • 30–60 cm high, 60–90 cm wide

Achillea sibirica
'Love Parade' • Large-clustered, pink flowers in late spring to fall • 45–60 cm high, 40–60+ cm wide

Achillea tomentosa
Lemon-yellow flowers in late spring to summer • Woolly foliage • 15–30 cm high, 30–45 cm wide

Acinos
p. 405

Genus Information
Origin: Europe and Asia
Selected Common Names: rock thyme
Nomenclature: From the Greek *akinos*, a name for an aromatic herb used by Pliny.

General Features
Height: 5–15 cm high
Spread: 30–45 cm wide
Habit: tufted, bushy or spreading mountainous perennial
Flowers: violet shades; early spring to summer
Hardiness: C–D
Warnings: not prone to insects or disease

Growing Requirements
Light: sun
Soil: well-drained, alkaline soil
Location: sunny, hot, dry areas in rock or alpine gardens; drought tolerant
Propagation: seed; division; cuttings
Expert Advice: Divide in spring. Take cuttings in summer.

Buying Considerations

Professionals
Popularity: relatively unknown
Availability: generally available from specialty growers
Size to Sell: sells best in mature sizes
On the Shelf: small market; appeals mostly to alpine collectors

Collectors
Popularity: of interest to alpine collectors; *A. alpinus* is unique

Gardeners
Ease of Growth: generally difficult to grow as it needs close attention to growing conditions
Start with: one mature plant for feature plant

What to Try First ...
Acinos alpinus

On the Market

Acinos (A. arugusis x A. corsidus)
Violet flowers in early spring • 5–15 cm high, 30–45 cm wide

Acinos alpinus
Red-violet flowers in summer • 5–15 cm high, 30–45 cm wide

Aconitum
p. 405

Genus Information
Origin: northern temperate regions
Selected Common Names: helmut flower, monkshood, climbing monkshood, wolfsbane
Nomenclature: The sepals of the flower form a hood, which was the inspiration for the English common name "monkshood" or "helmet flower."
Other Uses: *Aconitum* was used for acute illness and shock. Today it is used in Chinese medicine to relieve bruising, rheumatism and sciatica.

General Features
Height: 50 cm–6 m high
Spread: 45–90 cm wide
Habit: tall, upright, clump-forming or vining perennial
Flowers: (mostly) blue; summer to fall
Foliage: glossy-green
Hardiness: C
Warnings: all parts prone to leaf tier and caterpillars; prone to powdery mildew; contact with foliage may irritate skin; all plant parts are poisonous

Growing Requirements
Light: sun or shade
Soil: cool, evenly moist, fertile, organic soil
Location: woodland gardens; damp meadows; back of perennial border
Propagation: seed; division
Expert Advice: Blooms reliably with a half-day sun. Some species bloom later.

A

Buying Considerations

Professionals

Popularity: popular, old-fashioned

Availability: readily available as finished product

Size to Sell: sells best in mature sizes

On the Shelf: high ornamental appeal in bloom

Collectors

Popularity: of interest to collectors; *A. episopale, A. hemsleyanum* are unique due to their vining form

Gardeners

Ease of Growth: generally easy to grow

Start with: one mature plant for feature plant

What to Try First ...

Aconitum 'Stainless Steel', *Aconitum* x *cammarum* 'Bicolor', *Aconitum episcopale, Aconitum hemsleyanum, Aconitum napellus* 'Blue Valley'

On the Market

Aconitum

'Bressingham Spire' • Violet-blue flowers in summer • 90 cm high, 45–60 cm wide

'Eleanor' • White flowers with thin, blue edge in late summer • 90–100 cm high, 60 cm wide

'Stainless Steel' • Metallic lilac-blue flowers in midsummer • 90–100 cm high, 45–60 cm wide

Aconitum x *cammarum*

'Bicolor' • White flowers edged in blue in summer • 90–100 cm high, 45–60 cm wide

'Blue Sceptre' • White flowers with broad purple-blue edges in summer • 50–60 cm high, 40–50 cm wide

Aconitum carmichaelii

Blue flowers in late summer to fall • 1–2 m high, 45–60 cm wide

'Pink Sensation' • Soft-pink flowers in late summer to fall • 80–100 cm high, 45–60 cm wide

Aconitum episcopale • *Vine*

Blue-purple flowers in late summer • Rambling habit • 3–6 m high, 45–60 cm wide

Aconitum hemsleyanum • *Vine*

Purple-blue flowers in late summer • Rambling habit • 2–3 m high, 45–60 cm wide

Aconitum henryi

'Spark's Variety' • Violet-blue flowers in late summer to fall • 90–100 cm high, 60–90 cm wide

Aconitum lamarckii

Yellow flowers in summer • 90 cm high, 30–60 cm wide

Aconitum napellus

Indigo-blue flowers in late summer • 90–150 cm high, 30–60 cm wide

'Blue Valley' • Blue flowers in late summer • 75–100 cm high, 30–60 cm wide

'Newry Blue' • Deep violet-blue flowers in summer • 1.2 m high, 60 cm wide

'Rubellum' • Pink flowers in summer • 90–100 cm high, 60–90 cm wide

Aconitum napellus ssp. *compactum*

'Album' • White flowers in summer • 60–90 cm high, 30–45 cm wide

Acorus p. 405

Genus Information

Origin: the Northern Hemisphere and East Asia

Selected Common Names: sweet flag

Nomenclature: "Acorus" is from the name used by Theophrastus for a plant with aromatic rhizomes.

Other Uses: The plant was long used as a source of fragrant oils, medicines, rushes (for flooring), insecticides and liquor flavourings.

General Features

Height: 8–90 cm high

Spread: 10–60 cm wide

Habit: marginal aquatic, rhizomatous perennial

Flowers: insignificant; summer

Foliage: grass to iris-like; solid or variegated; lemon-scented when crushed

Hardiness: C–D

Warnings: not prone to pests or diseases

Expert Advice: The variegated leaf forms of this plant are the most attractive.

Growing Requirements

Light: sun to p.m. sun

Soil: moist to wet soil

Location: water gardens; bog gardens; waterside plantings

Propagation: division

Buying Considerations

Professionals

Popularity: gaining popularity as a foliage plant

Availability: readily available as finished product

Size to Sell: sells best in mature sizes as it matures slowly

Miscellaneous: grasses and grass-like plants are currently very popular

Collectors

Popularity: of interest to water garden enthusiasts

Gardeners

Ease of Growth: mostly easy to grow

Start with: one mature plant for feature plant and several for mass plantings

What to Try First ...

A. calamus 'Variegatus', *A. gramineus* 'Minimus Aureus'

On the Market

Acorus calamus
'**Variegatus**' • Seed heads in late spring • Narrow foliage with green-and-cream, vertical stripes • 60–90 cm high, 60 cm wide

Acorus gramineus
'**Minimus Aureus**' • Golden, weeping foliage • 8–10 cm high, 10–15+ cm wide

Actaea   p. 405

Genus Information

Origin: northern temperate regions

Selected Common Names: baneberry, black cohosh, bugbane, silver candle, snakeroot

Nomenclature: From the Greek *Aktea* (elder tree), because of its similar shaped leaves

Expert Advice: The genus *Cimicifuga* has recently been reclassified as *Actaea*. We divide *Actaea* into two sections for display and growing information purposes: ***Baneberry*** and ***Bugbane /Snakeroot.***

Actaea, Baneberry   p. 405

General Features

Height: 45–60 cm high

Spread: 45–60 cm wide

Habit: clump-forming woodland perennial

Flowers: white

Foliage: dark-green

Hardiness: A–B

Warnings: poisonous berries

Growing Requirements

Light: shade

Soil: moist soil

Location: woodland gardens

Propagation: seed; division

Expert Advice: Seed in fall. Divide in spring.

Buying Considerations

Professionals

Availability: generally available from specialty growers; native woodland plant

Size to Sell: sells best in mature sizes

Shrinkage: high; sensitive to overwatering; goes dormant in pot

Collectors

Popularity: of interest to collectors; *A. pachypoda*, *A. spicata* are unique, native plants

Gardeners

Ease of Growth: mostly easy to grow

Start with: one mature plant for feature plant

What to Try First ...

Actaea spicata, Actaea spicata ssp. *rubra*

On the Market

Actaea pachypoda
White flowers in spring • White berries • 60–90 cm high, 45–60 cm wide

Actaea spicata
White flowers in early spring • Black-red berries • 45–60 cm high, 45–60 cm wide

Actaea spicata ssp. *rubra*
White flowers in early spring • Red berries • 45–60 cm high, 45–60 cm wide

'**Neglecta**' • White flowers in spring • Red-orange berries • 45–50 cm high, 45 cm wide

Actaea, Bugbane/Snakeroot (formerly Cimicifuga)   p. 405

General Features

Height: 75–150 cm high

Spread: 45–90 cm wide

Habit: clump-forming woodland perennial

Flowers: white to creamy-white, bottlebrush-like; late summer to fall

Foliage: green to dark purple-bronze; toothed; interesting in cutflower arrangements

Hardiness: B–C

Warnings: not prone to insects or disease; prone to slugs

Growing Requirements

Light: shade

Soil: moist soil

Location: woodland gardens; back of shady border

Propagation: seed; division
Expert Advice: Seed in fall. Divide in spring. Can be grown in sun provided soil is kept moist.

Buying Considerations

Professionals
Popularity: gaining popularity as a foliage plant
Availability: generally available as bare root or finished product
Size to Sell: sells best in smaller sizes as it is expensive
On the Shelf: high ornamental appeal; keep stock rotated
Shrinkage: low; requires little maintenance

Collectors
Popularity: of interest to collectors; purple-leafed species are unique, have great contrast

Gardeners
Ease of Growth: mostly easy to grow
Start with: one mature plant for feature plant

What to Try First ...
Actaea 'Black Negligee'

On the Market

Actaea (syn. *Cimicifuga*)
  'Black Negligee' • Fragrant, bottlebrush-like, white flowers on arching stems in fall • Purple-black, lacy foliage • 1–1.5 m high, 60 cm wide
Actaea biternata (syn. *C. acerina*)
  Bottlebrush-like, white flowers on arching stems in late summer • Green foliage • 75–90 cm high, 50–75 cm wide
Actaea cordifolia (syn. *C. rubifolia*)
  Fragrant, bottlebrush-like, white flowers on arching stems in late summer • Purple foliage • 90–150 cm high, 60–90 cm wide
Actaea dahurica (syn. *Cimicifuga*)
  Bottlebrush-like, white flowers on arching stems in late summer • Green foliage • 90–100 cm high, 60–90 cm wide
Actaea matsumurae (syn. *C. simplex*)
  'Elstead Variety' • Bottlebrush-like flowers on arching stems in fall • 90–150 cm high, 45–90 cm wide
  'White Pearl' • Bottlebrush-like, white flowers on arching stems in late summer to fall • Green foliage • 90–100 cm high, 45–60 cm wide
Actaea podocarpa (syn. *C. americana*)
  Red-tinged, white flowers in late summer to fall • 60 cm–2.5 m high, 50–90 cm wide

Actaea racemosa (syn. *Cimicifuga*)
  Bottlebrush-like, creamy-white flowers on arching stems in late summer • Dark-green foliage • 90–150 cm high, 60–90 cm wide
Actaea simplex (syn. *Cimicifuga*)
  Fragrant, bottlebrush-like, white flowers on arching stems in late summer to fall • Green foliage • 60–90 cm high, 45–60 cm wide
Atropurpurea Group
  Fragrant, bottlebrush-like, white flowers on arching stems in fall • Purplish foliage • 1–1.5 m high, 60–90 cm wide
  'Brunette' • Bottlebrush-like, white flowers on arching stems in fall • Deep brown-red foliage • 1–1.5 m high, 60–90 cm wide
  'Hillside Black Beauty' • Fragrant, bottlebrush-like, white flowers on arching stems in fall • Purple-black foliage • 90–100 cm high, 45–60 cm wide
  'James Compton' • Bottlebrush-like, white flowers on arching stems in fall • Purple-bronze foliage • 1–1.5 m high, 45–60 cm wide
  'Pink Spike' • Bottlebrush-like, pale-pink flowers in fall • Bronze-purple foliage • 90–150 cm high, 45–90 cm wide

Adenophora
p. 406

Genus Information
Origin: temperate Europe and temperate Asia
Selected Common Names: ladybell
Nomenclature: From the Greek *aden* (gland) and *phoros* (bearing), referring to a gland that girds the base of the style.
Notes: Related to and closely resembling the bluebell or *Campanula* genus. Clump-forming unlike many of the bluebells.

General Features
Height: 10–45 cm high
Spread: 15–60 cm wide
Habit: clump-forming woodland perennial
Flowers: hanging bell-type; late spring to fall
Foliage: good fall colour
Hardiness: A–C
Warnings: not prone to insects or disease
Expert Advice: Good for naturalizing in gardens. Some varieties bloom later extending the season.

Growing Requirements
Light: sun to p.m. sun
Soil: fertile, moist, organic, well-drained soil
Location: woodland gardens
Propagation: seed; cuttings
Expert Advice: Take basal cuttings in spring. Resents being moved.

Buying Considerations

Professionals
Popularity: relatively unknown
Availability: generally available as finished product and bare root
Size to Sell: sells best in smaller sizes

Collectors
Popularity: not generally of interest to collectors

Gardeners
Ease of Growth: generally easy to grow
Start with: one mature plant or several small plants for mass plantings

What to Try First ...
Adenophora takedae var. *howozana*

On the Market

Adenophora lilifolia
Fragrant, blue flowers in summer • 30–45 cm high, 30–60 cm wide

Adenophora takedae **var.** *howozana*
Bell-like, violet-blue flowers in late summer to fall • 15 cm high, 15 cm wide

Adenophora tashiroi **(syn.** *A. polymorpha* **var.** *tashiroi)*
Bell-shaped, violet flowers in late summer • 10–30 cm high, 20–30 cm wide

---

Buying Considerations

Professionals
Popularity: popular foliage plant
Availability: readily available as finished product
Size to Sell: sells best in mature sizes
On the shelf: high ornamental appeal: foliage can break in wind
Shrinkage: low; requires little maintenance

Collectors
Popularity: of interest to collectors—native fern

Gardeners
Ease of Growth: generally easy to grow but requires close attention to growing conditions
Start with: one mature plant for instant visual effect

What to Try First ...
Adiantum pedatum

On the Market

Adiantum pedatum
Delicate, airy, green fronds • 45–60 cm high, 45–60 cm wide

'Miss Sharples' • Yellow-green, lacy fronds • 30–45 cm high, 45–60 cm wide

---

Adiantum
p. 406

Genus Information
Origin: tropical areas and temperate regions
Selected Common Names: maidenhair fern
Nomenclature: From the Greek *adiantos* (unwetted), referring to a name given to a plant with impermeable leaves.

General Features
Height: 30–60 cm high
Spread: 45–60 cm wide
Habit: woodland fern
Foliage: delicate, airy
Hardiness: C
Warnings: not prone to insects or disease
Expert Advice: For indoor and outdoor use.

Growing Requirements
Light: a.m. sun; prefers dappled shade; shelter from hot p.m. sun
Soil: cool, moist, organic soil
Location: woodland gardens; foliage may burn in windy locations
Propagation: spores; division of crown
Expert Advice: Cultivars may not come true from spore.

Adonis
p. 406

Genus Information
Origin: Europe and Asia
Selected Common Names: pheasant's eye, spring Adonis
Nomenclature: In Greek mythology, Adonis was the beautiful youth killed by a wild boar and turned into a flower by Aphrodite.
Notes: From Syria to Greece, people worshipped Adonis as the god of vegetation.

General Features
Height: 15–30 cm high
Spread: 20–30 cm wide
Habit: clump-forming perennial
Flowers: very showy, bright; early spring; floriferous
Foliage: fine, fern-like
Hardiness: A–B
Warnings: may go dormant by midsummer
Expert Advice: A genus of plants not readily available. Very expensive at the retail level but worth it. New varieties are being developed in Europe, Japan and China.

Growing Requirements
Light: sun
Soil: fertile, well-drained, alkaline soil
Location: rock gardens; alpine gardens

Propagation: seed
Expert Advice: Difficult to propagate. If seeding, sow immediately when ripe; germination is slow and erratic. Does not divide easily. Takes a long time to reach blooming size (5 years).

Buying Considerations

Professionals
Popularity: relatively unknown
Availability: occasionally available from specialty growers
Size to Sell: sells best in mature sizes as it matures slowly
On the Shelf: high ornamental appeal in bloom
Shrinkage: high; goes dormant in pot; can be overwintered for sale the following year
Miscellaneous: sells steadily when blooming, mature specimen is on display; may require import permit; expensive

Collectors
Popularity: of interest to collectors; *A. amurensis* 'Chichibubeni', *A. vernalis* are rare and exceptionally beautiful

Gardeners
Ease of Growth: generally easy to grow but needs close attention to growing conditions
Start with: one mature plant for feature plant

What to Try First ...
Adonis amurensis, Adonis amurensis 'Chichibubeni', *Adonis amurensis* 'Plena', *Adonis amurensis* 'Sandanzaki', *Adonis vernalis*

On the Market

Adonis
  'Orange Bowl' • Single to semi-double, orange flowers in early spring • 15–30 cm high, 20–30 cm wide

Adonis amurensis
  Golden-yellow flowers in early spring • 15–30 cm high, 20–30 cm wide
  'Beninadeshiko' • Semi-double, orange flowers in early spring • 15–30 cm high, 20–30 cm wide
  'Chichibubeni' • Orange-copper flowers in early spring • 15–30 cm high, 20–30 cm wide
  'Fukujukai' • Semi-double, sulphur-yellow flowers in early spring • 15–30 cm high, 20–30 cm wide
  'Plena' • Double, yellow flowers with green centres in early spring • 15–30 cm high, 20–30 cm wide

  'Rising Sun' • Scarlet-orange flowers in early spring • 15–30 cm high, 20–30 cm wide
  'Sandanzaki' • Double, yellow and green flowers in early spring • 15–30 cm high, 20–30 cm wide
  'Titibushinko' • Orange flowers in early spring • 15–30 cm high, 20–30 cm wide

Adonis sutchuenensis
  White flowers in early spring • 15–30 cm high, 20–30 cm wide

Adonis turkestanica
  Yellow flowers in early spring • 15–30 cm high, 20–30 cm wide

Adonis vernalis
  Yellow flowers in early spring • 15–30 cm high, 20–30 cm wide
  'Plena' • Double, yellow flowers in early spring • 15–30 cm high, 20–30 cm wide

Aegopodium   p. 406

Genus Information
Origin: Europe and West Asia
Selected Common Names: bishop's weed, goutweed, goat's foot, snow on the mountain
Nomenclature: From the Greek *aix* (goat) and *pous* (foot).

General Features
Height: 30–60 cm high
Spread: 30–60 cm wide; potentially unlimited width
Habit: aggressively spreading groundcover perennial
Flowers: white; early summer
Foliage: solid or variegated
Hardiness: B–C
Warnings: invasive
Expert Advice: Frequently used in tough, difficult locations. Grown mainly for its foliage. A very useful, but very aggressive plant that must be confined to contain its spread. Very difficult to eradicate once established.
The solid green form is more vigorous than the variegated form, but it is not readily available. Green form will sometimes appear randomly within variegated variety and should be removed.

Growing Requirements
Light: sun or shade
Soil: tolerant of wide range of soils
Location: alleyways; slopes; confined areas
Propagation: seed; division; cuttings

Buying Considerations

Professionals
Popularity: popular garden standard; old-fashioned foliage plant
Availability: readily available as finished product
Size to Sell: sells best in smaller sizes as it matures quickly
On the Shelf: keep stock rotated; rapidly overgrows pot

Collectors
Popularity: not generally of interest to collectors

Gardeners
Ease of Growth: very easy to grow
Start with: one small plant for feature plant and several for mass plantings

What to Try First ...
Aegopodium podagraria 'Variegatum'

On the Market

Aegopodium podagraria
'Variegatum' • Green-and-white-variegated foliage • 30–60 cm high, 60+ cm wide

Aethionema

p. 406

Genus Information
Origin: Turkey, Iraq, Iran, the Caucasus mountains of Europe and western Asia
Selected Common Names: stonecress
Nomenclature: From the Greek *aitho* (scorch) and *nema* (filament).

General Features
Height: 2–20 cm high
Spread: 15–30 cm wide
Habit: cushion-forming mountainous perennial
Flowers: spring to early summer; sometimes fragrant
Foliage: evergreen
Hardiness: C
Warnings: not prone to insects or diseases

Growing Requirements
Light: sun
Soil: sandy, well-drained, alkaline soil; tolerates poor, acidic soil
Location: rock gardens; wall crevices
Propagation: seed; cuttings
Expert Advice: Prefers warm, dry summers. Take cuttings in spring.

Buying Considerations

Professionals
Popularity: relatively unknown
Availability: occasionally available from specialty growers
Size to Sell: sells best in mature sizes as it matures slowly
On the Shelf: high ornamental appeal when in bloom
Shrinkage: high; sensitive to overwatering
Miscellaneous: moderately expensive; may require import permit

Collectors
Popularity: of interest to collectors; *A. oppositifolium* is an unique species, has stunning spring display

Gardeners
Ease of Growth: mostly easy to grow but needs close attention to growing conditions
Start with: one mature plant for feature plant

What to Try First ...
Aethionema oppositifolium

On the Market

Aethionema
'Olympus' • Pink flowers in early summer • Cushion-forming • 5 cm high, 15 cm wide
'Warley Rose' • Fragrant, rose flowers in spring to early summer • Blue-grey foliage • 15–20 cm high, 30 cm wide
'Warley Ruber' • Crimson-magenta flowers in spring to early summer • Blue-grey foliage • 15–20 cm high, 30 cm wide

Aethionema armenum
Rose-pink, sometimes white flowers in spring to early summer • 10–20 cm high, 30 cm wide

Aethionema caespitosum
Stemless, showy, pink flowers in late spring • Tuft-forming • 2–5 cm high, 15 cm wide

Aethionema coridifolium
Soft-pink flowers in late spring • 15–20 cm high, 30 cm wide

Aethionema grandiflorum
Lilac-pink flowers in spring • 15–20 cm high, 30 cm wide

Aethionema oppositifolium
Showy, pink flowers in spring • Cushion-forming • 2–5 cm high, 15 cm wide

Aethionema thomasianum
Pink flowers in spring • Cushion-forming • 10 cm high, 15 cm wide

Agastache
p. 406

Genus Information

Origin: North America, China and Japan
Selected Common Names: hyssop
Nomenclature: From the Greek *aga* (very much) and *stachys* (ears of wheat), referring to the many flower spikes.
Notes: Member of the mint family.

General Features

Height: 45–90 cm high
Spread: 45–90 cm wide
Habit: stiffly upright, short-lived perennial
Flowers: long blooming period; good for cutflowers; good for drying; attractive to butterflies and hummingbirds
Foliage: aromatic
Hardiness: D
Warnings: prone to powdery mildew and rust
Expert Advice: Resembles true hyssop.

Growing Requirements

Light: sun
Soil: fertile, well-drained soil
Location: herb gardens; mixed borders
Propagation: division; cuttings

Buying Considerations

Professionals
Popularity: popular
Availability: generally available as finished product
Size to Sell: sells best when blooming
On the Shelf: high ornamental appeal; keep stock rotated; rapidly overgrows pot

Collectors
Popularity: not generally of interest to collectors

Gardeners
Ease of Growth: generally easy to grow
Start with: one mature plant for feature plant

What to Try First ...
Agastache 'Blue Fortune'

On the Market

Agastache
'Apricot Sunrise' • Spiked, orange-apricot flowers in early summer to fall • Fragrant foliage • 45–75 cm high, 60 cm wide
'Blue Fortune' • Spiked, blue-violet flowers in early summer to fall • Fragrant foliage • 90 cm high, 90 cm wide
Agastache rugosa f. *albiflora*
'Honey Bee White' • Spiked, pure white flowers in early summer to fall • Fragrant foliage • 60–80 cm high, 45–60 cm wide

Agastache mexicana
'Mauve Beauty' • Spiked, deep-pink flowers continuously in summer • Very fragrant foliage • 60–90 cm high, 30–45 cm wide
Agastache urticifolia
Spiked, iridescent blue-violet flowers in midsummer to fall • Native to Alberta • Fragrant foliage • 60–90 cm high, 30–45 cm wide

Ajuga
p. 406

Genus Information

Origin: temperate Europe and Asia
Selected Common Names: carpet bugle, Geneva bugle, upright bugle
Nomenclature: From the Greek *a* (not) and *zugon* (yoke), referring to the shape of the calyx.
Notes: Member of the mint family.

General Features

Height: 8–30 cm high
Spread: 90+ cm wide
Habit: thickly matted groundcover perennial
Flowers: spring
Foliage: evergreen
Hardiness: C
Warnings: not prone to insects or disease
Expert Advice: Available in a wide range of foliage colours.

Growing Requirements

Light: a.m. sun; tolerates more sun with good soil moisture
Soil: fertile, moist, well-drained, alkaline-free soil
Location: front of mixed borders; rock gardens

Buying Considerations

Professionals
Popularity: popular foliage plant
Availability: readily available as finished product
Size to Sell: sells best in smaller sizes as it matures fast
Shrinkage: low; requires little maintenance

Collectors
Popularity: not generally of interest to collectors

Gardeners
Ease of Growth: generally easy to grow
Start with: one small plant for feature plant and several for mass plantings
Propagation: division
Expert Advice: Separate and replant runners or stolons.

What to Try First ...

Ajuga 'Bronze Beauty', *Ajuga* 'Royalty', *Ajuga reptans* 'Catlin's Giant', *Ajuga reptans* 'Pink Surprise', *Ajuga reptans* 'Valfredda'

On the Market

Ajuga
 'Arctic Fox' • Blue flowers in spring • Green-and-white-variegated foliage • 10–15 cm high, 45–60 cm wide

 'Bronze Beauty' • Spikes of blue flowers in spring • Waxy, bronze foliage • 10–15 cm high, 30+ cm wide

 'Royalty' • Spikes of blue flowers in spring • Purple-black foliage • 10–15 cm high, 30–45 cm wide

Ajuga genevensis
 Spikes of blue flowers in spring • 15–30 cm high, 30–60 cm wide

 'Pink Beauty' • Spikes of pink flowers in spring • Mat-forming • 15–30 cm high, 30–60 cm wide

Ajuga pyramidalis
 'Metallica Crispa' • Spikes of blue flowers in spring • Shiny, crinkled, bronze foliage • 15–30 cm high, 30–45+ cm wide

 'Mini Crispa Red' • Spikes of blue flowers in spring • Burgundy foliage • 10–15 cm high, 30–45+ cm wide

Ajuga reptans
 Spikes of blue flowers in spring • 10–30 cm high, 60–90+ cm wide

 'Atropurpurea' • Spikes of blue flowers in spring • Red-purple foliage • 10–30 cm high, 60+ cm wide

 'Burgundy Glow' • Spikes of violet-blue flowers in spring • White, green, pink and burgundy foliage • 15–20 cm high, 60+ cm wide

 'Catlin's Giant' • Spikes of blue flowers in spring • Purple-green foliage • 25 cm high, 45+ cm wide

 'Valfredda' (syn. 'Chocolate Chip') • Spikes of blue flowers in spring • Chocolate-coloured foliage • 8 cm high, 30+ cm wide

 'Mahogany' • Spikes of blue flowers in spring • Mahogany foliage • 10–15 cm high, 30+ cm wide

 'Pink Elf' • Spikes of deep-pink flowers in spring • Compact foliage • 10 cm high, 25 cm wide

 'Pink Surprise' • Spikes of purple-pink flowers in spring • Bronze foliage • 15–20 cm high, 45–60+ cm wide

 'Purple Torch' • Spikes of lavender flowers • 20–30 cm high, 45 cm+ wide

 'Silver Beauty' • Spikes of light-blue flowers in spring • Silver-green and white foliage • 10–30 cm high, 60–90+ cm wide

 'Variegata' • Spikes of blue flowers with pink edges in spring • Variegated foliage • 10–20 cm high, 45–60+ cm wide

Alcea
p. 406 📷

Genus Information

Origin: southwest to central Asia and Europe
Selected Common Names: hollyhock
Nomenclature: From the Greek *alkaia*, a type of mallow. Hollyhock comes from "holy hock" or "holy mallow."
Notes: Plants are said to have been brought back to England from the Crusades.

General Features

Height: 1–2 m high
Spread: 60–90 cm wide
Habit: upright biennial or perennial; may require staking
Flowers: single or double flowers on spikes; summer; attractive to butterflies and bees
Hardiness: C
Warnings: prone to powdery mildew, spider mites and hollyhock rust
Expert Advice: Most of the truly perennial varieties are single flowered. Most double-flowered varieties are biennial. Single varieties tend to be longer-lived.

Growing Requirements

Light: sun to p.m. sun
Soil: fertile, well-drained soil
Location: cottage gardens; English gardens
Propagation: seed (self-sows readily); division; cuttings

Buying Considerations

Professionals
Popularity: popular, old-fashioned garden standard
Availability: readily available as finished product
Size to Sell: sells best in smaller sizes
Shrinkage: requires little maintenance

Collectors
Popularity: not generally of interest to collectors

Gardeners
Ease of Growth: mostly easy to grow
Start with: one small plant for feature plant and several for mass plantings

What to Try First ...

Alcea ficifolia 'Indian Spring', *Alcea rosea*,
Alcea rosea 'Nigra'

On the Market

Alcea ficifolia
'Indian Spring' • Large, single, pink, rose or white flowers • 1.5–2 m high, 60–90 cm wide

Alcea rosea
Single or double, purple, pink, white or yellow flowers in summer • 1.5–2 m high, 60–90 cm wide

'Chater's Double Group' • Apricot, pink, purple, red, white or yellow, 10 cm, double, "powderpuff" flowers in summer • 1.5–2 m high, 90 cm wide

'Creme de Cassis' • Single, semi-double and double, black-purple flowers with yellow eye in summer • 1.5–2 m high, 60–90 cm wide

'Nigra' • Single, ruffled, maroon-black flowers in summer • 1.5–2 m high, 60–90 cm wide

Alcea rosea nigra plena
'Negrita' • Double, ruffled, purple-black flowers in summer • 1–1.5 m high, 60–90 cm wide

Alcea rugosa
Large, single, soft-yellow flowers in summer • 1.5–2 m high, 60–90 cm wide

Alchemilla

p. 406

Genus Information

Origin: northern temperate regions and the mountains of Africa, India and Indonesia
Selected Common Names: lady's mantle
Nomenclature: From the Arabic name *alkemelych*.
Notes: Pairs up well with roses and geraniums. The foliage often beads with dew drops after rain or from morning dew.

General Features

Height: 10–60 cm high
Spread: 15–60 cm wide
Habit: clump-forming or groundcover perennial
Flowers: greenish, long lasting; late spring to fall; good for cutflowers; good for drying
Foliage: palmate to lobed; attractive
Hardiness: B–C
Warnings: not prone to insects or disease

Growing Requirements

Light: sun to p.m. sun; tolerant of a wide range of light conditions

Soil: tolerant of wide range of soils
Location: rock gardens; front of mixed borders; between stepping stones
Propagation: seed (self-sows readily); division

Buying Considerations

Professionals
Popularity: popular garden standard; foliage plant
Availability: generally available as finished product; some species only available from specialty growers
Size to Sell: sells best in smaller sizes as it matures fast
On the Shelf: keep stock rotated; rapidly overgrows pot; deadhead regularly

Collectors
Popularity: of interest to collectors; *A. ellenbeckii*, *A. erythropoda* are unique

Gardeners
Ease of Growth: very easy to grow
Start with: one small plant for feature or several for mass plantings

What to Try First ...
Alchemilla ellenbeckii, *Alchemilla erythropoda*, *Alchemilla mollis* 'Thriller'

On the Market

Alchemilla alpina
Yellow-green flowers in summer • 10–15 cm high, 15–45 cm wide

Alchemilla ellenbeckii
Creamy-green flowers in late spring to early summer • 10–15 cm high, 30–60 cm wide

Alchemilla erythropoda
Green-yellow flowers in summer • 15–20 cm high, 20–30 cm wide

Alchemilla faeroensis **var.** *pumila*
'Pumila' • Chartreuse flowers in summer • 10 cm high, 15+ cm wide

Alchemilla lithophylla
Yellow flowers in summer • Purple-red foliage in spring • 50–65 cm high, 45–60 cm wide

Alchemilla mollis
Lime-green flowers in late spring to fall • 45 cm high, 45 cm wide

'Robusta' • Lime-green flowers in late spring to fall • 45–60 cm high, 45–60 cm wide

'Thriller' • Yellow-green flowers in late spring to fall • 50 cm high, 45–60 cm wide

Alchemilla saxatilis
Yellow flowers in summer • Blue-tinted foliage • 15 cm high, 15–45 cm wide

Allium
p. 406 📷

Genus Information

Origin: the Northern Hemisphere
Selected Common Names: chives, keeled garlic, ornamental onion, Persian onion, star of Persia, Turkestan onion
Nomenclature: From the Latin *Allium* and from the Celtic *all* (hot).
Notes: This genus has some 700 species. Ornamental *Alliums* are members of the same family as garlic, regular onions and chives.

General Features

Height: 10 cm–2 m high
Spread: 10–60 cm wide
Habit: bulbous perennial
Flowers: (most) ball-shaped; spring to fall; goes dormant after flowering; good for cutflowers and drying
Foliage: (most) narrow foliage; onion-scented when crushed
Hardiness: B–C
Warnings: not prone to pests or diseases

Growing Requirements

Light: sun
Soil: well-drained soil
Location: perennial border
Propagation: seed; division; offsets
Expert Advice: Plant bulbs three times as deep as their height. Many species self-sow readily; deadhead to prevent spread.

Buying Considerations

Professionals

Popularity: popular
Availability: generally available as bulbs from specialty growers
Size to Sell: sells best in mature sizes when blooming
On the Shelf: high ornamental appeal in bloom
Shrinkage: high; sensitive to overwatering; goes dormant in pot

Collectors

Popularity: of interest to collectors; *A. caeruleum*, *A. karataviense* have unique, exceptional beauty, high impact in bloom

Gardeners

Ease of Growth: mostly easy to grow but needs close attention to growing conditions
Start with: one mature plant or one bulb for feature plant or plant several bulbs of lower-growing varieties

What to Try First ...

Allium 'Globemaster', *Allium caeruleum*, *Allium karataviense*

On the Market

Expert Advice: *Allium* are available in fall as bulbs or in spring as potted plants. Species listed here are ones that we recommend for sale in pots.

Allium

'Globemaster' • Dark-purple flowers in late spring to early summer • 1 m high, 45 cm wide

'Lucy Ball' • Globe-like, dark-lilac flowers in late spring to early summer • 90 cm–2 m high, 60 cm wide

'Purple Sensation' • Dark-purple flowers in late spring to early summer • 60–90 cm high, 45 cm wide

Allium atropurpureum

Globe-like, wine-red flowers in spring • 60–75 cm high, 45–60 cm wide

Allium caeruleum

Globe-like, deep blue flowers in early summer • 20–30 cm high, 10–15 cm wide

Allium christophii

Globe-like, lilac flowers in late spring to early summer • 15–40 cm high, 30–40 cm wide

Allium giganteum

Globe-like, lilac flowers in late spring to early summer • 90 cm–2 m high, 30–35 cm wide

Allium karataviense

Globe-like, white flowers with purple midribs in spring • Metallic, blue-green foliage • 15–20 cm high, 25–30 cm wide

Allium moly

Star-like, yellow flowers in spring • Blue-green foliage • 10–35 cm high, 10–12 cm wide

Allium nigrum

White to pale-lilac flowers in summer • 40–70 cm high, 50 cm wide

Allium schoenoprasum

'Forescate' • Pink flowers in spring to late summer • 30 cm high, 30–45 cm wide

Althaea

Genus Information

Origin: Western Europe and central Asia
Selected Common Names: mallow
Nomenclature: From the Greek *althaia* (to cure).
Other Uses: Some species were used in herbal medicine. Mentioned in the Bible and in Arabic and Chinese history as a valuable food for the

poor. Ancient Greeks used it as medicine and for decorating graves. Widely used in European folk medicine.

General Features

Height: 90 cm–2 m high
Spread: 45–90 cm wide
Habit: clump-forming perennial
Flowers: small; summer to fall
Hardiness: C
Warnings: prone to powdery mildew; not prone to insects
Expert Advice: Similar to *Alcea* but with smaller flowers on strong stems that don't need support.

Growing Requirements

Light: sun
Soil: fertile, moist, organic soil; tolerates poor soil
Location: perennial borders
Propagation: seed; division

Buying Considerations

Professionals

Popularity: relatively unknown
Availability: occasionally available as bare root
Size to Sell: sells best in smaller sizes as it matures fast
On the Shelf: rapidly overgrows pot
Shrinkage: low
Miscellaneous: low ornamental value; some grown for medicinal use

Collectors

Popularity: not generally of interest to collectors

Gardeners

Ease of Growth: mostly easy to grow
Start with: one small plant

What to Try First ...

Althaea armeniaca, Althaea officinalis

On the Market

Althaea armeniaca
Rose-pink flowers in late summer
• 90–100 cm high, 45–60 cm wide
Althaea officinalis
Pale-rose flowers in early summer to fall
• Prefers moist soil • 90 cm–2 m high, 60–90 cm wide

Alyssum
p. 406

Genus Information

Origin: central and southern Europe, southwest and central Asia and North Africa
Selected Common Names: alpine alyssum, basket of gold, gold dust

Nomenclature: From the Greek *a* (without) and *lyssa* (rage), referring to the plant's reputed ability to stop anger.
Other Uses: Believed to cure rabies, which gave rise to the common name "madwort."
Notes: Member of the mustard family; many plants recently moved to *Aurinia*.

General Features

Height: 2–60 cm high
Spread: 2–90 cm wide
Habit: clump-forming alpine perennial
Flowers: yellow, apricot and white; late spring or summer
Foliage: silvery-grey; mostly evergreen
Hardiness: C–D
Warnings: prone to flea beetle infestations; not prone to disease

Growing Requirements

Light: sun
Soil: fertile, well-drained, alkaline-free soil
Location: rock gardens; front of mixed borders; wall crevices; cascading over walls or rocks
Propagation: seed; cuttings
Expert Advice: Overly rich soil produces lax, open growth.

Buying Considerations

Professionals

Popularity: gaining popularity
Availability: generally available as finished product
Size to Sell: sells best when blooming
On the Shelf: keep stock rotated; deadhead regularly
Shrinkage: high; sensitive to overwatering

Collectors

Popularity: of interest to collectors; *A. propinquum* is a unique, low, mat-forming species for alpine gardens

Gardeners

Ease of Growth: generally easy to grow
Start with: one small plant and several for mass plantings

What to Try First ...

Alyssum montanum 'Berggold', *Alyssum propinquum*

On the Market

Alyssum caespitosum
Yellow flowers in late spring • Silvery foliage • 5–10 cm high, 20–30 cm wide
Alyssum cuneifolium
Yellow flowers in late spring • Silvery foliage • 2–5 cm high, 15 cm wide
Alyssum idaeum
Yellow flowers • 8 cm high, 45 cm wide

Alyssum minutum **ssp.** *minutum*
Yellow flowers in late spring • Grey foliage •
10 cm high, 2 cm wide

Alyssum montanum
Fragrant, lemon-yellow flowers in late
spring • 15–25 cm high, 45 cm wide
  'Berggold' (Mountain Gold) • Fragrant,
  yellow flowers in late spring • 15 cm high,
  30 cm wide

Alyssum pateri
Yellow flowers in late spring • 5 cm high,
20 cm wide

Alyssum propinquum
Pale-yellow flowers in summer •
Grey foliage • 5 cm high, 25 cm wide

Alyssum repens
Golden-yellow flowers in late spring
• 40–60 cm high, 40–60 cm wide

Alyssum spinosum **(syn.** *Ptilotrichum
spinosa)*
White to off-white flowers in early summer
• Silver-grey evergreen foliage • 10–15 cm
high, 25–40 cm wide
  'Roseum' • Soft-pink to rose-pink flowers
  in early summer • Silver-grey evergreen
  foliage • 10–15 cm high, 25–40 cm wide

Ampelopsis
p. 406

Genus Information
Origin: North America and Asia
Selected Common Names: porcelain vine
Nomenclature: From the Greek *ampelos* (grape)
and *opsis* (appearance), referring to its
resemblance to the grape vine.

General Features
Height: 5 m high
Spread: 1 m wide
Habit: twining climber
Flowers: small, green, not showy; summer
Foliage: good fall colour
Fruit: bright-blue; fall
Hardiness: D
Warnings: prone to powdery mildew and flea
beetles; invasive in warmer climates
Expert Advice: Monecious. Dies back hard in
colder climates. Slow to emerge in spring.

Growing Requirements
Light: sun to p.m. sun
Soil: fertile, well-drained soil
Location: against south- or west-facing walls
or fences; against south- or west-facing heated
foundations in colder climates
Propagation: seed; cuttings

Buying Considerations
Professionals
Popularity: relatively unknown vine
Availability: generally available from
specialty growers
Size to Sell: sells best in mature sizes
Miscellaneous: not as popular or as showy
as *Clematis*
Collectors
Popularity: of interest to collectors in colder
climates; *A. brevipedunculata* is a challenge
Gardeners
Ease of Growth: easy to grow (more
challenging in colder climates)
Start with: one mature plant for feature plant
What to Try First ...
Ampelopsis brevipedunculata

On the Market
Ampelopsis brevipedunculata
Green flowers in summer • 5 m high,
1 m wide

Amsonia
p. 406

Genus Information
Origin: south Europe, Asia Minor, Japan and
North America
Selected Common Names: willow amsonia
Nomenclature: Named after Dr. Charles Amson,
a scientific traveller.

General Features
Height: 40–60 cm high
Spread: 30–45 cm wide
Habit: clump-forming perennial
Flowers: pale- to bright-blue; long lasting;
late spring to summer
Foliage: willow-like; contains milky sap
Hardiness: C–D
Warnings: sap may irritate skin

Growing Requirements
Light: sun to p.m. sun
Soil: moist, well-drained soil
Location: woodland gardens; streamsides;
mixed borders
Propagation: seed; division; cuttings
Expert Advice: Divide in spring. Take
cuttings in summer.

Buying Considerations

Professionals
Popularity: relatively unknown; underused garden perennial
Availability: generally available from specialty growers; occasionally available as finished product
Size to Sell: sells best in mature sizes as it matures slowly

Collectors
Popularity: of interest to collectors; *A. jonesii, A. tabernaemontana* have unique blue flowers, native plants

Gardeners
Ease of Growth: mostly easy to grow
Start with: one mature plant

What to Try First ...
Amsonia jonesii, Amsonia tabernaemontana

On the Market

Amsonia jonesii
Funnel-like, light-blue flowers in summer • Willow-like foliage • 45 cm high, 45 cm wide

Amsonia tabernaemontana
Pale blue flowers in late spring to midsummer • Willow-like foliage • 40–60 cm high, 30–45 cm wide

Anaphalis

Genus Information
Origin: northern temperate regions and tropical mountains
Selected Common Names: everlasting
Nomenclature: From the Greek name for a similar plant.

General Features
Height: 20–90 cm high
Spread: 30–60 cm wide
Habit: clump-forming perennial
Flowers: papery; summer; good for drying; attractive to butterflies
Foliage: woolly, grey; good for drying
Hardiness: C
Warnings: not prone to pests or disease

Growing Requirements
Light: sun
Soil: well-drained soil
Location: sunny, hot, dry areas
Propagation: seed; division
Expert Advice: Divide frequently to keep vigorous.

Buying Considerations

Professionals
Popularity: popular, old-fashioned, dried flower perennial
Availability: readily available as finished product
Size to Sell: sells best in smaller sizes
On the Shelf: low ornamental appeal

Collectors
Popularity: not generally of interest to collectors

Gardeners
Ease of Growth: generally easy to grow
Start with: one small plant

What to Try First ...
Anaphalis margaritacea

On the Market

Anaphalis margaritacea
White flowers in summer • 20–90 cm high, 60 cm wide

Anaphalis triplinervis
White flowers in summer • 30–60 cm high, 30–60 cm wide

Anchusa
p. 406

Genus Information
Origin: Europe, Asia Minor and Africa
Selected Common Names: bugloss, Italian bugloss
Nomenclature: From the Greek "to paint," referring to the use of the roots for dye. The common name is from the Greek for "ox tongue," which refers to the roughness and shape of the leaves.

General Features
Height: 20–150 cm high
Spread: 20–90 cm wide
Habit: short-lived, clump-forming perennial; may require staking
Flowers: brilliant blue; spring to fall; deadhead to extend growing season
Foliage: rough
Hardiness: C
Warnings: foliage prone to rust and powdery mildew; foliage irritates skin

Growing Requirements
Light: sun
Soil: gritty, sandy, well-drained soil
Location: hot, dry; does not like wet locations
Propagation: seed (some species self-sow readily); root cuttings; basal rosette cuttings
Expert Advice: Divide frequently to keep vigorous; short-lived—allow to self-seed.

Buying Considerations

Professionals

Popularity: popular; fast seller in bloom
Availability: generally available as bare root
Size to Sell: sells best in mature sizes
On the Shelf: high ornamental appeal in bloom only; impressive as a block of colour on display

Collectors

Popularity: not generally of interest to collectors

Gardeners

Ease of Growth: mostly easy to grow but needs close attention to growing conditions
Start with: one mature plant for instant visual effect and several for mass plantings; best when mass planted

What to Try First ...

Anchusa azurea 'Little John', *Anchusa azurea* 'Loddon Royalist', *Anchusa calcarea*

On the Market

Anchusa azurea
Blue flowers in late spring to late summer; deadhead to extend bloom • 90–100 cm high, 60–90 cm wide

'Little John' • Bright-blue flowers in late spring to late summer • 45–60 cm high, 30–45 cm wide

'Loddon Royalist' • Clustered, bright-blue flowers in late spring to late summer • 90–150 cm high, 60 cm wide

'Royal Blue' • Gentian-blue flowers in late spring to late summer • 45–60 cm high, 30 cm wide

Anchusa calcarea
Dark blue-purple flowers in summer • Grey-green foliage • Cushion-forming • 30–40 cm high, 20–30 cm wide

Anchusa capensis
'Blue Angel' • Spiked, bright-blue flowers in late spring to late summer • 20 cm high, 20 cm wide

Andropogon   p. 406 📷

Genus Information

Origin: tropical regions and temperate regions of both hemispheres, including Canada to Mexico
Selected Common Names: big bluestem
Nomenclature: From the Greek *aner* (man) and *pogon* (beard), referring to the silky hairs on the spikelets of some species.

Notes: A genus of some 100 species. Only a few species are garden worthy. Sometimes called "the King of the Grasses."

A

General Features

Height: 1.5–2.4 m high
Spread: 60 cm wide
Habit: long-lived, rhizomatous, clump-forming grass
Flowers: red-purple spikelets; late summer to fall
Foliage: arching, blue-green; good bronze-red fall colour
Hardiness: B–C
Warnings: not prone to pests or diseases

Growing Requirements

Light: sun; may become floppy in shade
Soil: prefers well-drained soil; tolerant of a wide range of soils
Location: grasslands; xeriscape gardens
Propagation: seed; division
Expert Advice: Avoid planting in soil that remains wet in winter. May take up to 3 years to develop to a mature size. Divide in mid spring.

Buying Considerations

Professionals

Popularity: gaining popularity as a foliage plant (tall grasses are currently among the most popular of perennials)
Availability: generally available as finished product
Size to Sell: sells best in mature sizes as it matures slowly
On the Shelf: high ornamental appeal
Shrinkage: low; requires little maintenance

Collectors

Popularity: of interest to collectors of native plants

Gardeners

Ease of Growth: generally easy to grow
Start with: one mature plant for feature plant or several mature plants for mass plantings

What to Try First ...

Andropogon gerardii, *Andropogon gerardii* 'Pawnee'

On the Market

Andropogon gerardii
Red-purple seed heads in late summer • Orange and copper foliage in fall • 1.5–2.4 m high, 60 cm wide

'Pawnee' • Red-purple seed heads in fall • Blue-green leaves change to bronze-red in fall • 1.5–2 m high, 60 cm wide

Androsace

p. 406 📷

Genus Information

Origin: Asia, Europe and North America
Selected Common Names: rock jasmine
Nomenclature: From the Greek *aner* (man) and *sakos* (buckler), referring to the plant's resemblance to an ancient buckler.
Notes: One of the largest genera of desirable alpine plants.

General Features

Height: 2–30 cm high
Spread: 5–45 cm wide
Habit: cushion-forming alpine perennial
Flowers: flat-faced with marked eyes; very fragrant; spring to early summer
Foliage: tight evergreen rosettes
Hardiness: A–C
Warnings: prone to aphids and downy mildew

Growing Requirements

Light: sun to p.m. sun
Soil: lean, well-drained soil; avoid winter wet
Location: rock gardens; scree; troughs; raised beds; tufa; provide good air circulation
Propagation: seed; division
Expert Advice: Separate and replant rooted rosettes.

Buying Considerations

Professionals

Popularity: relatively unknown
Availability: generally available from specialty growers
Size to Sell: sells best in smaller sizes
Shrinkage: requires little maintenance
Miscellaneous: may require import permit

Collectors

Popularity: of interest to collectors—unique

Gardeners

Ease of Growth: generally easy to grow but needs close attention to growing conditions
Start with: one small plant

What to Try First ...

Androsace 'Millstream Hybrid', *Androsace hedraeantha*, *Androsace muscoidea*, *Androsace sarmentosa* 'Chumbyi', *Androsace sempervivoides*, *Androsace villosa* f. *pyrenaica*

On the Market

Androsace
  'Millstream Hybrid' • Clustered, pink flowers in spring to early summer • 5–10 cm high, 30 cm wide
  'Millstream Hybrid' (white form) • Clustered, white flowers in spring to early summer • 5–10 cm high, 30 cm wide

  'Stardust' • White or soft pink flowers in spring to early summer • 10–15 cm high, 20–25 cm wide

Androsace (A. carnea x *A. pyrenaica)*
White to pink flowers in spring • Fertile, sharply drained, acidic soil • 2–5 cm high, 10–15 cm wide
  'Callisto' • White flowers with red eye in spring to early summer • Fertile, sharply drained, acidic soil • 2–5 cm high, 10–15 cm wide
  'Jupiter' • White flowers with red eye in spring to early summer • Fertile, sharply drained, acidic soil • 2–5 cm high, 10–15 cm wide
  'Rhapsody' • Fragrant, pink flowers in spring to early summer • Fertile, sharply drained, acidic soil • 12 cm high, 15 cm wide

Androsace (A. laevigata x *A. montana)*
Pink flowers in spring • Rosette foliage • 8 cm high, 10–15 cm wide

Androsace (A. mucronifolia x *A. sempervivoides)*
Fragrant, pink flowers in spring • 5 cm high, 16 cm wide

Androsace alpina
White or pink flowers in spring to early summer • Prefers sharply drained, fertile, alkaline-free soil • 5 cm high, 20 cm wide

Androsace armeniaca **var.** *macrantha*
Pink or white flowers in spring to early summer • 5–15 cm high, 30–40 cm wide

Androsace **aff.** *caduca*
White flowers in summer • Silvery, hairy foliage • 6 cm high, 10–15 cm wide

Androsace carnea
Pink or white flowers in spring to early summer • Fertile, sharply drained, acidic soil • 5–8 cm high, 10–15 cm wide
  'Alba' • White flowers in spring to early summer • Dark-green rosettes • Fertile, sharply drained, acidic soil • 6 cm high, 9 cm wide

Androsace carnea **ssp.** *brigantiaca*
Soft white flowers in spring to early summer • Fertile, sharply drained, acidic soil • 5–10 cm high, 5–10 cm wide

Androsace carnea **ssp.** *halleri*
Pink flowers in spring to early summer • Fertile, sharply drained, acidic soil • 15 cm high, 20 cm wide

Androsace carnea ssp. laggeri
Pink flowers in spring to early summer
• Fertile, sharply drained, acidic soil
• 8–10 cm high, 10–15 cm wide

Androsace chamaejasme
White flowers with yellow eye in spring to
early summer • 8 cm high, 15–30 cm wide

Androsace dasyphylla
Fragrant, white flowers in spring to early
summer • 3 cm high, 8 cm wide

Androsace geraniifolia
Fragrant, pink or white flowers in spring to
early summer • 15–20 cm high, 30–45+ cm
wide

Androsace hedraeantha
Pink flowers in spring to early summer
• 6 cm high, 9 cm wide

Androsace hirtella
White flowers in spring to early summer
• 2 cm high, 15 cm wide

Androsace incana
White flowers with yellow eye in spring
• 2–5 cm high, 10–15 cm wide

**Androsace laevigata (syn. Douglasia
laevigata)**
Rose-red flowers in spring • Rosette foliage
• 5 cm high, 20–25 cm wide

'Gothenburg' • Pink-red flowers in spring
• Evergreen rosettes • 10 cm high, 30 cm
wide

'Pin Eye Form' • Pink flowers in late spring
• Evergreen rosettes • 10 cm high, 30 cm
wide

Androsace laevigata var. ciliolata
Deep pink to rose-red flowers in spring
• Rosette foliage • 2–5 cm high, 10–15 cm
wide

Androsace laevigata var. laevigata
'Packwood' • Pink flowers in late spring
• Rosette foliage • 5–10 cm high

Androsace lanuginosa
Pink flowers with darker eye in late spring
to summer • 15 cm high, 30–45 cm wide

Androsace mathildae
White flowers with yellow eye in spring
• 2 cm high, 5–10 cm wide

Androsace montana
Pink flowers in spring • Rosette foliage
• 1 cm high, 5–8 cm wide

Androsace mucronifolia
Fragrant, white to pink flowers in spring
• 5 cm high, 16 cm wide

Androsace muscoidea
Pink flowers with greenish-yellow eye
in spring • 2–5 cm high, 15–20 cm wide

Androsace nivalis
Rose-purple flowers in spring • Silvery-grey
foliage • 5–8 cm high, 15–25 cm wide

Androsace obtusifolia
White flowers in spring • 5–8 cm high,
10–15 cm wide

Androsace pavlovsky
White flowers with yellow eye in summer
• Silvery foliage • 2–6 cm high, 10–15 cm
wide

Androsace pyrenaica
White flowers in spring • Sharply drained,
alkaline-free soil • 2–5 cm high, 10 cm wide

Androsace rotundifolia
Pink flowers with yellow eye in spring •
Sharply drained, acidic soil • 5–15 cm high,
5–10 cm wide

Androsace sarmentosa
Pink flowers with red eye in spring • Fuzzy
rosettes • Sharply drained, acidic soil •
10–15 cm high, 30–45 cm wide

'Chumbyi' • Pink flowers in spring • Sharply
drained, acidic soil • 10–15 cm high,
30–40 cm wide

'Sheppard's Form' • Pink flowers in spring
• Sharply drained, acidic soil • 5–10 cm
high, 15–25 cm wide

'Sherriffii' • Soft-pink flowers in spring •
Sharply drained, acidic soil • 10–15 cm
high, 30–45 cm wide

Androsace sarmentosa (MECC26)
Pink flowers in spring • Sharply drained,
acidic soil • 8–10 cm high, 30–35 cm wide

Androsace sarmentosa var. watkinsii
Bright-pink flowers in spring • Sharply
drained, acidic soil • 5–8 cm high,
30–45 cm wide

Androsace sempervivoides
Fragrant, lilac-pink flowers with yellow eye
in spring • 2–5 cm high, 20–30 cm wide

'Susan Joan' • Fragrant, bright-pink flowers
with yellow eye in spring • 2–7 cm high,
20–30 cm wide

Androsace strigillosa
White flowers in spring • 10–30 cm high,
20–30 cm wide

Androsace studiosorum
Pink flowers with yellow eye in spring
• 10–15 cm high, 30–40 cm wide

A

Androsace villosa (syn. *A. barbulata*)
Fragrant, white or pink flowers in spring to early summer • 5–8 cm high, 10–15 cm wide

  'Millstone' • Fragrant, rose-pink flowers in spring to early summer • 5–10 cm high, 15 cm wide

  (Select) • Fragrant, white or pink flowers in spring to early summer • 5–8 cm high, 10–15 cm wide

Androsace villosa var. *arachnoidea*
  'Superba' • Fragrant, white flowers fading to pink in late spring • Woolly foliage • 2–5 cm high, 10 cm wide

Androsace villosa var. *congesta*
Fragrant, white flowers with red eye in spring to early summer • 2 cm high, 5–8 cm wide

Androsace villosa ssp. *glabrata*
Pink flowers in spring to early summer • 5–8 cm high, 10–15 cm wide

Androsace villosa var. *jacquemontii*
Red-purple flowers with yellow eye in spring to early summer • 2–5 cm high, 15–20 cm wide

Androsace villosa ssp. *palandoken*
Fragrant, white flowers in spring to early summer • 10 cm high, 20 cm wide

Androsace villosa f. *pyrenaica*
White flowers in spring to early summer • 5 cm high, 15 cm wide

Androsace wulfeniana
Pink flowers with yellow or orange eye in spring to early summer • 5–7 cm high, 10–15 cm wide

Anemone   p. 407

Genus Information:
Origin: Europe and North America
Selected Common Names: windflower, anemone
Nomenclature: From the Greek *anemos* (wind)
Notes: According to ancient folklore, red-flowered anemones took their colour from the god Adonis' blood, and white flowers took their colour from the goddess Aphrodite's tears.
Expert Advice: We divide *Anemone* into two sections for display and information purposes: *Early Spring/Early Summer Blooming* or *Late Summer/Fall Blooming.*

General Features
Height: 45–150 cm high
Spread: 45–60 cm wide
Habit: upright, clump-forming or spreading perennial

Flowers: early spring to early summer or late summer to fall
Foliage: (some) deeply cut foliage
Hardiness: B–C; (some) D
Warnings: contact with sap may irritate skin

Growing Requirements
Light: sun to p.m. sun; *A. nemorsa* and *A.* x *seemannii* prefer shade to a.m. sun; shelter from hot p.m. sun; tolerates more sun with good soil moisture
Soil: moist, fertile, organic soil
Location: woodland gardens; mixed borders
Propagation: seed (self-sows readily); division; root cuttings

Buying Considerations
Professionals
Popularity: popular garden standard
Availability: readily available as finished product
Size to Sell: sells best in smaller sizes as it matures fast
On the Shelf: high ornamental appeal in bloom
Shrinkage: low; *A. nemorosa* goes dormant in pot
Miscellaneous: impressive as a block of colour on display
Collectors
Popularity: of interest to collectors; *A. nemorosa* 'Alba Plena', *A. sylvestris* 'Elise Fellmann' are unique, double-flowered woodland beauties
Gardeners
Ease of Growth: mostly easy to grow
Start with: one small plant for feature and several for mass plantings

What to Try First ...
Anemone nemorosa, Anemone sylvestris

On the Market

Anemone, Early Spring/ Early Summer Blooming   p. 407

Anemone blanda
  'White Splendour' • White flowers in early spring • 5–10 cm high, 10–15 cm wide

Anemone canadensis
White flowers in spring • 30–60 cm high, 30–45 cm wide

Anemone caroliniana
White-pink or purple flowers in spring • 5–15 cm high, 15–20 cm wide

Anemone x lesseri
Carmine-red flowers in late spring to early summer • 20–30 cm high, 20–25 cm wide

Anemone leveillei
White flowers flushed rose on outside in late spring to early summer • 30–50 cm high, 30–45 cm wide

Anemone multifida
Cream or pink to red-purple flowers in late spring to early summer • 20–30 cm high, 15–30 cm wide

Anemone multifida var. *globosa*
Red flowers in early summer • 20–30 cm high, 15–30 cm wide

Anemone multifida var. *magellanica*
Creamy-white flowers in spring • 20–30 cm high, 15–30 cm wide

Anemone narcissiflora
White flowers in late spring to early summer • 30–60 cm high, 30–50 cm wide

Anemone nemorosa
White flowers, sometimes flushed pink or blue in early spring • Goes dormant after blooming • 5–15 cm high, 30–45+ cm wide
'Alba Plena • Double, white flowers in spring • 5–15 cm high, 30–45+ cm wide
'Allenii' • Lavender-blue flowers in spring • 5–15 cm high, 30–45+ cm wide
'Bracteata' • Double, white flowers in spring • 5–15 cm high, 30–45+ cm wide
'Robinsoniana' • Lavender-blue flowers in spring • 5–15 cm high, 30–45+ cm wide

Anemone richardsonii
Yellow flowers in spring to summer • 4–6 cm high, 10–20 cm wide

Anemone rivularis
White flowers in late spring • 30–60 cm high, 30–45 cm wide

Anemone x *seemannii*
Creamy-yellow flowers in spring • 5–15 cm high, 30–45+ cm wide

Anemone sylvestris
Fragrant, pure white flowers in late spring to early summer • 30–50 cm high, 45–60+ cm wide
'Elise Fellmann' (syn. Flore Pleno, Elsie Feldman) • Double, white flowers in late spring to early summer • 30–50 cm high, 45–60+ cm wide

Anemone sylvestris var. *macrantha*
Fragrant, large, white flowers in late spring to early summer • 30–50 cm high, 45–60+ cm wide

Anemone virginiana
White flowers in late spring to late summer • 60–80 cm high, 45–60 cm wide

Anemone, Late Summer/ Fall Blooming
p. 407

Expert Advice: These take 2–3 years to comfortably establish themselves; best grown in a woodland situation for success in colder climates.

Anemone
'Honorine Jobert' • White flowers with yellow centre in late summer • 80–95 cm high, 60 cm wide
'Konigin Charlotte' (Queen Charlotte) • Semi-double, silvery-pink flowers in fall • 90–100 cm high, 60–90 cm wide
'Lady Gilmour' (syn. 'Crispa') • Semi-double, rose-pink flowers in late summer to fall • 80–95 cm high, 45–60 cm wide
'Loreley' (syn. 'Lorelei') • Semi-double, silvery-pink flowers in fall • 1 m high, 45–60 cm wide
'Elegans' (syn. 'Max Vogel') • Semi-double, pink-mauve flowers in late summer to fall • 80–95 cm high, 40–60 cm wide
'Serenade' • Semi-double, dark-pink flowers in late summer to fall • 90–100 cm high, 45–60 cm wide
'Whirlwind' • White flowers in late summer to fall • 90–100 cm high, 45–60 cm wide

Anemone hupehensis
White or pink flowers in late summer to fall • 45–90 cm high, 45–60 cm wide
'Pamina' • Semi-double, rosy-pink flowers in late summer to fall • 90–100 cm high, 45–60 cm wide
'Praecox' • Dark-pink flowers in late summer to fall • 90–100 cm high, 45–60 cm wide
'Prinz Heinrich' (Prince Henry) • Deep-pink flowers in late summer to fall • 60–90 cm high, 60–90 cm wide
'September Charm' • Rose-pink flowers in late summer to fall • 45–75 cm high, 45–60 cm wide

Anemone tomentosa
Mauve-pink flowers in late summer to fall • 60–90 cm high, 45–60 cm wide

Anemonella

A *(margin tab)*

p. 407

Genus Information

Origin: eastern North America
Selected Common Names: rue anemone
Nomenclature: From the Latin, the name
is a diminutive for *Anemone.*

General Features

Height: 10–20 cm high
Spread: 15–30+ cm wide
Habit: tuberous-rooted, spreading, woodland
perennial
Flowers: species plants—white to soft-mauve and
single; varieties include rare double forms—
long blooming period
Foliage: airy
Hardiness: C
Warnings: not prone to insects or disease

Growing Requirements

Light: shade
Soil: moist, well-drained soil
Location: woodland gardens
Propagation: seed; division
Expert Advice: Sow seed when ripe.
Divide in spring.

Buying Considerations

Professionals

Popularity: relatively unknown
Availability: generally available from specialty
growers
Size to Sell: sells best when blooming; even
when in bloom they are small in pot
Miscellaneous: some varieties tend to be
expensive

Collectors

Popularity: of interest to collectors;
A. thalictroides 'Cameo' is rare, with
exceptional beauty
Expert Advice: Rare flower forms in strong
pink and double forms are eagerly sought
after. Most are expensive.

Gardeners

Ease of Growth: generally easy to grow
Start with: several mature plants; needs
grouping for impact in garden; best when
mass planted

What to Try First ...

*Anemonella thalictroides, Anemonella
thalictroides* 'Cameo', *Anemonella thalictroides*
'Rosea'

On the Market

Anemonella thalictroides
White to pink-tinted flowers in early spring
• 10–20 cm high, 15–30+ cm wide

'Cameo' • Double, light-pink flowers in
spring • 10–15 cm high, 15–30+ cm wide
'Oscar Schoaff' (syn. Schoaff's Double) •
Double, pink flowers in spring • 10–12 cm
high, 15–30+ cm wide
'Rosea' • Single, rose-pink flowers in early
spring • 10–20 cm high, 15–30+ cm wide
'Rosea Plena' • Double, pink flowers in
spring • 10–20 cm high, 15–30+ cm wide

Angelica

p. 407

Genus Information:

Origin: Northern Hemisphere and includes
annuals, biennials and perennials
Nomenclature: From the Latin *angelus* (angel),
referring to the plant's angelic healing
properties.
Other Uses: In the 15th century, it was used
mainly against the plague and all epidemic
diseases. Young stems of *Angelica archangelica*
are used crystallized for confectionaries,
prepared the same as asparagus or cooked with
rhubarb to lessen tartness.

General Features

Height: 1–2.5 m high
Spread: 50–100 cm wide
Habit: clump-forming biennial or short-lived
perennial
Flowers: greenish-white umbels; attractive to
bees; early to midsummer
Foliage: large, coarse
Hardiness: C
Warnings: not prone to insects or disease
Expert Advice: Most impressive in the garden
when blooming.

Growing Requirements

Light: sun to p.m. sun; tolerates dappled shade
Soil: moist soil
Location: back of mixed borders; herb gardens
Propagation: seed
Expert Advice: Sow seed when ripe.

Buying Considerations

Professionals

Popularity: popular biennial
Availability: readily available as finished
product
Size to Sell: sells best in mature sizes

Collectors

Popularity: not generally of interest to
collectors

Gardeners

Ease of Growth: mostly easy to grow
Start with: one mature plant for instant
visual effect

On the Market

Angelica archangelica
Greenish-white flowers in early summer •
1–2.5 m high, 50–100 cm wide

Angelica gigas
Crimson-purple flowers in summer;
biennial • 1–2 m high, 60–90 cm wide

Antennaria p. 407

Genus Information

Origin: North America, Europe and Asia
Selected Common Names: pussy toes, woolly
everlasting
Nomenclature: From the Latin *antenna*, the
pappus hairs of male flowers resemble insect
antennae.

General Features

Height: 5–10 cm
Spread: 30–90+ cm
Habit: mat-forming groundcover perennial
Flowers: everlasting papery bracts; late spring
to early summer
Foliage: silver-grey; evergreen
Hardiness: A
Warnings: not prone to insects or disease
Expert Advice: Extremely hardy. Deadhead and
cut back to keep plant compact, encourage fresh
growth and extend blooming season. Can be
mown after flowering.

Growing Requirements

Light: sun
Soil: poor soil
Location: sunny, hot, dry areas; front of mixed
borders; rock gardens; wall crevices
Propagation: seed; cuttings; separate and replant
offshoots

Buying Considerations

Professionals
Popularity: popular foliage plant
Availability: readily available as finished
product
Size to Sell: sells best in smaller sizes as it
matures fast
On the Shelf: deadhead regularly
Shrinkage: requires little maintenance

Collectors
Popularity: not generally of interest to
collectors

On the Market

Antennaria
'McClintock' • Creamy-white flowers
in early summer • Silver-grey foliage
• 5–10 cm high, 30+ cm wide

Antennaria dioica
White or pink flowers in late spring to early
summer • 8–10 cm high, 45–90 cm wide
'Rubra' • Dark-red flowers in late spring
to early summer • 10 cm high, 45–90 cm
wide

Antennaria rosea (syn. *A. dioica* 'Rosea')
Pink flowers in late spring to early summer
• 10–15 cm high, 45–90 cm wide

Anthemis p. 407

Genus Information

Origin: Europe, North Africa and Iran
Selected Common Names: alpine Marguerite,
Marguerite daisy
Nomenclature: From the Greek *anthemon*
(flower), referring to the abundance of flowers
produced. Related to the herb chamomile.

General Features

Height: 10–90 cm high
Spread: 30–90 cm wide
Habit: clump-forming alpine perennial; may
require staking
Flowers: daisy-like; long blooming period
throughout summer; good for cutflowers
Foliage: ferny, aromatic
Hardiness: C
Warnings: prone to powdery mildew; not prone
to other diseases
Expert Advice: Most impressive when mature.
Deadhead to extend blooming season and to
keep plant compact.

Growing Requirements

Light: sun
Soil: moderately fertile, well-drained soil;
tolerant of a wide range of soils
Location: sunny, hot, dry areas
Propagation: seed; division
Expert Advice: Divide in spring.

Buying Considerations

Professionals
Popularity: popular, old-fashioned garden standard
Availability: readily available as finished product
Size to Sell: sells best in small sizes when blooming as it matures fast
On the Shelf: keep stock rotated; rapidly overgrows pot
Shrinkage: low; requires little maintenance

Collectors
Popularity: not generally of interest to collectors

Gardeners
Ease of Growth: very easy to grow
Start with: one small plant for feature plant

What to Try First ...
Anthemis tinctoria 'Kelwayi', *Anthemis tinctoria* 'Wargrave Variety'

On the Market

Anthemis carpatica
White flowers in early summer to summer • Fine, parsley-like foliage • 10–25 cm high, 30–40 cm wide

Anthemis sancti-johannis
Orange flowers in late spring to late summer • Fine, parsley-like foliage • 60–90 cm high, 45–60 cm wide

Anthemis tinctoria
Yellow flowers in summer • Fine, parsley-like foliage • 45–75 cm high, 60–75 cm wide
'Charme' • Bright-yellow flowers in late spring to summer • Fine, parsley-like foliage • 30–45 cm high, 45–60 cm wide
'E.C. Buxton' • White flowers in summer • Fine, parsley-like foliage • 75–90 cm high, 90 cm wide
'Kelwayi' • Dark-yellow flowers in summer • Fine, parsley-like foliage • 45–75 cm high, 60–90 cm wide
'Wargrave Variety' • Pale-yellow flowers in summer • 60-65 cm high, 30-45 cm wide

Anthericum

Genus Information
Origin: southern Europe, Turkey and Africa.
Selected Common Names: St. Bernard's lily
Nomenclature: From *antherikos*, the Greek name for the flowering stem of the asphodel.

General Features
Height: 50–75 cm high
Spread: 30–45 cm wide
Habit: rhizomatous or fleshy-rooted, clump-forming perennial
Flowers: lily-like; short blooming period; late spring to early summer
Foliage: grassy
Hardiness: C
Warnings: not prone to insects or disease

Growing Requirements
Light: sun
Soil: fertile, well-drained soil
Location: sunny mixed borders; rock gardens
Propagation: seed; division; cuttings
Expert Advice: Divide in spring or take basal cuttings.

Buying Considerations

Professionals
Popularity: relatively unknown
Availability: occasionally available from specialty growers
Size to Sell: sells best in mature sizes
Miscellaneous: tends to be expensive; interesting but not long blooming

Collectors
Popularity: of interest to collectors—rare

Gardeners
Ease of Growth: mostly easy to grow
Start with: one mature plant and several for mass plantings

What to Try First ...
Anthericum liliago, Anthericum ramosum

On the Market

Anthericum liliago
White flowers in late spring to early summer • 50–75 cm high, 30–45 cm wide

Anthericum ramosum
White flowers in late spring to early summer • 50–75 cm high, 30–45 cm wide

Anthyllis

Genus Information
Origin: the Mediterranean, Bulgaria and the mountains of southern Europe
Selected Common Names: lady's fingers
Nomenclature: Name used by Pliny and Dioscorides.
Notes: A member of the legume family.

General Features

Height: 10–75 cm high
Spread: 30–60 cm wide
Habit: mat-forming perennial
Flowers: attractive to bees and butterflies
Hardiness: B–C
Warnings: may be invasive
Expert Advice: An underused rock garden groundcover plant.

Growing Requirements

Light: sun
Soil: poor, sandy, well-drained soil
Location: sunny, hot, dry areas; dry banks; forage; rock gardens; rock walls; cascading over walls; between larger stepping stones
Propagation: seed; cuttings

Buying Considerations

Professionals

Popularity: relatively unknown
Availability: generally available as bare root from specialty growers
Size to Sell: sells best in smaller sizes as it matures fast
On the Shelf: keep stock rotated; roots into other pots
Shrinkage: low; requires little maintenance

Collectors

Popularity: of interest to collectors; *A. vulneraria* ssp. *alpestris* is unique, rare

Gardeners

Ease of Growth: generally easy to grow
Start with: one small plant

What to Try First ...

Anthyllis vulneraria ssp. *alpestris*

On the Market

Anthyllis montana
'Rubra' • Dark-pink to red flowers in late spring • Clump-forming • 10–15 cm high, 30–45 cm wide

Anthyllis vulneraria
Yellow to crimson-purple flowers in late spring to early summer • 25–30 cm high, 45–60 cm wide

Anthyllis vulneraria ssp. alpestris
Yellow flowers tinted red in late spring to early summer • 20–30 cm high, 45–60 cm wide

Anthyllis vulneraria ssp. pulchella
White-and-orange flowers in late spring to early summer • 30 cm high, 45 cm wide

Aquilegia
p. 407 📷 **A**

Genus Information

Origin: North America, Asia and Europe
Selected Common Names: columbine
Nomenclature: From the Latin *aquila* (eagle), referring to the shape of the spurs on the petals. The common name "columbine" means dove. The flowers are thought to resemble a flock of doves.

General Features

Height: 8–60 cm high
Spread: 10–45 cm wide
Habit: short-lived, clump-forming perennial
Flowers: late spring to summer
Foliage: soft-green to blue-green; delicate
Hardiness: A–C
Warnings: foliage prone to leaf miner, leaf tiers, aphids, slugs and powdery mildew; contact with sap may irritate skin

Growing Requirements

Light: sun to p.m. sun
Soil: fertile, organic, well-drained soil; alpine types need gritty soil (will not tolerate spring wet)
Location: mixed borders; rock gardens
Propagation: seed (self-sows); division
Expert Advice: Older plants do not transplant well. Hybridizes easily. May not come true from seed.

Buying Considerations

Professionals

Popularity: popular, old-fashioned garden standard; fast seller
Availability: readily available as finished product and bare root
Size to Sell: sells best in smaller sizes when blooming as it matures fast
On the Shelf: keep stock rotated; foliage breakage
Shrinkage: low; requires little maintenance

Collectors

Popularity: not generally of interest to collectors, except for the rare alpine types such as *A. jonesii*, *A. bertolonii*

Gardeners

Ease of Growth: mostly easy to grow but needs close attention to growing conditions
Start with: one small plant for feature plant

What to Try First ...

Aquilegia McKanna Group (mix), *Aquilegia* (*A. jonesii* x *A. saximontana*), *Aquilegia alpina*, *Aquilegia alpina* 'Hensol Harebell', *Aquilegia flabellata* 'Ministar', *Aquilegia flabellata* (mix)

On the Market

Aquilegia

'Crimson Star' • Red-and-white flowers in early spring to early summer • 60 cm high, 60 cm wide

'Dorothy Rose' • Rose-pink flowers in spring • 60–75 cm high, 30–45 cm wide

'Double Pleat' • Dark-burgundy flowers in summer • 60–75 cm high, 30–45 cm wide

'Dragonfly' • Flowers in late spring to early summer • 40–45 cm high, 40–45 cm wide

(ex. Pamir) • Violet flowers in spring • 30 cm high, 20 cm wide

'Hensol Harebell' • Blue flowers in late spring • 15–30 cm high, 30 cm wide

'Lime Frost' • Blue-purple flowers in late spring to early summer • Chartreuse-speckled foliage • 60–75 cm high, 45–60 cm wide

'Magpie' • Purple-black-and-white flowers in spring • 45–60 cm high, 45–60 cm wide

'Mrs. N. Nichols' • Deep blue-and-white flowers in late spring • 30–45 cm high, 45 cm wide

Beidermeier Group
Range of flower colours in spring • 25–40 cm high, 40–45 cm wide

(Clematiflora hybrids)
Spurless, deep red-purple flowers in summer • Blue-green foliage • 30 cm high, 20 cm wide

McKana Group
Mix of large flowers in late spring to early summer • 60–90 cm high, 60 cm wide

Music Series
Long-spurred, large flowers in early summer • 40–45 cm high

Origami Series
(yellow) • Yellow flowers in late spring to early summer • 35–40 cm high, 25–40 cm wide

Songbird Series
New series with large flowers on plants 40 cm tall. Blooms late spring to summer.

'Blue Jay' • Blue-and-white-bicoloured flowers in early summer • 60–75 cm high, 45–60 cm wide

'Cardinal' • Crimson-red-and-white flowers in spring • 45–60 cm high, 45–60 cm wide

'Dove' • Pure white flowers in spring • 45–60 cm high, 45–60 cm wide

'Goldfinch' • Golden-yellow flowers in spring • 45–60 cm high, 45–60 cm wide

'Robin' • Rose-pink-and-white-bicoloured flowers in late spring to early summer • 45–60 cm high, 45–60 cm wide

Aquilegia (A. jonesii x A. saximontana)
Blue flowers in spring • 8–10 cm high, 15 cm wide

Aquilegia alpina
Blue flowers in late spring • 30 cm high, 20–30 cm wide

Aquilegia barnebyi
Pink-and-yellow flowers in spring • 15–20 cm high, 10–15 cm wide

Aquilegia bertolonii
Rich-blue flowers in spring • 10–15 cm high, 10–15 cm wide

Aquilegia brevistyla
Blue-and-white flowers in spring • 30–60 cm high, 20–45 cm wide

Aquilegia coerulea
Blue-and-white-bicoloured flowers in late spring • 40–75 cm high, 45–60 cm wide

Aquilegia canadensis
Yellow-and-red flowers in spring • 30–40 cm high, 20–30 cm wide

Aquilegia chrysantha
Long-spurred, golden-yellow flowers in spring to early summer • 60–75 cm high, 30–45 cm wide

Aquilegia elegantula
Red-and-yellow-bicoloured flowers in spring • 25–30 cm high, 30 cm wide

Aquilegia flabellata
'Blue Angel' • Violet-blue flowers in late spring to early summer • Blue-green foliage • 15–20 cm high, 15–20 cm wide

'Ministar' • Deep-blue to purple-and-white flowers in late spring to early summer • 10–15 cm high, 15–20 cm wide

'Nana Rosea' • Pink flowers in late spring to early summer • 10–15 cm high, 15–20 cm wide

'Pink Frost' • Pink-and-white flowers in spring • 10–25 cm high, 20 cm wide

Cameo Series
Blue-and-white flowers in late spring • 10–25 cm high, 25–30 cm wide

Rose-and-white flowers in late spring • 10–25 cm high, 25–30 cm wide

Aquilegia flabellata (syn. A. akitensis)
Extra-large, soft blue-and-cream-bicoloured flowers in spring to early summer • Blue-green foliage • 15–25 cm high, 15–30 cm wide

Aquilegia flabellata var. pumila
Deep-blue or purple flowers with cream centres in late spring to early summer • 10–15 cm high, 15–20 cm wide

'Rosea' • Pale-pink flowers in late spring to early summer • Blue-green foliage • 10–15 cm high, 10–20 cm wide

Aquilegia flabellata var. pumila f. alba
White flowers in spring to early summer • 10–15 cm high, 10–20 cm wide

Aquilegia flabellata var. pumila f. kurilensis
Pink flowers in spring to early summer • 10–15 cm high, 10–20 cm wide

Aquilegia flavescens
Yellow flowers in late spring • 30–60 cm high, 30–45 cm wide

Aquilegia formosa
Red-and-yellow flowers in early spring to late summer • 30–75 cm high, 45–60 cm wide

Aquilegia fragrans
Fragrant, creamy-white to pale-purple flowers in spring • 30–60 cm high, 25–40 cm wide

Aquilegia glauca (syn. A. nivalis)
Deep purple-blue flowers in spring • Blue-green foliage • 15–30 cm high, 15–20 cm wide

Aquilegia jonesii
Large, purple to blue flowers in spring • 5–10 cm high, 10–15 cm wide

Aquilegia laramiensis
Creamy-white flowers in spring • 8–20 cm high, 8–15 cm wide

Aquilegia longissima
'Maxi' • Fragrant, long, thin-spurred, yellow flowers in late spring to early summer • 100 cm high, 45–60 cm wide

Aquilegia saximontana
Lavender-and-white flowers in spring • 10–15 cm high, 15 cm wide

Aquilegia scopulorum
Large, blue flowers in spring • 8–20 cm high, 15–20 cm wide

Aquilegia skinneri
Orange-red flowers in early spring to early summer • 45–60 cm high, 60 cm wide

Aquilegia viridiflora
Black-and-green flowers in late spring to early summer • 40–45 cm high, 40–45 cm wide

Aquilegia vulgaris
'Red Hobbit' • Red-and-white flowers in late spring to early summer • 25–30 cm high, 25–30 cm wide

Aquilegia vulgaris var. stellata
(Barlow mix) • Blue, dark-maroon and rose, double flowers in spring • 45–60 cm high, 30–45 cm wide

'Ruby Port' • Double, dark-ruby flowers in summer • 45–60 cm high, 45 cm wide

'Nora Barlow' • Double, pink-red-and-green flowers in spring • 45–60 cm high, 30–45 cm wide

Vervaeneana Group
Aquilegia vulgaris (syn. A. vulgaris 'Aureovariegata')
Large, blue flowers in spring • 40–45 cm high, 40–45 cm wide

'Woodside' • Large flowers in late spring • Variegated foliage • 45–60 cm high, 30–45 cm wide

Aquilegia vulgaris (syn. A. vulgaris 'Plena Variegata')
Double flowers in spring • Variegated foliage • 45–60 cm high, 30–45 cm wide

Aquilegia vulgaris (syn. A. vulgaris 'Variegata')
Blue-violet flowers in late spring to early summer • Variegated foliage • 40–45 cm high, 40–45 cm wide

Aquilegia vulgaris var. flore-pleno
Double flowers in late spring to early summer • 45–60 cm high, 30–45 cm wide

Arabis

p. 407

Genus Information

Origin: North America, Europe, the Caucasus and Iran
Selected Common Names: alpine rockcress, rockcress, wall rockcress
Nomenclature: From the Greek *arabis* (Arabia), referring to the dry locations preferred by many species.
Notes: A genus of some 120 species.

General Features

Height: 2–20 cm high
Spread: 20–30 cm wide
Habit: spreading, mat-forming alpine perennial
Flowers: spring blooming
Foliage: (some) evergreen
Hardiness: C–D
Warnings: prone to aphids, flea beetles and slugs; not prone to diseases
Expert Advice: Deadhead to extend blooming season and prune after flowering to keep plant compact.

Growing Requirements

Light: sun
Soil: well-drained soil
Location: alpine gardens; front of mixed borders; rock gardens
Propagation: seed; division; cuttings
Expert Advice: Double and variegated forms do not come true from seed.

Buying Considerations

Professionals

Popularity: gaining popularity; fast seller
Availability: generally available as finished product
Size to Sell: sells best in smaller sizes when blooming as it matures fast
On the Shelf: low ornamental appeal; keep stock rotated; rapidly overgrows pot

Collectors

Popularity: Not generally of interest to collectors

Gardeners

Ease of Growth: very easy to grow
Start with: one small plant for feature plant and several for mass plantings

What to Try First ...

Arabis alpina ssp. *caucasica*, *Arabis alpina* ssp. *caucasica* 'Rubin', *Arabis alpina* ssp. *caucasica* 'Schneehabe', *Arabis alpina* ssp. *caucasica* 'Variegata', *Arabis androsacea*, *Arabis* x *arendsii* 'Compinkie', *Arabis bryoides*, *Arabis* x *sturii*

On the Market

Arabis alpina
'Alba' • White flowers in spring • Evergreen • Mat-forming • 15 cm high, 90 cm wide

Arabis alpina ssp. *caucasica*
Pink or white flowers in spring • Evergreen • 20 cm high

'Flore Pleno' • Double, white flowers in spring • Evergreen • 15–25 cm high, 45–60 cm wide

'Red Sensation' • Red flowers in spring • Evergreen • 15–25 cm high, 45–60 cm wide

'Rubin' • Pink flowers in early spring • Evergreen • 15–25 cm high

'Schneehabe' (Snowcap) • White flowers in spring • Evergreen • 10–15 cm high, 30+ cm wide

'Variegata' • White flowers in spring • Evergreen • 10 cm high, 30–45 cm wide

Arabis androsacea
White flowers in spring • Evergreen • 2–5 cm high, 25–30 cm wide

Arabis x *arendsii*
'Compinkie' • Pink flowers in early spring • Evergreen • 15–25 cm high, 45–60 cm wide

Arabis aubrietioides
Rose flowers in spring to early summer • Evergreen • 10–15 cm high, 20–30 cm wide

Arabis bryoides
White flowers in spring • Evergreen • 5 cm high, 15–20 cm wide

Arabis caerulea
Soft-blue flowers in spring • Evergreen • 5–15 cm high, 25–30 cm wide

Arabis carduchorum
White flowers in early spring • Evergreen • 2–8 cm high, 30–45 cm wide

Arabis drabiformis
White flowers in summer • Evergreen • 8–15 cm high, 20–30 cm wide

Arabis procurrens (syn. *A. ferdinandi-coburgi*)
'Variegata' • White flowers in spring • Evergreen • 8–10 cm high, 20–30 cm wide

Arabis x *kellereri*
White flowers in spring • Evergreen, silver-green foliage • 5 cm high, 20 cm wide

Arabis lemmonii
Bright-purple flowers in spring • Evergreen • 15–30 cm high, 30+ cm wide

Arabis pumila
White flowers in spring • Evergreen • 10–15 cm high, 25–30 cm wide

Arabis purpurea
Rose-purple flowers in early spring • Evergreen • 10–15 cm high, 30–45 cm wide

Arabis sparsiflora rubra
Intense rose-pink flowers in spring • Evergreen • 5–10 cm high, 25–30 cm wide

Arabis x *sturii*
White flowers in spring • Evergreen • 15–20 cm high, 20–25 cm wide

Arctanthemum p. 407

Genus Information

Origin: Arctic; Subarctic
Selected Common Names: chrysanthemum
Nomenclature: From the Greek *arktos* (north) and *anthemon* (flower).

General Features

Height: 50 cm high
Spread: 30 cm wide
Habit: rhizomatous perennial

Flowers: daisy-like; late season; frost tolerant
Hardiness: A
Warnings: prone to aphids; prone to powdery mildew

Growing Requirements
Light: sun to p.m sun
Soil: moist, saline soil
Location: meadows; mixed borders; rock gardens
Propagation: seed; division; cuttings
Expert Advice: Divide every three years to maintain vigour.

Buying Considerations

Professionals
Popularity: relatively unknown; sells well when blooming late in season
Availability: occasionally available as finished product from specialty growers
Size to Sell: sells best in smaller sizes as it matures fast
On the Shelf: rapidly overgrows pot; keep stock rotated
Shrinkage: low shrinkage; requires little maintenance

Collectors
Popularity: not generally of interest to collectors

Gardeners
Ease of Growth: very easy to grow
Start with: one small plant for feature plant

What to Try First ...
Arctanthemum arcticum (syn. *Chrysanthemum arcticum*) 'Red Cheemo'

On the Market

Arctanthemum arcticum (syn. Chrysanthemum arcticum)
'Red Cheemo' • Large, daisy-like, pink flowers in late summer • 50 cm high, 30 cm wide

Arctostaphylos p. 407

Genus Information
Origin: North America, circumpolar
Selected Common Names: bear berry, kinnikinnik
Nomenclature: From the Greek *arktos* (bear) and *staphule* (grape). Bears are said to eat the fruit.

General Features
Height: 5–15 cm high
Spread: 20–60 cm wide
Habit: prostrate groundcover perennial
Flowers: white
Foliage: glossy; evergreen
Hardiness: C

Warnings: not prone to insects or diseases
Expert Advice: Grown for the foliage, flowers and fruit.

Growing Requirements
Light: sun to p.m. sun
Soil: moist, well-drained, fertile, acidic soil
Location: cool rock gardens; woodlands
Propagation: cuttings; rooted layering stems
Expert Advice: Take semi-ripe cuttings or layer stems in summer. Resents being disturbed.

Buying Considerations

Professionals
Popularity: popular native perennial
Availability: readily available as a finished product
Size to Sell: sells best in smaller sizes as it matures slowly
On the Shelf: keep stock rotated
Shrinkage: high; sensitive to overwatering

Collectors
Popularity: of interest to collectors; a native plant

Gardeners
Ease of growth: mostly easy to grow but needs close attention to growing conditions
Start with: many for mass plantings

What to Try First ...
Arctostaphylos alpina var. *rubra, Arctostaphylos uva-ursi*

On the Market

Arctostaphylos alpina var. rubra
Clustered, white flowers in early summer • 5–10 cm high, 20 cm wide
Arctostaphylos uva-ursi
White to soft-pink flowers in spring • Shiny, evergreen foliage • 10–15 cm high, 45–60 cm wide
'Massachusetts' • White to soft-pink flowers in spring • Shiny, evergreen foliage • 10–15 cm high, 45–50 cm wide
'Vancouver Jade' • White to soft-pink flowers in spring • Shiny, evergreen foliage • 10–15 cm high, 45–60 cm wide

Arenaria p. 407

Genus Information
Origin: the Northern Hemisphere
Selected Common Names: alpine sandwort, mountain sandwort, prairie sandwort, sandwort, Spanish sandwort
Nomenclature: From the Greek *arena* (sand), referring to growing in sandy soil.

General Features

Height: 1–15 cm high
Spread: 2–60 cm wide
Habit: mat- or cushion-forming groundcover perennial
Flowers: white
Foliage: mostly evergreen
Hardiness: C
Warnings: not prone to insects or diseases
Expert Advice: Most make excellent groundcovers and are very hardy.

Growing Requirements

Light: sun; *A. balearica* should be sheltered from hot p.m. sun
Soil: free-draining, gritty, lean, organic soil
Location: sunny, hot, dry areas; rock gardens; scree
Propagation: seed; division; cuttings
Expert Advice: Divide in early spring. Take cuttings in summer.

Buying Considerations

Professionals

Popularity: relatively unknown
Availability: occasionally available bare root from specialty growers
Size to Sell: sells best in smaller sizes when blooming as it matures fast
On the Shelf: keep stock rotated; rapidly overgrows pot
Shrinkage: low; requires little maintenance

Collectors

Popularity: of interest to collectors—a unique, rare plant

Gardeners

Ease of Growth: very easy to grow
Start with: one small plant for feature plant and several for mass plantings

What to Try First ...

Arenaria hookeri var. *desertorum*, *Arenaria lithops*, *Arenaria montana*, *Arenaria obtusiloba*, *Arenaria pseudo-acantholimon*, *Arenaria tetraquetra* var. *granatensis*

On the Market

Arenaria

'Blue Cascade' • White flowers in spring • Rich-blue, needle-like foliage, evergreen • Mound-forming • 5–10 cm high, 25–30 cm wide

Arenaria balearica

White flowers in spring to early summer • Evergreen • 2–6 cm high, 20–30 cm wide

Arenaria hookeri

White flowers in late spring • 10 cm high, 25–30 cm wide

Arenaria hookeri var. *desertorum*

White flowers in summer • 10 cm high, 25–30 cm wide

Arenaria lithops
(syn. *A. alfacarensis*; *A. pulvinata*)

White flowers in summer • 5–10 cm high, 30–60 cm wide

Arenaria montana

White flowers in spring • Evergreen • 8–12 cm high, 20–30 cm wide

Arenaria obtusiloba

White flowers in late spring to early summer • 10–15 cm high, 30 cm wide

Arenaria pseudo-acantholimon

White flowers in spring • Prickly, evergreen foliage • 1–5 cm high, 20–25 cm wide

Arenaria purpurascens

Pink-purple flowers in summer • Evergreen • 8 cm high, 15 cm wide

Arenaria recurva (syn. *Minuartia recurva*)

White flowers in late spring to early summer • 15 cm high, 8–12 cm wide

Arenaria roseaflora

Pink flowers in summer • 8 cm high, 10 cm wide

Arenaria scariosa

White flowers in late spring • Grey-green foliage • 10–15 cm high, 5–10 cm wide

Arenaria tetraquetra

Stemless, white flowers in summer • Evergreen • Densely cushion-forming • 2–5 cm high, 20–30 cm wide

Arenaria tetraquetra var. *granatensis*

White flowers in late summer • Evergreen • 2–5 cm high, 20–30 cm wide

Arisaema

p. 407

Genus Information

Origin: Africa, Asia and eastern North America
Selected Common Names: cobra lily, dragonroot Jack-in-the-pulpit
Nomenclature: From *Arum* and the Greek *aima* (blood-red), referring to the red-blotched leaves of some species.

General Features

Height: 15–90 cm high
Spread: 15–60 cm wide
Habit: tuberous or rhizomatous perennial
Flowers: hooded cups surround flower spikes; unisexual; one flower per corm; blooms in early spring to early summer in warm climates, can be delayed up to two months in colder climates

Foliage: dramatic
Fruit: orange-red colour
Hardiness: C–D
Warnings: prone to aphids and slugs
Expert Advice: Takes a few years to form a nice colony.

Growing Requirements
Light: shade to a.m. sun
Soil: cool, humus-rich, gritty, lean, neutral to acidic soil
Location: woodland gardens
Propagation: seed, separate and replant offsets

Buying Considerations

Professionals
Popularity: gaining popularity; fast seller when in bloom
Availability: occasionally available as bare root from specialty growers
Size to Sell: sells best in mature sizes when blooming as it matures slowly
On the Shelf: high ornamental appeal; keep stock rotated
Shrinkage: high; sensitive to overwatering; goes dormant in pot

Collectors
Popularity: of interest to collectors—a unique, rare, challenge; exceptional beauty; novelty plant

Gardeners
Ease of Growth: mostly difficult to grow as it needs close attention to growing
Start with: one mature plant for feature plant

What to Try First ...

Arisaema brevipes, Arisaema candidissimum, Arisaema dracontium, Arisaema elephas, Arisaema kiushianum, Arisaema ringens, Arisaema sikokianum, Arisaema thunbergii ssp. *urashima, Arisaema triphyllum*

On the Market

Arisaema brevipes
Purple, hooded spathe in summer • 40–50 cm high, 30–45 cm wide

Arisaema candidissimum
Fragrant, pink-striped, white spathe • 40–60 cm high, 30–45 cm wide

(White form) • Fragrant, white spathe • 40–60 cm high, 30–45 cm wide

(Yellow form) • Fragrant, butter-yellow spathe • 40–60 cm high, 30–45 cm wide

Arisaema ciliatum
Molasses-brown spathe with white stripes • 30–90 cm high, 30–50 cm wide

Arisaema concinnum
Green or sometimes purple spathe, often white-striped • 30–150 cm high, 25–60 cm wide

Arisaema consanguineum
Green spathe • 45–180 cm high, 25–60 cm wide

Arisaema dilatatum
Hooded spathe • Purple-marbled foliage • 30–45 cm high, 30–40 cm wide

Arisaema dracontium
Green spathe • 50–75 cm high, 25–40 cm wide

Arisaema du-bois-reymondiae
White-striped, red or green spathe • 45–50 cm high, 20–30 cm wide

Arisaema elephas
Liver-purple spathe • 30–50 cm high, 30–45 cm wide

Arisaema elphas var. handelii
Liver-purple spathe with white stripes • Purple foliage • 30–35 cm high, 40–45 cm wide

Arisaema erubescens
Blush-pink spathe • 80 cm high, 60 cm wide

Arisaema fargesii
Black-purple spathe with white stripes • 45–60 cm high, 30–45 cm wide

(Purple leaf) • Black-purple, hooded spathe • Purple foliage • 45–60 cm high, 30–45 cm wide

Arisaema franchettianum
Deep-maroon spathe with white stripes • 45–90 cm high, 30–90 cm wide

(Pink variety) • Pink spathe with white stripes • 45–90 cm high, 30–90 cm wide

Arisaema griffithii (syn. A. g. pradhanii)
Violet-purple spathe with green-and-white markings • 15–60 cm high, 30–80 cm wide

Arisaema inkiangense var. maculatum
Pale-green spathe • Evergreen • 40 cm high, 45–60 cm wide

Arisaema intermedium
Yellow-green, hooded spathe • 25–60 cm high, 25–60 cm wide

Arisaema jacquemontii (syn. A. cornutum)
Greenish-white, hooded spathe • 20–90 cm high, 40 cm wide

Arisaema kiushianum
White-striped, purple, hooded spathe in summer • 30–45 cm high, 15–40 cm wide

Arisaema lingyunense
Reversed, purple-brown, hooded spathe •
25–35 cm high, 25 cm wide

Arisaema nepenthoides
Green to bronze spathe with white stripes •
30–90 cm high, 15–30 cm wide

Arisaema propinquum (syn. *A. sikkimense*)
Green or purple spathe with white or purple
stripes • 60–80 cm high, 50 cm wide

Arisaema ringens
Green to purple spathe with green or white
stripes • 30–110 cm high, 25–80 cm wide

Arisaema serratum
Green to purple spathe, often white-striped
• 40–150 cm high, 25–60 cm wide

Arisaema sikkimense
Purple, hooded spathe with white stripes •
20–60 cm high

Arisaema sikokianum
White-striped, purple, hooded spathe •
30–70 cm high, 25–70 cm wide

Arisaema sikokianum var. *engleri*
Purple, hooded spathe with white stripes •
80 cm high, 30 cm wide

Arisaema speciosum
Purple, hooded spathe with white stripes •
45–60 cm high, 30–60 cm wide

Arisaema thunbergii
Bronze-purple spathe with white stripes •
30–60 cm high, 20–60 cm wide

Arisaema thunbergii ssp. *urashima*
Bronze-purple spathe with white stripes •
30–60 cm high, 20–60 cm wide

Arisaema tortuosum
Fragrant, green, or rarely purple, spathe •
50–60 cm high, 25 cm wide

Arisaema triphyllum
Green or purple spathe, usually striped
green or white • 30–80 cm high, 25–50 cm
wide

Arisaema utile
Purple, hooded spathe with white stripes •
30–50 cm high, 25–60 cm wide

Arisaema wattii (syn. *A.biauriculatum*)
Dark-spotted, reddish to green spathe •
80 cm high, 50 cm wide

Arisaema wilsonii
Black, hooded spathe with white stripe •
30–130 cm high, 30–90 cm wide

Arisaema yunnanense
Green, hooded spathe • 30–50 cm high,
25–30 cm wide

Aristolochia
p. 407

Genus Information
Origin: temperate regions and tropical regions
Selected Common Names: Dutchman's pipe
Nomenclature: From the Greek *aristos* (best) and
lochos (birth), referring to the traditional use of
some species for easing childbirth. The
common name "Dutchman's pipe" refers to the
shape of the flowers.

General Features
Height: 1–5 m high
Spread: 60 cm–3 m wide
Habit: climbing perennial
Flowers: unpleasant odour; flower shape traps
pollinating insects
Foliage: large; heart-shaped, tropical-looking
Hardiness: D
Warnings: prone to spider mites; not prone to
disease
Expert Advice: Dies back hard and is slow to
establish in colder areas.

Growing Requirements
Light: shade to a.m. sun
Soil: compost-rich, sandy soil
Location: screening; moist woodland gardens
Propagation: seed; cuttings; division
Expert Advice: Use rooting hormone on cuttings
and provide with gentle bottom heat.

Buying Considerations

Professionals
Popularity: gaining popularity
Availability: occasionally available as finished
product and bare root
Size to Sell: sells best in mature sizes and
matures slowly
On the Shelf: high ornamental appeal when in
bloom
Shrinkage: high; sensitive to underwatering

Collectors
Popularity: of interest to collectors—rare

Gardeners
Ease of Growth: mostly easy to grow
Start with: one mature plant for feature plant
and instant visual effect

What to Try First ...
Aristolochia macrophylla (Select)

On the Market

Aristolochia clematitis
Tubular, yellow-brown flowers in early
summer • 1 m high, 60 cm wide

Aristolochia macrophylla
(Select) • Pipe-shaped, maroon-and-white
flowers in early summer • Heart-shaped
foliage • 3–4.5 m high, 2–3 m wide

Armeria

p. 407

Genus Information

Origin: Asia Minor, North Africa, Europe and the Americas

Selected Common Names: alpine thrift, juniper thrift, sea pink, sea thrift, thrift

Nomenclature: From the Latin for *Dianthus barbatus* (sweet William), which it resembles.

General Features

Height: 2–25 cm high

Spread: 8–30 cm wide

Habit: cushion to clump-forming perennial

Flowers: ball-like flowers; spring to summer; deadhead to extend blooming season

Foliage: evergreen; grass-like

Hardiness: C–D

Warnings: not prone to insects or disease

Growing Requirements

Light: sun

Soil: well-drained soil

Location: front of mixed borders; rock gardens; troughs

Propagation: seed; division; cuttings

Expert Advice: May not come true from seed. Hybridizes easily. Divide in spring or take basal cuttings in summer.

Buying Considerations

Professionals

Popularity: popular; fast seller

Availability: readily available as finished product

Size to Sell: sells best in smaller sizes (when blooming) as it matures fast

Shrinkage: low; requires little maintenance

Collectors

Popularity: not generally of interest to collectors

Gardeners

Ease of Growth: very easy to grow

Start with: several small plants for instant visual effect

What to Try First ...

Armeria 'Nifty Thrifty', *Armeria juniperifolia*, *Armeria juniperifolia* 'Bevan's Variety', *Armeria maritima*, *Armeria maritima* 'Dusseldorfer Stolz' (Dusseldorf Pride)

On the Market

Armeria

'Nifty Thrifty' • Pink flowers in summer • Lime-green variegated foliage • 15–20 cm high, 20–30 cm wide

'Victor Rite' • Soft pink flowers in late spring • Clump-forming, compact habit • 10 cm high, 15–20 cm wide

---

Armeria girardii (syn. A. setacea)

Pink flowers intermittently in summer • 10 cm high, 15–20 cm wide

'Alba' • White flowers in spring • 8–10 cm high, 15–25 cm wide

Armeria juniperifolia

Pink-red flowers in late spring • Reddish foliage • 5–10 cm high, 20–30 cm wide

'Alba' • Pure white flowers in late spring • 5–10 cm high, 20–30 cm wide

'Bevan's Variety' • Bright-pink flowers in late spring • Short foliage • Clump-forming, compact habit • 2–5 cm high, 10–15 cm wide

'Rubra' • Pink-red flowers in late spring • Dark foliage • 5–10 cm high, 20–30 cm wide

Armeria maritima

Ball-like, pink flowers in spring • Grass-like foliage • 15–20 cm high, 30 cm wide

'Alba' • White flowers in summer • 10–15 cm high, 30 cm wide

'Dusseldorfer Stolz' (Dusseldorf Pride) • Deep-pink flowers in spring • 15–20 cm high, 30 cm wide

'Little Penny' • Rosy-pink flowers in late spring to summer • Red-purple, grass-like foliage • 5 cm high, 8 cm wide

'Pink Lusitanica' • Soft-pink flowers in late spring to summer • 15–25 cm high, 20–30 cm wide

'Red Fire' • Red-pink flowers in spring • 10 cm high, 30 cm wide

'Rubriflolia' • Pink flowers in summer • Purple-bronze foliage • 10–15 cm high, 30 cm wide

'Splendens' • Bright-pink flowers in late spring • 15–25 cm high, 20–30 cm wide

'Spring Charm' • Pink flowers in spring • 10 cm high, 30 cm wide

Armoracia

p. 407

Genus Information

Origin: Europe and Asia.

Selected Common Names: horseradish

Nomenclature: From the Greek name for horseradish.

General Features

Height: 75 cm high

Spread: 90 cm wide

Habit: weedy perennial

Flowers: spring

Foliage: solid or variegated
Hardiness: C
Warnings: invasive; not prone to insects or disease
Expert Advice: Considered invasive, but one species, *A. rusticana* 'Variegata,' is used as an ornamental and is less invasive than the green-leafed form.

Growing Requirements

Light: sun
Soil: tolerant of a wide range of soils
Location: mixed borders; difficult areas
Propagation: division; root cuttings

Buying Considerations

Professionals

Popularity: variegated form is grown as a foliage plant and is relatively unknown
Availability: occasionally available as bare root
Size to Sell: sells best in smaller sizes as it matures fast
Shrinkage: low; requires little maintenance

Collectors

Popularity: not generally of interest to collectors

Gardeners

Ease of Growth: very easy to grow
Start with: one small plant for instant visual effect

What to Try First ...

Armoracia rusticana 'Variegata'

On the Market

Armoracia rusticana
'**Variegata**' • White flowers in spring • Large, coarse foliage, variegation takes 2–3 years to appear• 75 cm high, 90 cm wide

Arnica   p. 407

Genus Information

Origin: northern temperate regions to the arctic hemisphere
Nomenclature: From the Greek *arnakis* (lambskin), referring to the leaf texture.

General Features

Height: 25–60 cm high
Spread: 45–60 cm wide
Habit: clump-forming, rhizomatous perennial
Flowers: yellow, daisy-like; summer
Foliage: woolly
Hardiness: A–C
Warnings: not prone to insects or disease; foliage and flowers will cause discomfort if swallowed; contact with sap may irritate skin

Growing Requirements

Light: sun
Soil: moist, organic, well-drained soil
Location: mixed borders; large rock gardens; wild gardens
Propagation: seed (self-sows readily), division
Expert Advice: Divide in spring.

Buying Considerations

Professionals

Popularity: relatively unknown
Availability: occasionally available from specialty growers
Size to Sell: sells best in smaller sizes when blooming as it matures fast
Shrinkage: low; requires little maintenance

Collectors

Popularity: of interest to collectors—prairie wildflower

Gardeners

Ease of Growth: very easy to grow
Start with: one small plant for feature plant and several for mass plantings

What to Try First ...

Arnica chamissonis, Arnica montana

On the Market

Arnica chamissonis
Yellow flowers in summer • 30–60 cm high, 45–60 cm wide

Arnica montana
Dark-yellow flowers in summer • Moist, well-drained, organic, alkaline-free soil • 25–60 cm high, 45–60 cm wide

Arrhenatherum   p. 408

Genus Information

Origin: Europe, North Africa and northwest Asia
Selected Common Names: variegated oat grass
Nomenclature: From the Greek *arren* (male) and *ather* (awn), referring to the bristled staminate flowers.

General Features

Height: 30 cm high
Spread: 30 cm wide
Habit: groundcover perennial grass
Flowers: oat-like spikelets; midsummer to fall; good for drying
Foliage: green or variegated
Hardiness: B–C
Warnings: green form is an aggressive spreader (keep contained and remove seed heads to prevent spread)

Expert Advice: *A. elatius* ssp. *bulbosum* 'Variegatum' forms bulbs that root readily on contact with the ground.

Growing Requirements
Light: sun
Soil: fertile, well-drained soil
Propagation: division
Expert Advice: Divide frequently to keep vigorous.

Buying Considerations

Professionals
Popularity: old-fashioned, garden standard foliage plant
Availability: readily available as finished product and bare root
Size to Sell: sells best in smaller sizes as it matures fast
On the Shelf: high ornamental appeal
Shrinkage: low; requires little maintenance

Collectors
Popularity: not generally of interest to collectors

Gardeners
Ease of Growth: very easy to grow
Start with: one small plant for feature plant and several for mass plantings

What to Try First ...
Arrhenatherum elatius ssp. *bulbosum* 'Variegatum'

On the Market
Arrhenatherum elatius ssp. *bulbosum*
'Variegatum' • Striped, green-and-white foliage • 30 cm high, 30 cm wide

Artemisia p. 408

Genus Information
Origin: the Northern Hemisphere, South Africa and western South America
Selected Common Names: old man, perennial dusty miller, sage, silver mound, wormwood
Nomenclature: The name is from the Greek goddess Artemis. The common name "wormwood" comes from its use by herbalists to kill parasitic worms.
Notes: This important plant has been grown since Roman times. Now mainly used for the foliage. The herb tarragon belongs in this family.

General Features
Height: 5–150 cm high
Spread: 8–100+ cm wide
Habit: creeping to clump-forming perennial; may require staking

Flowers: small and insignificant
Foliage: aromatic, silvery; shear in spring
Hardiness: C–D
Warnings: some species invasive (keep contained to prevent spread)
Expert Advice: Remove flowers to keep plant compact. Grown mainly for foliage.

Growing Requirements
Light: sun
Soil: lean, well-drained, alkaline soil: drought tolerant
Location: mixed borders
Propagation: seed; division; cuttings
Expert Advice: Take soft or semi-hardwood cuttings and divide regularly to maintain vigour.

Buying Considerations

Professionals
Popularity: popular, fast-selling foliage plant
Availability: readily available as finished product and bare root
Size to Sell: sells best in smaller sizes as it matures fast
On the Shelf: high ornamental appeal
Shrinkage: low; requires little maintenance

Collectors
Popularity: not generally of interest to collectors

Gardeners
Ease of Growth: very easy to grow
Start with: one small plant for instant visual effect and several for mass plantings

What to Try First ...
Artemisia 'Huntington', *Artemisia abrotanum*, *Artemisia ludoviciana* 'Silver King', *Artemisia ludoviciana* 'Valerie Finnis', *Artemisia schmidtiana*, *Artemisia stelleriana* 'Boughton Silver'

On the Market
Artemisia
'Huntington' • Silvery foliage • 60–120 cm high, 45–60 cm wide
'Powis Castle' • Fern-like, silvery foliage • 70–80 cm high, 90 cm wide
'Silver Frost' • Fine-cut silver-grey foliage • 75 cm high, 45–60+ cm wide
'Tiny Green' • Green foliage • 5–8 cm high
Artemisia abrotanum
Feathery, green, aromatic foliage • 90–100 cm high, 90–100 cm wide

Artemisia absinthium
Grey flowers in summer • Aromatic, silver-grey foliage • 75–100 cm high, 45–60 cm wide

Artemisia caucasica ssp. caucasica
Soft, ferny, silver-green foliage • 5–15 cm high, 30 cm wide

Artemisia frigida
Grey foliage • 40 cm high, 45–60 cm wide

Artemisia glacialis
Yellow florets in late summer • Silky, hairy, silver foliage • 8–18 cm high, 8–18 cm wide

Artemisia lactiflora
Cream-white flowers in summer • Clump-forming • Well-drained, moist soil • 1–1.5 m high, 60–90 cm wide

'Guizhou' • Fragrant, creamy-white flowers in summer to fall • Black-green foliage and mahogany stems • Clump-forming • Well-drained, moist soil • 1–1.5 m high, 45–60 cm wide

Artemisia ludoviciana
'Silver King' • Silver foliage • 60–90 cm high, 60–90+ cm wide

'Silver Queen' • Silver-grey foliage • 60–75 cm high, 60–90+ cm wide

'Valerie Finnis' • Silver foliage • 45–60 cm high, 60+ cm wide

Artemisia schmidtiana
Silky-soft, silver-grey foliage • 30–40 cm high, 60 cm wide

'Nana' • Silky-soft, silver-grey foliage • 8–10 cm high, 30 cm wide

Artemisia stelleriana
'Boughton Silver' (syn. Silver Brocade and Mori) • Silky-soft, silver-green, lobed foliage • 15–30 cm high, 60–75+ cm wide

Artemisia versicolor
Grey foliage • 30–45 cm high, 45–60 cm wide

'Sea Foam' • Feathery, grey foliage • 30–45 cm high, 45–60 cm wide

Artemisia vulgaris
'Cragg-Barber Eye' • White plumes in summer • Gold leaves with green pinstripes • 1–1.7 m high, 90–100 cm wide

'Golden Phoenix' • Flowers in late summer • Golden-yellow, lacy foliage • 30 cm high, 90–100 cm wide

'Oriental Limelight'™ ('Janlim') • Flowers in late summer • Variegated, cream-and-green foliage • 60–170 cm high, 30–100 cm wide

Aruncus
p. 408

Genus Information
Origin: the Northern Hemisphere
Selected Common Names: goat's beard
Nomenclature: Named by the Roman scientist Pliny.

General Features
Height: 30–150 cm high
Spread: 45–100 cm wide
Habit: clump-forming, rhizomatous perennial
Flowers: feathery; late spring to midsummer; good for drying
Foliage: finely cut; fall colour
Hardiness: B–C
Warnings: not prone to insects or disease

Growing Requirements
Light: shade
Soil: fertile, moist soil
Location: shady mixed borders
Propagation: seed (self-sows); division
Expert Advice: Taller varieties provide height in shade areas.

Buying Considerations
Professionals
Popularity: popular, old-fashioned perennial; fast seller in bloom
Availability: readily available as finished product and bare root
Size to Sell: sells best in smaller sizes as it matures fast
Shrinkage: low; requires little maintenance

Collectors
Popularity: of interest to collectors; A. aethusifolius

Gardeners
Ease of Growth: very easy to grow
Start with: one small plant for feature plant

What to Try First ...
Aruncus aethusifolius, Aruncus dioicus, Aruncus dioicus 'Kneiffii', Aruncus dioicus Zweiweltenkind'

On the Market
Aruncus aethusifolius
Creamy-white plumes in spring to early summer • Clump-forming, compact habit • 30–40 cm high, 45–60 cm wide

Aruncus dioicus
White plumes in late spring to early summer • Lush green foliage • 1–1.5 m high, 90–100 cm wide

'Kneiffii' • Cream plumes in late spring to early summer • Finely cut foliage • 60–90 cm high, 60–90 cm wide

'Zweiweltenkind' (Child of Two Worlds) •
Creamy-white plumes in summer to fall
• Dense, bronzy foliage • 1.5 m high,
60–90 cm wide

Asarum

p. 408

Genus Information

Origin: North America, Europe and East Asia
Selected Common Names: wild ginger
Nomenclature: From the Greek *asaron*,
the name used by Dioscorides.

General Features

Height: 10–20 cm high
Spread: 20–45 cm wide
Habit: rhizomatous woodland groundcover
perennial
Flowers: purple to brown; at ground level below
leaves; spring to early summer; pollinated by
flies
Foliage: leathery; ginger-like scent when crushed
Hardiness: C–D
Warnings: prone to slugs; not prone to disease

Growing Requirements

Light: shade; prefers dappled light
Soil: humus-rich, moist, well-drained, neutral
to acidic soil
Location: shady mixed borders; woodland
gardens
Propagation: seed (self-sows); division
Expert Advice: Divide in spring. Seeds dispersed
by ants. Crushed rhizomes scented like ginger.

Buying Considerations

Professionals

Popularity: gaining popularity as a foliage
plant
Availability: generally available as finished
product and bare root
Size to Sell: sells best in smaller sizes as it
matures slowly
On the Shelf: high ornamental appeal
Shrinkage: low; requires little maintenance

Collectors

Popularity: of interest to collectors—unique

Gardeners

Ease of Growth: generally easy to grow; *A.
canadense* or *A. europaeum*—very hardy
Start with: one small plant for feature and
several for mass plantings

What to Try First ...

*Asarum arifolium, Asarum canadense,
Asarum caulescens, Asarum europaeum*

On the Market

Asarum arifolium
Brown flowers in spring • Mottled foliage •
20 cm high, 30+ cm wide

Asarum campaniforme
Red-brown flowers with white eye •
15–20 cm high, 30–40 cm wide

Asarum canadense
Red-brown flowers in early summer •
15–20 cm high, 30–40 cm wide

Asarum caudatum
Red-brown flowers in spring • 15–20 cm
high, 30–40 cm wide

Asarum caulescens
Rose-pink flowers • Heart-shaped foliage •
10 cm high, 20–30 cm wide

Asarum delavayi
Black-brown flowers speckled white in
spring • Shiny foliage • 10–15 cm high,
20 cm wide

Asarum europaeum
Brown flowers in spring • Glossy, green
foliage • 15 cm high, 20–30 cm wide

Asarum hartwegii
Red-brown flowers in spring • Silver-
mottled, dark-green foliage • 15–20 cm
high, 30–40 cm wide

Asarum maximum
Violet-black flowers with white eye in late
spring • Emerald foliage with grey-blue
variegation • 15–20 cm high, 45 cm wide

Asarum megacalyx
Bell-like, black flowers in late summer •
Dark-green, glossy foliage • 20 cm high,
30 cm wide

Asarum shuttleworthii
Purple flowers in late spring • Silver-marked
foliage • 15–20 cm high, 20–30 cm wide

Asarum splendens
Dark-purple flowers in spring • Heart-
shaped foliage with silver markings •
10–16 cm high

Asarum tamaense
Brown flowers in spring • Leathery, glossy,
evergreen foliage • 20 cm high, 20–25 cm
wide

A

Asclepias

p. 408 📷

Genus Information

Origin: the Americas and Africa
Selected Common Names: butterfly flower
Nomenclature: Named for Asklepios, the Greek god of medicine, referring to the medicinal properties of some species.

General Features

Height: 20–120 cm high
Spread: 40–100 cm wide
Habit: tap-rooted, clump-forming perennial
Flowers: summer; attractive to butterflies
Hardiness: C
Warnings: not prone to insects or disease; contact with sap may irritate skin
Expert Advice: Produces ornamental fruits that split open to release seeds with silky hairs.

Growing Requirements

Light: sun
Soil: fertile, moist, organic, well-drained soil
Propagation: seed; division
Expert Advice: Resents being disturbed. *A. tuberosa* tends to rot in wet soil.

Buying Considerations

Professionals

Popularity: old-fashioned, garden standard
Availability: readily available as finished product and bare root
Size to Sell: sells best in mature sizes in bloom as it matures slowly
On the Shelf: rapidly becomes rootbound
Shrinkage: high; sensitive to overwatering

Collectors

Popularity: not generally of interest to collectors

Gardeners

Ease of Growth: generally easy to grow but needs close attention to growing conditions
Start with: one mature plant for feature plant

What to Try First ...

Asclepias incarnata, Asclepias incarnata 'Ice Ballet', *Asclepias tuberosa, Asclepias tuberosa* 'Rosea'

On the Market

Asclepias cryptoceras
Fuchsia-like, purple-maroon and cream flowers in summer • 20–25 cm high, 40–45 cm wide

Asclepias incarnata
Pink flowers in summer • 75–120 cm high, 90–100 cm wide

'Ice Ballet' • Fragrant, creamy-white flowers in summer • 75–120 cm high, 60–75 cm wide

'Soul Mate' • Fragrant, white flowers with red bracts in summer • 60–100 cm high, 90–100 cm wide

Asclepias tuberosa
Fragrant, orange-red flowers in summer • 60–90 cm high, 30 cm wide

'Orange Glory' • Orange-red flowers in summer • 60–90 cm high, 30 cm wide

'Rosea' • Pink flowers in summer • 50–90 cm high, 30 cm wide

Asparagus

p. 408 📷

Genus Information

Origin: Europe, Asia and Africa
Selected Common Names: climbing asparagus, asparagus
Nomenclature: The name used by Theophrastus.

General Features

Height: 2–4 m high
Spread: 1–2 m wide
Habit: climbing vine
Flowers: tiny, insignificant; white; bisexual or unisexual; summer
Foliage: fine, ferny, delicate; good for cutflower arrangements
Fruit: shiny red
Hardiness: C
Warnings: not prone to insects or disease

Growing Requirements

Light: sun
Location: on trellis or obelisk in perennial border
Soil: tolerates any soil
Propagation: seed; division
Expert Advice: Takes 3–4 years to reach notable size. Seed has low viability. Germination is slow and emergence poor under direct seeding; best to use a seeding bed. Germinate seed at 16°C. Divide in spring.

Buying Considerations

Professionals

Popularity: relatively unknown foliage plant
Availability: occasionally available bare root from specialty growers
Size to Sell: sells best in mature sizes as it matures slowly
On the Shelf: high ornamental appeal
Shrinkage: low; requires little maintenance

Collectors

Popularity: not generally of interest to collectors

Gardeners

Ease of Growth: very easy to grow
Start with: one mature plant for feature plant

What to Try First ...

Asparagus verticillatus

On the Market

Asparagus verticillatus
Inconspicuous white flowers • 2–4 m high, 1–2 m wide

Asperula

p. 408

Genus Information

Origin: Europe, Asia and Australia
Selected Common Names: alpine woodruff, Corsican woodruff
Nomenclature: From the Latin *asper* (rough).
Notes: Much of the taxonomy between this group and *Galium* is very confused.

General Features

Height: 2–15 cm high
Spread: 10–40 cm wide
Habit: cushion- to mat-forming or shrubby alpine perennial
Flowers: fragrant; late spring to early summer; long blooming period
Foliage: rosette-forming; evergreen
Hardiness: C–D
Warnings: not prone to insects or disease
Expert Advice: Blooms later than most alpine and rock garden plants and can help extend blooming period of these gardens.

Growing Requirements

Light: sun
Soil: cool, fertile, gritty, moist, sharply drained soil; tolerates alkaline soil; avoid winter wet
Location: rock gardens; front of mixed borders; troughs; tufa
Propagation: seed; division; cuttings
Expert Advice: Take cuttings of non-flowering shoots in early summer.

Buying Considerations

Professionals

Popularity: gaining popularity; has new varieties
Availability: occasionally available as bare root from specialty growers
Size to Sell: sells best in smaller sizes as it matures fast
Shrinkage: low; requires little maintenance

Collectors

Popularity: of interest to collectors—unique, rare

Gardeners

Ease of Growth: very easy to grow
Start with: several small plants for mass plantings

What to Try First ...

Asperula boisseri, Asperula gussonii, Asperula lilaciflora, Asperula nitida, Asperula nitida ssp. *hirtella, Asperula pontica, Asperula sintenisii* (Select), *Asperula suberosa*

On the Market

Asperula abchasica
Pink flowers in late spring to summer • 5 cm high, 20 cm wide

Asperula boisseri
Fragrant, pink flowers in late spring • 5 cm high, 10–20 cm wide

Asperula cyanchica (syn. *A. tenuiflora*)
Fragrant, pink flowers in summer • 2–5 cm high, 20–40 cm wide

Asperula daphneola
Pink flowers in late spring to summer • 2 cm high, 10–20 cm wide

Asperula gussonii
Fragrant, pink flowers in late spring • 2–5 cm high, 15–30 cm wide

Asperula lilaciflora
Fragrant, lilac-pink flowers in spring • 2–5 cm high, 25–30 cm wide

Asperula nitida
Tubular, rose flowers in early summer • 2–10 cm high, 10–30 cm wide

Asperula nitida ssp. *hirtella*
Rose-pink flowers in late spring • 2–10 cm high, 10–20 cm wide

Asperula nitida ssp. *nitida*
Pink flowers in summer • 5 cm high, 20 cm wide

Asperula nitida ssp. *subcapitellata*
Rose flowers in summer • 10 cm high, 20 cm wide

Asperula pontica
Fragrant, pink flowers in spring • 2 cm high, 20 cm wide

Asperula sintenisii
Pink flowers in summer • Blue-green foliage • 2 cm high, 15 cm wide

(Select) • Pink flowers in summer • 2–5 cm high, 10–20 cm wide

'What-a-Mess' • Pink flowers in early summer • Grey-green foliage • 2–5 cm high, 10–15 cm wide

Asperula suavis
Pink flowers in early summer • 15 cm high, 15 cm wide

Asperula suberosa
Fragrant, clear-pink flowers in spring • 2–8 cm high, 10–20 cm wide

Asplenium
p. 408

Genus Information

Origin: worldwide, except Antarctica
Selected Common Names: wavy hart's tongue fern
Nomenclature: From the Greek *a* (without) and *splien* (spleen), referring to the supposed medical effectiveness. The name used by Dioscorides.

General Features

Height: 30–45 cm
Spread: 50–60 cm
Habit: upright fern
Foliage: unusual leaf forms
Hardiness: C–D
Warnings: not prone to insects or disease
Expert Advice: An excellent shade fern for its upright form.

Growing Requirements

Light: shade
Soil: gritty, moist, organic, well-drained, alkaline soil
Location: woodland gardens; mixed borders; foliage breaks and burns in windy locations
Propagation: spores; division; leaf bases
Expert Advice: Maintain ripe spores at 15˚C (hardy varieties), 21˚C (tender varieties).

Buying Considerations

Professionals

Popularity: gaining popularity as a foliage plant
Availability: generally available as finished product from specialty growers
Size to Sell: sells best in mature sizes as it matures slowly
On the Shelf: high ornamental appeal; foliage breakage (display out of wind)
Shrinkage: low; requires little maintenance

Collectors

Popularity: not generally of interest to collectors

Gardeners

Ease of Growth: generally easy to grow but needs close attention to growing conditions
Start with: one mature plant for instant visual impact

What to Try First ...

Asplenium scolopendrium 'Undulatum'

On the Market

Asplenium platyneuron
Upright to prostrate fronds • 20–45 cm high, 40–60 cm wide

Asplenium scolopendrium
'Undulatum' • Wavy, solid, evergreen fronds • 30–45 cm high, 50–60 cm wide

Aster
p. 408

Genus Information

Origin: Europe, the Americas, Asia and Africa
Selected Common Names: bushy aster, Italian aster, New England aster, New York aster, aster
Nomenclature: From the Greek for "star."
Expert Advice: We divide *Asters* into two groups for information and display purposes: *Spring/Summer Blooming* and *Fall Blooming.*

General Features

Height: 10–100 cm high
Spread: 10–100 cm wide
Habit: clump-forming perennial; may require staking
Flowers: daisy-like; spring/summer or late summer to fall
Hardiness: B–D (may not bloom in B)
Warnings: Fall Blooming: prone to powdery mildew and aphids

Growing Requirements

Light: sun
Soil: fertile, moist, well-drained soil
Location: Spring/Summer Blooming: rock gardens, front of mixed borders; Fall Blooming: mixed borders
Propagation: seed; division; soft cuttings
Expert Advice: Hybridizes easily. May not come true from seed. Divide frequently to keep vigorous.

Buying Considerations

Professionals

Popularity: old-fashioned garden standard
Availability: readily available as finished product and bare root
Size to Sell: sells best in smaller sizes as it matures fast
On the Shelf: keep stock rotated; rapidly overgrows pot; may develop black spots on lower leaves; requires constant cleaning
Shrinkage: Spring/Summer Blooming: low, deadhead regularly; Fall Blooming: high, sensitive to underwatering

Collectors

Popularity: not generally of interest to collectors

Gardeners

Ease of Growth: very easy to grow

What to Try First ...

Aster 'Tiny Tot', *Aster amellus* 'Breslau',
Aster amellus 'Lady Hindlip', *Aster amellus*
'Veilchenkonigin', *Aster novae-angliae* 'Alma
Potschke', *Aster novi-belgii* 'Crimson Brocade',
Aster novi-belgii 'Patricia Ballard'

On the Market

Aster, Spring/Summer
Blooming   p. 408 📷

Aster alpinus
Shades of pink, blue or white flowers in
late spring • 10–20 cm high, 30 cm wide
  'Dunckle Schone' (Dark Beauty) • Dark-
  purple flowers in late spring • 15–20 cm
  high, 20–30 cm wide

Aster alpinus var. *dolomiticus*
Rose-red flowers in midsummer • Deep-
green foliage • Tuft-forming, compact habit
• 10–20 cm high, 10–20 cm wide

Aster coloradoensis
Lavender-pink flowers in early summer
• 15 cm high, 30 cm wide

Aster himalaicus
Lilac to bright-violet flowers with yellow
eye in spring • 15 cm high, 20 cm wide

Aster tongolensis
Lilac-blue flowers in late spring to early
summer • 30–45 cm high, 25–40 cm wide
  'Napsbury' • Dark-lavender flowers in
  summer • 25–40 cm high, 20–30 cm wide

Aster, Fall Blooming   p. 408 📷

Aster
  'Tiny Tot' • Deep-purple flowers with gold
  centres in late summer to fall • 10–15 cm
  high, 15–20 cm wide

Aster amellus
Blue flowers in late summer to fall • 45–60
cm high, 40 cm wide
  'Breslau' • Light-blue flowers in late summer
  to fall • 40 cm high, 40 cm wide
  'Lady Hindlip' • Pink flowers in late
  summer to fall • 45–50 cm high,
  45–50 cm wide
  'Loke Viking' • Light-raspberry flowers
  in late summer to fall • 45–60 cm high,
  30–45 cm wide
  'Mira' • Deep-violet flowers in late summer
  to fall • 40 cm high, 40 cm wide

A

  'Purple Beauty' • Deep-purple flowers in
  late summer to fall • 90–100 cm high,
  90–100 cm wide
  'Purple Monarch' • Medium-purple flowers
  in late summer to fall • 90–100 cm high,
  90–100 cm wide
  'Purple Viking' • Lavender-purple flowers
  in late summer to fall • 45–60 cm high,
  30–45 cm wide
  'Red Monarch' • Deep-pink flowers in
  late summer to fall • 90–100 cm high,
  90–100 cm wide
  'Rose Beauty' • Rose flowers in late summer
  to fall • 90–100 cm high, 90–100 cm wide
  'Thyra Viking' • Dark-pink flowers in late
  summer to fall • 45–60 cm high, 30–45 cm
  wide
  'Veilchenkonigin' (Violet Queen) • Violet
  flowers with yellow centres in late summer
  to fall • Well-drained, fertile, alkaline, moist
  soil • 45–60 cm high, 30–45 cm wide

Aster cordifolius
  'Ideal' • Lavender-blue flowers in fall
  • 75–90 cm high, 45–60 cm wide

Aster ericoides
White to lilac flowers in late summer to fall •
Clump-forming, bushy habit • 30–75 cm
high, 30–45 cm wide
  'Blue Star' • Blue flowers in late summer to
  fall • Clump-forming, bushy habit • 80 cm
  high, 60 cm wide
  'Pink Cloud' • Pink flowers in late summer
  to fall • Clump-forming, bushy habit
  • 60–75 cm high, 45–60 cm wide

Aster x *frikartii*
Lilac-blue flowers in late summer to fall
• 45–60 cm high, 45–60 cm wide
  'Monch' • Lilac-blue flowers in late summer
  to fall • 45–60 cm high, 60 cm wide

Aster laevis
Violet-blue flowers in late summer to fall
• 60–90 cm high, 45–60 cm wide

Aster lateriflorus
  'Coombe Fishacre' • Rose-pink flowers
  in late summer to fall • 60–90 cm high,
  45–60 cm wide
  'Horizontalis' • White flowers with reddish
  eye in late summer to fall • 60–75 cm high,
  60 cm wide
  'Lady in Black' • Clover-pink flowers in
  late summer to fall • Very dark foliage
  • 90–100 cm high, 45–60 cm wide
  'Prince' • Soft-pink flowers in late summer
  to fall • Purple-stained stems and foliage
  • 45–60 cm high, 30–45 cm wide

Aster novae-angliae

'Andenkenan Alma Potschke' (syn. 'Alma Potschke') • Salmon-pink flowers in late summer to fall • 60–90 cm high, 90 cm wide

'Harrington's Pink' • Salmon-pink flowers in late summer to fall • 75–100 cm high, 50–75 cm wide

'Pink Beauty' • Pink flowers in late summer to fall • 90–100 cm high, 90 cm wide

'Pink Parfait' • Pink flowers with deep-pink edges in late summer to fall • 60–90 cm high, 45–60 cm wide

'Pink Winner' • Salmon-pink flowers in late summer to fall • 1 m high, 90 cm wide

Aster novi-belgii

'Alice Haslam' • Double, rosy-red flowers in late summer to fall • 45–75 cm high, 50–75 cm wide

'Blue Gown' • Blue flowers in late summer to fall • 50–60 cm high, 60–90 cm wide

'Blue Lagoon' • Clear-blue flowers in late summer to fall • 30–40 cm high, 30–45 cm wide

'Crimson Brocade' • Semi-double, crimson flowers in late summer to fall • 60–90 cm high, 60–75 cm wide

'Fellowship' • Clear-pink flowers in late summer to fall • 60–90 cm high, 60–75 cm wide

'Freda Ballard' • Dark-raspberry flowers in late summer to fall • 45–60 cm high, 30–45 cm wide

'Jenny' • Double, red flowers in late summer to fall • 45–75 cm high, 50–75 cm wide

'Lady in Blue' • Semi-double, medium-blue flowers in late summer to fall • 45–75 cm high, 45–60 cm wide

'Patricia Ballard' • Lavender-pink flowers in late summer to fall • 60–75 cm high, 30–45 cm wide

'Professor Anton Kippenberg' • Semi-double, wisteria-blue flowers in late summer to fall • 45–75 cm high, 60 cm wide

'Purple Dome' • Rich-purple flowers in late summer to fall • 40–50 cm high, 45–60 cm wide

'Snowsprite' • Pure white flowers in late summer to fall • 45–75 cm high, 40–50 cm wide

'Starlight' • Wine-red flowers in late summer to fall • 40 cm high, 40–50 cm wide

'Winston S. Churchill' • Medium-red flowers in late summer to fall • 60–75 cm high, 45–60 cm wide

Aster sedifolius

Lilac flowers in late summer to fall • 45–75 cm high, 45–60 cm wide

'Nanus' • Lilac flowers in late summer to fall • 30–40 cm high, 45–60 cm wide

Astilbe

p. 408

Genus Information

Origin: China, Japan and North America
Selected Common Names: astilbe, false goatsbeard, false spirea
Nomenclature: From the Greek *a* (without) and *stilbe* (brightness), referring to the lack of brightness of the foliage of some species.
Notes: *A. simplicifolia* 'Sprite' was Perennial Plant of the Year for 1994 as chosen by the PPA (Perennial Plant Association).

General Features

Height: 10–100 cm high
Spread: 20–90 cm wide
Habit: clump-forming woodland perennial
Flowers: feathery panicles; summer
Foliage: feathery, divided
Hardiness: C
Warnings: prone to powdery mildew and aphids

Growing Requirements

Light: shade to a.m. sun; tolerates more sun with good soil moisture
Soil: cool, moist, organic, alkaline-free soil
Location: woodland gardens; foliage may burn in windy locations
Propagation: seed; division
Expert Advice: May not come true from seed. Divide frequently to keep vigorous.

Buying Considerations

Professionals

Popularity: popular, old-fashioned garden standard
Availability: readily available as finished product and bare root
Size to Sell: sells best in any size when blooming; matures fast
On the Shelf: high ornamental appeal; keep stock rotated; rapidly overgrows pot; never allow to dry on the shelf as leaves brown rapidly
Shrinkage: high; sensitive to underwatering

Collectors

Popularity: not generally of interest to collectors

Gardeners

Ease of Growth: generally easy to grow but needs close attention to growing conditions
Start with: one small plant for feature plant and several for mass plantings

What to Try First ...

Astilbe 'Bressingham Beauty', *Astilbe* 'Maggie Daley', *Astilbe* x *arendsii* 'Fanal', *Astilbe japonica* 'Deutschland', *Astilbe japonica* 'Federsee', *Astilbe* x *rosea* 'Peach Blossom'

On the Market

Astilbe

'Bressingham Beauty' • Pink plumes in summer • 60–90 cm high, 60–90 cm wide

'Bumalda' • White plumes in summer • 20–30 cm high, 25–30 cm wide

'Carnea' • Flesh pink plumes in summer • 30 cm high, 30–40 cm wide

'Darwin's Dream' • Deep-pink plumes in summer • 45 cm high, 40–50 cm wide

'Eden's Odysseus' • Soft-pink plumes in summer • Dark-green foliage • 60 cm high, 45–60 cm wide

'Elizabeth Bloom' • Rich-pink plumes in summer • 45–60 cm high, 30–45 cm wide

'Etna' • Dark-red plumes in summer • 45–55 cm high, 45–55 cm wide

'Fata Morgana' • Red plumes in summer • 45–60 cm high, 70–80 cm wide

'Federsee' • Carmine-red plumes in summer • 45–60 cm high, 30–45 cm wide

'Gloria Purpurea' • Carmine-rose plumes in summer • Bronze foliage • 45–60 cm high, 40–60 cm wide

'Hennie Graafland' • Clear-pink plumes in summer • 45–60 cm high, 30–45 cm wide

'Maggie Daley' • Purple-rose plumes in summer • 50–60 cm high, 30–45 cm wide

'Radius' • Bright-red plumes in summer • Dark-green foliage • 60 cm high, 45–60 cm wide

'Vesuvius' • Carmine-red plumes in summer • 45–60 cm high, 45–60 cm wide

'Washington' • White plumes in summer • 60 cm high, 40–50 cm wide

Astilbe x *arendsii*

'Amethyst' • Lilac-pink plumes in summer • 60–90 cm high, 45–60 cm wide

'Brautschleier' (syn. 'Bridal Veil') • Snow-white plumes in summer • 45–60 cm high, 40–50 cm wide

'Cattleya' • Soft-pink plumes in summer • 50–75 cm high, 45–60 cm wide

'Cotton Candy' • Deep-pink plumes in summer • 30–45 cm high, 25–40 cm wide

'Erica' • Heather-pink plumes in summer • 60–90 cm high, 45–60 cm wide

'Fanal' • Red plumes in summer • 45–60 cm high, 60 cm wide

'Feuer' (Fire) • Salmon-red plumes in summer • 60–75 cm high, 45–60 cm wide

'Gloria' • Dark-pink plumes in summer • 70–80 cm high, 45–60 cm wide

'Glut' (Glow) • Bright-red plumes in summer • 60 cm high, 45–60 cm wide

'Granat' • Carmine-red plumes in summer • 60 cm high, 45–60 cm wide

'Hyazinth' (Hyacinth) • Lavender plumes in summer • 75–90 cm high, 45–60 cm wide

'Showstar' • Plumes in a mix of colours in summer • 20–30 cm high, 25–30 cm wide

'W.E. Gladstone' • Creamy-white plumes in summer • 50 cm high, 60 cm wide

'Weisse Gloria' (White Gloria) • White plumes in summer • 60–90 cm high, 45–60 cm wide

Astilbe chinensis

Dense, pale-pink plumes in summer • Coarse foliage • 45 cm high, 30–45 cm wide

'Veronica Klose' • Dense, mauve-pink plumes in summer • Coarse foliage • 30–40 cm high, 20–25 cm wide

'Vision in Pink' • Dense, pink plumes in summer • Coarse foliage • 30–40 cm high, 30–40 cm wide

'Vision in Red' • Dense, pink-red plumes in summer • Coarse foliage • 30–40 cm high, 30–40 cm wide

'Visions' • Fragrant, dense, pink-purple plumes in summer • Coarse foliage • 30–40 cm high, 30–40 cm wide

Astilbe chinensis **var.** *pumila*

Dense, lilac plumes in summer • Coarse foliage • 20–30 cm high, 30–45 cm wide

Astilbe chinensis **var.** *taquetii*

'Purpurlanze' (Purple Lance) • Dense, purple-red plumes in summer • Coarse foliage • 60–90 cm high, 40–50 cm wide

'Superba' • Dense, lavender-pink plumes in summer • Coarse foliage • 60–90 cm high, 45–60 cm wide

Astilbe x *crispa*

'Liliput' • Salmon-rose plumes in summer • 20–25 cm high, 25–30 cm wide

'Perkeo' • Dark-pink plumes in summer • 10–15 cm high, 25–30 cm wide

Astilbe glaberrima **var.** *saxatilis*

Pink plumes in summer • 20–30 cm high, 25–30 cm wide

Astilbe japonica
 '**Bonn**' • Carmine-rose plumes in summer
  • 45–60 cm high, 45–60 cm wide
 '**Bremen**' • Rosy-red plumes in summer
  • 45–60 cm high, 45–60 cm wide
 '**Deutschland**' • White plumes in summer
  • 45–60 cm high, 40–60 cm wide
 '**Elisabeth van Veen**' • Intense purple plumes
  in summer • 45–60 cm high, 40–60 cm
  wide
 '**Ellie van Veen**' (syn. **Ellie**) • White plumes
  in summer • 45–60 cm high, 45–60 cm
  wide
 '**Europa**' • Soft pink plumes in summer
  • 50 cm high, 30–45 cm wide
 '**Koblenz**' • Salmon-red plumes in summer •
  60–75 cm high, 40–60 cm wide
 '**Lollipop**' • Fragrant, maroon plumes in
  summer • 50 cm high, 30–45 cm wide
 '**Mainz**' • Pink plumes in summer
  • 45–60 cm high, 40–60 cm wide
 '**Obergartner Jurgens**' • Carmine-red
  plumes in summer • 40–50 cm high,
  40–45 cm wide
 '**Peaches and Cream**' • White to pink
  plumes in summer • 60 cm high,
  30–45 cm wide
 '**Red Sentinel**' • Rich-red plumes in summer
  • 60–90 cm high, 60–90 cm wide
 '**Rheinland**' • Pink plumes in summer
  • 45–60 cm high, 30–45 cm wide

Astilbe x *rosea*
 '**Peach Blossom**' • Fragrant, soft peach-pink
  plumes in summer • 45–60 cm high,
  30–45 cm wide

Astilbe simplicifolia
 '**Aphrodite**' • Pink-red plumes in late
  summer • 40–50 cm high, 30–45 cm wide
 '**Bronce Elegans**' (Bronze Elegans) • Pink
  plumes in summer • Bronze foliage •
  30–45 cm high, 25–40 cm wide
 '**Pink Lightening**' • Red-purple plumes in
  summer • 30–35 cm high, 30–45 cm wide
 '**Sprite**' • Pale shell-pink plumes in summer
  • 30–45 cm high, 25–45 cm wide
 '**Touch of Pink**' • Fragrant, white plumes
  in summer • 35 cm high, 30–45 cm wide

Astilbe thunbergii
 '**Professor van der Wielen**' • Broad, white
  plumes in summer • 75 cm high,
  45–60 cm wide

'**Straussenfeder**' (Ostrich Plume) • Lilac-
 pink plumes in summer • 90–100 cm
 high, 60–90 cm wide

Astragalus   p. 408 📷

Genus Information
Origin: the Northern Hemisphere
Selected Common Names: milk vetch
Nomenclature: From the name used by
 Dioscorides.
Notes: Genus includes annuals, perennials and
 shrubs. Some are important economically for
 edible seeds and use in cosmetics.

General Features
Height: 2–100 cm high
Spread: 10–60 cm wide
Habit: mat- or clump-forming perennial
Flowers: pea-like, in terminal spikes; attractive
 to bees and butterflies
Foliage: silver-grey
Hardiness: B–C
Warnings: painful to handle
Expert Advice: Some produce unusual,
 inflated seed pods.

Growing Requirements
Soil: fertile, well- to sharply drained soil;
 drought tolerant
Location: rock gardens; dry sites
Propagation: seed; cuttings
Expert Advice: Germination is often erratic, even
 after stratification. Take cuttings in summer.
 Resents being disturbed.

Buying Considerations
Professionals
Popularity: relatively unknown
Availability: occasionally available as bare root
 from specialty growers
Size to Sell: sells best in smaller sizes as it
 matures fast
On the Shelf: holds well in mature sizes
Shrinkage: low; requires little maintenance
Collectors
Popularity: of interest to collectors—unique,
 rare
Gardeners
Ease of Growth: mostly easy to grow but
 needs close attention to growing conditions
Start with: many small plants for mass
 plantings
What to Try First ...
*Astragalus detritalis, Astragalus dolichocarpus,
Astragalus spathulatus, Astragalus utahensis*

On the Market

Astragalus alopecuroides
Yellow flowers in summer • 60–90 cm high

Astragalus alpinus
Blue-violet and white flowers in summer
• 10–15 cm high, 25–30 cm wide

Astragalus angustifolius
White flowers in late spring to early
summer • 20–30 cm high, 30–40 cm wide

Astragalus ceramicus var. *filifolius*
Creamy-white flowers in summer • 40–45
cm high, 20–30 cm wide

Astragalus detritalis
Vibrant magenta flowers in late summer
• Silver-grey foliage • 25–30 cm high,
25–30 cm wide

Astragalus dolichocarpus
Purple flowers in spring • 15–20 cm high,
15–20 cm wide

Astragalus glycyphyllos
Cream-white flowers in late summer
• 45–60 cm high, 60 cm wide

Astragalus kentrophyta
Rose-purple flowers with white tips in late
summer • 2 cm high, 15 cm wide

Astragalus megacarpus
White or lavender flowers in late summer
• 25–30 cm high, 40–45 cm wide

Astragalus propinquus
Pea-like, yellow flowers in late summer
• 90–100 cm high, 90–100 cm+ wide

Astragalus purshii var. *lectulus*
Purple flowers in early summer • Woolly,
silver-grey foliage • 2 cm high, 30+ cm wide

Astragalus simplicifolius
Magenta flowers in spring • 5 cm high,
15–20 cm wide

Astragalus spathulatus
Pale yellow to purple flowers in early
summer • 10 cm high, 10 cm wide

Astragalus utahensis
Pea-like, bright-red flowers in late spring to
early summer • 10–15 cm high, 30–45 cm
wide

Astragalus whitneyi var. *sonneanus*
• Cream flowers with lavender marks
in summer • 15 cm high, 15 cm wide

Astrantia   p. 408

Genus Information

Origin: Europe and Asia
Selected Common Names: great masterwort,
masterwort
Nomenclature: From the Latin "star," referring
to the star-like flowers, or a corruption of
magisterantia (masterwort).

General Features

Height: 25–90 cm high
Spread: 25–90 cm wide
Habit: upright, clump-forming perennial
Flowers: star-like; good for drying; good for
cutflowers
Foliage: airy, delicate
Hardiness: C
Warnings: not prone to insects or disease;
purported to repel slugs
Expert Advice: Interplant among hostas and
other perennials that are prone to slugs.

Growing Requirements

Light: sun or shade; tolerant of wide range of
conditions
Soil: fertile, evenly moist, organic soil
Location: woodland gardens; mixed borders
Propagation: seed; division

Buying Considerations

Professionals

Popularity: gaining popularity; new varieties
available
Availability: readily available as finished
product and bare root—avoid root washed
plants (best bought finished)
Size to Sell: sells best in smaller sizes in
bloom as it matures fast
On the Shelf: keep stock rotated; rapidly
overgrows pot
Shrinkage: high; sensitive to underwatering

Collectors

Popularity: not generally of interest to
collectors

Gardeners

Ease of Growth: very easy to grow
Start with: one small plant for feature plant

What to Try First ...

Astrantia 'Hadspen Blood', *Astrantia carniolica*
'Rubra', *Astrantia major* 'Lars', *Astrantia major*
'Ruby Wedding', *Astrantia major* 'Sunningdale
Variegated'

On the Market

Astrantia
'Hadspen Blood' • Dark-red flowers in
summer • Purple foliage • 60 cm high,
30 cm wide

A

Astrantia carniolica
'Rubra' • Maroon flowers in summer • 30–45 cm high, 25–40 cm wide

Astrantia major
Whitish-green to rose-red flowers in summer • 40–60 cm high, 60–90 cm wide
'Claret' • Dark-red flowers in summer • 60–75 cm high, 45–60 cm wide
'Lars' • Wine-red flowers in summer • 50–65 cm high, 45–60 cm wide
'Primadonna' • Purple flowers in late spring to early summer • 60–75 cm high, 45–60 cm wide
'Roma' • Pink flowers in summer • 70 cm high, 45–60 cm wide
'Rosea' • Deep rose-red flowers in late spring to early summer • 60–90 cm high, 45–60 cm wide
'Ruby Wedding' • Dark-red flowers in summer • 60–75 cm high, 45–60 cm wide
'Sunningdale Variegated' (syn. 'Variegata') • Pale-pink flowers in summer • Creamy-yellow, variegated foliage • Requires full sun • 45–75 cm high, 30–45 cm wide

Astrantia maxima
Large, rose flowers in late spring to early summer • 45–60 cm high, 60 cm wide

Asyneuma  p. 408

Genus Information
Origin: the Mediterranean, Europe and the Caucasus
Selected Common Names: harebell
Nomenclature: From the Greek *a* (without) and *syn* (together) and *Phyteuma* (a genus), referring to the lack of a joined corolla lobe during flowering.
Notes: Closely related to *Phyteuma*. Member of the *Campanula* genus.

General Features
Height: 15–90 cm high
Spread: 10–30 cm wide
Habit: clump-forming perennial
Flowers: bell-like; spring to summer
Hardiness: C–D
Warnings: Not prone to insects or disease

Growing Requirements
Light: sun
Soil: well-drained soil
Location: mixed borders; rock gardens
Propagation: seed; division; cuttings
Expert Advice: Take basal cuttings in spring.

Buying Considerations
Professionals
Popularity: relatively unknown; sells well in bloom
Availability: occasionally available as bare root from specialty growers
On the Shelf: keep stock rotated; rapidly overgrows pot
Shrinkage: low; requires little maintenance
Collectors
Popularity: of interest to collectors—unique, rare, novelty plant
Gardeners
Ease of Growth: generally easy to grow
Start with: several small plants for instant visual effect
What to Try First ...
Asyneuma limonifolium, Asyneuma trichostegium

On the Market
Asyneuma limonifolium
Violet-blue flowers in summer • 60–90 cm high, 30 cm wide
Asyneuma limonifolium ssp. *olympicum*
Dark-blue flowers in summer • 60–90 cm high, 30 cm wide
Asyneuma trichostegium
Star-shaped, blue to purple flowers in spring • 15 cm high, 10–15 cm wide

Athyrium p. 408

Genus Information
Origin: temperate and tropical regions
Selected Common Names: Japanese painted fern, lady fern
Nomenclature: From the Greek *athoros* (good at breeding), referring to the diverse forms of the sori.

General Features
Height: 30–150 cm high
Spread: 30–150 cm wide
Habit: creeping, rhizomatous fern
Foliage: pinnately leaved, deciduous
Hardiness: B–C
Warnings: not prone to insects or disease

Growing Requirements
Light: shade
Soil: humus-rich, moist, neutral to acidic soil
Location: woodland; shade gardens; foliage breaks and burns in windy locations
Propagation: spores; division
Expert Advice: Cultivars may not come true from spores.

Buying Considerations

Professionals

Popularity: fast-selling, garden standard foliage plant

Availability: readily available as finished product and bare root (bare roots are slow to emerge in pot)

Size to Sell: sells best in mature sizes as it matures slowly

On the Shelf: high ornamental appeal; keep stock rotated; foliage breakage (display out of wind); keep plants spaced and cleaned

Shrinkage: low

Collectors

Popularity: not generally of interest to collectors

Gardeners

Ease of Growth: mostly easy to grow but needs close attention to growing conditions

Start with: one mature plant for feature plant and several for mass plantings

What to Try First ...

Athyrium 'Ghost', *Athyrium filix-femina* 'Vernoniae Cristatum', *Athyrium niponicum* var. *pictum* 'Silver Falls', *Athyrium niponicum* var. *pictum*

On the Market

Athyrium

'Ghost' • Silvery-white fronds mature to green • 45–60 cm high, 30–45 cm wide

Athyrium filix-femina

Fine, lacy foliage • 30–60 cm high, 30–40 cm wide

'Frizelliae' • Fine, lacy foliage • 35–40 cm high, 30–40 cm wide

'Lady in Red' • Burgundy stemmed, mint-green foliage • 60–75 cm high, 60–150 cm wide

'Vernoniae Cristatum' • Fine, lacy foliage with red-brown stems • 60–150 cm high, 60 cm wide

Athyrium niponicum var. *pictum* (syn. 'Metallicum')

Metallic-grey foliage with purple veins • 30–45 cm high, 30–45 cm wide

'Burgundy Lace' • Metallic-burgundy foliage with purple veins • 30–45 cm high, 30–45 cm wide

'Silver Falls' • Silvery foliage with red veins • 40 cm high, 30 cm wide

'Wildwood Twist' • Smoky-grey and green twisted fronds • 45 cm high, 30 cm wide

Aubrieta

p. 408

A

Genus Information

Origin: southern Europe, Iran and Lebanon

Selected Common Names: alpine rockcress, false rockcress, rockcress

Nomenclature: Named for Claude Aubriet, a French botanical artist.

Notes: Closely related to and resembling *Arabis*.

General Features

Height: 5–20 cm high

Spread: 20–60 cm wide

Habit: groundcover alpine perennial

Flowers: spring to early summer

Foliage: evergreen

Hardiness: C

Warnings: not prone to disease; prone to slugs and flea beetles

Expert Advice: Deadhead to extend blooming season, to keep plant compact and to encourage fresh growth.

Growing Requirements

Light: sun; low tolerance for shade

Soil: lean, well-drained soil

Location: rock gardens; walls; front of mixed borders; early dormancy may occur in hot locations

Propagation: seed; division; cuttings

Expert Advice: Hybridizes easily. May not come true from seed. Divide in spring. Take cuttings after flowering.

Buying Considerations

Professionals

Popularity: popular garden standard; fast seller

Availability: readily available as finished product from specialty growers

Size to Sell: sells best in smaller sizes when blooming as it matures fast

On the Shelf: high ornamental appeal; keep stock rotated: centres tend to brown if overwatered

Shrinkage: low; requires little maintenance

Collectors

Popularity: of interest to collectors—unique

Gardeners

Ease of Growth: very easy to grow

Start with: one small plant for feature plant and several for mass plantings

What to Try First ...

Aubrieta 'Blaue Schonheit', *Aubrieta* 'Blaumeise', *Aubrieta* 'Purple Heart', *Aubrieta* 'Schloss Eckberg', *Aubrieta canescens*, *Aubrieta deltoidea* 'Tauricola'

On the Market

Aubrieta
White, red or purple flowers in spring
• 10–15 cm high, 45–60 cm wide

'Argenteovariegata' • Purple flowers
in spring • Gold, variegated foliage
• 5–10 cm high, 60 cm wide

'Bengal' • Semi-double, red or purple
flowers in spring • 10 cm high, 30–40 cm
wide

'Blaumeise' • Violet-blue flowers in spring •
10 cm high, 30 cm wide

'Blue Beauty' (Blaue Schonheit) • Purple-
blue flowers in spring • 10 cm high, 30 cm
wide

'Blue Emperor' • Blue flowers in spring to
early summer • 5–10 cm high, 45–60 cm
wide

'Gurgedyke' • Flowers in spring to early
summer • 8–10 cm high, 30–40 cm wide

'Purple Heart' • Royal-purple flowers in
spring • 10 cm high, 30 cm wide

'Schloss Eckberg' • Red-purple flowers in
spring • 10–15 cm high, 45–60 cm wide

'Variegata' • Lavender-purple flowers in
spring • Variegated foliage • 10–15 cm
high, 45–60 cm wide

Cascade Series
'Blue Cascade' • Violet-blue flowers in
spring • 10–20 cm high, 25–30 cm wide

'Purple Cascade' • Purple flowers in spring •
10–20 cm high, 25–30 cm wide

'Red Cascade' • Red-purple flowers in
spring • 10–20 cm high, 25–30 cm wide

Aubrieta canescens
Bright mauve-pink flowers in spring
• 8–10 cm high, 30–40 cm wide

Aubrieta canescens ssp. canescens
Violet flowers in spring • Silvery, evergreen
foliage • 5–15 cm high, 30–45 cm wide

Aubrieta deltoidea
Red-purple to violet flowers in spring
• 8–15 cm high, 45–60 cm wide

'Blue Indigo' • Clear-blue flowers in spring •
Green foliage • 8 cm high, 45 cm wide

'Borsch's White' • White flowers tinged with
pink in spring • 8 cm high, 45 cm wide

'Tauricola' (f. Greece) • Purple-blue flowers
in spring • 15–20 cm high, 45–60 cm wide

Aubrieta gracilis
Purple flowers in spring • 5–8 cm high,
20–30 cm wide

Aubrieta olympica
Soft-purple flowers in spring • 5 cm high,
30–40 cm wide

Aubrieta pinardii
Purple flowers in spring • 5–7 cm high,
30–60 cm wide

Aubrieta scardica
Lavender flowers in spring • 5 cm high,
20–30 cm wide

Aurinia

p. 409

Genus Information

Origin: central and southern Europe
Selected Common Names: basket of gold,
alyssum
Nomenclature: From the Latin *aureus* (golden),
referring to the flower colour.
Notes: Closely related to and formerly part of
the genus *Alyssum*. A member of the mustard
family.

General Features

Height: 5–30 cm high
Spread: 15–90 cm wide
Habit: groundcover perennial
Flowers: (most) yellow; spring
Foliage: evergreen
Hardiness: C
Warnings: prone to flea beetles; not prone
to disease

Growing Requirements

Light: sun
Soil: lean, well-drained soil
Location: rock gardens; front of mixed borders;
rock edges; cascading over walls
Propagation: seed; cuttings
Expert Advice: Take cuttings in early summer.

Buying Considerations

Professionals
Popularity: old-fashioned garden standard
Availability: readily available as finished
product
Size to Sell: sells best in smaller sizes when
blooming as it matures fast
On the Shelf: keep stock rotated; rapidly
overgrows pot: clean regularly
Shrinkage: high; sensitive to overwatering

Collectors
Popularity: not generally of interest to
collectors

Gardeners
Ease of Growth: very easy to grow
Start with: one small plant for feature plant
and several for mass plantings

What to Try First ...
Aurinia 'Tom Thumb', *Aurinia saxatilis*

On the Market

Aurinia

'Tom Thumb' • Golden-yellow flowers in spring • Evergreen • 5–8 cm high, 30 cm wide

Aurinia saxatilis **(syn.** *Alyssum saxatile*)
Bright-yellow flowers in spring • 20–30 cm high, 45–90 cm wide

'Citrina' • Lemon-yellow flowers in spring • Evergreen • 20–30 cm high, 45–90 cm wide

'Compacta' • Bright-yellow flowers in late spring • Silvery-grey foliage • 10–20 cm high, 30–45 cm wide

'Dudley Nevill' • Primrose-yellow flowers in spring • Silvery foliage • 15–30 cm high, 15–30 cm wide

'Dudley Nevill Variegated' • Primrose-yellow flowers in spring • Grey and white foliage • 20–30 cm high, 45 cm wide

'Flore Pleno' • Double, golden-yellow flowers in spring • 20–25 cm high, 30 cm wide

'Sunny Border Apricot' • Apricot flowers in spring • 25–30 cm high, 30–45 cm wide

Azorella

p. 409 A

Genus Information

Origin: the Andes and the Falkland Islands
Selected Common Names: unknown
Nomenclature: Name is a diminutive of Azores; exact origin is unknown.

General Features

Height: 2 cm high
Spread: 30–40 cm wide
Habit: mat- to cushion-forming perennial
Flowers: late spring
Foliage: rosettes
Hardiness: C
Warnings: Not prone to insects or disease

Growing Requirements

Light: sun
Soil: lean, well-drained soil
Location: between paving stones; rock gardens; scree; raised beds
Propagation: seed; cuttings
Expert Advice: Remove and replant rosettes. An underused perennial.

Buying Considerations

Professionals

Popularity: relatively unknown foliage plant
Availability: occasionally available from specialty growers
Size to Sell: sells best in smaller sizes as it matures fast
Shrinkage: low; requires little maintenance

Collectors

Popularity: of interest to collectors—unique, rare

Gardeners

Ease of Growth: very easy to grow
Start with: several small plants for instant visual effect

What to Try First ...

Azorella trifurcata 'Nana'

On the Market

Azorella trifurcata
'Nana' • Yellow flowers in late spring • 2 cm high, 30–40 cm wide

Baptisia

p. 409

Genus Information

B

Origin: North America
Selected Common Names: false indigo
Nomenclature: From the Greek for "to dye."
Other Uses: Used by Native Americans as a dye and in medicine.
Notes: Member of the legume (pea) family.

General Features

Height: 40–100 cm high
Spread: 45–90 cm wide
Habit: upright, tap-rooted perennial
Flowers: lupine-like
Foliage: divided, palmate
Hardiness: C
Warnings: not prone to insects or disease
Expert Advice: Produces ornamental seed pods.

Growing Requirements

Light: sun
Soil: gravelly, lean, poor, sandy, well-drained soil
Location: wild gardens; mixed borders; slopes; tolerates sunny, hot, dry areas
Propagation: seed; division
Expert Advice: Resents being disturbed.

Buying Considerations

Professionals

Popularity: gaining popularity
Availability: readily available as finished product and bare root
Size to Sell: sells best in smaller sizes as it matures fast
On the Shelf: keep stock rotated; rapidly overgrows pot
Shrinkage: low; requires little maintenance

Collectors

Popularity: not generally of interest to collectors

Gardeners

Ease of Growth: very easy to grow
Start with: one small plant for feature plant

What to Try First ...

Baptisia 'Carolina Moonlight', *Baptisia* 'Purple Smoke', *Baptisia australis*, *Baptisia australis* v. *minor*

On the Market

Baptisia
'Carolina Moonlight' • Lupine-like, yellow flowers in spring • Upright habit • Neutral to slightly acidic, moist soil • 90–100 cm high, 45–60 cm wide

'Purple Smoke' • Lupine-like, blue-purple flowers in spring • Upright habit • Neutral to slightly acidic soil • 90–100 cm high, 45–60 cm wide

Baptisia australis
Lupine-like, blue flowers in late spring to early summer • 60–90 cm high, 60–90 cm wide

Baptisia australis alba
Lupine-like flowers in summer • 60–90 cm high, 60–90 cm wide

Baptisia var. *minor*
Lupine-like, rich-blue flowers in spring • 40–50 cm high, 45–60 cm wide

Bellis

p. 409

Genus Information

Origin: Europe and the Mediterranean
Selected Common Names: English daisy
Nomenclature: From the Latin *bellus* (pretty).

General Features

Height: 15–25 cm high
Spread: 15–30 cm wide
Habit: clump-forming biennial or short-lived perennial
Flowers: spring
Hardiness: C
Warnings: prone to powdery mildew and aphids
Expert Advice: Does best in cool summers. Deadhead to extend blooming season.

Growing Requirements

Light: shade to a.m. sun; tolerates more sun with good soil moisture
Soil: evenly moist soil
Location: front of mixed borders; rock gardens; mass plantings
Propagation: seed (self-sows readily); division
Expert Advice: Hybrids will not come true from seed. Divide frequently to keep vigorous.

Buying Considerations

Professionals

Popularity: popular, old-fashioned garden standard; fast seller
Availability: readily available as finished product
Size to Sell: sells best in smaller sizes when blooming as it matures fast
On the Shelf: keep stock rotated; rapidly overgrows pot; deadhead regularly
Shrinkage: high; sensitive to overwatering or underwatering

Collectors
Popularity: not generally of interest to collectors

Gardeners
Ease of Growth: mostly easy to grow but needs close attention to growing conditions
Start with: several small plants for mass plantings

What to Try First ...
Bellis perennis, Bellis perennis 'Habanera Pink', *Bellis perennis* 'Habanera Red', *Bellis perennis* 'Habanera Rose', *Bellis perennis* 'Habanera White with Red Tips', *Bellis perennis* 'Monstrosa' (Mix)

On the Market

Bellis perennis
Pink, red or white flowers in summer • 15–25 cm high, 25–30 cm wide

'Habanera Pink' • Large, pink flowers in summer • 15–25 cm high, 30 cm wide

'Habanera Red' • Large, red flowers in summer • 15–25 cm high, 30 cm wide

'Habanera Rose' • Large, rose flowers in summer • 15–25 cm high, 25–30 cm wide

'Habanera White' • Large, white flowers in summer • 15–25 cm high, 30 cm wide

'Habanera White with Red Tips' • White flowers with red tips in summer • 15–25 cm high, 30 cm wide

'Monstrosa' (Mix) • White flowers in summer • 15–25 cm high, 25–30 cm wide

'Monstrosa Rose' • Large, double, rose flowers in summer • 15–20 cm high, 25–30 cm wide

'Monstrosa White' • Large, double, white flowers in summer • 15–20 cm high, 25–30 cm wide

'Super Enorma' • Large, red, white or pink flowers in summer • 15–20 cm high, 15 cm wide

'Tasso Deep Rose' • Large, rose flowers in summer • 15–20 cm high, 25–30 cm wide

'Red Buttons' • Button-like, red flowers in summer • 15–20 cm high, 20–25 cm wide

'Robella' • Double, salmon-pink flowers in spring • 15–20 cm high, 20–25 cm wide

'Rose Buttons' • Button-like, rose flowers in summer • 15–20 cm high, 20–25 cm wide

'White Buttons' • Button-like, white flowers in summer • 15–20 cm high, 20–25 cm wide

Bellis **Pomponette Series**
Double, pink, white or red flowers in summer • 15–25 cm high, 25–30 cm wide

Bergenia p. 409

Genus Information
Origin: East Asia
Selected Common Names: bergenia, elephant ears, giant rockfoil, heart-leaf bergenia, leatherleaf, rockfoil, saxifrage
Nomenclature: Named for Karl von Bergen, a German botany professor.
Notes: Member of the saxifrage family.

General Features
Height: 20–60 cm high
Spread: 25–60 cm wide
Habit: rhizomatous, clump-forming groundcover perennial
Flowers: early spring
Foliage: leathery, semi-evergreen, paddle-shaped; good fall colour; foliage may die back over winter; do not cut back in fall
Hardiness: B–D
Warnings: not prone to insects or disease
Expert Advice: Good for both residential and commercial applications. Has tough, thick rhizomes.

Growing Requirements
Light: sun or shade; tolerant of wide range of conditions
Soil: tolerant of wide range of soils; tolerates acidic soils
Location: mixed borders
Propagation: seed; division
Expert Advice: Hybridizes easily. May not come true from seed.

Buying Considerations

Professionals
Popularity: popular, old-fashioned garden standard; fast-selling foliage plant
Availability: readily available as finished product and bare root
Size to Sell: sells best in smaller sizes when blooming as it matures fast
On the Shelf: high ornamental appeal; keep stock rotated; rapidly overgrows pot
Shrinkage: low; requires little maintenance

Collectors
Popularity: not generally of interest to collectors

Gardeners
Ease of Growth: very easy to grow
Start with: one small plant for feature plant or several for mass planting—best when mass planted

What to Try First ...
Bergenia 'Abendglut', *Bergenia* 'Appleblossom', *Bergenia* 'Baby Doll', *Bergenia* 'Morgenrote', *Bergenia* 'Perfect', *Bergenia cordifolia* 'Bressingham Ruby', *Bergenia cordifolia* 'Glockenturm'

On the Market

Bergenia

'Abendglut' (Evening Glow) • Deep magenta-crimson flowers in early spring • Evergreen foliage • 25–40 cm high, 45–60 cm wide

'Appleblossom' • Light-pink flowers in early spring • Evergreen foliage • 30–45 cm high, 45–60 cm wide

'Baby Doll' • Pink flowers in spring • Evergreen foliage • 20–30 cm high, 45–60 cm wide

'Ballawley' • Bright-rose-pink flowers in spring • Shiny, evergreen foliage • 30–40 cm high, 45–60 cm wide

'Bressingham Ruby' • Red flowers in spring • Evergreen foliage, turns red in fall • 40–45 cm high, 45–60 cm wide

'Bressingham Salmon' • Salmon flowers in spring • Evergreen foliage • 45–60 cm high, 45–60 cm wide

'Bressingham White' • White flowers in early spring • Green, evergreen foliage • 30–45 cm high, 45–60 cm wide

'Britten' • Waxy, white flowers ageing to pink in spring • Evergreen foliage • 30–40 cm high, 45–60 cm wide

'Eden's Dark Margin' • Purple-red flowers in spring • Shiny, maroon, evergreen foliage • 30–40 cm high, 45–60 cm wide

'Eden's Magic Giant' • Purple-red flowers in spring • Shiny, maroon foliage in fall • 40 cm high, 45–60 cm wide

'Eroica' • Dark-purple flowers in spring • Copper-coloured foliage in fall • 30 cm high, 45–60 cm wide

'Glockenturm' (Bell Tower) • Pink-red flowers in spring • Large, glossy, evergreen foliage • 40–50 cm high, 45–60 cm wide

'Morgenrote' (Morning Red) • Dark purple-red flowers in spring • Bronze-green, evergreen foliage • 25–40 cm high, 45–60 cm wide

'Perfect' • Rose-red flowers in spring • Purple evergreen foliage • 40–50 cm high, 45–60 cm wide

'Pink Dragonfly' • Coral-pink flowers in spring • Pink-veined, plum-red foliage in fall • 30–40 cm high, 30–45 cm wide

'Rosi Klose' • Rose-pink flowers in early spring • Evergreen foliage • 30 cm high, 45–60 cm wide

'Rotblum' • Rose-pink flowers in spring • Evergreen foliage • 30 cm high, 45–60 cm wide

'Silberlicht' (Silverlight) • White flowers in spring • Evergreen foliage • 40–45 cm high, 45–60 cm wide

'Wintermarchen' (Winter Fairy Tales) • Rosy-red flowers in spring • Lance-shaped, evergreen foliage • 30 cm high, 45–60 cm wide

Bergenia ciliata

White or pink flowers in early spring • Evergreen foliage • 20–35 cm high, 30 cm wide

Bergenia cordifolia

Pale to dark-pink flowers in spring • Evergreen foliage • 40–45 cm high, 60 cm wide

'Winterglut' • Rose-red flowers in spring • Evergreen foliage • 30 cm high, 30 cm wide

Bergenia purpurascens

Dark-pink flowers in spring • Mahogany-red foliage in fall • 30–45 cm high, 45–60 cm wide

Bergenia stracheyi

White and pink flowers in early spring • Evergreen foliage • 30 cm high, 30 cm wide

Blechnum

p. 409

Genus Information

Origin: the Southern Hemisphere.
Selected Common Names: deer fern
Nomenclature: From the Greek *blechnon*, the old name for fern.

General Features

Height: 20–50 cm high
Spread: 45–60 cm wide
Habit: rhizomatous fern
Foliage: evergreen to semi-evergreen fronds
Hardiness: C–D
Warnings: not prone to insects or disease

Growing Requirements

Light: shade
Soil: moist, organic, well-drained, acidic soil
Location: woodland gardens; shady mixed borders; rock gardens; foliage may break and burn in windy locations
Propagation: spores; division
Expert Advice: Flick the foliage with a finger and if a cloud of dust emerges, the spores are ripe and ready for propagation.

Buying Considerations

Professionals

Popularity: popular foliage plant
Availability: generally available as a finished product from specialty growers
Size to Sell: sells best in small sizes
On the Shelf: high ornamental appeal; foliage breakage (display out of wind)
Shrinkage: low; requires little maintenance

Collectors

Popularity: of interest to collectors—unique

Gardeners

Ease of Growth: mostly easy to grow but requires attention to growing conditions
Start with: one plant for feature plant and several for mass plantings

What to Try First ...

Blechnum spicant

On the Market

Blechnum spicant
Deep-green, leathery, evergreen fronds • 20–50 cm high, 45–60 cm wide

Bolax

p. 409

Genus Information

Origin: South America
Selected Common Names: plastic plant
Nomenclature: From the Greek *bolax* (clod).
Notes: Closely related to *Azorella*.

General Features

Height: 2–5 cm high
Spread: 15–25 cm wide
Habit: cushion-forming groundcover perennial
Flowers: greenish-white, insignificant; summer
Foliage: evergreen
Hardiness: D
Warnings: not prone to insects or disease
Expert Advice: Can form large mounds in the wild, up to 60 cm tall and 120 cm wide, though this is rarely obtained in cultivation.

Growing Requirements

Light: sun
Soil: lean, well-drained soil
Location: between paving stones; rock gardens; alpine gardens; scree
Propagation: seed; cuttings
Expert Advice: Sow fresh seed. Take cuttings in summer. An underused perennial.

Buying Considerations

Professionals

Popularity: relatively unknown foliage plant
Availability: occasionally available from specialty growers
Size to Sell: sells best in smaller sizes
Shrinkage: low; requires little maintenance

Collectors

Popularity: of interest to collectors—unique, rare

Gardeners

Ease of Growth: generally easy to grow
Start with: one small plant or several for instant visual effect

What to Try First ...

Bolax gummifera

On the Market

Bolax gummifera
(syn. B. glebaria, Azorella glebaria)
Greenish-white flowers in summer • Glossy, evergreen foliage • 2–5 cm high, 15–25 cm wide

'Nana' • Small, greenish-white flowers in summer • Glossy, green, evergreen foliage • 2 cm high, 15–25 cm wide

Boltonia

p. 409

Genus Information

Origin: the United States and East Asia
Selected Common Names: thousand-flowered aster
Nomenclature: Named for James Bolton, 1758–1799, a British botanist. Common name is literally from how heavily it blooms.

General Features

Height: 45 cm–2 m high
Spread: 60–100 cm wide
Habit: clump-forming perennial; may require staking
Flowers: aster-like; late blooming (very late on the Prairies); good for cutflowers
Foliage: good fall colour
Hardiness: C
Warnings: prone to aphids

Growing Requirements

Light: sun
Soil: fertile, moist, well-drained soil
Location: mixed borders; wild gardens
Propagation: seed; division; cuttings
Expert Advice: Seed in fall. Divide in spring; divide frequently to keep vigorous.

Buying Considerations

Professionals

Popularity: relatively unknown, old-fashioned perennial

Availability: generally available as bare root

Size to Sell: sells best in smaller sizes as it matures fast

On the Shelf: rapidly overgrows pot; requires cleaning and staking

Shrinkage: high; sensitive to underwatering

Collectors

Popularity: not generally of interest to collectors

Gardeners

Ease of Growth: very easy to grow

Start with: one small plant for feature plant

What to Try First ...

Boltonia asteroides 'Pink Beauty', *Boltonia asteroides* var. *latisquama* 'Snowbank'

On the Market

Boltonia asteroides
  White to pink flowers in late summer to fall
  • 1.5–2 m high, 90–100 cm wide
  'Pink Beauty' • Soft-pink flowers in late summer • 90–150 cm high, 1 m wide

Boltonia asteroides var. *latisquama*
  'Nana' • Blue-purple flowers in summer to fall • 45–75 cm high, 60–75 cm wide
  'Snowbank' • White flowers • 90–150 cm high, 1 m wide

Bouteloua

Genus Information

Origin: United States, Central America, South America and the West Indies

Selected Common Names: blue grama grass, mosquito grass

Nomenclature: Named for Claudio and Esteban Boutelou (brothers), Spanish botanists.

General Features

Height: 20–40 cm

Spread: 30–40 cm

Habit: stoloniferous or rhizomatous annual or perennial grass

Flowers: unique seed heads on wiry stems

Foliage: good for drying

Hardiness: D

Warnings: not prone to insects or disease

Expert Advice: A great clump-forming grass that behaves in the garden. Can be mown.

Growing Requirements

Light: sun

Soil: well-drained soil; tolerates poor soil; drought tolerant

Location: mixed borders; rock gardens; wild gardens; xeriscaping

Propagation: seed; division

Buying Considerations

Professionals

Popularity: gaining popularity as foliage plant

Availability: occasionally available as finished product

Size to Sell: sells best in smaller sizes as it matures fast

On the Shelf: keep stock rotated; rapidly overgrows pot

Shrinkage: low shrinkage; requires little maintenance

Collectors

Popularity: of interest to collectors—native prairie grass

Gardeners

Ease of Growth: very easy to grow

Start with: one small plant as a feature plant, several small plants for instant visual effect and mass plantings

What to Try First ...

Bouteloua gracilis

On the Market

Bouteloua gracilis
  Brush-like, red seed heads in summer
  • 20–40 cm high, 30–40 cm wide

Boykinia

Genus Information

Origin: Japan and North America

Selected Common Names: boykinia

Nomenclature: Named for Dr. Samuel Boykin of the United States.

Notes: Closely related to *Telesonix*, *Heuchera*, *Tiarella* and *Peltoboykinia*.

General Features

Height: 60 cm high

Spread: 60 cm wide

Habit: clump-forming perennial

Flowers: bell-like; early summer

Foliage: kidney-shaped, leathery, glossy dark-green

Hardiness: B–C

Warnings: not prone to insects or disease

Growing Requirements

Light: shade

Soil: fertile, acidic, moist, gritty, well-drained soil; prefers cool roots

Location: wild gardens; woodland gardens

Propagation: seed; division

Expert Advice: Crowns tend to push up out of soil. Replant every 3 years.

Buying Considerations

Professionals
Popularity: relatively unknown
Availability: occasionally available bare root from specialty growers
Size to Sell: sells best in small sizes (when blooming) as it is expensive
Shrinkage: low; becomes rootbound fast

Collectors
Popularity: of interest to collectors—unique, rare

Gardeners
Ease of Growth: generally easy to grow but requires attention to growing conditions
Start with: one small plant for feature

What to Try First ...
Boykinia jamesii, Boykinia richardsonii

On the Market

***Boykinia jamesii* (syn. *Telesonix jamesii*)**
Purplish-rose flowers in early summer • Kidney-shaped, leathery foliage • 15–20 cm high, 15–20 cm width

Boykinia richardsonii
White flowers with purple centre • Kidney-shaped, dark-green foliage • 60 cm high, 60 cm wide

Buying Considerations

Professionals
Popularity: gaining popularity; old-fashioned foliage plant
Availability: occasionally available as finished product or bare root from specialty growers
Size to Sell: sells best in smaller sizes as it matures fast
On the Shelf: high ornamental appeal; rapidly overgrows pot: plants brown if allowed to dry out
Shrinkage: high; sensitive to underwatering

Collectors
Popularity: not generally of interest to collectors

Gardeners
Ease of Growth: very easy to grow
Start with: one small plant for feature plant and several for mass plantings

What to Try First ...
Bromus inermis 'Skinner's Gold'

On the Market

Bromus inermis* • *Grass
'Skinner's Gold' • Seed heads in summer • Bright-green and gold foliage • 60–90 cm high, 60+ cm wide

Bromus p. 409

Genus Information
Origin: Europe, Asia and North America
Selected Common Names: brome grass
Nomenclature: From the Latin *bromos* (oat).

General Features
Height: 60–90 cm high
Spread: 60+ cm wide
Habit: creeping rhizomatous grass
Flowers: seed heads in summer; good for drying
Foliage: solid and variegated
Hardiness: B–C
Warnings: spreading (keep contained and remove seed heads to prevent spread)
Expert Advice: Ruggedly hardy—great for tough areas (alleyways, etc.). Great groundcover or background plant to showcase other perennials.

Growing Requirements
Light: sun
Soil: fertile, well-drained soil
Location: alleyways; difficult locations; meadows; pasture
Propagation: seed; division

Bruckenthalia p. 409

Genus Information
Origin: southern Europe and Asia Minor
Selected Common Names: spike heath
Nomenclature: Named after Samuel Baron von Bruckenthal, an Austrian nobleman.
Notes: Closely related to *Calluna* and *Erica*.

General Features
Height: 15–20 cm high
Spread: 20–30 cm wide
Habit: shrubby perennial
Flowers: spring to early summer
Foliage: evergreen
Hardiness: D
Warnings: not prone to bugs or disease
Expert Advice: Try it planted around evergreens.

Growing Requirements
Light: sun
Soil: humus-rich, lean, well-drained, acidic soil
Location: rock gardens; alpine gardens
Propagation: seed; cuttings
Expert Advice: Seed in spring. Take semi-ripe cuttings in summer and provide cuttings with gentle bottom heat.

Buying Considerations

Professionals

Popularity: relatively unknown foliage plant
Availability: occasionally available from specialty growers
Size to Sell: sells best in smaller sizes (when blooming)
Shrinkage: low; requires little maintenance; sensitive to underwatering

Collectors

Popularity: of interest to collectors—unique, rare

Gardeners

Ease of Growth: generally easy to grow but needs close attention to growing conditions
Start with: one small plant for feature plant and several for mass plantings

What to Try First ...

Bruckenthalia spiculifolia

On the Market

Bruckenthalia spiculifolia
Bell-shaped, pink flowers in spring to early summer • Evergreen • 15–20 cm high, 20–30 cm wide

Brunnera

p. 409

Genus Information

Origin: eastern Europe and western Siberia
Selected Common Names: heartleaf forget-me-not, variegated heartleaf forget-me-not
Nomenclature: Named for Swiss botanist Samuel Brunner.
Notes: Closely related to *Anchusa* and *Myosotis*.

General Features

Height: 30–45 cm high
Spread: 30–60 cm wide
Habit: rhizomatous perennial
Flowers: blue; spring
Foliage: green or variegated
Hardiness: C
Warnings: prone to aphids; prone to powdery mildew

Growing Requirements

Light: shade to a.m. sun; shelter from hot p.m. sun; tolerates more sun with good soil moisture; variegated varieties prone to scorching
Soil: moist, organic, well-drained soil; provide consistent moisture—do not allow to dry out
Location: shady mixed borders; woodland gardens; sheltered locations—foliage may burn in windy locations
Propagation: seed; division; cuttings
Expert Advice: Variegated forms may not come true from seed. Separate and replant rooted pieces.

Buying Considerations

Professionals

Popularity: popular, old-fashioned foliage plant
Availability: readily available as finished product and bare root
Size to Sell: sells best in mature sizes (when blooming); matures fast
On the Shelf: (some) high ornamental appeal; keep stock rotated; rapidly overgrows pot; variegated cultivars burn in full sun on shelves
Shrinkage: low; sensitive to underwatering

Collectors

Popularity: of interest to collectors; can be expensive

Gardeners

Ease of Growth: generally easy to grow but needs close attention to growing conditions
Start with: one mature plant for feature plant and several for mass plantings

What to Try First ...

Brunnera macrophylla, *Brunnera macrophylla* 'Betty Bowring', *Brunnera macrophylla* 'Dawson's White', *Brunnera macrophylla* 'Jack Frost'

On the Market

Brunnera macrophylla
Forget-me-not, blue flowers • Heart-shaped foliage • 30–40 cm high, 40–45 cm wide
'Betty Bowring' • Forget-me-not, white flowers • Rounded foliage • 30–40 cm high, 30–45 cm wide
'Dawson's White' (syn. Variegata)• Forget-me-not, blue flowers in spring • Heart-shaped foliage is green with wide cream margins • 30–40 cm high, 40–45 cm wide
'Hadspen Cream' • Forget-me-not, blue flowers • Heart-shaped, variegated foliage • 30–40 cm high, 35–40 cm wide
'Jack Frost' • Forget-me-not, blue flowers • Heart-shaped, silvery-green foliage • 35 cm high, 45–60 cm wide
'Langtrees' • Forget-me-not, sky-blue flowers • Heart-shaped, silver-dotted foliage • 30–40 cm high, 40 cm wide
'Looking Glass' • Blue flowers in spring • Silvery-green foliage ages to solid silver • 30–35 cm high, 45–60 cm wide
'Silver Wings' • Forget-me-not, sky-blue flowers • Heart-shaped, silvery-green foliage • 30–45 cm high, 45–60 cm wide

Buphthalmum

p. 409

Genus Information

Origin: Europe and Asia Minor
Selected Common Names: oxeye daisy
Nomenclature: From the Greek *bous* (ox) and *opthalmos* (eye), referring to the daisy-like flowers.
Notes: Closely related to *Inula*.

General Features

Height: 45–60 cm high
Spread: 45–60 cm wide
Habit: clump-forming perennial
Flowers: yellow, daisy-like; summer; good for cutting; good for drying; long blooming period
Foliage: willow-like; dark-green
Hardiness: C
Warnings: prone to powdery mildew and aphids

Growing Requirements

Light: sun
Soil: moist, well-drained soil; tolerates lean soil once established; drought tolerant
Location: mixed borders; rock gardens; wild gardens
Propagation: seed; division
Expert Advice: Rich soil produces excessive growth at the expense of flowers. Divide in spring.

Buying Considerations

Professionals
Popularity: relatively unknown old-fashioned perennial
Availability: occasionally available from specialty growers; older species not readily available
Shrinkage: low; requires little maintenance

Collectors
Popularity: of interest to collectors—rare

Gardeners
Ease of Growth: very easy to grow
Start with: one small plant for feature plant

What to Try First ...
Buphthalmum salicifolium

On the Market

Buphthalmum salicifolium
Yellow flowers in summer • Willow-like, dark-green foliage • 45–60 cm high, 45–60 cm wide

Calamagrostis p. 409 📷

Genus Information

Origin: Northern Hemisphere
Selected Common Names: feather reed grass
Nomenclature: From the Greek *calamos* (reed) and *agrostis* (grass).

General Features

Height: 75–150 cm high
Spread: 30–45 cm wide
Habit: strong-growing, upright, cold-season, clump-forming or creeping grass; does not need staking
Flowers: plumes; summer; good for drying
Foliage: good for winter interest
Hardiness: C
Warnings: prone to aphids and rust
Expert Advice: Very hardy on the Prairies. Excellent choice for commercial applications. Provides height in borders.

Growing Requirements

Light: sun
Soil: moist, organic soil
Location: mixed borders
Propagation: division
Expert Advice: Divide in spring.

Buying Considerations

Professionals

Popularity: popular garden standard; fast-selling foliage plant
Availability: readily available as finished product and bare root
Size to Sell: sells best in smaller sizes as it matures fast
On the Shelf: high ornamental appeal; keep stock rotated; rapidly overgrows pot
Shrinkage: low; requires little maintenance

Collectors

Popularity: not generally of interest to collectors

Gardeners

Ease of Growth: very easy to grow
Start with: one small plant for feature plant

What to Try First ...

Calamagrostis x *acutiflora* 'Avalanche',
Calamagrostis x *acutiflora* 'Karl Foerster',
Calamagrostis x *acutiflora* 'Overdam'

On the Market

Calamagrostis x *acutiflora*
   'Avalanche' • Seed heads in late summer • White-centred, green foliage • 90–150 cm high, 30–45 cm wide
   'Karl Foerster' • Light-pink seed heads, fading to tan in late summer • 90–150 cm high, 30–45 cm wide
   'Overdam' • Pink seed heads in late summer • Variegated foliage • 75–120 cm high, 30–45 cm wide

Calamagrostis brachytricha
   Reddish seed heads in fall • Arching foliage • 90–100 cm high, 30–45 cm wide

Callianthemum p. 409 📷

Genus Information

Origin: Europe and Asia
Selected Common Names: unknown
Nomenclature: From the Greek *kallos* (beauty) and *anthemon* (flower).

General Features

Height: 10 cm
Spread: 20 cm
Habit: clump-forming alpine perennial
Flowers: delicate, buttercup-like; white to pink; large flower for a small plant; spring, reblooms in fall
Foliage: rosettes; finely divided
Hardiness: C
Warnings: not prone to insects or disease

Growing Requirements

Light: sun
Soil: cool, moist, gritty, well-drained soil
Location: scree; rock gardens; alpine gardens
Propagation: seed; division
Expert Advice: Sow seed when ripe and keep cool and shaded until germination. Divide in spring.

Buyer Advice

Professionals

Popularity: relatively unknown, fast seller in bloom
Availability: occasionally available from specialty growers
Size to Sell: sells best in smaller sizes
Shrinkage: low shrinkage; requires little maintenance

Collectors

Popularity: of interest to collectors—unique, rare

On the Market

Callianthemum kernerianum
Pale-pink flowers flushed rosy-purple with green eye in early spring • Fern-like foliage • 10 cm high, 20 cm wide

Callirhoe

p. 409

Genus Information

Origin: the United States and Mexico
Selected Common Names: poppy mallow, winecups
Nomenclature: From the Greek mythological name for the daughter of the river god Achelous.

General Features

Height: 20–45 cm high
Spread: 30–100 cm wide
Habit: tap-rooted, clump-forming groundcover perennial
Flowers: large, showy; summer
Foliage: deeply palmated
Hardiness: D
Warnings: prone to spider mites, rust and powdery mildew

Growing Requirements

Light: sun
Soil: lean, organic, sandy, well-drained soil
Location: rock gardens; front of mixed borders; rock walls; raised beds; cascading over walls; wildflower gardens
Propagation: seed (self-sows); division; cuttings
Expert Advice: Seed in spring. Division is difficult because of the long taproot. Softwood cuttings are best taken in summer.

Buying Considerations

On the Market

Callirhoe alcaeoides
'Logan Calhoun' • Cup-shaped, white flowers in summer • 20–30 cm high, 90–100 cm wide

Callirhoe involucrata
Large, wine-red flowers in summer • 30–45 cm high, 30–45 cm wide

Calluna

p. 409

Genus Information

Origin: Europe, Turkey, Siberia, Morocco and the Azores
Selected Common Names: Scotch heather
Nomenclature: From the Greek *kallunein* (to beautify), referring to the use of the stems for sweeping.
Other Uses: Produces honey, which is highly valued in some parts of the world.

General Features

Height: 10–60 cm
Spread: 25–60 cm
Habit: small shrub
Flowers: shades of pink, white, red and purple; darker varieties flower later than pastels; attractive to bees
Foliage: evergreen
Hardiness: D
Warnings: not prone to insects or disease
Expert Advice: Grow in a sheltered location on the Prairies as it is prone to winter desiccation.

Growing Requirements

Light: sun
Soil: moist, organic, well-drained, acidic soil
Location: rockeries; feature shrub; groundcover; cool roots
Propagation: cuttings; layering
Expert Advice: Take cuttings in summer. Layering is best done in spring.

Buying Considerations

Professionals

Popularity: fast-selling foliage plant

Availability: readily available as finished product

Size to Sell: sells best in smaller sizes (when blooming); matures slowly

On the Shelf: high ornamental appeal; keep stock rotated

Shrinkage: low; requires little maintenance

Collectors

Popularity: not generally of interest to collectors

Gardeners

Ease of Growth: mostly easy to grow but needs close attention to growing conditions

Start with: one small plant for feature plant and several for mass plantings

What to Try First ...

Calluna vulgaris 'Alba Plena', *Calluna vulgaris* 'Darkness', *Calluna vulgaris* 'J.H. Hamilton', *Calluna vulgaris* 'Spring Torch'

On the Market

Calluna vulgaris
Pink to purple flowers in midsummer to fall • 10–45 cm high, 25–45 cm wide

'**Alba Plena**' • White flowers in midsummer to fall • 30 cm high, 45 cm wide

'**Darkness**' • Dark-red flowers in midsummer to fall • 30 cm high, 45 cm wide

'**Elsie Purnell**' • Double, pink flowers in midsummer to fall • 30 cm high, 45 cm wide

'**Goldsworth Crimson**' • Deep-pink flowers in midsummer to fall • 60 cm high, 60 cm wide

'**J.H. Hamilton**' • Pink flowers in midsummer to fall • 10–15 cm high, 20–30 cm wide

'**Spring Torch**' • Mauve flowers in midsummer to fall • 45 cm high, 60 cm wide

Calopogon

Genus Information

Origin: North America

Selected Common Names: grass pink orchid

Nomenclature: From the Greek *kalos* (beautiful) and *pogon* (beard), referring to the beard on the lip.

General Features

Height: 30–45 cm high

Spread: 30 cm wide

Habit: clump-forming, terrestrial orchid

Flowers: purple-pink; late spring

Foliage: grass-like

Hardiness: C

Warnings: not prone to insects or disease

Expert Advice: Goes dormant after flowering. Are CITES plants, meaning that they are illegal to dig up from the wild. We only sell plants that are CITES certified.

Growing Requirements

Light: shade to a.m. sun

Soil: lean, moist, peaty, acidic soil

Location: bog gardens; woodland gardens; warm, sheltered areas

Propagation: division

Buying Considerations

Professionals

Popularity: relatively unknown

Availability: occasionally available from specialty growers

Size to Sell: sells best in mature sizes (when blooming) as it matures slowly

Shrinkage: high shrinkage; goes dormant in pot after flowering

Collectors

Popularity: of interest to collectors—unique, rare

Gardeners

Ease of Growth: mostly easy to grow but needs close attention to growing conditions

Start with: several mature plants for instant visual effect

What to Try First ...

Calopogon tuberosus

On the Market

Calopogon (C. tuberosus x *C. multiflorus)*
Purple-pink flowers in late spring • 30–45 cm high, 30 cm wide

Calopogon tuberosus
Purple-pink flowers in late spring • 30–45 cm high, 30 cm wide

Caltha
p. 410

Genus Information

Origin: northern temperate regions in Asia, North America and Europe

Selected Common Names: marsh marigold

Nomenclature: From the name of a yellow flower that was used by Pliny and Virgil.

General Features
Height: 15–30 cm high
Spread: 15–45 cm wide
Habit: clump-forming or creeping aquatic perennial
Flowers: bright; early spring; may rebloom in fall
Foliage: shiny green, heart- or kidney-shaped
Hardiness: B
Warnings: prone to aphids; not prone to disease
Expert Advice: plant with other perennials that bloom later.

Growing Requirements
Light: shade
Soil: moist to boggy, neutral to acidic soil
Location: shallow ponds; pond edges; bog gardens; moist, shady rock gardens; front of mixed borders
Propagation: seed; division
Expert Advice: May self-sow if conditions are correct, especially in bogs. Keep moist at all times.

Buying Considerations

Professionals
Popularity: old-fashioned perennial
Availability: readily available as finished product
Size to Sell: sells best in smaller sizes (when blooming) as it matures fast
On the Shelf: keep stock rotated; rapidly overgrows pot; requires regular cleaning (lower leaves tend to brown)
Shrinkage: low; sensitive to underwatering

Collectors
Popularity: not generally of interest to collectors

Gardeners
Ease of Growth: generally easy to grow but needs close attention to growing conditions
Start with: one small plant for feature plant

What to Try First ...
Caltha palustris, Caltha palustris 'Plena'

On the Market

Caltha leptosepala
Cream-white flowers with yellow centre in spring to early summer • 15–30 cm high, 15–30 cm wide

Caltha palustris
Single, yellow-buttercup flowers in early spring • Kidney-shaped, dark-green foliage • 15–25 cm high, 30–45 cm wide

Caltha palustris
'Plena' • Double, yellow-buttercup flowers in early spring • Kidney-shaped, dark-green foliage • 15–25 cm high, 30–45 cm wide

Calypso
p. 410

Genus Information
Origin: Scandinavia, Russia and North America
Selected Common Names: calypso orchid
Nomenclature: From the Greek *Calypso,* referring to the sea nymph famed for her elusiveness.

C

General Features
Height: 10–15 cm high
Spread: 15–20 cm wide
Habit: terrestrial orchid
Flowers: rosy-pink; single; spring
Hardiness: B–C
Warnings: not prone to insects or disease
Expert Advice: Many are endangered and are CITES plants, meaning that they are illegal to dig up from the wild. We sell plants that are of blooming size and CITES certified.

Growing Requirements
Light: shade to a.m. sun
Soil: humus-rich, moist, organic, acidic soil
Location: alpine house; cool rockeries; woodland gardens; bog gardens
Propagation: seed; offsets
Expert Advice: Separate and replant offsets.

Buying Considerations

Professionals
Popularity: relatively unknown
Availability: occasionally available from specialty growers
Size to Sell: sells best in mature sizes (when blooming); matures slowly
On the Shelf: keep stock rotated; very sensitive and needs very specific growing media
Shrinkage: high; goes dormant in pot

Collectors
Popularity: of interest to collectors—unique, rare, challenging

Gardeners
Ease of Growth: very difficult to grow and needs close attention to specific growing conditions
Start with: one mature plant for feature plant

What to Try First ...
Calypso bulbosa

On the Market

Calypso bulbosa
White to purple flowers in spring • 10–15 cm high, 15–20 cm wide

Calypso bulbosa occidentalis
Small, pink flowers in early summer • 10–15 cm high, 15–20 cm wide

Calyptridium

p. 410 📷

Genus Information

Origin: South America and North America
Selected Common Names: pussy paws
Nomenclature: From the Greek *kaluptra* (a cap or covering), referring to the way the petals close over the caps.

General Features

Height: 10–15 cm high
Spread: 30–40 cm wide
Habit: short-lived perennial
Flowers: late spring to early summer
Hardiness: D
Warnings: prone to aphids; not prone to disease

Growing Requirements

Light: sun
Soil: sharply drained soil; protect from excess rain
Location: alpine house; raised beds; scree
Propagation: seed (self-sows readily)

Buying Considerations

Professionals

Popularity: relatively unknown
Availability: occasionally available from specialty grower
Size to Sell: sells best in mature sizes (when blooming); matures fast
On the Shelf: rapidly overgrows pot
Shrinkage: low; requires little maintenance

Collectors

Popularity: not generally of interest to collectors

Gardeners

Ease of Growth: very easy to grow
Start with: one small plant for feature plant

What to Try First ...

Calyptridium umbellatum

On the Market

Calyptridium umbellatum
Pink flowers (rarely white) in late spring to early summer • 10–15 cm high, 30–40 cm wide

'Powder Puffs' • Pink or white flowers in late spring to early summer • 10–15 cm high, 30–40 cm wide

Calystegia

p. 410 📷

Genus Information

Origin: tropical regions and temperate regions
Selected Common Names: morning glory, perennial morning glory
Nomenclature: From the Greek *kalyx* (calyx) and *stege* (covering), referring to the bracteoles that partly or wholly cover the calyx.
Notes: The genus includes some troublesome weeds. Closely related to *Convolvulus*.

General Features

Height: 40 cm–3 m high
Spread: 2–3+ m wide
Habit: climbing, rhizomatous or aggressively spreading perennial
Flowers: late spring to fall
Hardiness: B–C
Warnings: prone to aphids and powdery mildew; very invasive—large root system spreads over great distances (provide a barrier to keep roots in check)
Expert Advice: Dies back to the ground each year. Not a bush vine but an excellent plant to help prevent erosion on banks.

Growing Requirements

Light: sun or shade; best in sun
Soil: well-drained soil; tolerant of wide range of soils
Location: banks; slopes
Propagation: seed; division

Buying Considerations

Professionals

Popularity: gaining popularity; old-fashioned perennial
Availability: generally available as finished product from specialty growers
Size to Sell: sells best in smaller sizes (when blooming)
On the Shelf: rapidly overgrows pot
Shrinkage: low; requires little maintenance

Collectors

Popularity: not generally of interest to collectors

Gardeners

Ease of Growth: very easy to grow
Start with: one small plant for feature plant

What to Try First ...

Calystegia sepium

On the Market

Calystegia hederacea • *Vine*
'Flore Pleno' • Double, soft-pink flowers in late spring to fall • 3–4 m high, 2–3+ m wide

Calystegia sepium • *Vine*
 White or pink flowers in late spring to
 late summer • 1–2 m high, 40–50 cm wide

Camassia
p. 410

Genus Information
Origin: North America and South America
Selected Common Names: Quamash, camas
Nomenclature: From *Quamash*, a native
 American name for this plant.

General Features
Height: 30–120 cm
Spread: 30 cm or more
Habit: bulbous, clump-forming perennial
Flowers: late spring to early summer; short
 blooming period; good for cutflowers
Foliage: narrow, grey-green
Expert Advice: A long-lived native plant for
 meadows and gardens. Multiplies quickly.

Growing Requirements
Light: sun; shelter from hot afternoon sun
Soil: humus-rich, moist soil
Location: mixed borders; meadow borders;
 wild gardens
Propagation: seed; division; offsets
Expert Advice: Seedlings may take several years
 to reach blooming size.

Buying Considerations

Professionals
Popularity: gaining popularity; sells well
 in bloom
Availability: occasionally available in fall
 as bulb from specialty grower
Size to Sell: sells best in small sizes
 (when blooming) as it matures fast
Shrinkage: low but goes dormant in pot

Collectors
Popularity: of interest to collectors—unique,
 rare

Gardeners
Ease of Growth: generally easy to grow
Start with: one small plant for feature plant

What to Try First ...
Camassia leichtlinii 'Semiplena', *Camassia
quamash*

On the Market

Camassia leichtlinii
 Semi-double, dark-purple flowers in late
 spring • 80–120 cm high, 30+ cm wide
 'Semiplena' • Semi-double, creamy-white
 flowers in late spring • 80–120 cm high,
 30+ cm wide

Camassia quamash
 Purple-blue flowers in late spring •
 30–70 cm high, 30+ cm wide
 'Blue Melody' • Blue flowers in late spring •
 45 cm high, 30+ cm wide

Campanula
p. 410

Genus Information
Origin: Europe, but it is grown worldwide
Selected Common Names: bellflower, Canterbury
 bells, Carpathian bellflower, Carpathian
 harebell, clustered bellflower, fairy thimble,
 peachleaf bellflower, Persian bellflower, spiral
 bellflower
Nomenclature: From *campana* (bell), referring
 to the bell-shaped flowers.
Expert Advice: We divide *Campanula* into 3
 sections for information and display purposes:
 Alpine/Rockery, *Tall Growing* and *Biennial*.

Campanula,
Alpine/Rockery
p. 410

General Features
Height: 5–25 cm high
Spread: 15–60 cm wide
Habit: clump-forming, spreading mat-forming
 or tap-rooted perennial
Flowers: generally blue or white; spring to early
 fall
Foliage: (some) evergreen
Hardiness: B–D
Warnings: prone to slugs; not prone to insects
 or diseases
Expert Advice: Some make excellent
 groundcovers.

Growing Requirements
Light: sun to p.m. sun
Soil: fertile, gritty, moist, well-drained soil;
 tolerant of a wide range of soils: some require
 acidic, others require alkaline; avoid winter wet
Location: rockery; scree; raised beds; tufa
Propagation: seed (some self-sow)
Expert Advice: Seed requires light to germinate.
 May not come true from seed. *C. carpatica* will
 bloom the first year from seed.

Buying Considerations

Professionals
Popularity: popular, old-fashioned garden
 standard; sells well in bloom
Availability: readily available as finished
 product; some from specialty growers
Size to Sell: sells best in smaller sizes
 (when blooming) as it matures fast
On the Shelf: rapidly overgrows pot
Shrinkage: low; requires little maintenance

C

Collectors

Popularity: not generally of interest to collectors except for species

Gardeners

Ease of Growth: generally easy to grow but needs close attention to growing conditions

Start with: one small plant for feature plant and several for mass plantings

What to Try First ...

Campanula 'Hilltop Snow', *Campanula carpatica, Campanula cochlearifolia, Campanula portenschlagiana*

On the Market

Campanula
  'Birch Hybrid' • Tiny, mauve-blue flowers in summer • Vigorous spreading habit • 10–15 cm high, 30–50 cm wide

  'Bumblebee' • Bell-shaped, blue flowers in summer • Spreading habit • Fertile, well-drained, moist, sandy, gritty soil • 2–5 cm high, 20–30 cm wide

  'Glandore' • Star-like, dark blue-violet flowers in summer to fall • Vigorous spreading habit • 8–15 cm high, 30–45 cm wide

  'Heaven' • Single, large, bell-shaped, white flowers in late spring to early summer • 15 cm high

  'Hilltop Snow' • Single, bell-shaped, white flowers in spring to early summer • Tiny foliage • 15–20 cm high, 20 cm wide

  'Samantha' • Fragrant, blue-violet flowers in early summer • Spreading habit • 8–15 cm high, 30+ cm wide

  'Tymonsii' • Soft-mauve flowers in late summer • 10–15 cm high, 15–20 cm wide

Campanula (C. tridentata x *C. bellidifolia)*
Blue-violet flowers in late spring to early summer • 5–10 cm high, 15–20 cm wide

Campanula alpestris
Bell-shaped, purple-blue flowers in spring • Colony-forming • Fertile, well-drained, moist, gritty soil • 5–8 cm high, 25–30 cm wide

Campanula alpina
Bell-shaped, rich-blue flowers in late spring to late summer • 10–15 cm high, 30–45 cm wide

Campanula alpina **ssp.** *bucegiensis*
Blue flowers in late spring to late summer • 10 cm high, 30–45 cm wide

Campanula ardonensis
Blue flowers in summer • Alkaline, moist, well-drained soil • Occasionally grouped with *C. tridenta* • 3–10 cm high, 15–20 cm wide

Campanula argyroticha
Funnel-shaped, powder-blue flowers in late summer • 8–15 cm high, 20–30 cm wide

Campanula aucheri
Bell-shaped, blue flowers in late spring to early summer • Colony-forming • Alkaline, well-drained, gritty soil • 5–15 cm high, 15–20 cm wide

Campanula bellidifolia
Blue flowers in late spring to early summer • 8–15 cm high, 15–20 cm wide

Campanula betulifolia
Bell-shaped, white flowers (sometimes soft-pink flowers) in late spring to summer • 15–20 cm high, 25–40 cm wide

Campanula carnica
Rich purple-blue flowers in summer • 15–25 cm high, 20–25 cm wide

Campanula carpatha
Violet-blue flowers in spring to late summer • 10–15 cm high, 25–30 cm wide

Campanula carpatica
  'Blaue Clips' (Blue Clips) • Bell-shaped, blue to violet flowers in summer • 15–25 cm high, 30 cm wide

  'Blue Moonlight' • Bell-shaped, pale-blue flowers in summer • 20–25 cm high, 20–25 cm wide

  'Blue Uniform' • Bell-shaped, blue flowers in summer • 10–15 cm high, 25–30 cm wide

  'Thor-Pedo Blue Ball' • Double, blue flowers in late spring to summer • 10–15 cm high, 30 cm wide

  'White Uniform' • Bell-shaped, white flowers in summer • 10–15 cm high, 25–30 cm wide

Campanula carpatica **f.** *alba*
Bell-shaped, white flowers in summer • 20–25 cm high, 30 cm wide

  'Weisse Clips' (White Clips) • Bell-shaped, white flowers in summer • 20–25 cm high, 30 cm wide

Campanula carpatica **var.** *turbinata*
Violet-blue flowers in summer • 10–20 cm high, 20–25 cm wide

  'Georg Arends' • Deep-blue flowers in summer • 15–20 cm high, 20–25 cm wide

  'Jewel' • Extra-large, dark-mauve flowers in summer • 10–15 cm high, 15–20 cm wide

'Karl Foerster' • Cobalt-blue flowers in summer • 15–20 cm high, 15–25 cm wide

Campanula cashmeriana
Delicate, soft-blue flowers in summer • 5–10 cm high, 20 cm wide

Campanula cenisia
Slate-blue flowers in late spring to early summer • 5–10 cm high, 15–25 cm wide

Campanula cespitosa
Bell-like, blue flowers in early summer • Moist, well-drained, gritty, alkaline soil • 10–12 cm high, 10–15 cm wide

Campanula chamissonis **(syn. *C. dasyantha*)**
Bell-shaped, blue flowers in late spring to early summer • Colony-forming • Alkaline-free, well-drained, organic, gritty soil • 10–15 cm high, 25–30 cm wide

'Oyobeni' • Bell-shaped, striped blue flowers in late spring to early summer • Colony-forming • Well-drained, gritty, alkaline-free, organic soil • 10–15 cm high, 25–30 cm wide

Campanula choruhensis
White flowers from pink buds in spring • 10–15 cm high, 15–20 cm wide

Campanula cochlearifolia
Dainty clusters of bell-shaped, blue flowers in summer • Tuft-forming, creeping habit • 10–15 cm high, 30–45+ cm wide

'Alba' • Dainty, nodding, white flowers in summer • Tuft-forming, creeping habit • 10 cm high, 15–30+ cm wide

'Bavaria White' • White flowers in summer • Tuft-forming, creeping habit • 10–15 cm high, 45–60 cm wide

'Elizabeth Oliver' • Dainty, double, bell-shaped, blue flowers in summer • Tuft-forming, creeping habit • 10–15 cm high, 30–45+ cm wide

'R.B. Loder' • Blue flowers in summer • Tuft-forming, creeping habit • 10–15 cm high, 45–60 cm wide

'Sleigh Bells' • Dainty clusters of bell-shaped, white flowers in summer • Tuft-forming, creeping habit • 10–15 cm high, 30–45+ cm wide

Campanula collina
Various shades of blue flowers in late spring to early summer • Upright, creeping habit • 20–25 cm high, 20–25 cm wide

Campanula elatines
Various shades of blue flowers in late spring to early summer • Spreading habit • 15–20 cm high, 40–45 cm wide

Campanula excisa
Bell-shaped, lilac-blue flowers in summer • Moist, fertile, well-drained, alkaline-free soil • 10–15 cm high, 25–30+ cm wide

Campanula fenestrellata
Deep-blue flowers in summer • 10 cm high, 30 cm wide

Campanula garganica
Blue to lilac flowers in late spring to summer • Cushion-forming, spreading habit • 5–15 cm high, 20–30+ cm wide

'Dickson's Gold' (syn. Aurea) • Mid-blue flowers in late spring to summer • Yellow-green foliage • Cushion-forming, spreading habit • 8–15 cm high, 20–30+ cm wide

Campanula hakkiarica
Narrow, bell-shaped, blue flowers in late summer • Alkaline, moist, well-drained soil • 6–10 cm high, 15–20 cm wide

Campanula x *haylodgensis*
'Blue Wonder' • Double, nodding, blue flowers in early summer to fall • 10 cm high, 25–35 cm wide

'Marion Fisher' • Double, white flowers in early summer to fall • 8–15 cm high, 25–35 cm wide

'Plena' • Double, light-blue flowers in summer • 10–15 cm high, 10–15 cm wide

'Warley White' • Double, white flowers in early summer to fall • 8–15 cm high, 25–35 cm wide

Campanula hercegovina
Blue-violet flowers in late spring to early summer • 15–30 cm high, 30–40 cm wide

Campanula incurva
Upward-facing, bell-shaped, lavender-blue or sometimes white flowers in summer • Hairy, grey foliage • 10–15 cm high, 30–35 cm wide

Campanula jaubertiana
Bell-like, violet-blue flowers in summer • Colony-forming • 10 cm high, 25–30 cm wide

Campanula kemulariae
Large, bell-shaped, blue flowers in late spring to early summer • 25–30 cm high, 30–40 cm wide

Campanula ledebouriana pulvinata
Violet-blue flowers in late spring • 2–5 cm high, 10–15 cm wide

Campanula massalvskyi
Pale-blue or white flowers in spring • Grey foliage • 5–15 cm high, 5–15 cm wide

Campanula pallida
Soft-lilac to soft-purple flowers in summer •
15–25 cm high, 25–30 cm wide

Campanula patula ssp. abietina
Red-purple flowers in summer • 20–30 cm
high, 20–30 cm wide

Campanula persicifolia var. planiflora
Bell-shaped, blue flowers in summer •
15 cm high, 15–20 cm wide

**Campanula persicifolia var. planiflora
f. alba**
Large, white flowers in summer • 15 cm
high, 15–20 cm wide

Campanula piperi
Purple-blue flowers • 2–5 cm high,
10–25 cm wide

**Campanula portenschlagiana
(syn. C. muralis)**
Purple flowers in summer • Evergreen •
Alkaline, well-drained, moist soil •
15–20 cm high, 30–45+ cm wide

'Get Me' • Blue flowers in summer •
Evergreen • Alkaline, well-drained, moist
soil • 10–15 cm high, 40–45 cm wide

'Hoffman's Blue' • Violet-blue flowers in
summer • Evergreen • Alkaline, well-
drained, moist soil • 15 cm high, 30+ cm
wide

'Resholdt's Variety' • Deep-blue flowers in
summer • Evergreen • Alkaline, well-
drained, moist soil • 20–25 cm high,
40–45 cm wide

Campanula poscharskyana
Pale-lavender flowers in summer to fall •
Vigorous spreading habit • 10–20 cm high,
30–60 cm wide

'Blue Cascade' • Violet-blue flowers in
summer to fall • Vigorous spreading habit
• 15–25 cm high, 45–60 cm wide

'Blue Gown' • Soft-blue flowers with white
eye in summer to fall • Vigorous spreading
habit • 10–15 cm high, 45–60 cm wide

'Blue Waterfall' • Blue flowers in summer to
fall • Vigorous spreading habit • 8–15 cm
high, 30–60 cm wide

'E.H. Frost' • Milk-white flowers in summer
to fall • Vigorous spreading habit •
15–25 cm high, 45–60 cm wide

'Stella' • Bright-blue flowers in summer to
fall • Vigorous spreading habit • 10–15 cm
high, 45–60 cm wide

Campanula x pseudoraineri
Large, upward-facing, mid-blue flowers in
summer • Yellow-green foliage • 5–10 cm
high, 10–20 cm wide

Campanula pulla
Bell-shaped, dark-blue flowers in late
spring to early summer • Clump-forming
• Sharply drained, fertile, alkaline, moist soil
• 10–15 cm high, 10–30 cm wide

Campanula x pulloides
Bell-shaped, dark-blue flowers in early
summer • Moist, sharply drained, alkaline,
gritty soil • 10–15 cm high, 20–30 cm wide

'G.F. Wilson' • Deep-violet flowers in
summer • 10–15 cm high, 20–30 cm wide

Campanula raddeana
Nodding, violet-purple flowers in summer
• 15–20 cm high, 30+ cm wide

Campanula raineri
Large, bell-shaped, lavender-blue flowers
• 5–10 cm high, 10–15 cm wide

'Alba' • Large, bell-shaped, white flowers •
Spreading habit • 5–10 cm high, 10–15 cm
wide

Campanula ruprechtii
Blue flowers in summer • 10 cm high, 20 cm
wide

Campanula samarkandensis
Pale-blue flowers in late spring to early
summer • Creeping habit • 10 cm high,
15–20 cm wide

Campanula scabrella
Light-blue flowers in summer • 6–12 cm
high, 10–15 cm wide

Campanula sporadum
Pale-violet flowers in summer • 20–30 cm
high, 20–30 cm wide

Campanula teucrioides
Lilac-blue flowers in summer • 5 cm high,
10 cm wide

Campanula tommasiniana
Bell-shaped, blue flowers in late summer •
Colony-forming • Alkaline, well-drained,
gritty, organic soil • 10–15 cm high,
15–20 cm wide

Campanula tridens
Pale-blue flowers in summer • Fertile,
well-drained location with alkaline soil •
Occasionally grouped with C. tridenata
• 5–10 cm high, 10–15 cm wide

Campanula tridentata
Bell-shaped, lavender-blue flowers in late
spring to early summer • 10–15 cm high,
15–20 cm wide

Campanula troegerae
Pale-pink to white flowers in spring •
10–15 cm high, 15–25 cm wide

Campanula waldsteiniana
Saucer-like, blue flowers in summer
• 10–15 cm high, 30–40 cm wide
Campanula witasekiana
Purple-blue flowers in summer • Colony-forming • 20–40 cm high, 30–45+ cm wide
Campanula zoysii
Shades of blue in summer • 5–8 cm high, 15–25 cm wide

Campanula, Tall Growing p. 410

General Features
Height: 30–120 cm high
Spread: 30–90 cm wide
Habit: spreading to clump-forming perennial; some need staking
Flowers: blue, mauve, pink, red or white; mostly single (some varieties double or semi-double); spring to late summer
Hardiness: B–D
Warnings: prone to powdery mildew and aphids
Expert Advice: Water well prior to freeze-up.

Growing Requirements
Light: sun
Soil: moist, well-drained soil; tolerant of wide range of soils
Location: cottage gardens; mixed borders; woodland gardens; wildflower gardens
Propagation: seed (some self-sow readily); division
Expert Advice: Seed requires light to germinate. May not come true from seed.

Buying Considerations

Professionals
Popularity: popular, old-fashioned garden standards
Availability: readily available as finished product and bare root
Size to Sell: sells best in smaller sizes (when blooming) as it matures fast
On the Shelf: rapidly overgrows pot; (some) requires constant cleaning
Shrinkage: low

Collectors
Popularity: not generally of interest to collectors

Gardeners
Ease of Growth: very easy to grow
Start with: one small plant for feature plant and several for mass plantings

What to Try First ...
Campanula lactiflora 'Prichard's Variety',
Campanula persicifolia 'Alba', *Campanula punctata* f. *rubriflora* 'Bowl of Cherries',
Campanula rotundifolia 'Olympica'

On the Market

Campanula
'Kent Belle' • Large, glossy, tubular, violet flowers in summer • Toothed, heart-shaped foliage • Moist, well-drained, neutral to alkaline soil • 45–60 cm high, 45–60 cm wide
'Mystery' • Pink flowers in late spring to early summer • 75–80 cm high

Campanula alliariifolia
White flowers in summer • 45–60 cm high, 45–60 cm wide

Campanula formanekiana
Near white flowers in summer • 30–45 cm high, 30–45 cm wide

Campanula glomerata
Clusters of bell-shaped, blue flowers in summer • Clump-forming, spreading habit • 45–60 cm high, 45–60 cm wide
'Alba' • White flowers in summer • 45–60 cm high, 30–45 cm wide
'Caroline' • Clusters of star-shaped, mauve flowers with a purple edge in spring to fall • Clump-forming, spreading habit • 40–50 cm high, 30–45 cm wide
'Schneekrone' (Crown of Snow) • Dense clusters of bell-shaped, white flowers in summer • Clump-forming, spreading habit • 45–60 cm high, 45–60 cm wide
'Superba' • Clusters of bell-shaped, violet-purple flowers in summer • Coarse, heart-shaped foliage • 45–60 cm high, 45–60 cm wide

Campanula glomerata var. *acaulis*
Violet-blue flowers in summer • Clump-forming, vigorous spreading habit • 8–15 cm high, 20–30 cm wide

Campanula x *haylodgensis*
Double, nodding, blue flowers in early summer to fall • 10 cm high, 25–35 cm wide

Campanula lactiflora
Various shades of blue flowers in summer • 90–100 cm high, 90 cm wide
'Loddon Anna' • Soft-pink flowers in late spring to late summer • 90–100 cm high, 60–90 cm wide
'Prichard's Variety' • Purple-blue flowers in late spring to late summer • 50–75 cm high, 45–60 cm wide

Campanula latifolia
Bell-shaped, purple-blue flowers in summer • Stoloniferous, clump-forming • 90–100 cm high, 90 cm wide

'Gloaming' • Bell-shaped, smoke-blue flowers in summer • Stoloniferous, clump-forming • 45–60 cm high, 45–60 cm wide

Campanula latifolia **var.** *macrantha*
Bell-shaped, deep-blue flowers in summer • Stoloniferous, clump-forming • 90–100 cm high, 60 cm wide

'Alba' • White flowers in summer • Stoloniferous, clump-forming • 90–100 cm high, 60 cm wide

Campanula latifolia **var.** *macrantha* **x** *C. punctata*
'Stevie Ray' • Large, pendant, pale blue flowers in summer • Stoloniferous, upright habit • 60–90 cm high, 60 cm wide

Campanula patula
Blue-violet flowers in late spring to fall • 60–90 cm high, 60–75 cm wide

Campanula persicifolia
Single, bell-shaped, blue flowers in summer • 60–90 cm high, 30–60 cm wide

'Alba' • Single, bell-shaped, white flowers in summer • 60–90 cm high, 60 cm wide

'Alba Plena' • Large, double, white flowers in midsummer • 75–90 cm high, 60 cm wide

'Chettle Charm' • Single, bell-shaped, white flowers with a tinted blue edge in summer • 60–90 cm high, 30–60 cm wide

'Flore Pleno' • Large, double, blue flowers in midsummer • 75–90 cm high, 60 cm wide

'Kelly's Gold' • Single, white flowers, tinged blue, in summer • Gold foliage • 60–65 cm high, 30 cm wide

Campanula punctata
Tubular, creamy-white to pink flowers with spotted interiors in early summer • Clump-forming, spreading habit • 30–45 cm high, 30–45+ cm wide

'Alina's Double' • Semi-double, rose flowers in early summer • Clump-forming, spreading habit • 40–45 cm high, 30–45+ cm wide

'Cherry Bells' • Tubular, red flowers, spotted inside, in early summer • Clump-forming, spreading habit • 30–45 cm high, 30–45+ cm wide

'Hot Lips' • Pale-pink flowers, spotted inside, in early summer • Clump-forming, compact spreading habit • 15 cm high, 25 cm wide

'Pink Chimes' • Pink flowers • Clump-forming, compact spreading habit • 30–45 cm high, 30–45+ cm wide

'Wedding Bells' • Double, white flowers in early summer • Clump-forming, spreading habit • 30–45 cm high, 30–45+ cm wide

Campanula punctata **f.** *rubriflora*
Creamy-red flowers with red veins and spots • Clump-forming, spreading habit • 30–45 cm high, 45–60+ cm wide

'Bowl of Cherries' • Tubular, cherry-red flowers in early summer • 30–45 cm high, 30–45+ cm wide

Campanula raineri
Large, bell-shaped, lavender-blue flowers • 5–10 cm high, 10–15 cm wide

Campanula rotundifolia
Bell-shaped, shades of blue flowers in summer • Spreading habit • 30–40 cm high, 15–30 cm wide

'Alba' • White flowers in spring to early summer • 30–40 cm high, 15–30 cm wide

Campanula sarmatica
Shades of blue flowers in summer • 30–50 cm high, 45–60 cm wide

Campanula takesimana
Pale-pink flowers with maroon specks in summer to late summer • Spreading habit • 45–60 cm high, 45–60+ cm wide

'Elizabeth' • Purple-pink flowers with maroon marks in summer to late summer • Rapid spreading habit • 30–40 cm high, 30–40 cm wide

Campanula trachelium
'Bernice' • Double, cupped, blue-purple flowers in summer • 60–75 cm high, 30–45 cm wide

'Snowball' • Double, white flowers in summer • 50–60 cm high, 35 cm wide

Campanula versicolor (MESE 648)
Fragrant, saucer-shaped, pale blue-and-violet bicoloured flowers in summer • 40 cm high, 30 cm wide

Campanula, Biennial
p. 410

General Features
Height: 30–90 cm high
Spread: 25–90 cm wide
Habit: rosette-forming biennial
Flowers: pink, blue or white; spring to late summer
Foliage: evergreen
Hardiness: C–D
Warnings: prone to powdery mildew and aphids

Growing Requirements

Light: sun
Soil: fertile, moist, well-drained soil; tolerant of a wide range of soils
Location: sheltered locations; cottage gardens; mixed borders
Propagation: seed
Expert Advice: Seed requires light to germinate. May not come true from seed. Water plants well prior to freeze-up and mulch.

Buying Considerations

Professionals

Popularity: popular, old-fashioned garden standard; sells well in bloom
Availability: *C. medium* readily available as finished product; other biennial types are occasionally available as finished products
Size to Sell: sells best in smaller sizes (when blooming) as it matures fast
On the Shelf: rapidly overgrows pot: requires constant cleaning
Shrinkage: high; sensitive to overwatering or underwatering

Collectors

Popularity: not generally of interest to collectors

Gardeners

Ease of Growth: mostly easy to grow but needs close attention to growing conditions
Start with: one small plant for feature plant

What to Try First ...

Campanula medium, Campanula medium 'Calycanthema'

On the Market

Campanula barbata
China-blue flowers in spring to early summer • 30–45 cm high, 25–40 cm wide

Campanula medium
Large, bell-shaped, pink, white or blue flowers in late spring to early summer • Hairy foliage • 60–90 cm high, 45–60 cm wide

'Calycanthema' • Cup and saucer, pink, white or blue flowers in late-spring to early summer • 60–90 cm high, 30 cm wide

Campanula primulifolia
Blue flowers with a white centre in summer • 60–90 cm high, 60–90 cm wide

Campanula thrysoides
Cream-yellow flowers in summer to late summer • 40–70 cm high, 30–45 cm wide

Campsis

p. 410

Genus Information

Origin: China and North America
Selected Common Names: hummingbird vine, trumpet creeper
Nomenclature: From the Greek *kampsis*.

General Features

Height: 3–6 m high
Spread: 90 cm wide
Habit: weedy, woody shrub or climbing perennial vine; needs sturdy staking or support
Flowers: colourful, honeysuckle-like; summer; attractive to hummingbirds
Hardiness: D
Warnings: prone to aphids and spider mites
Expert Advice: Mulch for winter, and where marginally hardy, place against a warm, sunny wall. It can take up to 7 years to flower in colder climates.

Growing Requirements

Light: sun
Soil: fertile, moist, well-drained soil
Location: sheltered locations; moist woodlands
Propagation: seed; layering; cuttings
Expert Advice: Seed in fall for best germination results.

Buying Considerations

Professionals

Popularity: popular; fast seller
Availability: readily available as finished product
Size to Sell: sells best in mature sizes as it matures slowly
Shrinkage: low; requires little maintenance

Collectors

Popularity: not generally of interest to collectors

Gardeners

Ease of Growth: mostly easy to grow but needs close attention to growing conditions
Start with: one small plant for feature plant

What to Try First ...

Campsis radicans

On the Market

Campsis radicans • Vine
Red-orange flowers in summer • 3–6 m high, 90 cm wide

Campsis radicans f. flava • Vine
Yellow flowers in summer • 6 m high, 90 cm wide

Carex
p. 410

Genus Information

Origin: temperate regions
Selected Common Names: sedge
Nomenclature: From the Latin *keiro* (to cut), which refers to the sharp leaf margins.
Other Uses: *Carex* is important as both a food source and as cover for wildlife.
Notes: A large genus of some 1500 species.

General Features

Height: 8–75 cm high
Spread: 10–90 cm wide
Habit: spreading and clump-forming aquatic grass
Flowers: unisexual seed heads
Foliage: solid and variegated; sharp-edged
Hardiness: C–D
Warnings: not prone to insects or disease
Expert Advice: Produces ornamental seed pods.

Growing Requirements

Light: sun or shade
Soil: fertile, moist to wet soil
Location: bog gardens; moors; woodland gardens; pond gardens; soil erosion control on banks
Propagation: seed; division
Expert Advice: Plant seeds in fall to stratify.

Buying Considerations

Professionals

Popularity: gaining popularity as a foliage plant; slow to sell (colourful varieties sell better, but their hardiness varies)
Availability: readily available as finished product and bare root
Size to Sell: sells best in smaller sizes; some mature slowly
On the Shelf: (some) high ornamental appeal
Shrinkage: low; requires little maintenance

Collectors

Popularity: not generally of interest to collectors

Gardeners

Ease of Growth: mostly easy to grow but needs close attention to growing conditions
Start with: one small plant for feature plant

What to Try First ...

Carex elata 'Aurea', *Carex morrowii* 'Aureo-variegata', *Carex muskingumensis* 'Ice Fountains', *Carex oshimensis* 'Evergold', *Carex siderosticha* 'Island Brocade'

On the Market

Carex albula
'Frosted Curls' • Green seed heads in summer • Silvery-green foliage with curled tips • 45–60 cm high, 30–45 cm wide

Carex aurea
Showy, yellow plumes in summer
• 10–15 cm high, 20 cm wide

Carex buchananii
Evergreen, orange-brown foliage
• 45–60 cm high, 45–60 cm wide

Carex dolichostachya
'Kaga-nishiki' (Gold Fountains) • Gold-edged, green foliage • 30–45 cm high, 45–60 cm wide

Carex elata
'Aurea' • Arching, brilliant yellow foliage
• 45–60 cm high, 45 cm wide

Carex firma
'Variegata' • Deep-green foliage with thin, gold edges • 8 cm high, 10 cm wide

Carex flacca
Purple-tinted seed heads in summer • Blue foliage • 15–40 cm high, 30–45+ cm wide

Carex flacca ssp. flacca (syn. C. glauca)
Broad, blue-grey foliage • 25–30 cm high, 45 cm wide

Carex grayi
Spiked seed heads in summer • Rich-green foliage • 35–50 cm high, 30–45 cm wide

Carex morrowii
'Aureo-variegata' • Green-and-yellow-variegated foliage • Evergreen • 30–45 cm high, 20–30 cm wide

'Ice Dance' • Green-and-white-variegated foliage • Evergreen • 30–45 cm high, 20–30 cm wide

'Variegata' • Rich-green-and-white-variegated foliage • Evergreen • 30–45 cm high, 20–30 cm wide

Carex muskingumensis
'Ice Fountains' • White, spring foliage fades to light green • 70–75 cm high, 45 cm wide

Carex nigra
Black-brown to red-brown flower spikes
• Evergreen • 30 cm high, 30–40 cm wide

'Variegata' • Blue-green foliage with a gold edge • Evergreen • 20–30 cm high, 30–40 cm wide

Carex oshimensis
'Evergold' • Green foliage with a broad, cream-yellow stripe • Evergreen • 30 cm high, 30–45 cm wide

Carex pendula
Arching flower spikes in early summer
• Evergreen • 60 cm high, 90 cm wide

Carex petriei
Copper-coloured foliage with curly tips •
Evergreen • 20–25 cm high, 20–30 cm wide

Carex remota
Fine-textured foliage • 45–60 cm high,
45 cm wide

Carex riparia
Arching green foliage • Aggressive spreader
• 60–100 cm high, 20–30 cm wide

Carex siderosticha
'Island Brocade' • Green foliage with a
broad, cream-yellow stripe • 15 cm high,
30 cm wide

Carlina p. 410

Genus Information
Origin: Asia and Europe (southern and eastern)
Selected Common Names: acanthus leaved
thistle, stemless carline thistle
Nomenclature: From *Carolus* (Charlemagne),
whose army is said to have been cured of the
plague by a plant of this genus.

General Features
Height: 15–20 cm high
Spread: 30 cm wide
Habit: short-lived or monocarpic perennial
Flowers: large, nearly stemless heads; summer;
good for drying
Foliage: prickly or spiny
Hardiness: C
Warnings: prone to rust; spiny foliage is painful
to handle

Growing Requirements
Light: sun
Soil: lean, well-drained soil; drought tolerant
Location: rock gardens; raised beds; sunny, hot,
dry areas
Propagation: seed
Expert Advice: Sow seed in situ. Seed is ripe
when it detaches easily.

Buying Considerations

Professionals
Popularity: relatively unknown
Availability: occasionally available as bare root
from specialty grower
Size to Sell: sells best in smaller sizes (when
blooming) as it matures fast
On the Shelf: rapidly overgrows pot
Shrinkage: low; requires little maintenance

Collectors
Popularity: not generally of interest to
collectors

Gardeners
Ease of Growth: mostly easy to grow but
needs close attention to growing conditions
Start with: one small plant for feature plant

What to Try First ...
Carlina acanthifolia, Carlina acaulis

On the Market

Carlina acanthifolia
Straw-coloured flowers in summer
• 15–20 cm high, 30 cm wide

Carlina acaulis
White and pale-pink flowers in summer
• 15–20 cm high, 30 cm wide

Cassiope p. 410

Genus Information
Origin: Japan, northern Asia, northern Europe
and North America
Selected Common Names: mountain heather,
white mountain heather
Nomenclature: Named for Cassiope, the wife
of Cepheus, King of Aethiopia.

General Features
Height: 6–40 cm high
Spread: 15–45 cm wide
Habit: heather-like small shrub
Flowers: some species flower only sporadically
at lower elevations
Foliage: heather-like; evergreen
Hardiness: B–D
Warnings: not prone to insects or diseases
Expert Advice: Primarily grown by collectors.

Growing Requirements
Light: sun
Soil: humus-rich, moist, well-drained, acidic soil
Location: cool rock garden
Propagation: seed; cuttings; layering
Expert Advice: Sow seeds in fall. This plant is very
slow to come from seed, and cultivars may not
come true from seed. Propagate cuttings under
mist.

Buying Considerations

Professionals
Popularity: relatively unknown foliage plant
Availability: occasionally available from
specialty growers
Size to Sell: sells best in mature sizes (when
blooming) as it matures slowly
Shrinkage: high; requires specific soil in pots

Collectors
Popularity: of interest to collectors—unique,
rare

Gardeners

Ease of Growth: mostly difficult to grow as it needs close attention to growing conditions
Start with: one mature plant for feature plant

What to Try First ...

Cassiope 'Kathleen Dryden', *Cassiope lycopodioides*

On the Market

Cassiope
'Kathleen Dryden' • Bell-like, white flowers in spring • Evergreen • 25–40 cm high, 40–45 cm wide

'Muirhead' • Bell-like, white flowers in spring • Evergreen • 15 cm high, 15–30 cm wide

Cassiope lycopodioides
Bell-like, white flowers in spring • Evergreen • 6–10 cm high, 15–25 cm wide

Cassiope mertensiana
Bell-like, white flowers in spring • Evergreen • 15–30 cm high, 25–40 cm wide

(Pink form) • Bell-like, pink flowers in spring • Evergreen • 15–30 cm high, 25–40 cm wide

Cassiope wardii
Bell-like, white flowers in spring • Evergreen • 15–30 cm high, 30–45 cm wide

Castilleja
p. 410

Genus Information

Origin: North America, South America, Asia and Europe
Selected Common Names: Indian paintbrush
Nomenclature: From Domingo Castillejo, an 18th-century Spanish botanist.

General Features

Height: 15–60 cm high
Spread: 20–45 cm wide
Habit: semi-parasitic perennial
Flowers: coloured bracts
Hardiness: A–C
Warnings: prone to aphids
Expert Advice: Forms a symbiotic relationship with grasses and leguminous perennials. Plant with native grasses in a meadow garden or with legumes, such as native lupines. Some species seem to be able to grow without a host, but they tend to be smaller. Some sources suggest that the parasitism is related to water uptake.

Growing Requirements

Light: sun
Soil: moist, organic, well-drained soil
Location: grass meadows; native wildflower gardens

Propagation: seed
Expert Advice: Sow seed in situ in fall. Difficult to establish.

Buying Considerations

Professionals

Popularity: relatively unknown
Availability: occasionally available as finished product from specialty grower
Size to Sell: sells best in mature sizes (when blooming) as it matures slowly
On the Shelf: needs cleaning and cutting back
Shrinkage: high; sensitive to overwatering

Collectors

Popularity: of interest to collectors— challenging (not for the novice gardener)

Gardeners

Ease of Growth: mostly difficult to grow as it needs close attention to growing conditions
Start with: one mature plant for feature plant

What to Try First ...

Castilleja intrega, Castilleja miniata

On the Market

Castilleja applegatei **var. *viscida***
Spiked, bright-orange-red flowers in summer • 20–45 cm high, 20–25 cm wide

Castilleja chromosa
Scarlet flowers in early summer • 15–40 cm high, 30–45 cm wide

Castilleja intrega
Bright orange-red flowers in late spring to late summer • 30–45 cm high, 30 cm wide

Castilleja linarifolia
Brick-red to rose flowers in late summer • 30–60 cm high, 30 cm wide

Castilleja miniata
Red to orange-red flowers in summer • 45–60 cm high, 30–45 cm wide

Celastrus
p. 410

Genus Information

Origin: South America, North America, Oceania and Africa
Selected Common Names: American bittersweet
Nomenclature: From the Greek *kelastros*, the old Greek name for *Phillyrea latifolia*.

General Features

Height: 5 m high
Spread: 2+ m wide
Habit: woody climbing perennial vine; requires sturdy support
Flowers: dioecious; yellow-green

Foliage: toothed; medium-green
Hardiness: C
Warnings: prone to aphids; powdery mildew and fungal leaf spots

Growing Requirements

Light: sun
Soil: tolerant of a wide range of soils
Location: climbing through trees; against walls
Propagation: seed; cuttings
Expert Advice: Plants from seed will be of unknown sex until blooming. After blooming, there is ornamental, orange, late-season fruit that splits when ripe to reveal brightly coloured seed. Birds are not attracted to the fruit, so it stays on the plant for a long period. Needs male and female plants to set fruit.

Buying Considerations

Professionals

Popularity: relatively unknown; slow seller
Availability: readily available as finished product
Size to Sell: sells best in smaller sizes as it matures fast
Shrinkage: low; requires little maintenance

Collectors

Popularity: not generally of interest to collectors

Gardeners

Ease of Growth: mostly easy to grow
Start with: one small plant for feature plant

What to Try First ...

Celastrus scandens

On the Market

Celastrus scandens
  Yellow-green flowers in summer • 5+ m high, 2+ m wide

Centaurea

p. 410

Genus Information

Origin: Europe, North America and tropical regions
Selected Common Names: cornflower, mountain bluet, perennial bachelor's button
Nomenclature: From the Greek mythological centaur. When centaurs felt poorly they grazed on cornflowers to restore their vigour.

General Features

Height: 8–100 cm high
Spread: 20–100 cm wide
Habit: clump-forming, long-lived perennial
Flowers: short blooming period; good for cutflowers and drying
Foliage: light- to medium-green

Hardiness: C–D
Warnings: prone to aphids and powdery mildew
Expert Advice: Deadhead to extend blooming season and cut back to keep plant compact.

Growing Requirements

Light: sun
Soil: moist, fertile, well-drained soil; tolerant of poor soil; dislikes winter wet
Location: rock gardens; mixed borders; wild gardens; scree; tolerant of fairly dry locations
Propagation: seed (some self-sow readily); division

Buying Considerations

Professionals

Popularity: old-fashioned garden standard
Availability: readily available as finished product and bare root
Size to Sell: sells best in smaller sizes (when in bloom) as it matures fast
On the Shelf: keep stock rotated; rapidly overgrows pot; needs regular cleaning
Shrinkage: low

Collectors

Popularity: not generally of interest to collectors

Gardeners

Ease of Growth: very easy to grow
Start with: one small plant for feature plant

What to Try First ...

Centaurea dealbata, Centaurea dissecta, Centaurea macrocephala, Centaurea montana, Centaurea montana 'Alba', Centaurea montana 'Gold Boullion', Centaurea simplicicaulis

On the Market

Centaurea dealbata
  Fringed, pink flowers in summer • 60–90 cm high, 45–60 cm wide

Centaurea dissecta
  Thistle-like, rosy-purple flowers in summer • Near white foliage • 15 cm high, 20 cm wide

Centaurea hypoleuca
  'John Coutts' • Rose-pink flowers in late spring to late summer • 30–45 cm high, 45–60 cm wide

Centaurea macrocephala
  Large, fuzzy, thistle-like, yellow flowers in mid- to late summer • 90–100 cm high, 90–100 cm wide

Centaurea montana
  Star-shaped, deep-blue flowers in late spring to late summer • 60–90 cm high, 60–90 cm wide

'Alba' • White flowers in late spring to early summer • 60–90 cm high, 60–90 cm wide

'Gold Boullion' • Deep-blue flowers in late spring to summer • Chartreuse foliage • 30–40 cm high, 30–45 cm wide

'Jordy' • Star-shaped, black-purple flowers in late spring to late summer • 25–30 cm high, 45–60 cm wide

Centaurea nigra
Purple flowers in late spring to fall • Grey-green foliage • 60–75 cm high, 45–60 cm wide

Centaurea nigrofimbria
Purple flowers in late spring to fall • Grey-green foliage • 60–75 cm high, 45–60 cm wide

Centaurea pestalozzae
Fringed, bright-yellow flowers in summer • Deeply lobed, silver-green foliage • 8 cm high, 20–25 cm wide

Centaurea aff. *pindicola*
White flowers with purple stamens • 10 cm high, 40 cm wide

Centaurea simplicicaulis
Rosy-pink flowers in late spring to early summer • Grey, felted foliage • 20–35 cm high, 30+ cm wide

Centaurea urvillei **ssp.** *hayekiana* Thistle-like, violet-purple flowers in summer • 8 cm high, 30 cm wide

Centranthus p. 410

Genus Information
Origin: Europe and the Mediterranean
Selected Common Names: Jupiter's beard
Nomenclature: From the Greek *kentron* (spur) and *anthos* (flowers), referring to the corolla that is spurred at the base.

General Features
Height: 60–90 cm high
Spread: 90 cm wide
Habit: clump-forming perennial
Flowers: fragrant; good for cutflowers; attractive to bees and butterflies
Hardiness: C
Warnings: prone to aphids
Expert Advice: Deadhead to extend blooming season and to keep plant compact. Short-lived, allow to self-seed if more plants desired.

Growing Requirements
Light: sun
Soil: lean soil
Location: mixed borders; dry slopes
Propagation: seed (self-sows readily)

Buying Considerations
Professionals
Popularity: old-fashioned garden standard
Availability: readily available as finished product and bare root
Size to Sell: sells best in smaller sizes as it matures fast
On the Shelf: keep stock rotated; rapidly overgrows pot; deadhead regularly
Shrinkage: low
Collectors
Popularity: not generally of interest to collectors
Gardeners
Ease of Growth: very easy to grow
Start with: one small plant for feature plant
What to Try First ...
Centranthus ruber

On the Market
Centranthus ruber
Carmine-red, fragrant flowers all summer • 60–90 cm high, 90 cm wide

Cerastium p. 411

Genus Information
Origin: temperate and arctic zones of Europe and North America
Selected Common Names: snow-in-summer
Nomenclature: From the Greek *keras* (horn), referring to the shape of the capsule.

General Features
Height: 15–20 cm high
Spread: 100+ cm wide
Habit: mat-forming or tufting perennial
Flowers: white; summer
Foliage: woolly, grey
Hardiness: A
Warnings: rapidly spreads, can be invasive
Expert Advice: Excellent groundcover. Can be mown in the spring.

Growing Requirements
Light: sun
Soil: well-drained; tolerant of a wide range of soils
Location: rock gardens; slopes; banks and borders
Propagation: seed (self sows readily); division

Buying Considerations

Professionals

Popularity: popular garden standard
Availability: readily available as finished product
Size to Sell: sells best in smaller sizes as it matures fast
On the Shelf: keep stock rotated; rapidly overgrows pot; requires trimming back frequently
Shrinkage: low; sensitive to underwatering

Collectors

Popularity: not generally of interest to collectors

Gardeners

Ease of Growth: very easy to grow
Start with: several plants for mass plantings

What to Try First ...

Cerastium tomentosum 'Yo-Yo'

On the Market

Cerastium tomentosum
White flowers in late spring to early summer • Woolly, grey foliage • 15–20 cm high, 90–100+ cm wide

'**Yo-Yo**' • White flowers in late spring to early summer • 15–20 cm high, 90–100+ cm wide

Chelone p. 411

Genus Information

Origin: North America
Selected Common Names: pink turtlehead, rose turtlehead, white turtlehead
Nomenclature: From *Chelone* (tortoise), referring to the flower, which resembles a tortoise head.

General Features

Height: 45–90 cm high
Spread: 40–60 cm wide
Habit: upright rhizomatous perennial
Flowers: late season; good for cutflowers
Foliage: strong, upright, wind resistant
Hardiness: C
Warnings: prone to aphids; not prone to diseases
Expert Advice: Produces ornamental seed pods. Good for drying.

Growing Requirements

Light: sun to p.m. sun
Soil: deep, fertile, moist soil
Location: bog gardens; moist woodland gardens; mixed borders
Propagation: seed; division; cuttings
Expert Advice: Seed in spring. Take tip cuttings in summer.

Buying Considerations

Professionals

Popularity: popular, old-fashioned garden standard
Availability: readily available as finished product and bare root
Size to Sell: sells best in smaller sizes (when blooming) as it matures fast
On the Shelf: keep stock rotated
Shrinkage: low; requires little maintenance

Collectors

Popularity: not generally of interest to collectors

Gardeners

Ease of Growth: very easy to grow
Start with: one small plant for feature plant

What to Try First ...

Chelone obliqua, Chelone obliqua 'Alba'

On the Market

Chelone lyonii
Purple to rose flowers in late summer • 45–75 cm high, 40–50 cm wide

'**Hot Lips**' • Deep hot-pink flowers in late summer • 60–120 cm high, 40–50 cm wide

Chelone obliqua
Rose-pink flowers in late summer • 45–75 cm high, 40–50 cm wide

'**Alba**' • White flowers in late summer • 60–90 cm high, 45–60 cm wide

Chrysanthemum p. 411

Genus Information

Origin: North America, Europe and Asia
Selected Common Names: Morden mum, fall mum
Nomenclature: From the Greek *chrysos* (gold) and *anthemos* (flower).
Notes: A very large and well-loved genus. It has, in recent years, been the subject of great debate over whether the genus should be split apart or not. You will find members of this family under a wide variety of names. There are hundreds of varieties available.

General Features

Height: 20–75 cm high
Spread: 30–75 cm wide
Habit: clump- or mound-forming perennial
Flowers: bright colours; long blooming period; good for cutflowers
Hardiness: C
Warnings: prone to powdery mildew and aphids

Growing Requirements
Light: sun
Soil: fertile, moist, well-drained soil
Location: rock gardens; mixed borders
Propagation: division; cuttings
Expert Advice: Divide frequently to keep vigorous.

Buying Considerations
Professionals
Popularity: old-fashioned, popular garden standard
Availability: readily available as finished product
Size to Sell: sells best in smaller sizes (when blooming) as it matures fast
On the Shelf: keep stock rotated; rapidly overgrows pot
Shrinkage: low; sensitive to overwatering or underwatering
Collectors
Popularity: not generally of interest to collectors
Gardeners
Ease of Growth: generally easy to grow
Start with: one small plant for feature plant

What to Try First ...
Chrysanthemum 'Clara Curtis', *Chrysanthemum* 'Duchess of Edinburgh', *Chrysanthemum* x *morifolium* 'Cameo', *Chrysanthemum* x *morifolium* 'Canary', *Chrysanthemum* x *morifolium* 'Candy', *Chrysanthemum* x *morifolium* 'Delight', *Chrysanthemum weyrichii*

On the Market
Chrysanthemum (syn. *Dendranthema*)
  'Clara Curtis' • Pink flowers in summer to fall • 50–75 cm high, 45–60 cm wide
  'Duchess of Edinburgh' • Daisy-like, bright bronze-crimson flowers in summer to fall • 50–75 cm high, 45–60 cm wide
  'Mary Stoker' • Yellow-orange flowers in summer to fall • 50–75 cm high, 45–60 cm wide

Chrysanthemum x *morifolium* (syn. *Dendranthema* x *morifolium*)
  'Aztec' • Orange-bronze flowers in late summer to fall • 45–60 cm high, 45–60 cm wide
  'Cameo' • White to cream flowers in late summer to fall • 45–60 cm high, 45–60 cm wide
  'Canary' • Bright-yellow flowers in late summer to fall • 50–60 cm high, 50–60 cm wide
  'Candy' • Candy-pink flowers in late summer to fall • 45–60 cm high, 45–60 cm wide
  'Delight' • Bronze flowers in late summer to fall • 45–60 cm high, 45–60 cm wide
  'Dreamweaver' • Mauve flowers with flared, trumpet-like petals in late summer to fall • 45–60 cm high, 45–60 cm wide
  'Fiesta' • Purple flowers in late summer to fall • 45–60 cm high, 45–60 cm wide
  'Eldorado' • Double, bright-yellow flowers in late summer to fall • 45–60 cm high, 45–60 cm wide
  'Everest' • Snow-white flowers in late summer to fall • 45–60 cm high, 45–60 cm wide
  'Gaiety' • Burnt-orange flowers in late summer to fall • 40–50 cm high, 45–60 cm wide
  'Garnet' • Garnet-red flowers in late summer to fall • 40–50 cm high, 45–60 cm wide
  'Jennifer Kristen' • Single, pink flowers in late summer to fall • 45–60 cm high, 45–60 cm wide
  'Lipstick' • Red flowers in late summer to fall • 45–60 cm high, 45–60 cm wide
  'Mertice Bottomley' • Rose-pink flowers in late summer to fall • 40–50 cm high, 45–60 cm wide
  'Suncatcher' • Double, bright-yellow flowers in late summer to fall • 45–60 cm high, 50–60 cm wide

Chrysanthemum weyrichii (syn. *Dendranthema weyrichii*)
  Large, daisy-like, pink flowers in fall • Mound-forming, slow-spreading habit • 20–30 cm high, 30 cm wide
  'White Bomb' • White flowers with a pink tint in fall • Mound-forming, slow-spreading habit • 20–30 cm high, 30 cm wide

Chrysogonum

Genus Information
Origin: eastern North America
Selected Common Names: goldenstar
Nomenclature: From the Greek *chrysos* (gold) and *gone* (joints), referring to the flowers being borne at the nodes.

General Features
Height: 15–25 cm high
Spread: 30–60 cm wide
Habit: rhizomatous groundcover perennial
Flowers: long blooming period; ray florets are female; disc florets are male
Hardiness: D
Warnings: prone to powdery mildew and aphids
Expert Advice: Much underused due to lack of availability.

Growing Requirements
Light: sun; tolerates shade but produces fewer flowers
Soil: moist, well-drained soil
Location: rock gardens; alpine gardens; sunny borders
Propagation: seed; division
Expert Advice: Propagation is easiest by division or runners.

Buying Considerations
Professionals
Popularity: relatively unknown
Availability: occasionally available from specialty growers
Size to Sell: sells best in smaller sizes (when blooming) as it matures fast
On the Shelf: keep stock rotated; deadhead regularly; rapidly overgrows pot
Shrinkage: low; sensitive to underwatering

Collectors
Popularity: not generally of interest to collectors

Gardeners
Ease of Growth: very easy to grow
Start with: one small plant for feature plant

What to Try First ...
Chrysogonus virginianum

On the Market
Chrysogonum virginianum
Gold-yellow flowers in late spring to summer • 15–25 cm high, 30–60 cm wide

Cimicifuga see *Actaea* p.7

Cirsium   p. 411 📷

Genus Information
Origin: northern temperate regions
Selected Common Names: Japanese thistle, plume thistle

Nomenclature: From the Greek *kiros* (a swollen vein), referring to the effect of being pricked by the spines.

General Features
Height: 60–100 cm high
Spread: 45–60 cm wide
Habit: spreading, rhizomatous, weedy biennial or perennial
Flowers: thistle-like; summer
Foliage: spiny
Hardiness: C
Warnings: prone to aphids; not prone to diseases; may be invasive (contain to prevent spread and deadhead to prevent self-seeding)

Growing Requirements
Light: sun
Soil: moist, well-drained soil; drought tolerant
Location: mixed borders; wild gardens; native gardens; sunny, hot, dry areas
Propagation: seed; division

Buying Considerations
Professionals
Popularity: relatively unknown
Availability: occasionally available as bare root from specialty growers
Size to Sell: sells best in smaller sizes (when blooming) as it matures fast
On the Shelf: rapidly overgrows pot
Shrinkage: low; sensitive to overwatering; requires little maintenance

Collectors
Popularity: not generally of interest to collectors

Gardeners
Ease of Growth: mostly easy to grow but needs close attention to growing conditions
Start with: one small plant for feature plant

What to Try First ...
Cirsium japonicum 'Early Rose Beauty', *Cirsium rivulare* 'Atropurpureum'

On the Market
Cirsium japonicum
'Early Rose Beauty' • Thistle-like, pink flowers in early summer • 60–75 cm high, 45–60 cm wide
'Rose Beauty' • Thistle-like, carmine-red flowers in summer • 90–100 cm high, 45–60 cm wide
Cirsium rivulare
'Atropurpureum' • Thistle-like, crimson flowers in summer • 60–90 cm high, 60 cm wide

Claytonia p. 411 📷

Genus Information

Origin: North America, Asia and Australia
Selected Common Names: Carolina spring beauty, leather leaf spring beauty, spring beauty
Nomenclature: Named for John Clayton, a pioneer American botanist.
Notes: Closely related to *Calandrinia* and *Lewisia*.

General Features

Height: 10–25 cm high
Spread: 10–25 cm wide
Habit: evergreen succulent
Flowers: white to pink; spring
Foliage: succulent
Hardiness: C–D
Warnings: not prone to insects or disease; prone to slugs
Expert Advice: *C. megarhiza* can be shy to bloom.

Growing Requirements

Light: Shade to a.m. sun
Soil: gritty, organic, well-drained soil
Location: alpine gardens; rock gardens
Propagation: seed; offsets

Buying Considerations

Professionals
Popularity: relatively unknown
Availability: occasionally available from specialty growers
Size to Sell: sells best in mature sizes (when blooming) as it matures slowly
On the Shelf: keep stock rotated

Collectors
Popularity: not generally of interest to collectors

Gardeners
Ease of Growth: generally easy to grow but needs close attention to growing conditions
Start with: one mature plant for feature plant

What to Try First ...
Claytonia megarhiza, Claytonia virginica

On the Market

Claytonia caroliniana
Pink to white flowers in early spring • Succulent foliage • 20–25 cm high, 20–25 cm wide

Claytonia megarhiza
White to pink flowers in early spring • Evergreen, succulent foliage • 10–15 cm high, 15 cm wide

Claytonia virginica
Pink flowers in spring • Evergreen, succulent foliage • 15–25 cm high, 10–15 cm wide

Clematis p. 411 📷

Genus Information

Origin: northern temperate regions, southern temperate zones and the mountains of tropical Africa
Selected Common Names: clematis
Nomenclature: From the Greek *clema* (a tendril), a name used by Dioscorides.
Notes: A very large, important and diverse genus that contains more than 200 species.
Expert Advice: We divide *Clematis* into 4 sections based on growing requirements and pruning advice: *Large Flowered Hybrids, Hardy from Old Wood, Hardy Herbaceous* and *Non-Vining.*

Clematis,
Large Flowered Hybrids p. 411 📷

General Features

Height: 1–4 m high
Spread: 1–2 m wide
Habit: climbing perennial vine
Flowers: blue, pink, purple, red or white; single, double or semi-double; spring to fall
Hardiness: C–D
Warnings: prone to clematis wilt, powdery mildew and aphids

Growing Requirements

Light: sun
Soil: cool, fertile, moist, well-drained soil; keep roots cool by growing a plant at base or mulching soil
Location: mixed borders on trellises, arbours or obelisks; against buildings
Propagation: cuttings; layering
Expert Advice: In colder climates plant against a south-or west-facing, heated foundation, with the base 10 cm below the soil surface. Cut back to 30 cm tall in fall or spring. Less dieback will occur in warmer climates and pruning may not be required. Hybrids may not come true from seed.

Buying Considerations

Professionals
Popularity: old-fashioned, popular garden standard; fast seller in bloom
Availability: readily available as a finished product and bare root from specialty growers
Size to Sell: sells best in smaller sizes (when in bloom) as it matures fast
On the Shelf: high ornamental appeal
Miscellaneous: To avoid clematis wilt, start with virus indexed stock

Collectors
Popularity: of interest to collectors—unique, rare, exceptional beauty

Gardeners

Ease of Growth: mostly easy to grow but needs close attention to growing conditions
Start with: one small plant for feature plant

What to Try First ...

Clematis 'Asao', *Clematis* 'Daniel Deronda', *Clematis* 'Elsa Spath', *Clematis* 'Jackmanii Superba', *Clematis* 'The President'

On the Market

Clematis • *Vine*

'Allanah' • Large, deep-red flowers in summer • 1.8–2.5 m high, 1–1.5 m wide

'Asao' • Deep-pink flowers in late spring to late summer • 1.8–2.5 m high, 2 m wide

'Barbara Jackman' • Mauve flowers with pink bars in summer • 1.8–2.5 m high, 1–2 m wide

'Blue Light' • Double, violet and blue flowers in summer • 2 m high, 1–1.5 m wide

'Blue Ravine' • Violet flowers with dark veins in spring to fall • 2–3 m high, 1.5 m wide

'Capitaine Thuilleaux' • Cream flowers with pink bars in late spring to summer • 2–3 m high, 1–2 m wide

'Carnaby' • Pink flowers with dark bars in summer • 1.8–2.5 m high, 1–2 m wide

'Comtesse de Bouchaud' • Mauve-pink flowers in summer • 1.8–2.5 m high, 1–2 m wide

'Countess of Lovelace' • Single and double, violet flowers in summer • 3 m high, 1.5 m wide

'Daniel Deronda' • Semi-double, purple-blue flowers in summer • 2–3 m high, 1–2 m wide

'Dr. Ruppel' • Deep rose-pink flowers with darker bars in summer • 3 m high, 1–2 m wide

'Duchess of Edinburgh' • Single and double, white flowers in summer • 1.8–2.5 m high, 1–2 m wide

'Elsa Spath' • Blue flowers in summer • 1.8–2 m high, 1–2 m wide

'Ernest Markham' • Magenta flowers in summer • 3 m high, 1–2 m wide

'Etoile de Malicorne' • Purple-blue flowers with maroon centre in summer • 3 m high, 1–2 m wide

'Fireworks' • Blue-mauve flowers with red bars in summer • 2–3 m high, 1–2 m wide

'General Sikorski' (syn. Jadwiga Teresa) • Large, deep blue flowers in summer • 1.8–2.5 m high, 1–2 m wide

'Gillian Blades' • Ruffled, white flowers in late spring to late summer • 1.8–2.5 m high, 1–2 m wide

'H.F. Young' • Wedgewood-blue flowers in summer • 3 m high, 1–2 m wide

'Hagley Hybrid' • Rosy-mauve flowers in summer • 1.8–2.5 m high, 1–2 m wide

'Hakuokan' (Haku Ookan) • Violet-blue flowers in summer • 2–3 m high, 1–2 m wide

'Henryi' • White flowers in summer • 3 m high, 1–2 m wide

'Huldine' • Single, pearl-white flowers in summer to fall • 2.5–3 m high, 1.5 m wide

'Jackmanii' • Dark-purple flowers in early to late summer • 3–4 m high, 1–2 m wide

'Jackmanii Alba' • White flowers in summer • 3–4 m high, 1–2 m wide

'Jackmanii Superba' • Deep-purple flowers in summer to fall • 3–4 m high, 1.5–2 m wide

'John Warren' • Red-edged, pink flowers with red bars in summer • 2.5–3 m high, 1–2 m wide

'Kakio' (Pink Champagne) • Purple-pink flowers in late spring to late summer • 1.8–2.5 m high, 1–1.5 m wide

'Lady Northcliffe' • Wedgewood-blue flowers in summer • 1.8–2.5 m high, 1–2 m wide

'Lilacina Floribunda' • Rich-purple flowers in summer • 3 m high, 1–2 m wide

'Marie Boisselot' (syn. Mme. Le Coultre) • White flowers in summer • 3 m high, 1.5 m wide

'Miss Bateman' • Fragrant, white flowers in summer • 1.8–2.5 m high, 1–2 m wide

'Mrs. Cholmondeley' • Lavender-blue flowers in summer • 3 m high, 1–2 m wide

'Mrs. N. Thompson' • Purple-blue flowers with pink bars in summer • 1.8–2.5 m high, 1–2 m wide

'Multi Blue' • Double, deep- and light-blue flowers in summer • 2–3 m high, 1–2 m wide

'Nelly Moser' • Pale-mauve flowers with lilac bars in summer • 3 m high, 1–2 m wide

'Niobe' • Deep-red flowers in summer • 1.8–2.5 m high, 1–2 m wide

'Piilu' (Little Duckling) • Double, purple-pink flowers with red bars in late spring to fall • 2–3 m high, 1–2 m wide

'Proteus' • Double, purple-pink flowers in summer • 1.5–2 m high, 1–2 m wide

'Rouge Cardinal' (Red Cardinal) • Velvet, crimson flowers in summer • 1.8–2.5 m high, 1–2 m wide

'Royalty' • Semi-double, purple-mauve flowers in summer • 3 m high, 1–2 m wide

'Silver Moon' • Silver-mauve flowers in late spring to late summer • 3 m high, 1–2 m wide

'Sylvia Denny' • Semi-double, clear-white flowers in summer • 1.8–2.5 m high, 1.5–2 m wide

'The President' • Rich-purple flowers in summer • 3 m high, 1–2 m wide

'Ville de Lyon' • Bright-crimson flowers in summer • 3–3.5 m high, 1–2 m wide

'Vino (Poulvo) • Petunia-red flowers in summer • 2.5–3 m high, 1–2 m wide

'Violet Charm' • Blue flowers in summer • 2.5–3 m high, 1–2 m wide

'Warszawska Nike' (Warsaw Nike) • Red-purple flowers in summer • 3 m high, 1–2 m wide

'Will Goodwin' • Mid-blue flowers in summer • 3–4 m high, 1–2 m wide

Clematis, Hardy from Old Wood

p. 411

General Features
Height: 1–8 m high
Spread: 1–5 m wide
Habit: low-growing to climbing perennial vine; may require staking rather than a trellis
Flowers: blue, deep red, pink or white; single, double or semi-double; (some) fragrant; spring to fall; (some) fluffy seed heads
Hardiness: B–D
Warnings: not prone to insects or disease
Expert Advice: Because of their size they are best grown on fences, trellisses or scrambling through trees. They are more tolerant of shade than hybrid clematis and do not require cool roots. Extremely hardy.

Growing Requirements
Light: sun to p.m. sun
Soil: fertile, moist, well-drained soil; tolerant of a wide range of soils; drought tolerant
Location: mixed border; as a groundcover; wind barrier; trailing over walls or fences; excellent screen
Propagation: seed (some self-sow readily); cuttings; layering (will often root where stems touch the ground)
Expert Advice: Do not cut back in fall as the old wood survives over winter. In colder areas they are pruned back by one third only if necessary. Some species may have more dieback than others—prune as needed in spring. To keep plants bushy at base they can be cut down.

Buying Considerations

Professionals
Popularity: gaining popularity; fast seller in bloom
Availability: readily available as a finished product
Size to Sell: sells best in smaller sizes (when blooming) as it matures fast
On the Shelf: high ornamental appeal; keep stock rotated; rapidly overgrows pot
Shrinkage: low shrinkage; requires little maintenance

Collectors
Popularity: of interest to collectors—unique, rare, exceptional beauty

Gardeners
Ease of Growth: very easy to grow
Start with: one small plant for feature plant

What to Try First ...
Clematis alpina 'Blue Dancer', *Clematis alpina* 'Constance', *Clematis macropetala* 'Lagoon', *Clematis macropetala* 'Pauline', *Clematis tangutica*

On the Market

Clematis • Vine
'Kugotia' (Golden Tiara) • Yellow flowers with dark-purple centre in summer to fall • 2–3 m high, 1.5 m wide

'Paul Farges' (syn. Summer Snow) • Fragrant, white flowers in summer • 5–6 m high, 2 m wide

'Prairie Traveller's Joy' • Star-like, white flowers in summer to fall • 3–4 m high, 2–3 m wide

Clematis alpina • Vine
Bell-shaped, blue, sometimes pink or white, flowers in late spring • 1–3 m high, 1 m wide

'Albiflora' • Nodding, white flowers in spring • 3 m high, 1.5–2 m wide

'Blue Dancer' • Nodding, soft-blue flowers in spring • 3 m high, 2 m wide

'Constance' • Semi-double, purple-pink flowers in spring • 2–3 m high, 2 m wide

'Frances Rivis' • Nodding, blue flowers with white centre in spring • 2–3 m high, 2 m wide

'Frankie' • Nodding, blue-purple flowers in spring • 3 m high, 2 m wide

'Helsingborg' • Nodding, purple-blue flowers in spring • 2.5–3 m high, 2 m wide

'Pamela Jackman' • Nodding, blue flowers in spring • 3 m high, 2 m wide

C

'**Pink Flamingo**' • Semi-double, nodding, pink flowers in spring • 2–3 m high, 2 m wide

'**Ruby**' • Nodding, rosy-red flowers in spring • 3 m high, 2 m wide

'**Tage Lundell**' • Nodding, rose-purple flowers in spring • 3 m high, 2 m wide

'**Willy**' • Nodding, soft mauve-pink flowers in spring • 2–3 m high, 1.5–2 m wide

Clematis koreana var. *fragrans* • *Vine*
Red-purple to violet-purple flowers in late spring to early summer • 2.5–3.5 m high, 1.5–2 m wide

Clematis ladakhiana • *Vine*
Yellow-green flowers in late summer • 2–3 m high, 1–2 m wide

Clematis ligusticifolia • *Vine*
Clustered, white flowers in summer to fall • 5–6 m high, 2–3 m wide

Clematis macropetala • *Vine*
Blue to blue-purple flowers in spring • 2–5 m high, 1–2 m wide

'**Blue Bird**' • Mauve-blue flowers in spring • 2.5–3 m high, 1–2 m wide

'**Jan Lindmark**' • Bell-shaped, mauve-purple flowers in spring • 2.5 m high, 1–2 m wide

'**Lagoon**' (Blue Lagoon) • Deep-blue flowers in spring • 2–3 m high, 1–2 m wide

'**Maidwell Hall**' • Double, pale-blue flowers in spring • 2–2.5 m high, 1–2 m wide

'**Markham's Pink**' (syn. *C. macropetala* var. *markhami*) • Double, open-faced, pink flowers in spring • 3–5 m high, 1–2 cm wide

'**Purple Spider**' • Open, bell-shaped, purple flowers in spring • 1.8–2.5 m high, 1.5–2 m wide

'**Rosy O'Grady**' • Pink-mauve flowers in spring • 3–5 m high, 1–2 m wide

'**White Swan**' • Bell-shaped, white flowers in spring • 1.8–2.5 m high, 1–2 m wide

Clematis occidentalis
Nodding, violet-blue flowers in spring to early summer • 1.5–2 m high, 1–2 m wide

Clematis potaninii ssp. *fargesii* • *Vine*
Anemone-like, cream-white flowers in summer to fall • 5–6 m high, 1–2 m wide

Clematis tangutica • *Vine*
Bright-yellow flowers in late spring to fall • 4–5 m high, 2–3 m wide

'**Golden Harvest**' • Gold-yellow flowers in midsummer to fall • 3–4 m high, 2–3 m wide

'**Radar Love**' • Gold-yellow flowers in midsummer to fall • 3–4 m high, 2–3 m wide

Clematis terniflora
(syn. *C. maximowicziana***)** • *Vine*
Star-like, white flowers in late summer to fall • 5–8 m high, 2–3 m wide

Clematis tibetana • *Vine*
Bell-like, yellow flowers in summer to fall • Well-drained, gritty soil • 3–4 m high, 1–2 m wide

Clematis, Hardy Herbaceous

p. 411

General Features
Height: 1.8–5 m high
Spread: 1–3 m wide
Habit: climbing perennial vine
Flowers: blue to purple, red, pink or white; single and double; (some) fragrant
Hardiness: B–D
Expert Advice: Generally die to ground each year. They are hardier than the Large Flowered Hybrids and can be planted in any location in the yard. Do not require mulching except in very cold climates. May regrow from old wood in warmer climates.

Growing Requirements
Propagation: cuttings; layering; seed (for non-hybrids)
Expert Advice: In colder climates plant with the base 10 cm below soil surface.

On the Market

Clematis campaniflora • *Vine*
Nodding, pale-blue flowers in summer to fall • 3–4 m high, 1 m wide

Clematis texensis • *Vine*
Nodding, red flowers in summer • 2–3 m high, 1–1.5 m wide

'**Duchess of Albany**' • Nodding, pink-red flowers in summer • 3 m high, 1–2 m wide

'**Etoile Rose**' • Nodding, deep-pink flowers in summer • 2–3 m high, 1–2 m wide

'**Gravetye Beauty**' • Nodding, ruby-red flowers in summer • 1.8–2.5 m high, 1–2 m wide

'**Pagoda**' • Pink flowers with mauve backs in summer • 3 m high, 1–2 m wide

'**Princess Diana**' (syn. The Princess of Wales) • Nodding, pink flowers in summer • 2–3 m high, 1–2 m wide

'**Sir Trevor Lawrence**' • Nodding, rose-red flowers in summer • 3 m high, 1–2 m wide

Clematis virginiana • *Vine*
Clustered, white flowers in summer • 4–5 m high, 2–3 m wide

Clematis viticella • Vine

'Abundance' • Rose-pink flowers in summer • 3 m high, 1–2 m wide

'Alba Luxurians' • White flowers with green tips in summer • 3 m high, 1–2 m wide

'Betty Corning' • Fragrant, nodding, blue flowers in summer • 2–3 m high, 1–2 m wide

'Blekitny Aniol' (Blue Angel) • Clear-blue flowers in summer to fall • 3–3.5 m high, 1–2 m wide

'Blue Belle' • Large, deep violet-blue flowers in summer • 3–4 m high, 1–2 m wide

'Etoile Violette' • Violet-purple flowers in summer • 3 m high, 1–2 m wide

'Kermesina' • Rich-red flowers in summer • 3–4 m high, 1–2 m wide

'Madame Julia Correvon' • Rosy-red flowers in summer • 3–4 m high, 1–2 m wide

'Margot Koster' • Bell-shaped, rose-pink flowers in summer • 2–3 m high, 1–2 m wide

'Minuet' • White flowers with maroon veining in summer • 3 m high, 1–2 m wide

'Negritjanka' (African Girl) • Dark-purple flowers in summer • 2.5–3.5 m high, 1–2 m wide

'Polish Spirit' • Purple-blue flowers in summer • 2.5–3 m high, 1–2 m wide

'Purpurea Plena Elegans' • Double, bluish-mauve flowers in summer • 2–3 m high, 1–2 m wide

'Royal Velours' • Black-red flowers in summer to fall • 3–4 m high, 1–2 m wide

'Rubra' • Bright-red flowers in summer • 2–3 m high, 1.5 m wide

'Venosa Violacea' • White flowers with purple veins in summer • 2–3 m high, 1–2 m wide

Clematis, Non-Vining   p. 411 📷

General Features

Height: 10 cm–3 m high
Spread: 15 cm–2 m wide
Habit: bushy to sprawling; non-clinging, most require support
Flowers: blue to purple, yellow, white or pink; late spring to fall; (some) fragrant; (some) fluffy seed heads
Hardiness: B–D
Warnings: Not prone to insects or diseases
Expert Advice: Can be grown in a perennial border. Most are treated like a perennial and cut down in fall.

On the Market

Clematis (C. integrifolia x C. viticella)
'Blue Boy' • Bell-shaped, hyacinth-blue flowers in early summer to fall • Sprawling habit • 1.5–1.8 m high, 1 m wide

Clematis columbiana
Nodding, purple-blue flowers in late spring • Rambling habit • 1–1.5 m high, 45–60 cm wide

Clematis columbiana var. tenuiloba (syn. C. tenuiloba)
Open, bell-shaped, violet-blue flowers in late spring • Creeping habit • 10–20 cm high, 1 m wide

Clematis x durrandii
Indigo-blue flowers in summer to fall • Rambling habit • 1–2 m high, 1 m wide

Clematis x eriostemon
'Hendersonii' • Purple-blue flowers in summer • 1.5–2 m high, 1 m wide

Clematis fremontii
Nodding, bell-shaped, purple flowers in summer • Rambling habit • Well-drained, dry, gritty soil • 15–40 cm high, 15–30 cm wide

Clematis fruticosa
'Mongolian Gold' • Yellow flowers in summer • Bushy habit • Well-drained, dry, gritty soil • 60 cm high, 60 cm wide

Clematis heracleifolia
Fragrant, wedgewood-blue flowers in late summer to fall • Bushy habit • 1 m high, 45–60 cm wide

'China Purple' • Fragrant, tubular, purple flowers in late summer to fall • Bushy habit • 1–1.5 m high, 60 cm wide

'New Love' • Fragrant, violet-blue flowers in late summer to fall • Bushy habit • 1–1.5 m high, 45–60 cm wide

Clematis heracleifolia var. davidiana
Fragrant, tubular, blue flowers in late summer to fall • Bushy habit • 90–100 cm high, 45–60 cm wide

'Wyevale' • Fragrant, wedgewood-blue flowers in late summer to fall • Bushy habit • 90–100 cm high, 45–60 cm wide

Clematis hirsutissima
Purple flowers in late spring to early summer • Tuft-forming • 15–60 cm high, 30–45 cm wide

'Sante Fe' • Purple-blue flowers in late spring to early summer • Tuft-forming • 60 cm high, 20 cm wide

Clematis hirsutissima var. scottii
Purple-blue flowers in mid- to late summer • Blue-green foliage • 30–45 cm high, 30–45 cm wide

Clematis integrifolia
Nodding, twisted, bell-shaped, dark-blue flowers in summer • Bushy habit • 90–100 cm high, 60–90 cm wide
'Alba' • Nodding, white flowers in late spring to late summer • Bushy habit • 60–90 cm high, 60–90 cm wide
'Arabella' • Semi-nodding, rosy-purple flowers in summer • Sprawling habit • 1.5–2 m high, 1–1.5 m wide
'Olgae' • Fragrant, nodding, mid-blue flowers in summer • Spreading, bushy habit • 60–90 cm high, 60–90 cm wide
'Pamiat Serdtsa' (Pamjat Serdtsa) • Nodding, violet-blue flowers in summer • Upright, bushy habit • 1.5–2 m high, 60–90 cm wide
'Rosea' • Nodding, pink flowers in late spring • Bushy habit • 60–90 cm high, 60–90 cm wide

Clematis x jouiniana
'Mrs. Robert Brydon' • Pale-mauve flowers in late summer • Yellow fall foliage • Upright habit • 2–3 m high, 1–2 m wide

Clematis mandschurica • Vine
Small, clustered, white flowers in summer • Sprawling habit • 1–1.2 m high, 60–90 cm wide

Clematis occidentalis
'Bighorns' • Nodding, violet-blue flowers in spring to early summer • Trailing habit • 8–15 cm high, 30–45 cm wide

Clematis recta
Fragrant, white flowers in midsummer to fall • Clump-forming habit • 1–2 m high, 1 m wide
'Purpurea' • Fragrant, white flowers in midsummer to fall • Bronze-purple foliage • Clump-forming habit • 90–100 cm high, 60–90 cm wide
'Velvet Night' • Fragrant, white flowers in midsummer to fall • Maroon foliage in spring • Clump-forming habit • 1–1.5 m high, 60–90 cm wide

Codonopsis
p. 411

Genus Information
Origin: Asia, the Himalayas, China and Japan
Selected Common Names: bonnet bellflower
Nomenclature: From the Greek *kodon* (bell) and *opsis* (appearance).
Notes: The taxonomy of this genus is quite confused and needs further clarification.

General Features
Height: 30 cm–3 m high
Spread: 30–60 cm wide
Habit: twining, scrambling or clump-forming perennial
Flowers: campanula-like; cream to soft blue; multi-coloured, with markings on the inside of each
Foliage: skunk-like scent when crushed
Hardiness: C–D
Warnings: prone to aphids; not prone to diseases
Expert Advice: May require staking or support.

Growing Requirements
Light: sun to p.m. sun
Soil: cool, fertile, moist, organic, well-drained soil
Location: woodland gardens; mixed borders; rock gardens
Propagation: seed; division

Buying Considerations
Professionals
Popularity: relatively unknown
Availability: occasionally available from specialty growers
Size to Sell: sells best in smaller sizes (when blooming) as it matures fast
On the Shelf: rapidly overgrows pot
Shrinkage: low; requires little maintenance
Collectors
Popularity: of interest to collectors—rare, exceptional beauty
Gardeners
Ease of Growth: very easy to grow
Start with: one small plant for feature plant

What to Try First ...
Codonopsis clematidea, Codonopsis dicentrifolia, Codonopsis mollis, Codonopsis ovata, Codonopsis pilosula

On the Market
Codonopsis clematidea
Star-like, soft-blue flowers in summer • 50–75 cm high, 45–60 cm wide
Codonopsis convolvulacea
Violet-blue, sometimes white flowers in late summer • 1–3 m high, 30–45 cm wide
Codonopsis dicentrifolia
Soft- to deep-blue flowers in early summer • 30–45 cm high, 45 cm wide
Codonopsis grey-wilsonii
'Himal Snow' • Star-like, white flowers in summer • 1–2 m high, 15–30 cm wide
Codonopsis mollis
Tubular, green-tinged, blue flowers in early summer • Grey-green, hairy foliage • 60–90 cm high, 30–45 cm wide

Codonopsis ovata
Star-like, soft-blue flowers in summer
• 30–45 cm high, 30–45 cm wide
Codonopsis pilosula (**Dang Shen**)
Purple flowers, flushed green, in early
summer • 1–1.7 m high, 45–60 cm wide

Convallaria

p. 411

Genus Information

Origin: North America, Europe and north Asia
Selected Common Names: lily-of-the-valley
Nomenclature: From the Latin *convallis* (a valley).
Other Uses: Apothecaries of the Middle Ages
recommended this plant in "disorders of the
heart and vital spirits." It is also renowned for
the treatment of fainting and poor memory.

General Features

Height: 15–20 cm high
Spread: 45–60+ cm wide
Habit: rhizomatous, spreading groundcover
perennial
Flowers: single and double; fragrant; good
cutflower; tiny; bell-shaped; pendant; spring
Foliage: solid or striped, glossy
Fruit: orange-red berries are produced by
midsummer
Hardiness: A–C
Warnings: prone to aphids and slugs; not prone
to diseases; flowers and foliage toxic; aggressive
spreader (contain to prevent spread)
Expert Advice: Unusual forms include double-
flowered, pink and striped-leaf varieties.

Growing Requirements

Light: sun or shade; tolerates more sun with good
soil moisture
Soil: moist, organic, well-drained soil; tolerates
poor soil
Location: shady woodland gardens; wild gardens
Propagation: species from seed; division
Expert Advice: Separate and replant rhizomes
in fall.

Buying Considerations

Professionals
Popularity: popular, old-fashioned garden
standard;
Availability: readily available as finished
product and bare root
Size to Sell: sells best in smaller sizes (when
blooming) as it matures fast
On the Shelf: keep stock rotated
Shrinkage: low; sensitive to overwatering

Collectors
Popularity: not generally of interest to
collectors except for striped foliage or
double varieties

Gardeners
Ease of Growth: very easy to grow
Start with: one small plant for feature and
several for mass plantings

What to Try First ...
Convallaria majalis, Convallaria majalis
'Albostriata', *Convallaria majalis* 'Variegata',
Convallaria majalis var. *rosea*

On the Market

Convallaria majalis
White flowers in spring • 15–20 cm high,
45–60+ cm wide
'**Albostriata**' • White flowers in spring •
White-and-green lengthwise striped
foliage • 15–25 cm high, 45–60+ cm wide
'**Flore Pleno**' • Double, white flowers in
spring • 15–20 cm high, 45–60+ cm wide
'**Variegata**' • White flowers in spring •
Yellow-striped, green foliage • 15–20 cm
high, 45–60+ cm wide
Convallaria majalis var. *rosea*
Pink flowers in spring • 15–20 cm high,
45–60+ cm wide

Coreopsis

p. 411

Genus Information

Origin: the Americas
Selected Common Names: tickseed, coreopsis
Nomenclature: From the Greek *koris* (bug) and
opsis (like), referring to the appearance of the
fruit.

General Features

Height: 15–75 cm high
Spread: 15–90 cm wide
Habit: short-lived (in colder areas), clump-
forming or rhizomatous perennial
Flowers: daisy-like; deadhead to extend blooming
season; good for cutflowers; attractive to bees
Foliage: airy, fine, fern-like
Hardiness: C–D
Warnings: prone to powdery mildew; not prone
to insects

Growing Requirements

Light: sun
Soil: fertile, well-drained soil; dislikes cold,
wet spring soil
Location: mixed borders
Propagation: seed; division; basal softwood
cuttings
Expert Advice: Often late to emerge in the spring
in colder areas. Often blooms the first year from
seed. Cut back midsummer after first bloom to
promote late summer blooming. Divide
frequently to keep vigorous.

C

Buying Considerations

Professionals

Popularity: gaining popularity; fast seller in bloom
Availability: readily available as finished product and bare root
Size to Sell: sells best in smaller sizes (when blooming) as it matures fast
On the Shelf: rapidly overgrows pot
Shrinkage: low; sensitive to overwatering; requires little maintenance

Collectors

Popularity: not generally of interest to collectors

Gardeners

Ease of Growth: generally easy to grow but needs close attention to growing conditions
Start with: one small plant for feature plant

What to Try First ...

Coreopsis grandiflora 'Flying Saucers', *Coreopsis lanceolata, Coreopsis lanceolata* 'Rotkehlchen', *Coreopsis rosea, Coreopsis verticillata, Coreopsis verticillata* 'Grandiflora', *Coreopsis verticillata* 'Moonbeam', *Coreopsis verticillata* 'Zagreb'

On the Market

Coreopsis
'Limerock Ruby' • Ruby-red flowers with a yellow eye in summer • 45–50 cm high, 80–90 cm wide
'Tequila Sunrise' • Yellow-orange flowers in summer • Olive-green-and-yellow-variegated foliage • 40–45 cm high, 30–40 cm wide

Coreopsis auriculata
'Nana' • Dark-yellow flowers in summer • Slow spreading habit • 15–20 cm high, 25–30 cm wide
'Zamfir' • Tubular, daisy-like, golden-orange flowers in summer • 45 cm high, 30–45 cm wide

Coreopsis grandiflora
'Calypso' • Yellow-orange flowers in summer • Olive-green-and-yellow-variegated foliage • 40–45 cm high, 30–40 cm wide
'Early Sunrise' • Large, semi-double, deep-yellow flowers in late spring to late summer • 30–45 cm high, 25–40 cm wide
'Flying Saucers™' (syn. 'Walcoreop') • Large, golden-yellow flowers in late spring to late summer • 45–60 cm high, 45 cm wide
'Goldfink' • Golden-yellow flowers in summer • 15–20 cm high, 15–25 cm wide

Coreopsis lanceolata
Bright-yellow flowers in early summer to fall • 45–60 cm high, 30–45 cm wide
'Double Sunburst' • Double, golden-yellow flowers in early summer to fall • 60–75 cm high, 45–60 cm wide
'Rotkehlchen' (Ruby Throat) • Double, bright-yellow flowers with rust-red eyes in early summer to fall • 15–30 cm high, 25–40 cm wide
'Sterntaler' • Large, gold flowers with brown centres in spring to fall • 30–45 cm high, 30–40 cm wide

Coreopsis rosea
Light-pink flowers in summer • Slow spreading habit • 30–60 cm high, 30–60 cm wide
'American Dream' • Rose-pink flowers in summer • Slow spreading habit • 30–45 cm high, 30–50 cm wide
'Sweet Dreams' • Pale-pink flowers with red ring around yellow eye in summer • Slow spreading habit • 45–60 cm high, 45–60 cm wide

Coreopsis tripteris
Brown-eyed, bright-yellow flowers in summer • Aromatic foliage • 60 cm–2 m high, 60 cm–2 m wide

Coreopsis verticillata
Starry, yellow flowers in midsummer to late summer • Slow spreading habit • 50–75 cm high, 30–45 cm wide
'Golden Gain' • Bright-yellow flowers in summer • Clump-forming, compact habit • 30–45 cm high, 30–45 cm wide
'Grandiflora' (syn. Golden Shower) • Large, deep-yellow flowers in summer • 45–60 cm high, 30–45 cm wide
'Moonbeam' • Icy-yellow flowers in summer • 45–60 cm high, 45–60 cm wide
'Zagreb' • Golden-yellow flowers in early summer to fall • Clump-forming, compact habit • 25–40 cm high, 30 cm wide

Cornus p. 411

Genus Information

Origin: northern temperate regions, circumpolar
Selected Common Names: bunchberry
Nomenclature: From the Latin for *Cornus mas*, the cornel or Cornelian cherry dogwood.
Notes: A large, well-known genus, including highly ornamental shrubs and trees.

General Features

Height: 10–20 cm high
Spread: 30+ cm wide
Habit: non-woody, creeping, rhizomatous perennial
Flowers: showy; creamy-white
Foliage: ornamental, evergreen; good fall colour
Fruit: orange-red; persists through winter
Hardiness: A–C
Warnings: prone to slugs; not prone to diseases
Expert Advice: This plant is grown for its showy flowers, fruits and foliage. Much underused woodland groundcover that naturalizes well.

Growing Requirements

Light: shade
Soil: moist, acidic soil
Location: woodland gardens; under plantings
Propagation: seed; cuttings; division; grafting
Expert Advice: Seed germination can take up to 18 months.

Buying Considerations

Professionals

Popularity: gaining popularity; fast seller in bloom
Availability: generally available as finished product
Size to Sell: sells best in smaller sizes
On the Shelf: rapidly overgrows pot
Shrinkage: low; requires little maintenance

Collectors

Popularity: not generally of interest to collectors

Gardeners

Ease of Growth: very easy to grow
Start with: several small plants for mass plantings

What to Try First ...

Cornus canadensis

On the Market

Cornus canadensis
Cream flowers in early summer • Evergreen • 10–20 cm high, 30+ cm wide

Coronilla

p. 411 📷

Genus Information

Origin: Europe, Asia and Africa
Selected Common Names: crown vetch
Nomenclature: From the Latin *coronilla* (a little crown), referring to the flowers.
Notes: A member of the legume family with the typical pea-like flowers.

General Features

Height: 10–60 cm high
Spread: 30–100+ cm wide
Habit: sprawling groundcover
Flowers: pea-like
Hardiness: C
Warnings: prone to aphids; not prone to diseases; aggressive spreader (contain to prevent spread)
Expert Advice: Excellent for erosion control on banks and slopes.

Growing Requirements

Light: sun
Soil: fertile, well-drained soil; tolerates poor soil; drought tolerant
Location: banks; slopes
Propagation: seed; cuttings

Buying Considerations

Professionals

Popularity: relatively unknown, somewhat weedy looking
Availability: occasionally available as finished product from specialty grower
Size to Sell: sells best in smaller sizes as it matures fast
On the Shelf: rapidly overgrows pot
Shrinkage: low; requires little maintenance

Collectors

Popularity: not generally of interest to collectors

Gardeners

Ease of Growth: very easy to grow
Start with: several for mass plantings

What to Try First ...

Coronilla minima, Coronilla varia

On the Market

Coronilla minima
Pea-like, fragrant, yellow flowers in summer to fall • Blue-green foliage • 10–20 cm high, 30+ cm wide

Coronilla varia
White, purple, or pink flowers in early summer to fall • 45–60 cm high, 60–100+ cm wide

Cortusa

p. 411 📷

Genus Information

Origin: Central Europe, Russia and Japan
Selected Common Names: bear's ear
Nomenclature: Named for Jacopo Cortusi, an Italian botanist.
Notes: Member of the primrose family.

General Features
Height: 15–35 cm high
Spread: 15–35 cm wide
Habit: long-lived, clump-forming woodland perennial
Flowers: nodding, bell-like
Hardiness: C
Warnings: prone to aphids; not prone to diseases

Growing Requirements
Light: shade
Soil: cool, moist, well-drained soil
Location: woodland gardens; lightly shaded rock gardens
Propagation: seed; division
Expert Advice: Easy to grow from seed. Divide after flowering and divide frequently to keep vigorous.

Buying Considerations
Professionals
Popularity: relatively unknown
Availability: occasionally available as a finished product from specialty growers
Size to Sell: sells best in smaller sizes (when blooming) as it matures fast
Shrinkage: low; requires little maintenance

Collectors
Popularity: of interest to collectors—unique, rare, exceptional beauty

Gardeners
Ease of Growth: very easy to grow
Start with: one small plant for feature plant and several for mass plantings; best when mass planted

What to Try First ...
Cortusa matthioli, Cortusa matthioli 'Alba', *Cortusa matthioli* ssp. *pekinensis, Cortusa turkestanica*

On the Market
Cortusa matthioli
  Bell-shaped, purple to magenta flowers in late spring • 20–35 cm high, 20–30 cm wide
'Alba' • Bell-shaped, white flowers in late spring • 15–35 cm high, 15–30 cm wide
Cortusa matthioli ssp. *brotheri*
  Bell-shaped, rose-purple flowers in late spring • 15–35 cm high, 15–30 cm wide
Cortusa matthioli ssp. *pekinensis*
  Bell-shaped, purple to magenta flowers in late spring • 15–35 cm high, 15–30 cm wide
Cortusa turkestanica
  Bell-shaped, purple-pink flowers in late spring • 20–35 cm high, 15–30 cm wide

'Alba' • Bell-shaped, white flowers in late spring • 15–35 cm high, 15–30 cm wide

Corydalis
p. 411

Genus Information
Origin: northern temperate regions, the Himalayas and South Africa
Selected Common Names: fumitory, blue fumitory
Nomenclature: From the Greek *korydalis* (the crested lark), which refers to the flowers resembling a lark's head.

General Features
Height: 10–40 cm high
Spread: 10–60 cm wide
Habit: bulbous, fibrous or tuberous perennial
Flowers: blue; early spring
Foliage: ferny
Hardiness: C–D
Warnings: prone to aphids and slugs; occasionally bothered by powdery mildew
Expert Advice: Some species go dormant after flowering. A nice addition to shade gardens.

Growing Requirements
Light: sun or shade; tolerant of a wide range of conditions
Soil: cool, fertile, moist, organic, well-drained soil
Location: rock gardens; woodland gardens
Propagation: seed (self-sows); division

Buying Considerations
Professionals
Popularity: gaining popularity
Availability: generally available as finished product and bare root from specialty growers
Size to Sell: sells best in smaller sizes (when blooming) as it matures fast
On the Shelf: rapidly overgrows pot; requires some cleaning; foliage breakage
Shrinkage: low; sensitive to overwatering

Collectors
Popularity: of interest to collectors; *C. solida*

Gardeners
Ease of Growth: generally easy to grow but needs close attention to growing conditions
Start with: one small plant for feature plant

What to Try First ...
Corydalis cashmeriana, Corydalis flexuosa, Corydalis flexuosa 'Blue Panda', *Corydalis flexuosa* 'China Blue', *Corydalis flexuosa* 'Purple Leaf', *Corydalis solida* 'George Baker'

On the Market

Corydalis

'Blackberry Wine' • Light-magenta flowers in late spring to summer • Fern-like foliage • 25–30 cm high, 45 cm wide

Corydalis (Ex Dufu Temple)
Blue-purple flowers in late spring to summer • Fern-like foliage • 15–25 cm high, 30–45 cm wide

Corydalis cashmeriana
Bright-blue flowers in summer • Fern-like foliage • 15–20 cm high, 15–30 cm wide

Corydalis elata
Fragrant, cobalt-blue flowers in late spring • Fern-like foliage • 20–40 cm high, 40–45 cm wide

Corydalis flexuosa
Blue flowers in late spring to summer • Fern-like foliage flushed purple • 20–30 cm high, 25–45 cm wide

'Blue Panda' • Fragrant, gentian-blue flowers in summer • Fern-like foliage • 15–25 cm high, 45–60 cm wide

'China Blue' • Purple-blue flowers in late spring to summer • Fern-like foliage • 20–30 cm high, 45–60 cm wide

'Golden Panda' • Fragrant, cobalt-blue flowers in late spring to summer • Green foliage aging to gold • 20–30 cm high, 30–45 cm wide

'Pere David' • Turquoise-blue flowers in late spring to summer • Fern-like foliage • 15–25 cm high, 30–45 cm wide

'Purple Leaf' • Fragrant, blue flowers in late spring to summer • Green foliage with purple tinge • 20–30 cm high, 45–60 cm wide

Corydalis glaucescens
Pink flowers in late spring to summer • Organic, well-drained, gritty soil • 10–15 cm high, 30–40 cm wide

Corydalis lutea
Yellow flowers in late spring to summer • Fern-like foliage • 20–40 cm high, 30 cm wide

Corydalis ochroleuca
Cream flowers with yellow spots in summer • 20–30 cm high, 30–40 cm wide

Corydalis solida
Pale pink to purple-red flowers in spring • Fern-like foliage • 10–20 cm high, 30–40 cm wide

'Dieter Schacht' • Soft-pink flowers with white spurs in spring • Fern-like foliage • Moist, sharply drained, organic, neutral to slightly acidic soil • 15–25 cm high, 20–30 cm wide

'George Baker' • Red flowers in early spring • Fern-like foliage • Moist, sharply drained, organic, neutral to slightly acidic soil • 15–25 cm high, 20–30 cm wide

(Penza strain) • Blue, pink, peach or red flowers in spring • Fern-like foliage • 10–20 cm high, 30–40 cm wide

Corydalis solida f. transsylvanica
Brick-red flowers in early spring • Fern-like foliage • Moist, sharply drained, organic, neutral to slightly acidic soil • 15–25 cm high, 20–30 cm wide

Corydalis stenantha
Lavender flowers with dark-purple tips in late spring • 30 cm high, 30+ cm wide

Corydalis wilsonii
Yellow flowers in spring • Silvery-grey foliage • Well-drained, organic, gritty soil • 15–20 cm high, 10–20 cm wide

Coryphantha p. 411

Genus Information

Origin: the southern United States and Mexico
Selected Common Names: nipple cactus, native pincushion cactus
Nomenclature: From the Greek *koryphe* (summit) and *anthos* (flower), referring to the flowers emerging from the stem apex.

General Features

Height: 4–10 cm high
Spread: 10–30 cm wide
Habit: cactus
Flower: pink to yellow-green; late spring to early summer
Foliage: fine, spiny needles
Hardiness: B–C
Warnings: not prone to insects or disease; painful to handle
Expert Advice: Can be grown indoors or outdoors.

Growing Requirements

Light: sun
Soil: dry, gritty, sharply drained soil; keep soil drier during dormancy
Location: sunny, hot, dry areas
Propagation: seed

Buying Considerations

Professionals
Popularity: gaining popularity; sells well in bloom
Availability: occasionally available from specialty growers
Size to Sell: sells best in mature sizes (when blooming) as it matures slowly
Shrinkage: low; requires little maintenance

Collectors
Popularity: not generally of interest to collectors

Gardeners
Ease of Growth: very easy to grow
Start with: one mature plant for feature plant or many small plants for instant visual impact

What to Try First ...
Coryphantha vivipara

On the Market

Coryphantha missouriensis
(syn. *Escobaria missouriensis***)**
Yellow-green or pink flowers in early summer • Organic, sharply drained, gritty soil in sheltered location • 4–5 cm high, 10–15 cm wide

Coryphantha vivipara **(syn.** *Escobaria vivipara***)**
Large, purple, pink or sometimes white flowers in late spring • Woolly cactus • Native to southern prairies • 5–10 cm high, 15–30 cm wide

Cotoneaster
p. 412

Genus Information
Origin: Europe, Africa, Asia, the Himalayas and Siberia.
Selected Common Names: cotoneaster
Nomenclature: From the Latin *cotoneum* (quince) and *aster*, referring to the incomplete resemblance applied to a wild or inferior kind. Refers to the similarity of the leaves to quince in some species.
Notes: A genus of some 200 species of deciduous, semi-evergreen or evergreen shrubs and trees. Some of the very small species are sold at the retail level as perennials.

General Features
Height: 15–30 cm high
Spread: 60+ cm wide
Habit: upright or prostrate shrub
Flowers: small; spring
Foliage: (some) evergreen; good fall colour

Fruit: ornamental
Hardiness: C
Warnings: not prone to insects or disease
Expert Advice: Smaller species are suitable for use in perennial beds and borders and are grown for their ornamental value.

Growing Requirements
Light: sun to p.m. sun
Soil: well-drained soil
Location: mixed borders; rock gardens
Propagation: seed; cuttings
Expert Advice: Sow ripe seed in fall—it can take two years to scarify.

C

Buying Considerations

Professionals
Popularity: gaining popularity as a foliage plant
Availability: generally available as finished product
Size to Sell: sells best in smaller sizes as it matures fast
On the Shelf: high ornamental appeal; keep stock rotated; rapidly overgrows pot
Shrinkage: low; requires little maintenance

Collectors
Popularity: not generally of interest to collectors

Gardeners
Ease of Growth: generally easy to grow but needs close attention to growing conditions
Start with: one small plant for feature plant or many for mass plantings

What to Try First ...
Cotoneaster adpressus, Cotoneaster apiculatus 'Tom Thumb'

On the Market

Cotoneaster adpressus
Red-tinted, white flowers in summer • Shiny, green foliage • 15–30 cm high, 60+ cm wide

'Compacta' • Red-tinted, white flowers in summer • Crinkled foliage • 15–30 cm high, 60+ cm wide

Cotoneaster apiculatus
'Tom Thumb' • Red-tinted, white flowers in summer • Shiny, green foliage • Low-spreading, shrubby habit • 10–15 cm high, 45–60+ cm wide

Cotoneaster dammeri
'Strieb's Findling' • White flowers in spring • Shiny, dark-green foliage • 15–25 cm high, 45–60+ cm wide

Cryptogramma p. 412 📷

Genus Information

Origin: northern temperate regions and the mountains of southern temperate regions
Selected Common Names: parsley fern
Nomenclature: From the Greek *kryptos* (hidden) and *gramme* (line), referring to the lines of sori that are concealed before maturity.

General Features

Height: 15–25 cm high
Spread: 15–30 cm wide
Habit: colonizing or spreading fern
Foliage: parsley-like
Hardiness: C–D
Warnings: not prone to insects or disease

Growing Requirements

Light: shade; tolerates more sun than many ferns; shelter from hot p.m. sun
Soil: acidic, free-draining soil
Location: woodland gardens; foliage may break in windy locations
Propagation: spores
Expert Advice: Fertile fronds are narrower than the non-fertile fronds. Propagation difficult unless acid medium is used.

Buying Considerations

Professionals

Popularity: relatively unknown; foliage plant
Availability: occasionally available as finished product
Size to Sell: sells best in smaller sizes as it matures fast
On the Shelf: high ornamental appeal; keep stock rotated; foliage breakage (display out of wind)
Shrinkage: low; sensitive to underwatering; requires little maintenance

Collectors

Popularity: not generally of interest to collectors

Gardeners

Ease of Growth: generally easy to grow but needs close attention to growing conditions
Start with: one small plant for feature plant

What to Try First ...

Cryptogramma crispa

On the Market

Cryptogramma crispa
Fronds turn rusty-brown in fall • 15–25 cm high, 15–30 cm wide

Cyananthus p. 412 📷

Genus Information

Origin: China and the Himalayas
Selected Common Names: trailing bellflower
Nomenclature: From the Greek *kyanos* (blue) and *anthos* (flower).

General Features

Height: 2–15 cm high
Spread: 10–30 cm wide
Habit: mat-forming or spreading perennial
Flowers: vibrant blue; mid- to late summer
Hardiness: C
Warnings: not prone to insects or disease
Expert Advice: A relatively unknown perennial that is excellent for rock gardens. Deadhead and cut back in midsummer to promote fresh growth.

Growing Requirements

Light: sun
Soil: cool, moist, organic, well-drained soil
Location: rock gardens; troughs; raised beds; alpine gardens; scree
Propagation: seed; cuttings

Buying Considerations

Professionals

Popularity: relatively unknown; sells well in bloom
Availability: occasionally available from specialty growers
Size to Sell: sells best in smaller sizes (when blooming); matures slowly
Shrinkage: low; requires little maintenance

Collectors

Popularity: not generally of interest to collectors

Gardeners

Ease of Growth: generally easy to grow but needs close attention to growing conditions
Start with: one small plant for feature plant or many for mass plantings

What to Try First ...

Cyananthus lobatus, Cyananthus macrocalyx, Cyananthus microphyllus

On the Market

Cyananthus lobatus
Blue flowers in late summer • 8–10 cm high, 30 cm wide

Cyananthus macrocalyx
Blue flowers in late summer • 10–15 cm high, 10–15 cm wide

Cyananthus microphyllus
Violet-blue flowers in midsummer to fall • Thyme-like foliage • 2–5 cm high, 20–25 cm wide

Cyclamen

p. 412

Genus Information

Origin: Europe, the Mediterranean and Somalia
Selected Common Names: cyclamen
Nomenclature: From the Greek *kylos* (circular), referring to the spiralling of the peduncle in some species.

General Features

Height: 8–15 cm high
Spread: 10–40 cm wide
Habit: colony-forming, tuberous perennial
Flowers: fall; goes dormant after flowering
Foliage: rounded to heart-shaped; (some) toothed or lobed
Hardiness: C–D
Warnings: prone to slugs; not prone to diseases
Expert Advice: This plant is not often available in retail greenhouses because it blooms in fall when the selling season is over. Best purchased in fall as a corm and planted at that time. The showy cyclamen from a florist comes from *C. persicum*.

Growing Requirements

Light: shade to a.m. sun
Soil: fertile, organic, well-drained soil; keep soil drier during dormancy and moist in fall when blooming begins
Location: woodland gardens; rock gardens; raised beds; naturalizes easily
Propagation: seed (self-sows); division of corms
Expert Advice: Seeds should be soaked for 12 hours and rinsed before planting. Plant tubers deeper in the garden (2–2.5 cm).

Buying Considerations

Professionals
Popularity: relatively unknown; fast seller in bloom
Availability: occasionally available as bare root from specialty growers
Size to Sell: sells best in mature sizes (when blooming) as it matures slowly
Shrinkage: high; sensitive to overwatering; goes dormant in pot

Collectors
Popularity: of interest to collectors—unique

Gardeners
Ease of Growth: mostly easy to grow but needs close attention to growing conditions
Start with: one mature plant for feature plant

What to Try First ...

Cyclamen coum, Cyclamen coum 'Rubrum', *Cyclamen hederifolium, Cyclamen purpurascens*

On the Market

Cyclamen coum
White to crimson flowers in late summer to fall • 8–10 cm high, 15–20 cm wide
'Album' • White flowers with purple blotch at base in late summer to fall • 8–10 cm high, 15–20 cm wide
'Rubrum' • Red flowers in late summer to fall • 8–10 cm high, 15–20 cm wide

Cyclamen coum ssp. caucasicum
White to pink flowers in late summer to fall • 8–10 cm high, 15–20 cm wide

Cyclamen hederifolium (syn. C. neapolitanum)
Pink flowers in late summer to fall • 10 cm high, 10–15 cm wide
'Perlenteppich' • Cream-white flowers in late summer to fall • 10 cm high, 10–15 cm wide
'Rosenteppich' • Pink-rose flowers in late summer to fall • 10 cm high, 10–15 cm wide

Cyclamen hederifolium var. hederifolium
Nodding, pink flowers in late summer to fall • 8–10 cm high, 10–15 cm wide

Cyclamen hederifolium var. hederifolium f. albiflorum
White flowers in late summer to fall • 8–10 cm high, 10–15 cm wide

Cyclamen purpurascens
Fragrant, carmine to rose-red flowers in summer to fall • 10–15 cm high, 15–20 cm wide

Cypripedium

p. 412

Genus Information

Origin: Asia and North America
Selected Common Names: lady's slipper, showy lady's slipper
Nomenclature: From the Greek *kypris* (Venus) and *pous* (foot).

General Features

Height: 10–60 cm high
Spread: 10–45 cm wide
Habit: colony-forming, terrestrial orchid
Flowers: spring
Foliage: fan-shaped to ovate
Hardiness: C–D
Warnings: not prone to insects or disease; prone to slugs
Expert Advice: Many are endangered and are CITES plants, meaning that they are illegal to dig up from the wild. We sell plants that are of blooming size and CITES certified.

Growing Requirements

Light: shade to a.m. sun
Soil: well-drained, organic, neutral to acidic, gritty soil; all require slightly differing soil conditions
Location: shady rock gardens; woodland gardens; peat beds; bog gardens
Propagation: division (but resents being disturbed)
Expert Advice: Some species can take up to 8 years to flower from seed. Some require specific growing conditions, which makes them difficult to establish.

Buying Considerations

Professionals

Popularity: gaining popularity; sells well in bloom
Availability: occasionally available as finished product or bare root from specialty growers; purchase only CITES certified stock; very expensive due to long, involved cultural methods
Size to Sell: sells best in larger sizes, however, due to cost, smaller sizes are usually more available; use good signage to show blooms
On the Shelf: keep stock rotated
Shrinkage: high; sensitive to overwatering; goes dormant in pot

Collectors

Popularity: of interest to collectors—unique, rare, challenge

Gardeners

Ease of Growth: mostly difficult to grow as it needs close attention to growing conditions
Start with: one small plant for feature plant

What to Try First ...

Cypripedium calceolus, Cypripedium calceolus var. *parviflorum, Cypripedium calceolus* var. *pubescens, Cypripedium guttatum, Cypripedium guttatum* var. *yatabeanum, Cypripedium montanum*

On the Market

Cypripedium
'Gisela' • Purple flowers with rose pouch in spring • 30–40 cm high, 40 cm wide
'Gisela' (Yellow form) • Purple flowers with yellowish-pink pouch in spring • 30–40 cm high, 40 cm wide
'Michael' • Purple-red flowers with darker veining in spring • 25–55 cm high, 30 cm wide
'Ulla Silkens' • White flowers with red spotting on the lip in spring • 25–35 cm high, 30–45 cm wide

Cypripedium acaule
Slipper-like, soft-pink flowers in spring • 15–45 cm high, 20–30 cm wide

Cypripedium bardolphianum
Yellow-green or maroon flowers with maroon marks in late spring • 10–15 cm high, 15–18 cm wide

Cypripedium calceolus
Slipper-like, yellow flowers in spring • 15–20 cm high, 20–30 cm wide

Cypripedium calceolus var. *kentuckiense*
Yellow flowers with brown wings in spring • 45–60 cm high, 25–40 cm wide

Cypripedium calceolus var. *parviflorum*
Slipper-like, yellow flowers in spring • 15–20 cm high, 20–30 cm wide

Cypripedium calceolus var. *pubescens*
Slipper-like, yellow flowers in spring • 25–40 cm high, 30–45 cm wide

Cypripedium cordigerum
Slipper-like, white to green flowers in late spring • 25–50 cm high, 30–40 cm wide

Cypripedium corrugatum
Slipper-like, maroon flowers in spring • 18–30 cm high, 10 cm wide

Cypripedium debile
Green flowers marked with purple in late spring • 10–20 cm high, 20–25 cm wide

Cypripedium franchetii
Pink or purple flowers in late spring • 15–30 cm high, 25–30 cm wide

Cypripedium guttatum
White flowers spotted pink-red in late spring • 10–35 cm high, 25–30 cm wide

Cypripedium guttatum var. *guttatum*
White flowers with rose marks in late spring • 15–35 cm high, 25–30 cm wide

Cypripedium guttatum var. *yatabeanum*
White flowers with brown marks in late spring • 10–35 cm high, 25–30 cm wide

Cypripedium henryi
White to yellow flowers in spring • 45–60 cm high, 20–30 cm wide

Cypripedium himalaicum
Slipper-like, flushed and marked red-purple flowers in spring • 30–45 cm high, 30 cm wide

Cypripedium japonicum
Green-yellow flowers flushed rose on the pouch in spring • 30–45 cm high, 30 cm wide

Cypripedium macranthos
Large, pink-fuchsia flowers in spring • 30–45 cm high, 30 cm wide

(Lake Baykal) • Purple-fuchsia flowers in spring • 30–45 cm high, 30 cm wide

(Light pink) • Slipper-like, soft-pink flowers in spring • 30–45 cm high, 30 cm wide

'Man-Chu' • Slipper-like, soft-pink flowers in spring • 30–45 cm high, 30 cm wide

(Reddish form) • Slipper-like, reddish flowers in spring • 30–45 cm high, 30 cm wide

'Wou-Long' • Slipper-like, dark-pink flowers in spring • 30–45 cm high, 30 cm wide

Cypripedium macranthos f. *albiflorum*
Slipper-like, pure white flowers in spring • 30–45 cm high, 30 cm wide

Cypripedium margaritaceum
Yellow-green flowers blotched purple in spring • 10–15 cm high, 20–30 cm wide

Cypripedium margaritaceum f. *Vietnam*
Cream flowers with purple spots and marks in spring • 15 cm high, 25–30 cm wide

Cypripedium montanum
White flowers with brown wings in spring • 30–45 cm high, 30 cm wide

Cypripedium passerinum
Fragrant, green-and-white flowers in late spring • 20–30 cm high, 20–30 cm wide

Cypripedium plectrochilum
White flowers, flushed pink, with brown wings in spring • 15–20 cm high, 30 cm wide

Cypripedium reginae
Fragrant, white-and-rose flowers in spring • 30–60 cm high, 30–45 cm wide

Cypripedium reginae var. *hubei*
Fragrant, pink flowers in spring • 30–45 cm high, 30–45 cm wide

Cypripedium segawai
Yellow flowers with a brighter, rarely marked pouch in spring • 10–15 cm high, 15–20 cm wide

Cypripedium tibeticum
Pink flowers with maroon marks in summer • 20–40 cm high, 20–30 cm wide

Cypripedium ventricosum
(syn. *C. manchuricum*)
White to rose flowers in spring • 45–60 cm high, 30–45 cm wide

Cypripedium wardii
Creamy-white flowers spotted purple in late spring • 8–15 cm high, 10–20 cm wide

Cypripedium yunnanense
Pink or red-purple flowers with darker veins in late spring • 20–35 cm high, 15–25 cm wide

Dactylorhiza

p. 412

Genus Information

Origin: Europe, Asia, North America and Africa

Selected Common Names: marsh orchid, spotted orchid

Nomenclature: From the Greek *daktylos* (finger) and *rhiza* (root), referring to the finger-like tubers.

Notes: Until recently, the plant was part of the genus *Orchis*.

Expert Advice: Not often commercially available. Plants are becoming rare in the wild and are protected. We sell plants that are of blooming size and CITES certified.

General Features

Height: 15–60 cm high

Spread: 15–40 cm wide

Habit: upright, colony-forming perennial

Flowers: late spring to early summer

Foliage: grass-like

Hardiness: C–D (most are hardy on the Prairies)

Warnings: not prone to insects or disease; prone to slugs

Growing Requirements

Soil: humus-rich, moist, well-drained soil; tolerant of most soils and a wide range of soil pH

Location: moist meadows; rock gardens; orchid gardens; marsh edges

Propagation: seed (self-sows, especially in peat beds); division

Expert Advice: Takes a long time from seed to reach blooming size. Takes 4 to 5 years to colonize nicely in colder areas—much sooner in warmer areas.

Buying Considerations

Professionals

Popularity: relatively unknown; sells well in bloom

Availability: occasionally available as finished product or bare root from specialty growers; purchase only CITES certified stock

Size to Sell: sells best in mature sizes (when blooming) as it matures slowly

On the Shelf: keep stock rotated

Shrinkage: low; goes dormant in pot after blooming

Collectors

Popularity: of interest to collectors—unique, rare, exceptional beauty

Gardeners

Ease of Growth: mostly easy to grow but needs close attention to growing conditions

Start with: one mature plant for feature plant

What to Try First ...

Dactylorhiza foliosa, Dactylorhiza fuchsii, Dactylorhiza maculata, Dactylorhiza praetermissa, Dactylorhiza purpurella

On the Market

Dactylorhiza (D. majalis x D. sambucina)
Spiked, cream flowers with purple veins in late spring • 45–60 cm high, 30 cm wide

Dactylorhiza (D. purpurella x D. fuchsii)
Violet-purple, spiked flowers in early summer • 45–60 cm high, 30 cm wide

Dactylorhiza foliosa
Spiked, dark-spotted, rose-purple flowers in late spring • 45–60 cm high, 15–25 cm wide

Dactylorhiza fuchsii
Spiked, soft to dark violet-pink flowers in late spring • 30–60 cm high, 15–25 cm wide

Dactylorhiza fuchsii alba
Spiked, white flowers in late spring • 25–50 cm high, 15–25 cm wide

Dactylorhiza incarnata
Spiked, pink-lilac flowers with dark-lined lips in late spring • 25–50 cm high, 15–25 cm wide

Dactylorhiza maculata
Spiked, pink to purple flowers with spots in late spring • 30–45 cm high, 20–30 cm wide

Dactylorhiza maculata ssp. *ericetorum*
Spiked, white to pink flowers with purple-red marks in late spring • Well-drained, organic, moist, acid soil • 30–40 cm high, 30 cm wide

Dactylorhiza majalis
Spiked, purple flowers with dark marks in early summer • 30–60 cm high, 20–30 cm wide

Dactylorhiza praetermissa
Spiked, rich-purple flowers in early summer • 30–50 cm high, 30 cm wide

Dactylorhiza purpurella
Spiked, deep-purple flowers in early summer • 30–45 cm high, 30 cm wide

(Tall form) • Spiked, deep-purple flowers in early summer • 45–60 cm high, 30 cm wide

Darmera
p. 412 📷

Genus Information

Origin: the western United States
Selected Common Names: umbrella plant
Nomenclature: Named for Karl Darmer, a 19th-century horticulturist in Berlin.

General Features

Height: 60–90 cm high
Spread: 60–90+ cm wide
Habit: rhizomatous perennial
Flowers: white to pink; fragrant; flower stems emerge before foliage in early spring
Foliage: large, rounded
Hardiness: C
Warnings: not prone to insects or disease

Growing Requirements

Light: sun
Soil: moist, boggy soil; tolerant of dry periods
Location: waterside plantings; shade gardens
Propagation: seed; division
Expert Advice: Thick root mass can aid in stabilizing marshy sites.

Buying Considerations

Professionals
Popularity: relatively unknown foliage plant
Availability: occasionally available as finished product and bare root from specialty growers
Size to Sell: sells best in smaller sizes
On the Shelf: high ornamental appeal; keep stock rotated; rapidly overgrows pot
Shrinkage: low; requires little maintenance

Collectors
Popularity: of interest to collectors—unique, rare

Gardeners
Ease of Growth: very easy to grow
Start with: one small plant for feature plant

What to Try First ...
Darmera peltata

On the Market

Darmera peltata
White to pink flowers in early spring • Large, rounded, dark-green foliage • 60–90 cm high, 60–90+ cm wide

Degenia
p. 412 📷

Genus Information

Origin: Yugoslavia
Selected Common Names: None
Nomenclature: Named for Arpad von Degen, 1866–1934, who was the director of the Budapest Seed Testing Station.

General Features

Height: 5–10 cm high
Spread: 25–30 cm wide
Habit: cushion-forming
Flowers: yellow
Foliage: silvery-grey
Hardiness: D
Warnings: not prone to insects or disease
Expert Advice: Very hardy if grown in lean soil. Rich soil produces soft, tender growth.

Growing Requirements

Light: sun to p.m. sun
Soil: lean, sharply drained soil; avoid winter wet; drought tolerant
Location: troughs; raised beds; scree
Propagation: seed

Buying Considerations

Professionals
Popularity: relatively unknown
Availability: occasionally available from specialty growers
Size to Sell: sells best in smaller sizes (when blooming) as it matures fast
On the Shelf: rapidly overgrows pot
Shrinkage: low; sensitive to overwatering

Collectors
Popularity: of interest to collectors—unique, rare

Gardeners
Ease of Growth: mostly easy to grow but needs close attention to growing conditions
Start with: one small plant for feature plant

What to Try First ...
Degenia velebitica

On the Market

Degenia velebitica
Yellow flowers in spring • Silver-grey, hairy foliage • 5–10 cm high, 25–30 cm wide

D

Delosperma

p. 412

Genus Information

Origin: Africa and Arabia
Selected Common Names: ice plant
Nomenclature: From the Greek *delos* (visible) and *sperma* (seed), referring to the seed capsules not having tops so that the seeds are visible.

General Features

Height: 2–15 cm high
Spread: 20–60 cm wide
Habit: spreading perennial
Flowers: daisy-like; single; open on sunny days and close at night
Foliage: evergreen to semi-evergreen; succulent
Hardiness: D
Warnings: not prone to insects or disease

Growing Requirements

Light: sun
Soil: extremely lean, gritty, well-drained soil
Location: rock gardens; raised beds; dry wall; alpine house
Propagation: seed; cuttings
Expert Advice: Keep soil moist when blooming and drier during dormancy. Will not survive winter in ground unless grown under cactus-like conditions. Take cuttings in summer.

Buying Considerations

Professionals

Popularity: relatively unknown; sells well in bloom
Availability: occasionally available as finished product from specialty growers
Size to Sell: sells best in smaller sizes (when blooming) as it matures fast
On the Shelf: rapidly overgrows pot
Shrinkage: high; sensitive to overwatering

Collectors

Popularity: not generally of interest to collectors

Gardeners

Ease of Growth: mostly difficult to grow as it needs close attention to growing conditions
Start with: one small plant for feature plant

What to Try First ...

Delosperma (ex Drakensberg Mountains), *Delosperma cooperi*, *Delosperma nubigenum*

On the Market

Delosperma (ex Drakensberg Mountains)
White flowers in summer • Succulent foliage • 5–10 cm high, 45–60 cm wide

Delosperma basuticum
Yellow flowers with white eye in summer • Succulent foliage • 2–5 cm high, 20–30 cm wide

Delosperma congestum
Yellow flowers with white eye in summer • Succulent foliage • 2–5 cm high, 20–30 cm wide

Delosperma cooperi
Purple-carmine flowers in summer • Succulent foliage • 5–10 cm high, 45–60 cm wide

Delosperma floribundum
'Starburst' • Bright-pink flowers with white centres in summer • Succulent foliage • 15 cm high, 45 cm wide

Delosperma nubigenum
Orange-red to yellow flowers in summer • Succulent foliage • 5–10 cm high, 40–45 cm wide

Delphinium

p. 412

Genus Information

Origin: North America, Asia and Europe.
Selected Common Names: candle larkspur, delphinium
Nomenclature: From the Greek for "dolphin." *Delphinion* was a name used by Discorides.

General Features

Height: 25 cm–2 m high
Spread: 15–90 cm wide
Habit: upright, clump-forming biennial or perennial; may require staking
Flowers: spikes of blue, pink, white or yellow (new additions in red shades); summer; excellent cutflower
Hardiness: B–D
Warnings: prone to powdery mildew, leaf tier and aphids; poisonous (flowers and foliage may cause discomfort if swallowed); contact with foliage may irritate skin
Expert Advice: Can be short-lived in humid climates. Cutback after flowering; water and fertilize to encourage repeat bloom.

Growing Requirements

Light: sun
Soil: fertile, well-drained soil; keep soil moist when blooming and during active growth
Location: cottage gardens
Propagation: seed; division
Expert Advice: Seed viability decreases when stored too warmly.

Buying Considerations

Professionals

Popularity: old-fashioned, popular garden standard; fast seller; many new varieties
Availability: readily available as finished product and bare root
Size to Sell: sells best in smaller sizes (when blooming) as it matures fast
On the Shelf: keep stock rotated; rapidly overgrows pot; foliage breakage
Shrinkage: high; due to powdery mildew

Collectors

Popularity: of interest to collectors—unusual varieties

Gardeners

Ease of Growth: very easy to grow
Start with: one small plant for feature plant

What to Try First ...

Delphinium 'Atlantis', *Delphinium* 'Blushing Bride', *Delphinium* 'Fernzuender', *Delphinium* 'Finsteraarhorn', *Delphinium* 'Pagan Purples', *Delphinium* 'Polar Night', *Delphinium* 'Royal Aspirations', *Delphinium* 'Volkerfrieden Improved', *Delphinium grandiflorum* 'Blue Butterfly'

On the Market

Delphinium
'Benary Red' • Spikes of scarlet-orange flowers in summer • 60–75 cm high, 45–60 cm wide

'Blue Mirror' • Spikes of vivid-blue flowers in summer • Fern-like foliage • 30–45 cm high, 30–40 cm wide

'Chelsea Star' • Spikes of violet flowers with white "bee" in summer • 1–1.5 m high, 75–90 cm wide

'Cherry Blossom' • Spikes of dusty-rose flowers with a white "bee" in summer • 1–1.5 m high, 75–90 cm wide

'Clear Springs Blue' • Spikes of sky-blue flowers in summer • 90–120 cm high, 60 cm wide

'Pink Dream' • Spikes of true pink flowers in summer • 1–1.5 m high, 75–90 cm wide

'Polar Night' • Spiked, gentian-blue flowers with white "bee" in summer • 1–1.7 m high, 75–90 cm wide

'Red Caroline' • Spiked, light rose-red flowers in summer • 90–100 cm high, 45–60 cm wide

'Red Princess' • Spikes of rose-red flowers in summer • 60–90 cm high, 45–60 cm wide

'Red Rocket' • Spikes of cerise-red flowers in summer • 75–100 cm high, 45–60 cm wide

'Strawberry Fair' • Spikes of rich mulberry-rose flowers in summer • 90–150 cm high, 75–90 cm wide

'Sundance' • Spikes of dusty-rose flowers in summer • 75–100 cm high, 75–90 cm wide

'Sungleam' • Spikes of cream flowers with sulphur "bee" in summer • 75–100 cm high, 75–90 cm wide

'Turkish Delight' • Spikes of dusky-pink flowers with a white "bee" in summer • 75–100 cm high, 60–75 cm wide

'Volkerfrieden Improved' (International Peace Improved) • Spikes of electric-blue flowers in summer • 90–120 cm high, 45–60 cm wide

'West End Blue' • Spikes of single, sky-blue flowers with darker "bee" in summer • 90–120 cm high, 45–60 cm wide

Blue Fountains Series
Spikes of blue shades of flowers in summer • 75–100 cm high, 60–75 cm wide

Clansman Series
Spikes of flowers in summer, colours include dark-blue with dark eye, dark-lilac with dark eye, clear-white with dark eye, light-blue with white eye • 1–1.5 m high, 75–90 cm wide

Belladonna Group
'Atlantis' • Spikes of blue flowers in summer • 90–120 cm high, 45–60 cm wide

'Bellamosum' • Spikes of dark-blue flowers in early summer • 90–120 cm high, 45–60 cm wide

'Sky Lady' • Spikes of sky-blue flowers in summer • 90–120 cm high, 45–60 cm wide

Guardian Series
Spiked, blue, pink or white flowers in summer • 1–1.5 m high, 50–75 cm wide

Magic Fountains Series
Spikes of flowers in shades of blue, pink and white in summer • 1–1.5 m high, 50–75 cm wide

New Millennium Series
Formerly known as New Zealand Series
'Blushing Bride' • Spiked, pink flowers in summer • 1–2 m high, 90 cm wide

'Innocence' • Spiked, white flowers in summer • 1–2 m high, 90 cm wide

'Pagan Purples' • Spiked, dark blue-and-purple flowers, sometimes white to mauve, in summer • 1.5–2 m high, 75–90 cm wide

'Royal Aspirations' • Spiked, shades of pink flowers in summer • 1–2 m high, 90 cm wide

Pacific Giant Series

'Astolat' • Spikes of lavender flowers in summer • 1–2 m high, 75–90 cm wide

'Black Knight' • Spikes of deep-purple flowers with black "bee" in summer • 1–2 m high, 75–90 cm wide

'Blue Bird' • Spikes of sky-blue flowers with white "bee" • 1–2 m high, 75–90 cm wide

'Blue Jay' • Spikes of dark-blue flowers in summer • 1–2 m high, 75–90 cm wide

'Camelaird' • Spikes of lavender-blue flowers with cream "bee" in summer • 1–2 m high, 75–90 cm wide

'Galahad' • Spikes of pure white flowers in summer • 1–2 m high, 75–90 cm wide

'Guinevere' • Spikes of pale-lilac flowers with white "bee" in summer • 1–2 m high, 75–90 cm wide

'King Arthur' • Spikes of royal-violet flowers with white "bee" in summer • 1–2 m high, 75–90 cm wide

'Summer Skies' • Spikes of light-blue flowers in summer • 1–2 m high, 75–90 cm wide

Delphinium brunonianum
Spikes of blue to purple flowers in summer • 25–40 cm high, 15–20 cm wide

Delphinium cashmerianum
Spikes of deep-blue flowers in summer • 25–40 cm high, 25 cm wide

Delphinium elatum
Spikes of various colours of flowers in summer • 1–2 m high, 75–90 cm wide

Delphinium glaucum
Spikes of blue-purple flowers in summer • 90–150 cm high, 60–90 cm wide

Delphinium grandiflorum (syn. D. chinense)
Spikes of blue, sometimes white, flowers in summer • Ferny foliage • 40–60 cm high, 30–45 cm wide

'Blue Butterfly' • Spikes of dark-blue flowers in summer • Ferny foliage • 40–60 cm high, 40–60 cm wide

'Summer Nights' • Spikes of blue flowers in early summer • Ferny foliage • 20–30 cm high, 30–45 cm wide

Delphinium nuttallianum
Spikes of deep blue-and-white flowers in summer • 20–40 cm high, 20–30 cm wide

Delphinium pylzowii
Spikes of blue flowers in summer • 20–30 cm high, 20 cm wide

Delphinium semibarbatum (syn. D. zalil)
Spikes of light-yellow flowers in summer • 75–100 cm high, 45–60 cm wide

Delphinium tricorne
Spikes of violet-blue flowers with white in early summer • 50–90 cm high, 30–45 cm wide

Delphinium x ruysii
'Pink Sensation' • Spikes of pink flowers in summer • 75–90 cm high, 45–60 cm wide

Dennstaedtia
p. 412

Genus Information
Origin: tropical regions; subtropical regions
Selected Common Names: hay scented fern
Nomenclature: Named for August Dennstedt, 1776–1826, a German botanist and physician.

General Features
Height: 45–90 cm
Spread: 45–90 cm
Habit: colony-forming, rhizomatous, slow-creeping fern
Foliage: interesting; hay-scented when crushed
Hardiness: B–C
Warnings: not prone to insects or disease; prone to slugs

Growing Requirements
Light: shade
Soil: humus-rich, moist, acidic soil
Location: shady mixed borders; wild gardens; woodland gardens: foliage may break and burn in windy locations
Propagation: spores; division in spring
Expert Advice: Germinate ripe spores at 15˚C for hardy types.

Buying Considerations

Professionals
Popularity: relatively unknown foliage plant
Availability: generally available as finished product from specialty growers
Size to Sell: sells best in smaller sizes
On the Shelf: high ornamental appeal; foliage breakage (display out of wind)
Shrinkage: low shrinkage; requires little maintenance

Collectors
Popularity: not generally of interest to collectors

Gardeners
Ease of Growth: generally easy to grow
Start with: one small plant for feature plant

What to Try First ...
Dennstaedtia punctiloba

On the Market
Dennstaedtia punctiloba
Colony-forming, slow creeper • 45–90 cm
high, 45–90 cm wide

Deschampsia
p. 412

Genus Information
Origin: temperate regions
Selected Common Names: tufted hair grass, wavy
hair grass
Nomenclature: Named for Louis Deschamps,
1765–1842, a French naturalist.

General Features
Height: 20–100 cm high
Spread: 20–90 cm wide
Habit: clump- or tussock-forming perennial grass
Flowers: light, airy seed heads; good for
cutflowers; good for drying
Foliage: solid and variegated
Hardiness: C
Warnings: prone to aphids and rust
Expert Advice: A non-invasive grass available in a
range of heights. Valued for its graceful, arching
plumes—good ornamental value.

Growing Requirements
Light: sun
Soil: moist, organic, neutral to acidic soil
Location: mixed borders; woodland gardens
Propagation: seed; division
Expert Advice: Propagate named varieties by
division.

Buying Considerations

Professionals
Popularity: gaining popularity as a foliage
plant
Availability: generally available as finished
product and bare root
Size to Sell: sells best in smaller sizes as it
matures fast
On the Shelf: high ornamental appeal; rapidly
overgrows pot
Shrinkage: low; requires little maintenance

Collectors
Popularity: of interest to collectors—
interesting seed heads

Gardeners
Ease of Growth: generally easy to grow but
needs close attention to growing conditions
Start with: one small plant for feature plant

What to Try First ...
Deschampsia cespitosa 'Bronzeschleier',
Deschampsia cespitosa 'Northern Lights',
Deschampsia cespitosa 'Tautrager', *Deschampsia
flexuosa nana*, *Deschampsia flexuosa* 'Tatra
Gold'

On the Market
Deschampsia cespitosa
Green-gold flowers followed by gold seed
heads in summer • 60–100 cm high,
45–60 cm wide

'Bronzeschleier' (Bronze Veil) • Silvery seed
heads turn to purple-bronze in summer •
60–100 cm high, 45–60 cm wide

'Goldschleier' (Golden Veil) • Narrow,
arching seed heads turn to gold in
summer • 60–100 cm high, 45–60 cm
wide

'Northern Lights' • Pink seed heads in
summer • Gold-white longitudinal stripes
• 30–45 cm high, 45–60 cm wide

'Schottland' (Scotland) • Silky, green seed
heads in summer • 60–100 cm high,
45–60 cm wide

'Tautrager' (Dew Carrier) • Shiny, silvery
seed heads in summer • 60–100 cm high,
45–60 cm wide

Deschampsia flexuosa
'Tatra Gold' (syn. Aurea) • Silver-purple
seed heads in summer • Bluish-green
foliage • 45–60 cm high, 20–30 cm wide

Deschampsia flexuosa nana
Purplish seed heads in summer • Yellow-
green foliage • 20–35 cm high, 20–25 cm
wide

Dianthus
p. 412

Genus Information
Origin: Asia, Europe and North America
Selected Common Names: alpine pink, carnation,
maiden pink, pink, red caesar, sweet William
Nomenclature: For the Greek *Dios* (genitive of
Zeus) and *anthos* (flower), the flower of the
gods. A plant name used by Theophrastus.
Notes: A genus of over 300 species.

General Features

Height: 2–75 cm high
Spread: 5–60 cm wide
Habit: clump-forming biennial to perennial; (some) short-lived
Flowers: many colours; (most) fragrant; single to double; late spring to fall; good for cutflowers; (most) long blooming period
Foliage: evergreen
Hardiness: A–D
Warnings: prone to crown rot and rust in poorly drained soils or humid regions
Expert Advice: A versatile addition to gardens. Deadhead to extend blooming season (do not deadhead biennial types).

Growing Requirements

Light: sun
Soil: cool, well-drained, lean, alkaline to neutral soil; avoid winter wet; drought tolerant; Alpine types: sharp to well-drained, generally lean, alkaline to neutral soil; avoid winter wet; Maiden Pink types: tolerate dry, sandy soil
Location: alpine gardens; rock gardens; mixed borders; Alpine types: scree
Propagation: seed; self-sows; cuttings
Expert Advice: Keep roots of Alpine types cool by growing near rocks or applying rock mulch. Sweet William/Carnation types benefit from protective winter mulch. Named *Dianthus* cultivars may not come true from seed.

Buying Considerations

Professionals

Popularity: popular garden standard; Alpine types • gaining popularity; all are fast sellers in bloom
Availability: readily available as finished product; Alpine types: from specialty growers
Size to Sell: sells best in smaller sizes (when blooming)
On the Shelf: high ornamental appeal; keep stock rotated; deadhead regularly
Shrinkage: low; sensitive to overwatering

Collectors

Popularity: of interest to collectors; Alpine types: rare, exceptional beauty

Gardeners

Ease of Growth: (most) very easy to grow; Alpine and Sweet William/Carnation types: need close attention to growing conditions
Start with: one small plant for feature plant or several for instant visual effect; Maiden Pink types: best for mass planting
Expert Advice: We divide *Dianthus* into 4 groups for display and growing information purposes: **Alpine/Species, Garden Pinks, Maiden Pinks** and **Sweet William/ Carnations.**

What to Try First ...

Dianthus 'G. Bentham', *Dianthus* 'Licinata', *Dianthus* 'Mini Mounds', *Dianthus alpinus*, *Dianthus alpinus* 'Joan's Blood', *Dianthus brevicaulis, Dianthus callizonus*

On the Market

Dianthus, Alpine/Species p. 412

Dianthus
'G. Bentham' • Pink flowers in early summer • Evergreen • 8–10 cm high, 20–30 cm wide

'Licinata' • Rose-red flowers in summer • Blue-grey foliage • 5–10 cm high, 15–20 cm wide

'Mini Mounds' • Pink flowers in early summer • Evergreen • 5 cm high, 5–10 cm wide

Dianthus alpinus
Crimson flowers with dark centre in summer • Evergreen • Organic, sharply drained, fertile soil • 8–10 cm high, 10–20 cm wide

'Albus' • White flowers with pink centres in summer • Evergreen • Organic, sharply drained, fertile soil • 8–10 cm high, 10–20 cm wide

'Big Cups' • Single, pink flowers in summer • Evergreen • Organic, sharply drained, fertile soil • 5–10 cm high, 10–25 cm wide

'Joan's Blood' • Fragrant, large, red-purple flowers in summer • Evergreen • Sharply drained, fertile soil • 8–10 cm high, 10–20 cm wide

'Little Joe' • Fragrant, crimson flowers in summer • Steel-blue, evergreen foliage • Organic, sharply drained, fertile soil • 8–10 cm high, 10–20 cm wide

Dianthus amurensis
Rose-purple flowers with darker centres in summer • 20–30 cm high, 20–30 cm wide

'Siberian Blues' • Blue flowers in summer • 20–30 cm high, 20–30 cm wide

Dianthus arenarius
Fragrant, white to pink flowers in summer • Evergreen • 15–30 cm high, 20–30 cm wide

Dianthus arpadianus **ssp. *pumilus***
Rose flowers in summer • Evergreen • 1–5 cm high, 15–20 cm wide

Dianthus brevicaulis
Large, deep-pink to purple flowers in summer • Evergreen • 5–10 cm high, 10–25 cm wide

Dianthus brevicaulis ssp. *brevicaulis*
Rose-pink flowers in summer • Evergreen •
5–10 cm high, 10–25 cm wide

Dianthus callizonus
Pink to carmine flowers in summer •
5–10 cm high, 10–15 cm wide

Dianthus carthusianorus
Clustered, pink to purple flowers in summer
• Evergreen • 40–60 cm high, 30–40 cm
wide

Dianthus dentosus
Violet to pink, dark-eyed flowers in summer
• Blue-green foliage • 15–30 cm high,
20–30 cm wide

Dianthus erinaceus
Pink flowers in summer • Evergreen •
5–12 cm high, 10–25 cm wide

Dianthus erinaceus var. *alpinus*
Pink flowers in summer • Evergreen •
5–12 cm high, 10–25 cm wide

Dianthus freynii
Bright-pink flowers in midsummer •
5–10 cm high, 10–20 cm wide

Dianthus giganteus
Purple-pink flowers in summer •
40–75 cm high, 30–45 cm wide

Dianthus glacialis
Soft- to dark-pink flowers in summer •
Evergreen • Slightly acidic, sharply drained
soil • 5–10 cm high, 10–15 cm wide

Dianthus glacialis ssp. *gelidus*
Carmine to red-pink flowers in summer •
Evergreen • Slightly acidic, sharply drained
soil • 5–10 cm high, 10–15 cm wide

Dianthus gracilis
Deep-pink to red flowers in late spring •
Evergreen • 10–30 cm high, 15–25 cm wide

Dianthus haematocalyx
Rose-red flowers in summer • Grey-green
evergreen foliage • 10–25 cm high,
15–20 cm wide

Dianthus haematocalyx ssp. *pindicola*
Purple-red flowers in summer • Grey-green
evergreen foliage • 5–10 cm high, 10–20 cm
wide

Dianthus haematocalyx var. *alpinus*
Rose flowers in summer • Grey-green
evergreen foliage • 10–15 cm high,
10–15 cm wide

Dianthus knappii
Small, sulphur-yellow flowers in summer •
25–40 cm high, 30–40 cm wide

Dianthus leucophaeus var. *leucophaeus*
Yellow to white flowers with reddish reverse
sides in summer • Blue-green foliage •
1–5 cm high, 10–20 cm wide

'Blue Lagoon' • Yellow to white flowers with
reddish reverse sides in summer • Blue-
green foliage • 5 cm high, 10–20 cm wide

Dianthus microlepis
Pink to purple flowers in summer • Blue-
grey evergreen foliage • Sharply drained,
acidic soil • 5–10 cm high, 10–20 cm wide

'Albus' • White flowers in summer • Blue-
grey evergreen foliage • Sharply drained,
acidic soil • 5–10 cm high, 10–20 cm wide

(Czech form) • Pink to purple flowers in
summer • Blue-grey evergreen foliage •
Sharply drained, acidic soil • 1–5 cm high,
10–20 cm wide

(Select) • Pink to purple flowers in summer
• Blue-grey evergreen foliage • Sharply
drained, acidic soil • 1–10 cm high,
10–20 cm wide

Dianthus microlepis var. *degenii*
Pink-purple flowers in early summer • Blue-
grey evergreen foliage • Sharply drained,
acidic soil • 5–10 cm high, 10–20 cm wide

Dianthus monspessulanus ssp. *sternbergii*
Fragrant, large, pink-purple flowers in
summer • Silvery evergreen foliage •
10–15 cm high, 10–15 cm wide

Dianthus myrtinervius
Bright-pink flowers in summer • Evergreen
• 5 cm high, 10–20 cm wide

Dianthus myrtinervius ssp. *caespitosus*
Rose-pink flowers in summer • Olive-green
evergreen folaige • 5 cm high, 10–15 cm wide

'Geri' • Pink flowers in summer • Silver-
green evergreen foliage • 2–5 cm high,
10–15 cm wide

Dianthus nitidus
Pink flowers with red veins in summer •
3–5 cm high, 5–15 cm wide

Dianthus pamiroalaicus
Single, yellow flowers in summer • 5–10 cm
high, 10–15 cm wide

Dianthus pavonius
Soft-red to cherry-red flowers in summer •
Evergreen • Sharply drained, acidic soil •
5–10 cm high, 20–30 cm wide

Dianthus petraeus
Fringed, white flowers in summer •
Evergreen • 15–20 cm high, 20–30 cm wide

Dianthus petraeus ssp. *noeanus*
Fragrant, white flowers in summer •
Evergreen • 10–15 cm high, 15–20 cm wide

Dianthus pinifolius
Rose-purple to pink flowers in summer •
Evergreen • 5–10 cm high, 20–30 cm wide

D

Dianthus seguieri
Rose-pink flowers in midsummer to fall • Evergreen • 40–50 cm high, 30–45 cm wide

Dianthus simulans
Rose-red flowers in late spring to early summer • Evergreen • 5–10 cm high, 15–20 cm wide

'Sugared Sweetie' • Pink flowers in summer • Evergreen • 5–10 cm high, 15–20 cm wide

(Tight form) • Rose-red flowers in summer • Evergreen • 5–10 cm high, 15–20 cm wide

Dianthus squarrosus
Fragrant, deeply fringed, feathery, white flowers in summer • Grey-green foliage • 2–5 cm high, 10–15 cm wide

Dianthus stenocalyx
Rich-pink flowers in summer • Evergreen • 15–20 cm high, 20–30 cm wide

Dianthus subacaulis
Carmine-pink to soft-pink flowers in summer • Evergreen • 5–20 cm high, 15–25 cm wide

'Punnett's Tight Blue' • Soft-pink to carmine-pink flowers in summer • Blue-grey evergreen foliage • 5–20 cm high, 15–25 cm wide

Dianthus subacaulis ssp. brachyanthus
Soft pink to carmine-pink flowers in summer • Evergreen • 5–15 cm high, 10–20 cm wide

Dianthus superbus
'Crimsonia' • Fragrant, fringed, crimson flowers in summer • Evergreen • 40–50 cm high, 40–50 cm wide

Dianthus sylvestris
Pink to rose flowers in summer • Evergreen • 15–40 cm high, 20–40 cm wide

Dianthus zederbaueri
White or pink flowers with red reverse sides in summer • Silver-grey foliage • 10–20 cm high, 10–15 cm wide

Dianthus, Garden Pinks   p. 412

Dianthus
'Aqua' • Fragrant, white flowers in summer • Evergreen • 15–25 cm high, 30–40 cm wide

'Aunt Rose' • Semi-double, white flowers in summer • Blue-green, evergreen foliage • 15–25 cm high, 20–30 cm wide

'Badenia' • Red flowers in early summer • Evergreen • 10 cm high, 15–20 cm wide

'Bat's Double Red' • Large, semi-double, deep ruby-red flowers in late spring to early summer • 25–40 cm high, 30–45 cm wide

'Bath's Pink' • Fragrant, pink flowers in early summer • Evergreen • 15–20 cm high, 20–25 cm wide

'Blue Hills' • Crimson flowers in early spring to early summer • Evergreen • 15–25 cm high, 25–40 cm wide

'Brilliant Star' • Fragrant, white flowers with a magenta eye in summer • Blue-grey, evergreen foliage • 15–20 cm high, 15–20 cm wide

'Candy Dish' • Frilly, double, pink flowers with red streaks in summer • Evergreen • 25–30 cm high, 30–45 cm wide

'Cheyenne' • Fragrant, rose-pink flowers in summer • Evergreen • 30–60 cm high, 30–45 cm wide

'Crimson Treasure' • Crimson flowers with gold flecks in summer • Evergreen • 10–15 cm high, 20–30 cm wide

'Doris' • Fragrant, double, pink flowers with salmon-pink eye in summer • Evergreen • 20–30 cm high, 30–45 cm wide

'Dottie' • Fragrant, white flowers with pink eye in late spring • Evergreen • 10–15 cm high, 15–20 cm wide

Eastern Star™ (Red Dwarf) • Fragrant, deep-pink flowers with a maroon eye in spring to late summer • Silver-gray, evergreen foliage • 5 cm high, 15–20 cm wide

'European Kopo Cardinal' • Bright-red flowers in summer • Evergreen • 20–30 cm high, 20–30 cm wide

'European Pink Dancer' • Soft-pink flowers with red eye in summer • Evergreen • 20–30 cm high, 20–30 cm wide

'European Showgirl' • Salmon flowers in summer • Evergreen • 20–30 cm high, 20–30 cm wide

Fire Star™ (Devon Xera) • Fragrant, fire-red flowers with a crimson eye in spring to late summer • Blue-grey, evergreen foliage • 15–20 cm high, 15–20 cm wide

'First Love' • Fragrant, white to rose flowers in summer • Evergreen • 15–30 cm high, 40–45 cm wide

'Frosty Fire' • Double, red flowers in late spring to summer • Blue-grey, evergreen foliage • 15 cm high, 20–30 cm wide

'Gaiety' • Fragrant, double, rose-pink flowers in summer • Evergreen • 25–30 cm high, 30–45 cm wide

'Gold Dust' • Red flowers with gold flecks in summer • Evergreen • 15–20 cm high, 20–25 cm wide

'Helen' • Double, deep-salmon flowers in summer • Evergreen • 25–30 cm high, 40–45 cm wide

'Itsaul White' • Fragrant, white flowers in summer • Evergreen • 20–30 cm high, 30–40 cm wide

'La Bourboule' • Fragrant, pink flowers in summer • Evergreen • 10–15 cm high, 15 cm wide

'Laced Hero' • Burgundy-and-white flowers in summer • Evergreen • 20–30 cm high, 30–45 cm wide

'Laced Romeo' • Fringed, red flowers with cream centre in summer • Evergreen • 30–40 cm high, 30–40 cm wide

'Little Blue Boy' • Single, soft-pink flowers with burgundy centre in summer • Fine, blue-grey foliage • 20–25 cm high, 30–40 cm wide

'Little Bobby' • Fragrant, soft-pink flowers in summer • Silver-blue, evergreen foliage • 10–15 cm high, 30–45 cm wide

'Little Jock' • Fragrant, pale-pink flowers with maroon eye in summer • Evergreen • 8–10 cm high, 20–30 cm wide

'Mars' • Fragrant, double, red flowers in summer • Blue, evergreen foliage • 10–15 cm high, 15–30 cm wide

'McMurtrie Seedling' • Mottled red, white and maroon flowers in summer • Evergreen • 20–25 cm high, 15–20 cm wide

'Mountain Mist' • Dark-pink flowers in early spring to early summer • Evergreen • 30–40 cm high, 25–40 cm wide

'Neon Star' • Hot-pink flowers in summer • Blue-grey, evergreen foliage • 15–20 cm high, 15–20 cm wide

'Peppermint Patty' • Fragrant, semi-double, pink flowers in early summer • Blue-grey, evergreen foliage • 20–30 cm high, 15–25 cm wide

'Pike's Pink' • Fragrant, double, soft-pink flowers in summer • Evergreen • 10 cm high, 15–20 cm wide

'Pink Princess' • Fragrant, coral-pink flowers in summer • Evergreen • 30–45 cm high, 30–45 cm wide

'Pixie' • Pink flowers with deeper pink accent in summer • Blue-grey, evergreen foliage • 15–20 cm high, 15–20 cm wide

'Pixie Star' • Bright-pink flowers with a rose-pink eye in summer • Blue-grey, evergreen foliage • 15–20 cm high, 15–20 cm wide

'Prairie Pink' • Fragrant, pink flowers in summer • Evergreen • 40–60 cm high, 25–40 cm wide

'Queen of Sheba' • Fragrant, frilled, single, pink-red flowers in spring • Evergreen • 15–20 cm high, 20–30 cm wide

'Rachel' • Fragrant, large, double, pink flowers in early summer • Evergreen • 20–30 cm high, 20–30 cm wide

'Rainbow Loveliness' • Fragrant, single, white, pink or rose flowers in summer • Evergreen • 30–40 cm high, 15–25 cm wide

'Raspberry Parfait' • Bluish-pink flowers with crimson eye in summer • Evergreen • 10–15 cm high, 15–20 cm wide

'Red Head' • Red flowers in summer • Evergreen • 20–25 cm high, 15–20 cm wide

'Rubin' • Fragrant, single, deep-red flowers in spring • Steel-blue, evergreen foliage • 10 cm high, 15–20 cm wide

'Snow White with a Red Eye' • Pink flowers in summer • Blue-green, evergreen foliage • 15–20 cm high, 30 cm wide

'Spangled Star' • Red flowers with pink blotches in summer • Blue-grey, evergreen foliage • 15–20 cm high, 15–20 cm wide

'Spotty' • Fragrant, white-spotted, red flowers in early summer • Evergreen • 10–15 cm high, 15–20 cm wide

'Stripes and Picotee' • Red-striped-and-splashed flowers in summer • Evergreen • 40–45 cm high, 20–30 cm wide

'Sweet Memory' • Semi-double, white flowers with pink eye in summer • Evergreen • 15–20 cm high, 30–40 cm wide

'Velvet and Lace' • Fragrant, black-purple flowers with white edge in summer • Evergreen • 30–40 cm high, 40–45 cm wide

'War Bonnet' • Fragrant, double, deep-red flowers in summer • Evergreen • 25–30 cm high, 30–45 cm wide

'Whatfield Mini' • Fragrant, white to pink flowers in summer • Evergreen • 15–20 cm high, 30–40 cm wide

'Whatfield Pom-Pom' • Fragrant, double, fringed, deep-pink flowers in summer • Evergreen • 10–15 cm high, 15–25 cm wide

D

'Whitehills' • Single, white flowers in summer • Evergreen • 5–10 cm high, 25–30 cm wide

Dianthus gratianopolitanus
Fragrant flowers in summer • Evergreen • 10–20 cm high, 30–40 cm wide

'Bourbon' • Fragrant, pink flowers in summer • Evergreen • 5–10 cm high, 10–15 cm wide

'Emmen' • Fragrant, red flowers in summer • Evergreen • 15–20 cm high, 15–20 cm wide

'Firewitch' • Fragrant, magenta flowers in early summer • Evergreen • 15–45 cm high, 30–40 cm wide

'French Kiss' • Fragrant, burgundy flowers with white in summer • Evergreen • 20–25 cm high, 20–30 cm wide

'Petite' • Fragrant, bright-pink flowers in summer • Evergreen • 10–15 cm high, 15–20 cm wide

'Sternkissen' • Fragrant, rose-pink flowers in summer • Evergreen • 5–10 cm high, 10–15 cm wide

'Tiny Rubies' • Fragrant, double, deep pink flowers in spring • Evergreen • 10–15 cm high, 30–40 cm wide

Dianthus plumarius
Fragrant, white to rose flowers in late spring to early summer • 20–40 cm high, 30–40 cm wide

'Roseus Plenus' • Fragrant, double, medium-pink flowers in summer • Evergreen • 25–40 cm high, 40–45 cm wide

Dianthus, Maiden Pinks   p. 412

Dianthus deltoides
Flowers in summer • Evergreen • 10–20 cm high, 25–45 cm wide

'Albus' • White flowers in summer • Evergreen • 10–20 cm high, 25–45 cm wide

'Arctic Fire' • White flowers with red eye in summer • Evergreen • 10–20 cm high, 25–45 cm wide

'Brilliant' • Double, bright-crimson flowers in summer • Evergreen • 15–20 cm high, 25–45 cm wide

'E.A. Bowles' • Rose-red flowers in summer • Evergreen • 10–20 cm high, 25–45 cm wide

'Erectus' • Bright-red flowers in summer • Evergreen • 10–20 cm high, 25–45 cm wide

'Flashing Light' • Hot-pink flowers in summer • Evergreen • 10–20 cm high, 25–45 cm wide

'Microchip' • White flowers with red stripes in summer • Evergreen • 10–15 cm high, 30–45 cm wide

'Samos' • Intense red flowers in summer • Evergreen • 10–20 cm high, 25–45 cm wide

'Snow Fire' • Red flowers with white eye in summer • Evergreen • 10–20 cm high, 25–45 cm wide

'Zing Rose' • Single, rose-red flowers in summer • Evergreen • 10–20 cm high, 25–45 cm wide

Dianthus, Sweet William/ Carnations   p. 412

Dianthus barbatus
Fragrant, clustered, white, pink, red and purple flowers in late spring to late summer • 30–60 cm high, 30–45 cm wide

'Alba' • Fragrant, clustered, white flowers in late spring to late summer • 30–60 cm high, 30–45 cm wide

'Double Dwarf' • Fragrant, clustered, bicoloured flowers in late spring to late summer • 15–20 cm high, 20–30 cm wide

(Dwarf Single mix) • Fragrant, clustered flowers in late spring to late summer • 15–25 cm high, 20–30 cm wide

(Indian Carpet mix) • Fragrant, clustered flowers in late spring to late summer • 15–30 cm high, 20–40 cm wide

(Messinger mix) • Fragrant, clustered flowers in late spring to late summer • 30–40 cm high, 40–45 cm wide

'Oeschberg' • Fragrant, clustered, purple-red flowers in late spring to late summer • 35–45 cm high, 30–45 cm wide

'Sooty' • Fragrant, clustered, velvety, burgundy flowers in late spring to late summer • 40–50 cm high, 25–40 cm wide

(Tall Double mix) • Fragrant, clustered flowers in late spring to late summer • 45–60 cm high, 30–45 cm wide

Nigrescens group
Fragrant, clustered, black-red flowers in late spring to late summer • 30–60 cm high, 30–45 cm wide

Dianthus caryophyllus
'King of the Blacks' • Long-stemmed, fragrant, double, deep-red flowers in summer • Evergreen • 45–60 cm high, 45–60 cm wide

'Shadow Valley' • Long-stemmed, fragrant, bright-red flowers in summer • Evergreen • 60–75 cm high, 45–60 cm wide

Grenadin Series
The best large-flowered carnation for the Prairies • 45–60 cm high, 30–45 cm wide

'Grenadin Pink' • Fragrant, double, pink flowers in summer • 45–60 cm high, 45–60 cm wide

'Grenadin Red' • Fragrant, double, red flowers in summer • 45–60 cm high, 45–60 cm wide

'Grenadin White' • Fragrant, double, white flowers in summer • 45–60 cm high, 45–60 cm wide

'Grenadin Yellow' • Fragrant, double, yellow flowers in summer • 45–60 cm high, 45–60 cm wide

Dicentra

p. 413

Genus Information

Origin: Asia and North America
Selected Common Names: bleeding heart, climbing bleeding heart, fernleaf bleeding heart, pacific bleeding heart, Valentine flower
Nomenclature: From the Greek *dis* (two) and *kentron* (spur), referring to the two spurred flowers.

General Features
Height: 15–90 cm high
Spread: 15–90 cm wide
Habit: rhizomatous or tuberous spreading perennial
Flowers: long blooming period; spring to late summer; *D. spectabilis* goes dormant in summer
Foliage: fern-like
Hardiness: B–D
Warnings: not prone to insects or disease; ingesting flowers and foliage may cause stomach upset; contact with foliage may irritate skin
Expert Advice: *D. spectabilis* has a yellow dye in the root that will discolour skin on contact.

Growing Requirements
Light: shade to a.m. sun
Soil: fertile, moist, organic, well-drained soil
Location: mixed borders; rock gardens; wild gardens; woodland gardens; avoid hot, windy sites
Propagation: seed; division
Expert Advice: Germinate seed at 16°C. Divide in spring. *D. spectabilis* can be divided by root cuttings.

Buying Considerations

Professionals
Popularity: popular, old-fashioned garden standard; fast-selling foliage plant
Availability: readily available as finished product and bare root
Size to Sell: sells best in smaller sizes (when blooming)—*D. spectablis* matures quickly
On the Shelf: keep stock rotated; foliage breakage
Shrinkage: (most) high; sensitive to overwatering; (*D. spectabilis*) low; little maintenance

Collectors
Popularity: not generally of interest to collectors

Gardeners
Ease of Growth: very easy to grow
Start with: one small plant for feature plant

What to Try First ...
Dicentra 'Adrian Bloom', *Dicentra* 'King of Hearts', *Dicentra* 'Luxuriant', *Dicentra formosa* 'Aurora', *Dicentra formosa* 'Ruby Marr', *Dicentra formosa* 'Zestful'

On the Market

Dicentra

'Adrian Bloom' • Deep-red flowers in spring to summer • Blue-green fern-like foliage • 30–40 cm high, 30–45 cm wide

'Bacchanal' • Red-pink flowers in spring to summer • Fern-like foliage • 25–45 cm high, 30–45 cm wide

'Bountiful' • Purple-red flowers in late spring to late summer • Fern-like foliage • 25–35 cm high, 30–45 cm wide

'Candy Hearts' • Red flowers in spring to summer • Blue-green foliage • 20–30 cm high, 30–45 cm wide

'Ivory Heart' • White flowers in spring to summer • Blue-green foliage • 20–30 cm high, 30–45 cm wide

'King of Hearts' • Dark-rose flowers in spring to summer • Fern-like foliage • 15–25 cm high, 30–45 cm wide

'Langtrees' • White flowers in spring to summer • Blue-green foliage • 20–40 cm high, 30–45 cm wide

'Luxuriant' • Carmine-pink flowers in spring to late summer • Fern-like foliage • 25–30 cm high, 30–45 cm wide

'Snowflakes' • White flowers in spring to summer • Fern-like foliage • 25–30 cm high, 30–45 cm wide

'Stuart Boothman' (syn. Boothman's Variety) • Flesh-pink flowers in summer • Fern-like foliage • 20–30 cm high, 40–45 cm wide

Dicentra canadensis
White flowers in spring • Grey-green foliage • 20–30 cm high, 20–30 cm wide

Dicentra cucullaria
White flowers in spring • Fern-like foliage • 15–30 cm high, 20–30 cm wide

Dicentra eximia
Pink flowers in spring to summer • Fern-like foliage • 30–45 cm high, 30–45 cm wide

'Alba' • White flowers in spring to summer • Fern-like foliage • 30–45 cm high, 30–45 cm wide

'Snowdrift' • White flowers in early spring to summer • Fern-like foliage • 20–30 cm high, 30–45 cm wide

Dicentra formosa
Pink flowers in spring to summer • Fern-like foliage • 30–45 cm high, 45–60 cm wide

'Aurora' • White flowers in spring to summer • Blue-green, fern-like foliage • 20–30 cm high, 30–45 cm wide

'Margery Fish' • White flowers in spring to summer • Blue-green foliage • 30–45 cm high, 30–45 cm wide

'Ruby Marr' • Ruby-red flowers in spring to summer • Fern-like foliage • 25–35 cm high, 30–45 cm wide

'Zestful' • Pink flowers in spring to summer • Fern-like foliage • 30–45 cm high, 30–45 cm wide

Dicentra macrantha
Creamy-yellow flowers in late spring to early summer • Moist, well-drained, sandy, fertile soil • 40–50 cm high, 30–45 cm wide

Dicentra peregrina
Lyre-shaped, pink flowers in early summer • Blue-green foliage • 5–10 cm high, 15–20 cm wide

Dicentra scandens
Yellow to white flowers in summer • Climber • 1–3 m high, 60–100 cm wide

Dicentra spectabilis
Pink flowers with white tips in spring to early summer • May go dormant in summer • 75–90 cm high, 75–90 cm wide

'Alba' • White flowers in spring to early summer • 75–90 cm high, 75–90 cm wide

'Gold Heart' • Pink flowers in spring to early summer • Lime-green foliage • 75–90 cm high, 75–90 cm wide

Dictamnus

p. 413

Genus Information

Origin: Europe, Asia, China and Korea
Selected Common Names: burning bush, dittany, gas plant, purple gas plant
Nomenclature: From the Greek *diktamnon* (Dittany), *Dictamnus* is another name for Oregano.
Notes: The flowers exude a volatile gas on warm, windless evenings—when lit, the gas creates a blue glow over the bush for a split second, hence its common name, "purple gas plant."

General Features

Height: 60–90 cm high
Spread: 60–75 cm wide
Habit: very long-lived, tap-rooted perennial
Flowers: purple or white; borne on spikes
Foliage: very aromatic (lemon-scented)
Hardiness: C
Warnings: not prone to insects or disease; contact with foliage may irritate skin
Expert Advice: A very long-lived, underused and hardy perennial that make take up to 3 years to bloom. Flowers emit flammable oil—a match held just below the blossom will ignite it with a soft "pop."

Growing Requirements

Light: sun
Soil: dry, moderately fertile, well-drained soil; drought tolerant
Location: mixed borders
Propagation: seed; division
Expert Advice: This plant takes a long time to reach blooming size from seed. Division can be difficult as it resents being disturbed.

Buying Considerations

Professionals

Popularity: gaining popularity; fast seller in bloom
Availability: occasionally available as bare root from specialty growers
Size to Sell: sells best in mature sizes (when blooming); matures slowly
Shrinkage: low; requires little maintenance

Collectors

Popularity: not generally of interest to collectors

Gardeners

Ease of Growth: very easy to grow
Start with: one mature plant for feature plant

What to Try First ...

Dictamnus albus 'Albiflorus', *Dictamnus albus* var. *purpureus*

On the Market

Dictamnus albus
'**Albiflorus**' • Fragrant, white flowers in late spring to early summer • 75–90 cm high, 60–75 cm wide

Dictamnus albus **var.** *caucasicus*
Fragrant, dark-pink flowers in late spring to early summer • 60–90 cm high, 60–75 cm wide

Dictamnus albus **var.** *purpureus*
Fragrant, pink flowers in late spring to early summer • 75–90 cm high, 60–75 cm wide

Digitalis

p. 413

Genus Information

Origin: Europe, Asia and North Africa
Selected Common Names: foxglove
Nomenclature: From the Latin *digitus* (finger), referring to the flower shape. The common name is from the Anglo-Saxon, meaning *foxes* (glew) or *fox* (music), which refers to the shape of an ancient instrument.
Other Uses: European herbalists used the leaves purely for healing wounds and skin diseases. Later, it was discovered to have value for the treatment of heart disease. Today, glycosides are extracted from *D. purpurea* and *D. lanata* by the pharmaceutical industry to produce digitoxin and digoxin, the heart drugs.

General Features
Height: 30 cm–2 m high
Spread: 20–75 cm wide
Habit: short-lived, clump-forming biennial or perennial; may require staking
Flowers: tall, spikes; tubular; (some) spotted; good for cutflowers; deadhead to extend blooming season; attracts hummingbirds
Foliage: hairy; peanut butter–scented
Hardiness: C–D
Warnings: prone to powdery mildew and aphids; not bothered by mammals; flowers and foliage are poisonous; contact with foliage may irritate skin
Expert Advice: In colder areas water well in fall and mulch with spruce boughs.

Growing Requirements
Light: sun to p.m. sun
Soil: fertile, moist, well-drained soil; avoid wet spring soil; mulch to keep cool roots
Location: borders; woodland gardens; wild gardens;, cottage gardens
Propagation: seed (self-sows); division
Expert Advice: Seed needs light to germinate. Sow outdoors in fall or spring. Often blooms the first year from seed. Do not cut back biennial plants.

Buying Considerations

Professionals
Popularity: popular, old-fashioned garden standard
Availability: readily available as finished product
Size to Sell: sells best in smaller sizes (when blooming) as it matures fast
On the Shelf: keep stock rotated; rapidly overgrows pot; needs regular cleaning
Shrinkage: high; sensitive to underwatering

Collectors
Popularity: not generally of interest to collectors

Gardeners
Ease of Growth: generally easy to grow but needs close attention to growing conditions
Start with: one small plant for feature plant and several for mass plantings

What to Try First ...
Digitalis grandiflora, Digitalis grandiflora 'Dropmore Yellow', *Digitalis* x *mertonensis*, *Digitalis purpurea* (mix), *Digitalis thapsi* 'Spanish Peaks'

On the Market

Digitalis grandiflora
Brown-spotted, yellow flowers in summer • 75–100 cm high, 30–45 cm wide

'**Carillon**' • Pale-yellow flowers with brown overtones in summer • 75–100 cm high, 30–45 cm wide

'**Dropmore Yellow**' • Soft-yellow flowers with brown speckled throats in summer • 75–100 cm high, 30–45 cm wide

Digitalis lanata
Yellow flowers in summer • 50–75 cm high, 30–45 cm wide

Digitalis x *mertonensis*
Strawberry-pink flowers in summer • 75–90 cm high, 30–45 cm wide

Digitalis obscura
Amber-orange flowers in summer • 30–60 cm high, 30–45 cm wide

Digitalis purpurea
Flowers in mixed colours in summer • 1–2 m high, 60–75 cm wide

'**Apricot**' • Apricot-pink flowers in summer • 1–2 m high, 60–75 cm wide

(**Peloric mixed**) • Large, open flowers in summer • 1–2 m high, 60–75 cm wide

Excelsior Group
Flowers in a variety of mixed colours in summer • 1–2 m high, 60–75 cm wide

Foxy Group
Spikes of carmine, pink, white or cream flowers in summer • 60–90 cm high, 30–45 cm wide

Gloxiniodes Group
Large, yellow, purple or pink flowers in summer • 1–2 m high, 60–75 cm wide

Digitalis thapsi
'Spanish Peaks' • Raspberry-rose flowers in early summer • 30–60 cm high, 30 cm wide

Dipsacus

Genus Information
Origin: Europe, Asia and North Africa
Selected Common Names: common teasel
Nomenclature: From the Greek *dipsa* (thirst), referring to the attached leaf bases found in some species that can hold water.

General Features
Height: 1.5–2 m high
Spread: 50–75 cm wide
Habit: upright, biennial or short-lived perennial
Flowers: excellent for drying
Hardiness: C
Warnings: prone to powdery mildew and aphids; painful to handle

Growing Requirements
Light: sun
Soil: lean, well-drained soil; drought tolerant
Location: wild gardens; mixed borders
Propagation: seed (self-sows readily)

Buying Considerations

Professionals
Popularity: relatively unknown
Availability: occasionally available from specialty growers
Size to Sell: sells best in smaller sizes as it matures fast
On the Shelf: rapidly overgrows pot
Shrinkage: high; sensitive to overwatering

Collectors
Popularity: not generally of interest to collectors

Gardeners
Ease of Growth: generally easy to grow but needs close attention to growing conditions
Start with: one small plant for feature plant

What to Try First ...
Dipsacus fullonum

On the Market
Dipsacus fullonum
Lilac flowers in midsummer • 1.5–2 m high, 50–75 cm wide

Disporopsis
p. 413

Genus Information
Origin: China and Asia
Selected Common Names: None
Nomenclature: From the Greek referring to the flowers having paired ovules. Resembles the related genus *Disporum*.
Notes: This genus is brand new, with the taxonomy still in dispute.

General Features
Height: 15–20 cm high
Spread: 15–20+ cm wide
Habit: rhizomatous perennial
Flowers: hanging, bell-like; spring
Foliage: dark-green, waxy
Fruit: deep-blue, ornamental
Hardiness: C–D
Warnings: prone to aphids and slugs; not prone to diseases

Growing Requirements
Light: shade
Soil: cool, moist, organic, well-drained soil
Location: woodland gardens; mixed borders
Propagation: seed; division
Expert Advice: Seeds are double-dormant (stay dormant for two growing seasons). Divide in spring.

Buying Considerations

Professionals
Popularity: relatively unknown
Availability: occasionally available from specialty growers
Size to Sell: sells best in smaller sizes (when blooming) as it matures fast
On the Shelf: keep stock rotated
Shrinkage: high; sensitive to overwatering; goes dormant in pot

Collectors
Popularity: not generally of interest to collectors

Gardeners
Ease of Growth: mostly easy to grow but needs close attention to growing conditions
Start with: one small plant for feature plant

What to Try First ...
Disporopsis arisanensis

Disporopsis arisanensis
Drooping, creamy-white flowers with blackish basal marks in late spring • 15–20 cm high, 15–20+ cm wide

Disporum

Genus Information

Origin: North America, east Asia and the Himalayas
Selected Common Names: fairy bells
Nomenclature: From the Greek *di* (two) and *spora* (seed), referring to the fruit that normally bears 2 seeds.
Notes: A newly created genus of plants that should become popular for the shade garden. Closely related to *Tricyrtis*.

General Features

Height: 30–75 cm high
Spread: 25–60 cm wide
Habit: slow-spreading, rhizomatous perennial
Flowers: hanging, bell-like; spring
Foliage: dark-green; ovate to lance-shaped
Fruit: orange, red or black
Hardiness: C–D
Warnings: prone to aphids and slugs; not prone to diseases
Expert Advice: Ornamental orange, black or red berries in fall.

Growing Requirements

Light: shade
Soil: cool, moist, organic, well-drained soil
Location: rock gardens; woodland gardens
Propagation: seed; division of rhizomes

Buying Considerations

Professionals
Popularity: relatively unknown
Availability: occasionally available from specialty growers
Size to Sell: sells best in smaller sizes as it matures fast
On the Shelf: keep stock rotated
Shrinkage: low; requires little maintenance

Collectors
Popularity: not generally of interest to collectors

Gardeners
Ease of Growth: mostly easy to grow but needs close attention to growing conditions
Start with: one small plant for feature plant

What to Try First ...
Disporum flavens, Disporum sessile 'Variegatum'

On the Market

Disporum cantoniense
'Variegated' • Lily-like, purple or white flowers in spring • 45–75 cm high, 45–60 cm wide

Disporum flavens
Creamy-white, bell flowers in spring • 45–60 cm high, 25–40 cm wide

Disporum hookeri
White bell flowers in spring • 30–60 cm high, 30–45 cm wide

Disporum sessile
'Variegatum' • White flowers in spring • Slow-spreading habit • 30–60 cm high, 30–45 cm wide

Disporum smilacinum
'Morning Glow' • White flowers in spring • Foliage has white centre • 30–45 cm high, 20–30 cm wide

'Silver Moon' • White flowers in spring • Foliage has white centre • 10 cm high, 10 cm wide

Disporum smithii
White flowers in spring • 30–50 cm high, 25–40 cm wide

Dodecatheon   p. 413

Genus Information

Origin: North America and Siberia
Selected Common Names: shooting star
Nomenclature: From the Greek and Latin, meaning the 12 gods; a compliment to the grandeur of the Pantheon.
Notes: A member of the primrose family.

General Features

Height: 10–40 cm high
Spread: 10–30 cm wide
Habit: clump-forming perennial
Flowers: shooting star-like; goes dormant after flowering; spring
Hardiness: B–C
Warnings: prone to slugs; not prone to insects or disease

Growing Requirements

Light: sun
Soil: moist, organic, well-drained soil; early dormancy may occur in dry soil
Location: rock gardens; shady woodland gardens
Propagation: seed; division
Expert Advice: Seeding can be difficult—requires stratification. Divide in spring every 3 or 4 years to keep vigorous.

Buying Considerations

Professionals

Popularity: gaining popularity; fast seller in bloom

Availability: generally available as finished product from specialty growers

Size to Sell: sells best in mature sizes (when blooming) as it matures slowly

On the Shelf: keep stock rotated

Shrinkage: high; sensitive to overwatering; goes dormant in pot

Collectors

Popularity: of interest to collectors—some native species

Gardeners

Ease of Growth: mostly easy to grow but needs close attention to growing conditions

Start with: one small plant for feature plant and several for instant visual effect

What to Try First ...

Dodecatheon alpinum, Dodecatheon dentatum, Dodecatheon hendersonii, Dodecatheon jeffreyi, Dodecatheon meadia, Dodecatheon pulchellum

On the Market

Dodecatheon alpinum
Magenta to lavender flowers in spring • 10–20 cm high, 10–20 cm wide

Dodecatheon dentatum
White flowers in spring • 15–30 cm high, 10–20 cm wide

Dodecatheon hendersonii
Pink flowers in spring • 20–40 cm high, 15–20 cm wide

Dodecatheon jeffreyi (syn. D. lancifolium)
Fragrant, magenta to white flowers in spring • 20–40 cm high, 20–30 cm wide

'Rotlicht' (Red Light) • Deep-red flowers in spring • 20–40 cm high, 20–30 cm wide

Dodecatheon meadia
Deep-rose flowers in spring • 20–40 cm high, 20–30 cm wide

'Album' • White flowers in spring • 30–40 cm high, 20–30 cm wide

Dodecatheon pulchellum
Dark-red flowers in spring • 15–25 cm high, 20–30 cm wide

Dodecatheon pulchellum ssp. *macrocarpum*
Pink flowers in spring • 10–20 cm high, 10–20 cm wide

'Sooke's Variety' • Purple, pink or white flowers in spring • 10–20 cm high, 15–25 cm wide

Doronicum

p. 413

Genus Information

Origin: Asia, Europe and Siberia

Selected Common Names: leopard's bane

Nomenclature: From the Arabic, *Doronigi.*

General Features

Height: 25–75 cm high

Spread: 25–60 cm wide

Habit: upright, rhizomatous or tuberous perennial; goes dormant in summer

Flowers: daisy-like; single, double or semi-double; spring; good cutflower

Hardiness: C

Warnings: some prone to leaf spot, powdery mildew and root rot

Expert Advice: Tends to brown off and go dormant in summer if not planted in moist location. Plant among perennials that will disguise foliage. A much underused perennial.

Growing Requirements

Light: p.m. sun

Soil: moist, organic, well-drained soil; not drought tolerant

Location: borders; woodland gardens

Propagation: seed; cuttings; division

Buying Considerations

Professionals

Popularity: gaining popularity; sells well in bloom

Availability: generally available as finished product

Size to Sell: sells best in smaller sizes (when blooming)

On the Shelf: keep stock rotated; requires regular cleaning

Shrinkage: high; sensitive to overwatering

Collectors

Popularity: not generally of interest to collectors

Gardeners

Ease of Growth: very easy to grow

Start with: one small plant for feature plant or several for instant visual effect

What to Try First ...

Doronicum orientale, Doronicum plantagineum

On the Market

Doronicum columnae
Yellow flowers in spring • 30–60 cm high, 30–45 cm wide

Doronicum orientale
Semi-double to double, yellow flowers in spring • 45–60 cm high, 30–45 cm wide

'Fruhlingspracht' (Spring Beauty) • Double, yellow flowers in spring • 25–40 cm high, 25–40 cm wide

'Gold Cut' • Yellow flowers in spring • 40 cm high, 25–40 cm wide

Doronicum plantagineum
Double, yellow flowers in late spring • 50–75 cm high, 45–60 cm wide

Draba

p. 413

Genus Information

Origin: northern temperate regions and the mountains of South America
Selected Common Names: whitlow grass
Nomenclature: Name used by Discorides for *Lepidium draba.*
Notes: One of the largest genera in the alpine garden, this plant is one that no alpine enthusiast should be without.

General Features

Height: 1–20 cm high
Spread: 5–30 cm wide
Habit: cushion- to mat-forming perennial
Flowers: very early spring; may rebloom in late summer; blooms completely cover foliage
Foliage: evergreen or semi-evergreen
Hardiness: A–D
Warnings: not prone to insects or disease

Growing Requirements

Light: sun
Soil: lean, gravelly, gritty, well-drained alkaline soil
Location: rock gardens; scree; tufa; alpine houses; troughs
Propagation: seed; cuttings; division
Expert Advice: Avoid planting where soil is wet in winter.

Buying Considerations

Professionals

Popularity: relatively unknown
Availability: occasionally available from specialty growers
Size to Sell: sells best in smaller sizes (when blooming) as it matures fast
On the Shelf: keep stock rotated
Shrinkage: low; sensitive to overwatering; requires little maintenance

Collectors

Popularity: Of interest to collectors—unique, rare

Gardeners

Ease of Growth: very easy to grow, great in rock gardens
Start with: one small plant for feature plant and several for instant visual effect

What to Try First ...

Draba (Bolkar Dag), *Draba acaulis, Draba aizoides, Draba bruniifolia, Draba cappadocica, Draba dedeana, Draba hispanica, Draba hoppeana, Draba mollissima, Draba ossetica* var. *racemosa, Draba paysonii, Draba polytricha, Draba rigida* var. *bryoides, Draba rigida* var. *imbricata, Draba sibirica, Draba* aff. *sphaeroides*

D

On the Market

Draba
(Bolkar Dag) • Yellow flowers in spring • 2–5 cm high, 8–10 cm wide

Draba acaulis
Stemless, gold-yellow flowers in late spring • 2–5 cm high, 15–25 cm wide

'Dick's Select • Yellow flowers in late spring • 2–5 cm high, 30 cm wide

Draba aizoides
Hot-yellow flowers in spring • Lance-shaped, grey-green foliage • 5–10 cm high, 15–20 cm wide

Draba aretioides
Yellow flowers • 2–5 cm high, 15–20 cm wide

Draba athoa
Bright-yellow flowers in spring • 5–10 cm high, 10–15 cm wide

Draba borealis
White flowers in early spring • 10–20 cm high, 30 cm wide

Draba bruniifolia
Gold-yellow flowers in early spring • Woolly foliage • 5–10 cm high, 25–30 cm wide

Draba cappadocica
Yellow flowers in spring • 5–10 cm high, 10 cm wide

Draba compacta
Deep-yellow flowers in spring • 2–4 cm high, 10–15 cm wide

Draba condensata
Gold-yellow flowers in spring • Grey-green foliage • 5–8 cm high, 10 cm wide

Draba crassifolia
Soft-yellow flowers in spring • 8–10 cm high, 10–15 cm wide

Draba dedeana
White flowers in spring • Evergreen foliage
• 5–10 cm high, 10 cm wide

Draba densifolia
Yellow flowers in spring • Evergreen foliage
• 5–15 cm high, 10–15 cm wide

Draba graminea
Yellow flowers in spring • 5–15 cm high,
10–20 cm wide

Draba grayana
Yellow flowers in spring • 5–15 cm high,
10–20 cm wide

Draba hispanica
Yellow flowers in spring • 5–10 cm high,
10 cm wide

Draba hoppeana
Soft-yellow flowers in spring • Evergreen
foliage • 5–8 cm high, 10–15 cm wide

Draba lasiocarpa (syn. D. aizoon)
Deep-yellow flowers in spring • 10–15 cm
high, 10–20 cm wide

Draba mollissima
Gold-yellow flowers in early spring •
Silvery-grey foliage • 5–10 cm high,
15–20 cm wide

Draba norvegica
White flowers in spring • Dark-green,
evergreen foliage • 4–6 cm high, 10–20 cm
wide

Draba oligosperma
Yellow flowers in early spring • Evergreen
foliage • 5–10 cm high, 10–25 cm wide

(Longleaf Clone 1) • Yellow flowers in
spring • Long, narrow foliage • 5–10 cm
high, 10–25 cm wide

Draba oligosperma ssp. subsessilis
Yellow flowers in spring • 3–8 cm high,
10–20 cm wide

Draba ossetica var. racemosa
White flowers in spring • Fuzzy, evergreen
foliage • 2–5 cm high, 10–15 cm wide

Draba parnassica
Yellow flowers in spring • 5–8 cm high,
10–15 cm wide

Draba paysonii
White flowers in spring • Silvery-grey,
evergreen foliage • Gritty, fertile, sharply
drained, neutral soil • 5–8 cm high,
5–10 cm wide

Draba paysonii var. treleasei
(Select form) • Mustard-yellow flowers in
spring • Silvery-grey, evergreen foliage •
1–5 cm high, 5–10 cm wide

Draba polytricha
Yellow flowers in early spring • Evergreen
foliage • 5–10 cm high, 10–15 cm wide

Draba rigida
Bright-yellow flowers in early spring •
5–10 cm high, 10–20 cm wide

Draba rigida var. bryoides (syn. D. bryoides)
(Clone 1) • Bright-yellow flowers • Moss-
like foliage • 1–2 cm high, 5–15 cm wide

'Tiny Balls' • Yellow flowers in spring •
2–5 cm high, 10–15 cm wide

Draba rigida var. imbricata
(syn. D. bryoides var. imbricata)
Bright-yellow flowers in early spring •
1–2 cm high, 5–10 cm wide

Draba rosularis
Yellow flowers in spring • 5–12 cm high,
10–15 cm wide

Draba x salomonii
Yellow flowers in spring • 5–10 cm high,
10 cm wide

Draba sibirica (syn. D. repens)
Yellow flowers in spring • 2–5 cm high,
10–15 cm wide

Draba aff. sphaeroides
Yellow flowers in spring • 5 cm high, 15 cm
wide

Draba thymbriphyrestus
Yellow flowers in early spring • 2–8 cm
high, 10–25 cm wide

Draba ventosa
Bright-yellow flowers in spring • 4–8 cm
high, 10–15 cm wide

Dracocephalum   p. 413

Genus Information
Origin: North America, North Africa and Eurasia
Selected Common Names: dragon's head
Nomenclature: From the Greek *drakon* (dragon)
and *kephale* (head), referring to the shape of the
corolla.
Notes: Related to *Nepeta* (catmint).

General Features
Height: 1–45 cm high
Spread: 10–60 cm wide
Habit: clump- or mat-forming perennial
Flowers: blue to purplish-blue; helmet-shaped
Hardiness: C–D
Warnings: prone to powdery mildew and aphids

Growing Requirements
Light: sun
Soil: fertile, moist, sharply drained soil; drought
tolerant
Location: rock gardens; mixed borders

Propagation: seed (self-sows readily); division; cuttings in spring

Expert Advice: Can become weedy as they self-sow freely. Tolerates dry soil once established.

Buying Considerations

Professionals
Popularity: relatively unknown
Availability: occasionally available from specialty growers
Size to Sell: sells best in smaller sizes (when blooming) as it matures fast
On the Shelf: rapidly overgrows pot
Shrinkage: low; requires little maintenance

Collectors
Popularity: not generally of interest to collectors

Gardeners
Ease of Growth: mostly easy to grow
Start with: one small plant for feature plant

What to Try First ...

Dracocephalum altaicum, Dracocephalum botryoides, Dracocephalum imberbe, Dracocephalum aff. *paulsenii*

On the Market

Dracocephalum altaicum
Bright-blue flowers in late spring • 15–25 cm high, 45–60 cm wide

Dracocephalum argunense
'Fuji White' • White flowers in early summer • 25 cm high, 35–60 cm wide

Dracocephalum botryoides
Fragrant, lavender-purple flowers in summer • 10–15 cm high, 30 cm wide

Dracocephalum aff. *discolor*
Violet-blue flowers in late spring • Shiny green foliage • 8 cm high, 10–20 cm wide

Dracocephalum imberbe
Lilac-blue flowers in summer • 25–30 cm high, 25–40 cm wide

Dracocephalum origanoides
Tubular, rose-violet flowers in summer • Aromatic foliage • Alkaline soil • 1–2 cm high, 15–20 cm wide

Dracocephalum aff. *paulsenii*
Helmet-shaped, stemless, blue flowers in summer • Grey foliage • 2 cm high, 10–15 cm wide

Dracocephalum purdomii
Spiked, blue-violet flowers in summer • 15–20 cm high, 25–30 cm wide

Dracocephalum wallichii
Purple-blue flowers in summer • 30–45 cm high, 45 cm wide

Dryas
p. 413

Genus Information
Origin: the Arctic, Canada and the Northern Hemisphere
Selected Common Names: mountain avens, yellow mountain avens
Nomenclature: From the Greek *Dryas* (wood nymph), referring to the resemblance of the leaves to an oak. The oak was a sacred plant for this nymph.

D

General Features
Height: 5–15 cm high
Spread: 20–60 cm wide
Habit: mat-forming alpine groundcover
Flowers: small, daisy-like; spring; wispy ornamental seed heads
Foliage: shiny; evergreen
Hardiness: A
Warnings: not prone to insects or disease
Expert Advice: A very easy-to-grow but underused perennial.

Growing Requirements
Light: sun
Soil: gritty, organic, well-drained, slightly acidic soil
Location: alpine gardens; rock gardens; troughs; pathways
Propagation: seed; semi-ripe cuttings; division
Expert Advice: Division can be difficult as it resents being disturbed.

Buying Considerations

Professionals
Popularity: gaining popularity as a foliage plant
Availability: occasionally available from specialty growers
Size to Sell: sells best in smaller sizes (when blooming) as it matures fast
On the Shelf: high ornamental appeal; rapidly overgrows pot
Shrinkage: low; requires little maintenance

Collectors
Popularity: of interest to collectors—native plant

Gardeners
Ease of Growth: very easy to grow
Start with: one small plant for feature plant and several for mass plantings

What to Try First ...

Dryas drummondii, Dryas integrifolia, Dryas octopetala

On the Market

Dryas drummondii
Soft-yellow flowers in summer • 10–15 cm high, 30–60 cm wide

Dryas integrifolia
White flowers in spring • Alkaline soil • 8–10 cm high, 30–45 cm wide

Dryas octopetala
White flowers in late spring • 10–15 cm high, 30–60 cm wide

'Minor' • Large, white flowers in late spring • 5 cm high, 20–30 cm wide

Dryas octopetala ssp. *hookeriana*
Creamy-white flowers in late spring • 5 cm high, 45–60 cm wide

Dryas octopetala var. *angustifolia*
White flowers in late spring • 5–10 cm high, 45–60 cm wide

Dryopteris   p. 413 📷

Genus Information

Origin: the temperate regions of the Northern Hemisphere
Selected Common Names: shield fern
Nomenclature: From the Greek *Dryas* (oak) and *pteris* (fern).

General Features
Height: 20–120 cm high
Spread: 30–100 cm wide
Habit: rhizomatous, creeping, terrestrial fern
Foliage: beautiful, waxy fronds
Hardiness: C–D
Warnings: not prone to insects or disease

Growing Requirements
Light: shade; tolerates more sun with good soil moisture
Soil: moist, humus-rich soil; drought tolerant; tolerant of acidic soil
Location: cool woodland gardens; foliage may burn and break in windy locations
Propagation: spores; division
Expert Advice: Specific varieties are propagated by division only.

Buying Considerations

Professionals
Popularity: gaining popularity as a foliage plant
Availability: generally available as a finished product from specialty growers

Size to Sell: sells best in smaller sizes as it matures fast
On the Shelf: high ornamental appeal; keep stock rotated; foliage breakage (display out of wind)
Shrinkage: low; requires little maintenance

Collectors
Popularity: not generally of interest to collectors

Gardeners
Ease of Growth: generally easy to grow
Start with: one small plant for feature plant

What to Try First ...
Dryopteris affinis 'Cristata the King', *Dryopteris carthusiana* (syn. *D. spinulosa*), *Dryopteris dilatata* 'Recurvata', *Dryopteris filix-mas*, *Dryopteris filix-mas* 'Crispa Cristata',

On the Market

Dryopteris affinis
'Cristata the King' • Dark-green, elegant foliage • 70–100 cm high, 30–45 cm wide

Dryopteris x *bootii*
Dark-green, elegant foliage • 45–90 cm high, 45–90 cm wide

Dryopteris carthusiana (syn. *D. spinulosa*)
Soft, feathery foliage • 45–60 cm high, 30–45 cm wide

Dryopteris cycadina
Dark-green, elegant foliage • 45–60 cm high, 30–45 cm wide

'Lepidota Cristata' • Dark-green, elegant foliage • 20–45 cm high, 45–60 cm wide

Dryopteris dilatata
'Recurvata' • Dark-green, elegant foliage • 50–90 cm high, 75–100 cm wide

Dryopteris erythrosora
Coppery-pink foliage in spring changing to dark-green • 45–60 cm high, 30–50 cm wide

Dryopteris filix-mas
Dark-green, elegant foliage • 60–90 cm high, 60–100 cm wide

'Crispa Cristata' • Dark-green, crested foliage • 40–60 cm high, 30–40 cm wide

Dryopteris marginalis
Spear-shaped, leathery foliage • 45–60 cm high, 45–60 cm wide

Duchesnea

p. 413

Genus Information

Origin: Asia
Selected Common Names: mock strawberry
Nomenclature: Named for Antoine Duchessne, 1747–1827, a French horticulturalist.
Notes: Related to the real strawberry.

General Features

Height: 5–10 cm high
Spread: 45–60+ cm wide
Habit: stoloniferous groundcover perennial
Flowers: yellow; late spring to summer
Foliage: evergreen
Hardiness: C
Warnings: prone to powdery mildew and aphids; rampant spreader (easily controlled by removing above-ground runners)
Expert Advice: Fruit is red, strawberry-like and edible, but rather tasteless.

Growing Requirements

Light: sun
Soil: well-drained soil; tolerates poor soil; drought tolerant
Location: banks; slopes
Propagation: division; seed

Buying Considerations

Professionals

Popularity: relatively unknown
Availability: occasionally available as finished product
Size to Sell: sells best in smaller sizes as it matures fast
On the Shelf: rapidly overgrows pot; trim frequently in pot
Shrinkage: low; sensitive to underwatering

Collectors

Popularity: not generally of interest to collectors

Gardeners

Ease of Growth: very easy to grow
Start with: several for mass plantings

What to Try First ...

Duchesnea indica

On the Market

***Duchesnea indica* (syn. *Fragaria indica*)**
Yellow flowers in late spring to early summer • 5–10 cm high, 45–60+ cm wide

D

Echinacea

Genus Information

Origin: central to eastern North America
Selected Common Names: coneflower, purple coneflower
Nomenclature: From the Greek *echinos* (hedgehog or sea urchin), the name refers to the prickly, spiky central cone of the coneflower.
Other Uses: *E. angustifolia* was used by Native Americans and early settlers to clean and heal wounds and as a guard against infectious diseases—even to cure snake bites. Scientific research has confirmed its stimulatory effects on white blood cells, which fight infection.
Notes: A genus of some 9 species and many new cultivars. Closely related to *Rudbeckia*.

General Features

Height: 30–150 cm high
Spread: 30–60 cm wide
Habit: upright, clump-forming, tap-rooted perennial
Flowers: large; daisy-like; broad petals, (some) reflexed, surround prominent protruding orange-brown, cone-shaped centres; single or double; blooms midsummer to frost; good for cutflowers and dried flowers; attracts butterflies
Foliage: rough, hairy
Hardiness: C
Warnings: prone to aphids; not prone to diseases
Expert Advice: Hybridization work is producing a wide range of colours and forms. In fall goldfinches and sparrows love the seeds. It looks great planted with *Rudbeckia* and *Perovskia*, which require similar cultural conditions.

Growing Requirements

Light: sun to p.m. sun
Soil: poor, well-drained soil; drought tolerant once established
Location: open woodlands; mixed borders; cutflower borders; hot, dry windy areas
Propagation: seed; division; root cuttings
Expert Advice: Seed indoors in February or March. Sow outdoors in early spring. Plants bloom the second year. Slow to form large clumps. Division can be difficult as it resents being disturbed. For success in colder areas, mix coarse sand around and under the plant's roots.

Buying Considerations

Professionals

Popularity: popular; fast seller in bloom
Availability: readily available as finished product and bare root
Size to Sell: sells best in smaller sizes (when blooming); matures slowly
On the Shelf: keep stock rotated
Shrinkage: low; sensitive to overwatering

Collectors

Popularity: of interest to collectors—native plant, unique new varieties

Gardeners

Ease of Growth: mostly easy to grow but needs close attention to growing conditions
Start with: one small plant for feature plant and several for mass plantings

What to Try First ...

Echinacea 'Kim's Knee High', *Echinacea* 'Little Giant', *Echinacea purpurea* 'Leuchtstern', *Echinacea purpurea* 'Magnus', *Echinacea purpurea* 'Ruby Giant', *Echinacea purpurea* 'White Swan'

On the Market

Echinacea
'Kim's Knee High' • Fragrant, reflexed, pink flowers with red-orange disks in summer • 50–60 cm high, 30–45 cm wide
'Little Giant' • Fragrant, red-purple flowers with dark-orange cones in summer to late summer • 30–45 cm high, 30 cm wide

Echinacea angustifolia
Purple-rose flowers in summer to fall • 90–120 cm high, 45 cm wide

Echinacea pallida
Purple-rose flowers in summer to fall • 90 cm high, 45 cm wide

Echinacea paradoxa
Bright-yellow flowers with brown disks in early summer • 60–90 cm high, 45 cm wide

Echinacea purpurea
Reflexed, purple flowers in summer to fall • 90–150 cm high, 45 cm wide
'Alba' • Reflexed, white flowers in summer to fall • 60–90 cm high, 45 cm wide
'Bravado' • Reflexed, rose-purple flowers in summer to fall • 45–60 cm high, 45 cm wide
'Crimson Star' • Flat, deep crimson-purple flowers in summer to fall • 45–60 cm high, 45 cm wide
'Doppelganger' (Double Walker) • Unusual, double, rosy-purple flowers in summer to fall • 70–80 cm high, 45 cm wide
'Kim's Mop Head' • Reflexed, white flowers with greenish disks in summer to fall • 30–60 cm high, 45 cm wide
'Leuchtstern' (Bright Star) • Reflexed, purple-red flowers in summer to fall • 60–80 cm high, 45 cm wide

118 Hole's Dictionary of Hardy Perennials

'**Magnus**' • Flat, purple flowers with dark-orange disks in summer to fall • 60–90 cm high, 45 cm wide

'**Mango Meadowbrite**' • Reflexed, mustard-orange flowers in summer to fall • 60–90 cm high, 45 cm wide

Orange Meadowbrite™ ('Art's Pride') • Reflexed, tangerine-orange flowers in summer to fall • 60–90 cm high, 45 cm wide

'**Prairie Frost**' • Reflexed, rose-pink flowers in summer to fall • Variegated foliage • 30–45 cm high, 45 cm wide

'**Razzamatazz**' • Fragrant, double pom-pom, purple-pink flowers in summer to fall • 85–90 cm high, 45 cm wide

'**Rubinstern**' (**Ruby Star**) • Reflexed, carmine-red flowers with brown disks in summer to fall • 90–100 cm high, 45 cm wide

'**Ruby Giant**' • Reflexed, wine-red flowers in summer to fall • 60–90 cm high, 45 cm wide

'**The King**' • Reflexed, lilac flowers with an orange-yellow centre in summer to fall • 45 cm high, 30–45 cm wide

'**Vintage Wine**' • Reflexed, raspberry-red flowers in summer to fall • 65–70 cm high, 45 cm wide

'**White Lustre**' • Reflexed, creamy-white flowers in summer to fall • 60–80 cm high, 45 cm wide

'**White Swan**' • Fragrant, reflexed, pure white flowers in summer to fall • 45–60 cm high, 30–45 cm wide

Big Sky Series
'**Sunrise**' • Fragrant, single, reflexed, lemon-yellow flowers in summer to fall • 75–90 cm high, 45 cm wide

'**Sunset**' • Fragrant, single, reflexed, salmon-coral flowers in summer to fall • 75–90 cm high, 45 cm wide

Echinacea tennesseensis
Upward-facing, mauve flowers with green-pink disks in summer • 60–90 cm high, 45 cm wide

'**Rocky Top Hybrids**' • Upward-facing, bright-pink flowers in summer to fall • 60–75 cm high, 45 cm wide

Echinocereus p. 413 📷

Genus Information

Origin: the south to southwest United States and Mexico
Selected Common Names: hedgehog cactus
Nomenclature: From the Greek *echinos* (hedgehog), referring to its spiny nature.
Notes: The genus comprises about 45 species of cacti.

General Features

Height: 5–30 cm high
Spread: 8–25 cm wide
Habit: cactus
Flowers: colourful; spring to early summer
Foliage: ribbed stems
Hardiness: C–D
Warnings: painful to handle; not prone to insects or disease
Expert Advice: These plants occur in a wide range of habitats and vary in their ability to tolerate low temperatures. Only a few are considered hardy for northern climates.

Growing Requirements

Light: sun
Soil: dry, lean, sharply drained soil; drought tolerant
Location: alpine gardens; deserts; dry uplands; rock gardens
Propagation: seed; stem cuttings

Buying Considerations

Professionals
Popularity: relatively unknown
Availability: occasionally available from specialty growers
Size to Sell: sells best in mature sizes as it matures slowly
Shrinkage: low; requires little maintenance
Miscellaneous: may require an import permit

Collectors
Popularity: of interest to collectors—unique

Gardeners
Ease of Growth: very easy to grow
Start with: one mature plant for feature plant

What to Try First ...

Echinocereus triglochidiatus, Echinocereus viridiflorus

On the Market

Echinocereus fendleri ssp. *fendleri*
Violet-red flowers in spring to early summer • Ribbed stems • 10 cm high, 8–10 cm wide

Echinocereus triglochidiatus
Crimson flowers in spring to early summer • Ribbed stems • 20–30 cm high, 15–20 cm wide

Echinocereus viridiflorus
Fragrant, green to yellow-green flowers in spring • Ribbed stems • 5–10 cm high, 20–25 cm wide

Echinops
p. 413

Genus Information
Origin: Europe, Mediterranean, Central Asia and the mountains of tropical Africa
Selected Common Names: globe thistle, small globe thistle
Nomenclature: From the Greek *Echinos* (sea urchin or hedgehog) and *opsis* (resemblance).

General Features
Height: 60–100 cm
Spread: 45–100 cm
Habit: sturdy, upright, clump-forming perennial; taller types may require staking
Flowers: spiky globes; long blooming; good for cutflowers and drying; attractive to butterflies
Foliage: bold, thistle-like; silver-grey
Hardiness: C
Warnings: prone to powdery mildew; not generally prone to insects although may be prone to aphids in greenhouse situations; contact with foliage may irritate skin
Expert Advice: Unusual and striking. Combines well with other drought-tolerant perennials. Deadhead to prevent self-seeding.

Growing Requirements
Light: sun to p.m. sun
Soil: lean, well-drained soil; in fertile soil becomes floppy and may require staking; dislikes wet spring soil; drought tolerant once established
Location: sunny, hot, dry areas; mixed borders; wild gardens; hot, dry grasslands; dry, gravelly slopes
Propagation: seed (self sows); division; root cuttings
Expert Advice: Seed indoors in February or March. Seed needs light to germinate. Sow outdoors in early spring. Plants will bloom the second year.

Buying Considerations
Professionals
Popularity: popular
Availability: readily available as finished product and bare root
Size to Sell: sells best in smaller sizes as it matures fast
On the Shelf: keep stock rotated; rapidly overgrows pot

Shrinkage: low; sensitive to overwatering; requires little maintenance
Collectors
Popularity: not generally of interest to collectors
Gardeners
Ease of growth: mostly easy to grow but needs close attention to growing conditions
Start with: one small plant for feature plant

What to Try First ...
Echinops ritro 'Veitch's Blue', *Echinops sphaerocephalus*, *Echinops sphaerocephalus* 'Arctic Glow'

On the Market
Echinops ritro
Blue flowers in late summer • Silver-grey foliage • 60 cm high, 45 cm wide
'Veitch's Blue' • Steel-blue flowers in late summer • Silver-grey foliage • 60–100 cm high, 60–90 cm wide
Echinops sphaerocephalus
Grey-blue flowers in summer • Silver-grey foliage • 1.5–2 m high, 60–100 cm wide
'Arctic Glow' • Round, white flowers in summer • Silver-grey foliage and red-brown stems • 60–75 cm high, 60 cm wide

Edraianthus
p. 413

Genus Information
Origin: the Mediterranean and the central and western Balkan Peninsula
Selected Common Names: grassy bells
Nomenclature: From the Greek *edraios* (sessile) and *anthos* (flower).
Notes: This plant belongs to a genus of some 24 species.

General Features
Height: 2–15 cm high
Spread: 5–30 cm wide
Habit: low, mat-forming perennial
Flowers: *Campanula*-like; early summer; short blooming period
Foliage: grassy
Hardiness: C
Warnings: not prone to insects or disease

Growing Requirements
Light: sun
Soil: lean, organic, sharply drained, alkaline soil; drought tolerant
Location: rock gardens; scree; troughs
Propagation: seed; cuttings
Expert Advice: Avoid planting in areas where soil is cold and remains wet. Generally short-lived.

Buying Considerations

Professionals

Popularity: relatively unknown
Availability: occasionally available from specialty growers
Size to Sell: sells best in smaller sizes (when blooming) as it matures fast
On the Shelf: rapidly overgrows pot
Shrinkage: low; requires little maintenance

Collectors

Popularity: not generally of interest to collectors

Gardeners

Ease of Growth: generally easy to grow but needs close attention to growing conditions
Start with: one small plant for feature plant

What to Try First ...

Edraianthus dalmaticus, Edraianthus graminifolius (syn. *E. kitaibelii*), *Edraianthus pumilio, Edraianthus tenuifolius*

On the Market

Edraianthus dalmaticus
Bell-shaped, violet flowers in early summer • 5–10 cm high, 20–30 cm wide

Edraianthus graminifolius (syn. *E. kitaibelii*)
Violet-blue flowers in early summer • 5–15 cm high, 15–20 cm wide

Edraianthus graminifolius ssp. *niveus*
White flowers in early summer • 15 cm high, 15–20 cm wide

Edraianthus pumilio
Violet flowers in early summer • 3 cm high, 15 cm wide

Edraianthus serpyllifolius
Dark-violet flowers in early summer • Evergreen • 2–5 cm high, 10–15 cm wide

Edraianthus tenuifolius
Blue-violet flowers in early summer • 10–15 cm high, 15 cm wide

Elymus

p. 413 📷

Genus Information

Origin: northern and southern temperate regions
Selected Common Names: Magellan wheatgrass, blue wild rye
Nomenclature: From the Greek *elymos*, the classical name for millet.
Notes: A genus of some 150 species. Nomenclature of this genus and the genus *Leymus* is confused at present. The family includes some troublesome weeds, including quack grass.

General Features

Height: 45–130 cm high
Spread: 40–130 cm wide
Habit: tufted, rhizomatous perennial
Flowers: upright, slender spikes of seed heads; summer
Foliage: linear, flat or rolled; intense blue; good for winter interest
Hardiness: C–D
Warnings: not prone to insects or disease; some varieties are invasive but *E. magellanicus* is not
Expert Advice: One of the bluest ornamental grasses. Wait until spring to cut back.

Growing Requirements

Light: sun to p.m. sun; most prefer filtered p.m. sun
Soil: fertile, moist, organic, well-drained soil; tolerant of wide range of soils
Location: mixed borders; woodland gardens
Propagation: seed (self-sows); division
Expert Advice: Divide frequently to keep vigorous.

Buying Considerations

Professionals

Popularity: gaining popularity as a foliage plant
Availability: generally available as finished product
Size to Sell: sells best in smaller sizes as it matures fast
On the Shelf: high ornamental appeal; keep stock rotated; rapidly overgrows pot
Shrinkage: low; requires little maintenance

Collectors

Popularity: not generally of interest to collectors

Gardeners

Ease of Growth: very easy to grow
Start with: one small plant for feature plant

What to Try First ...

Elymus magellanicus, Elymus magellanicus 'Blue Tango'

On the Market

Elymus hispidus (syn. *E. glaucus*)
Seed heads in summer • Arching, blue-grey foliage • 75–120 cm high, 40–60 cm wide

Elymus magellanicus
Seed heads in summer • Intense blue foliage • 45–130 cm high, 45–60 cm wide

'Blue Tango' • Seed heads in summer • Grey-blue foliage • 45–130 cm high, 45–60 cm wide

Epimedium

p. 414 📷

Genus Information

Origin: Japan, China, India, Europe and North Africa

Selected Common Names: barrenwort, red barrenwort, bishop's hat

Nomenclature: From the Greek, an ancient plant name of unknown derivation.

General Features

Height: 10–75 cm high
Spread: 30–60 cm wide
Habit: rhizomatous, clump-forming perennial; slow-spreader
Flowers: spring
Foliage: deciduous or evergreen; fall colour
Hardiness: C
Warnings: not prone to insects or disease
Expert Advice: Excellent groundcover for difficult areas. For flowers to be visible in spring, cut back foliage in fall or very early spring; new leaves will appear during and after blooming period.

Growing Requirements

Light: shade
Soil: moist, organic, well-drained soil; drought tolerant once established; tolerant of acidic soil
Location: mixed borders; under plantings in evergreen gardens; woodland gardens
Propagation: seed; division; cuttings
Expert Advice: Two different clones of the same species or two different species are needed to set seed. Divide in spring. Take cuttings in summer.

Buying Considerations

Professionals

Popularity: gaining popularity; fast seller; has new varieties
Availability: generally available as finished product; bare root from specialty growers
Size to Sell: sells best in smaller sizes (when blooming) as it matures fast
On the Shelf: high ornamental appeal; keep stock rotated
Shrinkage: low; requires little maintenance

Collectors

Popularity: of interest to collectors—unique, rare species, exceptional beauty

Gardeners

Ease of Growth: generally easy to grow but needs close attention to growing conditions
Start with: one small plant for feature plant and several for mass plantings

What to Try First ...

Epimedium 'Black Sea', *Epimedium brachyrrhizum* 'Elfin Magic', *Epimedium epsteinii*, *Epimedium grandiflorum* 'Lilafee', *Epimedium* x *perralchicum* 'Frohnleiten', *Epimedium* x *rubrum*, *Epimedium* x *versicolor* 'Sulphureum', *Epimedium* x *warleyense*, *Epimedium* x *youngianum* 'Roseum'

On the Market

Epimedium
'Black Sea' • Cream-yellow flowers in spring • 30–50 cm high, 30–50 cm wide

Epimedium brachyrrhizum
'Elfin Magic' • Rose-pink bicoloured flowers in spring • 20–25 cm high, 30–50 cm wide

Epimedium epsteinii
Red-and-white bicoloured flowers in spring • 10–15 cm high, 30–50+ cm wide

Epimedium franchetii
Cream-yellow flowers in spring • Coppery-bronze foliage • 60 cm high, 30–60 cm wide
'Brimstone Butterfly' • Red-brown and yellow flowers in spring • Coppery-bronze foliage • 60 cm high, 30–60 cm wide

Epimedium grandiflorum
White, yellow, rose or violet flowers in spring • 10–35 cm high, 30–45 cm wide
'Lilafee' (Lilac Fairy) • Lavender flowers in spring • 10–35 cm high, 30–45 cm wide
'Saxton's Purple' • Red-purple flowers in spring • Blue-green foliage • 10–35 cm high, 30–45 cm wide
'Yubae' (syn. Rose Queen) • Glossy, red-violet flowers in spring • 10–35 cm high, 30–45 cm wide

Epimedium lishihchenii
Yellow flowers in spring • 30–40 cm high, 30–50 cm wide

Epimedium x *perralchicum*
'Frohnleiten' • Gold-yellow flowers in spring • Foliage tinged red in fall • 15–40 cm high, 30–45 cm wide

Epimedium platypetalum
Spurless, yellow flowers in spring • 30–40 cm high, 30–50 cm wide

Epimedium pubigerum
Creamy-white flowers in spring • 25–75 cm high, 30–50 cm wide

Epimedium x *rubrum*
Ruby-red flowers in spring • Young foliage tinted red • 25–40 cm high, 30–45 cm wide

E

Epimedium x *versicolor*
'Sulphureum' • Lemon-yellow flowers in spring • 25–30 cm high, 30–45 cm wide

Epimedium x *warleyense*
(syn. E. Ellen Willott)
Copper-red flowers in spring • 20–50 cm high, 30–45 cm wide

Epimedium x *youngianum*
'Niveum' • White flowers in spring • 10–30 cm high, 30–50 cm wide

'Roseum' • Purple-mauve flowers in spring • 10–30 cm high, 30–50 cm wide

Epipactis   p. 414

Genus Information

Origin: Eurasia, North America and North Africa
Selected Common Names: bog orchid, chatterbox orchid
Nomenclature: From the Greek name for this plant.

General Features
Height: 25–60 cm high
Spread: 90–150 cm wide
Habit: rhizomatous, colony-forming perennial
Flowers: summer; valued for their flowers
Foliage: grass-like
Hardiness: D
Warnings: not prone to insects or disease

Growing Requirements
Light: shade
Soil: fertile, moist, organic, boggy soil
Location: marshes; alpine meadows; woodland gardens; stream sides
Propagation: seed; division
Expert Advice: These collectors' plants have specific soil requirements.

Buying Considerations

Professionals
Popularity: relatively unknown
Availability: occasionally available from specialty growers. May require CITES permits.
Size to Sell: sells best in mature sizes (when blooming) as it matures slowly
Shrinkage: high; sensitive to overwatering; goes dormant in pot

Collectors
Popularity: of interest to collectors—unique, rare, challenge

Gardeners
Ease of Growth: very difficult to grow as it needs close attention to growing conditions
Start with: one mature plant for feature plant

What to Try First ...
Epipactis gigantea, Epipactis palustris, Epipactis thunbergii

On the Market

Epipactis gigantea
Nodding, green flowers veined with red in early summer • 30–40 cm high, 90–150 cm wide

Epipactis palustris
Nodding, cream flowers with reddish interior in summer • 25–50 cm high, 90 cm wide

Epipactis thunbergii
Golden-bronze flowers with maroon spots in summer • 30–60 cm high, 90 cm wide

Eragrostis   p. 414

Genus Information

Origin: North America
Selected Common Names: blue love grass, sand grass
Nomenclature: From the Greek *eros* (love) and *agrostis* (grass), referring to the plant's beauty.

General Features
Height: 90–120 cm
Spread: 90–100 cm
Habit: clump-forming grass
Flowers: seed heads; late summer
Foliage: blue to blue-green
Hardiness: D
Warnings: not prone to insects or disease
Expert Advice: This native woodland grass makes an elegant feature in mixed borders.

Growing Requirements
Light: sun
Soil: sandy, well-drained soil; drought tolerant
Location: woodland gardens
Propagation: seed (self sows); division

Buying Considerations

Professionals
Popularity: relatively unknown foliage plant
Availability: occasionally available as finished product
Size to Sell: sells best in smaller sizes as it matures fast
On the Shelf: high ornamental appeal; keep stock rotated; rapidly overgrows pot
Shrinkage: low; requires little maintenance

Collectors
Popularity: not generally of interest to collectors

E

Gardeners

Ease of growth: very easy to grow

Start with: one small plant for feature plant

What to Try First ...

Eragrostis trichodes

On the Market

Eragrostis elliottii
Seed heads in late summer • Icy-blue foliage
• 1 m high, 1 m wide

Eragrostis trichodes
Olive-grey seed heads in late summer
• 90–120 cm high, 90–100 cm wide

Eremurus p. 414

Genus Information

Origin: western to central Asia

Selected Common Names: desert candle, foxtail lily, golden foxtail lily, Himalayan desert candle

Nomenclature: From the Greek *eremia* (desert) and *oura* (tail), referring to the flower's shape and the desert conditions it lives in.

Notes: A genus of some 40–50 species.

General Features

Height: 90 cm–3 m high

Spread: 30–60 cm wide

Habit: very tall, upright, fleshy-rooted perennial

Flowers: torch-like; early summer; goes dormant after flowering

Hardiness: D

Warnings: not prone to insects or disease

Expert Advice: This grassland, semi-desert plant is not suitable for frost-free zones as it requires a cold period to flower well.

Growing Requirements

Light: sun

Soil: fertile, well-drained, sandy soil; avoid winter wet

Location: sunny, hot, dry areas; sheltered locations; dry grasslands; rocky semi-desert areas

Propagation: seed; division

Expert Advice: In colder areas plant on the south side of buildings. Division is difficult as it resents being moved. The roots are fragile, so careful replanting of the crowns should be done when the plant goes dormant in late summer. Set crowns in sharp sand.

Buying Considerations

Professionals

Popularity: gaining popularity; fast seller in bloom

Availability: generally available as finished product and bare root

Size to Sell: sells best in larger sizes (when blooming) as it matures slowly

Shrinkage: high; sensitive to overwatering; goes dormant in pot

Collectors

Popularity: of interest to collectors—unique, challenge

Gardeners

Ease of Growth: mostly easy to grow but needs close attention to growing conditions

Start with: one small plant for feature plant

What to Try First ...

Eremurus 'Oase', *Eremurus himalaicus*,
Eremurus x *isabellinus* (Ruiter hybrids),
Eremurus x *isabellinus* (Shelford hybrids),
Eremurus robustus, Eremurus stenophyllus

On the Market

Eremurus
'**Brutus**' • White flowers in early summer •
1.5–2 m high, 45–60 cm wide
'**Oase**' • Salmon flowers in early summer •
1.5–2 m high, 45–60 cm wide
'**Romance**' • Red-tinged flowers in early
summer • 1.5–1.7 m high, 45–60 cm wide

Eremurus himalaicus
White flowers in early summer • 2–2.5 m
high, 45–60 cm wide

Eremurus x *isabellinus*
'**Cleopatra**' • Orange flowers in early
summer • 1.5 m high, 45–60 cm wide
'**Pinokkio**' • Orange flowers in early summer
• 1.5–2 m high, 45–60 cm wide
'**Tropical Dream**' • White flowers in early
summer • 1.5–2 m high, 45–60 cm wide
(**Ruiter hybrids**) • Pastel colours in early
summer • 1.5 m high, 45–60 cm wide
(**Shelford hybrids**) • Yellow, orange or
cream flowers in early summer • 3 m high,
45–60 cm wide

Eremurus robustus
Peach to pink flowers in early summer •
2–3 m high, 45–60 cm wide

Eremurus stenophyllus
Yellow to orange flowers in early summer •
90–100 cm high, 30–45 cm wide

E

Erigeron

p. 414 📷

Genus Information

Origin: the mountains of Western Canada and the United States

Selected Common Names: daisy fleabane, fleabane, Oregon fleabane

Nomenclature: From the Greek *eri* (early) and *geron* (an old man), referring to the hairy papus or the hoary appearance of the foliage of some species in summer.

Notes: Erigeron is a member of the daisy family.

General Features

Height: 2–80 cm high

Spread: 10–60 cm wide

Habit: clump- or mound-forming biennial or long-lived perennial; taller varieties may require staking (tomato cages work well)

Flowers: aster-like; spring through summer; (tall types) good for cutflowers and long blooming; deadhead to extend blooming season

Hardiness: B–D

Warnings: prone to powdery mildew and aphids

Expert Advice: Dwarf types make excellent groundcovers.

Growing Requirements

Light: sun to p.m. sun

Soil: fertile, moist, well-drained soil; tolerant of a wide range of soils (*E. aureus;* sharply drained, acidic, sandy soil)

Location: dry grassland areas; rocky areas; rock gardens; mixed borders

Propagation: seed; division

Expert Advice: Seed indoors in February or March. Sow seed outdoors in fall or early spring. Divide every 3 to 5 years to keep vigorous. Fertilize sparsely to prevent floppy growth.

Buying Considerations

Professionals

Popularity: gaining popularity; fast seller in bloom; new varieties available

Availability: generally available as finished product and bare root from specialty growers

Size to Sell: sells best in smaller sizes (when blooming) as it matures fast

On the Shelf: rapidly overgrows pot

Shrinkage: low; requires little maintenance

Collectors

Popularity: of interest to collectors—unique species, rare, exceptional beauty

Gardeners

Ease of Growth: generally easy to grow

Start with: one small plant for feature plant and several for mass plantings

What to Try First ...

Erigeron 'Azurfee', *Erigeron* 'Dunkelste Aller', *Erigeron aureus* 'Canary Bird', *Erigeron chrysopsidis* 'Grand Ridge', *Erigeron leiomerus, Erigeron linearis* 'Rimrock', *Erigeron pinnatisectus, Erigeron scopulinus, Erigeron speciosus* 'Grandiflorus'

On the Market

Erigeron

'Azurfee' (Azure Fairy) • Lavender-blue flowers with yellow centres in summer • 45 cm high, 45 cm wide

'Chameleon' • Yellow flowers age to white and then pink in spring to late summer • 5–15 cm high, 10–15 cm wide

'Dunkelste Aller' (Darkest of All) • Daisy-like, dark-violet flowers with yellow centres in summer • 45–60 cm high, 45 cm wide

'Foersters Liebling' • Semi-double, reddish-pink flowers with yellow centres in summer • 40–60 cm high, 45 cm wide

'Goat Rocks' • Bright-lemon-yellow flowers in summer • Silver-grey foliage • 8 cm high, 10–20 cm wide

'Prosperity' • Semi-double, mauve-blue flowers in summer • 45 cm high, 45 cm wide

'Rosa Juwel' (Pink Jewel) • Bright-pink flowers with yellow centres in summer • 45–60 cm high, 45 cm wide

'Rosa Triumph' (Pink Triumph) • Pink flowers in summer • 40–45 cm high, 45 cm wide

'Rotes Meer' (Red Sea) • Semi-double, rose-red flowers in summer • 40–60 cm high, 30–45 cm wide

'Schone Blaue' (Schone Blue) • Purple-blue flowers in summer • 60 cm high, 45 cm wide

'Sea Breeze' • Pale-purple flowers in summer • Succulent-like leaves • 10–30 cm high, 45 cm wide

'Sommerneuschnee' (Summer Snow) • Double, pinkish-white flowers with yellow centres in summer • 40–50 cm high, 30–45 cm wide

Erigeron aphanactis **var.** *congestus*
Yellow flowers in spring • 5–8 cm high, 25–30 cm wide

Erigeron aureus
'Canary Bird' • Creamy-yellow flowers in summer to fall • Sharply drained, fertile, moist, acidic soil • 8–10 cm high, 15 cm wide

E

'The Giant' • Golden-yellow flowers in spring to fall • Sharply drained, fertile, moist, organic, acidic soil • 8–15 cm high, 15–20 cm wide

Erigeron chrysopsidis
'Grand Ridge' • Bright-yellow flowers in spring to late summer • 5–10 cm high, 10–15 cm wide

Erigeron chrysopsidis var. brevifolius
Yellow flowers continuously in summer • 15 cm high, 30 cm wide

Erigeron compositus
White, bluish or pink flowers with a yellow eye in early summer • 5–20 cm high, 10–20 cm wide

Erigeron compositus var. discoideus
White, bluish or pink flowers with a yellow eye in summer • 5–15 cm high, 10–20 cm wide

Erigeron elegantulus
Blue or pink flowers in summer • Silver-green foliage • 10–20 cm high, 20–25 cm wide

Erigeron glaucus
Mauve flowers in summer • Succulent-like stems • 30–50 cm high, 30–45 cm wide

Erigeron lanatus
White flowers with yellow centres in early summer • Hairy stems and leaves • 5 cm high, 10–15 cm wide

Erigeron leiomerus
Deep-blue flowers in summer • 10 cm high, 15–20 cm wide

Erigeron linearis
'Rimrock' • Daisy-like, bright-yellow flowers in early summer • Silvery foliage • 3–15 cm high, 6–30 cm wide

Erigeron peregrinus
White to purple flowers in spring • 10–15 cm high, 30–40 cm wide

Erigeron pinnatisectus
Violet-purple flowers with yellow-orange centres in summer • 15–20 cm high, 15 cm wide

Erigeron scopulinus
Daisy-like, white to pinkish flowers in summer • Glossy, tiny leaves • 5 cm high, 30–60+ cm wide

Erigeron speciosus
Violet-purple flowers with yellow centres in summer • 60–80 cm high, 45–60 cm wide
'Grandiflorus' • Blue flowers with yellow centers in summer • 75–80 cm high, 45–60 cm wide

Erigeron spectabilis
Daisy-like, pink flowers in spring to late summer • Grey-green foliage • 6 cm high, 10–15 cm wide

Erinus

p. 414 📷

Genus Information

Origin: Europe and North Africa
Selected Common Names: alpine balsam, liver balsam
Nomenclature: The name is from the Greek *erinos.*
Other Uses: The plant was used by Dioscorides for a kind of basil.
Notes: The genus has only 2 species.

General Features

Height: 8–15 cm high
Spread: 10–20 cm wide
Habit: tuft-forming perennial; short-lived in cold areas
Flowers: spring to early summer
Foliage: evergreen
Hardiness: C–D
Warnings: prone to powdery mildew and aphids

Growing Requirements

Light: sun
Soil: fertile, well-drained soil; avoid winter wet
Location: sheltered areas; rock gardens; crevice plantings; raised beds; tufa; scree; troughs
Propagation: seed (self-sows)
Expert Advice: To promote hardiness in cold areas, grow in lean soil in a sheltered spot. Many cultivars come true from seed.

Buying Considerations

Professionals
Popularity: relatively unknown
Availability: occasionally available as finished product
Size to Sell: sells best in smaller sizes (when blooming) as it matures fast
On the Shelf: rapidly overgrows pot
Shrinkage: low; sensitive to underwatering; requires little maintenance

Collectors
Popularity: not generally of interest to collectors

Gardeners
Ease of Growth: mostly easy to grow but needs close attention to growing conditions
Start with: one small plant for feature plant

What to Try First ...
Erinus alpinus, Erinus alpinus 'Dr. Hahnle'

On the Market

Erinus alpinus
Rose-purple flowers in early summer •
10–15 cm high, 10–20 cm wide

'Dr. Hahnle' • Purple-pink flowers in early
summer • 10–15 cm high, 10–20 cm wide

Erinus alpinus var. *albus*
White flowers in spring • 10–15 cm high,
10–20 cm wide

Erinus alpinus var. *hirsutus*
Rosy-pink flowers in early summer •
Hairy, dark-green foliage • 8–15 cm high,
10–20 cm wide

Eriogonum

p. 414

Genus Information

Origin: North America and the western United
States
Selected Common Names: sulphur flower, wild
buckwheat
Nomenclature: From the Greek *erion* (wool) and
gonia (joint).
Other Uses: A genus of some 150 species.

General Features

Height: 1–30 cm high
Spread: 8–75 cm wide
Habit: mat- or cushion-forming groundcover
perennial
Flowers: long lasting; late blooming; good for
cutflowers; good for drying
Foliage: dense, woolly
Hardiness: C–D
Warnings: not prone to insects or disease
Expert Advice: A ruggedly hardy, underused
perennial, it requires a deep root run.

Growing Requirements

Light: sun
Soil: deep, gritty, sharply drained soil; tolerates
poor soil; drought tolerant (water well during
active growth and keep dry during fall and
winter dormancy); (woolly species) avoid
winter wet
Location: rock gardens; alpine houses; tolerates
exposed sites
Propagation: seed; root cuttings (resents being
disturbed)

Buying Considerations

Professionals
Popularity: relatively unknown
Availability: occasionally available from
specialty growers
Size to Sell: sells best in smaller sizes as it
matures fast
On the Shelf: rapidly overgrows pot

Shrinkage: low; requires little maintenance

Collectors
Popularity: not generally of interest to
collectors

Gardeners
Ease of Growth: very easy to grow
Start with: one small plant for feature plant
and several for mass plantings

What to Try First …
Eriogonum brevicaule var. *nanum, Eriogonum
caespitosum* ssp. *douglasii, Eriogonum flavum,
Eriogonum kennedyi* ssp. *alpigenum, Eriogonum
kennedyi* var. *kennedyi, Eriogonum ovalifolium,
Eriogonum umbellatum* var. *minus*

E

On the Market

Eriogonum brevicaule var. *nanum*
Yellow flowers in late summer • Grey foliage
• 2–5 cm high, 10–20 cm wide

Eriogonum caespitosum ssp. *douglasii*
Yellow flowers in summer • 10–15 cm high,
30 cm wide

Eriogonum compositum var. *leianthum*
White to yellow flowers in summer
• 15–25 cm high, 10–20 cm wide

Eriogonum douglasii var. *tenue*
Cream-yellow flowers in early summer
• 10–15 cm high, 20–30 cm wide

Eriogonum ericifolium var. *pulchrum*
White or red flowers in summer
• 12–20 cm high, 25–30 cm wide

Eriogonum flavum
Bright-yellow flowers in early summer
• Woolly foliage • 10–20 cm high,
20–30 cm wide

(Alpine form) • Yellow flowers, fading
to red, in spring • Silver-grey foliage
• 10–20 cm high, 20–30 cm wide

Eriogonum kennedyi ssp. *alpigenum*
Red-veined, white flowers in summer
• White, woolly foliage • 1–2 cm high,
10–15 cm wide

Eriogonum kennedyi var. *austromontanum*
Red-veined, white flowers in summer
• 15 cm high, 20–30 cm wide

Eriogonum kennedyi var. *kennedyi*
Red-veined, white flowers in summer
• 15 cm high, 15 cm wide

Eriogonum ovalifolium
Creamy-yellow flowers in summer • Silvery,
white, hairy foliage • 10–20 cm high, 30 cm
wide

Eriogonum ovalifolium var. *nivale*
Red-veined, white flowers in summer •
White-felted foliage • 2–5 cm high, 20 cm wide

Eriogonum saxatile
Pale-yellow to pink flowers in summer
• 15–30 cm high, 20–30 cm wide

Eriogonum siskiyouense
Yellow flowers in late summer • Woolly leaves, edged in red • 5–10 cm high, 15–20 cm wide

Eriogonum umbellatum
Yellow flowers in summer • 8–30 cm high, 30–45 cm wide

'Alturas Red' • Gold flowers, aging red, in summer • 20–25 cm high, 30–45 cm wide

(Bear Tooth Pass) • Cream flowers in summer • Silver-backed foliage • 15–25 cm high, 30–45 cm wide

'Silver Lake' • Ball-shaped, yellow flowers in summer • 30 cm high, 75 cm wide

'Siskiyou Gold' • Yellow-gold flowers in summer • Olive foliage • 20–30 cm high, 30–45 cm wide

Eriogonum umbellatum var. *haussknechtii*
Creamy-yellow flowers in summer • 2–8 cm high, 45–60 cm wide

Eriogonum umbellatum var. *minus*
Amethyst-red flowers in summer • 2–12 cm high, 8 cm wide

Eriogonum umbellatum var. *polyanthum*
Yellow flowers in summer • 10–30 cm high, 30–45 cm wide

Eriogonum umbellatum var. *subalpinum*
White-cream flowers in summer • 5–15 cm high, 30–45 cm wide

Eriophorum

Genus Information
Origin: North America, Europe and South Africa (some are native to the tundra)
Selected Common Names: cotton grass
Nomenclature: From the Greek *erion* (wool) and *phoero* (to bear), referring to the hairy fruits.
Notes: A genus of some 20 species.

General Features
Height: 30–45 cm high
Spread: 45–75 cm wide
Habit: borderline aquatic, native, tuft-forming, spreading grass
Flowers: cottony-plumed seed heads; summer
Foliage: grass-like; evergreen

Hardiness: C
Warnings: not prone to insects or disease
Expert Advice: Performs best in cool summers.

Growing Requirements
Light: sun
Soil: moist, organic, acidic soil
Location: marshes; bog gardens
Propagation: division

Buying Considerations

Professionals
Popularity: relatively unknown as a foliage plant
Availability: occasionally available from specialty growers
Size to Sell: sells best in smaller sizes as it matures fast
On the Shelf: high ornamental appeal when in bloom; rapidly overgrows pot
Shrinkage: low; requires little maintenance

Collectors
Popularity: not generally of interest to collectors

Gardeners
Ease of Growth: very easy to grow
Start with: one small plant for feature plant

What to Try First ...
Eriophorum angustifolium

On the Market
Eriophorum angustifolium
Pendant, downy, white spikelets in summer • Grass-like foliage • 30–45 cm high, 45–75+ cm wide

Eriophyllum   p. 414

Genus Information
Origin: western North America
Selected Common Names: golden yarrow, woolly sunflower
Nomenclature: From the Greek *erion* (woolly) and *phyllum* (leaf).
Notes: A genus of some 12 species.

General Features
Height: 20–60 cm high
Spread: 20–60 cm wide
Habit: vigorous, low-growing, mat-forming groundcover
Flowers: bright-yellow; daisy-like
Foliage: silvery-grey
Hardiness: C
Warnings: not prone to insects or disease

Growing Requirements

Light: sun
Soil: lean, sandy soil; (tolerates) poor, dry soil
Location: alleyways; rock gardens; mixed borders; between paving stones; cascading over walls
Propagation: seed; division
Expert Advice: Divide in spring.

Buying Considerations

Professionals
Popularity: relatively unknown
Availability: occasionally available as finished product from specialty growers
Size to Sell: sells best in smaller sizes (when blooming) as it matures fast
On the Shelf: high ornamental appeal; rapidly overgrows pot

Collectors
Popularity: not generally of interest to collectors

Gardeners
Ease of Growth: very easy to grow
Start with: one small plant for feature plant

What to Try First ...
Eriophyllum lanatum, Eriophyllum lanatum 'Siskiyou'

On the Market

Eriophyllum lanatum
Yellow flowers in summer • White, woolly, silver-grey leaves • 20–60 cm high, 20–60 cm wide
'Siskiyou' • Golden-yellow flowers in summer • 25 cm high, 20–60 cm wide

Eritrichium
p. 414

Genus Information

Origin: arctic regions, alpine regions, Europe, North America and the Himalayas
Selected Common Names: alpine forget-me-not
Nomenclature: From the Greek *erion* (wool) and *trichos* (hair).

General Features

Height: 6 cm high
Spread: 15–30 cm wide
Habit: short-lived, low-growing, cushion- or tuft-forming perennial
Flowers: blue; forget-me-not-like
Foliage: silky, silver
Hardiness: C
Warnings: not prone to insects or disease

Growing Requirements

Light: sun
Soil: lean, sharply drained, alkaline soil; avoid winter wet

Location: alpine gardens; scree; troughs; tufa
Propagation: seed; basal stem cuttings
Expert Advice: It is challenging to grow and can be difficult to bring to bloom.

Buying Considerations

Professionals
Popularity: relatively unknown
Availability: occasionally available from specialty growers
Size to Sell: sells best in mature sizes (when blooming) as it matures slowly
On the Shelf: low ornamental appeal
Shrinkage: low; requires little maintenance

Collectors
Popularity: of interest to collectors—unique, rare

Gardeners
Ease of Growth: difficult to grow; needs close attention to growing conditions
Start with: one mature plant for feature plant

What to Try First ...
Eritrichium howardii

On the Market

Eritrichium howardii
Blue flowers in early summer • Silky, silver leaves • 6 cm high, 15–30 cm wide

Erodium
p. 414

Genus Information

Origin: Europe, Asia, Australia and South America
Selected Common Names: heron's bill, stork's bill
Nomenclature: From the Greek *erodios* (heron), referring to the flowers' resemblance to the head and beak of a heron.

General Features

Height: 10–45 cm high
Spread: 15–45 cm wide
Habit: mat-forming, short-lived perennial
Flowers: geranium-like; long blooming period; summer
Foliage: silver
Hardiness: D
Warnings: prone to powdery mildew; not prone to insects

Growing Requirements

Light: sun
Soil: gritty, lean, organic, well-drained soil
Location: sheltered areas; alpine houses; rock gardens; troughs
Propagation: seed; division; stem cuttings
Expert Advice: Hybridization easily occurs if 2 species are close enough. Some are dioecious.

E

Buying Considerations

Professionals
Popularity: relatively unknown
Availability: occasionally available from specialty growers
Size to Sell: sells best in mature sizes (when blooming) as it matures slowly
Shrinkage: low; requires little maintenance

Collectors
Popularity: of interest to collectors—unique, rare

Gardeners
Ease of Growth: mostly difficult to grow as it needs close attention to growing conditions
Start with: one or more mature plants for feature plant and instant visual effect

What to Try First ...
Erodium manescaui, Erodium rupestre, Erodium x variabile 'Roseum'

On the Market

Erodium manescaui
Purple-red flowers with dark veins in summer • 20–45 cm high, 30–45 cm wide

Erodium rupestre (syn. E. supracanum)
Pale-pink flowers with dark veins in summer • Silvery foliage • 10–15 cm high, 20–30 cm wide

Erodium sibthorpianum ssp. sibthorpianum
White or pink flowers with pink veins in summer • Silver foliage • 10 cm high, 15 cm wide

Erodium x variabile
'Roseum' • Deep-pink flowers in summer • 8 cm high, 15–30 cm wide

Eryngium
p. 414 📷

Genus Information
Origin: Europe, central Asia, North Africa, Turkey, China, Mexico, Brazil, Argentina, temperate North America and temperate South America
Selected Common Names: sea holly, flat sea holly, alpine sea holly
Nomenclature: From the Greek *eyringion*, a name used by Theophrastus, the Greek philosopher and scientist.
Other Uses: This plant was used medicinally for centuries, but the roots of many species were used as candy. Some species have roots rich in iron and other minerals.
Notes: The genus includes annuals, biennials, deciduous and evergreen perennials.

General Features
Height: 15 cm–4 m high
Spread: 25 cm–2 m wide
Habit: tap-rooted perennial
Flowers: steel blue; thistle-like; midsummer to fall; good for cutflowers; good for drying; long lasting
Foliage: mid-green to silvery-green; deciduous to evergreen
Hardiness: C
Warnings: not prone to insects or disease
Expert Advice: A very useful and striking perennial. Self-sows readily if flowers are not harvested.

Growing Requirements
Light: sun
Soil: most require sharply drained soil; drought and salt tolerant; *E. giganteum* prefers moist but well-drained soil
Location: xeriscaping; well-drained sites
Propagation: seed (self-sows readily); division; root cuttings

Buying Considerations

Professionals
Popularity: gaining popularity; old-fashioned
Availability: readily available as finished product and bare root
Size to Sell: sells best in smaller sizes (when blooming); matures slowly
Shrinkage: low; sensitive to overwatering; requires little maintenance

Collectors
Popularity: not generally of interest to collectors

Gardeners
Ease of Growth: very easy to grow
Start with: one small plant for feature plant

What to Try First ...
Eryngium 'Sapphire Blue', *Eryngium alpinum* 'Blue Star', *Eryngium amethystinum*, *Eryngium giganteum*, *Eryngium planum* 'Blue Ribbon', *Eryngium variifolium*, *Eryngium yuccifolium*

On the Market

Eryngium
'Sapphire Blue' • Steel-blue flowers in summer • 60–90 cm high, 45 cm wide

Eryngium alpinum
Steel-blue flowers in midsummer to fall • 60–70 cm high, 45 cm wide
'Blue Star' • Large, feathery, steel-blue flowers in summer • 60–80 cm high, 45 cm wide

Eryngium amethystinum
Amethyst-blue flowers in summer • 40 cm high, 45 cm wide

E

Eryngium bourgatii
Steel-blue flowers in midsummer to fall
• 15–45 cm high, 30 cm wide

Eryngium giganteum
Prickly, steel-blue flowers in summer •
Fertile, well-drained, moist soil • 70–90 cm
high, 30 cm wide
'Ghost Hills' • Spiky, silver-grey flowers in
summer • 90–100 cm high, 30 cm wide

Eryngium planum
Small, blue flowers in midsummer to fall
• Evergreen • 75–90 cm high, 45 cm wide
'Blue Ribbon' • Double, pale blue flowers
in midsummer to fall • 75–90 cm high,
45 cm wide
'Silverstone' • Creamy-white flowers in
midsummer • Evergreen • 60 cm high,
45 cm wide

Eryngium x tripartitum
Metallic-blue flowers in midsummer to fall
• Blue stems • 60–90 cm high, 40–50 cm
wide

Eryngium variifolium
Grey-blue flowers in midsummer to fall
• Evergreen foliage blotched white •
30–40 cm high, 25 cm wide

Eryngium yuccifolium
White flowers tinted pink in summer
• Semi-evergreen • 75–180 cm high,
45–60 cm wide

Eryngium x zabelii
'Donard Variety' • Large, blue flowers in
summer • 45–60 cm high, 45 cm wide

Erysimum

p. 414

Genus Information
Origin: Europe, the Swiss Alps, North Africa
and North America
Selected Common Names: wallflower
Nomenclature: From the Greek *eryo* (to draw
out), referring to some species that produce
blisters on contact. The name was used by
Hippocrates.
Notes: A genus of some 80 species including
annuals, biennials and evergreen to woody
perennials.

General Features
Height: 5–60 cm high
Spread: 8–60 cm wide
Habit: evergreen or woody perennial or biennial
Flowers: fragrant; spring to summer; cut back
after blooming to keep plant compact
Foliage: (most) lance-shaped, toothed, hairy

Hardiness: D
Warnings: not prone to insects or disease

Growing Requirements
Light: sun
Soil: lean, well-drained, neutral to alkaline soil
Location: rock gardens; scree; raised beds
Propagation: seed; allow to self sow; division;
cuttings
Expert Advice: May not come true from seed.

Buying Considerations
Professionals
Popularity: gaining popularity
Availability: occasionally available as finished
product; from specialty growers
Size to Sell: sells best in smaller sizes (when
blooming) as it matures fast
Shrinkage: low; requires little maintenance
Collectors
Popularity: not generally of interest to
collectors
Gardeners
Ease of Growth: generally easy to grow but
needs close attention to growing conditions
Start with: one small plant for feature plant
What to Try First ...
Erysimum amoenum, Erysimum chieri 'Gold
Dust', *Erysimum decumbens, Erysimum
kotschyanum*

On the Market
Erysimum
'Bowles' Mauve' (syn. E.A. Bowles) • Purple
flowers in late spring to summer •
Evergreen • 45–75 cm high, 45–60 cm
wide

Erysimum x allionii
(syn. *Cheiranthus x allionii*)
Fragrant, orange flowers in late spring to
midsummer • Evergreen • 50–60 cm high,
30 cm wide

Erysimum capitatum
Fragrant, yellow-cream flowers in spring •
20–60 cm high, 45 cm wide

Erysimum chieri
'Gold Dust' • Flowers in spring to early
summer • 15–20 cm high, 20–25 cm wide

Erysimum decumbens (syn. *E. ochroleucum*)
Bright-yellow flowers in spring • 10–40 cm
high, 15–20 cm wide

Erysimum kotschyanum
Fragrant, orange-yellow to yellow flowers
in summer • 5–10 cm high, 15–20 cm wide

Erysimum nivale
Fragrant, yellow flowers in summer •
10 cm high, 8–10 cm wide

E

Erysimum torulosum (syn. *E. arenicola* var. *torulosum*)
Fragrant, orange-yellow flowers in summer
• 15–20 cm high, 25–45 cm wide

Erysimum wilczeckianum
Fragrant, yellow flowers in spring
• 10–15 cm high, 20 cm wide

Erythronium

E

p. 414

Genus Information

Origin: Europe, Asia and North America
Selected Common Names: trout lily, dogtooth violet
Nomenclature: From the Greek *erythros* (red), the colour of the European species. The common name "dog's tooth" refers to the shape of the bulb.

General Features

Height: 8–35 cm high
Spread: 8–25 cm wide
Habit: colony-forming perennial
Flowers: pendent; graceful, recurved petals; early spring; goes dormant after flowering
Foliage: glossy, mid- to dark-green; (some) marbled
Hardiness: C
Warnings: not prone to insects or disease; prone to slugs
Expert Advice: A very hardy plant that can bloom as soon as the snow melts. *E. grandiflorum* can bloom while there is still snow. *Erythronium* is an underused perennial that is excellent for alpine and woodland gardens. Allow it to colonize for best appearance. It is most often found in garden centres in the fall as a bare root or bulb.

Growing Requirements

Light: shade
Soil: evenly moist, fertile, organic, well-drained soil; keep soil moist during active growth and drier during dormancy
Location: alpine gardens; mixed borders; woodland gardens
Propagation: division
Expert Advice: Plant the bulb at least 10 cm deep to ensure flowering. If planted in too shallow, too warm or too dry soil, it will not flower. The bulb will pull itself downward to a point where it will find cooler, moister soil. While the bulb is finding the correct level, blooming is unlikely. Division can be difficult as it resents being disturbed. Do not delay replanting when dividing because the bulbs shouldn't dry out.

Buying Considerations

Professionals

Popularity: gaining popularity; sells well in bloom
Availability: generally available as bare root from specialty growers
Size to Sell: sells best in smaller sizes (when blooming)
Shrinkage: high; sensitive to overwatering; goes dormant in pot

Collectors

Popularity: of interest to collectors—unique, exceptional beauty, rare, new varieties

Gardeners

Ease of Growth: generally easy to grow but needs close attention to growing conditions
Start with: many small plants for mass plantings

What to Try First ...

Erythronium 'Citronella', *Erythronium* 'Kondo', *Erythronium* 'Pagoda', *Erythronium dens-canis*, *Erythronium dens-canis* 'Frans Hals', *Erythronium grandiflorum*

On the Market

Erythronium
'Citronella' • Bright-yellow flowers in spring • Bronze-mottled, green leaves • 20–35 cm high, 10–15 cm wide
'Kondo' • Lemon-yellow flowers with red-brown centres in spring • Bronze-mottled, green leaves • 15–35 cm high, 10–15 cm wide
'Pagoda' • Sulphur-yellow flowers in spring • Bronze-mottled, green leaves • 15–35 cm high, 10–15 cm wide

Erythronium albidum
White flowers, tinted pink, with a yellow throat in spring • Spotted, reddish-brown leaves • 10–30 cm high, 10–20 cm wide

Erythronium americanum
Fragrant, yellow flowers, tinged red, in spring • Brown-and-white-mottled leaves • 8–15 cm high, 10–20 cm wide

Erythronium californicum
'White Beauty' • White flowers with yellow centres in spring • Mottled leaves • 15 cm high, 10–15 cm wide

Erythronium dens-canis
Rose to mauve flowers in spring • Marbled, purplish-brown leaves • 10–15 cm high, 10 cm wide
'Frans Hals' • Pale-plum flowers in spring • 10–15 cm high, 10 cm wide

'Purple King' • Rich-plum flowers, striped white and brown in the centre, in spring • 10–15 cm high, 10 cm wide

Erythronium grandiflorum
Nodding, gold-yellow flowers in spring • 15–30 cm high, 10 cm wide

Erythronium japonicum
Large, pink-purple flowers in early spring • 10–15 cm high, 8–10 cm wide

Erythronium montanum
White flowers with an orange base in early spring • 20–30 cm high, 20–25 cm wide

Erythronium revolutum
Soft pink flowers in spring • 20–30 cm high, 10 cm wide

Erythronium tuolumnense
Deep yellow flowers with green veins in spring • 20–35 cm high, 8–10 cm wide

Eupatorium

p. 414

Genus Information

Origin: North America and South America
Selected Common Names: boneset, feverweed, hemp agrimony, mistflower, sweet Joe pye, white sanicle
Nomenclature: Named for Eupator, King of Pontus, who used one species as an antidote for poison.
Other Uses: North American native peoples boiled the roots and washed newborn infants in the water to give them strength and vigour.
Notes: It is known as "boneset" for its use as a treatment for broken bones.

General Features

Height: 90 cm–2 m high
Spread: 60–100 cm wide
Habit: upright, tall and wide-spreading, shrub-like perennial
Flowers: pink to white; large flowerheads; late summer to fall; long blooming period; good for cutflowers; attractive to bees and butterflies
Foliage: dark green, whorled
Hardiness: C–D
Warnings: prone to aphids; not prone to diseases

Growing Requirements

Light: sun
Soil: moist, alkaline soil
Location: mixed borders; woodland gardens; wild gardens; back of borders
Propagation: seed; division
Expert Advice: The more moisture and sun this plant receives, the larger it will grow (especially in rich soil).

Buying Considerations

Professionals
Popularity: popular; fast seller in bloom
Availability: readily available as finished product and bare root
Size to Sell: sells best in larger sizes (when blooming)
On the Shelf: rapidly overgrows pot
Shrinkage: low; requires little maintenance

Collectors
Popularity: not generally of interest to collectors

Gardeners
Ease of Growth: very easy to grow
Start with: one plant for feature plant

What to Try First ...
Eupatorium cannabinum, Eupatorium cannabinum 'Flore Pleno', *Eupatorium coelestinum, Eupatorium fistulosum* 'Atropurpureum', *Eupatorium purpureum, Eupatorium purpureum* 'Purple Bush', *Eupatorium purpureum* ssp. *maculatum* 'Atropurpureum'

On the Market

Eupatorium album
'Braunlaub' • Large clusters of white flowers in late summer to fall • 1 m high, 90–100 cm wide

Eupatorium aromaticum
'Joicus Variegated' • Fragrant, clustered, pink-and-cream flowers in late summer to fall • Green foliage spotted cream • 1.75 m high, 90–100 cm wide

Eupatorium cannabinum
Clustered, creamy-pink flowers in late summer to fall • 90–150 cm high, 90–100 cm wide

'Flore Pleno' • Double, purple-rose flowers in late summer to fall • 1–1.5 m high, 90 cm wide

Eupatorium coelestinum
Clustered, blue-violet flowers in late summer to fall • 90–100 cm high, 60–90 cm wide

Eupatorium dubium
'Little Joe' • Fragrant, clustered, rose-purple flowers in late summer to fall • 90–100 cm high, 90–100 cm wide

Eupatorium fistulosum
'Atropurpureum' • Clustered, dusty-rose flowers in late summer to fall • Purplish foliage • 1.5 m high, 60–90 cm wide

Eupatorium perfoliatum
Clustered, white flowers, tinged purple, in late summer to fall • 90–150 cm high, 60–90 cm wide

Eupatorium purpureum
Fragrant, clustered, rose-purple flowers in late summer to fall • 90–150 cm high, 90–100 cm wide

'Bartered Bride' • Fragrant, clustered, white flowers in late summer to fall • 1–2 m high, 90–100 cm wide

'Purple Bush' • Clustered, violet-red flowers in late summer to fall • 90–150 cm high, 60–90 cm wide

Eupatorium purpureum ssp. *maculatum*
'Album' • Clustered, white flowers in late summer to fall • 1–2 m high, 90–100 cm wide

'Atropurpureum' • Clustered, dark purple-rose flowers in late summer to fall • 1–1.5 m high, 90–100 cm wide

'Gateway' • Clustered, pink flowers in late summer to fall • Black stems • 1–2 m high, 90–100 cm wide

Eupatorium rugosum
'Chocolate' • Clustered, white flowers in late summer to fall • Cocoa-brown foliage • 1.5–1.8 m high, 90–100 cm wide

Euphorbia   p. 414

Genus Information
Origin: worldwide
Selected Common Names: cushion spurge, Cypress spurge, spurge, purple-leaf milkweed
Nomenclature: From the Latin *Euphorbea*, referring to Euphorbius, a Greek physician to King Juba II of Mauritania, who used the latex for medicinal purposes.
Other Uses: The plant contains a hot, acrid juice reputed to eat away warts and other growths, which gives rise to the common name "warteaters."
Notes: A genus of some 2000 species.

General Features
Height: 5 cm–2 m high
Spread: 30–100 cm wide
Habit: clump-forming or spreading subshrub or perennial
Flowers: specialized leaves (bracts) in yellow, chartreuse, orange or red; spring to early summer
Foliage: evergreen or succulent leaves

Hardiness: C
Warnings: not prone to insects or disease; occasionally bothered by powdery mildew; contact with sap may irritate skin; some species invasive (deadhead to prevent spread); very vigorous (some spread by roots).

Growing Requirements
Light: sun
Soil: lean, sandy, well-drained soil; (some) moist, well-drained, organic soil; drought tolerant
Location: sunny, hot, dry areas; rock gardens; mixed borders; woodland gardens
Propagation: seed; (some self-sow readily); division
Expert Advice: Divide every 3 to 4 years to keep vigorous.

Buying Considerations
Professionals
Popularity: popular, old-fashioned garden standard
Availability: readily available as finished product and bare root
Size to Sell: sells best in smaller sizes (when blooming) as it matures fast
On the Shelf: rapidly overgrows pot
Shrinkage: low; requires little maintenance
Collectors
Popularity: not generally of interest to collectors
Gardeners
Ease of Growth: very easy to grow
Start with: one small plant for feature plant
What to Try First ...
Euphorbia cyparissias, Euphorbia cyparissias 'Fens Ruby', *Euphorbia dulcis* 'Dixter', *Euphorbia polychroma*

On the Market
Euphorbia amygdaloides
Yellow bracts in spring • 40–80 cm high, 60 cm wide

Euphorbia amygdaloides **'Purpurea'** (syn. **'Rubra'**)
Yellow bracts in spring • Reddish-purple foliage • 30–45 cm high, 45 cm wide

Euphorbia characias ssp. *wulfenii*
Lime-green bracts in spring • Evergreen, grey-green leaves • 90–100 cm high, 90–100 cm wide

Euphorbia cyparissias
Yellow bracts in spring • Feathery, blue-green foliage • Self-sows readily • 20–40 cm high, 30–45+ cm wide

'Fens Ruby' • Yellow bracts aging to purplish-red in spring • Feathery, blue-green foliage • 20–40 cm high, 30–40+ cm wide

'Orange Man' • Clustered, orange-yellow bracts in spring • Feathery, blue-green foliage • 20–40 cm high, 30–45+ cm wide

Euphorbia dulcis
'Chameleon' • Yellow bracts in spring • Purple foliage • 25–50 cm high, 30–45 cm wide

'Dixter' • Burnt-apricot bracts in early summer • Copper-tinted, dark-green foliage • Well-drained, moist soil • 45–75 cm high, 90–100 cm wide

Euphorbia griffithii
Yellow-and-orange-red bracts in early summer • Green leaves turn red and yellow in fall • Well-drained, moist soil • 60–90 cm high, 60 cm wide

'Fireglow' • Orange-red bracts in early summer • Green leaves with pink midribs and red stems • Well-drained, moist, organic soil • 30 cm high, 90–100 cm wide

Euphorbia myrsinites
Pale-yellow bracts in spring • Blue-grey, evergreen, succulent leaves • 5–10 cm high, 30 cm wide

Euphorbia polychroma
Bright chartreuse-yellow bracts in spring • 40–60 cm high, 40–60 cm wide

'Candy' (syn. Purpurea) • Deep-yellow flowers in spring • Purple-green leaves and stems • 40–45 cm high, 40–60 cm wide

'First Blush' • White bracts in spring • Green and cream foliage • 30 cm high, 30–45 cm wide

Euphorbia seguieriana ssp. *niciciana*
Chartreuse bracts in early summer to fall • Semi-evergreen, needle-like foliage • 30–50 cm high, 45 cm wide

E

Fallopia

p. 414

Genus Information

Origin: northern temperate regions and the Northern Hemisphere
Selected Common Names: Japanese fleeceflower, low Japanese fleeceflower, silver lace vine
Nomenclature: Named for Gabriello Fallopia, a 16th century Italian anatomist who discovered Fallopian tubes.

General Features

Height: 60 cm–5 m high
Spread: 60 cm–2 m wide
Habit: rhizomatous climbing or spreading perennial; climbers require strong support
Flowers: white to rose; funnel-shaped; large panicles; summer
Foliage: green or variegated foliage
Hardiness: C
Warnings: not prone to insects or disease; occasionally leaf miners; *F. baldschuanica* aggressively spreads (contain to prevent spread)

Growing Requirements

Light: sun to p.m. sun
Soil: moist, poor to moderately fertile, well-drained soil
Location: banks (erosion control); climbers on walls, structures or through large trees
Propagation: seed; cuttings
Expert Advice: Sow seed in containers in cold frames in spring or as soon as ripe. Take semi-ripe cuttings in summer.

Buying Considerations

Professionals

Popularity: gaining popularity as a foliage plant
Availability: readily available as finished product and bare root
Size to Sell: sells best in smaller sizes as it matures fast
On the Shelf: variegated varieties, highly ornamental; rapidly overgrows pot
Shrinkage: low (shrinkage increases as plants become rootbound); requires little maintenance

Collectors

Popularity: not generally of interest to collectors

Gardeners

Ease of Growth: generally easy to grow
Start with: one small plant for feature plant

What to Try First ...

Fallopia baldschuanica, Fallopia japonica, Fallopia japonica var. *compacta, Fallopia japonica* var. *compacta* 'Milk Boy'

On the Market

Fallopia baldschuanica (syn. *F. aubertii)* •
Vine
White flowers, tinged pink, in late summer • Heart-shaped, mid-green foliage • rampant grower • 3–5 m high, 1–2 m wide
Fallopia japonica
White flowers, aging to rose, in summer • 60 cm–2 m high, 60–90+ cm wide
'Devon Cream' • White flowers in summer • 60–100 cm high, 60–90+ cm wide
'Spectabilis' • Flowers in summer • Showy, spotted foliage with red stems • 60 cm–2 m high, 60–90+ cm wide
Fallopia japonica var. *compacta*
White flowers, aging to rose, in summer • 60–120 cm high, 60–90+ cm wide
'Milk Boy' (syn. 'Variegata') • White flowers in summer • Light- and dark-green foliage with splashes of cream and pink • 60–120 cm high, 60–90+ cm wide
Fallopia japonica f. *rosea*
Rose flowers in summer • 60 cm–2 m high, 60–90+ cm wide

Festuca

p. 415

Genus Information

Origin: northern temperate regions
Selected Common Names: blue fescue, blue grass, fescue
Nomenclature: From the Latin *festuca*, meaning stalk or stem.

General Features

Height: 5–50 cm high
Spread: 10–40 cm wide
Habit: clump-forming or rhizomatous grass
Flowers: purple-tinged seed heads; summer
Foliage: blue, evergreen
Hardiness: C
Warnings: not prone to insects or disease
Expert Advice: Excellent alternative to *Artemisia*. Very attractive mass planted.

Growing Requirements

Light: sun
Soil: sandy, well-drained soil; drought tolerant
Location: mixed borders; turf; pasture
Propagation: seed; division
Expert Advice: Hybridizes easily. May not come true from seed. Divide frequently to keep vigorous.

Buying Considerations

Professionals

Popularity: popular garden standard; fast-selling foliage plant
Availability: readily available as finished product and bare root
Size to Sell: sells best in smaller sizes as it matures fast
On the Shelf: high ornamental appeal; keep stock rotated
Shrinkage: low; requires little maintenance

Collectors

Popularity: not generally of interest to collectors

Gardeners

Ease of Growth: generally easy to grow
Start with: one small plant for feature plant or several for visual impact and mass planting

What to Try First ...

Festuca glauca, *Festuca glauca* 'Azurit', *Festuca glauca* 'Blaufuchs', *Festuca glauca* 'Boulder Blue', *Festuca glauca* 'Elijah Blue', *Festuca glauca* 'Pepindale Blue'

On the Market

Festuca amethystina
Greenish-violet seed heads in late spring to early summer • Grey-green foliage • 25–50 cm high, 25–35 cm wide

Festuca glauca
Blue-green seed heads in summer • Blue-green foliage • 25–40 cm high, 25–30 cm wide

'Azurit' • Blue-green seed heads in summer • Blue-grey foliage • 20–35 cm high, 15–30 cm wide

'Blaufuchs' (Blue Fox) • Blue-green seed heads in summer • Blue-green foliage • 15–40 cm high, 25–30 cm wide

'Boulder Blue' • Blue-green seed heads in summer • Blue foliage • 20–30 cm high, 30–40 cm wide

'Elijah Blue' • Dainty, blue-green seed heads in summer • Fine-textured, powder-blue foliage • 15–20 cm high, 30–40 cm wide

'Golden Toupee' • Seed heads in summer • Golden foliage • 25–30 cm high, 30–40 cm wide

'Pepindale Blue' • Blue-green seed heads in summer • Icy-blue foliage • 30 cm high, 30 cm wide

'Seeigel' (Sea Urchin) • Blue-green seed heads in summer • Fine, spiky, green foliage • 20–30 cm high, 15 cm wide

Festuca glauca minima
Seed heads in summer • Blue-grey-green foliage • 5 cm high, 10 cm wide

Festuca idahoensis
'Siskiyou' • Blue-green to silver-blue foliage • 25–35 cm high, 25–30 cm wide

Festuca punctoria
Seed heads in late spring to early summer • Sharply pointed, blue-grey foliage • 15–30 cm high, 15–30 cm wide

Festuca valesiaca
'Silbersee' (Silver Sea; syn. Seven Seas) • Pale-green seed heads in summer • Silvery-blue foliage • 15–20 cm high, 15 cm wide

Filipendula   p. 415

Genus Information

Origin: Europe, Asia and North America
Selected Common Names: double queen of the meadow, queen of the meadow, queen of the prairie
Nomenclature: From the Latin *filum* (thread) and *pendulas* (drooping), which refer to the roots that hang together in threads.
Other Uses: This plant has been long used as an herbal medicine. Salicylic acid, the aspirin-like painkiller, can be extracted from it. It has been used by herbalists to alleviate the pain of arthritis and rheumatism as well as to treat stomach problems such as ulcers and heartburn.

General Features

Height: 15 cm–3 m high
Spread: 20–150 cm wide
Habit: rhizomatous or tuberous perennial
Flowers: tiny; fragrant; on tall stalks; summer
Foliage: green to golden
Hardiness: C
Warnings: prone to powdery mildew and aphids
Expert Advice: An excellent perennial for height at the back of borders.

Growing Requirements

Light: shade to a.m. sun; tolerates more sun with good soil moisture; golden foliage types perform better in shade
Soil: cool, damp, organic soil; *F. vulgaris* tolerates dry soil
Location: bog gardens; shady mixed borders; woodland gardens
Propagation: seed; division; root cuttings

Buying Considerations

Professionals
Popularity: old-fashioned perennial that is gaining popularity; fast seller in bloom
Availability: readily available as finished product and bare root
Size to Sell: sells best in smaller sizes (when blooming) as it matures fast
On the Shelf: rapidly overgrows pot
Shrinkage: low; requires little maintenance

Collectors
Popularity: not generally of interest to collectors

Gardeners
Ease of Growth: very easy to grow
Start with: one small plant for feature plant

What to Try First ...
Filipendula 'Kahome', *Filipendula palmata*, *Filipendula purpurea*, *Filipendula rubra*, *Filipendula rubra* 'Venusta', *Filipendula ulmaria* 'Aurea'

On the Market

Filipendula
  'Kahome' • Fragrant, rose-pink flowers in summer • 15–20 cm high, 20–30 cm wide

Filipendula camtschatica (syn. *F. kamtschatica*)
  Fragrant, large, white flowers in midsummer to fall • 2–3 m high, 1.2 m wide

Filipendula multijuga (syn. *F. palmata*)
  'Nana' • Fragrant, deep rose-pink flowers in summer • Fern-like foliage • 60–100 cm high, 45–60 cm wide

Filipendula palmata
  Fragrant, pale- to deep-pink flowers in midsummer • 90–100 cm high, 60 cm wide

Filipendula purpurea
  Fragrant, carmine-red flowers in summer • 75–120 cm high, 45–60 cm wide
  'Elegans' • Fragrant, carmine-pink flowers in summer • 80–130 cm high, 60 cm wide

Filipendula rubra
  Fragrant, deep peach-pink flowers in early summer • 1.5–2.5 m high, 90–120 cm wide
  'Venusta' (syn. Magnifica, Venusta Magnifica) • Fragrant, large, deep rose-pink flowers in summer • 90–150 cm high, 1 m wide

Filipendula ulmaria
  Fragrant, creamy-white flowers in late spring to early summer • 90 cm–2 m high, 60 cm wide
  'Aurea' • Fragrant, white flowers in summer • Gold-green foliage • 60–90 cm high, 40–60 cm wide

  'Flore Pleno' • Fragrant, double, creamy-white flowers in early summer • 60–90 cm high, 60 cm wide
  'Variegata' (syn. Aureo-Variegata) • Fragrant, white, feathery flowers in late spring • Green-and-yellow variegated foliage • 60–90 cm high, 60 cm wide

Filipendula vulgaris (syn. *F. hexapetala*)
  Fragrant, white flowers in early summer • Fern-like foliage • 60–80 cm high, 30–45 cm wide
  'Multiplex' (syn. Plena) • Fragrant, double, creamy-white flowers in early summer • 45–60 cm high, 30–45 cm wide

Fragaria
p. 415

Genus Information
Origin: North America, Europe, Asia and temperate regions
Selected Common Names: strawberry
Nomenclature: From the Latin *fragrans*, meaning fragrant, referring to the aroma of the fruit.

General Features
Height: 10–30 cm high
Spread: 30–60 cm wide
Habit: stoloniferous groundcover perennial
Flowers: pink to red; attractive
Foliage: dark-green
Hardiness: A–C
Warnings: prone to aphids, powdery mildew and leaf spot; *Fragaria* Pink Panda™ may become invasive (control spread by removing runners)
Expert Advice: Some produce ornamental fruit.

Growing Requirements
Light: sun
Soil: fertile, moist, well-drained, alkaline soil; tolerant of acidic soil
Location: rock gardens, edging, pathways
Propagation: seed; separate plantlets and replant runners

Buying Considerations

Professionals
Popularity: gaining popularity; fast seller in bloom
Availability: readily available as finished product
Size to Sell: sells best in smaller sizes as it matures fast
On the Shelf: high ornamental appeal: keep stock rotated; rapidly overgrows pot
Shrinkage: low; requires little maintenance

Collectors
Popularity: not generally of interest to collectors

F

On the Market

Fragaria
  'Lipstick' • Large, red flowers in late spring
  to summer • 10–15 cm high, 45–60 cm
  wide
  Pink Panda™ (Frel) • Large, bright-pink
  flowers in late spring to summer
  • 10–15 cm high, 45–60+ cm wide
  Red Ruby™ (Samba) • Large, deep
  rose flowers in late spring to summer
  • 15 cm high, 30+ cm wide

Fragaria vesca
  White flowers in late spring to summer
  • 30 cm high, 45–60 cm+ wide
  'Variegata' • White flowers in late spring to
  summer • Grey-green and cream foliage
  • 30 cm high, 45–60+ cm wide

Fragaria virginiana
  White or pink flowers in late spring to
  summer • 10–30 cm high, 30+ cm wide

F

Gaillardia

p. 415 📷

Genus Information

Origin: North America and South America
Selected Common Names: blanket flower
Nomenclature: Named for M. Gaillard de Charentoneau, a French patron of botany.
Notes: A genus of some 30 species of annual, biennial or short-lived perennials.

General Features

Height: 15–85 cm high
Spread: 15–60 cm wide
Habit: clump-forming biennial or (some) short-lived perennial
Flowers: colourful; prolific; long blooming; summer to fall; deadhead to extend blooming season
Foliage: rough
Hardiness: C
Warnings: prone to powdery mildew and aphids

Growing Requirements

Light: sun
Soil: fertile, well-drained soil; tolerates poor, salty soil; drought tolerant
Location: sunny, hot, dry areas; borders; wild gardens
Propagation: seed (self-sows readily); division, root cuttings
Expert Advice: Often blooms the first year from seed. Cut back in early fall to aid in overwintering.

Buying Considerations

Professionals
Popularity: popular, old-fashioned garden standard; fast seller in bloom
Availability: readily available as finished product and bare root
Size to Sell: sells best in smaller sizes (when blooming) as it matures fast
On the Shelf: keep stock rotated; rapidly overgrows pot; deadhead regularly
Shrinkage: high; sensitive to underwatering

Collectors
Popularity: not generally of interest to collectors

Gardeners
Ease of Growth: very easy to grow
Start with: one small plant for feature plant

What to Try First ...
Gaillardia 'Baby Cole', Gaillardia 'Fanfare', Gaillardia 'Kobold', Gaillardia 'Little Boy', Gaillardia aristata

On the Market

Gaillardia
Red, yellow and orange flowers in summer • 60–75 cm high, 30 cm wide
'Baby Cole' • Red-and-yellow flowers with maroon centres in summer • 15–20 cm high, 15–20 cm wide
'Bijou' • Red flowers with yellow tips in summer to fall • 25 cm high, 45–60 cm wide
'Burgunder' (Burgundy) • Fragrant, wine-red flowers in summer • 50–60 cm high, 45 cm wide
'Dazzler' • Golden-yellow flowers with maroon centres in summer • 60–85 cm high, 45 cm wide
'Fanfare' • Red petals with bright-yellow tips in summer • 45–60 cm high, 45–60 cm wide
'Kobold' (Goblin) • Red flowers with yellow tips in summer to fall • 30–40 cm high, 30–45 cm wide
'Little Boy' • Red-and-yellow flowers in summer • 25 cm high
'Mandarin' • Flame-orange flowers with yellow tips in summer • 45–60 cm high, 45–60 cm wide
'Summer's Kiss' • Golden-apricot flowers in summer • 45 cm high, 30–45 cm wide

Gaillardia aristata
Yellow, red-based flowers in summer • 45–75 cm high, 60 cm wide

Galearis

Genus Information

Origin: the eastern United States, eastern Canada and the Great Lakes region.
Selected Common Names: showy orchid
Nomenclature: From the Greek *galea* (helmut), referring to the helmet-like appearance of the flower.
Notes: Formerly part of the *Orchis* genus.

General Features

Height: 15–35 cm high
Spread: 20–25 cm wide
Habit: tuberous, terrestrial orchids
Flowers: mauve, orchid-like with hood, lip and short spur; early summer
Foliage: lance-shaped
Hardiness: D
Warnings: not prone to insects; requires specific cultural conditions

Expert Advice: This orchid has a symbiotic relationship with mycorrhizal fungi, and therefore may be a challenge to grow outside of its natural habitat. If this fungus is not present at the time of planting, the orchid may be short-lived. It would be popular if cultural conditions could be met. It is best left for collectors. Plants require CITES certification.

Growing Requirements
Light: shade
Soil: moist, organic, rich soil; pH sensitive
Location: woodland gardens
Propagation: separate and replant offsets

Buying Considerations
Professionals
Popularity: relatively unknown
Availability: occasionally available from specialty growers; purchase only CITES certified stock
Size to Sell: sells best in mature sizes (when blooming) as it matures slowly
On the Shelf: high ornamental appeal; keep stock rotated; very difficult to maintain in pots (needs specific potting soil)
Shrinkage: high; goes dormant in pot
Collectors
Popularity: of interest to collectors—unique, rare, challenge
Gardeners
Ease of Growth: very difficult to grow as it needs close attention to growing conditions
Start with: several mature plants for instant visual effect

What to Try First ...
Galearis spectabilis

On the Market
Galearis spectabilis (syn. *Orchis spectabilis*)
Mauve flowers with white lips in spring to early summer • 15–35 cm high, 20–25 cm wide

Galium
p. 415

Genus Information
Origin: temperate regions
Selected Common Names: bedstraw, lady's bedstraw, northern bedstraw, sweet woodruff, woodruff
Nomenclature: From the Greek *gala* (milk), referring to the former use of *G. vernum* in curdling milk for cheese.
Other Uses: Used in potpourris and sachets, and used as a moth repellent. Used as an herb to flavour wines, brandy and apple jellies.
Notes: A genus of some 400 species.

General Features
Height: 1–90 cm high
Spread: 15–90 cm wide
Habit: weedy, open-spreading groundcover perennial
Flowers: fragrant; late spring to fall
Foliage: green; fragrant
Hardiness: A
Warnings: prone to rust
Expert Advice: When dried, *G. odoratum* produces a fresh, grassy-like fragrance.

Growing Requirements
Light: sun to shade
Soil: moist, organic soil
Location: woodland gardens
Propagation: seed; division

G

Buying Considerations
Professionals
Popularity: gaining popularity as a foliage plant
Availability: generally available as finished product from specialty growers
Size to Sell: sells best in smaller sizes (when blooming) as it matures fast
On the Shelf: rapidly overgrows pot
Shrinkage: low; requires little maintenance
Collectors
Popularity: some of interest to collectors—unique, rare; *G. aretioides* is for the alpine collector
Gardeners
Ease of Growth: generally easy to grow
Start with: one small plant for feature plant and several for mass plantings

What to Try First ...
Galium aretioides, Galium odoratum, Galium verum

On the Market
Galium aretioides (ex jurasek)
White flowers in spring • 1 cm high, 15 cm wide

Galium boreale
Fragrant, white flowers in late spring to early summer • 30–80 cm high, 30–60+ cm wide

Galium odoratum
Fragrant, white flowers in spring to midsummer • 15–45 cm high, 30+ cm wide

Galium verum
Yellow flowers in summer to fall • 30–90 cm high, 90 cm wide

Gentiana

p. 415 📷

Genus Information

Origin: worldwide, except in Africa
Nomenclature: Named for Gentius, the King of ancient Illyria. He was said to have discovered the medicinal properties of the roots.

General Features

Height: 5–150 cm high
Spread: 10–60 cm wide
Habit: upright, tall to clump- or mat-forming groundcover perennial
Flowers: blue; spring to late fall
Foliage: glossy; (some) evergreen
Hardiness: C–D
Warnings: prone to aphids; not prone to disease
Expert Advice: Many are prized by collectors; among bluest flowers in perennial world.

Growing Requirements

Light: sun or shade
Soil: cool, moist, organic, well-drained soil; (some) specific pH requirements
Location: alpine gardens; rock gardens; woodland gardens
Propagation: seed; division; cuttings; layering
Expert Advice: Seeds of all species need light for germination, and seeds should be sown as fresh as possible as they have a short viability period. Fresh seed does not require a chilling period, but older seed does.

Buying Considerations

Professionals

Popularity: gaining popularity; fast seller in bloom
Availability: generally available as finished product and bare root from specialty growers
Size to Sell: sells best in smaller sizes (when blooming)
On the Shelf: keep stock rotated
Shrinkage: high; sensitive to overwatering

Collectors

Popularity: of interest to collectors—unique, rare

Gardeners

Ease of Growth: generally easy to grow
Start with: one mature plant for feature plant and several for mass plantings

What to Try First ...

Gentiana 'Susan Jane', *Gentiana acaulis*, *Gentiana cachemirica*, *Gentiana clusii*, *Gentiana dinarica*, *Gentiana septemfida*, *Gentiana septemfida* var. *lagodechiana*, *Gentiana sino-ornata*, *Gentiana sino-ornata* 'Azurhimmel', *Gentiana verna*

On the Market

Gentiana
'Alex Duguid' • Light-blue flowers with white throat in fall • 5–10 cm high, 30–40 cm wide

'Blauer Gnom' (Blue Gnome) • Trumpet-shaped, azure-blue flowers in fall • 5–10 cm high, 20–30 cm wide

'Blauer Zwerg' (Blue Dwarf) • Trumpet-shaped, blue flowers in fall • 5–10 cm high, 20–30 cm wide

'Blue Silk' • Trumpet-shaped, violet-blue to purple flowers in fall • 5–10 cm high, 20–30 cm wide

'Edith Sarah' • Deep blue flowers in fall • 8–15 cm high, 10–20 cm wide

(Hybrid 4) • Blue flowers in early summer to fall • 35–45 cm high, 45–60 cm wide

'Strathmore' • Trumpet-shaped, powder-blue flowers in late summer to fall • 5–10 cm high, 30–40 cm wide

'Susan Jane' • Azure-blue flowers with white throat in late summer to fall • 5–8 cm high, 20–30 cm wide

'Violette' • Trumpet-shaped, violet-blue flowers in fall • 5–10 cm high, 20–30 cm wide

Gentiana (G. septemfida x *G. paradoxa)*
Bright-blue flowers in summer • 15–30 cm high, 30 cm wide

Gentiana acaulis **(syn.** *G kochiana)*
Large, blue flowers in spring to summer • 10–15 cm high, 20–30 cm wide

'Coelestina' • Large, sky-blue flowers in spring to summer • 10–15 cm high, 20–30 cm wide

'Holzmannii' • Large, blue flowers in spring • 5–10 cm high, 20–30 cm wide

Gentiana affinis
Clustered, purple to blue flowers in summer • 20–30 cm high, 25–40 cm wide

Gentiana algida
Cream-white flowers with green or blue spots in summer • 10–20 cm high, 20–30 cm wide

Gentiana alpina
Deep blue, green-spotted flowers in summer • 5–10 cm high, 20–30 cm wide

Gentiana andrewsii
Rich-blue-purple flowers in summer to fall • 30–50 cm high, 30–45 cm wide

G

Gentiana angustifolia
Blue flowers with green spots in throat in summer • Organic, moist, well-drained, alkaline soil • 5–10 cm high, 20–30 cm wide
'**Alba**' • White flowers with green throat and blue marks in summer • 5–10 cm high, 20–30 cm wide

Gentiana asclepiadea
Blue flowers in summer to fall • Neutral to acidic soil • 40–60 cm high, 30–45 cm wide
'**Pink Swallow**' • Pink flowers in late summer to fall • 40–60 cm high, 30–45 cm wide

Gentiana asclepiadea var. **alba**
White flowers in late summer to fall • 45–60 cm high, 30–45 cm wide

Gentiana austromontana
Blue-violet flowers in fall • 30–45 cm high, 20–30 cm wide

Gentiana bavarica
Bright-blue flowers in summer • 5–15 cm high, 15–25 cm wide

Gentiana bigelovii
Medium-blue flowers in late summer • 20–30 cm high, 25–40 cm wide

Gentiana boissieri
Blue flowers in summer • 5–10 cm high, 20–30 cm wide

Gentiana brachyphylla
Deep-blue flowers in summer • 3–5 cm high, 10–15 cm wide
'**Alba**' • White flowers in summer • 3–5 cm high, 10–15 cm wide

Gentiana cachemirica
Clear azure-blue flowers in summer • 5–15 cm high, 20–30 cm wide

Gentiana calycosa
Bright-blue flowers in late summer • 15–30 cm high, 30–40 cm wide

Gentiana clusii
Sky-blue flowers in late spring to early summer • Evergreen foliage • 8–15 cm high, 15–25 cm wide

Gentiana clusii ssp. **rochelii**
Rich-blue flowers in late spring to early summer • 5–15 cm high, 20–30 cm wide

Gentiana clusii var. **alboviolacea**
Trumpet-shaped, white flowers with pink stripes in late spring to early summer • 5–15 cm high, 20–30 cm wide

Gentiana cruciata
Blue flowers in summer • 10–40 cm high, 25–40 cm wide

Gentiana dahurica
Rich-blue flowers in summer • 15–40 cm high, 25–40 cm wide

Gentiana decumbens
Blue to purple-blue flowers in summer • 15–25 cm high, 15–25 cm wide

Gentiana dendrologi
Clustered, white to off-white flowers in summer • 20–40 cm high, 20–30 cm wide

Gentiana dinarica
Blue flowers with no spots in the throat in late spring to early summer • Organic, moist, well-drained, neutral to alkaline soil • 8–15 cm high, 15–20 cm wide
'**Frohnleiten**' • Deep-blue flowers in late spring to early summer • 8–15 cm high, 15–20 cm wide

Gentiana freyniana
Purple-blue flowers in summer • 15–30 cm high, 30–40 cm wide

Gentiana gelida
Pale-yellow to cream flowers in late summer to fall • 25–40 cm high, 20–30 cm wide

Gentiana gracilipes
Purple-blue flowers in summer • 25–40 cm high, 20–25 cm wide

Gentiana x hexafarreri
Deep-blue flowers with white throats in summer to fall • 5–10 cm high, 15–20 cm wide
'**Dark Heart**' • Trumpet-shaped, deep-blue flowers with dark-purple throat in late summer • 10–15 cm high, 20–30 cm wide

Gentiana kurroo
Large, blue flowers in summer to fall • 10–25 cm high, 20–35 cm wide

Gentiana lawrencei
Cambridge-blue flowers with white throats in late summer to fall • 10–15 cm high, 15–20 cm wide

Gentiana ligustica
Bright sky-blue flowers with green-spotted throat in late spring to summer • Organic, moist, well-drained, alkaline soil • 5–10 cm high, 15–20 cm wide

Gentiana loderi
Rich-blue flowers in summer to fall • 10–15 cm high, 15–20 cm wide

Gentiana lutea
Gold-yellow flowers in summer • 75–150 cm high, 45–60 cm wide

Gentiana x macaulayi
'**Kidbrooke Seedling**' • Upturned, medium-blue flowers in late summer to fall • 10–15 cm high, 20–40 cm wide

G

'Kingfisher' • Upturned, bright-blue flowers in late summer to fall • 10–15 cm high, 20–40 cm wide

Gentiana makinoi
Purple-blue flowers with irregular spots in late summer to fall • Excellent cutflower • Acidic soil • 30–60 cm high, 30–45 cm wide
'Alba' • White flowers in late summer to fall • 30–60 cm high, 30–45 cm wide
'Royal Blue' • Bright-blue flowers in late summer to fall • 30–60 cm high, 30–45 cm wide

Gentiana newberryi
Large, upward-facing, dark- to mid-blue flowers in summer • 5–10 cm high, 15–20 cm wide

Gentiana nipponica
Blue flowers in summer • 3–10 cm high, 10–20 cm wide

Gentiana olivieri
Blue flowers with white throat in late spring to summer • 10–40 cm high, 20–30 cm wide

Gentiana orbicularis
Violet-blue flowers in summer • 3–5 cm high, 10–15 cm wide

Gentiana paradoxa
Rich-blue flowers in late summer to fall • 25–50 cm high, 30–45 cm wide
'Blauer Herold' • Large, rich-blue flowers in late summer to fall • 25–50 cm high, 30–45 cm wide

Gentiana parryi
Deep-blue, green-spotted flowers in late summer • 25–45 cm high, 15–20 cm wide

Gentiana punctata
Pale-yellow flowers with purple spots in summer • 20–60 cm high, 20–35 cm wide

Gentiana purpurea
Purple-red flowers with purple spots in summer • 20–60 cm high, 30–40 cm wide
'Nana' • Purple-red flowers in summer • 15–25 cm high, 15–25 cm wide

Gentiana scabra
Purple-blue flowers in late summer to fall • 20–30 cm high, 15–25 cm wide
'Fuji White' • White flowers in late summer to fall • 20–30 cm high, 15–25 cm wide
'Kutani Purple' • Blue flowers in late summer to fall • 20–30 cm high, 15–25 cm wide
'Pink Gal' • Blue flowers in late summer to fall • 20–30 cm high, 15–25 cm wide

'Zuki Rindo' • Rose flowers in late summer to fall • 20–30 cm high, 15–25 cm wide

Gentiana septemfida
Clustered, deep-blue flowers in summer • 15–30 cm high, 30–40 cm wide

Gentiana septemfida var. lagodechiana
Dark-blue flowers in summer to fall • 10–20 cm high, 30–40 cm wide
(Select) • Deep-blue flowers in early summer to fall • 10–20 cm high, 30–40 cm wide

Gentiana setigera
Deep blue flowers with white throat in summer • 5–20 cm high, 20–30 cm wide

Gentiana sino-ornata
Upturned, cobalt-blue flowers in late summer to fall • Needle-like foliage • 5–10 cm high, 30–40 cm wide
'Alba' • White flowers in late summer to fall • 5–10 cm high, 30–40 cm wide
'Azurhimmel' • Large, azure-blue flowers with vivid stripes in late summer to fall • 5–10 cm high, 30–40 cm wide
'Brin Form' • Upturned, blue flowers in late summer to fall • Needle-like foliage • 5–10 cm high, 30–40 cm wide
'Starlight' • Trumpet-shaped, azure-blue flowers in fall • 5–10 cm high, 20–30 cm wide

Gentiana x stevenagensis
Deep blue flowers in late summer to fall • Acidic soil • 5–10 cm high, 30–40 cm wide
'Bernardii' • Trumpet-shaped, azure-blue flowers with red and yellow markings in fall • 5–10 cm high, 20–30 cm wide

Gentiana straminea
Straw-yellow flowers in summer • 30–40 cm high, 20–25 cm wide

Gentiana terglouensis
Sky-blue flowers in summer • 5–8 cm high, 10–20 cm wide

Gentiana ternifolia
Soft blue flowers in late summer to fall • 5–8 cm high, 15–30 cm wide

Gentiana tianschanica
Purple-blue flowers in summer • 15–25 cm high, 20–40 cm wide

Gentiana tibetica
Greenish-white flowers in summer • 40–60 cm high, 25–35 cm wide

Gentiana triflora
Purple-blue flowers in late summer to fall • 40–90 cm high, 25–40 cm wide

G

'Royal Blue' • Blue flowers in late summer to fall • 60–90 cm high, 40–50 cm wide

Gentiana verna
Azure-blue flowers with white eye in spring • 5–10 cm high, 10–15 cm wide
'Alba' • White flowers in spring • 5–10 cm high, 10–15 cm wide

Gentiana verna ssp. *balcanica*
Dark-blue flowers in spring • Organic, moist, well-drained, alkaline soil • 5–10 cm high, 10–15 cm wide

Gentiana verna ssp. *oschtenica*
Soft-to lemon-yellow flowers in spring • 5–10 cm high, 10–15 cm wide

Gentiana verna ssp. *pontica*
Brilliant blue flowers in spring • 5–10 cm high, 10–15 cm wide

Gentiana verna ssp. *tergestina*
Tubular-shaped, dark-blue flowers in spring • 5–10 cm high, 10–15 cm wide

Geranium
p. 415

Genus Information

Origin: North America, Europe, the Himalayas and the Caucasus Mountains
Selected Common Names: cranesbill, geranium
Nomenclature: From the Greek *geranos* (crane). The unripe fruit of the geranium looks like the long beak of a crane—hence the common name "cranesbill."

General Features

Height: 10–75+ cm high
Spread: 10–120 cm wide
Habit: undemanding, long-lived, clump-forming or rhizomatous perennial
Flowers: white, pink, purple or blue; spring to fall; (some) long blooming
Foliage: range of shapes and textures; (some) aromatic; (some) superb fall colour
Hardiness: C–D
Warnings: prone to powdery mildew and aphids
Expert Advice: An excellent low-maintenance groundcover.

Growing Requirements

Light: sun to p.m. sun; tolerant of a wide range of light conditions
Soil: well-drained soil; tolerant of a wide range of soils; some tolerate dry periods once established
Location: mixed borders; rock gardens; woodland gardens
Propagation: seed; division; cuttings; separate and replant offshoots

Buying Considerations

Professionals

Popularity: popular, old-fashioned garden standard; fast-selling in bloom and as a foliage plant; sells well in fall colour
Availability: readily available as finished product and bare root
Size to Sell: sells best in smaller sizes (when blooming) as it matures fast
On the Shelf: keep stock rotated; rapidly overgrows pot; cutback regularly
Shrinkage: low

Collectors

Popularity: not generally of interest to collectors

Gardeners

Ease of Growth: very easy to grow
Start with: one small plant for feature plant or several for mass planting

What to Try First ...

Geranium 'Bertie Crug', *Geranium* 'Johnson's Blue', *Geranium* 'Phillippe Vapelle', *Geranium* 'Rozanne', *Geranium cinereum* 'Ballerina', *Geranium cinereum* 'Laurence Flatman', *Geranium cinereum* 'Purple Pillow', *Geranium himalayense* 'Plenum', *Geranium macrorrhizum* 'Ingwersen's Variety', *Geranium pratense* 'Okey Dokey', *Geranium pratense* 'Plenum Caeruleum', *Geranium x riversleaianum* 'Mavis Simpson', *Geranium sanguineum* 'Max Frei', *Geranium sanguineum* var. *striatum*

On the Market

Geranium

'Ann Folkard' • Magenta flowers in midsummer to fall • 45–60 cm high, 60–100+ cm wide

'Bertie Crug' • Deep-pink flowers in late spring to fall • Bronze foliage • 10–20 cm high, 20–30 cm wide

'Brookside' • Purple-veined, violet-blue flowers with small eye in late spring to fall • 45–60 cm high, 45–65 cm wide

'Chocolate Candy' • Pale-pink flowers in summer • Chocolate-brown foliage • 15 cm high, 20–30 cm wide

'Confetti' • Pink flowers in late spring to fall • Green and pink speckles on white foliage • 35–40 cm high, 40–50 cm wide

'Dilys' • Soft-purple flowers with purple veins in summer to fall • 25 cm high, 90 cm wide

'Johnson's Blue' • Lavender-blue flowers in summer • 30–45 cm high, 60–75 cm wide

'New Dimension' • Purple-blue flowers in summer • Bronze foliage • 30 cm high, 45–60 cm wide

'Philippe Vapelle' • Dark-veined, blue-purple flowers in summer • Velvety, grey-green foliage • 30–40 cm high, 30–40 cm wide

'Pink Spice' • Pink flowers in summer • Bronze foliage • 15 cm high, 30 cm wide

'Rozanne' • Violet-blue flowers with darker veins in late spring to fall • Red fall foliage • 45–50 cm high, 50–60 cm wide

'Salome' • Lilac flowers with black centre in summer • 30 cm high, 1.2 m wide

'Shocking Blue' • Purple-blue flowers with a white eye in late-spring to fall • 30 cm high, 45–60 cm wide

'Spinners' • Cup-shaped, deep-violet flowers in late spring to midsummer • 90–100 cm high, 90 cm wide

'Stanhoe' • Pink flowers in midsummer to fall • Silvery-green foliage • 10 cm high, 30 cm wide

'Strawberry Frost' • Coral flowers in late spring to fall • Silvery-brown foliage • 20–25 cm high, 20–30 cm wide

'Sue Crug' • Magenta flowers with darker veins and centre in late spring to fall • 50 cm high, 50–60 cm wide

Geranium bicknellii
Large, rose-purple flowers • 25–40 cm high, 45 cm wide

Geranium x *cantabrigiense*
'Biokovo' • White, pink-tinged flowers in spring to early summer • Aromatic foliage • 15–25 cm high, 75–90 cm wide

'Biokovo Karmina' • Deep-pink flowers in spring to early summer • Aromatic foliage • 15–25 cm high, 45–60 cm wide

'St. Ola' • Fragrant, white flowers in spring to early summer • Aromatic foliage • 20–30 cm high, 45–60 cm wide

Geranium cinereum
'Ballerina' • Red-veined, lilac-pink flowers with red centres in late spring to summer • Grey-green foliage • 10–15 cm high, 20–30 cm wide

'Carol' • Bright-pink flowers with dark veins in late spring to summer • Grey-green foliage • 10–15 cm high, 20–30 cm wide

'Laurence Flatman' • Dark-veined, deep-pink flowers with dark eye in late spring

to summer • Grey-green foliage • 10–15 cm high, 30–45 cm wide

'Purple Pillow' • Dark-veined, red-purple flowers in late spring to summer • Grey-green foliage • 15–20 cm high, 30–45 cm wide

Geranium clarkei
'Kashmir Pink' • Soft-pink flowers in summer • Deeply cut foliage • 30–45 cm high, 30–45+ cm wide

'Kashmir Purple' • Large, violet-blue flowers in summer • Deeply cut foliage • 30–45 cm high, 45+ cm wide

'Kashmir White' • White flowers with pink-lilac veins in summer • 30–45 cm high, 45+ cm wide

Geranium dalmaticum
Shell-pink flowers in midsummer • Glossy, aromatic foliage • 10–15 cm high, 45–60 cm wide

Geranium endressii
Dark-veined, pink flowers in late spring to fall • Evergreen foliage • 30–45 cm high, 45–60 cm wide

Geranium erianthum
Large, blue flowers with dark veins in summer • 45–60 cm high, 30 cm wide

Geranium farreri
Clear-pink flowers with dark veins in early summer • Kidney-shaped foliage with red stems • 10–15 cm high, 10–15 cm wide

Geranium himalayense
Violet-blue flowers in early summer to fall • 30–45 cm high, 45–60 cm wide

'Gravetye' • Large, deep-blue flowers with reddish centre in early summer to fall • Finely cut foliage • 30 cm high, 30–60 cm wide

'Plenum' (syn. **Birch Double**) • Double, purplish-pink, blue-shaded flowers in early summer to fall • 25–30 cm high, 45–60 cm wide

Geranium lambertii
Nodding, pink flowers in midsummer to fall • Soft, wrinkled, green foliage • 30–45 cm high, 90 cm wide

Geranium x *lindavicum*
'Fairy Cups' • Pink flowers with dark-pink veins in summer • 10–15 cm high, 20–25 cm wide

'Lissadell' • Plum flowers in early summer • Blue-grey foliage • 15 cm high, 20–25 cm wide

Geranium macrorrhizum
Pink to purplish-pink flowers in early summer • Aromatic foliage • 30–45 cm high, 45–60 cm wide
'Bevan's Variety' • Deep-magenta flowers with red sepals in early summer • Aromatic foliage • 25–45 cm high, 45–60 cm wide
'Camce' • Pink flowers in early summer • Aromatic foliage • 25–30 cm high, 45–60 cm wide
'Czakor' • Magenta flowers in early summer • Aromatic foliage • 25–30 cm high, 45–60 cm wide
'Ingwersen's Variety' • Soft-pink flowers in early summer • Light-green, aromatic foliage • 30–45 cm high, 45–60 cm wide
'Spessart' • White to pink flowers in early summer • Aromatic foliage • 30–45 cm high, 45–60 cm wide
'Variegatum' • Bright-magenta flowers in early summer • Splashes of cream on greyish-green foliage • 30–45 cm high, 45–60 cm wide

Geranium maculatum
Lavender-pink flowers in late spring to summer • 45–70 cm high, 30–45 cm wide
'Chatto' • Intense pink flowers in early spring to early summer • 50 cm high, 30–45 cm wide
'Espresso' • Purple-pink flowers in late spring • Green to chocolate-brown foliage • 30-60 cm high, 30–45 cm wide

Geranium x *magnificum*
Blue-violet flowers in midsummer • 45–70 cm high, 45–60 cm wide
'Rosemoor' • Blue-violet flowers in midsummer • 40–45 cm high, 45–60 cm wide

Geranium orientalitibeticum
Deep purplish-pink flowers in summer • Marbled, green foliage • 20–30 cm high, 1+ m wide

Geranium x *oxonianum*
'Bressingham Delight' • Soft-pink flowers in spring to fall • Evergreen • 25–40 cm high, 45–60 cm wide
'Claridge Druce' • Rosy-pink flowers in spring • Evergreen • 45–75 cm high, 45–60 cm wide
'Pearl Boland' • Dark rose-pink flowers, fading to white, in early spring to fall • Evergreen • 45 cm high, 90 cm wide

'Phoebe Noble' • Dark-pink flowers in summer to fall • Evergreen • 35–45 cm high, 45–60 cm wide
'Rose Clair' • Rosy-pink flowers in summer to fall • Evergreen • 35–40 cm high, 45–60 cm wide
'Wargrave Pink' (syn. G. endressii 'Wargrave Pink') • Salmon-pink flowers in late spring to fall • Evergreen • 40–60 cm high, 60–90 cm wide

Geranium x *oxonianum* f. *thurstonianum*
Unusual, twisted, red flowers in summer • Evergreen • 45–60 cm high, 45–60 cm wide

Geranium phaeum
Nodding, blackish-purple flowers in late spring to summer • 80 cm high, 45 cm wide
'Samobor' • Nodding, dark-purple flowers with white eye in late spring to summer • Foliage blotched with dark mahogany • 80 cm high, 45 cm wide

Geranium platypetalum
Violet-blue flowers in midsummer • Hairy, wrinkled leaves • 30–45 cm high, 45 cm wide

Geranium pratense
Blue-violet flowers in early summer • 60–90 cm high, 60 cm wide
'Hocus Pocus' • Blue-violet flowers in early summer • Dark-bronze foliage • 40–45 cm high, 60 cm wide
(Midnight Reiter strain) • Dark-lilac flowers in early summer • Purple foliage • 25 cm high, 25 cm wide
'Mrs Kendall Clark' • White-veined, violet-blue flowers in early summer • 60–90 cm high, 60 cm wide
'Okey Dokey' • Steel-blue flowers in summer • Purple foliage • 35 cm high, 45–60 cm wide
'Plenum Caeruleum' • Double, violet-blue flowers in summer • 60–90 cm high, 60 cm wide
'Plenum Violaceum' • Double, blue-violet flowers in summer • 45–90 cm high, 60 cm wide
'Speckled and Striped' • Blue-purple, striped and speckled flowers in summer • 30–40 cm high, 40–45 cm wide
'Splish-splash' • White flowers with blue splashes in early summer • 30–40 cm high, 20–30 cm wide
'Striatum' (syn. Bicolor) • White flowers streaked with violet-blue in early summer • 45–60 cm high, 60–90 cm wide

G

Geranium psilostemon
Bright-magenta flowers in summer • Deeply cut foliage • 60–120 cm high, 60 cm wide
'Bressingham Flair' • Magenta-red flowers in summer • 45–60 cm high, 45–60 cm wide
'Patricia' • Large, magenta-red flowers continuously in summer • 60–120 cm high, 60 cm wide
Geranium renardii
White, purple-veined flowers in summer • Velvet, sage-green leaves • 25–30 cm high, 25–30 cm wide
'Orchid Blue' • Orchid-like, violet-blue flowers with darker veins in summer • 25–30 cm high, 25–30 cm wide
Geranium x riversleaianum
'Mavis Simpson' • Shell-pink flowers with darker veins in summer to fall • Silvery, silky, pale-green leaves • 15–30 cm high, 45–100 cm wide
'Russell Prichard' • Magenta-pink flowers in summer to fall • 15–30 cm high, 45–100 cm wide
Geranium sanguineum
Magenta-red flowers in summer • 20–30 cm high, 30–45 cm wide
'Alan Bloom' • Pink flowers in summer • 20–30 cm high, 30–40 cm wide
'Album' • White flowers in summer • 15–30 cm high, 30–40 cm wide
'Alpenglow' • Carmine-red flowers in late spring to summer • 20–45 cm high, 25–30 cm wide
'Ankum's Pride' • Fluorescent pink flowers in late spring to summer • 15–20 cm high, 30–45 cm wide
'Apfelblute' (Apple Blossom) • Pink flowers in spring to fall • 15–20 cm high, 25–40 cm wide
'Glenluce' • Bright-carmine flowers in late spring to summer • 15–30 cm high, 30–45 cm wide
'John Elsley' • Dark-magenta flowers in summer • 10–15 cm high, 30–45 cm wide
'Max Frei' • Deep-magenta flowers continuously in summer • 15–20 cm high, 25–30 cm wide
'New Hampshire' • Magenta-purple flowers in summer • 15–30 cm high, 30–45 cm wide
'Purple Trailer' • Large, purple-red flowers in summer • 20–25 cm high, 30–45 cm wide

'Shepherd's Warning' • Magenta-red flowers in summer • 15 cm high, 15 cm wide
Geranium sanguineum var. striatum (syn. G. sanguineum var. lancastriense)
Pale-pink flowers veined with dark-pink in summer • 10 cm high, 30–45 cm wide
Geranium sessiliflorum
'Dusky Rose' • Hot-pink flowers in spring • Bronze foliage • 2–5 cm high, 30–45 cm wide
Geranium sessiliflorum ssp. novae-zelandiae
'Nigricans' • White flowers in summer • Bronze foliage • 5–8 cm high, 6–10 cm wide
Geranium subcaulescens
Magenta-red flowers with black centres in late spring to summer • Dark-green leaves • 15–20 cm high, 25–40 cm wide
'Giuseppii' • Magenta flowers with purple veins in late spring to summer • Dark-green leaves • 10–15 cm high, 30–45 cm wide
'Splendens' • Bright magenta-pink flowers with dark-red centre in late spring to summer • Dark-green leaves • 15 cm high, 30–40 cm wide
Geranium sylvaticum
Bright-lavender flowers in late spring • 45–75 cm high, 45–60 cm wide
'Album' • White flowers in late spring • 45–75 cm high, 45–60 cm wide
'Mayflower' • Violet-blue flowers with white eye in late spring • 45–75 cm high, 45–60 cm wide
'Silva' • Upward-facing, purple flowers in late spring • 45–75 cm high, 45–60 cm wide
Geranium versicolor
White flowers with magenta veins in early summer to fall • 45 cm high, 40–50 cm wide
Geranium viscosissimum
Pink-purple flowers with white centre in summer • 30–75 cm high, 30–60 cm wide
Geranium wallichianum
Purple-lilac flowers with white centre in midsummer to fall • 30 cm high, 90–120 cm wide
Geranium wallichianum
'Buxton's Variety' • Blue flowers with white centre in midsummer to fall • 30 cm high, 90–120 cm wide
'Syabru' • Magenta-purple flowers in summer • Reddish-green foliage • 20 cm high, 90–120 cm wide

Geranium wlassovianum
Dusky, magenta-purple flowers in summer to fall • Velvety, dusky-green leaves • 30–60 cm high, 45–60 cm wide

Geum
p. 415

Genus Information
Origin: North America, South America, Europe, Asia, New Zealand and Africa
Selected Common Names: avens, prairie smoke
Nomenclature: A name used by Pliny.
Notes: A genus of some 50 species.

General Features
Height: 10–100 cm high
Spread: 30–90 cm wide
Habit: stoloniferous perennial; (some) short-lived
Flowers: colourful; single to semi-double; summer; good for cutting
Foliage: (some) evergreen or variegated
Hardiness: A–D; mulch for winter
Warnings: prone to powdery mildew and aphids

Growing Requirements
Light: full sun
Soil: fertile, moist, organic, well-drained soil
Location: woodland gardens; rock gardens; wild gardens
Propagation: seed; division; separate and replant offshoots
Expert Advice: Hybridizes easily. Divide frequently to keep vigorous.

Buying Considerations
Professionals
Popularity: garden standard; sells well in bloom
Availability: readily available as finished product
Size to Sell: sells best in smaller sizes (when blooming) as it matures fast
On the Shelf: rapidly overgrows pot; requires constant cleaning
Shrinkage: high; sensitive to underwatering
Collectors
Popularity: not generally of interest to collectors
Gardeners
Ease of Growth: generally easy to grow
Start with: one small plant for feature plant
What to Try First ...
Geum 'Lady Stratheden', *Geum* 'Waight', *Geum triflorum*

On the Market
Geum
'Beech House Apricot' • Apricot-orange flowers with yellow centre in spring • 10 cm high, 30 cm wide
'Borisii' • Orange-scarlet flowers in early summer • 30–50 cm high, 30 cm wide
'Lady Stratheden' • Yellow flowers in summer • 45–60 cm high, 45–60 cm wide
'Mrs. J. Bradshaw' • Semi-double, carmine-red flowers in summer • Hairy foliage • 30–60 cm high, 45–60 cm wide
'Waight' • Orange-red flowers in summer to fall • 15 cm high, 30 cm wide
Geum aleppicum
Orange to yellow flowers in summer • 60–100 cm high, 90 cm wide
Geum chiloense
'Sunsplash Orange' • Orange-red flowers in summer • Cream-and-white-variegated foliage • 40 cm high, 40–45 cm wide
Geum triflorum
Purplish to straw-coloured flowers in summer • 30–40 cm high, 60–90 cm wide
Geum urbanum sibiricum
Pale-yellow flowers in early summer • 50–60 cm high, 30–45 cm wide

G

Gillenia
p. 415

Genus Information
Origin: eastern, central and southeast North America
Selected Common Names: bowman's root
Nomenclature: Named for Arnold Gille, a 17th century German botanist.
Notes: This genus has only 2 species.

General Features
Height: 90–100 cm high
Spread: 60 cm wide
Habit: woodland; rhizomatous perennial
Flowers: star-shaped; good for cutflowers; late spring to summer
Foliage: willow-like
Hardiness: C
Warnings: prone to aphids
Expert Advice: May take 2 years to look its best.

Growing Requirements
Light: shade; shelter from hot p.m. sun
Soil: fertile, moist, well-drained soil
Location: woodland gardens; shady mixed borders
Propagation: seed; division

Buying Considerations

Professionals
Popularity: relatively unknown
Availability: generally available as bare root
Size to Sell: sells best in smaller sizes (when blooming) as it matures fast
On the Shelf: rapidly overgrows pot
Shrinkage: low; requires little maintenance

Collectors
Popularity: not generally of interest to collectors

Gardeners
Ease of Growth: generally easy to grow
Start with: one mature plant for feature plant

What to Try First ...
Gillenia trifoliata

On the Market

Gillenia trifoliata
Star-shaped, white flowers in late spring to late summer • Red-tinted stems • 90–100 cm high, 60 cm wide

Glaucidium
p. 415

Genus Information
Origin: northern Japan
Selected Common Names: unknown
Nomenclature: Named from the resemblance to *Glaucium*, referring to the similar flower form.
Notes: A genus of only one species. Member of the peony family.

General Features
Height: 40–50 cm high
Spread: 45 cm wide
Habit: clump-forming perennial
Flowers: peony- or poppy-like; spring
Foliage: large; palmately lobed
Hardiness: C
Expert Advice: Does best in cool, moist climates.

Growing Requirements
Light: shade
Soil: cool, moist, organic, well-drained soil
Location: woodland gardens; shady mixed borders
Propagation: seed; division
Expert Advice: Difficult and very slow to propagate. Foliage may burn in windy locations.

Buying Considerations

Professionals
Popularity: relatively unknown
Availability: occasionally available from specialty growers; very expensive
Size to Sell: sells best in mature sizes (when blooming) as it matures slowly
On the Shelf: keep stock rotated
Shrinkage: high; sensitive to overwatering; goes dormant in pot

Collectors
Popularity: of interest to collectors—unique, rare

Gardeners
Ease of Growth: mostly difficult to grow as it needs close attention to growing conditions
Start with: one mature plant for feature plant

What to Try First ...
Glaucidium palmatum, Glaucidium palmatum var. *leucanthum*

On the Market

Glaucidium palmatum
Lavender-blue flowers in early summer • 40–50 cm high, 45 cm wide
Glaucidium palmatum var. *leucanthum* (syn. *G. palmatum* 'Album')
White flowers in early summer • 40–45 cm high, 45 cm wide

Glechoma
p. 415

Genus Information
Origin: North America and Europe
Selected Common Names: creeping Charlie, ground ivy
Nomenclature: From the Greek *glechon* for a plant in pseudo-Dioscorides.

General Features
Height: 2–5 cm
Spread: 45–90 cm
Habit: creeping groundcover perennial
Flowers: tiny; blue to purple; summer
Foliage: variegated
Hardiness: C
Warnings: prone to aphids; invasive (contain to prevent spread)
Expert Advice: This old-fashioned perennial is sometimes substituted for lawn in areas where grass will not grow. Can be mowed.

Growing Requirements
Light: sun or shade
Soil: fertile, well-drained soil; tolerates poor soil; drought tolerant

G

Location: wild gardens; between pavers; banks;
slopes; difficult areas
Propagation: division; runners

Buying Considerations

Professionals
Popularity: gaining popularity as a foliage
plant
Availability: readily available as finished
product
Size to Sell: sells best in smaller sizes as it
matures fast
On the Shelf: rapidly overgrows pot
Shrinkage: low shrinkage; requires little
maintenance

Collectors
Popularity: not generally of interest to
collectors

Gardeners
Ease of growth: very easy to grow
Start with: several for mass plantings

What to Try First ...
Glechoma hederacea

On the Market
Glechoma hederacea
Blue to purple flowers in summer •
Variegated foliage • 2–5 cm high,
45–90 cm+ wide

Globularia p. 415

Genus Information
Origin: Turkey and the mountains of
southwestern Europe
Selected Common Names: creeping globeflower,
globeflower, heartleaf globeflower
Nomenclature: From the Latin *globulus* (small,
round head), referring to the tiny, globe-like
flowerheads.
Notes: A genus of some 20 species.

General Features
Height: 2–30 cm high
Spread: 15–40 cm wide
Habit: mat-forming, woody groundcover
perennial
Flowers: tiny, globe-like; summer
Foliage: evergreen; leathery
Hardiness: C–D
Warnings: prone to aphids; not prone to disease

Growing Requirements
Light: sun
Soil: gritty, well-drained, alkaline soil; avoid
winter wet; adapts to most soils; drought
tolerant

Location: rock gardens; troughs
Propagation: seed; division; cuttings
Expert Advice: Sow seed when ripe.

Buying Considerations

Professionals
Popularity: relatively unknown
Availability: occasionally available from
specialty growers
Size to Sell: sells best in smaller sizes as it
matures fast
Shrinkage: low; requires little maintenance

Collectors
Popularity: of interest to collectors—unique,
rare

Gardeners
Ease of Growth: mostly easy to grow
Start with: one small plant for feature plant

What to Try First ...
*Globularia cordifolia, Globularia incanescens,
Globularia repens*

On the Market
Globularia cordifolia
Lavender-blue flowers in summer • Woody-
based evergreen • 2–10 cm high, 20–30 cm
wide
Globularia incanescens
Globe-shaped, soft-blue flowers in summer
• 5–10 cm high, 20–40 cm wide
Globularia meridionalis
Lavender-blue flowers in summer • Woody-
based evergreen • 8–10 cm high, 15–30 cm
wide
Globularia nudicaulis
Globe-shaped, blue flowers in summer •
15–30 cm high, 20–30 cm wide
Globularia punctata
Globe-shaped, violet-blue flowers in
summer • 25–30 cm high, 30–40 cm wide
Globularia repens
Deep-blue flowers in spring • Evergreen
foliage • 5 cm high, 15 cm wide
Globularia repens (syn. G. nana)
Round, blue flowers in early summer •
Spoon-shaped, glossy, evergreen foliage •
2.5–5 cm high, 15 cm wide
Globularia stygia
Bright-blue flowers in summer • Woody-
based evergreen • 8 cm high, 20 cm wide
Globularia trichosantha
Soft-blue flowers in summer • Evergreen
foliage • 15–20 cm high, 25–40 cm wide

G

Glyceria

p. 415 📷

Genus Information

Origin: north temperate regions, Australia, New Zealand and South America
Selected Common Names: manna grass
Nomenclature: From the Greek *glykys* (sweet), referring to the flavour of some seeds of this genus.

General Features

Height: 45–80 cm high
Spread: 45–60 cm wide
Habit: aquatic, rhizomatous grass
Flowers: purple-pink spikelets; mid- to late summer
Foliage: variegated
Hardiness: C–D
Warnings: prone to aphids; aggressive spreader (contain to prevent spread)

Growing Requirements

Light: sun
Soil: moist soil
Location: bog gardens; moist mixed borders; waterside plantings, in water up to 75 cm deep; river banks
Propagation: division

Buying Considerations

Professionals

Popularity: relatively unknown as a foliage plant
Availability: generally available as finished product
Size to Sell: sells best in smaller sizes as it matures fast
On the Shelf: high ornamental appeal; rapidly overgrows pot; browns if allowed to dry out
Shrinkage: high; sensitive to underwatering

Collectors

Popularity: not generally of interest to collectors

Gardeners

Ease of Growth: mostly easy to grow but needs close attention to growing conditions (keep moist at all times)
Start with: one small plant for feature plant

What to Try First ...

Glyceria maxima var. *variegata*

On the Market

Glyceria maxima* var. *variegata
Purplish-pink spikelets in midsummer • Cream-and-green-striped foliage • 45–80 cm high, 45–60+ cm wide

Goniolimon

p. 415 📷

Genus Information

Origin: Europe, central Asia and northwest Africa
Selected Common Names: dwarf statice, German statice
Nomenclature: From the Greek *gonio* (angled), referring to the branches, and from *limon*, after *Limonium*, a related genus.
Notes: A genus of some 20 species.

General Features

Height: 30–45 cm high
Spread: 30–45 cm wide
Habit: clump-forming perennial
Flowers: tiny blooms on upright stems; mid- to late summer; good for cutflowers; good for drying
Foliage: grows from base
Hardiness: C
Warnings: prone to aphids; not prone to disease

Growing Requirements

Light: sun
Soil: poor, sandy, well-drained soil
Location: sunny, hot, dry areas; mixed borders; cutting gardens
Propagation: seed; root cuttings
Expert Advice: Will not thrive in wet soil.

Buying Considerations

Professionals

Popularity: popular old-fashioned perennial
Availability: readily available as finished product
Size to Sell: sells best in smaller sizes as it matures fast
On the Shelf: rapidly overgrows pot
Shrinkage: low; requires little maintenance

Collectors

Popularity: not generally of interest to collectors

Gardeners

Ease of Growth: mostly easy to grow
Start with: one small plant for feature plant

What to Try First ...

Goniolimon tartaricum

On the Market

***Goniolimon incanum* (syn. *G. speciosum*)**
White or cream flowers in summer • 20–45 cm high, 30–45 cm wide

***Goniolimon tartaricum* (syn. *Limonium tartaricum*)**
Rose-blue and white flowers in midsummer to late summer • Stiff stems • 30–45 cm high, 30–45 cm wide

Gymnocarpium

Genus Information

Origin: Europe, North America and Asia
Selected Common Names: oak fern
Nomenclature: From the Greek *gymnos* (naked) and *karpos* (fruit), referring to the lack of an indusium.

General Features

Height: 20–50 cm high
Spread: 30–60 cm wide
Habit: creeping, low-growing rhizomatous fern
Foliage: arching, lacy, deciduous
Hardiness: C
Warnings: not prone to insects or disease
Expert Advice: Although the fronds are long, they tend to arch over low across the ground.

Growing Requirements

Light: shade to a.m. sun
Soil: humus-rich, moist, neutral to acidic soil
Location: woodland gardens; may burn and break in windy locations
Propagation: spores; division

Buying Considerations

Professionals
Popularity: gaining popularity as a foliage plant
Availability: readily available as finished product
Size to Sell: sells best in smaller sizes as it matures fast
On the Shelf: high ornamental appeal; keep stock rotated; foliage breakage (display out of wind)

Collectors
Popularity: not generally of interest to collectors

Gardeners
Ease of Growth: mostly easy to grow but needs close attention to growing conditions
Start with: one small plant for feature plant

What to Try First ...
Gymnocarpium dryopteris

On the Market

Gymnocarpium dryopteris
Yellow-green, lacy fronds age to dark-green
• 20–50 cm high, 30–60+ cm wide

Gypsophila

p. 415

Genus Information

Origin: Eurasia and southeast Europe
Selected Common Names: baby's breath, chalk plant
Nomenclature: From the Greek *gypso* (chalk) and *philos* (loving), referring to the plant's preference for alkaline soil.

General Features

Height: 3–120 cm high
Spread: 15–120 cm wide
Habit: tap-rooted, upright or creeping to cushion- or mat-forming perennial
Flowers: tiny blooms form airy masses; late spring to early summer; good for cutflowers; good for drying
Foliage: (some) evergreen or semi-evergreen
Hardiness: C

Growing Requirements

Light: sun
Soil: deep, sharply drained, alkaline soil; tolerates poor soil; alpine types prefer lean soil
Location: rock gardens; raised beds
Propagation: seed; root cuttings
Expert Advice: Avoid planting where soil is wet in winter. Resents being disturbed (except for *G. repens*).

Buying Considerations

Professionals
Popularity: popular old-fashioned garden standard; fast seller; alpine types are relatively unknown
Availability: readily available as finished product; alpine types are occasionally available from specialty growers
Size to Sell: sells best in smaller sizes (when blooming) as it matures fast
On the Shelf: keep stock rotated; rapidly overgrows pot; cutback *G. paniculata* (foliage breakage)
Shrinkage: low; requires little maintenance

Collectors
Popularity: of interest to collectors; *G. aretioides*, *G. cerastioides* are unique, rare; alpine types; *G. nana*, *G. petraea*, *G. tenuifolia*

Gardeners
Ease of Growth: mostly easy to grow
Start with: one small plant for feature plant or mature plant for alpine gardens

What to Try First ...
Gypsophila 'Rosenschleier', *Gypsophila aretioides*, *Gypsophila cerastioides*, *Gypsophila fastigiata* 'Festival Pink', *Gypsophila fastigiata* 'Festival White', *Gypsophila paniculata* 'Bristol Fairy', *Gypsophila paniculata* 'Compacta Plena', *Gypsophila paniculata* 'Perfekta', *Gypsophila repens*

G

On the Market

Gypsophila
'Jolien' • Pale-pink flowers in summer • Variegated foliage • 50–60 cm high, 60–100 cm wide

'Rosenschleier' (Rosy Veil) • Double, soft-pink flowers in midsummer to fall • 40–50 cm high, 60–100 cm wide

Gypsophila aretioides
Pale-pink to white flowers in early summer • Grey-green evergreen • 5–8 cm high, 15–30 cm wide

'Caucasica' • White flowers with pinkish veins in early summer • Evergreen foliage • 4–8 cm high, 15 cm wide

Gypsophila briquetiana
White to pale-pink flowers with purple veining in early summer • 3–10 cm high, 15–20 cm wide

Gypsophila bungeana
Lilac to white flowers in summer • 10–15 cm high, 15 cm wide

Gypsophila cephalotes
White to soft-pink flowers in summer • 20–50 cm high, 20–50 cm wide

Gypsophila cerastioides
White flowers with red veins in late spring to summer • Downy, grey-green foliage • 5–10 cm high, 20–30 cm wide

Gypsophila fastigiata
Festival Series
'Festival Pink' • Double, pale-pink flowers in late spring to fall • 45–60 cm high, 45–60 cm wide

'Festival White' • Double, white flowers in late spring to fall • 45–60 cm high, 45–60 cm wide

Gypsophila nana
Alpine type • Pale-purple flowers in summer • 4 cm high, 15 cm wide

Gypsophila pacifica
Single, pale-pink flowers in summer • 65–100 cm high, 90–100 cm wide

Gypsophila paniculata
Single, white flowers in summer • 90–120 cm high, 90–100 cm wide

'Bristol Fairy' • Double, pure white flowers in summer to fall • 60–75 cm high, 30–60 cm wide

'Compacta Plena' • Double, white flowers in summer • 20–30 cm high, 30–45 cm wide

'Flamingo' • Double, soft-pink flowers in summer • 60–90 cm high, 60–90 cm wide

'Perfekta' (Perfecta) • Double, white flowers in summer • 90–120 cm high, 60–90 cm wide

'Pink Fairy' • Double, pale-pink flowers in summer • 45 cm high, 45–60 cm wide

'Schneeflocke' (Snowflake) • Double, white flowers in late spring to summer • 90 cm high, 90 cm wide

'Viette's Dwarf' • Double, pink to white flowers in summer • 30–40 cm high, 30–45 cm wide

Gypsophila petraea
Alpine type • White to soft-purple flowers in summer • 10–20 cm high, 10–20 cm wide

Gypsophila repens
White flowers in late spring to early summer • 15–20 cm high, 30–50 cm wide

'Dubia' • White flowers with pink veins in summer • Dark-red stems • 5–8 cm high, 15–25 cm wide

'Rosa Schonheit' (Rose Beauty) • Rose-pink flowers in late spring to early summer • 15–20 cm high, 30–50 cm wide

'Rosea' • Pink flowers in late spring to summer • 15–20 cm high, 30–50 cm wide

Gypsophila tenuifolia
Alpine type • White to pink flowers in early summer • 10–20 cm high, 15–20 cm wide

Haberlea

p. 415 📷

Genus Information

Origin: Balkans
Selected Common Names: unknown
Nomenclature: Named for Karl Haberle, 1764–1832, a professor of botany in Perth.
Notes: *Haberlea* is related to African violets.

General Features

Height: 10–15 cm high
Spread: 15–30 cm wide
Habit: clump- or rosette-forming perennial
Flowers: African violet-like; late spring to early summer
Foliage: hairy; evergreen
Hardiness: C
Warnings: prone to aphids; not prone to diseases

Growing Requirements

Light: shade to a.m. sun; shelter from hot p.m. sun
Soil: cool, moist, organic, well-drained soil
Location: scree; wall crevices; dry walls; raised beds; foliage may burn in windy locations
Propagation: seed; division
Expert Advice: Do not plant in areas where water pools and avoid soils that are wet in winter. Division is difficult as it resents being disturbed.

Buying Considerations

Professionals
Popularity: relatively unknown as a flowering plant
Availability: occasionally available from specialty growers
Size to Sell: sells best in smaller sizes (when blooming)
Shrinkage: high; sensitive to overwatering

Collectors
Popularity: of interest to collectors—unique, rare

Gardeners
Ease of Growth: mostly easy to grow, needs close attention to growing conditions
Start with: one small plant for feature plant

What to Try First ...
Haberlea ferdinandi-coburgii, Haberlea rhodopensis

On the Market

Haberlea ferdinandi-coburgii
Pale-lavender flowers in spring to early summer • Evergreen • 10–15 cm high, 15–25 cm wide

Haberlea rhodopensis
Lilac-violet flowers in late spring to early summer • Evergreen • 10–15 cm high, 20–30 cm wide

'Virginalis' • White flowers in late spring to early summer • Evergreen • 10–15 cm high, 20–30 cm wide

Hakonechloa

p. 416 📷

Genus Information

Origin: Japan
Selected Common Names: golden Hakone grass, Hakone grass
Nomenclature: Named for the Japanese region of Hakone.

General Features

Height: 30–40 cm high
Spread: 30–50 cm wide
Habit: rhizomatous, slow-spreading grass
Flowers: green to purple seed heads; late summer
Foliage: variegated, arching; good fall colour
Hardiness: D
Warnings: not prone to insects or disease

Growing Requirements

Light: sun to p.m. sun; light shade intensifies foliage colour
Soil: cool, fertile, moist, organic, well-drained soil
Location: woodland gardens; rock gardens; shady mixed borders
Propagation: seed; division
Expert Advice: Seed rarely ripens on plant. May take up to 3 years to fully mature from seed.

Buying Considerations

Professionals
Popularity: gaining popularity as a foliage plant
Availability: generally available as finished product and bare root from specialty growers
Size to Sell: sells best in smaller sizes; matures slowly
On the Shelf: high ornamental appeal; prone to rust in pots
Shrinkage: low; requires little maintenance

Collectors
Popularity: not generally of interest to collectors

Gardeners
Ease of Growth: mostly easy to grow
Start with: one larger plant for feature plant and several for mass plantings

What to Try First ...
Hakonechloa macra 'Albovariegata', *Hakonechloa macra* 'Aureola'

H

On the Market

Hakonechloa macra
Green seed heads, turning purple, in late summer • Arching foliage • 30–40 cm high, 30–50 cm wide

'Albovariegata' (syn. Albostriata) • Green seed heads, turning purple, in late summer • Arching, white-striped foliage • 30–40 cm high, 30–50 cm wide

'All Gold' • Green seed heads, turning purple, in late summer • Golden foliage • 30–40 cm high, 30–50 cm wide

'Aureola' • Green seed heads, turning purple, in late summer • Arching, gold-striped foliage • 30–40 cm high, 30–50 cm wide

Collectors
Popularity: not generally of interest to collectors
Gardeners
Ease of Growth: mostly easy to grow but needs close attention to growing conditions
Start with: one small plant for feature plant
What to Try First ...
Hedera helix 'Super Hardy English'

On the Market

Hedera helix
'Baltica' • Glossy deep-green foliage • 5–10 cm high, 60–90+ cm wide

'Super Hardy English' • Glossy deep-green foliage • 5–10 cm high, 60–90+ cm wide

H

Hedera   p. 416 📷

Genus Information
Origin: Europe, Asia and North Africa
Selected Common Names: Baltic ivy, English ivy
Nomenclature: From the Latin name for ivy.

General Features
Height: 5–10 cm high
Spread: 60–90 cm wide
Habit: self-clinging, climbing or groundcover perennial
Foliage: evergreen; prominently viened
Hardiness: D
Warnings: prone to aphids; not prone to disease
Expert Advice: Grown as a sheltered ground ivy in colder areas. Not able to withstand cold, dry winter winds. Mulch for winter.

Growing Requirements
Light: shade
Soil: fertile, moist, organic, well-drained soil
Location: Avoid hot, dry, sunny, windy locations in all climates; in warm climates grow on walls fences, pergolas, cascading; in cold climates grow as a groundcover in sheltered location
Propagation: stem cuttings

Buying Considerations

Professionals
Popularity: relatively unknown as a foliage plant
Availability: occasionally available as finished product
Size to Sell: sells best in smaller sizes as it matures fast
On the Shelf: high ornamental appeal; rapidly overgrows pot
Shrinkage: low; requires little maintenance

Hedysarum   p. 416 📷

Genus Information
Origin: northern temperate regions; native to Alberta
Selected Common Names: sweet vetch
Nomenclature: From the Greek *hedys* (sweet) and *arum* (aroma).
Notes: A member of the legume family.

General Features
Height: 25–50 cm high
Spread: 20–35 cm wide
Habit: shrubby perennial
Flowers: pea-like; late spring to early summer; attracts bees
Foliage: pea-like
Hardiness: C
Warnings: prone to aphids; not prone to disease
Expert Advice: The honey collected from some species is very sweet.

Growing Requirements
Light: sun
Soil: sandy, well-drained, neutral to alkaline soil; tolerant of a wide range of soils; drought tolerant
Location: erosion control; banks; slopes
Propagation: seed (self-sows readily); division; layering
Expert Advice: Division is difficult as it resents being disturbed.

Buying Considerations
Professionals
Popularity: relatively unknown
Availability: occasionally available from specialty growers
Size to Sell: sells best in smaller sizes as it matures fast
On the Shelf: rapidly overgrows pot
Shrinkage: low; requires little maintenance

What to Try First ...

Hedysarum alpinum

On the Market

Hedysarum alpinum
Red-violet flowers in late spring to early
summer • 25–50 cm high, 20–35 cm wide

Helenium

p. 416

Genus Information

Origin: Americas
Selected Common Names: golden star, Helen's
flower, sneezeweed
Nomenclature: From the Greek *helenion* for an
old world plant. It is said to be named for Helen
of Troy.

General Features

Height: 60–150 cm high
Spread: 30–60 cm wide
Habit: upright, clump-forming perennial
Flowers: yellow to deep orange-red blooms
on sturdy stems; summer to fall; good for
cutflowers; deadhead to extend blooming season;
attracts bees and butterflies
Hardiness: C
Warnings: prone to aphids; contact with foliage
may irritate skin
Expert Advice: A reliable bloomer that provides
late-summer and fall colour to the garden.

Growing Requirements

Light: sun
Soil: fertile, moist, well-drained soil; drought
tolerant once established
Location: mixed borders
Propagation: seed; division; basal cuttings
Expert Advice: Divide frequently to keep vigorous.

Buying Considerations

What to Try First ...

Helenium 'Baudirektor Linne', *Helenium*
'Crimson Beauty', *Helenium* 'Konigstiger',
Helenium 'Margot', *Helenium* 'Moerheim
Beauty', *Helenium* 'Rubinzwerg', *Helenium*
'Waldtraut'

On the Market

Helenium
'Baudirektor Linne' • Large, bronze-red
flowers in mid-summer to fall
• 75–120 cm high, 45–60 cm wide

'Bronzed Beauty' • Large, bronze-red
flowers in midsummer to fall • 75–100 cm
high, 45–60 cm wide

'Bruno' • Copper-red flowers with brown
centre in late summer to fall • 90–120 cm
high, 45–60 wide

'Coppelia' • Large, copper-orange flowers
with brown centre in midsummer to fall •
75–90 cm high, 45–60 cm wide

'Crimson Beauty' • Crimson-brown flowers
with brown centre in summer • 60–75 cm
high, 45–60 cm wide

'Indian Summer' • Copper-red flowers with
yellow centre in summer • 75–100 cm
high, 45–60 cm wide

'Konigstiger' (King's Tiger) • Large,
red-brown, edged-yellow flowers in
midsummer to fall • 75 cm–1.2 m high,
45–60 cm wide

'Margot' • Red-brown flowers with yellow
edges in midsummer to fall • 75–100 cm
high, 45–60 cm wide

'Moerheim Beauty' • Mahogany-red flowers
with brown centres in midsummer •
60–90 cm high, 45–60 cm wide

'Red Army' • Yellow-tipped, red flowers
with brown to gold centres in late summer
to fall • 60–65 cm high, 30 cm wide

'Riverton Beauty' • Lemon-yellow flowers
with bronze centres in late summer to fall
• 1–1.5 m high, 45–60 cm wide

'Rubinzwerg' • Burnt-red flowers with
yellow and brown centres in summer •
60–75 cm high, 45–60 cm wide

'Waldtraut' • Gold-brown flowers in late
summer to fall • 75–100 cm high,
45–60 cm wide

H

Helenium autumnale
Daisy-like, golden-yellow to copper-red
flowers in late summer to fall • 90–150 cm
high, 45–60 cm wide

Helenium hoopesii
Yellow to orange flowers in summer
• 60–90 cm high, 30–45 cm wide

Helianthemum   p. 416 📷

Genus Information

Origin: Europe, the Americas, North Africa and
East Asia
Selected Common Names: rock rose, sun rose
Nomenclature: From the Greek *helios* (sun) and
anthemon (flower), referring to the opening of
the flowers only in sunshine.

General Features

Height: 10–30 cm high
Spread: 25–45 cm wide
Habit: short-lived, mat-forming, small shrub
Flowers: yellow to orange-red; single or double;
deadhead to extend blooming season; long
blooming period
Foliage: evergreen to semi-evergreen
Hardiness: C
Warnings: prone to aphids; not prone to disease

Growing Requirements

Light: sun
Soil: moderately fertile, well-drained, neutral to
alkaline soil; drought tolerant once established
Location: rock gardens; front of mixed borders
Propagation: seed (some self sow); softwood
cuttings
Expert Advice: Sow seed of species and take
softwood cuttings in early spring.

Buying Considerations

Professionals

Popularity: gaining popularity
Availability: readily available as finished
product
Size to Sell: sells best in smaller sizes (when
blooming) as it matures fast
On the Shelf: rapidly overgrows pot
Shrinkage: low; requires little maintenance

Collectors

Popularity: not generally of interest to
collectors

Gardeners

Ease of Growth: mostly easy to grow
Start with: one small plant for feature plant
and several for mass plantings

What to Try First ...

Helianthemum 'Ben Nevis', *Helianthemum*
'Henfield Brilliant', *Helianthemum* 'Wisley
Primrose'

On the Market

Helianthemum
'Annabel' • Double, pink flowers in late
spring to summer • 10–30 cm high,
25–40 cm wide

'Belgravia Rose' • Single, rose-pink flowers
in late spring to summer • 10–30 cm high,
25–40 cm wide

'Ben Nevis' • Fiery-orange flowers in late
spring to summer • 10–30 cm high,
25–40 cm wide

'Boule de Feu' • Red flowers in summer •
10–30 cm high, 25–40 cm wide

'Dazzler' • Single, magenta-red flowers in
late spring to summer • 20–30 cm high,
30 cm wide

'Fire Dragon' • Orange-red flowers in late
spring to summer • 10–30 cm high,
25–40 cm wide

'Henfield Brilliant' • Single, brick-red
flowers in late spring to summer • Grey-
green foliage • 10–30 cm high, 25–40 cm
wide

'Raspberry Ripple' • Raspberry-red and
white flowers in late spring to late summer
• 10–30 cm high, 25–40 cm wide

'St. Mary's' • Single, white flowers in late
spring to summer • 10–30 cm high,
25–40 cm wide

'Stoplight' • Single, red flowers in late spring
to summer • 10–30 cm high, 25–40 cm
wide

'Wisley Primrose' • Single, soft-yellow
flowers in summer • 20–30 cm high,
25–45 cm wide

Helianthemum nummularium
Single or double, yellow flowers in late
spring to summer • 10–30 cm high,
25–40 cm wide

Helianthus   p. 416 📷

Genus Information

Origin: Americas
Selected Common Names: dark-eyed sunflower,
thin leaf sunflower
Nomenclature: From the Greek *helios* (sun) and
anthos (flower).
Other Uses: *Helianthus* is a source of vegetable
oil.
Notes: The Jerusalem artichoke is also a member
of this family.

General Features
Height: 30 cm–3 m high
Spread: 45–120 cm wide
Habit: upright, tuberous or spreading perennial
Flowers: yellow; single or double; good for cutting; late summer to fall
Foliage: sunflower-like; rough
Hardiness: C
Warnings: prone to powdery mildew and aphids; some self-sow aggressively (deadhead to prevent spread)
Expert Advice: The wide range of heights available means that this perennial can be grown in a variety of locations in the landscape.

Growing Requirements
Light: sun
Soil: fertile, moist, organic, well-drained, alkaline soil; (some) drought tolerant; tolerant of a wide range of soils
Location: dry woodlands; mixed borders; swampy locations
Propagation: seed; division; basal cuttings

Buying Considerations

Professionals
Popularity: old-fashioned garden standard
Availability: readily available as finished product and bare root
Size to Sell: sells best in smaller sizes (when blooming) as it matures fast
On the Shelf: rapidly overgrows pot
Shrinkage: high; sensitive to underwatering

Collectors
Popularity: not generally of interest to collectors

Gardeners
Ease of Growth: generally easy to grow
Start with: one small plant for feature plant

What to Try First ...
Helianthus 'Capenoch Star', *Helianthus* 'Lemon Queen', *Helianthus* 'Loddon Gold', *Helianthus decapetalus*, *Helianthus maximilliani*

On the Market

Helianthus
'Capenoch Star' • Lemon-yellow flowers in late summer to fall • 1–1.5 m high, 60–90 cm wide

'Lemon Queen' • Double, pale-yellow flowers in late summer to fall • 1–1.5 m high, 60–90 cm wide

'Loddon Gold' • Double, vivid-yellow flowers in late summer to fall • 1–1.5 m high, 60–90 cm wide

'Low Down' • Yellow flowers in late summer to fall • Fertile, well-drained, dry soil • 30 cm high, 45–55 cm wide

'Soleil d'Or' • Double, yellow flowers in late summer to fall • 1–1.5 m high, 60–90 cm wide

Helianthus angustifolius
Yellow flowers in late summer to fall • 1.5–2 m high, 60–90 cm wide

Helianthus atrorubens
Deep-yellow flowers with dark-red centre in late summer • 90–120 cm high, 60–90 cm wide

Helianthus decapetalus
Bright-yellow flowers in late summer to fall • 1–1.5 m high, 60–90 cm wide

'Maximus Flore Pleno' • Double, bright-yellow flowers in late summer to fall • 1–1.5 m high, 60–90 cm wide

Helianthus maximilliani
Fragrant, yellow flowers in late summer • 1.5–3 m high, 60–90 cm wide

Helianthus pauciflorus (syn. *H. rigidus*)
Fragrant, yellow flowers in late summer • spreading habit • 1.5–2 m high, 60–90 cm wide

Helianthus x *multiflorus* 'Flore Pleno'
Double, bright-yellow flowers in summer to fall • 1–2 m high, 60–90 cm wide

Helianthus salicifolius
'First Light' • Yellow flowers in late summer to fall • Fertile, well-drained, dry soil • 1–1.2 m high, 90–120 cm wide

Helictotrichon　　p. 416

Genus Information
Origin: temperate Northern Hemisphere and South Africa
Selected Common Names: blue oat grass
Nomenclature: From the Greek *heliktos* (twisted) and *trichos* (spine), referring to the shape of the awn on the seed.

General Features
Height: 45–120 cm high
Spread: 45–60 cm wide
Habit: clump-forming grass
Flowers: seed heads; summer; good for winter interest
Foliage: blue to blue-grey
Hardiness: C
Expert Advice: An attractive grass that provides contrast in the perennial border. Although this grass does self-sow, it is easily managed.

Growing Requirements

Light: sun
Soil: fertile, well-drained, alkaline soil; tolerates poor soil; prefers cool, moist springs, but dislikes winter wet; drought tolerant once established
Location: mixed borders; specimen plant
Propagation: seed; division

Buying Considerations

Professionals
Popularity: popular as a foliage plant
Availability: readily available as finished product and bare root
Size to Sell: sells best in smaller sizes as it matures fast
On the Shelf: high ornamental appeal; keep stock rotated
Shrinkage: low; requires little maintenance

Collectors
Popularity: not generally of interest to collectors

Gardeners
Ease of Growth: very easy to grow
Start with: one small plant for feature plant

What to Try First ...

Helictotrichon sempervirens, Helictotrichon sempervirens 'Saphirsprudel'

On the Market

Helictotrichon sempervirens
Arching, tan seed heads in summer • Blue, spiky foliage • 90–100 cm high, 60 cm wide
'Saphirsprudel' (Sapphire)• Nodding seed heads in summer • Intense blue foliage • 60–120 cm high, 45–60 cm wide

Heliopsis　　　　　p. 416　📷

Genus Information

Origin: North America
Selected Common Names: false sunflower, ox eye, sunflower heliopsis
Nomenclature: From the Greek *helois* (sun) and *opsis* (appearance), referring to the noticeable capitula.

General Features

Height: 60–150 cm high
Spread: 30–60 cm wide
Habit: upright, clump-forming perennial; may require staking
Flowers: bright, daisy-like; very floriferous; midsummer to fall; good for cutflowers; long blooming period
Foliage: (some) variegated
Hardiness: B–C

Warnings: prone to aphids; not prone to diseases
Expert Advice: Extremely cold hardy.

Growing Requirements

Light: sun
Soil: fertile, moist, organic, well-drained soil; tolerates poor soil; drought tolerant
Location: mixed borders
Propagation: seed (self-sows readily); division
Expert Advice: Growing in poorer soil produces more compact growth. Divide frequently to keep vigorous.

Buying Considerations

Professionals
Popularity: popular garden standard
Availability: readily available as finished product and bare root
Size to Sell: sells best in smaller sizes (when blooming) as it matures fast
On the Shelf: rapidly overgrows pot
Shrinkage: low; requires little maintenance

Collectors
Popularity: not generally of interest to collectors

Gardeners
Ease of Growth: very easy to grow
Start with: one small plant for feature plant

What to Try First ...

Heliopsis 'Loraine Sunshine', *Heliopsis helianthoides, Heliopsis helianthoides* var. *scabra* 'Summer Nights'

On the Market

Heliopsis
'Loraine Sunshine' (Helhan) • Golden-yellow flowers in midsummer to fall • Green-and-white-variegated foliage • 60–90 cm high, 30–45 cm wide

Heliopsis helianthoides
Single or double, golden-yellow flowers in midsummer to fall • 1–1.5 m high, 60 cm wide
'Hohlspiegel' (Concave Mirror) • Semi-double, dark-orange flowers in midsummer to fall • Dark foliage • 90–120 cm high, 45–60 cm wide
'Patula' • Semi-double, orange-yellow flowers in midsummer to fall • 90–120 cm high, 45–60 cm wide
'Prairie Sunset' • Yellow flowers with wine-coloured eye in midsummer to fall • Purple stems • 90–120 cm high, 45–60 cm wide

Heliopsis helianthoides var. *scabra*
'Goldgefieder' (Golden Plume) • Double, deep-yellow flowers in midsummer to fall • 90–120 cm high, 45–60 cm wide

H

'Goldgrunherz' (Goldgreenheart) • Double, lemon-yellow flowers in midsummer to fall • 60–90 cm high, 45–60 cm wide

'Sommersonne' (Summer Sun) • Single, golden-yellow flowers in midsummer to fall • 75–90 cm high, 45–60 cm wide

'Spitzentanzerin' (Toe Dancer) • Semi-double, bright-yellow flowers in midsummer to fall • 90–120 cm high, 45–60 cm wide

'Summer Nights' • Yellow flowers with mahogany eye in midsummer to fall • Purple stems • 90–120 cm high, 45–60 cm wide

Helleborus   p. 416

Genus Information

Origin: Europe, Turkey, Russia and western China
Selected Common Names: Christmas rose, Lenten rose, hellebore
Nomenclature: *Helleborus* was a name used by Theophrastus, 370–287 BC, for medicinal herbs, which was later applied to this genus.
Notes: This plant is well known in England, where it can bloom in late winter, hence some of the common names. Some of the new hybrids have become collector's plants. Enthusiasts are coming up with black and double-flowered strains.

General Features

Height: 20–75 cm high
Spread: 20–45 cm wide
Habit: clump-forming perennial
Flowers: green to purple; spring; prone to cold damage
Foliage: evergreen; prone to desiccation
Hardiness: C–D
Warnings: prone to aphids and spider mites; not prone to diseases; contact with sap may irritate skin
Expert Advice: Very difficult to grow on the Prairies as it tends to desiccate in harsh winter winds. The varieties listed here are the hardiest. Mulch for winter.

Growing Requirements

Light: shade
Soil: fertile, moist, organic, neutral to alkaline soil
Location: rock gardens; woodland gardens; mixed borders; avoid windy, exposed sites
Propagation: seed; division
Expert Advice: Use fresh seed because older seed can take up to 1.5 years to germinate. May take 2–3 years from seed to flowering. Division is difficult as it resents being disturbed.

Buying Considerations

Professionals

Popularity: popular, fast-selling plant
Availability: readily available as finished product and bare root from specialty growers
Size to Sell: sells best in smaller sizes (when blooming)
On the Shelf: keep stock rotated
Shrinkage: low; requires little maintenance

Collectors

Popularity: of interest to collectors—unique, challenge

Gardeners

Ease of Growth: generally easy to grow in warmer climates but needs close attention to growing conditions; mostly difficult to grow in colder climates as it needs close attention to growing conditions
Start with: one small plant for feature plant

What to Try First …

Helleborus atrorubens, Helleborus niger, Helleborus orientalis, Helleborus purpurascens

On the Market

Helleborus **Ballard's Group**
Large flowers in early spring • Evergreen foliage • 30–45 cm high, 30–45 cm wide

Helleborus **Lady Series**
'White Lady Spotted' • White flowers with red spots in early spring • Evergreen foliage • 25–30 cm high, 30–45 cm wide

Helleborus **Wester Flisk Group**
Green flowers with red veins in early spring • Rhubarb-red stems • 45–75 cm high, 30–45 cm wide

Helleborus atrorubens
Green- or purple-backed flowers in early spring • 30–45 cm high, 30–45 cm wide

Helleborus foetidus
Purple-edged, green flowers in early spring • 45–75 cm high, 30–45 cm wide

Helleborus lividus
Green flowers, flushed pink on the outside, in early spring • Silvery-veined, mottled foliage • 20–35 cm high, 20–30 cm wide

Helleborus niger
White flowers in early spring • Evergreen foliage • 20–30 cm high, 30–45 cm wide
'Potter's Wheel' • Large, white flowers with green eye in early spring • 20–30 cm high, 30–45 cm wide

Helleborus niger ssp. *macranthus*
White flowers in early spring • Evergreen foliage • 20–30 cm high, 30–45 cm wide

H

Helleborus orientalis
White to purple flowers, often spotted, in early spring • Evergreen foliage • 30–45 cm high, 30–45 cm wide
'Blue Lady' • Dark blue-red flowers in early spring • Evergreen foliage • 30–45 cm high, 30–45 cm wide
'Metallic Blue' • Purple, heavily spotted flowers in early spring • Evergreen foliage • 30–45 cm high, 30–45 cm wide
Orientalis hybrids • Mixed-colour flowers in early spring • Evergreen foliage • 30–45 cm high, 30–45 cm wide
'Pink Lady' • Soft pink flowers in early spring • Evergreen foliage • 30–45 cm high, 30–45 cm wide
Red hybrids • Reddish flowers in early spring • Evergreen foliage • 30–45 cm high, 30–45 cm wide
'Ruse Black' • Dark blue-black flowers in early spring • Evergreen foliage • 30–45 cm high, 30–45 cm wide
'Sparkling Red Eyes' • Off-white flowers with red eye in early spring • Evergreen foliage • 30–45 cm high, 30–45 cm wide
Helleborus orientalis ssp. *guttatus*
White flowers with maroon spots in early spring • Evergreen foliage • 30–45 cm high, 30–45 cm wide
Helleborus purpurascens
Purple, often flushed rose, flowers in early spring • 20–30 cm high, 20–30 cm wide

Hemerocallis p. 416

Genus Information
Origin: Asia
Selected Common Names: daylily
Nomenclature: From the Greek *hemero* (one day) and *callis* (beauty), referring to each flower lasting about 1 day, which is also the origin of the common name "daylily."
Notes: There are thousands of *Hemerocallis* varieties available today, bred from a base of 13–15 species. A very popular plant for the amateur breeder. *Hemerocallis* is often organized into 3 categories: dormant (the hardiest and most vigorous for cold-winter areas), semi-evergreen and evergreen (the most tender). We generally recommend the dormant or semi-evergreen, early to mid-season bloomers for northern climates. *Hemerocallis* is further divided into diploid (Dip.) or tetraploid (Tet.). Simply put, daylilies that are diploid have 22 chromosomes and tetraploid daylilies

have 44 chromosomes. Diploids are crossed with other diploids and tetraploids with other tetraploids. Professional and amateur breeders use these classifications to successfully produce new plants with desired characteristics.

General Features
Height: 25–100 cm high
Spread: 30–90 cm wide
Habit: clump-forming, (some) rhizomatous perennial
Flowers: single, double or spider forms; early to late summer; (some) fragrant; (some) nocturnal; extended, repeat or continuously blooming
Foliage: arching, grass-like; deciduous, semi-evergreen or evergreen
Hardiness: A–C
Warnings: prone to aphids; not prone to diseases
Expert Advice: Recently, horticulturalists have developed cultivars that are extended bloomers, which means the flower lasts longer than one day, and cultivars that are repeat bloomers, which means the plant will flower again later in the season. Continuous bloomers flower for the entire summer. Usually most *Hemerocallis* flowers open only in the day, but there are some which are nocturnal (opening in the late afternoon and lasting through the night). Daylilies are also grown as a foliage plant adding texture and height to the landscape.

Growing Requirements
Light: sun
Soil: fertile, moist, well-drained soil; tolerant of a wide range of soils
Location: mixed borders
Propagation: seed; division
Expert Advice: Divide every 3–5 years (or as needed) to keep vigorous.

Buying Considerations
Professionals
Popularity: popular, old-fashioned garden standard; fast seller in bloom; new varieties available
Availability: readily available as finished product and bare root from specialty growers
Size to Sell: sells best in smaller sizes (when blooming) as it matures fast
On the Shelf: high ornamental appeal when in bloom; keep stock rotated; rapidly overgrows pot
Shrinkage: low; requires little maintenance
Collectors
Popularity: of interest to collectors and breeders—*H. lilioasphodelus*, *H. minor*, *H. nana*

Gardeners

Ease of Growth: very easy to grow
Start with: one small plant for feature plant and several for mass plantings

What to Try First ...

Hemerocallis 'Bonanza', *Hemerocallis* 'Chicago Apache', *Hemerocallis* 'Dominic', *Hemerocallis* 'El Desperado', *Hemerocallis* 'Fire Music', *Hemerocallis* 'Flasher', *Hemerocallis* 'Golden Prize', *Hemerocallis* 'Holiday Delight', *Hemerocallis* 'Hudson Valley', *Hemerocallis* 'Stella de Oro'

On the Market

Hemerocallis

'Abraham' • Crimson-red flowers in mid-season • Tetraploid • 65 cm high, 45–75 cm wide

'Acapulco Night' • Velvety, mahogany-black flowers in early season • Evergreen, tetraploid, extended and repeat bloomer • 70 cm high, 45–75 cm wide

'Addie Branch Smith' • Orchid-rose flowers with purple eye in mid-season (may rebloom in fall) • Diploid, extended bloomer • 50 cm high, 45–75 cm wide

'Admiral's Braid' • Fragrant, ivory flowers with a gold-braided edge in mid-season • Tetraploid • 55 cm high, 45–75 cm wide

'Alaqua' • Fragrant, yellow-cream flowers with burgundy eye in mid-season • Tetraploid, extended bloomer • 60 cm high, 45–75 cm wide

'Alexander the Great' • Velvet-red flowers with green-yellow throat in mid-season • 85 cm high, 45–75 cm wide

'All American Tiger' • Burnt-orange flowers with red eye in mid-season (may rebloom in fall) • Tetraploid • 60 cm high, 45–75 cm wide

'American Revolution' • Black-red flowers in mid-season (may rebloom in fall) • Diploid • 70 cm high, 45–75 cm wide

'Apollodorus' • Violet-purple flowers with darker halo in mid-season (may rebloom in fall) • Tetraploid • 70 cm high, 45–75 cm wide

'Baja' • Bright-red flowers with green throat in early season • Tetraploid • 45–60 cm high, 45–60 cm wide

'Bali Hai' • Melon flowers with ochre midribs in mid-season • Diploid • 55 cm high, 45–75 cm wide

'Barbara Mitchell' • Pink flowers in mid-season (may rebloom in fall) • Diploid • 50 cm high, 45–75 cm wide

'Barbary Corsair' • Rich-violet-plum flowers in mid-season (may rebloom in fall) • Diploid • 40 cm high, 30–60 cm wide

'Beauty to Behold' • Lemon-yellow flowers in mid-season • Diploid • 60 cm high, 45–75 cm wide

'Becky Lynn' • Fragrant, brilliant rose flowers with green throat in early season • Diploid • 50 cm high, 45–75 cm wide

'Bel Air Dawn' • Pink flowers with lime throat in mid-season (may rebloom in fall) • 70 cm high, 45–75 cm wide

'Bela Lugosi' • Deep purple flowers in mid-season • 85 cm high, 45–90 cm wide

'Better Believe It' • Pink flowers with rose-red eye in mid season • 60–90 cm high, 45–75 cm wide

'Bibbity Bobbity Boo' • Lavender flowers with dark grape-purple eye in early season • 45 cm high, 30–60 cm wide

'Big Bird' • Fragrant, yellow flowers in midsummer • 50–90 cm high, 45–90 cm wide

'Big Smile' • Ruffled, sun-yellow flowers with blue-pink edge in early season • 45–60 cm high, 45–75 cm wide

'Black Ambrosia' • Black-purple flowers in mid-season • 70 cm high, 45–75 cm wide

'Black Eyed Stella' • Gold flowers with dark-red eye in early season • 35 cm high, 30–60 cm wide

'Black Prince' • Orange-brown flowers in early season • 1 m high, 45–90 cm wide

'Blackberry Candy' • Fragrant, lemon-yellow flowers with dark-red eye in mid-season • 65 cm high, 45–75 cm wide

'Blackjack Cherry' • Fragrant, red-black flowers with burgundy watermark in mid-season • 50 cm high, 45–75 cm wide

'Bloodline' • Hot-ember-red flowers with yellow-green throat in mid-season • 70 cm high, 45–75 cm wide

'Blue Sheen' • Black-blended flowers with yellow throat in mid-season • 50 cm high, 45–75 cm wide

'Boardwalk Cafe' • Fragrant, pink-mauve flowers with a magenta-purple edge in mid-season • 60 cm high, 45–75 cm wide

'Bonanza' • Fragrant, yellow flowers with red halo in mid-season • 85 cm high, 45–90 cm wide

'Bozo' • Red flowers in mid-season • 45 cm high, 30–60 cm wide

'Bright Side' • Flame-red flowers with olive-green throat in mid-season • 55 cm high, 45–75 cm wide

'Broadway Pink Slippers' • Deep-pink flowers with rose halo in mid-season (may rebloom in fall) • 40 cm high, 30–60 cm wide

'Bubbly' • Double, apricot flowers in mid-season • 50 cm high, 45–75 cm wide

'Bug's Hug' • Pink flowers with red eye in early season • 40 cm high, 30–60 cm wide

'Buttered Popcorn' • Fragrant, butter-yellow flowers in mid-season • 80 cm high, 45–90 cm wide

'Butterscotch Ruffles' • Peach-blended flowers in early season • 60 cm high, 45–75 cm wide

'Buzzbomb' • Red flowers with gold throat in mid-season • 50 cm high, 45–60 cm wide

'Cameron Quantz' • Large, almost white flowers, with pink tones, in mid-season • 70 cm high, 45–75 cm wide

'Cameroons' • Red flowers in mid-season • 70 cm high, 45–75 cm wide

'Cameroons Twister' • Fragrant, wine-purple flowers with pale watermark in mid-season (may rebloom in fall) • 1 m high, 75–90 cm wide

'Canadian Border Patrol' • Cream flowers with purple eye and purple edge in early season (may rebloom in fall) • 70 cm high, 45–75 cm wide

'Capernaum Sin' • Fragrant, burgundy-purple flowers in early season • 65 cm high, 45–75 cm wide

'Caprician Honeygold' • Soft-yellow flowers in mid-season to late season • 45 cm high, 45 cm wide

'Catherine Neal' • Deep-purple flowers in late season • 75 cm high, 45–75 cm wide

'Caviar' • Deep maroon-black flowers in mid-season • 65 cm high, 45–75 cm wide

'Chamonix' • Pink flowers in early season to mid-season • 75 cm high, 45–75 cm wide

'Chance Encounter' • Fragrant, raspberry-rose flowers with a gold edge in early season • 50–65 cm high, 50–75 cm wide

'Charles Johnston' • Fragrant, rose-red flowers in early season • 60 cm high, 45–75 cm wide

'Charming Heart' • Dark-red flowers with cream midribs in early season • 1 m high, 45–90 cm wide

'Chartwell' • Fragrant, grape-plum flowers in early season • 75 cm high, 45–75 cm wide

'Cherry Eyed Pumpkin' • Pumpkin-orange flowers with red eye in early season • 70 cm high, 45–75 cm wide

'Chicago Apache' • Ruffled, deep scarlet-red flowers in mid-season • 70 cm high, 45–75 cm wide

'Chicago Blackout' • Black-red flowers in mid-season • 75 cm high, 45–75 cm wide

'Chicago Brave' • Deep-red flowers in mid-season • 70 cm high, 45–75 cm wide

'Chicago Cattleya' • Lavender flowers with deep-purple halo in mid-season • Grass-like foliage • 60–70 cm high, 45–75 cm wide

'Chicago Cherry' • Cherry-red flowers in early season • 60 cm high, 45–75 cm wide

'Chicago Fire' • Fire-engine-red flowers in mid-season • 85 cm high, 45–90 cm wide

'Chicago Heirloom' • Lavender flowers with purple eye in mid-season • 55 cm high, 45–75 cm wide

'Chicago Picotee Lace' • Cream flowers with lavender edge in mid-season • 55 cm high, 45–75 cm wide

'Chicago Picotee Memories' • Cream flowers with purple eye in early season • 70 cm high, 45–75 cm wide

'Chorus Line' • Fragrant, soft-pink flowers with rose band in early season • 50 cm high, 45–75 cm wide

'Christmas Carol' • Crimson-red flowers with green throat in early season • 75 cm high, 45–75 cm wide

'Christmas Is' • Scarlet-red flowers in early season • 65 cm high, 45–75 cm wide

'Cinnamon Roll' • Bright-yellow flowers edged in cinnamon in mid-season • 75 cm high, 45–75 cm wide

'Cosmic Hummingbird' • Fragrant, peach flowers with red eye in early season • 65 cm high, 45–75 cm wide

'Country Charmer' • Rose-pink flowers with cream midribs in mid-season • 80 cm high, 45–75 cm wide

'Country Club' • Pink flowers with lavender edge in mid-season • 45 cm high, 30–60 cm wide

'Cragmoor Sweetheart' • Fragrant, deep-yellow flowers with green throat in mid-season • 65 cm high, 65 cm wide

'Creative Edge' • Fragrant, lavender flowers with purple-gold edge in mid-season • 60 cm high, 45–75 cm wide

'Crimson Shadows' • Crimson-red flowers in mid-season • 60–70 cm high, 45–75 cm wide

'Daring Deception' • Cream-pink flowers with purple eye and purple edge in early season • 60 cm high, 45–75 cm wide

'Daring Dilemma' • Cream-tinted flowers with plum edge and eye in mid-season • 75 cm high, 45–75 cm wide

'Dark Ruby' • Round, velvety, ruby-red flowers with green throat in early season • 60 cm high, 45–75 cm wide

'Dash Dash' • Fragrant, cream-yellow flowers with yellow-purple eye in early season • 40 cm high, 30–60 cm wide

'David Kirchhoff' • Lavender flowers in mid- season • 65 cm high, 45–75 cm wide

'Decatur Dictator' • Red flowers with plum eye in early season • 60 cm high, 45–75 cm wide

'Dominic' • Red flowers in early season • 75 cm high, 45–75 cm wide

'Dorethe Louise' • Fragrant, yellow-green flowers in mid-season • 45 cm high, 30–60 cm wide

'Double Bold One' • Double, gold flowers with burgundy eye in early season • 80 cm high, 45–75 cm wide

'Double Charm' • Double, lemon-yellow flowers in mid-season • 60 cm high, 45–75 cm wide

'Double Firecracker' • Double, red flowers in early season • 60 cm high, 45–75 cm wide

'Double Pompom' • Double, pink flowers in mid-season • 85 cm high, 45–90 cm wide

'Double River Wye' • Double, lemon-yellow flowers in mid-season • 75 cm high, 45–75 cm wide

'Dream Blue' • Grape-purple flowers with darker eye in early season • 65 cm high, 45–75 cm wide

'Ed Murray' • Black-red flowers with yellow-green throat in mid-season • 75 cm high, 45–75 cm wide

'Edge of Darkness' • Fragrant, lavender flowers with purple eye and edge in early season • 65 cm high, 45–75 cm wide

'Eenie Fanfare' • Red flowers in early season • 25–40 cm high, 45–60 cm wide

'Eenie Weenie' • Yellow flowers with green throat continuously in early season • 25 cm high, 30–60 cm wide

'El Desperado' • Mustard-yellow flowers with maroon eye and tips in late season • 70 cm high, 45–75 cm wide

'Elegant Candy' • Fragrant, ruffled, pink flowers with red eye in early season • 65 cm high, 45–75 cm wide

'Elfin Stella' • Yellow flowers continuously in summer • 25 cm high, 25–40 cm wide

'Elizabeth Salter' • Ruffled, melon-pink flowers in mid-season • 55 cm high, 45–75 cm wide

'Emperor's Dragon' • Silvery-mauve flowers with raisin-plum eye in mid-season • 65 cm high, 45–75 cm wide

'Exotic Echo' • Double, cream and melon flowers with purple eye in mid-season • 40 cm high, 30–60 cm wide

'Exotic Love' • Golden-yellow flowers with maroon eye and red edge in mid-season • 75 cm high, 45–75 cm wide

'Eye-Yi-Yi' • Bronze flowers with red eye in early season • 75 cm high, 45–75 cm wide

'Ezekiel' • Double, black-red flowers in mid-season • 70 cm high, 45–75 cm wide

'Fair Isabel' • Peach-orange flowers in mid-season • 75 cm high, 45–75 cm wide

'Fairy Tale Pink' • Pink flowers with green throat in mid-season • 60 cm high, 45–75 cm wide

'Fan Club' • Lavender flowers with purple eye in mid-season • 70 cm high, 45–75 cm wide

'Fire Music' • Fiery-red flowers with dark-red eye in mid-season • 75 cm high, 45–75 cm wide

'Fires of Fuji' • Double, orange-tan flowers with red edge in mid-season • 70 cm high, 45–75 cm wide

'Flasher' • Bright-tangerine flowers in early season • 60 cm high, 45–75 cm wide

'Flower Basket' • Double, coral-pink flowers in mid-season • 50 cm high, 45–75 cm wide

'Forsyth Jimmy Cricket' • Purple flowers with black halo in mid-season • 60 cm high, 40–75 cm wide

'Friar's Lantern' • Fragrant, purple flowers with lemon-yellow watermark in early season • 60 cm high, 45–75 cm wide

'Frosted Velvet' • Rich, dark-red flowers with red eye in early season • 60 cm high, 45–75 cm wide

'Frosty Beauty' • Peach flowers with a darker edge in mid-season • 80 cm high, 45–90 cm wide

'Gentle Shepherd' • Cream-white flowers in early season • 75 cm high, 45–75 cm wide

'Golden Prize' • Golden-yellow flowers in late season • 65 cm high, 45–75 cm wide

'Golden Scroll' • Fragrant, melon flowers in early season • 50 cm high, 45–75 cm wide

'Gordon Biggs' • Raspberry-red flowers with bright-red eye in early season • 60 cm high, 45–75 cm wide

'Grape Season' • Ruffled, plum flowers with darker eye in mid-season • 75 cm high, 45–75 cm wide

'Green Eyes Wink' • Rust-red flowers with rose halo in early season • 55 cm high, 45–75 cm wide

'Hamlet' • Fragrant, purple flowers with purple halo in early season • 45 cm high, 30–60 cm wide

'Happy Returns' • Fragrant, canary-yellow flowers in early season • Grass-like foliage • 45 cm high, 45–90 cm wide

'Hey There' • Crimson-red flowers in mid-season • 75 cm high, 50–75 cm wide

'Highland Lord' • Double, wine-red flowers with thin, white edges in mid-season • 55 cm high, 45–75 cm wide

'Hobkirk Inn' • Fragrant, red-purple flowers with apricot midribs in late season • 1 m high, 45–90 cm wide

'Holiday Delight' • Orange flowers with red eye in mid-season • 70 cm high, 45–75 cm wide

'Houdini' • Violet flowers with cream eye in mid-season • 60 cm high, 45–75 cm wide

'Hudson Valley' • Yellow-green flowers in mid-season • 80 cm high, 45–90 cm wide

'Hyperion' • Fragrant, lemon-yellow flowers in mid-season • 95 cm high, 45–90 cm wide

'Ice Carnival' • Fragrant, almost white flowers in mid-season • 70 cm high, 45–75 cm wide

'Ida's Magic' • Amber-peach flowers with a gold edge in early season • 70 cm high, 45–75 cm wide

'Indian Paintbrush' • Tangerine flowers with burnt-orange veins and tangerine throat in mid-season • 65–75 cm high, 45–75 cm wide

'Indigo Moon' • Fragrant, purple flowers with black eye in early season • 60 cm high, 45–75 cm wide

'Inspired Edge' • Fragrant, gold-edged, maroon flowers with purple eye in early season • 65 cm high, 45–75 cm wide

'Integrity' • Pink-apricot and yellow flowers in early season • 65 cm high, 45–75 cm wide

'Jalapeno Pepper' • Showy, apricot flowers with red eye in mid-season • 55 cm high, 50–75 cm wide

'Jamaican Jammin' • Fragrant, silvery rose-purple flowers in mid-season • 70 cm high, 45–75 cm wide

'Janice Brown' • Bright-pink flowers with rose eye in early season • 55 cm high, 45–75 cm wide

'Jason Salter' • Yellow flowers with faded purple eye in early season • 45 cm high, 30–60 cm wide

'Jedi Brenda Spann' • Fragrant, ruffled, pink-apricot flowers in mid-season • 60 cm high, 45–75 cm wide

'Jewel Russell' • Light-yellow flowers in mid-season • 90 cm high, 60–90 cm wide

'Joan Senior' • Near white flowers with lime-green throat in early season • 65 cm high, 45–75 cm wide

'Jolyene Nichole' • Ruffled, rose-pink flowers with dark-rose veins in mid-season • 35 cm high, 30–60 cm wide

'Judith' • Ruffled, coral-pink flowers with rose eye in early season • 65 cm high, 45–75 cm wide

'Kimmswick' • Cream flowers with lavender midribs in mid-season • 60 cm high, 45–75 cm wide

'Kwanzo Flore Pleno' • Double, bright-orange flowers in mid-season • 60–90 cm high, 45–90 cm wide

'Lady Elizabeth' • White flowers in mid-season • 40–60 cm high, 40–60 cm wide

'Lady Eva' • Maroon-purple flowers with dark-purple eye in early season • 75–85 cm high, 45–90 cm wide

'Lady Jackie' • Mulberry to buff-mauve flowers with plum eye in mid-season • 40–65 cm high, 45–55 cm wide

'Lady Lucille' • Bright-orange flowers in late season • 60–80 cm high, 45–75 cm wide

'Lady Maryland' • Near white flowers in early season • 65 cm high, 45–75 cm wide

'Lady Mischief' • Rose-pink flowers with darker eye in early season • 45 cm high, 30–60 cm wide

'Lady Scarlett' • True-red flowers with yellow-green throat in mid-season • 60–80 cm high, 45–75 cm wide

'Ladybug's Louise' • Pink flowers with cranberry eye in mid-season • 55 cm high, 45–75 cm wide

'Lahara' • Fragrant, deep-purple flowers with darker eye and chartreuse throat in mid-season • 55 cm high, 45–75 cm wide

'Lavender Dew' • Lavender flowers in mid-season • 60 cm high, 45–75 cm wide

'Lavender Whisper' • Fragrant, lavender flowers with darker veins in early season • 50 cm high, 45–75 cm wide

'Limited Edition' • Spider-like, lemon-yellow flowers in mid-season • 90 cm high, 45–90 cm wide

'Little Audrey' • Yellow flowers with red eye in mid-season • 50 cm high, 45–75 cm wide

'Little Fantastic' • Rose-pink flowers in early season • 50 cm high, 45–75 cm wide

'Little Grapette' • Red-purple flowers in early season • 30 cm high, 30–60 cm wide

'Little Gravetye' • Burgundy flowers with green eye in early season • 50 cm high, 45–75 cm wide

'Little Gypsy Vagabond' • Soft-yellow flowers with black-plum eye in early season • 45 cm high, 30–60 cm wide

'Little Joy' • Red flowers with darker eye • 70 cm high, 45–75 cm wide

'Little Missy' • Purple flowers with a white edge in early season • 40 cm high, 30–60 cm wide

'Little Mitzie' • Purple flowers with a lavender edge in early season • 45 cm high, 30–60 cm wide

'Little Moki' • Peach-and-cream flowers in mid-season • 50 cm high, 45–75 cm wide

'Little Pumpkin Face' • Butter-yellow flowers with maroon eye zone in mid-season • 45–55 cm high, 50–60 cm wide

'Little Squiz' • Dark-red flowers in mid-season • 65 cm high, 45–75 cm wide

'Little Witching Hour' • Rose-lavender flowers with pale-lavender eye in mid-season • 45 cm high, 30–60 cm wide

'Longfield's Purple Eye' • Plum-purple flowers with dark eye and green throat in mid-season • 60–70 cm high, 45–75 cm wide

'Lusty Lealand' • Red flowers with a lighter edge in mid-season • 70 cm high, 45–75 cm wide

'Magic Dawn' • Rose-pink flowers in early season • 95 cm high, 45–90 cm wide

'Magician's Mask' • Yellow-gold flowers with black eye in mid-season • 50 cm high, 45–75 cm wide

'Making Whoopee' • Fragrant, silvery-purple flowers with dark eye in early season • 50 cm high, 45–75 cm wide

'Mama's Cherry Pie' • Cherry-red flowers with yellow edges and red eye in mid-season • 65 cm high, 45–75 cm wide

'Manilla Moon' • Bright golden-yellow flowers in mid-season • 60–90 cm high, 60 cm wide

'Mardi Gras Parade' • Rose-lavender flowers with double, wine-coloured eye and green throat in mid-season • 65 cm high, 45–75 cm wide

'Mary Todd' • Yellow flowers in early season • 65 cm high, 45–75 cm wide

'Mary's Gold' • Golden-orange flowers in mid-season • 85 cm high, 45–75 cm wide

'Master Magician' • Creamy-pink flowers with red eye in mid-season • 55 cm high, 45–75 m wide

'Mateus' • Ruffled, rose-wine flowers with lighter-coloured midribs in early season • 75 cm high, 45–75 cm wide

'Mauna Loa' • Gold flowers with red edge in early season • 55 cm high, 45–75 cm wide

'May Colvin' • Rose-pink flowers with green throat in mid-season • 75 cm high, 45–75 cm wide

'Meadow Sprite' • Lavender flowers with rose eye in mid-season • 35 cm high, 30–60 cm wide

'Melon Balls' • Melon flowers with ochre overtones in mid-season • 80 cm high, 45–90 cm wide

'Moonlight Mist' • Peach-pink flowers in mid-season • 45 cm high, 30–60 cm wide

'Moonlit Masquerade' • Cream flowers with dark-purple eye in early season • 65 cm high, 45–75 cm wide

'Morning Cheerfulness' • Ruffled, pink flowers in early season • 55 cm high, 45–75 cm wide

'Mountain Heights' • Purple flowers with lavender midribs in mid-season • 60 cm high, 45–75 cm wide

H

'Mountain Violet' • Purple flowers with violet band in mid-season • 70 cm high, 45–75 cm wide

'Nairobi Night' • Violet-plum flowers with ivory halo in mid-season • 75 cm high, 45–75 cm wide

'Nefertiti' • Fragrant, yellow flowers with red eye in early season • 60 cm high, 45–75 cm wide

'Newberry Blue Eyes' • Fragrant, blue-purple flowers with blue eye in mid-season • 65 cm high, 45–75 cm wide

'Night Beacon' • Purple-red flowers with chartreuse centre in early season • 70 cm high, 45–75 cm wide

'Nile Crane' • Fragrant, blue-lavender flowers with cream throat in mid-season • 65 cm high, 45–75 cm wide

'Nordic Night' • Purple flowers with chalky red-purple eye in early season • 60 cm high, 45–75 cm wide

'Pandora's Box' • Fragrant, cream flowers with purple eye in early season • 50 cm high, 45–75 cm wide

'Paradise Pink' • Pink flowers in early season • 75 cm high, 45–75 cm wide

'Pardon Me' • Fragrant, bright-red flowers in mid-season • 45 cm high, 30–60 cm wide

'Peaks of Otter' • Fragrant, black flowers with grape-purple eye in early season • 45 cm high, 30–60 cm wide

'Pearl Jam' • Light lavender flowers with purple halo in mid-season • 65 cm high, 45–75 cm wide

'Pepper Sauce' • Red-black flowers with red halo in early season • 35 cm high, 30–60 cm wide

'Pink Lace' • Pink flowers in mid-season • 60 cm high, 45–75 cm wide

'Pink Playmate' • Pure rose-pink flowers in late season • 55 cm high, 45–75 cm wide

'Pinocchio' • Lavender-pink flowers in early season • 30–40 cm high, 30–60 cm wide

'Pizza Sauce' • Fiery-orange flowers in early season • 40 cm high, 30–60 cm wide

'Pocket Change' • Bright-red flowers with a lighter edge in early season • 45 cm high, 30–60 cm wide

'Prairie Blue Eyes' • Lavender flowers with blue eye in mid-season • 70 cm high, 45–75 cm wide

'Precious One' • Cream flowers with ochre midribs in early season • 70 cm high, 45–75 cm wide

'Prester John' • Fragrant, double, orange-gold flowers in early season • 65 cm high, 45–75 cm wide

'Ptarmigan' • White flowers with green throat in mid-season • 50 cm high, 45–75 cm wide

'Pure Bliss' • Yellow flowers with green throat in mid-season • 55 cm high, 45–75 cm wide

'Purple de Oro' • Purple flowers with dark midribs in mid-season • 65–70 cm high, 45–90 cm wide

'Pyewacket' • Rose flowers with plum eye in mid-season • 35 cm high, 30–60 cm wide

'Quinn Buck' • Lavender-blue flowers with darker halo in mid-season • 65 cm high, 45–75 cm wide

'Rainbow Candy' • Fragrant, cream flowers with purple-lavender-grey eye in early season • 70 cm high, 45–75 cm wide

'Rambo' • Blue or blood-red flowers with lime-coloured throat in early season • 55 cm high, 45–75 cm wide

'Raspberry Pixie' • Fragrant, raspberry-red flowers in mid-season • 30 cm high, 30–60 cm wide

'Raspberry Ripple' • Raspberry-red flowers with darker eye in mid-season • 60–90 cm high, 45–90 cm wide

'Rectory Square' • Fragrant, rose flowers with cherry halo in mid-season • 85 cm high, 45–90 cm wide

'Red Rum' • Bright-red flowers in early season • 40 cm high, 30–60 cm wide

'Red Select' • Deep-red flowers in early season • 70 cm high, 45–75 cm wide

'Respighi' • Wine-purple flowers with lighter eye in early season • 50 cm high, 45–75 cm wide

'Robbie Bush' • Fragrant, double, melon-coloured flowers in early season • 65 cm high, 45–75 cm wide

'Rogue's Masquerade' • Ivory flowers with burgundy eye in mid-season • 40–50 cm high, 45–75 cm wide

'Rojo Alto' • Bright-red flowers in early season • 50–100+ cm high, 45–90 cm wide

'Rooten Tooten Red' • Fragrant, rich-red flowers in mid-season • 60 cm high, 45–60 cm wide

'Rosella Sheridan' • Pink flowers with a green throat in mid-season • 55 cm high, 45–75 cm wide

'Rosy Returns' • Fragrant rose-pink flowers with a deeper rose eye-zone in late spring to fall • 40–45 cm high, 45–90 cm wide

'Route Sixty Six' • Black-wine-red flowers in mid-season • 60 cm high, 45–75 cm wide

'Royal Braid' • Fragrant, silver-edged, lavender flowers with purple eye in mid-season • 65 cm high, 45–75 cm wide

'Ruffled Storm' • Fragrant, maroon-red flowers in mid-season • 75 cm high, 45–75 cm wide

'Russian Rhapsody' • Violet-purple flowers with darker eye in mid-season • 75 cm high, 45–75 cm wide

'Sabine Baur' • Cream flowers with purple eye and edge in early season • 65 cm high, 45–75 cm wide

'Scaramouche' • Red flowers with purple eye in mid-season • 70 cm high, 45–75 cm wide

'Scatterbrain' • Fragrant, double, light-peach-pink flowers in mid-season • 80 cm high, 45–90 cm wide

'Seductor' • Fragrant, apple-red flowers with green throat in early season • 45 cm high, 30–60 cm wide

'Shady Lady' • Yellow flowers with wine-red eye in mid-season • 85 cm high, 45–90 cm wide

'Sherwood Gladiator' • Bright-yellow flowers in mid-season • 90–100 cm high, 45–90 cm wide

'Sherwood Lemon Drop' • Lemon-yellow flowers in mid-season • 60 cm high, 45–75 cm wide

'Silent Sentry' • Purple flowers in early season • 60 cm high, 45–75 cm wide

'Siloam Allison Perry' • Fragrant, rose-coral flowers in mid-season • 65 cm high, 45–60 cm wide

'Siloam Button Box' • Cream flowers with maroon eye in early season • 50 cm high, 45–75 cm wide

'Siloam Bye Lo' • Fragrant, rose flowers with rose-red eye in mid-season • 40 cm high, 30–60 cm wide

'Siloam David Kirchhoff' • Orchid flowers with faded cerise, pencil-lined eye in early season • 40 cm high, 30–60 cm wide

'Siloam Double Classic' • Fragrant, double, pink flowers in early season • 40 cm high, 30–60 cm wide

'Siloam Ethel Smith' • Beige-pink flowers with rose eye in mid-season • 50 cm high, 45–75 cm wide

'Siloam Fine Art' • Fragrant, rose-purple flowers with smoky-purple eye in early season • 50 cm high, 45–75 cm wide

'Siloam French Marble' • Ivory-white flowers with cherry-red eye in mid-season • 40 cm high, 30–60 cm wide

'Siloam Grace Stamile' • Fragrant, red flowers with red halo in early season • 35 cm high, 30–60 cm wide

'Siloam June Bug' • Gold flowers with a maroon eye in early to mid-season • 55–60 cm high, 45–60 cm wide

'Siloam Little Girl' • Shrimp-pink flowers with rose eye in mid-season • 45 cm high, 30–60 cm wide

'Siloam New Toy' • Fragrant, orchid flowers with purple eye in early season • 45 cm high, 30–60 cm wide

'Siloam Plum Tree' • Deep purple flowers with green throat in early season • 60 cm high, 45–75 cm wide

'Siloam Red Ruby' • Ruby-red flowers in mid-season • 45 cm high, 30–60 cm wide

'Siloam Red Toy' • Ruby-red flowers in early season • Grass-like foliage • 50 cm high, 30–60 cm wide

'Siloam Shocker' • Cream-pink flowers with red eye in mid-season • 70 cm high, 45–75 cm wide

'Siloam Show Girl' • Deep-red flowers with darker eye in mid-season • 45 cm high, 45–75 cm wide

'Siloam Tee Tiny' • Orchid flowers with purple eye in mid-season • 50 cm high, 45–75 cm wide

'Siloam Tiny Tears' • Pastel, creamy-pink flowers with yellow eye and green throat in early season • 40–50 cm high, 45–60 cm wide

'Siloam Tiny Tim' • Blue-lavender flowers with blue eye in mid-season • 35 cm high, 30–60 cm wide

'Siloam Tom Howard' • Cream flowers with rose-red eye in early season • 40 cm high, 30–60 cm wide

'Siloam Ury Winniford' • Dainty, cream flowers with purple eye in early season • 60 cm high, 45–75 cm wide

H

'Sings the Blues' • Fragrant, lavender-rose flowers with violet eye in mid-season • 65 cm high, 45–75 cm wide

'So Excited' • Rose flowers with large, raspberry eye in early season • 65 cm high, 45–75 cm wide

'So Sweet' • Fragrant, lemon-yellow flowers in early season • 55 cm high, 45–75 cm wide

'Song Sparrow' • Ruffled, dazzling gold-orange flowers in mid-season • 60 cm high, 45–75 cm wide

'Starling' • Chocolate-red flowers with green throat in early season • 60–70 cm high, 50–65 cm wide

'Startle' • Red bi-tone with a cream halo in summer • 60–65 cm high, 45–90 cm wide

'Stella de Oro' • Fragrant, golden-yellow flowers continuously in summer to fall • 30 cm high, 30–60 cm wide

'Strawberry Candy' • Strawberry-pink flowers with rose-red eye in early season • 65 cm high, 45–75 cm wide

'Strawberry Fields Forever' • Fragrant, pink flowers with a red-rose edge and eye in early season • 65 cm high, 45–75 cm wide

'Strutter's Ball' • Rich plum-purple flowers with white watermark in mid-season • 70 cm high, 45–75 cm wide

'Summer Wine' • Deep-violet flowers in mid-season • 60 cm high, 45–75 cm wide

'Super Purple' • Fragrant, rich-purple flowers in mid-season • 70 cm high, 45–75 cm wide

'Swirling Water' • Lavender-purple flowers with white watermark in early season • 55 cm high, 45–75 cm wide

'Terminator' • True-red flowers in early season • 90 cm high, 90 cm wide

'Texas Sunlight' • Pure gold flowers in mid-season • 70 cm high, 45–75 cm wide

'Tiger Kitten' • Light-orange flowers with bold red eye in mid-season • 55 cm high, 45–75 cm wide

'Tigger' • Copper-orange flowers with red eye in mid-season • 60 cm high, 45–75 cm wide

'Tom Collins' • Lemon-yellow flowers with green throat in early season • 65 cm high, 45–75 cm wide

'Too Marvelous' • Ruffled, melon-and-pink flowers in mid-season • 60 cm high, 45–75 cm wide

'Tootsie Rose' • Rose-pink flowers with deeper halo in early season • 35 cm high, 30–60 cm wide

'Tour de Force' • Fragrant, double, rose flowers in early season • 50 cm high, 45–75 cm wide

'Tundra' • Near white flowers in mid-season • 60 cm high, 45–75 cm wide

'Tuscawilla Tigress' • Orange-red flowers with darker eye in early season • 65 cm high, 45–75 cm wide

'Tweety' • Yellow flowers in mid-season • 20 cm high, 30–45 cm wide

'Twiggy' • Spider-like, orange flowers with wine eye in mid-season • 45 cm high, 30–60 cm wide

'Vanilla Fluff' • Fragrant, double, cream flowers in mid-season • 85 cm high, 45–90 cm wide

'Velveteen' • Rich-royal-red flowers in mid-season • 60–70 cm high, 50–75 cm wide

'Victorian Days' • Grape-purple flowers with a gold edge in mid-season • 60 cm high, 45–75 cm wide

'Vintage Bordeaux' • Cherry-red flowers with a yellow edge in early season • 70 cm high, 45–75 cm wide

'Voluptuous Pink' • Fragrant, rose-pink flowers with pink watermark in mid-season • 50 cm high, 45–75 cm wide

'Watermelon' • Pale-pink flowers with darker eye in mid-season • 45–60 cm high, 45–75 cm wide

'Wayside King Royale' • Fragrant, purple flowers in early season • 90 cm high, 45–90 cm wide

'Wedding Band' • Fragrant, cream flowers with a gold edge in mid-season • 65 cm high, 45–75 cm wide

'Which Way Jim' • Fragrant, dark-purple flowers with dusty-purple eye in mid-season • 65 cm high, 45–75 cm wide

'White Temptation' • Near white flowers with green throat in mid-season • 80 cm high, 45–90 cm wide

'Wineberry Candy' • Fragrant, orchid flowers with purple eye in early season • 55 cm high, 45–75 cm wide

'Wings of Chance' • Yellow flowers with wide, rose halo in mid-season • 40 cm high, 30–60 cm wide

'Yellow Explosion' • Crinkled, bright-yellow flowers in mid-season • 70 cm high, 45–75 cm wide

Hemerocallis lilioasphodelus (syn. *H. flava*)
Fragrant, star-shaped, bright-yellow flowers in early season • 60–90 cm high, 60–90 cm wide

Hemerocallis minor
Fragrant, lemon-yellow flowers in early season • 60 cm high, 30–60 cm wide

Hemerocallis multiflora
Chrome-yellow flowers in late summer to fall • 50–75 cm high, 30–60 cm wide

Hemerocallis nana
Clear-orange flowers in mid-season • 30 cm high, 30–60 cm wide

Hepatica

p. 416

Genus Information

Origin: northern temperate regions
Selected Common Names: noble liverleaf, sharp lobed liverleaf
Nomenclature: From the Latin *hepar* (liver), referring to the leaves, which resemble the liver in outline.
Other Uses: *Hepatica* was said to cure liver diseases.
Notes: Some species are collector's plants, especially the new double forms that have sold as high as 50,000–60,000 yen (over $500) in Japan. They have fully double, pom-pom like flowers. New single-flowered strains are being bred for their clarity and intensity of flower colour. Some new strains also have mottled leaves.

General Features

Height: 10–25 cm high
Spread: 15–30 cm wide
Habit: clump-forming spreading perennial
Flowers: blue, white or pink; single or double; bowl- to star-shaped; early spring; reblooms in fall
Foliage: kidney-shaped, evergreen
Hardiness: C
Warnings: prone to aphids; prone to slugs; not prone to diseases

Growing Requirements

Light: shade; tolerates more sun with good soil moisture
Soil: humus-rich, moist, neutral to alkaline soil; thrives in heavy soil
Location: shady rock gardens; woodland gardens
Propagation: seed; division
Expert Advice: Sow fresh seed in early summer to germinate the following spring. Division is difficult as it resents being disturbed.

On the Market

Hepatica acutiloba
Blue, sometimes white or pink, flowers in spring • 15–25 cm high, 15–30 cm wide

Hepatica americana
Blue, sometimes white or pink, flowers in spring • 10–15 cm high, 20–30 cm wide

Hepatica x *media*
Large, blue flowers in spring • 10–15 cm high, 15–20 cm wide

Hepatica nobilis
Blue, sometimes white or pink, flowers in spring • 10–15 cm high, 15–20 cm wide

'Alba' • White flowers in spring • 10–15 cm high, 15–20 cm wide

'Babiyrosa' • Bright-rose flowers in spring • 10–15 cm high, 15–20 cm wide

'Caerulea' • Blue-violet flowers in spring • 10–15 cm high, 15–20 cm wide

'Cobalt' • Dark-blue flowers in spring • 10–15 cm high, 15–20 cm wide

(Double Blue form) • Double, blue flowers in spring • 10–15 cm high, 15–20 cm wide

'Pink Persuasion' • Pink flowers in spring • 10–15 cm high, 15–20 cm wide

'Rosea' • Rose flowers in spring • 10–15 cm high, 15–20 cm wide

'Rubra Plena' • Double, red flowers in spring • 10–15 cm high, 15–20 cm wide

'Walter Peters' • Dark-blue flowers in spring • 10–15 cm high, 15–20 cm wide

H

Hepatica nobilis var. *japonica*
Blue, pink or white flowers in spring •
10–15 cm high, 15–20 cm wide
'Akafuka' • Single, burgundy flowers,
edged in white, in spring • 10–15 cm high,
15–20 cm wide
'Akanezora' • Semi-double, purple-pink
flowers in spring • 10–15 cm high,
15–20 cm wide
'Aofuku' • Semi-double, white flowers with
bluish edges in spring • 10–15 cm high,
15–20 cm wide
Curly Leaf • Flowers in spring • Curled
and twisted leaf forms • 10–15 cm high,
15–20 cm wide
'Fujimusume' • Double, blue flowers,
fading to white, in spring • 10–15 cm
high, 15–20 cm wide
'Orihime' • Double, rose-pink flowers,
fading to white, in spring • 10–15 cm
high, 15–20 cm wide
'Shirayuki' • Fully double, white flowers in
spring • 10–15 cm high, 15–20 cm wide
Hepatica nobilis var. *japonica* f. *magna*
Pink, blue or sometimes white, flowers in
spring • 10–15 cm high, 15–20 cm wide
Hepatica transsilvania
Blue, white or sometimes pink, flowers in
spring • 10–15 cm high, 15–20 cm wide

Hernieria   p. 416 📷
Genus Information
Origin: Eurasia and Africa
Selected Common Names: common rupturewort
Nomenclature: The name is from the Latin *hernia*
(rupture).
Other Uses: The plant was first used in the
16th century for ruptured hernias.
General Features
Height: 5–10 cm high
Spread: 30–45 cm wide
Habit: annual or perennial groundcover;
long lived
Flowers: white; summer
Hardiness: D
Warnings: not prone to insects or disease
Growing Requirements
Light: sun
Soil: neutral to alkaline soil; drought tolerant
Location: front of mixed borders; between
stepping stones
Propagation: seed; division; cuttings
Expert Advice: Seed in spring. Divide in fall. Take
cuttings in summer.

Buying Considerations
Professionals
Popularity: relatively unknown foliage plant
Availability: occasionally available as finished
product from specialty growers
Size to Sell: sells best in smaller sizes as it
matures fast
On the Shelf: rapidly overgrows pot
Shrinkage: low; requires little maintenance
Collectors
Popularity: not generally of interest to
collectors
Gardeners
Ease of Growth: mostly easy to grow
Start with: several for mass plantings
What to Try First ...
Hernieria glabra

On the Market
Hernieria glabra
White flowers in summer • 5–10 cm high,
30–45 cm wide

Hesperis   p. 416 📷
Genus Information
Origin: Asia and Europe
Selected Common Names: sweet rocket, dame's
rocket
Nomenclature: From *hesperos* (evening), referring
to when the plant's fragrance is at its peak.
Notes: Genus includes annuals, biennials and
perennials.
General Features
Height: 60–90 cm high
Spread: 30–45 cm wide
Habit: biennial or short-lived perennial
Flowers: fireweed-like; fragrant
Hardiness: A
Warnings: prone to powdery mildew and aphids;
self-sows aggressively (deadhead to prevent
spread)
Expert Advice: Replace plants every 2–3 years as
flowering diminishes with age (although if left
to seed, there will be plenty of new plants).
Growing Requirements
Light: sun
Soil: fertile, moist, well-drained, neutral to
alkaline soil
Location: meadows; wild gardens; cutting gardens
Propagation: seed (self-sows readily); division;
basal cuttings

Buying Considerations

Professionals

Popularity: popular, old-fashioned garden standard

Availability: readily available as finished product

Size to Sell: sells best in smaller sizes as it matures fast

On the Shelf: rapidly overgrows pot

Shrinkage: low; requires little maintenance

Collectors

Popularity: not generally of interest to collectors

Gardeners

Ease of Growth: very easy to grow

Start with: one small plant for feature plant

What to Try First ...

Hesperis matronalis

On the Market

Hesperis matronalis
Fragrant, lilac flowers in late spring to summer • 75–90 cm high, 30–45 cm wide

'Lilacina Flore Pleno' • Fragrant, double, lilac flowers in late spring to summer • 75–90 cm high, 30–45 cm wide

Hesperis steveniana
Fragrant, large flowers in late spring to summer • 60–90 cm high, 30–45 cm wide

Heuchera

p. 416

Genus Information

Origin: North America, the Rocky Mountains and Mexico

Selected Common Names: alumroot, American alumroot, coralbells

Nomenclature: Named for Johann von Heucher, 1677–1747, a German professor of medicine.

Notes: The genus has some 55 species.

General Features

Height: 5–75 cm high

Spread: 10–90 cm wide

Habit: clump-forming perennial

Flowers: cream to red blooms on tall stalks; tiny, bell-shaped; late spring to fall

Foliage: green, gold, purple, silver-veined or pink

Hardiness: C

Warnings: prone to aphids and rust

Expert Advice: Many selections have been developed by US tissue culture labs and are making waves worldwide for their intense foliage colours.

Growing Requirements

Light: purple-leafed *Heuchera* require shade to a.m. sun as foliage edges brown in bright sunlight (*H. micrantha* var. *diversifolia* 'Palace Purple' is quite sun tolerant); green-leafed *Heuchera* prefer sun

Soil: fertile, moist, well-drained soil

Location: woodland gardens; rock gardens

Propagation: seed; cuttings

Expert Advice: *Heuchera* crowns tend to push themselves up out of the ground, and they need to be replanted every 2–3 years—mulching before winter may help to prevent this problem.

Buying Considerations

Professionals

Popularity: popular garden standard; new varieties available

Availability: readily available as finished product and bare root

Size to Sell: sells best in smaller sizes (when blooming) as it matures fast

On the Shelf: high ornamental appeal; rapidly overgrows pot

Shrinkage: low; requires little maintenance

Collectors

Popularity: of interest to collectors—new colourful varieties

Gardeners

Ease of Growth: generally easy to grow

Start with: one small plant for feature plant

What to Try First ...

Heuchera 'Amethyst Myst', *Heuchera* 'Cherries Jubilee', *Heuchera* 'Chocolate Ruffles', *Heuchera* 'Florist's Choice', *Heuchera* 'Green Spice', *Heuchera* 'Lime Rickey', *Heuchera* 'Obsidian', *Heuchera* 'Petite Pearl Fairy'

On the Market

Heuchera
'Amber Waves' • Tiny, light-rose flowers on 30-cm stalks in summer • Ruffled, amber-gold foliage • 20 cm high, 45 cm wide

'Amethyst Myst' • Tiny, cream flowers on 65-cm stalks in late spring • Silvery-amethyst foliage • 25 cm high, 45–60 cm wide

'Black Beauty' • Tiny, cream flowers on 60-cm stalks in summer • Huge, ruffled, chocolate and ruby foliage • 25 cm high, 45 cm wide

Bressingham hybrids • Tiny, white flowers on delicate stalks in early summer • Grey-marbled foliage • 45–75 cm high, 45–60 cm wide

'Canyon Pink' • Tiny, deep pink flowers on delicate stalks in summer • Green foliage • 30–50 cm high, 30 cm wide

'Cappuccino' • White flowers on 65-cm stalks in early summer • Ruffled, tan foliage • 20 cm high, 45 cm wide

'Cathedral Windows' • Purple-white flowers on 65-cm stalks in late spring to summer • Purple foliage • 20 cm high, 40 cm wide

'Champagne Bubbles' • Tiny, white to rose-red flowers on 75-cm stalks in summer • Green foliage • 25 cm high, 45 cm wide

'Cherries Jubilee' • Cherry-red flowers on 40-cm stalks in late spring to summer • Ruffled, green foliage • 20 cm high, 40 cm wide

'Chocolate Ruffles' • Tiny, cream flowers on 75-cm stalks in summer • Huge, ruffled, chocolate-and-burgundy foliage • 25 cm high, 45 cm wide

'Constance' • Tiny, pink-and-white flowers on 35-cm stalks in summer • Green foliage • 10–15 cm high, 10–15 cm wide

'Coral Bouquet' • Tiny, coral flowers on 30-cm stalks in late spring • Green foliage • 15 cm high, 20–35 cm wide

'Ebony and Ivory' • Tiny, ivory flowers on 55-cm stalks in summer • Ruffled, ebony foliage • 25 cm high, 40 cm wide

'Eco Magnififolia' • Tiny, cream flowers on 60-cm stalks in summer • Brown leaves tinged purple and veined silvery-grey • 35–45 cm high, 60 cm wide

'Fireworks' • Tiny, pale-coral flowers in summer • Ruffled, bronze foliage • 20–50 cm high, 40–45 cm wide

'Florist's Choice' • Tiny, rich-red flowers on 80-cm stalks in summer • Green foliage • 50 cm high, 60 cm wide

'Green Spice' (Eco-Improved) • Tiny, cream flowers on 70-cm stalks in early summer • Silver, green-veined, purple foliage • 25 cm high, 40 cm wide

'Helen Dillon' • Tiny, red flowers on delicate stalks in late spring • Cream-speckled, green foliage with reddish veins • 30–50 cm high, 40–50 cm wide

'Leuchtkafer' (Firefly) • Fragrant, tiny, red flowers on stalks in summer • Dark-green foliage • 50–60 cm high, 30–45 cm wide

'Lime Rickey' • Tiny, white flowers on 45-cm stalks in summer • Ruffled, chartreuse, spring foliage • 20 cm high, 45 cm wide

'Magic Wand' • Tiny, cerise flowers on 75-cm stalks in summer • Green foliage • 20 cm high, 40 cm wide

'Mardi Gras' • Tiny, red-brown flowers on 70-cm stalks in summer • Variegated coral, orange, green and grey foliage • 20 cm high, 45 cm wide

'Marmalade' • Tiny, red-brown flowers on 30-cm stalks in summer • Ruffled, umber to deep-sienna foliage • 25 cm high, 45 cm wide

'Mayfair' • Tiny, rose flowers on delicate stalks in late spring to summer • Green foliage • 15–25 cm high, 10–20 cm wide

'Midnight Claret' • Tiny, green flowers on 65-cm stalks in summer • Dark-purple foliage with patches of light-grey • 25 cm high, 45 cm wide

'Night Watch' • Tiny flowers on delicate stalks in early summer • Dark-purple foliage • 45–60 cm high, 60 cm wide

'Northern Fire' • Tiny, scarlet-red flowers on 80-cm stalks in summer • Silver-mottled foliage • 40–45 cm high, 30 cm wide

'Oakington Jewel' • Tiny, shell-pink flowers on 1-m stalks in late spring to summer • Metallic foliage • 60–75 cm high, 45 cm wide

'Obsidian' • Tiny, green-white flowers on 60-cm stalks in summer • Shiny, very black, rounded foliage • 25 cm high, 30–40 cm wide

'Palace Passion' • Tiny, cream flowers on stalks in summer • Purple foliage • 35–40 cm high, 60 cm wide

'Persian Carpet' • Tiny, white flowers on 65-cm stalks in summer • Silvery, rose-burgundy foliage with dark-purple edges • 20 cm high, 40 cm wide

'Petite Marbled Burgundy' • Tiny, soft-pink flowers on 30-cm stalks in summer • Burgundy leaves with silver markings • 30 cm high, 30–40 cm wide

'Petite Pearl Fairy' • Tiny, pink flowers on 35-cm stalks in early summer • Dark-green foliage sprinkled with silver • 15–20 cm high, 30 cm wide

'Pewter Moon' • Tiny, creamy-pink flowers on 55-cm stalks in summer • Silvery foliage with maroon underside • 25 cm high, 30 cm wide

'Pewter Veil' • Tiny, cream flowers on 70-cm stalks in late spring • Maple leaf–shaped, metallic-silver foliage • 20 cm high, 35 cm wide

'Plum Pudding' • Tiny, cream flowers on 65-cm stalks in late spring • Shimmering, plum-purple foliage • 20 cm high, 40 cm wide

'Purple Petticoats' • Tiny, purple to white flowers on 70-cm stalks in summer • Purple foliage • 30 cm high, 60 cm wide

'Purple Sails' • Tiny flowers on 65-cm stalks in summer to fall • Dark-purple, maple-shaped foliage • 20 cm high, 45 cm wide

'Raspberry Ice' • Tiny, pink flowers on 60-cm stalks in summer • Dark-veined, raspberry and frosty-silver foliage with burgundy undersides • 30 cm high, 30 cm wide

'Regal Robe' • Tiny, cream flowers on 65-cm stalks in summer • Silver-and-lavender foliage • 15 cm high, 40 cm wide

'Rosemary Bloom' (Heuros) • Tiny, coral-pink flowers on delicate stalks in early summer • Rich-green foliage • 45–60 cm high, 20–30 cm wide

'Ruby Bells' • Fragrant blood-red flowers on stalks in late-spring to summer • Marbled light-and dark-green foliage • 45 cm high, 30 cm wide

'Ruby Mist' • Tiny, pink flowers on 45–60-cm stalks in late spring to summer • Marbled light-and dark-green foliage • 20–25 cm high, 30–60 cm wide

'Ruby Veil' • Tiny, cream flowers on 65-cm stalks in summer • Maple leaf–shaped foliage with metallic-copper sheen • 15 cm high, 40 cm wide

'Sashay' • Tiny, greenish flowers on 55-cm stalks in early summer • Green, ruffled foliage and burgundy underside • 20 cm high, 40 cm wide

'Silver Shadows' • Tiny, cream flowers on 65-cm stalks in summer • Dark, silvery foliage with rosy tinge • 15 cm high, 40 cm wide

'Silver Veil' • Tiny, cerise-rose flowers on delicate stalks in summer • Foliage has metallic sheen • 30–50 cm high, 60 cm wide

'Smokey Rose' • Rose flowers on 50-cm red stalks in summer • Purple foliage • 20 cm high, 40 cm wide

'Snow Angel' • Rose-pink flowers on stalks in late spring to early summer • Frosted, variegated foliage • 25–45 cm high, 25–40 cm wide

'Splendens' • Scarlet-red flowers on stalks in late spring to midsummer • Marbled light-and dark-green foliage • 60–70 cm high, 30 cm wide

'Splish Splash' • Tiny, rich-red flowers on 50-cm stalks in summer • Variegated foliage looks splashed • 15 cm high, 35 cm wide

'Stormy Seas' • Tiny, white to pink flowers on 90-cm stalks in summer • Ruffled, silver-grey foliage • 45–60 cm high, 90 cm wide

'Strawberry Candy' • Tiny, pink flowers on 40-cm stalks in summer • Silver-marbled, green foliage • 25 cm high, 45 cm wide

'Strawberry Swirl' • Tiny, pink flowers on 70-cm stalks in late spring to summer • Silvery-ruffled foliage • 25 cm high, 45 cm wide

'Swirling Fantasy' • Tiny, red flowers on stalks in late spring to early summer • Pewter-red foliage with dark veins • 20–30 cm high, 20–30 cm wide

'Veil of Passion' • Tiny, red flowers on 65-cm stalks in summer • Purple foliage • 25 cm high, 45 cm wide

'Vesuvius' • Tiny, orange-red flowers on 60-cm stalks in summer • Rounded, purple foliage • 20 cm high, 45 cm wide

'Winter Red' • Tiny, pink flowers on delicate stalks in late spring to summer • Maple-shaped, deep green foliage • 40 cm high, 45 cm wide

Dancer Series
'Tango' • Bright-pink flowers in late spring • Metallic-purple foliage • 20–40 cm high, 25–30 cm wide

Heuchera americana
Dale's strain • Tiny, greenish-white flowers on stalks in early summer • Silver-mottled foliage • 60–75 cm high, 25–30 cm wide

'Velvet Night' • Tiny, cream flowers on 65-cm stalks in midsummer • Metallic-purple foliage over slate-black underlay • 20 cm high, 45 cm wide

Heuchera x brizoides
'Mt. St. Helens' • Cardinal-red flowers on 55-cm stalks in late spring to summer • 30 cm high, 30–45 cm wide

Heuchera grossulariifolia
Tiny, white flowers in early summer • Maple-shaped, green foliage • 10 cm high, 15 cm wide

H

Heuchera hallii
Tiny, creamy-white flowers on delicate stalks in summer • 20–30 cm high, 10 cm wide

Bressingham Bronze ('Absi') • Tiny, white flowers on stalks in late spring to summer • Crinkled, bronze foliage • 45–60 cm high, 45–60 cm wide

Heuchera micrantha var. *diversifolia*
'Palace Purple' • Tiny, greenish-cream flowers on 50-cm stalks in summer • Jagged, shiny, bronze-purple foliage • Takes more sun than other purple-leafed varieties • 20 cm high, 45 cm wide

Heuchera parishii
'Chiquita' • Tiny, white-pink flowers on 10-cm stalks in summer • Grey-green foliage • 5 cm high, 10–15 cm wide

Heuchera pulchella
Tiny, pale-pink flowers on stalks in late spring to summer • Green foliage • 7–10 cm high, 20–30 cm wide

Heuchera sanguinea
Tiny, red, pink or white flowers on 45–50-cm stalks in late spring to summer • Marbled light-and dark-green foliage • 25–30 cm high, 30 cm wide

'Brandon Glow' • Tiny, red flowers on delicate stalks in late spring to summer • Green foliage • 45–60 cm high, 30 cm wide

'Brandon Pink' • Tiny, rose-pink flowers on delicate stalks in late spring • Green-and-white foliage • 40–60 cm high, 60 cm wide

'Firesprite' • Tiny, bright rose-red flowers on 50-cm stalks in summer • 30 cm high, 30 cm wide

'Frosty' • Tiny, bright-red flowers on 50-cm stalks in summer • Silver, variegated foliage • 20 cm high, 40 cm wide

'Geisha's Fan' • Tiny, pink flowers on 45-cm stalks in summer • Charcoal-veiled, silver-purple foliage • 20 cm high, 30–40 cm wide

'Monet' • Tiny, deep-red flowers on 50-cm stalks in late spring to summer • Marbled green-and-cream foliage • 20 cm high, 35 cm wide

'Morden Pink' • Tiny, rich-pink flowers on stalks in late spring to summer • Green foliage • 45–60 cm high, 30 cm wide

'Sioux Falls' • Tiny, bright-red flowers on stalks in late spring to summer • Marbled light-and dark-green foliage • 60–75 cm high, 40–45 cm wide

'Snow Storm' • Tiny, bright-red flowers on 50-cm stalks in summer • Variegated foliage • 15 cm high, 35 cm wide

'Vivid Crimson' • Tiny, crimson-red flowers on 45 cm stalks in summer • Scalloped foliage • 25–30 cm high, 30 cm wide

'White Cloud' • Tiny, white flowers on stalks in late spring to summer • Green foliage with silver-white mottling • 45 cm high, 30 cm wide

Heucherella   p. 416

Genus Information
Origin: man made cross
Selected Common Names: foamy bells
Nomenclature: A combination of the words *Heuchera* and *Tiarella*.
Notes: A sterile, intergeneric cross between *Heuchera* and *Tiarella*.

General Features
Height: 30–60 cm high
Spread: 30–45 cm wide
Habit: clump-forming or spreading groundcover perennial
Flowers: plume-like; late spring to early summer; long blooming
Foliage: heart-shaped or ovate; evergreen; good fall colour
Hardiness: C
Warnings: prone to aphids and rust
Expert Advice: An excellent edging or groundcover for the herbaceous border.

Growing Requirements
Light: shade to a.m. sun
Soil: evenly moist, fertile, neutral to alkaline, well-drained soil
Location: front of mixed borders; woodland gardens
Propagation: division; separate and replant stolons
Expert Advice: Divide in spring or fall.

Buying Considerations
Professionals
Popularity: gaining popularity as a foliage plant
Availability: generally available as bare root from specialty growers
Size to Sell: sells best in smaller sizes (when blooming) as it matures fast
On the Shelf: high ornamental appeal; rapidly overgrows pot
Shrinkage: low; requires little maintenance

H

Collectors
Popularity: not generally of interest to collectors

Gardeners
Ease of Growth: generally easy to grow
Start with: one small plant for feature plant and several for mass plantings

What to Try First ...
Heucherella 'Burnished Bronze', *Heucherella* 'Cinnamon Bear', *Heucherella* 'Dayglow Pink', *Heucherella* 'Sunspot', *Heucherella alba* 'Rosalie'

On the Market

Heucherella
'**Burnished Bronze**' • Tawny flowers in late spring to summer • Burnished-bronze, evergreen foliage • 30–45 cm high, 30–40 cm wide

'**Chocolate Lace**' • Pink flowers in late spring to summer • Purple-bronze, evergreen foliage • 30–45 cm high, 30–40 cm wide

'**Cinnamon Bear**' • Tawny flowers in late spring to summer • Cinnamon-brown, evergreen foliage • 40–50 cm high, 30–40 cm wide

'**Crimson Clouds**' • Pink flowers in late spring to summer • Evergreen leaves with crimson dots • 30–45 cm high, 30–40 cm wide

'**Dayglow Pink**' • Pink flowers in late spring to summer • Evergreen foliage has chocolate inlay • 30–45 cm high, 30–40 cm wide

'**Heart of Darkness**' • White flowers in late spring to summer • Silver-grey, maroon foliage • 30–45 cm high, 30–40 cm wide

'**Kimono**' • Tawny flowers in late spring to summer • Silvery foliage with purple veins • 30–45 cm high, 30–40 cm wide

'**Strike It Rich Gold**' • Flowers in summer • Lime-gold foliage with purple-tinged centre vein • 25–40 cm high, 30–40 cm wide

'**Sunspot**' • Pink flowers in late spring to summer • Electric yellow foliage with red centre patch • 30–45 cm high, 30–40 cm wide

'**Viking Ship**' • Coral-pink flowers in late spring to summer • Maple leaf–shaped, silvery, evergreen foliage • 30–45 cm high, 30–40 cm wide

Heucherella alba
'**Bridget Bloom**' • Shell-pink flowers in early spring to summer • Evergreen foliage • 30–45 cm high, 30–40 cm wide

'**Pink Frost**' • Pink flowers in early spring to summer • Evergreen foliage • 30–60 cm high, 30–40 cm wide

'**Rosalie**' • Ice-pink flowers in late spring to summer • Evergreen foliage with dark patch • 30–45 cm high, 30–40 cm wide

Hibiscus
p. 416

Genus Information
Origin: temperate and tropical regions
Selected Common Names: common rose mallow, hibiscus
Nomenclature: From the Greek name for mallow.

General Features
Height: 90–150 cm high
Spread: 45–75 cm wide
Habit: short-lived, clump-forming, woody perennial
Flowers: late summer to fall
Foliage: very slow to emerge in spring (as late as July in colder climates)
Hardiness: D
Warnings: prone to aphids; not prone to diseases
Expert Advice: Performs best in long, hot summers. Gardeners often mistakenly think the plant has not overwintered. Mulch for winter. Plant against the south side of a building.

Growing Requirements
Light: sun
Soil: moist, organic, well-drained soil
Location: mixed borders
Propagation: seed; division; cuttings
Expert Advice: Sow seed in spring at 13–18°C. Divide in spring. Take semi-ripe cuttings in summer.

Buying Considerations

Professionals
Popularity: relatively unknown
Availability: occasionally available as finished product and bare root
Size to Sell: sells best in smaller sizes (when blooming) as it matures fast
On the Shelf: rapidly overgrows pot
Shrinkage: low; requires little maintenance

Collectors
Popularity: not generally of interest to collectors

Gardeners
Ease of Growth: mostly difficult to grow as it needs close attention to growing conditions
Start with: one small plant for feature plant

On the Market

Hibiscus

'Kopper King' • Red-eyed, white flowers in late summer to fall • Coppery foliage • 90–120 cm high, 45–60 cm wide

'Old Yella' • Pale-yellow flowers in late summer to fall • 90–120 cm high, 45–60 cm wide

Hibiscus moscheutos

White, pink or rose flowers in late summer to fall • 1–1.5 m high, 50–75 cm wide

'Blue River II' • Large, white flowers in late summer to fall • 90–120 cm high, 45–60 cm wide

'Lady Baltimore' • Large, pink flowers in late summer to fall • 90–120 cm high, 45–60 cm wide

'Lord Baltimore' • Large, red flowers in late summer to fall • 90–120 cm high, 45–60 cm wide

Hierochloe
p. 417

Genus Information
Origin: North America and Eurasia
Selected Common Names: sweet grass
Nomenclature: From the Greek *hieros* (sacred) and *chloe* (grass).
Other Uses: It was used by native peoples as incense and to make baskets.
Notes: It is not grown for its ornamental qualities, but rather for its association with the culture of native peoples. It is also grown for ceremonial purposes.

General Features
Height: 45–60 cm high
Spread: 45–60+ cm wide
Habit: weedy, spreading, rhizomatous native grass
Foliage: quack grass-like; scented when crushed
Hardiness: B–C
Warnings: prone to aphids and rust; invasive (keep contained to prevent spread)
Expert Advice: This grass is not really grown for the ornamental garden.

Growing Requirements
Light: sun
Soil: moist soil; drought tolerant; tolerates poor soil
Location: native plant gardens
Propagation: seed; division

Buying Considerations

Professionals
Popularity: relatively unknown as a foliage plant
Availability: occasionally available as finished product
Size to Sell: sells best in smaller sizes as it matures fast
On the Shelf: low ornamental appeal; rapidly overgrows pot; prone to rust in pot
Shrinkage: low; requires little maintenance

Collectors
Popularity: not generally of interest to collectors

Gardeners
Ease of Growth: very easy to grow
Start with: one small plant for feature plant

What to Try First ...
Hierochloe odorata

On the Market

Hierochloe odorata
Aromatic foliage • 45–60 cm high, 45–60+ cm wide

Holcus
p. 417

Genus Information
Origin: Europe, temperate Asia and Africa
Selected Common Names: creeping soft grass, velvet grass, Yorkshire fog
Nomenclature: From the Greek *holkos*, a type of cereal.

General Features
Height: 30–100 cm high
Spread: 40–60+ cm wide
Habit: rhizomatous, creeping annual or perennial grass
Flowers: summer
Foliage: soft, velvety; solid green or variegated
Hardiness: C
Warnings: prone to aphids and rust; invasive (deadhead and contain to prevent spread)

Growing Requirements
Light: sun
Soil: moist to wet soil
Location: avoid sunny, hot, dry areas
Propagation: seed (self-sows readily); division
Expert Advice: An excellent groundcover if contained. Seedlings from the variegated *H. mollis* will be solid green. Propagate by division only for this type.

Buying Considerations

Professionals

Popularity: relatively unknown as a foliage plant
Availability: occasionally available as finished product
Size to Sell: sells best in smaller sizes as it matures fast
On the Shelf: high ornamental appeal; rapidly overgrows pot
Shrinkage: high; sensitive to underwatering

Collectors

Popularity: not generally of interest to collectors

Gardeners

Ease of Growth: very easy to grow
Start with: one small plant for feature plant

What to Try First ...

Holcus mollis 'Aureovariegatus', *Holcus mollis* 'Variegatus'

On the Market

Holcus lanatus
'Variegatus' • Pale green-and-white, pink-tinted foliage • 75–100 cm high, 45–60 cm wide

Holcus mollis
'Aureovariegatus' • White to green plumes in summer • Cream-and-green foliage • 30–45 cm high, 40–60+ cm wide
'Variegatus' (Albovariegatus) • White to green plumes in summer • White-and-green foliage • 30–45 cm high, 40–60+ cm wide

Horminum

Genus Information

Origin: Pyrenees
Selected Common Names: dragon's mouth
Nomenclature: From the Greek *hormao* (excite), referring to its use as an aphrodisiac.

General Features

Height: 20–30 cm high
Spread: 20–30 cm wide
Habit: low-growing, creeping rhizomatous perennial
Flowers: violet spikes; short blooming period; summer
Foliage: dark-green; basal rosettes
Hardiness: D
Warnings: prone to aphids and slugs

Growing Requirements

Light: sun
Soil: moist, moderately fertile, well-drained, neutral to alkaline soil
Location: mixed borders; rock gardens
Propagation: seed (self-sows readily); division
Expert Advice: Best propagated from seed in autumn. Divide in spring.

Buying Considerations

Professionals

Popularity: relatively unknown
Availability: occasionally available from specialty growers
Size to Sell: sells best in smaller sizes (when blooming) as it matures fast
On the Shelf: rapidly overgrows pot
Shrinkage: low; requires little maintenance

Collectors

Popularity: not generally of interest to collectors

Gardeners

Ease of Growth: mostly easy to grow
Start with: one small plant for feature plant

What to Try First ...

Horminum pyrenaicum

On the Market

Horminum pyrenaicum
Rich-purple to blue flowers in summer • 20–30 cm high, 20–30 cm wide

Hosta p. 417

Genus Information

Origin: Japan, Korea and China.
Selected Common Names: hosta, funkia, plantain lily
Nomenclature: Named for Nicolaus Host, 1761–1834, physician to the Austrian Emperor.
Notes: This member of the lily family was called *Funkia* until the 1970s when *Hosta* became the only name. With hundreds of cultivars available, this hardy herbaceous perennial is grown in almost every temperate climate worldwide mainly for its foliage.

General Features

Height: 20–80 cm high
Spread: 15–150 cm wide
Habit: mounding, clump-forming, long-lived perennial
Flowers: lily-like, bell-shaped; white to lilac; (some) fragrant; stalks rise above foliage; summer
Foliage: yellows, greens to blue-greens; distinctive veining or variegation; narrow elliptic to very broad ovate or heart-shaped
Hardiness: B

Warnings: prone to aphids, spider mites and slugs
Expert Advice: Excellent feature plants that do not require dividing to maintain vigour. For deep shade, select a *Hosta* with large, dark-green or blue leaves. For a sunnier site, choose a *Hosta* with yellow or creamy-white variegation. It is slow to emerge in spring, but it will provide plenty of enjoyment for the entire growing season. Some consider the flowers to be insignificant, and cut them back to keep the plant neat and tidy.

Growing Requirements

Light: shade to a.m. sun; filtered sun; tolerates deep shade but grows best in dappled light
Soil: deep, moist, fertile, organic, well-drained soil; tolerant of wide range of soils
Location: rock gardens; mixed borders; woodland gardens; under plantings
Propagation: seed for species; division

Buying Considerations

Professionals

Popularity: popular, old-fashioned, garden standard foliage plant; fast seller; has new varieties
Availability: readily available as finished product and bare root from specialty growers
Size to Sell: sells best in smaller sizes as it matures fast
On the Shelf: high ornamental appeal; keep stock rotated
Shrinkage: low; requires little maintenance

Collectors

Popularity: of interest to collectors—rare species and varieties, including many miniature and dwarf types

Gardeners

Ease of Growth: very easy to grow
Start with: one small plant for feature plant and several for mass plantings

What to Try First ...

Hosta 'Abiqua Drinking Gourd', *Hosta* 'August Moon', *Hosta* 'Blue Mammoth', *Hosta* 'Carol', *Hosta* 'Cherry Berry', *Hosta* 'Fire and Ice', *Hosta* 'Fortunei Albomarginata', *Hosta* 'Fragrant Blue', *Hosta* 'June'

On the Market

Hosta
'Abba Dabba Do' • Deep-green foliage with gold margins • 70 cm high, 1.5 m wide
'Abiqua Ariel' • Gold, puckered, thick foliage • 45 cm high, 95 cm wide
'Abiqua Blue Edger' • Blue-green, heart-shaped foliage • 20 cm high, 40 cm wide
'Abiqua Blue Krinkles' • Puckered, intense blue foliage • 45–60 cm high, 45–60 cm wide
'Abiqua Delight' • Green foliage with creamy-white margins • 40–50 cm high, 1 m wide
'Abiqua Drinking Gourd' • Large, cupped, thick, blue-green foliage • 60 cm high, 1 m wide
'Abiqua Hallucination' • Gold foliage with corrugated, green edges • 40 cm high, 45 cm wide
'Abiqua Moonbeam' • Green foliage with wide, gold margins • 50 cm high, 1.4 m wide
'Abiqua Parasol' • Blue-green foliage with ruffled margins • 65 cm high, 1.2 m wide
'Abiqua Recluse' • Large, golden-yellow foliage • 60 cm high, 1 m wide
'Abiqua Trumpet' • Cupped, blue-green foliage • 25 cm high, 55 cm wide
'Alex Summers' • Green-centred, gold-margined leaves • 80–85 cm high, 1.5 m wide
'Alvatine Taylor' • Blue-green foliage with wide, gold margins • 60 cm high, 1 m wide
'Antioch' • Lavender flowers in summer • Green foliage with white margins • 60 cm high, 1.4 m wide
'Aristocrat' • Blue-green foliage with creamy edge • 25–35 cm high, 45–55 cm wide
'August Moon' • Broad, golden foliage with good substance • 50 cm high, 1 m wide
'Baby Bunting' • White flowers in summer • Blue-green, heart-shaped foliage • 30 cm high, 65 cm wide
'Big Daddy' • Cupped, quilted, thick, blue-green foliage • 65 cm high, 1.5 m wide
'Birchwood Parky's Gold' • Lavender flowers in summer • Gold foliage • 45 cm high, 1 m wide
'Black Hills' • Shiny, dark-green, puckered, round foliage • 55 cm high, 1 m wide
'Blonde Elf' • Wavy, gold, lance-shaped foliage • 20 cm high, 60 cm wide
'Blue Angel' • Deep blue-green, thick foliage • 80 cm high, 1.5+ m wide
'Blue Cadet' • Blue-green, heart-shaped foliage • 40 cm high, 95 cm wide
'Blue Jay' • Deep blue, heart-shaped, cupped foliage • 40 cm high, 90 cm wide
'Blue Mammoth' • Blue-green, puckered, thick foliage • 85 cm high, 1.5 m wide

'Blue Seer' • Deep-blue, puckered foliage • 40–50 cm high, 45 cm wide

'Blue Umbrellas' • Shiny, dark-green, inversely cupped foliage • 85 cm high, 1.5+ m wide

'Blue Vision' • Intense blue, thick foliage • 65 cm high, 1 m wide

'Blue Wedgwood' • Thick, deep-blue, wedge-shaped foliage • 50 cm high, 95 cm wide

'Blue Whirls' • Lavender flowers in summer • Thick, wavy, blue-green foliage • 60 cm high, 1 m wide

'Bright Lights' • Mottled-yellow foliage with green edges • 50 cm high, 1 m wide

'Brim Cup' • Cupped, green foliage edged in white • 35 cm high, 1 m wide

'Cadillac' • Corrugated, gold-centred leaves with wide, green edges • 40–50 cm high, 50 cm wide

'Camelot' • Heart-shaped, thick, bright-blue foliage • 45 cm high, 95 cm wide

'Canadian Blue' • Blue-green, oval-shaped, thick foliage • 45 cm high, 45 cm wide

'Candy Hearts' • White flowers in summer • Heart-shaped, blue-green foliage • 45 cm high, 1 m wide

'Captain Kirk' • Gold-centred, wide, dark green leaves • 50–55 cm high, 1.5 m wide

'Carnival' • Lavender flowers in summer • Oval leaves with yellow edges • 45 cm high, 95 cm wide

'Carol' • Green foliage edged in cream • 55 cm high, 1.5 m wide

'Cherry Berry' • White-centred foliage with dark-green edges • 30 cm high, 70 cm wide

'Chinese Sunrise' (syn. *H. lancifolia* 'Chinese Sunrise') • Shiny, lemon-green foliage with green margins • 45 cm high, 95 cm wide

'Christmas Tree' • Corrugated, green foliage with creamy-white margins • 60 cm high, 1.5 m wide

'Colour Glory' • Greenish-yellow foliage with blue-green margins • 75 cm high, 1 m wide

'Crispula' • Green, wavy foliage edged in white • 65 cm high, 1.3 m wide

'Crowned Imperial' • Dark-green foliage with white margins • 65 cm high, 80 cm wide

'Crusader' • Dark-green foliage with white edges • 45 cm high, 1 m wide

'Cynthia' • Green foliage with chartreuse streaks • 70 cm high, 1.5 m wide

'Dancing in the Rain' • White-centred leaf with blue-green streaks and margins • 80–85 cm high, 1.5+ m wide

'Daybreak' • Shiny, gold foliage • 60 cm high, 1.5 m wide

'Decorata' • Matte, green foliage with silver edge • 40 cm high, 95 cm wide

'Dorset Blue' • Thick, corrugated, turquoise-blue foliage • 25 cm high, 60 cm wide

'Dream Weaver' • Cream foliage with wide, blue-green edge • 45–70 cm high, 70–80 cm wide

'Eleanor Lachman' • White-centred foliage with green margins • 25–30 cm high, 55–60 cm wide

'El Nino' • Lilac flowers in summer • Blue leaves with bright-white edge • 40–50 cm high, 45–60 cm wide

'Elisabeth' • Solid green foliage • 65 cm high, 95 cm wide

'Elizabeth Campbell' • Green-yellow foliage with deep-green margins • 30–45 cm high, 30–45 cm wide

'Embroidery' • Green foliage with puckered and twisted margins • 40 cm high, 75 cm wide

'Emerald Tiara' • Gold-centred foliage with green edges • 45 cm high, 90 cm wide

'Fair Maiden' • Heart-shaped, dark-green foliage with creamy-white margin • 40–60 cm high, 90–100 cm wide

'Feather Boa' • Yellow, wavy, narrow foliage • 30 cm high, 70 cm wide

'Fire and Ice' • White-centred, thick foliage with green edges • 20–25 cm high, 30–40 cm wide

'Fortunei Albomarginata' (Silver Crown) • Green foliage with white edges • 60 cm high, 1.3 m wide

'Fortunei Albopicta' • Gold-centred foliage with green margins • 60 cm high, 1 m wide

'Fortunei Aurea' • Gold-centred foliage that turns green • 50 cm high, 1 m wide

'Fortunei Aureomarginata' • Deep-green foliage with gold margins • 60 cm high, 1 m wide

'Fragrant Blue' • Heart-shaped, frosty blue-green foliage with fragrant flowers • 50 cm high, 1 m wide

H

'Fragrant Bouquet' • Apple-green foliage with creamy edges with fragrant flowers • 55 cm high, 1 m wide

'Francee' • Forest-green, heart-shaped foliage edged in white • 55 cm high, 1 m wide

'Fried Green Tomatoes' • Lavender flowers in summer • Rich-green, heart-shaped foliage • 65 cm high, 1.5 m wide

'Fringe Benefit' • Flowers in summer • Green foliage with creamy-white margins • 60 cm high, 90 cm wide

'Frosted Jade' • Heart-shaped, grey-green foliage with white margins • 80 cm high, 1.5 m wide

'Ginko Craig' • Narrow, dark-green foliage with white edges • 35 cm high, 1 m wide

'Gloriosa' • Green foliage with thin, white edges • 45 cm high, 1 m wide

'Gold Edger' • Heart-shaped, light-green, aging to gold, foliage • 35 cm high, 95 cm wide

'Gold Standard' • Light-green foliage edged in green • 55 cm high, 1.5 m wide

'Golden Medallion' • Bright-gold, corrugated, thick foliage • 40 cm high, 95 cm wide

'Golden Tiara' • Light-green foliage with gold margins • 40 cm high, 95 cm wide

'Grand Master' • Blue-green foliage with white margins • 60 cm high, 95 cm wide

'Grand Tiara' • Dark-green foliage with wide, gold margins • 40 cm high, 1 m wide

'Great American Expectations' • Yellow leaves with wide, blue-green edges • 75 cm high, 1.5 m wide

'Great Expectations' • Thick, green, corrugated foliage with cream centres • 75 cm high, 1.5 m wide

'Green Acres' • Heart-shaped, green, wavy foliage • 90 cm high, 1.5+ m wide

'Ground Master' • Long, green foliage with creamy-white edges • 40 cm high, 95 cm wide

'Guacamole' • Apple-green foliage edged in dark-green • 60 cm high, 1 m wide

'Hadspen Blue' • Blue-green, thick foliage • 45 cm high, 1 m wide

'Hadspen Hawk' • Thick, blue-green, slightly wavy foliage • 45 cm high, 1 m wide

'Halcyon' • Thick, spear-shaped, ribbed, blue-green foliage • 45 cm high, 95 cm wide

'Hi Ho Silver' • Lance-shaped, green foliage with white edges • 20–25 cm high, 20–30 cm wide

'Ice Cream' • Green foliage with lighter-green edges • 20–30 cm high, 45–60 cm wide

'Independence' • Dark-green foliage with creamy-white, green-speckled margins • 55–60 cm high, 40–50 cm wide

'Inniswood' • Gold, corrugated foliage with green margins • 55 cm high, 1 m wide

'Invincible' • Fragrant, lilac flowers in summer • Shiny, bright-green foliage • 50 cm high, 1 m wide

'Iona' • Lavender flowers in summer • Green foliage with wide, yellowish margin • 45–60 cm high, 1–1.5 m wide

'Island Charm' • Green-edged, yellow-centred foliage • 25 cm high, 55 cm wide

'Jade Lancer' • Large, green foliage with white edges • 60 cm high, 1.5+ m wide

'Jade Scepter' • Green leaves • 40 cm high, 1 m wide

'Janet' • Gold foliage with slender, green margins • 45 cm high, 95 cm wide

'Joker' • Grey-green foliage with chartreuse edge • 45–60 cm high, 60 cm wide

'June' • Thick, narrow, gold-centred foliage with blue-green margins • 40 cm high, 95 cm wide

'Kifukurin Ko Mame' • Green foliage with gold margins • 8 cm high, 20 cm wide

'King Tut' • Thick, heart-shaped, corrugated, bright-gold foliage • 50 cm high, 1 m wide

'Kirishima' • Purple flowers in summer • Spear-shaped, light-green foliage • 20 cm high, 35–45 cm wide

'Knockout' • Puckered, blue-green foliage with cream margins • 45 cm high, 85 cm wide

'Krossa Regal' • Greyish, blue-green, thick foliage • 85 cm high, 1.5 m wide

'Lakeport Blue' • Blue-green, thick foliage, heavily corrugated • 70 cm high, 1.5 m wide

'Lakeside Kaleidoscope' • Streaked, blue-green foliage with white margin • 20–30 cm high, 35–40 cm wide

'Leather Sheen' • Shiny, dark-green, narrow foliage • 45 cm high, 1 m wide

'Lemon Lime' • Lavender flowers in summer • Narrow, wavy, lemon-green foliage • 30 cm high, 90 cm wide

'Liberty' • Thick, green leaves with wide yellow margins, fading to white • 65–70 cm high, 1.5 m+ wide

'Little Sunspot' • Gold-centred foliage with dark-green margin • 30–40 cm high, 60–70 cm wide

'Love Pat' • Thick, quilted, blue foliage • 50 cm high, 95 cm wide

'Loyalist' • White-centred foliage with green edges • 30–45 cm high, 40–60 cm wide

'Maruba Iwa' (syn. *H. longipes* 'Maruba Iwa') • Round, green, thick, wavy foliage • 20 cm high, 50 cm wide

'Mary Marie Ann' • Yellow-green foliage with wavy, green margins • 35 cm high, 75 cm wide

'Masquerade' • White-centred foliage with green edges • 15 cm high, 45 cm wide

'Medusa' • Narrow, white-centred foliage with green margins • 15 cm high, 40 cm wide

'Midas Touch' • Cupped, thick, corrugated, bright-gold foliage • 55 cm high, 100 cm wide

'Mildred Seaver' • Green foliage with creamy-white edges • 70 cm high, 1.5 m wide

'Minuteman' • Dark-green foliage with white margin • 60 cm high, 1 m wide

'Morning Light' • Lavender flowers in summer • Gold leaves with irregular, green edges • 50–60 cm high, 50–75 cm wide

'Mr. Big' • Large, blue-green, seer-suckered foliage • 90 cm high, 90 cm wide

'Night Before Christmas' • White-centred foliage with green margins • 65 cm high, 1.5 m wide

'On Stage' • Yellow foliage with irregular, green edges • 35 cm high, 60 cm wide

'Pacific Blue Edger' • Lavender flowers in summer • Heart-shaped, blue-green foliage • 30–45 cm high, 60 cm wide

'Pandora's Box' • White-centred foliage with green edges • 10 cm high, 25 cm wide

'Paradigm' • Lavender flowers in summer • Gold foliage with green margins • 45–60 cm high, 30–45 cm wide

'Paradise Joyce' • Gold-centred foliage with blue-green edges • 40–50 cm high, 40–60 cm wide

'Patriot' • Dark-green foliage with white margins • 60 cm high, 1 m wide

'Paul's Glory' • Golden, heart-shaped foliage with blue-green edges • 65 cm high, 1.3 m wide

'Peedee Gold Flash' • Narrow, gold-centred, green foliage • 30 cm high, 70 cm wide

'Perry's True Blue' • Powder-blue, corrugated foliage • 75 cm high, 1.5+ m wide

'Piedmont Gold' • Bright-gold foliage • 65 cm high, 1.5 m wide

'Pineapple Poll' • Lavender flowers in summer • Narrow, rippled, green foliage • 50 cm high, 1.5+ m wide

'Pineapple Upsidedown Cake' • Narrow, green-gold foliage with rippled, green margins • 30–45 cm high, 90–150 cm wide

'Pizzazz' • Blue, thick foliage with wavy, white edges • 55 cm high, 1 m wide

'Platinum Tiara' • Lilac flowers in summer • Chartreuse foliage with white edges • 30 cm high, 75 cm wide

'Potomac Pride' • Shiny, dark-green, puckered foliage • 60 cm high, 1 m wide

'Queen Josephine' • Glossy, green, thick foliage with yellow edges • 45 cm high, 95 cm wide

'Red October' • Lavender flowers in summer • Green foliage with prominent red stems • 20–30 cm high, 45–60 cm wide

'Regal Splendor' • Thick, frosty-blue foliage with creamy-white margins • 75 cm high, 1.5+ m wide

'Remember Me' • White-centred, green foliage • 30 cm high, 40–45 cm wide

'Reversed' • Creamy-white foliage with green margins • 40 cm high, 1 m wide

'Revolution' • Yellow-green leaves with grey-blue edges • 30–40 cm high, 40–50 cm wide

'Robert Frost' • Thick, blue-green foliage with wide, streaky, white margins • 60 cm high, 1.5 m wide

'Rock Princess' • Purple flowers in summer • Green foliage • 10–20 cm high, 60–75 cm wide

'Royal Standard' • Shiny, bright-green foliage • 65 cm high, 1.5 m wide

'Ryan's Big One' • White flowers in summer • Blue-green, corrugated foliage • 70 cm high, 1.5+ m wide

'Sagae' (syn. *H. fluctuans* 'Variegated') • Thick, green foliage with creamy-yellow edges • 80 cm high, 1.5+ m wide

H

'Saint Elmo's Fire' • Gold foliage with white edges • 45 cm high, 45 cm wide

'Saishu Jima' • Purple flowers in summer • Narrow, wavy, green foliage • 20 cm high, 50 cm wide

'Sea Lotus Leaf' • Blue-green, thick, corrugated, cupped foliage • 65 cm high, 1.5 m wide

'Sea Thunder' • Cream-centred foliage with green-streaked margins • 40 cm high, 85 cm wide

'September Sun' • Blooms in summer • Gold-centred foliage with green edges • 55 cm high, 1 m wide

'Shade Fanfare' • Blooms in summer • Chartreuse foliage with creamy margins • 55 cm high, 1.2 m wide

'Sharmon' • Blooms in summer • Green foliage with a chartreuse centre • 60 cm high, 1 m wide

'So Sweet' • Fragrant flowers • Grass-green foliage with white edges • 55 cm high, 1 m wide

'Spilt Milk' • White streaks on green, heart-shaped, thick foliage • 60 cm high, 1 m wide

'Spritzer' • Shiny, gold foliage with lime-green edges • 55 cm high, 1 m wide

'Stained Glass' • Gold leaves with wide, dark-green margins • 35–40 cm high, 1 m wide

'Stiletto' • Narrow, wavy, green foliage with white edges • 30 cm high, 80 cm wide

'Striptease' • Gold-centred leaf with wide, green margin • 50 cm high, 1 m wide

'Sugar and Cream' • Wavy, green foliage with creamy edges • 70 cm high, 1.5 m wide

'Sum and Substance' • Thick, lemon-green, cupped foliage • 75 cm high, 1.5+ m wide

'Sum of All' • Green-centred foliage with wide, gold edges • 90–150 cm high, 80–150+ cm wide

'Summer Music' • White-centred foliage with chartreuse margins • 45 cm high, 95 cm wide

'Sun Power' • Narrow, wavy, twisted, golden foliage • 70 cm high, 1.5+ m wide

'Sunshine Glory' • Gold-centred foliage with creamy edges • 70 cm high, 1.5 m wide

'Tambourine' • Heart-shaped, green foliage with white edges • 55 cm high, 1 m wide

'Tattoo' • Gold-centred foliage with lime-green edges • 20–30 cm high, 60–90 cm wide

'Teaspoon' • Cupped-green foliage on long stems (resembles a teaspoon) • 25–30 cm high, 60 cm wide

'Tiny Tears' • Purple flowers in summer • Green, teardrop-shaped foliage • 15 cm high, 55 cm wide

'Titanic' • Green-centred foliage with a wide yellow-green margin • 80 cm-1 m high, 1.5 m+ wide

'Tokudama' • Thick, cupped, seer-suckered, blue foliage • 45 cm high, 95 cm wide

'Tokudama Aureonebulosa' • Pale-yellow foliage with sea-green margins • 45 cm high, 95 cm wide

'Tokudama Flavocircinalis' • Blue-green foliage with chartreuse margins • 45 cm high, 1 m wide

'Tortifrons' • Lilac flowers in summer • Twisted, narrow, green foliage • Collector's plant • 20 cm high, 45 cm wide

'Tot Tot' • Dwarf variety with small, green leaves • 20 cm high, 55 cm wide

'True Blue' • Blue-green foliage • 60 cm high, 1.2 m wide

'Undulata' • White-centred foliage with green margins • 30 cm high, 80 cm wide

'Undulata Albomarginata' • Olive-green foliage with white edges • 45 cm high, 1 m wide

'Undulata Univittata' • Twisted, green foliage with white centres • 45 cm high, 1 m wide

'Uzo-no-Mai' • Lilac flowers in summer • Tiny rosettes of green foliage • Collector's plant • 4 cm high, 15 cm wide

'Vanilla Cream' • Lavender flowers in summer • Light-green to bright-gold foliage • 30 cm high, 65 cm wide

'Warwick Delight' • Creamy-white-centred foliage with dark-green edges • 25–40 cm high, 30–45 cm wide

'Whirlwind' • Wavy foliage with greenish-white centre and green margins • 50 cm high, 95 cm wide

'White Christmas' • White-centred foliage with wavy, green edges • 40 cm high, 90 cm wide

'Wide Brim' • Green-centred foliage with creamy margins • 45 cm high, 1 m wide

'Winfield Blue' • Blue-green foliage • 45 cm high, 1 m wide

'Wolverine' • Blue foliage edged in gold • 45 cm high, 85 cm wide

'Woolly Mammoth' • Puckered, thick, blue-green foliage with a wide gold margin • 70–75 cm high, 1–1.5 m wide

'Yellow River' • Dark-green foliage with yellow edges • 75 cm high, 1.5+ m wide

'Zager's White Edge' • Forest-green foliage with wide, white edges • 50 cm high, 1 m wide

Hosta 'Zounds' • Thick, glossy, puckered, golden foliage • 55 cm high, 1 m wide

Hosta kikutii
'Kifukurin Hyuga' • Green foliage with gold margins • 45 cm high, 70–85 cm wide

Hosta lancifolia
Lavender flowers in summer • Shiny, narrow, green foliage • 50 cm high, 95 cm wide

Hosta longissima
Violet flowers in summer • Narrow, glossy, dark-green foliage • 35 cm high, 75 cm wide

Hosta minor (Keirin Giboshi)
Green foliage • 20 cm high, 55 cm wide

Hosta minuta
Green foliage • 15–20 cm high, 60–75 cm wide

Hosta montana
'Aureomarginata' • Blooms in summer • Green foliage with golden-yellow margins • 70 cm high, 1.5+ m wide

'Mountain Snow' • Green foliage with white margins • 70–75 cm high, 1.5m+ wide

Hosta montana macrophylla
Heart-shaped, green foliage, deeply veined • 90 cm high, 1.5+ m wide

Hosta nakaiana (Kanzashi Giboshi)
Heart-shaped, green foliage • 30 cm high, 80 cm wide

Hosta plantaginea
'Aphrodite' • Fragrant, double flowers in summer • Shiny, green foliage • 60 cm high, 1.5 m wide

Hosta pygmaea
Mauve flowers in summer • Green foliage • 25 cm high, 15–20 cm wide

Hosta rectifolia
'Chionea' • Purple flowers in summer • Green foliage with white edges • 45–60 cm high, 45 cm wide

Hosta sieboldiana (To Giboshi)
White flowers in summer • Thick, green foliage • 60 cm high, 1.5+ m wide

'Blue Giant' • Large, blue-toned foliage • 60 cm high, 60–90 cm wide

'Elegans' • Waxy, puckered, thick, blue-grey foliage • 70 cm high, 1.5 m wide

'Frances Williams' • Thick, puckered, blue-green foliage with gold margins • 70 cm high, 1.5 m wide

'Golden Sunburst' • Gold, thick, heavily corrugated foliage • 50 cm high, 1 m wide

'Northern Exposure' • Puckered, blue foliage with creamy margins • 70 cm high, 1.5+ m wide

'Northern Halo' • Blue-green, thick, corrugated foliage with white edges • 70 cm high, 1.5+ m wide

Hosta sieboldii
'Kabitan' • Narrow, lemon-yellow foliage with green margins • 35 cm high, 80 cm wide

'Shiro Kabitan' (Silver Kabitan) • Narrow, white-centred, green foliage • 15 cm high, 45 cm wide

Hosta tsushimensis (Tsushima Giboshi)
Purple flowers in summer • Wavy, green foliage • 30 cm high, 80 cm wide

Hosta ventricosa (Murasaki Giboshi)
Lavender flowers in summer • Shiny, dark-green foliage • 55 cm high, 1 m wide

'Aureomaculata' • Gold-centred foliage with green edges • 45 cm high, 70 cm wide

'Aureomarginata' • Green foliage with cream-white margins • 55 cm high, 1 m wide

Hosta venusta (Otome Giboshi)
Mauve flowers in summer • Teardrop-shaped, olive-green foliage • 20 cm high, 75 cm wide

'Cat's Eyes' • Greenish-yellow, teardrop-shaped foliage with green margins • 5 cm high, 20 cm wide

Houstonia

p. 417

Genus Information

Origin: North America
Selected Common Names: mountain bluet
Nomenclature: Named for Dr. William Houston, 1695–1733, a British botanist.
Notes: Some botanists still lump these species in with *Hedyotis*.

General Features

Height: 10–45 cm high
Spread: 10–45 cm wide
Habit: clump- to mat-forming perennial
Flowers: dainty; blue or white; long blooming; spring to summer; deadhead to extend blooming period

Foliage: tiny
Hardiness: D
Warnings: prone to aphids; not prone to diseases

Growing Requirements
Light: shade
Soil: lean, moist, organic soil
Location: rock crevices
Propagation: seed; division
Expert Advice: Prefers cool roots and lean soil, which promotes a denser growth habit.

Buying Considerations
Professionals
Popularity: gaining popularity; fast seller in bloom
Availability: generally available as finished product and bare root from specialty growers
Size to Sell: sells best in smaller sizes (when blooming) as it matures fast
On the Shelf: rapidly overgrows pot
Shrinkage: low; requires little maintenance
Collectors
Popularity: not generally of interest to collectors
Gardeners
Ease of Growth: mostly easy to grow
Start with: one small plant for feature plant and several for mass plantings
What to Try First ...
Houstonia caerulea, Houstonia caerulea var. *alba, Houstonia michauxii*

On the Market
Houstonia acerosa
Cream flowers in spring to summer •
10–15 cm high, 10–15 cm wide
Houstonia caerulea
Blue star flowers in spring to summer •
10–15 cm high, 25–40 cm wide
Houstonia caerulea var. *alba*
White star flowers in spring to summer •
10–15 cm high, 25–40 cm wide
Houstonia michauxii (syn. *H. serpyllifolia*)
Deep-blue star flowers in spring to summer
• 10–15 cm high, 25–40 cm wide
'Fred Mullard' (Fred Millard, Millard's Variety) • Clear-blue star flowers in spring to summer • 10–15 cm high, 25–40 cm wide
Houstonia purpurea var. *tenuifolia*
White, lilac or purple flowers in spring to summer • 25–45 cm high, 40–45 cm wide

Humulus p. 417

Genus Information
Origin: North America, Europe and Asia
Selected Common Names: bear hops, common hops, hop vine
Nomenclature: From the Latin *humus* (soil), referring to the low growth habit.
Other Uses: *Humulus* was first used in beer-making in 14th-century Flanders. It reached Britain 2 centuries later where it was used to cure insomnia and calm nervous stomachs. Young shoots can be used in salads or cooked and used like spinach.

General Features
Height: 2–6 m high
Spread: 2–3 m or more wide
Habit: quick-growing, climbing perennial
Flowers: loose bunches (male) or yellowish-green, cone-like (female); summer; good for drying; good for brewing beer
Foliage: green to gold; rough
Hardiness: C
Warnings: prone to powdery mildew, aphids and leaf hoppers; may choke out trees that it climbs on
Expert Advice: Monecious. A rapid spreader that grows outward as much as it climbs. A quick-covering vine; useful as a groundcover on banks. It dies back to the ground each year but quickly springs up to cover supports. Tender tips are edible. Only the female plants have cones (used for making beer) but there is no way to sex the plants ahead of time.

Growing Requirements
Light: sun
Soil: moderately fertile, moist, well-drained soil; tolerates poor soil; drought tolerant
Location: groundcover on banks and slopes; on trellises, pergolas, walls, unsightly structures
Propagation: seed; cuttings
Expert Advice: Germinate seed in spring at 15–18°C. Take root or green shoot cuttings in midsummer.

Buying Considerations
Professionals
Popularity: popular, old-fashioned, garden standard foliage plant
Availability: readily available as finished product and bare root
Size to Sell: sells best in smaller sizes as it matures fast
On the Shelf: rapidly overgrows pot
Shrinkage: low; requires little maintenance
Collectors
Popularity: not generally of interest to collectors

On the Market

Humulus lupulus
Green, female, cone-like flowers in summer • Coarse, large, light-green foliage • 4–6 m high, 2–3+ m wide
'Aureus' • Cone-like, green, female flowers in summer • Coarse, large, gold-yellow foliage • 3–4 m high, 2–3+ m wide
'Magnum' • Cone-like, green, female flowers in summer • 3–4 m high, 2–3+ m wide
'Nordbrau' • Cone-like, green, female flowers in summer • 4–6 m high, 2–3+ m wide
'Taff's Variegated' • Cone-like, green, female flowers in summer • Variegated foliage • 2–3 m high, 2–3+ m wide
'Target' • Cone-like, green, female flowers in summer • 4–6 m high, 2–3+ m wide
'Yeoman' • Cone-like, green, female flowers in summer • 4–6 m high, 2–3+ m wide

Hypericum p. 417 📷

Genus Information

Origin: worldwide, except in Arctic and desert regions
Selected Common Names: St. John's wort
Nomenclature: From the Greek *hyper* (above) and *eikon* (image), the names used by Dioscorides.
Notes: The magical properties of this plant were supposed to drive away evil spirits through the smell. The yellow flower petals turn red when crushed, which, in folklore, indicated blood. Many of these plants flowered around June 24, the date St. John was beheaded, which gave rise to the common name "St. John's wort" or herb of St. John. It is a large, diverse genus.

General Features

Height: 2–90 cm high
Spread: 30–60 cm wide
Habit: shrubby, spreading groundcover perennial
Flowers: tiny; yellow; summer; long-blooming
Foliage: (most) downy; grey-green
Hardiness: C
Warnings: prone to aphids; not prone to diseases; (some) aggressive spreaders (contain and deadhead to prevent spread)

Expert Advice: Suitable for use in a variety of situations—very low-maintenance. Some varieties produce red berries in fall.

Growing Requirements

Light: sun or shade
Soil: moderately fertile, moist, sharply drained soil; tolerates poor soil; drought tolerant
Location: mixed borders; rock gardens
Propagation: seed (self-sows); division; semi-ripe cuttings

Buying Considerations

Professionals

Popularity: gaining popularity
Availability: occasionally available from specialty growers
Size to Sell: sells best in smaller sizes (when blooming) as it matures fast
On the Shelf: rapidly overgrows pot
Shrinkage: low; requires little maintenance

H

Collectors

Popularity: not generally of interest to collectors (although it is of interest to herbalists)

Gardeners

Ease of Growth: very easy to grow
Start with: one small plant for feature plant and several for mass plantings

What to Try First ...

Hypericum kiusianum var. *yakusimense*, *Hypericum perforatum*

On the Market

Hypericum androsaemum
Reddish-yellow flowers in summer • 30–75 cm high, 45–60 cm wide

Hypericum ascyron
Bright-yellow flowers in summer • 45–90 cm high, 30–45 cm wide

Hypericum buckleyi
Yellow flowers in summer • 20–30 cm high, 45–60+ cm wide

Hypericum cerastioides
Bright-yellow flowers in midsummer • 10–20 cm high, 30–45+ cm wide

Hypericum kiusianum var. *yakusimense* (syn. *H. yakusimense*)
Yellow flowers in summer • 2–8 cm high, 30–45+ cm wide

Hypericum perforatum
Bright-yellow flowers in summer • 60–90 cm high, 45–60+ cm wide

Hypsela

p. 417

Genus Information

Origin: Andes, New Zealand and Australia
Selected Common Names: unknown
Nomenclature: From the Greek *hypselos* (high), referring to the species found in the Andes.

General Features

Height: 2–5 cm high
Spread: 30–45 cm wide
Habit: low, spreading, creeping perennial
Flowers: white to pale pink; star-like; early summer
Foliage: mid- to dark-green
Hardiness: D
Warnings: not prone to insects or disease

Growing Requirements

Light: shade
Soil: evenly moist, well-drained soil
Location: shady rock gardens; between paving stones
Propagation: seed; division

Buying Considerations

Professionals
Popularity: relatively unknown
Availability: occasionally available as bare root from specialty growers
Size to Sell: sells best in smaller sizes as it matures fast
On the Shelf: rapidly overgrows pot
Shrinkage: low; requires little maintenance

Collectors
Popularity: of interest to collectors—rare

Gardeners
Ease of Growth: mostly easy to grow
Start with: one small plant for feature plant and several for mass plantings

What to Try First ...
Hypsela reniformis

On the Market

Hypsela reniformis **(syn. *H. longiflora*)**
White to pale-pink flowers in early summer
• 2–5 cm high, 30–45+ cm wide

Hyssopus

p. 417

Genus Information

Origin: Mediterranean to central Asia
Selected Common Names: hyssop
Nomenclature: From the Greek name used by Dioscorides.
Notes: This genus includes herbaceous perennials and semi-evergreen to evergreen shrubs grown for their aromatic foliage and flowers.

General Features

Height: 60 cm
Spread: 60 cm
Habit: dense, upright, shrubby perennial
Flowers: dark-blue; on slender spikes; fragrant; midsummer to fall; attracts bees and butterflies
Foliage: blue-green; aromatic (mint-like)
Hardiness: C
Warnings: not prone to pests or diseases
Expert Advice: *Hyssopus* is an excellent alternative to lavender on the Prairies. *H. officinalis* ssp. *aristatus* makes a striking and unusual hedge.

Growing Requirements

Light: sun
Soil: fertile, well-drained, acid-free soil; tolerant of sandy, dry soil
Location: wild gardens; meadows; rock garden; herb garden
Propagation: seed; cuttings
Expert Advice: Sow seeds in autumn. Take softwood cuttings in summer.

Buying Considerations

Professionals
Popularity: relatively unknown
Availability: occasionally available as finished product
Size to Sell: sells best in smaller sizes (when blooming) as it matures fast
On the Shelf: rapidly overgrows pot
Shrinkage: low shrinkage; requires little maintenance

Collectors
Popularity: not generally of interest to collectors

Gardeners
Ease of growth: very easy to grow
Start with: one small plant for feature plant and several for mass plantings

What to Try First ...
Hyssopus officinalis ssp. *aristatus*

On the Market

Hyssopus officinalis ssp. *aristatus*
Dark-blue flower spikes in midsummer to fall • Aromatic foliage • 60 cm high, 60 cm wide

Iberis

p. 417

Genus Information

Origin: Southern Europe, Western Asia and Iberia
Selected Common Names: candytuft, evergreen candytuft
Nomenclature: From Iberia in Spain, where most of the species occur.

General Features

Height: 5–30 cm
Spread: 15–45 cm
Habit: low-growing, compact, shrubby perennial
Flowers: white to lilac; spring; deadhead flowers to keep plant compact
Foliage: evergreen; prone to desiccation
Hardiness: C–D
Warnings: prone to aphids; not prone to diseases
Expert Advice: Short-lived if not provided with snow cover in winter. Provides a mass of colour in early spring.

Growing Requirements

Light: sun
Soil: moist, poor to moderately fertile, well-drained, neutral to alkaline soil
Location: rock gardens; walls
Propagation: seed; cuttings
Expert Advice: Seed in fall. Take softwood cuttings in late spring and semi-ripe cuttings in summer.

Buying Considerations

Professionals

Popularity: popular, old-fashioned garden standard
Availability: readily available as finished product
Size to Sell: sells best in smaller sizes (when blooming) as it matures fast
On the Shelf: deadhead regularly
Shrinkage: low shrinkage; requires little maintenance; after blooming it tends to lose foliage making it unsaleable

Collectors

Popularity: not generally of interest to collectors

Gardeners

Ease of growth: very easy to grow
Start with: one small plant for feature plant and several for mass plantings

What to Try First ...

Iberis saxatilis, Iberis sempervirens, Iberis sempervirens 'Purity', *Iberis sempervirens* 'Weisser Zwerg'

On the Market

Iberis aurosiaca
'**Sweetheart**' • Lilac-pink flowers in summer • Evergreen foliage • 5–15 cm high, 20–30 cm wide

Iberis gibraltarica
Lilac flowers in late spring to summer • Evergreen foliage • 15–30 cm high, 30–45 cm wide

Iberis pruitii (syn. *I. candolleana*)
White flowers in spring • Evergreen foliage • 5–15 cm high, 15–20 cm wide

Iberis saxatilis
White flowers in spring • Evergreen foliage • 15 cm high, 30 cm wide

Iberis sayana
White flowers in spring • Evergreen foliage • 5–10 cm high, 20–30 cm wide

Iberis sempervirens
White flowers, sometimes flushed with lilac, in spring • Evergreen foliage • 15–30 cm high, 30–45 cm wide

'**Purity**' • Large, white flowers in spring • Evergreen foliage • 10–20 cm high, 20–30 cm wide

'**Schneeflocke**' (**Snowflake**) • White flowers in spring • Evergreen • 15–25 cm high, 30–45 cm wide

'**Weisser Zwerg**' (**Little Gem**) • White flowers in spring • Evergreen foliage • 10–15 cm high, 15–25 cm wide

Imperata

p. 417

Genus Information

Origin: Japan and Southeast Asia
Selected Common Names: Japanese blood grass
Nomenclature: Name means "imperial" or "regal."
Notes: It is long known and grown in Japan where it has been used in bonsai.

General Features

Height: 30–45 cm high
Spread: 30–45 cm wide
Habit: rhizomatous, slow-spreading grass
Flowers: short, silvery spikelets; summer (rarely seeds in cooler climates)
Foliage: blood-red to ruby-red
Hardiness: D; not recommended for the Prairies
Warnings: prone to aphids; not prone to diseases

Expert Advice: Grown by gardening enthusiasts across Canada for its striking foliage (although it is not hardy in colder areas). In colder areas it is slow to emerge in spring and will be sparse. Try overwintering by planting in a sheltered site, next to a heated foundation with good snow coverage. Best for warmer climates.

Growing Requirements

Light: sun
Soil: moist, organic, well-drained soil
Location: mixed borders; woodland gardens; sheltered locations
Propagation: seed; division

Buying Considerations

Professionals

Popularity: popular as a foliage plant
Availability: readily available as finished product
Size to Sell: sells best in larger sizes; matures slowly
On the Shelf: high ornamental appeal
Shrinkage: high; sensitive to overwatering

Collectors

Popularity: not generally of interest to collectors (although it is of interest to Japanese garden enthusiasts)

Gardeners

Ease of Growth: difficult to estabish on the prairies
Start with: one small plant for feature plant

What to Try First ...

Imperata cylindrica 'Rubra'

On the Market

Imperata cylindrica
'Rubra' (Red Baron) • Silver plumes in late summer • Blood-red foliage • 30–45 cm high, 30–45 cm wide

Incarvillea

Genus Information

Origin: central Asia, East Asia and the Himalayas
Selected Common Names: Sometimes called "garden gloxinia" because of the floral display.
Nomenclature: Named for Pierre d'Incarville, 1706–1757, a French missionary in China.

General Features

Height: 10–15 cm high
Spread: 20–30 cm wide
Habit: tap-rooted perennial
Flowers: gloxinia-like; large; summer
Hardiness: C
Warnings: prone to aphids

Growing Requirements

Light: sun
Soil: fertile, organic soil; keep soil moist during active growth and drier during dormancy; avoid winter wet
Propagation: seed
Expert Advice: Plant the crowns 8–10 cm deep. Avoid damaging the fleshy roots. Seed in fall or spring. Seedlings take 3 years to reach blooming size. Division is possible, but very difficult—resents being disturbed.

Buying Considerations

Professionals

Popularity: relatively unknown
Availability: occasionally available from specialty growers
Size to Sell: sells best in smaller sizes (when blooming); matures slowly
Shrinkage: high; sensitive to overwatering

Collectors

Popularity: of interest to collectors—rare, novelty plant

Gardeners

Ease of Growth: mostly easy to grow but needs close attention to growing conditions
Start with: one small plant for feature plant

What to Try First ...

Incarvillea zhongdianensis

On the Market

Incarvillea zhongdianensis
Trumpet-like, very large, purple-pink flowers in early summer • 20–30 cm high, 20–30 cm wide

Indigofera

Genus Information

Origin: tropics and subtropics
Selected Common Names: indigo
Nomenclature: From the Latin *indigus* (indigo) and *ferus* (bearing), referring to the blue dye from the leaves and young stems.

General Features

Height: 10–15 cm high
Spread: 30–45 cm high
Habit: subshrub
Flowers: pea-like; summer
Hardiness: C
Warnings: prone to aphids; not prone to diseases
Expert Advice: This plant is often grown as a novelty.

Growing Requirements

Light: sun to p.m. sun
Soil: fertile, well-drained soil
Location: mixed borders; rock gardens
Propagation: seed; cuttings
Expert Advice: Seed in fall. Take root cuttings in spring and semi-ripe cuttings in summer.

Buying Considerations

Professionals

Popularity: relatively unknown
Availability: occasionally available from specialty growers
Size to Sell: sells best in smaller sizes (when blooming) as it matures fast
On the Shelf: rapidly overgrows pot
Shrinkage: low; requires little maintenance

Collectors

Popularity: not generally of interest to collectors

Gardeners

Ease of Growth: mostly easy to grow
Start with: one small plant for feature plant

What to Try First ...

Indigofera pseudotinctoria

On the Market

Indigofera pseudotinctoria
Pea-like, pink to rose flowers in summer •
10–15 cm high, 30–45 cm wide

Inula

p. 417 📷

Genus Information

Origin: Caucasus Mountains and Southern Europe
Selected Common Names: yellow sunray, sunray
Nomenclature: From the name used by Pliny for *Helenium*, which it resembles.
Other Uses: *Inula* was used by the Romans and Greeks as a digestive tonic after feasts.

General Features

Height: 30–180 cm high
Spread: 20–120 cm wide
Habit: large, upright, tap-rooted or rhizomatous, clump-forming perennial
Flowers: daisy-like; mid-to late summer; good for cutflowers
Foliage: hairy foliage
Hardiness: C
Warnings: prone to aphids

Growing Requirements

Light: sun to p.m. sun; tolerates some shade
Soil: fertile, moist, well-drained soil; tolerates sandy soil; drought tolerant once established

Location: back of mixed borders; wild gardens; herb gardens; rock gardens
Propagation: seed; division
Expert Advice: Lean soils promote compact growth.

Buying Considerations

Professionals

Popularity: relatively unknown
Availability: occasionally available from specialty growers
Size to Sell: sells best in smaller sizes (when blooming) as it matures fast
On the Shelf: rapidly overgrows pot
Shrinkage: high; sensitive to underwatering

Collectors

Popularity: not generally of interest to collectors

Gardeners

Ease of Growth: very easy to grow
Start with: one small plant for feature plant

What to Try First ...

Inula ensifolia, Inula magnifica, Inula orientalis

On the Market

Inula ensifolia
Yellow, daisy-like flowers in summer •
30–60 cm high, 20–30 cm wide
Inula magnifica
Golden-yellow flowers in mid-to late summer • 1–1.8 m high, 1–1.2 m wide
Inula orientalis
Yellow, daisy-like flowers in summer •
45–60 cm high, 30–45 cm wide

Iris

p. 417 📷

Genus Information

Origin: throughout the Northern Hemisphere
Selected Common Names: bearded iris, fleur-de-Lis, German iris, poor man's orchid, Siberian iris
Nomenclature: *Iris* comes from the Greek word for rainbow.
Notes: In mythology, the goddess Iris, who was Juno's personal messenger, travelled over the rainbow to reach Earth. Brightly coloured flowers sprang up from her footsteps. *Iris* are prized by gardeners and breeders for their stunning flowers and some for their foliage. *Iris* are divided botanically in a fairly complicated fashion. We divide *Iris* into 3 categories for display and growing information purposes: **Bearded (Dwarf and Tall), Species** and **Water/Siberian.**

Iris, Bearded

p. 417

General Features

Height: 10–100 cm high
Spread: 10–60 cm wide
Habit: upright, clump-forming or spreading rhizomatous perennial
Flowers: wide range of colours; large; (some) very fragrant; late spring to early summer; good cutflowers; (most) short-blooming period; deadhead to extend blooming period
Foliage: attractive, flat, fan-shaped
Hardiness: C–D
Warnings: prone to aphids and iris borer (in warmer climates); not prone to diseases; crown rot if grown too wet
Expert Advice: A large amount of breeding has taken place, making bearded iris very far removed from the original species. There are lots of divisions (classes) in this type based mostly on plant height. Extend the blooming season by choosing cultivars accordingly. Short to medium height plants tend to be hardier than taller varieties.

Growing Requirements

Light: sun
Soil: moist, sharply-drained, neutral to alkaline soil; avoid fall and winter wet
Location: sheltered beds against the west or south side of a building; mixed borders; raised beds; rock gardens
Propagation: seed for species types; division
Expert Advice: Plant with the flat side of leaves facing the direction from which you want to view the flowers. Seed is very difficult to germinate and plants will take 3–4 years to reach blooming size. Good-sized rhizomes will produce some flowers the 1st year. In light soil, plant so that the top of the rhizome is barely covered. In heavier soils, leave rhizome barely exposed. Deep planting can retard blooming and result in rot. Divide rhizomes every 3–4 years (or as the centres die out) right after flowering. Cut the fans back by half at time of transplanting.

Buying Considerations

Professionals

Popularity: popular garden standard; sells well in bloom; nice foliage plant
Availability: readily available as finished product and bare root from specialty growers
Size to Sell: sells best in smaller sizes (when blooming) as it matures fast
On the Shelf: high ornamental appeal
Shrinkage: low; sensitive to overwatering; requires little maintenance

Collectors

Popularity: of interest to collectors—unique, exceptional beauty

Gardeners

Ease of Growth: generally easy to grow but needs close attention to growing conditions
Start with: one small plant for feature plant

What to Try First ...

Iris 'Batik', *Iris* 'Cherry Garden', *Iris* 'Yo Yo', *Iris* 'Alpine Lake', *Iris* 'Black Dragon', *Iris* 'Beverly Sills', *Iris* 'Bengal Tiger', *Iris* 'Acapulco Gold'

On the Market

Iris, Dwarf

Flowers in late spring • 10-25 cm high, 30–45 cm wide

'Alpine Lake' • Blue-tinted, white standards and blue falls in late spring • 15 cm high, 30–45 cm wide

'Banbury Ruffles' • Rich-blue standards and darker-spotted falls in late spring • 20–25 cm high, 30–45 cm wide

'Be Dazzled' • Yellow flowers with dark-brown markings in late spring • 10–20 cm high, 30–45 cm wide

'Bloodstone' • Burgundy flowers in late spring • 20–25 cm high, 30–45 cm wide

'Bright White' • Pure white flowers in late spring • 15–20 cm high, 30–45 cm wide

'Button Box' • Fragrant, rosy-purple flowers in late spring • 30–40 cm high, 30–45 cm wide

'Candy Fluff' • Soft-pink flowers in late spring • 20–30 cm high, 30–45 cm wide

'Captured Spirit' • Milk-white flowers in late spring • 25 cm high, 30–45 cm wide

'Cherry Garden' • Velvety, burgundy flowers in late spring • 40 cm high, 30–45 cm wide

'Emily Grey' • Purple flowers with yellow streaks in late spring • 10–20 cm high, 30–45 cm wide

'Eyebright' • Yellow flowers with brown lines in late spring • 20–30 cm high, 30–45 cm wide

'Fairy Face' • Dark-purple flowers with white veins in late spring • 10–20 cm high, 10–20 cm wide

'French Wine' • Deep wine-coloured flowers in late spring • 15–25 cm high, 30–45 cm wide

'Galleon Gold' • Pure gold flowers with blue beards in late spring • 30 cm high, 30–45 cm wide

'Golden Fair' • Golden-yellow flowers in late spring • 30 cm high, 30–45 cm wide

'Hazel's Pink' • Salmon-pink flowers in late spring • 25–40 cm high, 30–45 cm wide

'Hee Haw' • Red-edged, cream flowers in late spring • 15–20 cm high, 30–45 cm wide

'Jamari' • Dark cherry-red flowers in late spring • 22 cm high, 30–45 cm wide

'Knick Knack' • White flowers with light purple veins in late spring • 10–20 cm high, 30–45 cm wide

'Lenna M' • Beige-pink flowers in late spring • 20–25 cm high, 30–45 cm wide

'Little Black Belt' • Purple-black flowers with blue beards in late spring • 30 cm high, 30–45 cm wide

'Little Buccaneer' • Red flowers with orange beards in late spring • 30 cm high, 30–45 cm wide

'Little Dream' • Orchid-pink flowers in late spring • 15–20 cm high, 30–45 cm wide

'Little Sapphire' • Silver-blue flowers in late spring • 20–25 cm high, 30–45 cm wide

'Michael Paul' • Fragrant, ruffled, black-purple flowers in late spring • 25 cm high, 30–45 cm wide

'Music Box' • Lavender and tan flowers in late spring • 15–20 cm high, 30–45 cm wide

'Orange Caper' • Deep-gold flowers in late spring • 20–25 cm high, 30–45 cm wide

'Orange Tiger' • Fragrant, orange flowers in late spring • 30 cm high, 30–45 cm wide

'Peach Bavarian' • Light-peach flowers with white beards in late spring • 30–35 cm high, 30–45 cm wide

'Petite Polka' • White flowers with purple stitching in late spring • 25 cm high, 30–45 cm wide

'Pink Amber' • Pink and amber flowers in late spring • 25 cm high, 30–45 cm wide

'Pink Cushion' • Pink flowers in late spring • 25–30 cm high, 30–45 cm wide

'Pixie Princess' • White flowers edged blue in late spring • 20–40 cm high, 30–45 cm wide

'Pumpin' Iron' • Dark red-black flowers in late spring • 35 cm high, 30–45 cm wide

'Red Dandy' • Wine-red flowers in late spring • 25–30 cm high, 30–45 cm wide

'Ritz' • Yellow flowers with maroon blotch in late spring • 20–25 cm high, 30–45 cm wide

'Ruby Contrast' • Fragrant, maroon flowers in late spring • 35 cm high, 30–45 cm wide

'Sail Away' • Blue flowers in late spring • 20–25 cm high, 30–45 cm wide

'Sapphire Gem' • Sapphire-blue flowers in late spring • 20–25 cm high, 30–45 cm wide

'Sarah Taylor' • Cream-yellow flowers with blue beards in late spring • 20–25 cm high, 30–45 cm wide

'Sky Scraper' • Pale-blue flowers in late spring • 15 cm high, 30–45 cm wide

'Sleepytime' • Light-blue flowers in late spring • 15–20 cm high, 30–45 cm wide

'Small Flash' • Yellow flowers with red blotch in late spring • 20–25 cm high, 30–45 cm wide

'Smell the Roses' • Fragrant, violet-blue flowers in late spring • 35 cm high, 30–45 cm wide

'Sprite' • Bright-yellow flowers in late spring • 20–25 cm high, 30–45 cm wide

'Sun Doll' • Fragrant, ruffled, yellow flowers in late spring • 35 cm high, 30–45 cm wide

'Tillie' • Peach-pink flowers in late spring • 20–25 cm high, 30–45 cm wide

'Tinkerbell' • Mid-blue standards and dark-blue falls in late spring • 35 cm high, 30–45 cm wide

'Tippy' • Blue and violet flowers in late spring • 20–35 cm high, 30–45 cm wide

'Toots' • Velvety, wine-coloured flowers in late spring • 20–25 cm high, 30–45 cm wide

'Wake Up' • Fragrant, bright-yellow flowers in late spring • 35 cm high, 30–45 cm wide

'White Gem' • White flowers in late spring • 30 cm high, 30–45 cm wide

'Yo Yo' • Orchid-coloured flowers with purple blotch in late spring • 25–40 cm high, 30–45 cm wide

Iris, Tall

Flowers in early summer • 35–100 cm high, 45–60 cm wide

'Aachen Elf' • Fragrant, yellow standards and lavender falls in early summer • 50 cm high, 45–60 cm wide

'Acapulco Gold' • Fragrant, gold flowers in early summer • 70–100 cm high, 45–60 cm wide

'Aggressively Forward' • Fragrant, yellow-based standards and blue falls in early summer • 90 cm high, 45–60 cm wide

'All that Jazz' • Fragrant, gold standards and mahogany falls in early summer • 70–100 cm high, 45–60 cm wide

'American Sweetheart' • Fragrant, gold standards and red-brown falls in early summer • 90 cm high, 45–60 cm wide

'Amethyst Flame' • Fragrant, ruffled, amethyst-orchid flowers in early summer • 75 cm high, 45–60 cm wide

'Austrian Garnets' • Fragrant, garnet-red flowers in early summer • 1 m high, 45–60 cm wide

'Avalon Sunset' • Fragrant, ruffled, vibrant orange flowers in early summer • 90 cm high, 45–60 cm wide

'Az Ap' • Fragrant, cobalt-blue flowers in early summer • 55 cm high, 45–60 cm wide

'Batik' • Fragrant, purple flowers with white streaks in early summer • 65 cm high, 45–60 cm wide

'Batman' • Fragrant, ruffled, black-purple flowers in early summer • 90 cm high, 45–60 cm wide

'Before the Storm' • Fragrant, inky-black flowers in early summer • 90 cm high, 45–60 cm wide

'Bengal Tiger' • Fragrant, yellow-and-maroon-striped flowers in early summer • 95 cm high, 45–60 cm wide

'Beverly Sills' • Fragrant, ruffled, coral-pink flowers in early summer • 90 cm high, 45–60 cm wide

'Black Dragon' • Fragrant, velvety blue-black flowers in early summer • 90 cm high, 45–60 cm wide

'Blue Staccato' • Fragrant, white flowers with blue markings in early summer • 1 m high, 45–60 cm wide

'Bold Gold' • Fragrant, ruffled, gold flowers in early summer • 1 m high, 45–60 cm wide

'Breakers' • Fragrant, ruffled, blue flowers in early summer • 95 cm high, 45–60 cm wide

'Bright Fire' • Fragrant, flamingo-pink flowers in early summer • 90 cm high, 45–60 cm wide

'Broadway Star' • Fragrant, cream standards and rose-red falls in early summer • 75–90 cm high, 45–60 cm wide

'Burgundy Brown' • Fragrant, gold flowers with burgundy marks in early summer • 60–90 cm high, 45–60 cm wide

'Busy Being Blue' • Fragrant, sky-blue flowers with blue veins in early summer • 80 cm high, 45–60 cm wide

'Cable Car' • Fragrant, honey-brown flowers in early summer • 75–90 cm high, 45–60 cm wide

'Carolina Gold' • Fragrant, gold flowers in early summer • 85 cm high, 45–60 cm wide

'Carriage Trade' • Fragrant, white flowers with ice-blue tones in early summer • 60–75 cm high, 45–60 cm wide

'Champagne Elegance' • Fragrant, white standards and apricot falls in early summer • 85 cm high, 45–60 cm wide

'Chanteuse' • Fragrant, pink flowers in early summer • 90 cm high, 45–60 cm wide

'Chapeau' • Fragrant, cream standards and lavender falls in early summer • 60–90 cm high, 45–60 cm wide

'Chasing Rainbows' • Fragrant, beige and orchid-violet flowers in early summer • 80 cm high, 45–60 cm wide

'Cheesecake' • Fragrant, pink flowers in early summer • 60–75 cm high, 45–60 cm wide

'Cherub's Smile' • Fragrant, flamingo-pink flowers in early summer • 95 cm high, 45–60 cm wide

'China Dragon' • Fragrant, bright-orange flowers in early summer • 60–90 cm high, 45–60 cm wide

Chinese Treasure' • Fragrant, white standards and pink falls in early summer • 90 cm high, 45–60 cm wide

'Christmas Time' • Fragrant, pure white flowers in early summer • 70 cm high, 45–60 cm wide

'Cinnamon Girl' • Fragrant, red-cinnamon standards and ivory falls in early summer • 90 cm high, 45–60 cm wide

'Congratulations' • Fragrant, pansy-blue standards and violet falls in early summer • 90 cm high, 45–60 cm wide

'Coral Beads' • Fragrant, white standards and peach falls in early summer • 1 m high, 30–45 cm wide

'Coral Beauty' • Fragrant, white standards and peach falls in early summer • 85 cm high, 45–60 cm wide

'Cracklin' Burgundy' • Fragrant, ruffled, deep-burgundy flowers in early summer • 90 cm high, 45–60 cm wide

'Cranberry Ice' • Fragrant, cranberry-rose flowers in early summer • 45–60 cm high, 45–60 cm wide

'Crystal Glow' • Fragrant, white standards and lavender falls in early summer • 70–90 cm high, 45–60 cm wide

'Dappled Pony' • Fragrant, light-lavender, blue-dotted flowers in early summer • 40 cm high, 45–60 cm wide

'Dark Triumph' • Fragrant, dark royal-purple flowers in early summer • 95 cm high, 45–60 cm wide

'Dazzling Gold' • Fragrant, gold flowers with red veins in early summer • 75 cm high, 45–60 cm wide

'Distant Chimes' • Fragrant, yellow standards and lavender falls in early summer • 75–90 cm high, 45–60 cm wide

'Dusky Challenger' • Fragrant, silky, dark-purple flowers in early summer • 1 m high, 45–60 cm wide

'Eagle's Flight' • Fragrant, lavender and white flowers in early summer • 90 cm high, 45–60 cm wide

'Echo de France' • Fragrant, white and gold flowers in early summer • 85 cm high, 45–60 cm wide

'Edge of Winter' • Fragrant, blue standards and lighter falls in early summer • 95 cm high, 45–60 cm wide

'Edith Wolford' • Fragrant, yellow and violet-blue flowers in early summer • 1 m high, 45–60 cm wide

'Eleanor's Pride' • Fragrant, powder-blue flowers in early summer • 1 m high, 45–60 cm wide

'Enchanted Violet' • Fragrant, grey-blue and orchid flowers in early summer • 70–100 cm high, 45–60 cm wide

'Enchanted World' • Fragrant, rose-pink flowers in early summer • 90 cm high, 45–60 cm wide

'Entourage' • Fragrant, hazy-rose flowers in early summer • 70–90 cm high, 45–60 cm wide

'Epicentre' • Black-cherry standards and salmon falls in early summer • 1 m high, 45–60 cm wide

'Exactitude' • Antique-gold standards and blue-edged falls in early summer • 85 cm high, 45–60 cm wide

'Faded Denims' • Fragrant, orchid-blue flowers in early summer • 95 cm high, 45–60 cm wide

'Florentina' • Fragrant, white and blue-washed flowers in early summer • 70–100 cm high, 45–60 cm wide

'Fort Apache' • Fragrant, rich, maroon-red flowers in early summer • 1 m high, 45–60 cm wide

'Frequent Flyer' • Fragrant, ruffled, white flowers in early summer • 80 cm high, 45–60 cm wide

'Gallant Moment' • Fragrant, velvety, bronze-red flowers in early summer • 1 m high, 45–60 cm wide

'Gay Parasol' • Fragrant, white standards and rose-violet falls in early summer • 90 cm high, 45–60 cm wide

'Glacier Gold' • Fragrant, white standards and mid-yellow falls in early summer • 75 cm high, 45–60 cm wide

'Gnus Flash' • Purple-streaked, silver-tan standards and silver-streaked, purple falls in late spring • 95–100 cm high, 45–60 cm wide

'Go for Bold' • Yellow with white-centered purple falls in late spring • 40–70 cm high, 30–45 cm wide

'Going My Way' • Fragrant, purple-edged, white flowers in early summer • 95 cm high, 45–60 cm wide

'Goldkist' • White standards and purple-veined, white falls in early summer • 90 cm high, 45–60 cm wide

'Harbour Blue' • Fragrant, Wedgewood-blue flowers in early summer • 60–75 cm high, 45–60 cm wide

'Hell's Fire' • Fragrant, red-black flowers in early summer • 90 cm high, 45–60 cm wide

'Hemstitched' • Fragrant, violet-edged, white flowers in early summer • 80 cm high, 45–60 cm wide

'Heritage Lace' • Fragrant, creamy-yellow flowers in early summer • 90 cm high, 45–60 cm wide

'Hindenburg' • Fragrant, ruffled, pale-orange flowers in early summer • 70–100 cm high, 45–60 cm wide

'Honky Tonk Blues' • Fragrant, grey-edged, hyacinth-blue flowers in early summer • 95 cm high, 45–60 cm wide

'Hot Gossip' • Buff-pink standards and lavender-violet falls in early summer • 80–90 cm high, 45–60 cm wide

'Indulge' • Fragrant, orchid standards and orchid-rose falls in early summer • 70–100 cm high, 45–60 cm wide

'Infernal Fire' • Buff-gold flowers with random magenta streaking in early summer • 80 cm high, 45–60 cm wide

'Interpol' • Fragrant, velvet-black flowers in early summer • 90 cm high, 45–60 cm wide

'It's Magic' • Yellow flowers in early summer • 90 cm high, 45–60 cm wide

'Jazz Festival' • Fragrant, cream and cerise-rose flowers in early summer • 1 m high, 45–60 cm wide

'Jesse's Song' • Fragrant, violet-edged, white flowers in early summer • 90 cm high, 45–60 cm wide

'Jewel Tone' • Fragrant, dark ruby-red flowers in early summer • 70–100 cm high, 45–60 cm wide

'Jitterbug' • Fragrant, gold standards and russet-washed falls in early summer • 90 cm high, 45–60 cm wide

'Joyful News' • Fragrant, light-orange flowers in early summer • 90 cm high, 45–60 cm wide

'Jurassic Park' • Fragrant, yellow standards and violet falls in early summer • 90 cm high, 45–60 cm wide

'Juris Prudence' • Fragrant, white flowers with ice-blue tones in early summer • 90 cm high, 45–60 cm wide

'Kilt Lilt' • Fragrant, gold-brown flowers in early summer • 1 m high, 45–60 cm wide

'Laced Cotton' • Fragrant, ruffled, white flowers in early summer • 85 cm high, 45–60 cm wide

'Lacy Snowflake' • Fragrant, ruffled, white flowers in early summer • 95 cm high, 45–60 cm wide

'Latin Lover' • Fragrant, light-pink standards and wine falls in early summer • 90 cm high, 45–60 cm wide

'Lilac Wine' • Fragrant, lilac standards and red-plum falls in early summer • 70–90 cm high, 45–60 cm wide

'Live Music' • Fragrant, peach standards and rose falls in early summer • 75 cm high, 45–60 cm wide

'Loganberry Squeeze' • Fragrant, raspberry-violet flowers in early summer • 90 cm high, 45–60 cm wide

'Lorilee' • Fragrant, ruffled, rose-orchid flowers in early summer • 95 cm high, 45–60 cm wide

'Los Banos' • Fragrant, brown flowers with red tones in early summer • 70–100 cm high, 45–60 cm wide

'Love the Sun' • Fragrant, yellow standards and bronze falls in early summer • 90 cm high, 45–60 cm wide

'Loyalist' • Fragrant, ruffled, violet-blue flowers in early summer • 95 cm high, 45–60 cm wide

'Lullaby of Spring' • Fragrant, soft-yellow standards and mauve falls in early summer • 95 cm high, 45–60 cm wide

'Magic Man' • Fragrant, velvety-blue flowers in early summer • 95 cm high, 45–60 cm wide

'Margarita' • Fragrant, ice-white standards and blue-purple falls in early summer • 75 cm high, 45–60 cm wide

'Maria Tormena' • Fragrant, pink flowers with violet splashes in early summer • 80 cm high, 45–60 cm wide

'Maroon Caper' • Fragrant, velvety, deep red-purple flowers in early summer • 40–50 cm high, 45–60 cm wide

'Master Touch' • Fragrant, ruffled, purple flowers in early summer • 1 m high, 45–60 cm wide

'Matinata' • Fragrant, deep-purple flowers in early summer • 1 m high, 45–60 cm wide

'Memphis Blues' • Fragrant, ruffled, lobelia-blue flowers in early summer • 1 m high, 45–60 cm wide

'Merry Madrigal' • Fragrant, creamy-yellow and lavender flowers in early summer • 95 cm high, 45–60 cm wide

'Michigan Pride' • Fragrant, yellow standards and brown falls in early summer • 90 cm high, 45–60 cm wide

'Midnight Hour' • Fragrant, ruffled, purple-black flowers in early summer • 75 cm high, 45–60 cm wide

'Ming Dynasty' • Fragrant, ruffled, orange-gold flowers in early summer • 70–100 cm high, 45–60 cm wide

'Montevideo' • Fragrant, mid- to dark-orange flowers in early summer • 95 cm high, 45–60 cm wide

'Mystique' • Fragrant, soft-blue standards and darker falls in early summer • 90 cm high, 45–60 cm wide

'Olympiad' • Fragrant, elegant, pale-blue-violet flowers in early summer • 95 cm high, 45–60 cm wide

'Olympic Challenge' • Fragrant, ruffled, orange flowers in early summer • 1 m high, 45–60 cm wide

'One Desire' • Fragrant, deep-pink flowers in early summer • 75 cm high, 45–60 cm wide

'Ostentatious' • Red-black standards and maroon and yellow falls in early summer • 95 cm high, 45–60 cm wide

'Pagan Pink' • Fragrant, hot-pink standards and pale-pink falls in early summer • 90 cm high, 45–60 cm wide

'Palais Royale' • Fragrant, exotic, orchid-pink flowers in early summer • 70–100 cm high, 45–60 cm wide

'Paradise' • Fragrant, peach-pink flowers in early summer • 85 cm high, 45–60 cm wide

'Persian Berry' • Fragrant, blue-raspberry flowers in early summer • 90 cm high, 45–60 cm wide

'Pina Colada' • Fragrant, cream flowers with peach accents in early summer • 70–100 cm high, 45–60 cm wide

'Pinafore Pink' • Fragrant, shell-pink flowers in early summer • 90 cm high, 45–60 cm wide

'Pink Horizon' • Fragrant, flamingo-pink flowers in early summer • 75 cm high, 45–60 cm wide

'Pink Vanilla' • Fragrant, apricot-pink flowers in early summer • 75 cm high, 45–60 cm wide

'Pinnacle' • Fragrant, white and yellow flowers in early summer • 75 cm high, 45–60 cm wide

'Pride of Ireland' • Fragrant, chartreuse flowers in early summer • 90 cm high, 45–60 cm wide

'Princesse Caroline de Monaco' • Light-blue flowers in early season • 85–90 cm high, 45–60 cm wide

'Prom Night' • Fragrant, raspberry-red flowers in early summer • 1 m high, 45–60 cm wide

'Proud Tradition' • Fragrant, ice-blue standards and blue falls in early summer • 90 cm high, 45–60 cm wide

'Purple Streaker' • Fragrant, purple flowers with white streaks in early summer • 70–100 cm high, 45–60 cm wide

'Queen in Calico' • Fragrant, pale-orange flowers with violet markings in early summer • 85 cm high, 45–60 cm wide

'Rancho Rose' • Fragrant, light-pink and magenta flowers in early summer • 95 cm high, 45–60 cm wide

'Rare Edition' • Fragrant, white flowers with purple marks in early summer • 60 cm high, 45–60 cm wide

'Raspberry Ripples' • Fragrant, raspberry-rose flowers in early summer • 90 cm high, 45–60 cm wide

'Real Delight' • Fragrant, peach-apricot flowers in early summer • 90 cm high, 45–60 cm wide

'Red Zinger' • Fragrant, burgundy-wine flowers in early summer • 65 cm high, 45–60 cm wide

'Ringo' • Fragrant, white standards and grape falls in early summer • 90 cm high, 45–60 cm wide

'Riverboat Blues' • Fragrant, ruffled, sapphire-blue flowers in early summer • 95 cm high, 45–60 cm wide

'Rosy Wings' • Rosy-red flowers in early summer • 70–100 cm high, 45–60 cm wide

'Royal Crusader' • Fragrant, light-blue standards and darker falls in early summer • 75–90 cm high, 45–60 cm wide

'Shipshape' • Fragrant, mid-blue flowers in early summer • 95 cm high, 45–60 cm wide

'Silverado' • Fragrant, ruffled, pale-lavender-white flowers in early summer • 95 cm high, 45–60 cm wide

'Skyfire' • Fragrant, rich-orange flowers in early summer • 90 cm high, 45–60 cm wide

'Skylab' • Fragrant, light-blue standards and navy falls in early summer • 90 cm high, 45–60 cm wide

'Snow Cloud' • Fragrant, icy-white standards and blue falls in early summer • 75 cm high, 45–60 cm wide

'Snowmound' • Fragrant, white standards and purple falls in early summer • 90 cm high, 45–60 cm wide

'Soft Jazz' • Fragrant, gold standards and wine-coloured falls in early summer • 70–100 cm high, 45–60 cm wide

'Sparkle Berry' • Fragrant, white flowers with berry-red marks in early summer • 80 cm high, 45–60 cm wide

'Spellbreaker' • Fragrant, ruffled, cranberry-violet flowers in early summer • 90 cm high, 45–60 cm wide

'Spiced Tiger' • Light-brown standards and mahogany, white-streaked falls in early summer • 80 cm high, 45–60 cm wide

'Stairway to Heaven' • Near-white standards with medium-blue falls in early summer • 90–100 cm high, 45–60 cm wide

'Stepping Out' • Fragrant, white flowers with violet edges in early summer • 95 cm high, 45–60 cm wide

'Sultry Mood' • Fragrant, cerise-purple flowers in early summer • 90 cm high, 45–60 cm wide

'Summer Fiesta' • Fragrant, yellow standards and rose-violet falls in early summer • 70–100 cm high, 45–60 cm wide

'Sunkist Delight' • Light-yellow standards and gold-edged, white falls in early summer • 90 cm high, 45–60 cm wide

'Superstition' • Fragrant, ebony-black flowers in early summer • 90 cm high, 45–60 cm wide

'Supreme Sultan' • Fragrant, gold standards and mahogany-red falls in early summer • 1 m high, 45–60 cm wide

'Sweet Lena' • Fragrant, light-blue flowers with white edge in early summer • 70 cm high, 45–60 cm wide

'Sweet Musette' • Fragrant, pink standards and cerise falls in early summer • 95 cm high, 45–60 cm wide

'Sweeter than Wine' • Fragrant, white standards and wine-red falls in early summer • 90 cm high, 45–60 cm wide

'Sweetwater' • Fragrant, soft-blue flowers in early summer • 60 cm high, 45–60 cm wide

'Tangueray' • Fragrant, cream standards and white falls in early summer • 95 cm high, 45–60 cm wide

'Theatre' • Fragrant, soft-violet standards and dotted falls in early summer • 85 cm high, 45–60 cm wide

'Thriller' • Fragrant, bright-grape-red flowers in early summer • 90 cm high, 45–60 cm wide

'Tide's In' • Fragrant, ruffled, celestial-blue flowers in early summer • 90 cm high, 45–60 cm wide

'Tiffany' • Fragrant, burgundy-veined flowers in early summer • 70–100 cm high, 45–60 cm wide

'Titan's Glory' • Fragrant, deep-violet flowers in early summer • 95 cm high, 45–60 cm wide

'Total Recall' • Fragrant, soft-yellow flowers in early summer • 85 cm high, 45–60 cm wide

'Vanity' • Fragrant, soft-pink flowers in early summer • 90 cm high, 45–60 cm wide

'Vibrations' • Fragrant, burgundy-rose flowers in early summer • 85 cm high, 45–60 cm wide

'Victoria Falls' • Fragrant, violet-blue flowers in early summer • 1 m high, 45–60 cm wide

'War Chief' • Fragrant, rich-ruby flowers in early summer • 95 cm high, 45–60 cm wide

'Winter Olympics' • Fragrant, pure white flowers in early summer • 95 cm high, 45–60 cm wide

Iris germanica
Fragrant, blue-violet flowers with yellow beards in early summer • 70–120 cm high, 45–60 cm wide

Iris pallida
Fragrant, lavender-blue flowers in late spring to early summer • Silvery, grey-green foliage • 90–120 cm high, 45–60 cm wide

'Variegata' • Fragrant, violet-blue flowers in late spring • Gold-and-green-striped foliage • 90–120 cm high, 45–60 cm wide

Iris, Species p. 417

General Features
Height: 6–90 cm high
Spread: 15–60 cm wide
Habit: upright, clump-forming or stoloniferous perennial
Flowers: delicate-looking; (some) fragrant; spring to early summer; seed pods attractive for drying
Foliage: attractive; (some) variegated
Hardiness: C–D
Warnings: prone to aphids; not prone to diseases
Expert Advice: Most species *Iris* are unknown and deserve to be planted in the garden. They are hardy and require little care.

Growing Requirements
Light: sun; (*I. cristata*) shade
Soil: moist, well-drained, neutral to acidic soil (*I. stolonifera*; alkaline soil); (some) require moist soil; (some) require a moist spring followed by a dry summer
Location: mixed borders; raised beds; rock gardens
Propagation: seed; division
Expert Advice: A diverse group with a wide range of growing conditions. Seed is very difficult to germinate and plants will take 3–4 years to reach blooming size.

Buying Considerations

Professionals

Popularity: relatively unknown

Availability: occasionally available as finished product and bare root from specialty growers

Size to Sell: sells best in smaller sizes (when blooming) as it matures fast

On the Shelf: high ornamental appeal

Shrinkage: low; requires little maintenance

Collectors

Popularity: of interest to collectors—unique species, exceptional beauty

Gardeners

Ease of Growth: mostly easy to grow

Start with: one small plant for feature plant

What to Try First ...

Iris cristata, Iris setosa, Iris suaveolens, Iris suaveolens 'Rubromarginata'

On the Market

Iris aphylla
Pale-to dark-purple flowers in late spring • 15–30 cm high, 45–60 cm wide

Iris chrysographes
Fragrant, reddish-violet flowers with gold streaks on falls in early summer • Greyish-green foliage • 40–50 cm high, 30–45 cm wide

(**Black form**) • Fragrant, velvet-black flowers with gold veins on falls in early summer • Greyish-green foliage • 40–50 cm high, 30–45 cm wide

Iris cristata
Stemless, lilac-blue flowers in spring • Rich, peaty soil • Keep moist during active growth • 10–15 cm high, 20–30 cm wide

'**Alba**' • Fragrant, stemless, white flowers in spring • 10–15 cm high, 25–30 cm wide

'**Eco White Angel**' • Stemless, white flowers with yellow centres in spring • 10–15 cm high, 25–30 cm wide

Iris gracilipes
Lilac-blue flowers with violet-veined, white falls in late spring • Moist, well-drained soil • Protect from hot afternoon sun • 10–15 cm high, 30 cm wide

Iris graminea (syn. *I. colchica*)
Fragrant, purple flowers with violet-veined, white falls in early summer • Moist, well-drained, fertile soil • 20–40 cm high, 30 cm wide

Iris lactea
Fragrant, white or violet-blue flowers in late spring • Tough, leathery foliage • Well-drained soil • Clump-forming • 6–40 cm high, 30–40 cm wide

Iris longipetala
White flowers with lilac veins in spring • Alkaline-free, well-drained, gritty soil • Moist spring, dry summer • 30–60 cm high, 30–60 cm wide

Iris missouriensis (syn. *I. tolmeiana*)
Lilac-blue, strongly veined flowers in late spring • Well-drained soil • Moist spring, dry summer • Clump-forming • 20–50 cm high, 45–60 cm wide

Iris prismatica
Spidery-like, lilac-blue flowers with violet-veined falls in late spring • Moist, organic, sandy soil • Tolerates part shade • 40–80 cm high, 45–60 cm wide

Iris sanguinea
'**Snow Queen**' • Ivory-white flowers in late spring • Moist, well-drained, slightly acidic soil • Avoid dry sites • 60–90 cm high, 30–45 cm wide

Iris schachtii
Greenish-yellow or purple flowers in early spring • Grey-green foliage • Well-drained, gritty soil • Clump-forming • 10–30 cm high, 30–45 cm wide

Iris setosa
Purple-blue flowers with purple-veined falls in late spring • Reddish-tinged foliage at base • Moist, fertile alkaline-free soil • Avoid fall and winter wet • 15–90 cm high, 30–45 cm wide

'**Blaulicht**' • Pale blue flowers in late spring • 30–60 cm high, 30–45 cm wide

'**Nana Alba**' • White flowers in late spring • 15–30 cm high, 30–45 cm wide

Iris setosa var. *arctica* (syn. *I. arctica*)
Purple-violet flowers with white variegation in late spring • Moist, fertile, organic soil • Avoid fall and winter wet • 15–30 cm high, 30–45 cm wide

Iris sikkimensis
Blue or purple flowers in spring • Moist, organic, well-drained, gritty soil • Clump-forming • 15–25 cm high, 30–45 cm wide

Iris stolonifera
Blend of brown and purple flowers in spring • Moist, organic, well-drained, gritty, alkaline soil • Clump-forming • 30–60 cm high, 45–60 cm wide

Iris suaveolens (syn. *I. mellita*)
Soft-yellow flowers in spring • Sharply drained, fertile, alkaline soil • 8–15 cm high, 15–30 cm wide

Arch590.950 • Yellow to purple, bicoloured flowers in spring • Red-edged foliage • Sharply drained, fertile, alkaline soil • Clump-forming • 8–15 cm high, 15–30 cm wide

'Rubromarginata' • Bronze, brown or purple flowers in spring • Red-edged foliage • 10 cm high, 15–30 cm wide

Iris sweertii
White flowers with purple veins in early summer • Moist, fertile, organic soil • Clump-forming • Moist spring, dry summer • 60–90 cm high, 45–60 cm wide

Iris tectorum
Frilly, blue-violet flowers in spring • Well-drained, fertile, organic soil • Clump-forming • Avoid fall and winter wet • 25–35 cm high, 30–45 cm wide

Iris urumovii
Violet flowers in late spring to early summer • Narrow foliage • Clump-forming • 15–30 cm high, 30–45 cm wide

Iris verna
Clear-violet flowers with narrow, orange stripe on falls in early spring • Moist, acidic, well-drained, gritty, organic soil • 10–15 cm high, 25–30 cm wide

Iris, Water/Siberian   p. 417

General Features
Height: 20–160 cm high
Spread: 30–60 cm wide
Habit: upright, clump-forming perennial
Flowers: delicate-looking on tall stems; late spring to early summer
Foliage: long, grassy; (some) variegated
Hardiness: C–D
Warnings: not prone to diseases; *I. pseudacorus* is an aggressive-spreader
Expert Advice: Siberian *Iris* are among the hardiest of all irises, they are easy to grow and long-lived. These plants provide a strong vertical accent in the moist border, water-side or pond. Quite adaptable to most growing conditions but definitely performs best in moist conditions. *I. ensata*, while not as hardy, has the most blooms of the genus.

Growing Requirements
Light: sun to p.m. shade
Soil: moist, well-drained, neutral to slightly acidic soil
Location: moist mixed borders; ponds; water edges; bogs; *I. sibirica* in moist locations; *I laevigata*, *I. pseudacorus* and *I. spuria* in wet to moist locations; *I. ensata* in moist to wet locations with ample spring moisture is essential
Propagation: seed; division
Expert Advice: Seed is very difficult to germinate and plants will take 3–4 years to reach blooming size; seeds only come true from species. Plant in spring, with crowns at soil level. Plants bloom 1st year. May not require dividing for up to 10 years but are often divided every 3 years. *I. ensata* should be planted 5 cm deep and mulched for winter.

Buying Considerations

Professionals
Popularity: popular, garden standard; fast seller in bloom; interesting foliage plant
Availability: readily available as finished product and bare root from specialty growers
Size to Sell: sells best in smaller sizes (when blooming) as it matures fast
On the Shelf: high ornamental appeal; rapidly overgrows pot
Shrinkage: low; requires little maintenance

Collectors
Popularity: of interest to water garden enthusiasts

Gardeners
Ease of Growth: very easy to grow
Start with: one mature plant for feature plant

What to Try First ...
Iris ensata 'Agoga-Kujyo', *Iris ensata* 'Beni-Botan', *Iris pseudacorus* 'Variegata', *Iris sibirica* 'Big Blue', *Iris sibirica* 'Butter and Sugar'

On the Market

Iris ensata (Japanese Iris)
Flowers in early summer • Wet, acidic, organic soil • Clump-forming • Heavy feeder • Ample water in spring • 75–90 cm high, 45–60 cm wide

'Agoga-Kujyo' • Dark-purple flowers in early summer • 65–90 cm high, 45–60 cm wide

'Alba' • White flowers in early summer • 75–90 cm high, 45–60 cm wide

'Beni-Botan' • Maroon flowers with yellow throat marks in early summer • 65–90 cm high, 45–60 cm wide

'Caprician Butterfly' • Purple-striped, white flowers in early summer • 65–90 cm high, 45–60 cm wide

'Eden's Artist' • Pale-purple flowers with white speckling in early summer • 90 cm high, 45–60 cm wide

'Eden's Blue Pearl' • Sky-blue flowers with white veins in early summer • 90 cm high, 45–60 cm wide

'Eden's Delight' • Purple flowers with yellow throat marks in early summer • 90 cm high, 45–60 cm wide

'Eden's Paintbrush' • Purple-striped, white flowers in early summer • 90 cm high, 45–60 cm wide

'Eden's Picasso' • White-striped, purple flowers in early summer • 90 cm high, 45–60 cm wide

'Eden's Purple Glory' • Deep-blue flowers with yellow throat marks in early summer • 85 cm high, 45–60 cm wide

'Emotion' • Double, white flowers with soft blue edges in early summer • 90 cm high, 45–60 cm wide

'Gekkeikan' • Blue-purple flowers in early summer • 65–90 cm high, 45–60 cm wide

'Gracieuse' • White flowers edged in violet in early summer • 80 cm high, 45–60 cm wide

'Haku Botan' • White flowers with gold throat marks in early summer • 65–90 cm high, 45–60 cm wide

'Kogeso' • Lavender-blue flowers with white veins in early summer • 65–90 cm high, 45–60 cm wide

'Kumo-No-Obi' • Striped, lilac flowers in early summer • 90 cm high, 45–60 cm wide

'Laughing Lion' • Double, purplish-red flowers in early summer • 90 cm high, 45–60 cm wide

'Lavender Wash' • Purple flowers with white veins in early summer • 65–90 cm high, 45–60 cm wide

'Ocean Mist' • Violet-purple flowers with yellow throats in early summer • 70–80 cm high, 45–60 cm wide

'Oriental Fantasy' • Pink-striped, white flowers in early summer • 65–75 cm high, 45–60 cm wide

'Peacock Dance' • Red-purple flowers with white veins in early summer • 1+ m high, 45–60 cm wide

'Pink Dance' • Soft-pink flowers in early summer • 65–90 cm high, 45–60 cm wide

'Pink Lady' • Soft-pink flowers in early summer • 65–90 cm high, 45–60 cm wide

'Sanko Nishiki' • Pink and white flowers in early summer • 65–90 cm high, 45–60 cm wide

'Sensation' • Double, purple-red flowers in early summer • 90 cm high, 45–60 cm wide

'Thunder and Lightning' • White flowers with purple veins in early summer • 65–90 cm high, 45–60 cm wide

'Variegata' • Blue flowers in early summer • Variegated foliage • 90 cm high, 45–60 cm wide

'Velvety Queen' • Velvety dark-blue flowers in early summer • 65–90 cm high, 45–60 cm wide

Iris forrestii
Fragrant, yellow flowers with brown lines on falls in early summer • Grey-green foliage • Acidic, moist, organic soil • Avoid dry sites • 30–40 cm high, 45–60 cm wide

Iris laevigata
Rich-blue flowers in early summer • Fertile, boggy soil • Clump-forming • Plant rhizomes 2–3 cm deep • 80–100 cm high, 45–60 cm wide

'Variegata' • Pale-blue flowers in early summer • Variegated white-and-bright-green foliage • 80–100 cm high, 45–60 cm wide

Iris pseudacorus
Yellow flowers in early summer • Grey-green foliage • Wet, fertile, organic soil • Aggressive spreader • 75–160 cm high, 45–60 cm wide

'Ivory' • Ivory flowers in early summer • 90–150 cm high, 45–60 cm wide

'Sun Cascade' • Double, bright-yellow flowers in early summer • 90–120 cm high, 45–60 cm wide

'Variegata' • Yellow flowers in early summer • Gold-and-green-variegated foliage • 90–150 cm high, 45–60 cm wide

Iris sibirica (Siberian Iris)
Flowers in late spring • Well-drained, moist, slightly acidic soil • clump-forming • Avoid dry sites • 60 cm high, 30–45 cm wide

'Alba' • White flowers in late spring • 75–90 cm high, 30–45 cm wide

'Alba Nana' • White flowers in late spring • 30 cm high, 30–45 cm wide

'Big Blue' • Gentian-blue flowers in late spring • 60–70 cm high, 30–45 cm wide

'Blue Burgee' • Deep velvety-blue flowers in late spring • 60–75 cm high, 30–45 cm wide

'Blue King' • Light-blue flowers in late spring • 1 m high, 30–45 cm wide

'Butter and Sugar' • White flowers with yellow falls in late spring • 70 cm high, 30–45 cm wide

'Caesar's Brother' • Deep-purple flowers in late spring • 75–90 cm high, 30–45 cm wide

'Coronation Anthem' • Ruffled, blue flowers with creamy-yellow falls in late spring • 80 cm high, 30–45 cm wide

'Creme Chantilly' • Cream flowers fading to white in late spring • 65–90 cm high, 30–45 cm wide

'Dance Ballerina Dance' • Ruffled, white flowers with pink or violet markings in late spring • 80 cm high, 30–45 cm wide

'Dreaming Spires' • Lavender flowers with white streaking in early summer • 90 cm high, 30–45 cm wide

'Dreaming Yellow' • White flowers with creamy-yellow falls in late spring • 80 cm high, 30–45 cm wide

'Ego' • Azure-blue flowers with violet tones in late spring • 80 cm high, 30–45 cm wide

'Ewen' • Red-purple flowers in late spring • 80 cm high, 30–45 cm wide

'Forrest McCord' • Dark-blue flowers in late spring • 90 cm high, 30–45 cm wide

'Gelber Mantel' • Creamy-yellow flowers in late spring • 60–75 cm high, 30–45 cm wide

'Jamaican Velvet' • Velvety, red-violet flowers in late spring • 75 cm high, 30–45 cm wide

'Jewelled Crown' • Wine-red flowers with circular gold falls in late spring • 60 cm high, 30–45 cm wide

'Lavender Bounty' • Lavender-pink flowers in late spring • 90 cm high, 30–45 cm wide

'Lavender Light' • Lavender flowers with tan crest in late spring • 90 cm high, 30–45 cm wide

'Looks Mohrish' • Grey-white flowers with pink falls in late spring • 60–75 cm high, 30–45 cm wide

'Mildred Peck' • Pale-pink flowers in late spring • 90–100 cm high, 30–45 cm wide

'Moon Silk' • Cream-white flowers with pale yellow falls in late spring • 70 cm high, 30–45 cm wide

'Peg Edwards' • Violet-blue flowers in late spring • 90 cm high, 30–45 cm wide

'Pink Haze' • Lavender-pink flowers in late spring • 95 cm high, 30–45 cm wide

'Rimouski' • Creamy-white flowers in late spring • 75–90 cm high, 30–45 cm wide

'Rose Quest' • Pink flowers in late spring • 60–75 cm high, 30–45 cm wide

'Ruffled Velvet' • Velvety, red-purple flowers with darker falls in late spring • 55 cm high, 30–45 cm wide

'Salem Witch' • Blue-purple flowers with white spots in late spring • 90 cm high, 30–45 cm wide

'Sea Turn' • Yellow and orchid-pink flowers in late spring • 75–90 cm high, 30–45 cm wide

'Showdown' • Wine-red flowers with aqua-purple veins in late spring • 65 cm high, 30–45 cm wide

'Silver Edge' • Ruffled, blue flowers with silver-edged falls in late spring • 70 cm high, 30–45 cm wide

'Sky Wings' • Light-and dark-blue flowers with yellow falls in late spring • 90 cm high, 30–45 cm wide

'Spalding Rose' • Lavender-pink flowers in late spring • 60–100 cm high, 30–45 cm wide

'Sparkling Pink' • Lavender-pink flowers in late spring • 60 cm high, 30–45 cm wide

'Sparkling Rose' • Mauve flowers with yellow or purple veins in late spring • 90 cm high, 30–45 cm wide

'Steve' • Dark lavender-blue flowers in late spring • 60–80 cm high, 30–45 cm wide

'Strawberry Fair' • Ruffled, strawberry-pink flowers with yellow and white signals in late spring • 70–75 cm high, 30–45 cm wide

'Suji Uri' • White flowers with pale-blue spots in late spring • 90 cm high, 30–45 cm wide

'Tycoon' • Black-blue flowers in late spring • 70–90 cm high, 30–45 cm wide

'Welcome Return' • Ruffled, blue flowers with white-edged falls in late spring • 75–90 cm high, 30–45 cm wide

'White Swirl' • White flowers in late spring •
1 m high, 30–45 cm wide

Iris spuria
Violet-blue flowers in late spring • Sword-
like foliage • Moist, well-drained, alkaline-
free soil • Clump-forming • 45–60 cm high,
45–60 cm wide

'Miss Duluth' • Rich, deep-purple flowers in
late spring • 60–90 cm high, 45–60 cm
wide

'Missouri Gal' • Pale-blue and gold flowers
in late spring • Sword-like foliage • 1 m
high, 45–60 cm wide

Iris spuria ssp. *musulmanica*
Violet-blue, dark-veined flowers in late
spring • Moist, well-drained, alkaline-free,
organic soil • Avoid fall and winter wet •
40–90 cm high, 45–60 cm wide

Iris versicolor
Light-blue to purple flowers in late spring •
Alkaline-free, wet, organic soil • Clump-
forming • 20–80 cm high, 45–60 cm wide

'Gerald Darby' • Purple-blue flowers in late
spring • Foliage emerges purple and turns
green in summer • 60–90 cm high, 45–60
cm wide

'Kermesina' • Rose-purple flowers in late
spring • 60–90 cm high, 45–60 cm wide

Buying Considerations
Professionals
Popularity: gaining popularity
Availability: readily available as finished
product
Size to Sell: sells best in smaller sizes
(when blooming) as it matures fast
On the Shelf: rapidly overgrows pot
Shrinkage: low; requires little maintenance
Collectors
Popularity: not generally of interest to
collectors
Gardeners
Ease of Growth: mostly easy to grow
Start with: one small plant for feature plant
and several for mass plantings
What to Try First ...
Isotoma fulviatilis, Isotoma fulviatilis 'Kelsey
Blue'

On the Market
Isotoma fulviatilis
(syn. *Laurentia fulviatilis*)
Soft-to deep-blue, tiny, star-like flowers in
summer to fall • 3–5 cm high, 30–60 cm
wide

'Kelsey Blue' • Bright blue flowers in
summer to fall • 3–5 cm high, 30–60 cm
wide

Isotoma
Genus Information
Origin: Mediterranean, South Africa and North
America
Selected Common Names: blue star creeper
Nomenclature: *Isotoma* means "equal cut."
Notes: The genus was formerly *Laurentia*.
General Features
Height: 3–5 cm high
Spread: 30–60 cm wide
Habit: mat-forming, spreading perennial
Flowers: blue; star-like; tiny; summer to fall
Foliage: tiny; mid-green
Hardiness: D
Warnings: prone to aphids; not prone to diseases
Expert Advice: Can be short-lived on the Prairies.
Performs well in warmer climates.
Growing Requirements
Light: sun
Soil: well-drained, moist, neutral to acidic soil
Location: between paving stones; rock gardens;
edges
Propagation: seed; division; cuttings

Ivesia
Genus Information
Origin: western North America
Selected Common Names: mouse tail
Nomenclature: *Ivesia* was named for Lieutenant
Eli Ives, leader of one of the Pacific Railway
surveys.
Notes: It is closely related to *Potentilla*.
General Features
Height: 5–10 cm high
Spread: 10–15 cm wide
Habit: tuft-forming perennial
Flowers: yellow; late summer; short blooming
period
Foliage: deep-red fall colour
Hardiness: C
Warnings: not prone to insects or disease
Expert Advice: This tiny plant adds late-
summer colour to the alpine garden.
Growing Requirements
Light: sun
Soil: gritty, lean, well-drained soil
Location: alpine gardens; rock gardens
Propagation: seed; division

Buying Considerations

Professionals
Popularity: relatively unknown
Availability: occasionally available from specialty growers
Size to Sell: sells best in smaller sizes (when blooming) as it matures slowly
Shrinkage: low; requires little maintenance

Collectors
Popularity: of interest to alpine collectors— unique, rare

Gardeners
Ease of Growth: mostly easy to grow
Start with: one small plant for feature plant and several for mass plantings

What to Try First ...
Ivesia lycopodioides

On the Market

Ivesia lycopodioides
Yellow flowers in late summer •
5–10 cm high, 10–15 cm wide

Jasione

Genus Information

Origin: the Mediterranean and Europe
Selected Common Names: sheep's bit
Nomenclature: From the Greek, *Jasione* is the name given by Theophrastus for *Convolvulus*.

General Features

Height: 20–30 cm high
Spread: 15–25 cm wide
Habit: tuft-forming perennial
Flowers: bluish, scabiosa-like; summer; long blooming period
Foliage: tiny; mid-green
Hardiness: C–D
Warnings: prone to aphids; not prone to diseases

Growing Requirements

Light: sun
Soil: moderately fertile, well-drained, neutral to acidic soil
Location: rock gardens; mixed borders
Propagation: seed; division
Expert Advice: Divide in spring.

Buying Considerations

Professionals
Popularity: relatively unknown
Availability: occasionally available from specialty growers
Size to Sell: sells best in smaller sizes (when blooming) as it matures slowly
Shrinkage: low; requires little maintenance

Collectors
Popularity: of interest to collectors—unique

Gardeners
Ease of Growth: mostly easy to grow
Start with: one mature plant for feature plant

What to Try First ...

Jasione laevis 'Blaulicht'

On the Market

Jasione laevis (syn. *J. perennis*)
'Blaulicht' (Blue Light) • Pincushion-shaped, blue flowers in summer • 20–30 cm high, 15–25 cm wide

Jeffersonia
p. 417

Genus Information

Origin: North America and East Asia
Selected Common Names: American twinleaf, Asian twinleaf
Nomenclature: This plant was named for United States President Thomas Jefferson, 1743–1826.

General Features

Height: 15–25 cm high
Spread: 20–30 cm wide
Habit: clump-forming perennial
Flowers: white to lavender-blue; single; spring
Foliage: rounded, opposite
Hardiness: C
Warnings: prone to aphids; not prone to diseases

Growing Requirements

Light: shade
Soil: moist, rich soil
Location: rock gardens; woodland gardens
Propagation: seed (self-sows); division
Expert Advice: Prefers a cool root run.

Buying Considerations

Professionals
Popularity: relatively unknown
Availability: occasionally available as bare root from specialty growers
Size to Sell: sells best in smaller sizes (when blooming) as it matures slowly
Shrinkage: high; goes dormant in pot

Collectors
Popularity: of interest to collectors—unique, rare, expensive

Gardeners
Ease of Growth: generally easy to grow
Start with: one mature plant for feature plant

What to Try First ...

Jeffersonia diphylla, *Jeffersonia dubia*

On the Market

Jeffersonia diphylla
Single, white flowers in spring • 15–25 cm high, 20–30 cm wide
Jeffersonia dubia
Lavender-blue flowers in spring • 15–25 cm high, 20–30 cm wide

Jovibarba
p. 417

Genus Information

Origin: Europe
Selected Common Names: Jupiter's beard
Nomenclature: From the Latin *Iovis* (of Jupiter) and *barba* (beard).
Notes: Formerly part of the genus *Sempervivum*. The 2 genera look vegetatively the same, but there are differences in the flower structure.

General Features

Height: 4–30 cm high
Spread: 15–45 cm wide
Habit: mat-forming, stoloniferous groundcover perennial

Flowers: green to yellow; summer
Foliage: rosette-forming; succulent
Hardiness: C
Warnings: prone to aphids; not prone to diseases

Growing Requirements

Light: sun
Soil: gritty, lean, poor, alkaline, well-drained soil
Location: rock walls; rock gardens; troughs
Propagation: separate and replant offsets
Expert Advice: Avoid planting in areas where soil is wet in winter (i.e. low spots).

Buying Considerations

Professionals

Popularity: gaining popularity as a foliage plant
Availability: generally available as finished product from specialty growers
Size to Sell: sells best in smaller sizes as it matures fast
On the Shelf: rapidly overgrows pot
Shrinkage: low; sensitive to overwatering; requires little maintenance

Collectors

Popularity: of interest to collectors—rare

Gardeners

Ease of Growth: generally easy to grow
Start with: one small plant for feature plant and several for mass plantings

What to Try First ...

Jovibarba 'Athos', *Jovibarba heuffelii*, *Jovibarba hirta*, *Jovibarba sobolifera*

On the Market

Jovibarba
Greenish to yellow flowers in summer • Evergreen, succulent foliage • 5–30 cm high, 15–45 cm wide
  'Athos' • Flowers in summer • Evergreen, succulent foliage • 5–30 cm high, 15–45 cm wide

Jovibarba (J. sobolifera x *J. hirta)*
Greenish-yellow flowers in summer • Red-purple-backed, grey-green rosettes of evergreen, succulent foliage • 10–20 cm high, 15–45 cm wide

Jovibarba allionii
Green to yellow-white flowers in summer • Forms red rosettes of evergreen, succulent foliage • 10–15 cm high, 15–45 cm wide

Jovibarba arenaria
Greenish-white flowers in summer • Flushed-red rosettes of evergreen, succulent foliage • 5–12 cm high, 15–45 cm wide

Jovibarba heuffelii
Yellow flowers in summer • Evergreen-succulent foliage • 10–20 cm high, 15–45 cm wide
  'Avant Garde' • Yellow flowers in summer • Green, with dark-red shading, evergreen, succulent foliage • 10–20 cm high, 15–45 cm wide
  'Beacon Hill' • Yellow flowers in summer • Satiny, grey-green and rose-purple rosettes of evergreen, succulent foliage • 10–20 cm high, 15–45 cm wide
  'Chocolate Sundae' • Yellow flowers in summer • Chocolate-red-brick rosettes of evergreen, succulent foliage • 10–20 cm high, 15–45 cm wide
  'Chryseis' • Yellow flowers in summer • Purple rosettes of green-edged, evergreen, succulent foliage • 10–20 cm high, 15–45 cm wide
  'Elinor' • Yellow flowers in summer • Green, with dark-red shading, evergreen, succulent foliage • 4–7 cm high, 15–45 cm wide
  'Fandango' • Yellow flowers in summer • Green, with dark-red shading, evergreen, succulent foliage • 7+ cm high, 15–45 cm wide
  'Gommerina' • Yellow flowers in summer • Dark-green, purple-tinted, evergreen, succulent foliage • 10–20 cm high, 15–45 cm wide
  'Hot Lips' • Yellow flowers in summer • Dark-red rosettes of evergreen, succulent foliage • 10–20 cm high, 15–45 cm wide
  'Inferno' • Yellow flowers in summer • Red, green-centred rosettes of evergreen, succulent foliage • 10–20 cm high, 15–45 cm wide
  'Luna' • Yellow flowers in summer • Green, with dark-red shading, evergreen, succulent foliage • 4–7 cm high, 15–45 cm wide
  'Maggie' • Yellow flowers in summer • Dark red-purple rosettes of evergreen, succulent foliage • 10–20 cm high, 15–45 cm wide
  'Midori' • Yellow flowers in summer • Satiny, grey-green and rose-purple rosettes of evergreen, succulent foliage • 4–7 cm high, 15–45 cm wide
  'Mystique' • Yellow flowers in summer • Green, with dark-red shading, evergreen, succulent foliage • 4–7 cm high, 15–45 cm wide

J

'Nanette' • Yellow flowers in summer • Green, with dark-red shading, evergreen, succulent foliage • 4–7 cm high, 15–45 cm wide

'Torrid Zone' • Yellow flowers in summer • Copper-red rosettes of evergreen, succulent foliage • 10–20 cm high, 15–45 cm wide

'Violet' • Yellow flowers in summer • Violet-purple rosettes of evergreen, succulent foliage • 10–20 cm high, 15–45 cm wide

Jovibarba hirta
Green-white to pale yellow flowers in summer • Red-backed rosettes of evergreen, succulent foliage • 5–20 cm high, 15–45 cm wide

'Histoni' • Green-white to pale-yellow flowers in summer • Blond-red rosettes of evergreen, succulent foliage • 5–30 cm high, 15–45 cm wide

'Preissiana' • Green-white to pale-yellow flowers in summer • Green, red-tipped, evergreen, succulent foliage • 5–30 cm high, 15–45 cm wide

'Prussiana' • Green-white to pale-yellow flowers in summer • Light-green, red-tipped, evergreen, succulent foliage • 5–30 cm high, 15–45 cm wide

Jovibarba hirta ssp. *borealis*
Yellow to white flowers in summer • Orange-backed rosettes of evergreen, succulent foliage • 5–20 cm high, 15–45 cm wide

Jovibarba hirta ssp. *glabrescens*
Green-white to pale yellow flowers in summer • Hairless rosettes of evergreen, succulent foliage • 5–30 cm high, 15–45 cm wide

Jovibarba sobolifera
Greenish-yellow flowers in summer • Apple-green, red-backed, red-tipped, evergreen, succulent foliage • 10–20 cm high, 15–45 cm wide

Juncus   p. 418 📷

Genus Information

Origin: temperate regions
Selected Common Names: hard rush, spiral rush
Nomenclature: From the Latin *iuncus* (a rush) and *iungere* (to join), referring to the use of the stems in tying.

General Features

Height: 30–100 cm high
Spread: 30–100 cm wide

Habit: aquatic, clump-forming or spreading perennial
Flowers: onion-like seed heads; summer
Foliage: reed-like; spiral
Hardiness: C–D
Warnings: prone to aphids; not prone to diseases; invasive in warmer climates (keep contained to prevent spread)
Expert Advice: This plant's dense spiral blades add interesting shape to ponds and pond edges.

Growing Requirements

Light: sun
Soil: moist to wet, alkaline soil
Location: ponds; water gardens; waterside plantings; plant at or slightly above water level
Propagation: species by seed; division; cultivars by division
Expert Advice: Germinate seed at 6–12˚C.

Buying Considerations

Professionals

Popularity: gaining popularity as a foliage plant
Availability: readily available as finished product
Size to Sell: sells best in smaller sizes as it matures fast
On the Shelf: high ornamental appeal; rapidly overgrows pot
Shrinkage: low; requires little maintenance

Collectors

Popularity: of interest to water gardening enthusiasts—novelty plant

Gardeners

Ease of Growth: mostly easy to grow
Start with: one small plant for feature plant

What to Try First ...

Juncus effusus f. *spiralis*, *Juncus inflexus*, *Juncus inflexus* 'Lovesick Blues'

On the Market

Juncus effusus
'Unicorn' • Brown seed heads in summer • Dark-green spiral foliage • 30–45 cm high, 45–60 cm wide

Juncus effusus f. *spiralis*
Brown seed heads in summer • Spiral stems • 30–45 cm high, 45–60 cm wide

Juncus inflexus
Brown seed heads in late spring • Blue-green, spiral stems • 60–100 cm high, 45–60 cm wide

'Afro' • Brown seed heads in late spring • Blue-green, spiral stems • 45–60 cm high, 30–60 cm wide

'Lovesick Blues' • Steely-blue foliage • Spiral stems • 60 cm high, 90 cm wide

J

Junellia

p. 418

Genus Information

Origin: Patagonia
Selected Common Names: unknown
Nomenclature: From the Latin *iuncus* (a rush) from *iungere* (to join), referring to the use of the stems in tying.
Notes: Related to the genus *Verbena*. There has been debate as to whether or not *Junellia* should be independent of *Verbena*.

General Features

Height: 0.5–1 cm high
Spread: 60–100 cm wide
Habit: short-lived, mat-forming, sub-shrubby perennial
Foliage: tiny; mid-green
Flowers: lilac; honey-scented
Hardiness: D
Warnings: not prone to insects or disease

Growing Requirements

Light: sun
Soil: lean soil
Location: alpine gardens; between paving stones
Propagation: seed (self-sows)

Buying Considerations

Professionals
Popularity: relatively unknown
Availability: occasionally available from specialty growers
Size to Sell: sells best in smaller sizes (when blooming) as it matures fast
Shrinkage: low; requires little maintenance

Collectors
Popularity: of interest to collectors—unique, rare

Gardeners
Ease of Growth: mostly easy to grow
Start with: one small plant for feature plant

What to Try First ...
Junellia wilczeckii

On the Market

Junellia wilczeckii
Fragrant, lilac flowers in summer •
0.5–1 cm high, 60–100 cm wide

Kelseya   p. 418 📷

Genus Information
Origin: western United States
Selected Common Names: unknown
Nomenclature: Named for Harlan Kelsey, 1872–1958, a nurseryman in Massachusetts.

General Features
Height: 4–8 cm high
Spread: 10–15 cm wide
Habit: slow-growing subshrub
Flowers: white; early summer
Foliage: silvery; rosette-forming evergreen
Hardiness: A
Warnings: not prone to insects or disease

Growing Requirements
Light: sun
Soil: moist, organic, sharply drained, gritty, alkaline soil; avoid winter wet
Location: rock gardens; scree; troughs; tufa
Propagation: seed; division; softwood cuttings
Expert Advice: Seed can be difficult to locate. Best germinted in tufa. Cuttings are difficult to root.

Buying Considerations
Professionals
Popularity: relatively unknown
Availability: occasionally available from specialty growers
Size to Sell: sells best in mature sizes as it matures slowly
Shrinkage: low; requires little maintenance

Collectors
Popularity: of interest to alpine collectors— unique, rare, challenge

Gardeners
Ease of Growth: mostly easy to grow, but need close attention to growing conditions
Start with: one mature plant for feature plant

What to Try First ...
Kelseya uniflora

On the Market
Kelseya uniflora
White or pink-flushed flowers in early summer • 4–8 cm high, 10–15 cm wide

Kirengeshoma   p. 418 📷

Genus Information
Origin: Japan and Korea
Selected Common Names: Japanese waxbells, Korean waxbells
Nomenclature: From the Japanese *ki* (yellow) and *rengeshoma,* a native name for *Anemopsis,* which the plant is said to resemble.

General Features
Height: 75–130 cm high
Spread: 50–75 cm wide
Habit: upright, clump-forming perennial; may require staking
Flowers: waxy, creamy-yellow; late summer to fall
Foliage: maple leaf-like
Hardiness: D
Warnings: prone to aphids
Expert Advice: As this plant's bloom period is late in the season, early frost may damage flowers before they open open in colder climates. Plant in a sheltered site.

Growing Requirements
Light: shade
Soil: moist, organic, acidic soil
Location: woodland gardens; cottage gardens; wild gardens; shelter from wind
Propagation: seed; division
Expert Advice: Seed can take up to 10 months to germinate. Divide frequently to keep vigorous.

K

Buying Considerations
Professionals
Popularity: gaining popularity
Availability: generally available as finished product and bare root
Size to Sell: sells best in when blooming
On the Shelf: rapidly overgrows pot; foliage breakage
Shrinkage: low; requires little maintenance

Collectors
Popularity: not generally of interest to collectors

Gardeners
Ease of Growth: mostly easy to grow
Start with: one small plant for feature plant

What to Try First ...
Kirengeshoma palmata

On the Market
Kirengeshoma palmata
Waxy, bell-like, yellow flowers in late summer to fall • 75–130 cm high, 50–75 cm wide

Korean Group
Waxy, bell-like, yellow flowers in late summer to fall • 75–110 cm high, 50–75 cm wide

Knautia

p. 418

Genus Information

Origin: Siberia, the Caucasus, Europe and North Africa
Selected Common Names: crimson scabious, maroon scabious, scabious, pincushion plant
Nomenclature: Named for Christian Knaut, 1654–1716, a German botanist.

General Features

Height: 40–80 cm high
Spread: 30–50 cm wide
Habit: clump-forming, sprawling perennial; benefits from caging
Foliage: dark-green
Flowers: dark-red; pincushion-like; borne on tall stalks; summer
Hardiness: B–C
Warnings: prone to powdery mildew and aphids

Growing Requirements

Light: sun
Soil: moderately fertile, well-drained, alkaline soil
Location: wild gardens; cottage gardens
Propagation: seed; basal cuttings

Buying Considerations

Professionals

Popularity: gaining popularity
Availability: generally available as finished product and bare root
Size to Sell: sells best in smaller sizes (when blooming) as it matures fast
On the Shelf: rapidly overgrows pot; deadhead regularly; foliage breakage
Shrinkage: low; requires little maintenance

Collectors

Popularity: not generally of interest to collectors

Gardeners

Ease of Growth: very easy to grow
Start with: one small plant for feature plant

What to Try First ...

Knautia macedonica, Knautia macedonica 'Mars Midget'

On the Market

Knautia macedonica
Small, pincushion-like, dark-purple to red flowers in summer • 60–80 cm high, 30–45 cm wide

'Mars Midget' • Pincushion like, ruby-red flowers in summer • 40–45 cm high, 40–50 cm wide

Koeleria

p. 418

Genus Information

Origin: temperate regions and tropical Africa
Selected Common Names: blue hair grass
Nomenclature: Named for George Koeler, 1765–1806, a botanist who specialized in grasses.

General Features

Height: 40–60 cm high
Spread: 20–30 cm wide
Habit: clump-forming grass
Flowers: shiny spikes on slender stems; summer; good for cutflowers; good for drying
Foliage: silver-green
Hardiness: D
Warnings: prone to aphids and rust
Expert Advice: Deadhead to keep plant compact.

Growing Requirements

Light: sun
Soil: well-drained, alkaline soil
Location: rock gardens; mixed borders
Propagation: seed (self-sows); division

Buying Considerations

Professionals

Popularity: relatively unknown foliage plant
Availability: generally available as finished product
Size to Sell: sells best in smaller sizes as it matures fast
On the Shelf: prone to rust in pot
Shrinkage: low; requires little maintenance

Collectors

Popularity: not generally of interest to collectors

Gardeners

Ease of Growth: very easy to grow
Start with: one small plant for feature plant

What to Try First ...

Koeleria glauca

On the Market

Koeleria glauca
Shiny, silver-green, aging to buff, spikelets in summer • Grey-green foliage • 40–60 cm high, 20–30 cm wide

K

Lamium

p. 418 📷

Genus Information

Origin: Europe, North Africa and Asia
Selected Common Names: deadnettle, spotted deadnettle, white archangel
Nomenclature: From the Greek word for "throat," referring to the hooded flowers. A Latin name used by Pliny.

General Features

Height: 10–35 cm high
Spread: 20–100+ cm wide
Habit: spreading groundcover perennial
Flowers: pink, purple, yellow or white; tiny, snapdragon-like; spring to summer; deadhead to keep plant compact
Foliage: rough; green, gold or silver; (some) variegated
Hardiness: C
Warnings: prone to aphids; not prone to diseases
Expert Advice: *Lamium's* colourful, showy foliage brightens shady areas. An adaptable and non-invasive groundcover that roots at ground level. Deadhead and cutback to keep compact. Can be mowed.

Growing Requirements

Light: sun or shade
Soil: moist, well-drained soil; tolerant of a wide range of soils
Propagation: seed, division, basal cuttings
Expert Advice: Seeding can be difficult.

Buying Considerations

Professionals
Popularity: popular, garden standard foliage plant
Availability: readily available as finished product
Size to Sell: sells best in smaller sizes (when blooming) as it matures fast
On the Shelf: high ornamental appeal; keep stock rotated; rapidly overgrows pot; prone to powdery mildew in the pot
Shrinkage: low; requires little maintenance

Collectors
Popularity: not generally of interest to collectors

Gardeners
Ease of Growth: very easy to grow
Start with: one small plant for feature plant and several for mass plantings

What to Try First ...
Lamium armenum, Lamium galeobdolon 'Herman's Pride', *Lamium maculatum* 'Beacon Silver', *Lamium maculatum* 'Pink Pewter', *Lamium maculatum* 'Purple Dragon', *Lamium maculatum* 'White Nancy'

On the Market

Lamium album
'Friday' • White flowers in spring • Green foliage with gold centre • 30–60 cm high, 60–90+ cm wide

Lamium armenum
Ice-pink to white, hooded flowers in summer • Parsley-like foliage • 5–10 cm high, 30–45 cm wide

Lamium armenum ssp. *armenum*
White flowers in summer • Parsley-like, aromatic foliage • 5–10 cm high, 30–45 cm wide

Lamium armenum ssp. *sintenisii*
Pink and cream flowers in summer • Parsley-like, aromatic foliage • 5–10 cm high, 30–45 cm wide

Lamium eriocephalum ssp. *eriocephalum*
Pink flowers in summer • 10–15 cm high, 15–25 cm wide

Lamium galeobdolon (syn. *Galeobdolon luteum*)
'Herman's Pride' • Yellow flowers in summer • Green veins in silver foliage • 20–30 cm high, 45–60+ cm wide

Lamium galeobdolon ssp. *montanum*
'Florentinum' (Variegatum) • Lemon-yellow flowers in summer • Silver-centred foliage with green edges • 30–45 cm high, 60–100+ cm wide

Lamium garganicum ssp. *garganicum*
Pink-purple, sometimes white flowers in summer • 10–35 cm high, 30–45 cm wide

Lamium garganicum ssp. *laevigatum*
Hooded, pink flowers in summer • Crinkled, dark-green foliage • 10–35 cm high, 30–45 cm wide

Lamium maculatum
'Anne Greenaway' • Mauve flowers in spring to summer • Green foliage with chartreuse and silver • 15–25 cm high, 60–100+ cm wide

'Aureum' (Gold Leaf) • Pink flowers in spring to summer • Yellow foliage with white centre • 15–25 cm high, 60–100+ cm wide

'Beacon Silver' • Soft-pink flowers in spring to summer • Metallic-silver foliage with green edge • 15–25 cm high, 60–100+ cm wide

'Chequers' • Pink flowers in spring to summer • Dark-green foliage with silver stripe • 15–25 cm high, 60–100+ cm wide

L

'Golden Anniversary' (Dellam) • Pink flowers in spring to summer • Green foliage with gold splotches • 15–25 cm high, 60–100+ cm wide

'Orchid Frost' • Orchid-pink flowers in spring to summer • Silvery-blue-green foliage • 10–25 cm high, 60–100+ cm wide

'Pink Pewter' • Pink flowers in spring to summer • Silver and green foliage • 15–25 cm high, 60–100+ cm wide

'Purple Dragon' • Deep-purple flowers in spring to summer • Silver and green foliage • 10–25 cm high, 60–100 cm wide

'White Nancy' • White flowers in spring to summer • Silver foliage with green edge • 15–25 cm high, 60–100+ cm wide

Lathyrus

p. 418

Genus Information

Origin: northern temperate regions, temperate South America and the mountains of Africa
Selected Common Names: perennial sweet pea
Nomenclature: From *la* (very) and *thoures* (stimulant), referring to the seeds' having stimulant properties. Name used by Theophrastus from the ancient Greek name for "pea" or "pulse."
Notes: This genus includes the fragrant annual sweet pea.

General Features

Height: 2–3 m high
Spread: 60–90 cm wide
Habit: clump-forming perennial; climbing or sprawling but requires staking or support
Flowers: pea-like; summer to fall
Foliage: pea-like
Hardiness: C–D
Warnings: prone to aphids; invasive in warm climates
Expert Advice: Gardeners are often disappointed to learn that this plant bears very little resemblance to annual sweet peas in terms of amount, colour and fragrance of blooms.

Growing Requirements

Light: sun
Soil: fertile, organic, well-drained soil
Location: mixed borders on trellis or obelisk
Propagation: seed
Expert Advice: Presoak seed or plant on site in spring. Does not divide easily or transplant well.

Buying Considerations

Professionals

Popularity: old-fashioned garden standard
Availability: readily available as finished product
Size to Sell: sells best in smaller sizes (when blooming) as it matures fast
On the Shelf: requires staking
Shrinkage: low; requires little maintenance

Collectors

Popularity: not generally of interest to collectors

Gardeners

Ease of Growth: mostly easy to grow
Start with: one small plant for feature plant

What to Try First ...

Lathyrus latifolius

On the Market

Lathyrus latifolius
White, pink or rose-red flowers in summer to fall • Blue-green foliage • 2–3 m high, 60–90 cm wide

Lavandula

p. 418

Genus Information

Origin: India, West Asia, Arabia, the Mediterranean and tropical Africa
Selected Common Names: true lavender
Nomenclature: From the Latin *lavo* (I wash), referring to lavender water, which has been long used as a fragrant wash, made from oil of lavender.
Other Uses: This plant is grown commercially for the fragrance, and it is used in a wide variety of products from lavender cookies to sachets, potpourri and cosmetics.

General Features

Height: 30–45 cm high
Spread: 45–60 wide
Habit: short-lived, shrubby or woody perennial
Flowers: fragrant; good for drying; attractive to bees (high in nectar)
Foliage: silvery-green; evergreen; aromatic
Hardiness: D
Warnings: prone to aphids
Expert Advice: This popular plant desiccates on the Prairies and as a result is short-lived. Plant in a warm, protected site and provide winter protection. In warmer climates it can be grown as a striking fragrant hedge.

Growing Requirements

Light: sun
Soil: moderately fertile, well-drained soil; not tolerant of winter wet

Location: sheltered locations; borders; raised beds; hedging (warm climates)
Propagation: seed; cuttings
Expert Advice: Take cuttings in early summer and semi-ripe cuttings in late summer.

Buying Considerations

Professionals
Popularity: popular, old-fashioned garden standard; fast-selling foliage plant
Availability: readily available as finished product
Size to Sell: sells best in smaller sizes (when blooming) as it matures fast
On the Shelf: high ornamental appeal and fragrant
Shrinkage: low; requires little maintenance

Collectors
Popularity: not generally of interest to collectors (although of interest to herbalists)

Gardeners
Ease of Growth: mostly easy to grow
Start with: one small plant for feature plant and several for mass plantings

What to Try First ...
Lavandula angustifolia, *Lavandula angustifolia* 'Jean Davis', *Lavandula angustifolia* 'Martha Roderick', *Lavandula angustifolia* 'Munstead'

On the Market

Lavandula angustifolia
Fragrant, lavender-blue or pink flowers in summer • Evergreen foliage • 40–60 cm high, 45–60 cm wide

'Blue Cushion' (Lavandula Schola) • Fragrant, purple-blue flowers in summer • Evergreen foliage • 30–45 cm high, 45–60 cm wide

'Hidcote' (Hidcote Blue) • Fragrant, purple flowers in summer • Silver-grey, evergreen foliage • 45–60 cm high, 50–75 cm wide

'Jean Davis' • Fragrant, soft pink flowers in summer • Evergreen foliage • 35–45 cm high, 45–60 cm wide

'Martha Roderick' • Fragrant, blue flowers in summer • Evergreen foliage • 40 cm high, 60 cm wide

'Munstead' • Fragrant, lavender flowers in summer • Evergreen foliage • 30–45 cm high, 45–60 cm wide

'Rosea' • Fragrant, rose-lavender flowers in summer • Evergreen foliage • 30–45 cm high, 45–60 cm wide

Lavatera
p. 418

Genus Information
Origin: Asia, Australia, the Mediterranean, Macronesia and California
Selected Common Names: tree mallow
Nomenclature: Named for Johann Lavater, 1741–1801, a 16th century physician in Zurich.
Notes: The genus includes annuals, biennials and perennials.

General Features
Height: 90–150 cm high
Spread: 60–90 cm wide
Habit: bushy, upright, clump-forming biennial or perennial
Flowers: large, showy bunches; summer to fall
Hardiness: C–D
Warnings: prone to powdery mildew and aphids
Expert Advice: Species plants are hardiest but all require shelter from cold, drying winds. Requires warm springs. Mulch for winter. Not reliably hardy on the Prairies.

Growing Requirements
Light: sun
Soil: moderately fertile, well-drained soil
Location: mixed borders; avoid windy locations
Propagation: seed; cuttings
Expert Advice: Take softwood cuttings in spring to early summer.

Buying Considerations

Professionals
Popularity: popular garden standard; fast seller in bloom
Availability: readily available as finished product and bare root
Size to Sell: sells best in smaller sizes (when blooming) as it matures fast
On the Shelf: rapidly overgrows pot
Shrinkage: high; sensitive to overwatering

Collectors
Popularity: not generally of interest to collectors

Gardeners
Ease of Growth: mostly easy to grow but requires close attention to growing conditions
Start with: one small plant for feature plant

What to Try First ...
Lavatera 'Sweet Dreams', *Lavatera* x *clementii* 'Rosea', *Lavatera thuringiaca*

L

On the Market

Lavatera
'Summer Kisses' • Fragrant, soft red-pink flowers in summer to fall • 1.2–1.5 m high, 60–90 cm wide

'Sweet Dreams' • Hibiscus-like, white to pink flowers in summer to fall • 1.2–1.5 m high, 60–90 cm wide

'White Angel' • Large, soft-pink flowers in summer to fall • 1.2–1.5 m high, 60–90 cm wide

Lavatera x *clementii*
'Barnsley' • White flowers with crimson eye that fades pink in summer to fall • 1.2–1.5 m high, 60–90 cm wide

'Bredon Springs' • Mauve, flushed dusky-pink flowers in summer to fall • 1.2–1.5 m high, 60–90 cm wide

'Candy Floss' • Bright-pink flowers in summer to fall • 1.2–1.5 m high, 60–90 cm wide

'Eye Catcher' • Wine-red flowers with dark eye and veins in summer to fall • 1.2–1.5 m high, 60–90 cm wide

'Kew Rose' • Rose-pink flowers with darker veins in summer to fall • 1.2–1.5 m high, 60–90 cm wide

'Rosea' • Pink-mauve flowers in summer to fall • 1.2–1.5 m high, 60–90 cm wide

Lavatera maritima
White to pink flowers with purple base in late summer to fall • 90–100 cm high, 60–75 cm wide

Lavatera thuringiaca
Soft-pink flowers in summer to fall • 1.2–1.5 m high, 60–90 cm wide

Leontopodium   p. 418

Genus Information

Origin: Europe and Asia
Selected Common Names: edelweiss
Nomenclature: From the Greek Lion and *pous*, referring to the shape of the flower heads.
Notes: This plant is especially beloved by Austrians. It is grown for romantic associations rather than for the beauty of its flowers.

General Features

Height: 15–20 cm high
Spread: 20–30 cm wide
Habit: clump- to mat-forming perennial
Flowers: downy, silver-grey to white; spring
Foliage: downy; grey-green
Hardiness: B–C
Warnings: prone to aphids

Growing Requirements

Light: sun
Soil: dry, lean, well-drained to sharply drained, neutral to alkaline soil; tolerates acidic soil
Location: rock gardens; troughs; raised beds
Propagation: seed; division
Expert Advice: Avoid planting in soil that is wet in winter or has standing water in spring.

Buying Considerations

Professionals
Popularity: popular foliage plant
Availability: readily available as finished product
Size to Sell: sells best in smaller sizes as it matures fast
On the Shelf: rapidly overgrows pot
Shrinkage: low; requires little maintenance

Collectors
Popularity: not generally of interest to collectors

Gardeners
Ease of Growth: mostly easy to grow
Start with: one small plant for feature plant

What to Try First ...
Leontopodium alpinum

On the Market

Leontopodium alpinum
Silver-grey flowers in spring • Grey-green foliage • 15–20 cm high, 20–30 cm wide

Leonurus

Genus Information

Origin: Europe, temperate Asia and the tropics
Selected Common Names: common motherwort
Nomenclature: From *Leonurus,* referring to a lion's tail.
Other Uses: It has been used medicinally since medieval times. For example, it was used to treat pregnant women for anxiety, hence the use of the word "mother" in the common name.

General Features

Height: 75–150 cm high
Spread: 45–60 cm wide
Habit: upright, clump-forming perennial
Flowers: white or pink; summer
Hardiness: C
Warnings: prone to aphids; not prone to diseases
Expert Advice: Adapts well to most garden soils. Suited to herb or wild gardens.

Growing Requirements

Light: sun
Soil: well-drained soil; (tolerates) poor, dry soil; drought tolerant

Location: herb gardens; wild gardens
Propagation: seed (self-sows); division

Buying Considerations
Professionals
Popularity: relatively unknown
Availability: occasionally available from specialty growers
Size to Sell: sells best in smaller sizes (when blooming) as it matures fast
On the Shelf: rapidly overgrows pot
Shrinkage: low; requires little maintenance
Collectors
Popularity: not generally of interest to collectors
Gardeners
Ease of Growth: very easy to grow
Start with: one small plant for feature plant
What To Try First ...
Leonurus cardiaca

On the Market
Leonurus cardiaca
White or pink flowers in summer • 75–150 cm high, 45–60 cm wide

Lepidium

Genus Information
Origin: worldwide
Selected Common Names: pepperwort
Nomenclature: From the Greek *lepis* (scale), referring to the shape of the fruits. A name used by Dioscorides.
Other Uses: *L. sativum* has long been used as a green salad vegetable.
Notes: *Lepidium* is related to garden cress. The genus includes annuals, biennials and perennials.
General Features
Height: 2–4 cm high
Spread: 10–15 cm wide
Habit: dense, cushion-forming perennial
Flowers: cream-white; spring
Foliage: tiny; mid-green
Hardiness: D
Warnings: not prone to insects or disease
Growing Requirements
Light: sun
Soil: well-drained soil
Location: alpine gardens
Propagation: seed

Buying Considerations
Professionals
Popularity: relatively unknown
Availability: occasionally available from specialty growers
Size to Sell: sells best in mature sizes (when blooming) as it grows slowly
Shrinkage: low; requires little maintenance
Collectors
Popularity: of interest to collectors—unique, rare
Gardeners
Ease of Growth: mostly easy to grow
Start with: one small plant for feature plant
What to Try First ...
Lepidium nanum

On the Market
Lepidium nanum (Nevada Racemose form)
Cream-white flowers in spring • 2–4 cm high, 10–15 cm wide

Lesquerella   p. 418 📷

Genus Information
Origin: North America
Selected Common Names: bladder pod
Nomenclature: Named for Leo Lesquereux, 1806–1889, a 19th century American paleo-botanist.
Notes: Genus includes annuals and perennials.
General Features
Height: 10–15 cm high
Spread: 10–15 cm wide
Habit: clump- or tuft-forming perennial
Flowers: yellow; spring
Foliage: silvery-grey
Hardiness: C–D
Warnings: prone to aphids; not prone to disease
Expert Advice: Produces ornamental bladder-like seed pods.
Growing Requirements
Light: sun
Soil: lean, sharply drained soil
Location: rock gardens; raised beds; wall crevices; wild gardens
Propagation: seed

Buying Considerations
Professionals
Popularity: relatively unknown
Availability: occasionally available from specialty growers
Size to Sell: sells best in smaller sizes (when blooming) as it matures fast
On the Shelf: rapidly overgrows pot
Shrinkage: low; requires little maintenance

Collectors
Popularity: not generally of interest to collectors

Gardeners
Ease of Growth: mostly easy to grow
Start with: one small plant for feature plant

What to Try First ...
Lesquerella ovalifolia

On the Market

Lesquerella ovalifolia
Yellow flowers in spring • Grey foliage •
10–15 cm high, 10–15 cm wide

Leucanthemopsis p. 418

Genus Information

Origin: the mountains of Europe and North Africa
Selected Common Names: alpine daisy, alpine moon daisy
Nomenclature: This plant's name comes from *Leucanthemum*, which comes from the Greek *leukos* (white) and *anthemon* (flower), and the Greek *opsis* (appearance).

General Features
Height: 10–15 cm high
Spread: 20–30 cm wide
Habit: tuft- or clump-forming perennial
Flowers: daisy-like; summer
Foliage: tiny
Hardiness: D
Warnings: prone to powdery mildew and aphids

Growing Requirements
Light: sun
Soil: well-drained soil
Location: alpine gardens; rock gardens
Propagation: seed; division; basal cuttings

Buying Considerations

Professionals
Popularity: relatively unknown
Availability: occasionally available from specialty growers
Size to Sell: sells best in smaller sizes (when blooming) as it matures fast
On the Shelf: rapidly overgrows pot
Shrinkage: low; requires little maintenance

Collectors
Popularity: of interest to collectors—rare

Gardeners
Ease of Growth: mostly easy to grow
Start with: one small plant for feature plant

What to Try First ...
Leucanthemopsis alpina

On the Market

Leucanthemopsis alpina
Pink or white flowers in summer •
10–15 cm high, 20–30 cm wide

Leucanthemopsis pectinata
(syn. *L. radicans*)
Sulphur-yellow flowers, aging orange-red, in summer • 10–15 cm high, 20–30 cm wide

Leucanthemum p. 418

Genus Information

Origin: Europe and temperate Asia
Selected Common Names: Shasta daisy
Nomenclature: From the Greek *leukos* (white) and *anthemon* (flower). The name "Shasta," used for many in this genus, comes from the Shasta Mountains in California, where Luther Burbank had his horticultural test plots.
Notes: Genus includes annuals and perennials

General Features
Height: 25–90 cm high
Spread: 20–60 cm wide
Habit: upright, clump-forming, short-lived perennial
Flowers: single, semi-double or double; white with yellow centres; summer; good for cutflowers; deadhead to prolong blooming
Foliage: mid-green
Hardiness: B–C
Warnings: prone to powdery mildew and aphids; not bothered by deer
Expert Advice: Can become weedy. Single forms are somewhat hardier than double. Hybrids will not come true from seed.

Growing Requirements
Light: sun
Soil: fertile, moist, well-drained soil
Location: English gardens; cottage gardens; rock gardens; cutting gardens; wild gardens; mixed borders; herb borders
Propagation: seed (self-sows readily); division; cuttings
Expert Advice: Seed in spring. Divide frequently to keep vigorous.

Buying Considerations

Professionals

Popularity: popular, old-fashioned garden standard; fast seller in bloom
Availability: readily available as finished product
Size to Sell: sells best in smaller sizes (when blooming) as it matures fast
On the Shelf: rapidly overgrows pot
Shrinkage: low; requires little maintenance

Collectors

Popularity: not generally of interest to collectors

Gardeners

Ease of Growth: mostly easy to grow
Start with: one small plant for feature plant

What to Try First ...

Leucanthemum 'Sedgewick', *Leucanthemum* x *superbum* 'Esther Read', *Leucanthemum* x *superbum* 'Gruppenstolz', *Leucanthemum* x *superbum* 'Silberprinzesschen', *Leucanthemum* x *superbum* 'Snowcap'

On the Market

Leucanthemum
'Sedgewick' • Double, white flowers with yellow eye in summer • 30–40 cm high, 20–30 cm wide

Leucanthemum x *superbum*
Single or double, white flowers with yellow to orange eye in summer • 60–90 cm high, 45–60 cm wide

'Aglaia' • Fringed, semi-double, white flowers in summer • 45–60 cm high, 30–60 cm wide

'Alaska' • Single, white flowers with yellow centres in late spring to fall • 60–75 cm high, 30–60 cm wide

'Barbara Bush' • Single, white flowers in summer • Foliage has cream edge • 60–90 cm high, 45–60 cm wide

'Becky' • Single, white flowers in summer • 60–90 cm high, 30–60 cm wide

'Crazy Daisy' • Single, white flowers, yellow centres, in late spring to fall • 60–75 cm high, 30–60 cm wide

'Esther Read' • Fully double, white flowers in summer • 45–60 cm high, 45–60 cm wide

'Gruppenstolz' • Large, semi-double, white flowers in summer • 60–80 cm high, 30–45 cm wide

'Marconi' • Double, white flowers in summer • 60–90 cm high, 45–60 cm wide

'Silberprinzesschen' (Little Princess, Silver Princess) • White flowers with orange eye in summer • 20–30 cm high, 30–45 cm wide

'Snowcap' • Single, white flowers with yellow to orange eye in summer • 30–35 cm high, 30–35 cm wide

'Snow Lady' • Single, white flowers with yellow eye in summer • 25–45 cm high, 30–40 cm wide

'Summer Snowball' • Double, white flowers in summer • 60–90 cm high, 45–60 cm wide

'T.E. Killin' (Thomas Killin) • Double-petalled, white flowers with yellow centre in summer • 60–90 cm high, 45–60 cm wide

Lewisia
p. 418

Genus Information

Origin: western North America
Selected Common Names: bitterroot
Nomenclature: Named for Meriwether Lewis, 1774–1809, of the Lewis and Clark expeditions.

General Features

Height: 2–30 cm high
Spread: 10–30 cm wide
Habit: clump-forming perennial
Flowers: brightly coloured; spring to summer; some species may go dormant after flowering
Foliage: deciduous or evergreen
Hardiness: C–D
Warnings: not prone to insects or disease; prone to rot if wet during dormancy
Expert Advice: This tiny plant garners a lot of interest because of its beautiful, colourful blooms. Many are rare collector's species.

Growing Requirements

Light: evergreen types prefer sun to p.m. sun; shelter from hot p.m. sun; deciduous types prefer full sun
Soil: lean, dry, gritty soil; keep soil moist when blooming; soil must be drier during dormancy
Location: rock gardens; alpine gardens; slopes; wall crevices; scree
Propagation: seed; leaf cuttings; offshoots
Expert Advice: *Lewisia* hybridizes easily. May not come true from seed.

Buying Considerations

Professionals

Popularity: popular perennial; fast seller in bloom
Availability: readily available as finished product
Size to Sell: sells best in smaller sizes (when blooming) as it matures fast
On the Shelf: rapidly overgrows pot; foliage breakage
Shrinkage: low; sensitive to overwatering; requires little maintenance

Collectors

Popularity: of interest to collectors—unique

Gardeners

Ease of Growth: mostly easy to grow but requires close attention to growing conditions
Start with: one small plant for feature plant

What to Try First ...

Lewisia 'Little Plum', *Lewisia* 'Pinkie', *Lewisia brachycalyx*, *Lewisia columbiana*, *Lewisia columbiana* ssp. *rupicola*, *Lewisia cotyledon* (mix), *Lewisia longipetala*

On the Market

Lewisia
  'George Henley' • Magenta flowers in summer • Evergreen foliage • 10–15 cm high, 15–20 cm wide
  'Little Plum' • Rose-purple, orange-tinted flowers in spring • 8–10 cm high, 10–15 cm wide
  'Pinkie' • Soft rose-pink flowers in summer • Evergreen • 5–10 cm high, 10–15 cm wide

Lewisia (L. brachycalyx x *L. cotyledon)*
Range of flower colours: pinks, oranges and yellows • Flowers in summer • Evergreen foliage • 5–10 cm high, 10–15 cm wide

Lewisia
(L. cotyledon x *L. columbiana* ssp. *rupicola)*
Bright-pink flowers in summer • Evergreen foliage • 20–30 cm high, 15–25 cm wide

Lewisia brachycalyx
Large, soft-pink flowers in spring • 5–10 cm high, 10–15 cm wide
  'Alba' • White flowers in spring • 5–10 cm high, 10–15 cm wide

Lewisia cantelovii
White or soft-pink flowers with darker stripes in spring • 15–30 cm high, 10–15 cm wide

Lewisia columbiana
Pink or white flowers with pink veins in summer • Evergreen foliage • 20–30 cm high, 20–30 cm wide
  'Edithae' • Large, salmon-pink flowers in summer • Evergreen foliage • 20–30 cm high, 20–30 cm wide

Lewisia columbiana ssp. *columbiana*
Pink flowers or white flowers with pink veins in summer • Evergreen foliage • 20–30 cm high, 20–30 cm wide

Lewisia columbiana ssp. *rupicola*
(syn. 'Rosea')
Rose flowers in summer • Evergreen foliage • 10–20 cm high, 20–30 cm wide

Lewisia columbiana ssp. *wallowensis*
Pink flowers or white flowers with pink veins in summer • Evergreen foliage • 20–30 cm high, 20–30 cm wide

Lewisia cotyledon
  Ashwood strain • Shades of magenta, orange or yellow, double flowers in summer • Evergreen foliage • 20–30 cm high, 15–25 cm wide
  Birch strain • Rose-pink flowers in summer • Evergreen foliage • 20–30 cm high, 15–25 cm wide
  'Praline' • Semi-double flowers in summer • Evergreen foliage • 20–30 cm high, 15–25 cm wide
  'Regenbogen' (Rainbow) • Flowers in mixed colours in summer • Evergreen foliage • 20–30 cm high, 15–25 cm wide
  Shalpines hybrids • Flowers in summer • Evergreen foliage • 20–30 cm high, 15–25 cm wide

Sunset Group
Flowers in summer in shades of bright-magenta, bright-red, orange, pink, red-orange, salmon-pink, yellow and pink-and-white-stripes • Evergreen foliage • 20–30 cm high, 15–25 cm wide

Lewisia cotyledon f. *alba*
White flowers in summer • Evergreen foliage • 20–30 cm high, 20–30 cm wide

Lewisia cotyledon var. *heckneri*
Striped, pink to purple flowers in summer • Evergreen foliage • 20–30 cm high, 15–25 cm wide

Lewisia leeana (syn. *L. leana*)
Pink to purple, sometimes white flowers in summer • Evergreen foliage • 10–20 cm high, 10–15 cm wide

L

Lewisia longipetala
Star-shaped, pink or white flowers in summer • 5–10 cm high, 5–10 cm wide

Lewisia nevadensis
White flowers in summer • 10–20 cm high, 10–15 cm wide

'**Rosea**' • Rose-pink flowers with dark veins in summer • 10–15 cm high, 10–15 cm wide

Lewisia pygmaea
Large, pink to purple, sometimes white flowers in summer • 5–10 cm high, 8–12 cm wide

from **Colorado** • Large, white flowers in summer • 5–10 cm high, 8–12 cm wide

Mt. Tahoma form • Large, pink flowers in summer • 5–10 cm high, 8–12 cm wide

Lewisia rediviva
Huge, pink or white flowers in spring • Summer dormant • 2–5 cm high, 5–10 cm wide

Lewisia rediviva ssp. *minor*
White flowers in spring • 2–5 cm high, 5–10 cm wide

Lewisia sierrae
Dark-veined, pink, sometimes white flowers in summer • 2–5 cm high, 5–10 cm wide

Lewisia stebbinsii
Dark-veined, rose flowers in summer • 2–5 cm high, 5–10 cm wide

Lewisia tweedyi
Apricot, rarely white flowers in spring to early summer • Evergreen foliage • 10–20 cm high, 15–20 cm wide

'**Alba**' • White flowers in spring to early summer • Evergreen foliage • 10–20 cm high, 15–20 cm wide

'**Lovedream**' • Pink flowers in spring to early summer • Evergreen foliage • 10–20 cm high, 15–20 cm wide

Habit: rhizomatous, aggressively spreading grass
Flowers: seed heads; late summer to fall; deadhead to keep plant compact
Foliage: blue; long, sharp blades
Hardiness: B–C
Warnings: prone to aphids; invasive (keep contained and deadhead to prevent spread)
Expert Advice: *Leymus* can help anchor slopes and banks. Not to be confused with *Elymus* which is also blue, but far less aggressively spreading.

Growing Requirements
Light: sun
Soil: moderately fertile, well-drained soil; tolerates a wide range of soils; tolerates dry soil
Location: banks; slopes; contained beds
Propagation: division

Buying Considerations
Professionals
Popularity: gaining popularity as a foliage plant
Availability: readily available as finished product
Size to Sell: sells best in smaller sizes as it matures fast
On the Shelf: rapidly overgrows pot
Shrinkage: low; requires little maintenance

Collectors
Popularity: not generally of interest to collectors

Gardeners
Ease of Growth: very easy to grow
Start with: one small plant for feature plant

What to Try First ...
Leymus arenarius

On the Market
Leymus arenarius
(syn. *L. arenarius* 'Glaucus')
Beige seed heads in summer • Silver-blue foliage • 1.2–1.5 m high, 60–90+ cm wide

L

Leymus   p. 418 📷
Genus Information
Origin: northern temperate zones and Argentina
Selected Common Names: European dune grass
Nomenclature: From the Greek *elymos*, referring to a type of millet.
Notes: Many species were formerly included in the genus *Elymus*.

General Features
Height: 30–150 cm high
Spread: 30–90 cm wide

Liatris   p. 419 📷
Genus Information
Origin: North America
Selected Common Names: blazing star, button snakeroot, Kansas gayfeather, spiked gayfeather
Nomenclature: The name *Liatris* is of unknown origin.

General Features
Height: 45–90 cm high
Spread: 30–45 cm wide

Habit: upright, clump-forming, corm-like, tuberous perennial

Flowers: purple or white in spikes; late summer to fall; good for cutflowers; good for dried flowers; attractive to bees and butterflies

Foliage: lance-shaped, grass-like

Hardiness: B

Warnings: prone to powdery mildew and aphids

Expert Advice: Flowers open from the tip of the spike downward. Looks its best as a single plant rather than in groups, but is attractive dispersed throughout a bed or border.

Growing Requirements

Light: sun

Soil: moderately fertile, moist, well-drained soil; drought tolerant once established; avoid soils that remain wet in spring

Location: mixed borders; wild gardens; cottage gardens; cutting gardens

Propagation: seed (self-sows); division

Expert Advice: Seed in fall.

Buying Considerations

Professionals

Popularity: popular garden standard; fast seller in bloom

Availability: readily available as finished product and bare root

Size to Sell: sells best in smaller sizes (when blooming) as it matures fast

On the Shelf: rapidly overgrows pot

Shrinkage: low; requires little maintenance

Collectors

Popularity: not generally of interest to collectors

Gardeners

Ease of Growth: mostly easy to grow

Start with: one small plant for feature plant

What To Try First ...

Liatris punctata, Liatris spicata, Liatris spicata 'Floristan Violett', *Liatris spicata* 'Floristan Weiss', *Liatris spicata* 'Kobold'

On the Market

Liatris ligulistylis
Purple flowers in late summer • 45–60 cm high, 30–45 cm wide

Liatris punctata
Spiked, purple flowers in late summer to fall • 60–80 cm high, 30–45 cm wide

Liatris spicata
Spiked, purple flowers in late summer • 60–90 cm high, 30–45 cm wide

'Alba' • Spiked, white flowers in late summer • 60–90 cm high, 30–45 cm wide

'Floristan Violett' (Floristan Violet) • Spiked, violet-purple flowers in late summer • 60–90 cm high, 30–45 cm wide

'Floristan Weiss' (Floristan White) • Spiked, white flowers in late summer • 60–90 cm high, 30–45 cm wide

'Kobold' (Goblin) • Spiked, purple flowers in late summer • 45–60 cm high, 30–45 cm wide

Ligularia

p. 419

Genus Information

Origin: Asia and Europe

Selected Common Names: big leaf rayflower, elephant ears, goldenray, leopard plant, rayflower

Nomenclature: From the Latin *ligula* (little tongue), referring to the tongue shape of the ray florets.

Notes: This plant is closely related to the genus *Senecio*.

General Features

Height: 90 cm–3 m high

Spread: 50–120 cm wide

Habit: large, upright, clump-forming perennial

Flowers: bright yellow; borne on spikes or daisy-like atop stems; summer

Foliage: exotic, tropical-looking; (some) purple-leaved

Hardiness: C

Warnings: prone to aphids and slugs; not prone to diseases

Growing Requirements

Light: shade; tolerates more sun with good soil moisture

Soil: deep, moist, organic, rich soil

Location: mixed borders; woodland gardens; pond sides; stream sides

Propagation: seed; division

Expert Advice: Hybridizes easily. Can take 2–3 years to reach maturity but well worth the wait. Never allow to dry out.

Buying Considerations

Professionals

Popularity: popular, garden standard foliage plant

Availability: readily available as finished product and bare root

Size to Sell: sells best in smaller sizes (when blooming) as it matures fast

On the Shelf: high ornamental appeal; rapidly overgrows pot; must kept well watered on shelf

Shrinkage: low; requires little maintenance

On the Market

Ligularia
'Gregynog Gold' • Conical, clustered, orange-yellow flowers in midsummer • 1.2–2 m high, 60–90 cm wide

'Megamona' • Orange-yellow flowers in summer • 1–1.5 m high, 75–100 cm wide

'Lanternchen' (Little Rocket) • Large, spiked, bright-yellow flowers in summer • 50 cm high, 75–90 cm wide

'Sungold' • Clustered, 2-tone, yellow flowers in midsummer • 75–100 cm high, 50–75 cm wide

'The Rocket' • Spiked, bright-yellow flowers in summer • Large leaves with black stems • 1.2–1.8 m high, 75–90 cm wide

'Weihenstephan' • Large, spiked, yellow flowers in summer • 1.2–1.8 m high, 75–90 cm wide

'Zepter' • Spiked, bright-yellow flowers in summer • 2–2.5 m high, 75–100 cm wide

Ligularia amplectens var. holmii (syn. Senecio amplectens)
Pendant, daisy-like, light-yellow flowers in summer • Shiny, succulent foliage • 10–30 cm high, 15–20 cm wide

Ligularia dentata (syn. L. clivorum)
Clustered, orange-yellow, daisy flowers in summer • 90–120 cm high, 60–90 cm wide

'Brit-Marie Crawford' • Clustered, orange-yellow flowers in summer • Chocolate-maroon foliage • 90–120 cm high, 60–90 cm wide

'Desdemona' • Clustered, daisy-like, orange-yellow flowers in summer • Large, purple foliage • 90–120 cm high, 60–90 cm wide

'Othello' • Clustered, orange-yellow flowers in summer • Large, purple foliage • 90–120 cm high, 60–90 cm wide

Ligularia fischeri (syn. L. speciosa)
Spiked, orange-yellow flowers in summer
• 1.5–2 m high, 60–90 cm wide

Ligularia x hessei
Clustered, orange-yellow flowers in summer
• Large, toothed, green foliage • 1.2–1.8 m high, 60–90 cm wide

Ligularia japonica
Clustered, daisy-like, yellow-orange flowers in early summer • Deeply cut, large foliage • 1–1.5 m high, 75–100 cm wide

Ligularia macrophylla altaica
Spiked, rich-yellow flowers in summer • Large, green leaves • 1.5–3 m high, 1–1.2 m wide

Ligularia przewalskii
Fragrant, spiked, yellow flowers in summer • Deeply cut, green foliage with black stems • 1–2 m high, 75–100 cm wide

Ligularia x palmatiloba
Clustered, yellow flowers in summer • 1–1.5 m high, 60–90 cm wide

Ligularia sachalinensis
Large, spiked, bright-yellow flowers in summer • Purple-green foliage • 50 cm high, 75–90 cm wide

Ligularia sibirica
Spiked, bright-yellow flowers in summer • large leaves with black stems • 1.2–1.8 m high, 75–60 cm wide

Ligularia stenocephala
Spiked, yellow flowers in summer • Purple stems • 1.2–1.5 m high, 60–90 cm wide

Ligularia veitchiana
Spiked, yellow flowers in summer • 1.5–2 m high, 60–90 cm wide

Ligularia vorobievii
Fragrant, spiked, yellow flowers in summer • Large, deeply-cut, green foliage • 1.5–2.2 m high, 75–100 cm wide

Ligularia wilsoniana
Fragrant, spiked, golden-yellow flowers in summer • 1.2–2 m high, 1–1.2 m wide

L

Lilium
p. 419

Genus Information
Origin: Asia, Europe and North America
Selected Common Names: lily, Turk's cap lily
Nomenclature: From the Latin form of the Greek *leirion*, used by Theophrastus for the Madonna lily.
Notes: Some of the earliest images of lilies are on the tomb walls of the Egyptian Pharaohs. They

have also become a religious symbol in the art of early Christians, where they developed an association with the Virgin Mary as representing purity. A genus of over 100 species, botanically classified into 9 divisions with a wide selection of garden hybrids. We divide lilies into 4 categories for display and growing information purposes: *Asiatic* (includes L.A. Hybrids), *Martagon, Oriental & Other Hybrid* and *Species*.

Lilium, Asiatic   p. 419 📷

General Features
Height: 30–150 cm high
Spread: 30–45 cm wide
Habit: upright, bulbous, clump-forming perennial
Flowers: all colours except blue; (some) fragrant; upward-facing, outward-facing or pendant; late spring to summer; good for cutflowers
Foliage: narrow, dark-green
Hardiness: B–C
Warnings: prone to Botrytis; not prone to insects

Growing Requirements
Light: sun
Soil: fertile, well-drained soil; prefers cool roots
Location: mixed borders; cutting gardens
Propagation: seed; bulbils; bulblets; division
Expert Advice: May not come true from seed. Prefer to be deeply planted. Lily bulbs have exposed outer scales and can be easily damaged and lose moisture—do not leave exposed or allow to dry out during transplanting.

Buying Considerations

Professionals
Popularity: popular, old-fashioned, garden standard foliage plant; many new varieties available
Availability: readily available as finished product and bare root from specialty growers
Size to Sell: sells best in mature sizes (when blooming) as it matures quickly
On the Shelf: rapidly overgrows pot
Shrinkage: low; sales drop dramatically after blooming finishes

Collectors
Popularity: of interest to collector—unique, exceptional beauty

Gardeners
Ease of Growth: mostly easy to grow but needs close attention to growing conditions
Start with: one mature plant for feature plant

What to Try First ...
Lilium 'Aladdin's Beauty', *Lilium* 'Aladdin's Dazzle', *Lilium* 'Artistic', *Lilium* 'Bakersfield', *Lilium* 'Black Bird', *Lilium* 'Black Jack', *Lilium* 'Brenda Watts', *Lilium* 'Brushstroke', *Lilium* 'Butter Pixie'

On the Market

'Abba' • Orange-yellow flowers with light-orange tips in early summer • 75 cm high, 30–45 cm wide

'Aladdin's Beauty' (Ceb Beauty) • L.A. Hybrid • Upward-facing, vivid-orange flowers in early summer • 1.2 m high, 30–45 cm wide

'Aladdin's Dazzle' (Ceb Dazzle) • L.A. Hybrid • Upward-facing, clear-yellow flowers in early summer • 1 m high, 30–45 cm wide

'Aladdin's Quest' (Ceb Quest) • L.A. Hybrid • Upward-facing, purplish-pink flowers with pale-yellow throat in late spring • 80 cm high, 30–45 cm wide

'Aladdin's Sun' (Ceb Sun) • L.A. Hybrid • Upward-facing, vivid-yellow flowers in early summer • 1.5 m high, 30–45 cm wide

'Alexis' • Orange-yellow flowers in early summer • 1–1.2 m high, 30–45 cm wide

'Amarone' • Wine-red flowers with a purple midvein in midsummer • 1.5 m high, 30–45 cm wide

'Amberglow' • Creamy-yellow flowers in early summer • 1 m high, 30–45 cm wide

'America' (syn. **Holean**) • Dark-maroon flowers in early summer • 80 cm high, 30–45 cm wide

'Antartica' • Cream-white to pure white flowers in early summer • 90 cm high, 30–45 cm wide

'Apollo' • Pure white flowers in early summer • 60–90 cm high, 30–45 cm wide

'Artistic' • White flowers with purple markings in early summer • 1.2 m high, 30–45 cm wide

'Avignon' • Soft orange-red flowers in early summer • 1 m high, 30–45 cm wide

'Bakersfield' • Bright-yellow flowers with maroon brush marks in midsummer • 1–1.2 m high, 30–45 cm wide

'Barcelona' • Yellow flowers with outer dark-red petals in early summer • 90 cm high, 30–45 cm wide

'Barricade' • Pepper-red flowers with outer mandarin-red petals in early summer • 1.5 m high, 30–45 cm wide

'Belle Ami' • Clear-white flowers in early summer • 45–50 cm high, 30–45 cm wide

'Black Bird' • Dark-red flowers in summer • 35–40 cm high, 30–45 cm wide

'Black Butterfly' • Crimson-black flowers in early summer • 1.2 m high, 30–45 cm wide

'Black Jack' • Dark mahogany-red flowers in summer • 1 m high, 30–45 cm wide

'Black Out' • Red-black flowers in late spring • 1.2 m high, 30–45 cm wide

'Black Velvet' • Crimson flowers with purple-grey centres in early summer • 1 m high, 30–45 cm wide

'Blizzard' • White flowers with red tips and yellow throat in early summer • 1 m high, 30–45 cm wide

'Blue Eyes' • Purplish-red and ivory flowers in early summer • 1.2 m high, 30–45 cm wide

'Bold Knight • Deep orange-red flowers in early summer • 1 m high, 30–45 cm wide

'Bonnie' • Outward-facing, shell-pink flowers in summer • 90–100 cm high, 30–45 cm wide

'Brenda Watts' • Orange-red flowers in early summer • 1–1.5 m high, 30–45 cm wide

'Bright Eyes' • Yellow flowers with red tips and purple throat in early summer • 1 m high, 30–45 cm wide

'Brushstroke' • Soft-yellow flowers with magenta brush marks in early summer • 1.5 m high, 30–45 cm wide

'Buff Pixie' • Soft buff-orange flowers in late spring • 30 cm high, 30–45 cm wide

'Butter Pixie' • Butter-yellow flowers in late spring • 40 cm high, 30–45 cm wide

'California' • L.A. Hybrid • Deep-red flowers in early summer • 1 m high, 30–45 cm wide

'Cancun' • Canary-yellow flowers with orange tips in summer • 90 cm high, 30–45 cm wide

'Candy Dulfer' • Deep-pink flowers with golden throat in summer • 90 cm high, 30–45 cm wide

'Caress' • Downward-facing, light-yellow flowers in early summer • 60–100 cm high, 30–45 cm wide

'Catalina' • Fragrant, bright-yellow flowers with orange tints in early summer • 1.5 m high, 30–45 cm wide

'Centre Stage' • Peach-pink flowers with yellowish base in late spring • 1–1.2 m high, 30–45 cm wide

'Centurion' • Orange-red flowers in late spring • 1 m high, 30–45 cm wide

'Clubhouse' • L.A. Hybrid • Melon-coloured flowers in early summer • 75 cm high, 30–45 cm wide

'Connecticut Beauty' • Large, soft-yellow flowers in late spring • 1 m high, 30–45 cm wide

'Connecticut King' • Yellow-orange flowers in early summer • 1 m high, 30–45 cm wide

'Conquistador' • Reddish-orange flowers in midsummer • 85 cm high, 30–45 cm wide

'Coral Sunrise' • Peach-pink flowers with ivory centre in early summer • 1 m high, 30–45 cm wide

'Corianne' • Pink and cream flowers with red tips in early summer • 90–100 cm high, 30–45 cm wide

'Corina' • Glowing red flowers with brown spots in early summer • 60–90 cm high, 30–45 cm wide

'Corrida' • Greenish-yellow flowers with reddish tips, throat and back in midsummer • 1 m high, 30–45 cm wide

'Corsica' • Purple-pink flowers with light-red centres in early summer • 1.3 m high, 30–45 cm wide

'Country Star' • L.A. Hybrid • Upward-facing, pale orange-yellow flowers in early summer • 1 m high, 30–45 cm wide

'Crete' • Bright purple-pink flowers in late spring • 90 cm high, 30–45 cm wide

'Crimson Pixie' • Upward-facing, reddish-orange flowers in spring • 40 cm high, 30–45 cm wide

'Delta' • Yellow flowers with burgundy brush marks in early summer • 90–100 cm high, 30–45 cm wide

'Denia' • Purple-pink flowers with yellow centres in early summer • 45 cm high, 30–45 cm wide

'Don Quichotte' • L.A. Hybrid • Purplish-pink flowers with white centres in early summer • 55 cm high, 30–45 cm wide

'Donna Sylvester' • Yellow-gold flowers (reddish on outside) in midsummer • 1 m high, 30–45 cm wide

'Dreamland' • Large, sulphur-yellow flowers with orange throat in summer • 75–90 cm high, 30–45 cm wide

'Dynamico' • L.A. Hybrid • Deep purplish-red flowers with pale-yellow throat in summer • 80 cm high, 30–45 cm wide

'Eleanor Yates' • Pink flowers in summer • 90–150 cm high, 30–45 cm wide

L

'Electric' • Orange-red flowers with lilac edges in early summer • 1–1.3 m high, 30–45 cm wide

'Embarrassment' • Red flowers in early summer • 1.2 m high, 30–45 cm wide

'Fangio' • L.A. Hybrid • Purplish-red flowers in midsummer • 1.5 m high, 30–45 cm wide

'Fata Morgana' • Double, yellow flowers with dark-red spots in summer • 75 cm high, 30–45 cm wide

'Firecracker' • Cherry-red flowers in early summer • 1–1.2 m high, 30–45 cm wide

'Flirt' • Green-yellow flowers with pencil-stripe brush mark in early summer • 75–120 cm high, 30–45 cm wide

'Fuego' • Green-yellow flowers with orange flame in early summer • 1.2 m high, 30–45 cm wide

'Fuzzy Wuzzy' • Orange flowers from fuzzy, white flower buds in early summer • 90 cm high, 30–45 cm wide

'Gardenja' • Yellow-orange flowers with red tips in early spring • 1.2 m high, 30–45 cm wide

'Giant Ruby' • Dark-red-burgundy flowers in early summer • 85–95 cm high, 30–45 cm wide

'Glossy Wings' • L.A. Hybrid • Pink-red flowers in midsummer • 90–100 cm high, 30–45 cm wide

'Gold Lode' • Yellow-orange flowers with gold stripes in midsummer • 1.2 m high, 30–45 cm wide

'Good Night' • Dark-red flowers with yellow centre in midsummer • 1–1.2 m high, 30–45 cm wide

'Gran Cru' • Gold-yellow flowers with red centres in spring • 1–1.2 m high, 30–45 cm wide

'Gran Paradiso' • Orange-red flowers in early summer • 1.5 m high, 30–45 cm wide

'Granny' • Yellow flowers with red-pink edges in early summer • 1 m high, 30–45 cm wide

'Haidee' • Soft-yellow flowers in early summer • 1 m high, 30–45 cm wide

'Harmony' • Orange flowers with maroon spots in early summer • 60–100 cm high, 30–45 cm wide

'Hodge Podge' • Raspberry-pink and creamy-yellow flowers in summer • 90 cm high, 30–45 cm wide

'House of Orange' • Orange-red flowers with red spots in early summer • 1.5 m high, 30–45 cm wide

'Ibarra' • L.A. Hybrid • Medium purplish-red flowers with red throat in summer • 1.4 m high, 30–45 cm wide

'Imperial Love' • L.A. Hybrid • Variegated, light purplish-red flowers in early summer • 1 m high, 30–45 cm wide

'Indian Maid' • Yellow flowers with yellow-green throat in midsummer • 1 m high, 30–45 cm wide

'Innocence' • Large, smooth, pink flowers in early summer • 60–100 cm high, 30–45 cm wide

'Italia' • Pink flowers with red-orange edges in early summer • 1.5 m high, 30–45 cm wide

'Jaunty' • Red-orange flowers with yellow centres in late spring • 65 cm high, 30–45 cm wide

'Jubileo' • White flowers with purple-pink tips in early summer • 80 cm high, 30–45 cm wide

'Kaz Mynett' • Bright orange-red flowers in early summer • 1–1.5 m high, 30–45 cm wide

'Kimberly Ann' • Deep blood-red flowers in midsummer • 90 cm high, 30–45 cm wide

'La Paz' • L.A. Hybrid • Pale-yellow flowers with yellowish-pink throat in early summer • 1.2 m high, 30–45 cm wide

'Latoya' • Purplish-red flowers in early summer • 75 cm high, 30–45 cm wide

'Lemon Pixie' • Lemon-yellow flowers in spring • 40 cm high, 30–45 cm wide

'Lippizaner' • White flowers with yellow-green tinge at base in early summer • 75 cm high, 30–45 cm wide

'Little Yellow Kiss' • Double, yellow flowers with few spots in early summer • 80–90 cm high, 30–45 cm wide

'Lollypop' • Cream flowers with rose-red tips in early summer • 55 cm high, 30–45 cm wide

'Loreto' • Orange flowers with red flame in early summer • 60 cm high, 30–45 cm wide

'Mamaska' • Deep-red flowers with black spots in midsummer • 1.3 m high, 30–45 cm wide

'Marlene' • Light pink-tipped flowers with white centre in early summer • 95 cm high, 30–45 cm wide

'Marseille' • Large, cream flowers with pink throat in late spring • 1.3 m high, 30–45 cm wide

'Melissa Jamie' • Soft-pink flowers with cream centre in early summer • 50–60 cm high, 30–45 cm wide

'Melody' • Yellow flowers with rust-red outer petals in early summer • 1.1 m high, 30–45 cm wide

'Milano' • Orange-red flowers with brown tips and spots in early summer • 1.2 m high, 30–45 cm wide

'Modern Style' • L.A. Hybrid • Upward-facing, peach to cream flowers with orange throat in early summer • 1 m high, 30–45 cm wide

'Monaco' (Mona) • Unspotted, yellow flowers with green throat in late spring • 60 cm high, 30–45 cm wide

'Moneymaker' • L.A. Hybrid • Upward-facing, purplish-pink flowers in midsummer • 1 m high, 30–45 cm wide

'Monte Negro' • Blood-red flowers with violet-red glow in early summer • 1 m high, 30–45 cm wide

'Montreux' • Rose-pink flowers with yellow-brown flame in early summer • 1 m high, 30–45 cm wide

'Moon Baby' • Creamy-yellow flowers with maroon brush marks and red throat in midsummer • 60 cm high, 30–45 cm wide

'Napoli' • Orange flowers with dark throat in early summer • 1.1 m high, 30–45 cm wide

'Navona' • Yellowish-white flowers in early summer • 85 cm high, 30–45 cm wide

'Oprah Winfrey' • Upward-facing, solid, deep-red flowers in early summer • 80–90 cm high, 30–45 cm wide

'Orange Pixie' • Orange-red flowers in early summer • 30–40 cm high, 30–45 cm wide

'Parfait Frost' • Pink-and-yellow-bicoloured flowers in early summer • 1 m high, 30–45 cm wide

'Parisienne' • Mandarin-red flowers with rose tips in late spring • 1 m high, 30–45 cm wide

'Parkland Orange' • Flat, clear-orange flowers with paler outside petals in midsummer • 1 m high, 30–45 cm wide

'Pasteur' • Purple-red flowers with dark-pink centre in early summer • 90–100 cm high, 30–45 cm wide

'Paulus Potter' • Pale yellow-green flowers with dark-red spots in late spring • 70 cm high, 30–45 cm wide

'Peach Butterflies' • Nodding, recurved, peach-apricot flowers in late spring • 1–1.2 m high, 30–45 cm wide

'Peach Pink' • Peach-pink flowers in summer • 60–90 cm high, 30–45 cm wide

'Peach Pixie' • Peach-pink flowers in late spring • 40 cm high, 30–45 cm wide

'Philos' • Apricot-gold flowers with rose tips and cream centre in midsummer • 1 m high, 30–45 cm wide

'Pink Chique' • Pink and white flowers in early summer • 1 m high, 30–45 cm wide

'Pink Pagoda' • Soft-pink flowers with rose eye in early summer • 60 cm high, 30–45 cm wide

'Pink Pixie' • Creamy flowers with pink tips in late spring • 40 cm high, 30–45 cm wide

'Pink Trophy' • Soft-pink flowers in midsummer • 1 m high, 30–45 cm wide

'Presto' • L.A. Hybrid • Deep-pink flowers edged in medium-red in summer • 1 m high, 30–45 cm wide

'Prunus' • Cream to coral-pink flowers with spots in summer • 60–90 cm high, 30–45 cm wide

'Pulsar' • Yellowish-white flowers with light red-orange tips in late spring • 75 cm high, 30–45 cm wide

'Red Carpet' • Bright-red flowers in early summer • 30 cm high, 30–45 cm wide

'Red Juanita' • Orange-red flowers in early summer • 60–75 cm high, 30–45 cm wide

'Red Raven' • Black-red flowers in midsummer • 1 m high, 30–45 cm wide

'Red Ticklers' • Pollen-free, bright-red flowers in early summer • 1–1.2 m high, 30–45 cm wide

'Red Velvet' • Rich, deep-red flowers in early summer • 1.5 m high, 30–45 cm wide

'Reinesse' • Greenish-white flowers with yellow-green throat in late spring • 65 cm high, 30–45 cm wide

'Rembrandt' • Shades of purple, yellow, orange and pink flowers in late spring • 1.2 m high, 30–45 cm wide

'Rhodes' • Deep-red flowers in early summer • 60–90 cm high, 30–45 cm wide

'Rocky Mountain' • Soft-yellow flowers with orange-yellow throat in early summer • 70 cm high, 30–45 cm wide

L

'Rodeos' (Rodeo) • L.A. Hybrid • Lavender-pink flowers with white centres in early summer • 75 cm high, 30–45 cm wide

'Rosa Linda' • Strong pink flowers with creamy centres in early summer • 1 m high, 30–45 cm wide

'Rosabelle #2' • Downward-facing, rose flowers in early summer • 1 m high, 30–45 cm wide

'Rosefire' • Orange-red flowers with yellow blush on centre of petals in late spring • 1.2 m high, 30–45 cm wide

'Rosepoint Lace' • Creamy-pink to ivory, heavily marbled flowers in early summer • 1–1.5 m high, 30–45 cm wide

'Royal Cinnabar' • L.A. Hybrid • Burnt-orange and red flowers in early summer • 75–100 cm high, 30–45 cm wide

'Royal Dream' • L.A. Hybrid • Creamy-white flowers in early summer • 45 cm high, 30–45 cm wide

'Royal Lace' • L.A. Hybrid • Ruffled, creamy-white flowers with dark-red spots in summer • 75 cm high, 30–45 cm wide

'Royal Love' • L.A. Hybrid • Soft-pink flowers with yellow centres in early summer • 90 cm high, 30–45 cm wide

'Royal Parade' • L.A. Hybrid • Unspotted, red flowers in midsummer • 1 m high, 30–45 cm wide

'Royal Paradise' • L.A. Hybrid • Bright watermelon-red flowers in early summer • 90–100 cm high, 30–45 cm wide

'Royal Present' • L.A. Hybrid • Upward-facing, medium purplish-red flowers with yellow centres in summer • 1.25 m high, 30–45 cm wide

'Royal Sunset' • L.A. Hybrid • Red flowers with orange centres in early summer • 75–90 cm high, 30–45 cm wide

'Royal Trinity' • L.A. Hybrid • Upward-facing, brilliant orange-yellow flowers in midsummer • 1 m high, 30–45 cm wide

'Royal Victory' • L.A. Hybrid • Solid creamy-yellow flowers without spots in early summer • 50 cm high, 30–45 cm wide

'Salem' • Orange, red-edged flowers in late spring • 1 m high, 30–45 cm wide

'Sally' • Orange-red flowers with orange tips and brown spots in early summer • 1.5 m high, 30–45 cm wide

'Sancerre' • Yellowish-white flowers in early summer • 75 cm high, 30–45 cm wide

'Science Fiction' • L.A. Hybrid • Pure red flowers with maroon shading in early summer • 1 m high, 30–45 cm wide

'Shirley' • Greenish-yellow flowers with light-red flame on petals in late spring • 1.5 m high, 30–45 cm wide

'Shocking Pink' • Bright-pink flowers in late spring • 1 m high, 30–45 cm wide

'Showbiz' • L.A. Hybrid • Clear-pink flowers in midsummer • 1.2 m high, 30–45 cm wide

'Snow Storm' • Yellowish-white flowers with yellow-green throat in early summer • 1 m high, 30–45 cm wide

'Sonnentiger' (Sun Tiger) • Yellow flowers with yellow-orange centre and brown spots in midsummer • 1.2 m high, 30–45 cm wide

'Sorbet' • Greenish-white flowers with purple-red edges in early summer • 75–90 cm high, 30–45 cm wide

'Spark' • Pink flowers with yellow centre in early summer • 1 m high, 30–45 cm wide

'Sphinx' • Double, vivid-red flowers in early summer • 1 m high, 30–45 cm wide

'Spirit' • L.A. Hybrid • Yellowish-white flowers with pink blush in early summer • 50 cm high, 30–45 cm wide

'Starchild' • Canary-yellow flowers without spots in summer • 1 m high, 30–45 cm wide

'Summer Night' • Recurved, black-red flowers in early summer • 1.2 m high, 30–45 cm wide

'Suncrest' • L.A. Hybrid • Speckled, soft-yellow flowers in midsummer • 90–100 cm high, 30–45 cm wide

'Tiger Babies' • Fragrant, peach-pink flowers with orange throat in early summer • 90–120 cm high, 30–45 cm wide

'Top Gun' • L.A. Hybrid • Large, purplish-pink flowers in early summer • 1.4 m high, 30–45 cm wide

'Towering Turk' • Downward-facing, glossy, red flowers with darker throat in early summer • 1.2 m high, 30–45 cm wide

'Trenwell' • Buttercup-yellow flowers with few spots in summer • 1 m high, 30–45 cm wide

'Tresor' • Red-orange flowers with orange midveins in summer • 1.2 m high, 30–45 cm wide

L

'Twilight Life' • L.A. Hybrid • Upward-facing, maroon flowers with pink shading in early summer • 1.3 m high, 30–45 cm wide

'Ventoux' • Yellowish-white flowers with pink centres in late spring • 1.5 m high, 30–45 cm wide

'Venture' • Intense red flowers in early summer • 1.5 m high, 30–45 cm wide

'Vermeer' • Purple-pink flowers with white throat in summer • 1.3 m high, 30–45 cm wide

'Vivaldi' • Bright-pink flowers with yellow-green tips in early summer • 85 cm high, 30–45 cm wide

'White Pixie' (Snow Crystal) • Yellowish-white flowers in midsummer • 25 cm high, 30–45 cm wide

'Yellow Hornet' • Bright-yellow flowers with dark-red brush marks in midsummer • 1 m high, 30–45 cm wide

'Yellow Present' • Bright-yellow flowers in early summer • 90–100 cm high, 30–45 cm wide

'Yellow Princess' • Yellow flowers with orange throat and red-brown brush mark in early summer • 90–100 cm high, 30–45 cm wide

Lilium, Martagon   p. 419

General Features
Height: 90–150 cm high
Spread: 30–45 cm wide
Habit: upright, bulbous, clump-forming perennial
Flowers: many colours; strongly recurved (turkscap); (some) unpleasantly aromatic; late spring; good for cutflowers
Foliage: dark-green
Hardiness: B–C
Warnings: prone to Botrytis; not prone to insect damage

Growing Requirements
Light: a.m. sun; tolerates more sun in cool soil with good moisture
Soil: moist, organic soil
Location: mixed borders; cutting gardens; woodland gardens; wild gardens
Propagation: seed; bulblets; division; scaling
Expert Advice: Named varieties will not come true from seed. Can take years to develop into a nice clump. Can take 5–10 years to bloom from scale.

Buying Considerations

Professionals
Popularity: gaining popularity; fast seller in bloom
Availability: generally available from specialty growers
Size to Sell: sells best in mature sizes (when blooming) as it matures slowly
On the Shelf: rapidly overgrows pot
Shrinkage: low; sales drop dramatically after blooming finishes

Collectors
Popularity: of interest to collectors—unique, challenge, exceptional beauty; can be expensive

Gardeners
Ease of Growth: very easy to grow
Start with: one mature plant for feature plant, grows slowly

What to Try First ...
Lilium martagon 'Attiwaw', *Lilium martagon* 'Bornholm', *Lilium martagon* 'Brocade', *Lilium martagon* 'Claude Shride', *Lilium martagon* 'Jacques S. Dijt', *Lilium martagon* 'Lois Hole', *Lilium martagon* 'Maroon King', *Lilium martagon* 'Moonyeen'

On the Market   L

Lilium x *dalhansonii*
Recurved, maroon flowers with gold spots in early summer • 1–1.5 m high, 30–45 cm wide

Lilium hansonii
Fragrant, pendant, orange-red flowers with brown spots in late spring • 60–150 cm high, 30–45 cm wide

Lilium martagon
Recurved, light-purple flowers in early summer • 90–150 cm high, 30–45 cm wide

'Akimina' • Recurved, light-yellow flowers with spots in late spring • 95 cm high, 30–45 cm wide

'Attiwaw' • Fragrant, recurved, pink flowers with spots in late spring • 90 cm high, 30–45 cm wide

'Autumn Colour' • Recurved, yellow flowers with maroon spots in early summer • 1.2–1.4 m high, 30–45 cm wide

'Bornholm' • Recurved, cream flowers, unspotted, in early summer • 1–1.5 m high, 30–45 cm wide

'Brocade' • Recurved, buff-yellow flowers with brown spots in late spring • 1–1.5 m high, 30–45 cm wide

'Brotsing' • Unspotted, pale-yellow flowers in early summer • 90–110 cm high, 30–45 cm wide

'Cadense' • Recurved, yellow flowers with dark spots in early summer • 1 m high, 30–45 cm wide

'Claude Shride' • Recurved, grey-purple flowers with yellow spots in late spring • 1–1.5 m high, 30–45 cm wide

'Early Bird' • Recurved, sunflower-yellow flowers that flush rose in early summer • 90–150 cm high, 30–45 cm wide

'Gay Lights' • Recurved, yellow-brown flowers with maroon spots in early summer • 1.2–1.5 m high, 30–45 cm wide

'Glynis' • Recurved, red flowers with dark stripes and spots in early summer • Dark stems • 1–1.5 m high, 30–45 cm wide

'Guinea Gold' • Recurved, yellow flowers with brown spots in early summer • 1.2–1.5 m high, 30–45 cm wide

'Hantsing' • Recurved, light-red flowers with yellow centres in early summer • 1.2–1.5 m high, 30–45 cm wide

'Jacques S. Dijt' • Recurved, cream-yellow flowers with purple spots in early summer • 1.5 m high, 30–45 cm wide

Komet hybrids • Shades of yellow, apricot or red flowers in early summer • Stems dotted purple • 1–1.2 m high, 30–45 cm wide

'Larissa' • Outward-facing, yellow flowers with red spots in early summer • 90–100 cm high, 30–45 cm wide

'Lois Hole' • Recurved, yellow flowers with a white outer petal in early summer • 90 cm–1.5 m high, 30–45 cm

'Maroon King' • Maroon flowers with light centres in late spring • 1–1.4 m high, 30–45 cm wide

'Moonyeen' • Recurved, purple-pink flowers with spots in late spring • 1 m high, 30–45 cm wide

'Mrs. R.O. Backhouse' • Recurved, orange-yellow flowers flushed with pink in early summer • 1–1.5 m high, 30–45 cm wide

'Orange Marmalade' • Outward-facing, dark orange-red flowers, without spots, in early summer • 1.2–1.5 m high, 30–45 cm wide

Paisley hybrids • Yellow-orange, lilac-purple or mahogany flowers in early summer • 1–1.5 m high, 30–45 cm wide

'Port Wine' • Recurved, red-purple flowers in early summer • 1–1.2 m high, 30–45 cm wide

'Raspberry Delight' • Recurved, raspberry-pink flowers with some spots in early summer • 90–150 cm high, 30–45 cm wide

'Redman' • Recurved, dark-red flowers in early summer • 1–1.2 m high, 30–45 cm wide

'Sweet Betsy' • Recurved, silver-pink flowers with maroon spots in early summer • 1–1.5 m high, 30–45 cm wide

'Towering Delight' • Recurved, mauve-pink flowers with some spots in early summer • 1.5 m high, 30–45 cm wide

'Tsingense' • Recurved, bright-orange flowers with some spots in early summer • 1–1.5 m high, 30–45 cm wide

Lilium martagon **var.** *album*
Dainty, recurved, white flowers in early summer • 90–150 cm high, 30–45 cm wide

Lilium martagon **var.** *pilosiusculum*
Recurved, purple-red flowers with spots in early summer • Woolly stems • 45–90 cm high, 30–45 cm wide

Lilium, Oriental & Other Hybrid

p. 419

General Features

Height: 45–150 cm high
Spread: 10–45 cm wide
Habit: bulbous, clump-forming perennial
Flowers: many colours; (most) fragrant; trumpet-shaped, flat-faced, bowl-shaped or distinctly recurved; early to late summer; good for cutflowers
Foliage: lance-shaped
Hardiness: C–D
Warnings: prone to Botrytis; not prone to insect damage
Expert Advice: Provide good snow coverage.

Growing Requirements

Light: sun to p.m. sun
Soil: Oriental lilies prefer fertile, well-drained, organic soil; shade base; Hybrid lilies prefer fertile well-drained organic soil; tolerates alkaline soil
Location: mixed borders; cutting gardens; sheltered locations
Propagation: seed; bulbils; bulblets; division; scaling

L

Buying Considerations

Professionals

Popularity: gaining popularity
Availability: occasionally available from specialty growers
Size to Sell: sells best in mature sizes (when blooming) as it matures slowly
On the Shelf: low ornamental appeal except when in bloom
Shrinkage: low; sales drop dramatically after blooming finishes; requires little maintenance

Collectors

Popularity: of interest to collectors—unique, challenge, exceptional beauty

Gardeners

Ease of Growth: mostly easy to grow but needs close attention to growing conditions
Start with: one small plant for feature plant

What to Try First ...

Lilium 'Bright Star', *Lilium* 'Casa Blanca', *Lilium* 'Medusa', *Lilium* 'Northern Beauty', *Lilium* 'Standing Ovation', *Lilium* 'Star Gazer'

On the Market

Lilium Hybrid

'**Bright Star**' • Fragrant, orange-centred, ivory-white flowers in summer • 1–1.5 m high, 30–45 cm wide

'**Fiery Belles**' • Down-facing, orange flowers in late summer• 60–90 cm high, 30–45 cm wide

'**Ivory Belles**' • Down-facing, ivory-white flowers in late summer • 60–90 cm high, 30–45 cm wide

'**Northern Beauty**' • Fragrant, gold-throated, white flowers in summer • 75–90 cm high, 30–45 cm wide

'**Northern Carillon**' • Fragrant, dark-red-throated, white flowers in summer • 90–100 cm high, 30–45 cm wide

'**Northern Sensation**' • Fragrant, bright-red-throated, white flowers in summer • 90–100 cm high, 30–45 cm wide

'**Royal Fantasy**' • Cream-yellow flowers in summer • 60–75 cm high, 30–45 cm wide

'**Silky Belles**' • Down-facing, white to cream flowers in summer • 60–90 cm high, 30–45 cm wide

'**Standing Ovation**' • Yellow-banded, white flowers in summer • 90–100 cm high, 30–45 cm wide

'**Starburst Sensation**' • Fragrant, dark-red-throated, pink flowers in summer • 75–90 cm high, 30–45 cm wide

Lilium Oriental Hybrids

'**Bergamo**' • Soft-pink flowers with red margins in late summer • 1–1.5 m high, 30–45 cm wide

'**Birma**' (**Miss Burma**) • Pink flowers with orange-red spots in early summer • 60 cm high, 30–45 cm wide

'**Casa Blanca**' • Pure white flowers in late summer • 1 m high, 30–45 cm wide

'**Ed**' (**Mr. Ed**) • Greenish-white flowers with red spots in midsummer • 45 cm high, 30–45 cm wide

'**Grayswood**' • Magenta-pink flowers in late summer • 45 cm high, 30–45 cm wide

'**Jet Set**' • Yellowish-white flowers with gold midvein in late summer • 55 cm high, 30–45 cm wide

'**Medusa**' • Purplish-pink flowers with yellow centres in midsummer • 1–1.3 m high, 30–45 cm wide

'**Miami**' • Purplish-pink flowers in early summer • 80 cm high, 30–45 cm wide

'**Miss Iceland**' • Soft pink flowers with pink-orange band in early summer • 50 cm high, 30–45 cm wide

'**Miss Oregon**' • Bright-pink flowers in early summer • 45 cm high, 30–45 cm wide

'**Mona Lisa**' • Ivory-white flowers with a red-purple blush in summer • 45 cm high, 30–45 cm wide

'**Mr. Ruud**' • White flowers with gold midvein in midsummer • 40–45 cm high, 30–45 cm wide

'**Mr. Sam**' • Fragrant, pink-red flowers edged in white in midsummer • 40–45 cm high, 30–45 cm wide

'**Picture**' • Raspberry-pink flowers with white edges in summer • 45 cm high, 30–45 cm wide

'**Pompei**' • White flowers with narrow, yellow flame in summer • 65 cm high, 30–45 cm wide

'**Star Gazer**' • Red flowers with dark spots in early summer • 1–1.5 m high, 30–45 cm wide

'**White Star Gazer**' • White flowers with yellow-green throat in late summer • 70 cm high, 30–45 cm wide

Lilium, Species   p. 419 📷

General Features
Height: 10 cm–3 m high
Spread: 15–60 cm wide
Habit: (most) clump-forming or spreading, stoloniferous perennial
Flowers: many colours, except blue; (some) fragrant; upward-facing, pendant, bowl-shaped or strongly recurved (turkscap); late spring to summer; good for cutflowers
Foliage: lance-shaped
Hardiness: B–D
Warnings: prone to Botrytis; not prone to insects

Growing Requirements
Light: sun or a.m. sun; specific to species
Soil: well-drained soil; other requirements specific to species
Location: mixed borders; cutting gardens; wild gardens; woodland gardens; rock gardens
Propagation: seed; bulbils; bulblets; division; scaling
Expert Advice: Species lilies come true from seed. Some species do not form bulbils. Plant deeply in colder climates.

Buying Considerations

Professionals
Popularity: gaining popularity
Availability: occasionally available from specialty growers
Size to Sell: sells best in mature sizes (when blooming) as it matures slowly
Shrinkage: low; sales drop dramatically after blooming finishes; requires little maintenance

Collectors
Popularity: of interest to collectors—unique, challenge, exceptional beauty

Gardeners
Ease of Growth: mostly easy to grow but needs close attention to growing conditions
Start with: one small plant for feature plant

What to Try First ...
Lilium medeoloides, Lilium michiganense, Lilium pardalinum, Lilium philadelphicum, Lilium pumilum, Lilium regale, Lilium rubellum

On the Market

Lilium bakerianum
Fragrant, nodding, white flowers with maroon spots in early summer • Clump-forming • 60–90 cm high, 30–45 cm wide

Lilium bakerianum var. *aureum*
Pale-yellow flowers with purple spots in early summer • Clump-forming • 60–90 cm high, 30–45 cm wide

Lilium brownii
Fragrant, trumpet-shaped, creamy-white inside and green to purple outside flowers in early summer • 90–120 cm high, 45–60 cm wide

Lilium canadense
Red or yellow flowers with dark spots in early summer • Acidic, moist, well-drained, sandy, organic soil • Clump-forming • 60–150 cm high, 45–60 cm wide

Lilium cernuum
Fragrant, recurved, plum flowers in early summer • Moist, well-drained, sandy, organic soil • Cool site • Dry fall • 30–80 cm high, 30–45 cm wide

Lilium columbianum
Golden-yellow to orange-red flowers in late spring • Acidic, moist, well-drained, sandy, organic soil • Moist spring • Dry summer • 1–2 m high, 45–60 cm wide

Lilium concolor
Recurved, upward-facing, glossy, scarlet-red flowers in early summer • Fertile, well-drained, sandy, organic soil • Clump-forming • 30–90 cm high, 60 cm wide

Lilium dauricum
Upward-facing, cup-shaped, orange-red flowers with spots in early spring • Well-drained, moist, fertile, alkaline-free soil • 50–70 cm high, 30–45 cm wide

Lilium davidii
Nodding, orange-red flowers with purple spots in midsummer • Hairy stems • Well-drained soil • Shade base • 1–1.2 m high, 45–60 cm wide

Lilium distichum
Pale orange-red flowers with plum spots in early summer • Moist, acidic, well-drained, organic soil in shady woodland location • 30–90 cm high, 30–45 cm wide

Lilium duchartrei
Fragrant, nodding, white flowers with purple spots in early summer • Requires well-drained, moist, organic, boggy, cool soil • 45–150 cm high, 45–60 cm wide

Lilium formosanum
'Snow Queen' • Fragrant, creamy-white flowers in early summer • Fertile, well-drained, organic soil • 30–40 cm high, 30–45 cm wide

Lilium forrestii
Fragrant, white flowers with purple spots in late spring to early summer • 45–60 cm high, 20–30 cm wide

Lilium gloriosoides
White flowers with yellow-green throat and scarlet base in late spring to early summer • 40 cm high, 30–45 cm wide

Lilium henrici
White flowers with dark centre in early summer • Organic, moist, acidic soil • 90–120 cm high, 45–60 cm wide

Lilium henryi
Recurved, orange flowers with black spots in summer • Deep, fertile, neutral to alkaline soil • Clump-forming • 1–3 m high, 45–60 cm wide

White Henryi clone • White flowers with orange throat in summer • Deep, fertile, neutral to alkaline soil • Clump-forming • 1–2 m high, 45–60 cm wide

Lilium henryi var. *citrinum*
Nodding, yellow flowers with brown spots in late-season • Strong-stemmed • 1–2 m high, 30–45 cm wide

Lilium japonicum f. *albomarginatum*
Trumpet-shaped, pale pink flowers in early summer • Fine, white margin on foliage • Moist woodland location • Filtered p.m. sun • 30–90 cm high, 30–45 cm wide

Lilium lancifolium (syn. *L. tigrinum*)
Nodding, recurved, orange flowers with spots in midsummer • Lance-shaped foliage • Fertile, well-drained, acidic, moist soil • 1–2 m high, 45–60 cm wide

'Flore Pleno' • Nodding, double, bright-orange flowers in midsummer to late summer • Lance-shaped foliage • Fertile, well-drained, moist, acidic soil • 1–2 m high, 45–60 cm wide

Lilium leichtlinii
Outward-facing, spotted, yellow flowers in late summer • Fertile, well-drained, moist soil • Shade base • 60 cm–2 m high, 45–60 cm wide

Lilium leichtlinii var. *maximowiczii*
Pendant, orange-red flowers with brown spots in late summer • Fertile, well-drained, moist soil • Shade base • 60 cm–2 m high, 45–60 cm wide

Lilium leucanthum
Fragrant, trumpet-shaped, white to pale-yellow flowers in summer • Fertile, well-drained soil • 60–150 cm high, 45–60 cm wide

Lilium lophophorum
Yellow to green-yellow flowers with faint spots in late spring to early summer •

Organic, well-drained, moist soil • Shade base • 10–45 cm high, 30 cm wide

Lilium medeoloides
Orange to apricot flowers with dark spots in summer • Well-drained, organic, sandy soil • Filtered p.m. sun • Mulch for winter • 25–70 cm high, 30–45 cm wide

Lilium meleagrina
White to rose flowers with purple base in summer • Organic, well-drained, moist soil • 40–60 cm high, 30–45 cm wide

Lilium michiganense
Reflexed, red-orange flowers with red-brown spots in mid-season • Well-drained, moist soil • 60–150 cm high, 45–60 cm wide

Lilium monadelphum
Fragrant, trumpet-like, yellow to cream flowers in late spring • Organic, well-drained, fertile soil • 60–80 cm high, 30–45 cm wide

Lilium nanum
Pale-pink or creamy-yellow flowers with purple spots in late spring to early summer • Sandy, well-drained, organic, acidic soil • 15–40 cm high, 20–30 cm wide

Lilium nepalense
Fragrant, lemon-green flowers with purple throat in early summer • Acidic, moist, well-drained soil • Dry fall and winter • 90–120 cm high, 45–60 cm wide

Lilium oxypetalum var. *insigne*
Large, pendant, purplish-pink and green flowers in early summer • Clump-forming • 30 cm high, 20–40 cm wide

Lilium pardalinum
Orange or gold flowers with spots in early summer • Cool, well-drained, organic, moist soil in woodland location • 1–2 m high, 45–60 cm wide

Lilium parryi var. *kessleri*
Fragrant, yellow flowers with spots in summer • Organic, sharply drained, gritty soil • Do not plant too deeply • 60–180 cm high, 45–60 cm wide

Lilium philadelphicum
Fragrant, red-orange flowers in early summer • Sandy, well-drained, organic soil • Clump-forming • 45–90 cm high, 30–45 cm wide

Lilium primulinum
Fragrant, green-yellow flowers with purple spots in summer • 1–2 m high, 45–60 cm wide

L

Lilium pumilum
Fragrant, waxy, recurved, scarlet-red flowers with black spots in spring • Sandy, well-drained, organic soil • 45–120 cm high, 30–45 cm wide

Lilium regale
Fragrant, trumpet-shaped, white flowers in early summer • Well-drained, organic soil • 80–120 cm high, 45–60 cm wide

Lilium aff. rosthornii
Pendant, orange flowers with spots in summer • 1–1.5 m high, 45–60 cm wide

Lilium rubellum
Fragrant, funnel-shaped, soft-pink flowers in late spring • Organic, moist, acidic, well-drained soil • 30–80 cm high, 30–45 cm wide

Lilium sempervivoideum
Nodding, white flowers with purple spots in late spring • Grass-like foliage • Sandy, well-drained, organic soil • 15 cm high, 15 cm wide

Lilium speciosum var. rubrum
Fragrant, carmine-red flowers in late summer • Dark-purple stems • Well-drained, organic, moist, acidic soil • 90 cm–2 m high, 45–60 cm wide

Lilium superbum
Pendant, orange flowers with dark spots in midsummer • Organic, alkaline-free, moist soil • 1.5–3 m high, 45–60 cm wide

Lilium taliense
Fragrant, pendant, white flowers in early summer • Alkaline, well-drained soil • 1.5–3 m high, 45–60 cm wide

Lilium tsingtauense
Orange-red flowers with spots in early summer • Moist, acidic, organic, well-drained soil • 40–90 cm high, 30–45 cm wide

Lilium xanthellum var. luteum
Yellow-green flowers with purple spots in late spring • Clump-forming • 30–60 cm high, 30–45 cm wide

Limonium   p. 419 📷

Genus Information
Origin: worldwide
Selected Common Names: caspia, dwarf statice, golden statice, matted sea lavender, perennial statice, sea lavender
Nomenclature: From the Greek *leimon* (meadow), referring to the plant commonly growing in salt meadows.

Notes: Genus includes annuals, biennials, perennials and subshrubs.

General Features
Height: 10–60 cm high
Spread: 10–60 cm wide
Habit: rosette-forming perennial
Flowers: airy; long blooming period; summer; good for cutflowers; good for drying
Foliage: rosette-forming; evergreen
Hardiness: C–D
Warnings: prone to aphids

Growing Requirements
Light: sun
Soil: dry, sandy, well-drained soil; best in lean soil; avoid winter wet; tolerates saline soil
Location: sunny, hot, dry areas; rock gardens; raised beds; scree; mixed borders; wild gardens
Propagation: seed; division; root cuttings
Expert Advice: Grow in containers so that the plant can easily be moved to the garden with an intact root and soil ball.

Buying Considerations
Professionals
Popularity: popular garden standard; fast seller in bloom
Availability: readily available as finished product
Size to Sell: sells best in smaller sizes as it matures fast
On the Shelf: rapidly overgrows pot
Shrinkage: low; requires little maintenance
Collectors
Popularity: not generally of interest to collectors
Gardeners
Ease of Growth: mostly easy to grow
Start with: one small plant for feature plant
What to Try First ...
Limonium platyphyllum

On the Market
Limonium bellidifolium
Smoky-lilac flowers in summer • Evergreen foliage • 10–25 cm high, 15–20 cm wide

'Spangle' • Soft-blue flowers in summer • 10–25 cm high, 15–20 cm wide

Limonium minutum (syn. Statice minuta)
Violet flowers in early summer • Evergreen foliage • 10–15 cm high, 10–15 cm wide

Limonium platyphyllum (syn. L. latifolium)
Tiny, light-violet flowers in midsummer to late summer • 45–60 cm high, 45–60 cm wide

'Violetta' • Deep-violet flowers in midsummer to late summer • 45–60 cm high, 45–60 cm wide

Linanthus

p. 419

Genus Information
Origin: North America and Chile
Selected Common Names: Nuttall's desert trumpet, desert trumpet
Nomenclature: From the Greek *linon* (flax) and *anthos* (flower), referring to the plant's resemblance to the flowers of the *Linum* family.
Notes: A member of the *Phlox* family.

General Features
Height: 15–30 cm high
Spread: 20–25 cm wide
Flowers: fragrant; phlox-like; spring to fall; heavy blooming; deadhead to extend blooming season
Hardiness: D
Warnings: prone to aphids; not prone to disease

Growing Requirements
Light: full sun
Soil: deep, well-drained, sandy soil
Location: rock gardens
Propagation: seed; cuttings
Expert Advice: Take stem-tip cuttings.

Buying Considerations
Professionals
Popularity: relatively unknown
Availability: occasionally available from specialty growers
Size to Sell: sells best in smaller sizes (when blooming) as it matures fast
On the Shelf: rapidly overgrows pot
Shrinkage: low; requires little maintenance
Collectors
Popularity: of interest to collectors—unique, rare
Gardeners
Ease of Growth: mostly easy to grow
Start with: one small plant for feature plant
What to Try First ...
Linanthus nuttallii

On the Market
Linanthus nuttallii
Fragrant, white to cream flowers with a yellow eye in early summer to fall • 15–30 cm high, 20–25 cm wide

Linaria

p. 419

Genus Information
Origin: northern temperate regions and Europe
Selected Common Names: alpine snapdragon, spurred snapdragon
Nomenclature: From the Latin *linum* (flax), referring to the flax-like leaves of some species.
Notes: Genus includes annuals, biennials and perennials.

General Features
Height: 10–60 cm high
Spread: 10–60 cm wide
Habit: erect or low-growing, short-lived perennial
Flowers: snapdragon-like; summer to fall
Hardiness: C–D
Warnings: prone to aphids
Expert Advice: *Linaria* can get loose and sparse; cut back to keep plant compact. Allow to self-sow as it is short-lived.

Growing Requirements
Light: sun
Soil: lean, sandy, well-drained soil
Location: cutting gardens; mixed borders; raised beds; rock gardens
Propagation: seed in spring (self-sows readily); division; basal cuttings

Buying Considerations
Professionals
Popularity: relatively unknown
Availability: generally available from specialty growers
Size to Sell: sells best in smaller sizes (when blooming) as it matures fast
On the Shelf: rapidly overgrows pot; requires regular cutting back
Shrinkage: low; requires little maintenance
Collectors
Popularity: not generally of interest to collectors
Gardeners
Ease of Growth: mostly easy to grow
Start with: one small plant for feature plant
What to Try First ...
Linaria alpina, *Linaria purpurea* 'Canon Went'

On the Market
Linaria aeruginea
Snapdragon-like, yellow flowers, with purple-brown tint, in summer • 10–20 cm high, 15–25 cm wide
Linaria alpina
Violet flowers in summer to fall • 10–20 cm high, 20–30 cm wide

Linaria purpurea

'Canon Went' (Canon J. Went) •
Snapdragon-like, soft-pink flowers in early
summer to late summer • 30–60 cm high,
30–45 cm wide

Linaria vulgaris

'Fairy Bouquet' • Snapdragon-like flowers
in mixed colours in summer • 20–30 cm
high, 15–20 cm wide

Linnaea

p. 419 📷

Genus Information

Origin: circumboreal from Alaska to
Newfoundland
Selected Common Names: twinflower
Nomenclature: Named for Carolus Linnaeus,
1707–1778, who was the father of the Latin
classification system. One of his favourite
flowers.

General Features

Height: 5–8 cm high
Spread: 45–90+ cm wide
Habit: mat-forming, native, subshrub
groundcover
Flowers: delicate; pink; in pairs; spring
Foliage: evergreen
Hardiness: A
Warnings: not prone to insects or disease
Expert Advice: A useful groundcover in shady,
moist locations.

Growing Requirements

Light: shade
Soil: cool, moist to wet, organic, acidic soil
Location: woodland gardens; rock gardens
Propagation: division; separate and replant
rooted layers

Buying Considerations

Professionals

Popularity: relatively unknown
Availability: occasionally available as finished
product from specialty growers
Size to Sell: sells best in smaller sizes
Shrinkage: low; requires little maintenance

Collectors

Popularity: not generally of interest to
collectors

Gardeners

Ease of Growth: mostly easy to grow
Start with: plant many for mass planting

What to Try First ...

Linnaea borealis

On the Market

Linnaea borealis
Fragrant, nodding, pink flowers (always
in pairs) in spring • Evergreen foliage •
5–8 cm high, 45–90+ cm wide

Linum

p. 419 📷

Genus Information

Origin: northern temperate regions
Selected Common Names: blue flax, golden flax,
perennial flax, yellow flax
Nomenclature: From the Latin *Linum* (flax).
Notes: Genus includes annuals, biennials and
perennials.

General Features

Height: 2–60 cm high
Spread: 10–45 cm wide
Habit: tap-rooted, clump-forming biennial or
perennial
Flowers: blue, white or clear yellow; delicate;
spring to summer; long blooming period;
deadhead to extend blooming season
Foliage: needle-like; blue-green
Hardiness: B–D
Warnings: prone to aphids; not prone to diseases
Expert Advice: *L. perenne* (blue flax) only lives for
2–3 years but self-sows readily. *L. flavum* lives
much longer but self-sows reluctantly.
Expert Advice: Some species produce ornamental
seed heads that are good for drying.

Growing Requirements

Light: sun to p.m. sun
Soil: moist, well-drained, alkaline soil; tolerates
wide range of soils; avoid winter wet
Location: rock gardens; mixed borders
Propagation: seed (*L. perenne* self-sows readily);
basal cuttings
Expert Advice: Can not be easily divided nor
moved. Move only when very small.

Buying Considerations

Professionals

Popularity: popular, old-fashioned garden
standard
Availability: readily available as finished
product
Size to Sell: sells best in smaller sizes (when
blooming) as it matures fast
On the Shelf: rapidly overgrows pot
Shrinkage: low; sensitive to overwatering

Collectors

Popularity: of interest to alpine collectors—
unique, rare, challenge

What to Try First ...

Linum capitatum, Linum flavum 'Compactum',
Linum perenne 'Diamant', *Linum perenne* ssp.
lewisii

On the Market

Linum alexenkoanum
Large, bright-yellow flowers in late spring
to early summer • 10–15 cm high,
15–20 cm wide

Linum aretioides
Bright-yellow flowers in summer •
2–5 cm high, 20–25 cm wide

Linum capitatum
Yellow flowers in summer • 15–40 cm high,
15–25 cm wide

Linum flavum
Golden-yellow flowers in late spring to
summer • 30–45 cm high, 20–30 cm wide

'Compactum' • Yellow flowers in late
spring to late summer • 10–15 cm high,
10–15 cm wide

Linum hirsutum
Large, blue flowers in summer • Hairy
foliage • 30–45 cm high, 20–30 cm wide

Linum kingii
Clear-yellow flowers in spring • Blue-grey
foliage • 5–10 cm high, 10–15 cm wide

Linum mucronatum ssp. armenum
Golden-yellow flowers in summer •
5–8 cm high, 10–15 cm wide

Linum perenne
Dainty, sky-blue flowers in summer •
40–60 cm high, 30–45 cm wide

'Album' • White flowers in summer •
45–60 cm high, 30–45 cm wide

'Diamant' (Diamond) • Sky-blue flowers in
summer • 45–60 cm high, 30–45 cm wide

Linum perenne ssp. lewisii
Blue flowers in summer • 45–60 cm high,
30–45 cm wide

Linum rhodopeum
Bright-yellow flowers in late spring to early
summer • 10–20 cm high, 15–25 cm wide

Linum tenuifolium
Blush to pink flowers, sometimes with
purple veins, in summer • 30–45 cm high,
25–40 cm wide

Linum uninerve
Golden-yellow flowers in summer •
10–15 cm high, 10–20 cm wide

Lobelia

p. 419

Genus Information

Origin: temperate regions, tropical regions and
the Americas
Selected Common Names: cardinal flower, great
blue lobelia
Nomenclature: Named for Matthias de l'Obel,
1538–1616, a botanist and physician to King
James I.
Other Uses: Native North Americans used to
smoke 1 species to cure asthma and respiratory
problems.
Notes: Genus includes annuals, biennials and
perennials.

General Features

Height: 45–60 cm high
Spread: 25–60 cm wide
Habit: clump-forming biennial or short-lived
perennial; (some) semi-aquatic
Flowers: range of colours; summer to fall
Foliage: maroon or dark green
Hardiness: D
Warnings: prone to aphids; contact with foliage
or sap may irritate skin

Growing Requirements

Light: shade to a.m. sun; tolerates more sun
with good soil moisture
Soil: deep, fertile, moist to wet, organic soil
Location: mixed borders; pond sides
Propagation: seed (self-sows); division; bud
cuttings
Expert Advice: Germinate seed at 13–18°C in
late winter or as seed ripens. Divide in spring.
L. cardinalis can be propagated by taking bud
cuttings in midsummer.

Buying Considerations

Professionals
Popularity: popular; sells well in bloom
Availability: readily available as finished
product
Size to Sell: sells best in smaller sizes (when
blooming) as it matures fast
On the Shelf: rapidly overgrows pot
Shrinkage: low; requires little maintenance

Collectors
Popularity: not generally of interest to
collectors

Gardeners
Ease of Growth: mostly easy to grow
Start with: one small plant for feature plant

L

What to Try First ...

Lobelia 'Queen Victoria', *Lobelia cardinalis*, *Lobelia siphilitica*

On the Market

Lobelia

'Cotton Candy' • Pale-pink flowers in summer • 60–90 cm high, 30–45 cm wide

'Dark Crusader' • Magenta-purple flowers in summer • Maroon foliage • 60–90 cm high, 30–45 cm wide

'Eulalia Berridge' • Red flowers with white centres in summer • 60–75 cm high, 30–45 cm wide

'Grape Knee-Hi' • Deep-purple flowers in summer • 40–70 cm high, 30–45 cm wide

'Monet Moment' • Rose-pink flowers in summer • 60–90 cm high, 30–45 cm wide

'Queen Victoria' • Scarlet flowers in summer to fall • Deep-burgundy foliage • 60–90 cm high, 30–45 cm wide

'Rose Beacon' • Rose flowers in summer • 60–90 cm high, 30–45 cm wide

'Ruby Slippers' • Ruby-red flowers in summer • 60–90 cm high, 45–60 cm wide

'Russian Princess' • Fuchsia flowers in summer • 50–75 cm high, 30–45 cm wide

'Sparkle DeVine' • Fuchsia, blue-tinged flowers in summer • 60–90 cm high, 30–45 cm wide

'Tania' • Magenta flowers in summer • 60–75 cm high, 30–45 cm wide

'Wildwood Splendour' • Amethyst flowers in summer • 60–90 cm high, 30–45 cm wide

Compliment Series

'Kompliment Scharlach' (Compliment Scarlet) • Scarlet flowers in summer to fall • Dark-green foliage • Biennial • 60–90 cm high, 25–40 cm wide

'Kompliment Tiefrot' (Compliment Deep Red) • Royal-red flowers in summer to fall • Dark-green foliage • Biennial • 60–90 cm high, 25–40 cm wide

Fan Series

'Fan Orchidrosa' (Fan Deep Rose) • Deep rose flowers in summer to fall • Bronze foliage • Biennial • 45–60 cm high, 25–40 cm wide

'Fan Scharlach' (Fan Scarlet) • Scarlet-red flowers in summer to fall • Bronze foliage • Biennial • 45–60 cm high, 25–40 cm wide

Lobelia cardinalis

Bright-red flowers in summer to fall • Dark-burgundy foliage • Semi-aquatic • 60–90 cm high, 30–45 cm wide

'Atropurpurea' • Red flowers in summer to fall • 60–90 cm high, 30–45 cm wide

Lobelia siphilitica

Bright-blue flowers in late summer to fall • 60–90 cm high, 30–45 cm wide

'Alba' • White flowers in late summer to fall • 60–90 cm high, 30–45 cm wide

Lonicera   p. 419

Genus Information

Origin: Northern Hemisphere
Selected Common Names: climbing honeysuckle, scarlet honeysuckle vine, scarlet trumpet honeysuckle
Nomenclature: Named for Adam Lonitzer, 1528–1586, a German naturalist.
Notes: A genus of some 180 species of deciduous and evergreen shrubs and twining climbers.

General Features

Height: 3–8 m high
Spread: 1–2 m wide
Habit: twining, climbing vine; requires support
Flowers: tubular; (most) fragrant; on new wood; (some) long blooming; attractive to hummingbirds and butterflies
Foliage: deciduous; green to green with yellow markings
Hardiness: B–C
Warnings: prone to powdery mildew and aphids
Expert Advice: An excellent vine for the shady side of a building. Do not cut back in fall.

Growing Requirements

Light: shade or sun
Soil: fertile, moist, organic, well-drained soil
Location: trellises against buildings or up arbours or fences
Propagation: seed; cuttings; layering
Expert Advice: Germinate seed at 19–24°C.

Buying Considerations

Professionals

Popularity: popular, old-fashioned garden standard; fast seller in bloom
Availability: readily available as finished product
Size to Sell: sells best in smaller sizes (when blooming) as it matures fast
On the Shelf: high ornamental appeal; rapidly overgrows pot
Shrinkage: low; requires little maintenance

Collectors

Popularity: not generally of interest to collectors

Gardeners

Ease of Growth: generally easy to grow
Start with: one small plant for feature plant

What to Try First ...

Lonicera 'Mandarin', *Lonicera pericylmenum* 'Belgica Select', *Lonicera* x *brownii* 'Dropmore Scarlet'

On the Market

Lonicera • Vine
'Mandarin' • Long, trumpet-shaped, sweetly-scented, red-orange flowers in June • 3–4 m high, 1–2 m wide

Lonicera japonica • Vine
'Aureoreticulata' • Fragrant, white flowers in spring • Yellow-netted markings on foliage • 5–8 m high, 2–3 m wide

Lonicera pericylmenum • Vine
'Belgica Select' • Fragrant, pink, yellow and red flowers from June to September • 5–6 m high, 1 m wide

Lonicera x *brownii • Vine*
'Dropmore Scarlet' • Long, trumpet-shaped, bright scarlet to orange-scarlet flowers from June to September • 3–4 m high, 1–2 m wide

Lotus p. 419

Genus Information

Origin: Europe, Asia, Australia, North America and Africa
Selected Common Names: canary clover, bird's foot trefoil
Nomenclature: From the Greek *lotos*, which was the name used by Discorides for some members of the legume family.

General Features

Height: 5–10 cm high
Spread: 45–60 cm wide
Habit: mat-forming, groundcover perennial
Flowers: single to double; long blooming period; late spring to summer; attractive to bees and butterflies
Foliage: tiny; mid-green
Hardiness: B–D
Warnings: not prone to insects or disease
Expert Advice: A care-free, reliable groundcover that tolerates a wide range of conditions.

Growing Requirements

Light: sun
Soil: sharply drained soil; (tolerates) dry soil
Location: rock gardens; wild gardens; mixed borders
Propagation: seed; division; cuttings
Expert Advice: Take semi-ripe cuttings in summer.

Buying Considerations

Professionals

Popularity: gaining popularity
Availability: generally available as bare root
Size to Sell: sells best in smaller sizes (when blooming) as it matures fast
On the Shelf: rapidly overgrows pot
Shrinkage: low; requires little maintenance

Collectors

Popularity: not generally of interest to collectors

Gardeners

Ease of Growth: generally easy to grow
Start with: one small plant for feature plant

What to Try First ...

Lotus corniculatus, Lotus corniculatus 'Plenus'

On the Market

Lotus corniculatus
Bright-yellow flowers in late spring to summer • 5–10 cm high, 45–60 cm wide

'Plenus' (Flore Pleno) • Double, bright-yellow, red-tinted flowers in late spring to summer • 5–10 cm high, 45–60 cm wide

Lotus hirsutus (syn. *Dorycnium hirsutum*)
White or pink-flushed flowers in summer to fall • 40–50 cm high, 45–60 cm wide

Lupinus p. 419

Genus Information

Origin: North America, South America, Europe and Africa
Selected Common Names: lupine
Nomenclature: From the Latin *lupus* (wolf).
Other Uses: Seeds of some species were used to make flour.
Notes: A genus of some 200 species of annual, perennials and semi-evergreen to evergreen subshrubs or shrubs.

General Features

Height: 20–150 cm high
Spread: 10–75 cm wide
Habit: tap-rooted, dense clump-forming, short-lived perennial; tall plants may need staking
Flowers: densely packed blooms on long spikes; summer; deadhead to extend blooming season; may rebloom in fall; excellent cutflowers
Foliage: tropical-looking; short-stemmed; mid-green
Hardiness: C–D
Warnings: prone to powdery mildew, rust and aphids; ingesting seed will cause discomfort
Expert Advice: Lupines are a beloved perennial across Canada and grow best where summers are cool. They provide upright form in the perennial border. Hybrids may rebloom in fall if cut back after first flush of bloom.

Growing Requirements

Light: sun to p.m. sun
Soil: moderately fertile, slightly sandy, neutral to slightly acidic soil; tolerates poor soil; tolerates periods of dryness
Location: mixed borders; wild gardens; rock gardens, scree
Propagation: seed (self-sows readily); basal cuttings
Expert Advice: Sow seed in spring or late autumn. Seed requires scarification. Soak seed for 24 hours in warm water before planting. Take basal cuttings of cultivars in mid-spring. Resents being disturbed. Generally looses vigour after 3–4 years (allow to self-sow).

Buying Considerations

Professionals

Popularity: popular, old-fashioned garden standard; fast seller in bloom
Availability: readily available as finished product
Size to Sell: sells best in smaller sizes (when blooming) as it matures fast
On the Shelf: rapidly overgrows pot; deadhead regularly
Shrinkage: low but prone to breakage; requires maintenance

Collectors

Popularity: not generally of interest to collectors

Gardeners

Ease of Growth: generally easy to grow
Start with: one small plant for feature plant and several for mass plantings

What to Try First ...

Lupinus Band of Nobels Series, *Lupinus* Gallery Series, *Lupinus* Russell Hybrids

On the Market

Lupinus

'Chandelier' • Spikes of cream-coloured flowers in summer • 60–90 cm high, 50–75 cm wide

'Cherry Pink' • Spikes of cherry-pink and white flowers in summer • 45–60 cm high, 30–45 cm wide

'Tutti Frutti' • Spikes of mixed, bicoloured flowers in summer • 75–100 cm high, 45–60 cm wide

Band of Nobles Series
Spikes of flowers in mixed colours in summer • 1–1.2 m high, 45–60 cm wide

'Noble Maiden' • Spikes of creamy-white flowers in summer • 75–100 cm high, 45–60 cm wide

'Sundown' • Spikes of flowers in red shades in summer • 1–1.2 m high, 45–60 cm wide

'The Chatelaine' • Spikes of blush-pink flowers in summer • 75–90 cm high, 50–75 cm wide

'The Page' • Spikes of carmine-red flowers in summer • 75–90 cm high, 50–75 cm wide

Gallery Series
Spikes of flowers in summer in shades of blue, pink and red • 40–50 cm high, 30–45 cm wide

Russell Hybrids
Spikes of flowers in summer in blue, pink, red, white or yellow • 75–90 cm high, 30–40 cm wide

Lupinus arcticus
Spikes of blue to purple flowers in summer • 20–30 cm high, 10–15 cm wide

Lupinus argenteus
Spikes of white, rose, blue or violet flowers in summer • 30–60 cm high, 30–45 cm wide

Lupinus hartwegii ssp. *cruickshankii*
Spikes of white, gold and blue flowers in summer • 75–100 cm high, 60–75 cm wide

Lupinus lepidus
Spikes of violet-blue flowers in summer • 15–30 cm high, 15–25 cm wide

Lupinus lepidus var. *aridus*
Spikes of deep-blue flowers in summer • Soft, grey-green foliage • 10–20 cm high, 15–25 cm wide

Lupinus nootkatensis
Spikes of blue flowers in summer • 45–60 cm high, 30–45 cm wide

L

Lupinus x *regalis*
'Morello Cherry' • Spikes of cherry-red flowers in summer • 75–100 cm high, 45–60 cm wide

Lupinus texensis
Spikes of purple-blue and white flowers in summer • 20–30 cm high, 15–25 cm wide

Lychnis
p. 419 📷

Genus Information

Origin: Northern Hemisphere
Selected Common Names: alpine campion, catchfly, Maltese cross, rose campion, scarlet lightning, soldier's coat
Nomenclature: The name is from the Greek *lychnos* (lamp) and was used by Theophrastus.
Other Uses: The grey, felt-like foliage of *L. coronaria* was used for lamp wicks.
Notes: Related to *Dianthus* and very closely related to *Silene*.

General Features

Height: 10–120 cm high
Spread: 10–45 cm wide
Habit: clump-forming biennial or perennial
Flowers: in clusters; spring to summer; deadhead to extend blooming season
Foliage: sticky, hairy (*L. coronaria*; grey, felt-like)
Hardiness: B–C
Warnings: prone to powdery mildew and aphids

Growing Requirements

Light: sun to p.m. sun
Soil: fertile, moist, well-drained soil; tolerant of wide range of soils, including clay; drought tolerant
Location: larger perennials and biennials in border gardens, wild gardens; smaller alpine species in rock gardens, alpine gardens
Propagation: seed (self-sows readily); division; basal cuttings
Expert Advice: Grey-leaved species produce the best colour in full sun in dry soil.

Buying Considerations

Professionals
Popularity: popular, old-fashioned garden standard; fast seller in bloom
Availability: readily available as finished product
Size to Sell: sells best in smaller sizes (when blooming) as it matures fast
On the Shelf: rapidly overgrows pot
Shrinkage: low; requires little maintenance

Collectors
Popularity: not generally of interest to collectors

On the Market

Lychnis alpina
'Alba' • White flowers in spring to summer • 10–15 cm high, 10–15 cm wide
'Rosea' • Rose-pink flowers in spring to summer • 10–15 cm high, 10–15 cm wide

Lychnis x *arkwrightii*
Large, orange-red flowers in early summer to midsummer • 30–45 cm high, 20–30 cm wide
'Orange Zwerg' • Large, orange-red flowers in early summer to midsummer • 30–45 cm high, 20–30 cm wide
'Vesuvius' • Orange-scarlet flowers in early summer to midsummer • Burgundy foliage • 30–45 cm high, 20–30 cm wide

Lychnis chalcedonica
Cross-shape, scarlet-red flowers in early summer to midsummer • Upright, stiff stems • 90–120 cm high, 20–30 cm wide
'Rosea' • Cross-shape, rose-pink flowers in early summer to midsummer • 90–120 cm high, 20–30 cm wide
'Rubra Plena' • Cross-shape, deep-red flowers in early summer to midsummer • Upright, stiff stems • 90–120 cm high, 20–30 cm wide

Lychnis chalcedonica var. *albiflora*
Cross-shape, white flowers in early summer to midsummer • Upright, stiff stems • 90–120 cm high, 20–30 cm wide

Lychnis coronaria
Magenta flowers in summer • Woolly, grey foliage • 60–90 cm high, 30–45 cm wide
'Angel's Blush' • White flowers, flushed pink, in summer • Woolly, grey foliage • 60–90 cm high, 30–45 cm wide
'Gardener's World' • Sterile, double, deep-red flowers in summer • Woolly, grey foliage • 60–90 cm high, 30–45 cm wide
'Hutchinson's Cream' • White flowers in summer • Woolly, variegated cream and grey-green foliage • 60–90 cm high, 30–45 cm wide

Lychnis flos-cuculi
Rose-pink flowers in late spring to early summer • 50–75 cm high, 30–45 cm wide

L

Lychnis flos-jovis
Pink-purple flowers in late spring to early summer • Grey, woolly foliage • 30–50 cm high, 30–45 cm wide
'Nana' • Pink-purple flowers in late spring to early summer • Grey, woolly foliage • 15–25 cm high, 15–20 cm wide

Lychnis x haageana
Orange-red flowers in summer • 30–50 cm high, 20–30 cm wide
'Molten Lava' • Orange-red flowers in summer • 30–50 cm high, 20–30 cm wide

Lychnis viscaria
Purple-red flowers in late spring to summer • 45–60 cm high, 30–45 cm wide
'Snowbird' • Snow-white flowers in late spring to early summer • 45–60 cm high, 30–45 cm wide
'Splendens Plena' • Double, purple-red flowers in late spring to summer • 45–60 cm high, 30–45 m wide

Lychnis viscaria ssp. atropurpurea
Deep-magenta flowers in late spring to summer • 45–60 cm high, 30–45 cm wide

Lychnis yunnanensis
White flowers in summer • 15–20 cm high, 10–15 cm wide

Lysimachia
p. 420

Genus Information
Origin: North America, Europe and Africa
Selected Common Names: circle flower, creeping Jenny, moneywort, goose-neck loosestrife
Nomenclature: The name is from the Greek *lysis* (releasing) and *mache* (strife), referring to the plant's reputation of having calming abilities for angry oxen.

General Features
Height: 2–90 cm high
Spread: 30–60 cm wide
Habit: upright or spreading, rhizomatous perennial
Flowers: (most) white or yellow; star-shaped to cup-shaped; spring to summer
Foliage: scalloped, often hairy; (some) evergreen
Hardiness: C
Warnings: prone to aphids, rust and leaf spot; *L. nummularia* is a rampant spreader, easy to remove; *L. punctata* may be invasive (contain and deadhead to prevent spread)
Expert Advice: Low-growing species make a great groundcover.

Growing Requirements
Light: sun to p.m. sun
Soil: moist, organic, well-drained soil; tolerates dry soil but most vigorous in moist soil
Location: moist herbaceous border; bog gardens; pond sides; wild gardens; woodland gardens
Propagation: seed (some self-sow readily); division; cuttings
Expert Advice: Sow seed in spring. Divide in autumn. Take softwood cuttings midsummer.

Buying Considerations
Professionals
Popularity: popular; fast seller in bloom
Availability: readily available as finished product
Size to Sell: sells best in smaller sizes (when blooming) as it matures fast
On the Shelf: keep stock rotated; rapidly overgrows pot
Shrinkage: low; requires little maintenance
Collectors
Popularity: not generally of interest to collectors
Gardeners
Ease of Growth: generally easy to grow
Start with: one small plant for feature plant

What to Try First ...
Lysimachia ciliata, Lysimachia clethroides, Lysimachia nummularia, Lysimachia nummularia 'Aurea', Lysimachia punctata, Lysimachia punctata 'Alexander'

On the Market
Lysimachia atropurpurea
'Beaujolais' • Spiked, wine-red flowers in summer • 25–60 cm high, 30–45 cm wide

Lysimachia ciliata
Bright-yellow flowers in summer • Erect, vigorous form • 75–100 cm high, 45–60 cm wide
'Firecracker' • Yellow flowers in summer • Dark-burgundy foliage • 50–75 cm high, 45–60 cm wide

Lysimachia clethroides
Arching, spiked, white flowers in summer • Erect form • 60–90 cm high, 45–60 cm wide

Lysimachia nummularia
Golden-yellow flowers in late spring to summer • Evergreen foliage • Rampant spreader (roots along ground) • 2–5 cm high, 45–60+ cm wide
'Aurea' • Yellow flowers in late spring to summer • Golden foliage • 2–5 cm high, 45–60+ cm wide

L

'Goldilocks' • Golden-yellow flowers in late spring to summer • Yellow-green foliage • 2–5 cm high, 45–60+ cm wide

Lysimachia punctata
Star-shaped, bright-yellow flowers in midsummer to late summer • May be invasive • 60–90 cm high, 45–60+ cm wide

'Alexander' • Gold flowers in midsummer to late summer • White-and-green-variegated foliage • 50–75 cm high, 45–60+ cm wide

'Golden Alexander' • Yellow flowers in mid-summer to late summer • Gold-edged, green foliage • 50–60 cm high, 45–60+ cm wide

Macleaya

p. 420

Genus Information

Origin: China and Japan
Selected Common Names: plume poppy, small-fruited plume poppy
Nomenclature: Named for Alexander Macleay, 1767–1848, a colonial secretary for New South Wales in Australia.
Notes: A genus of some 3 species.

General Features

Height: 1.5–3 m high
Spread: 90 cm–2.5 m wide
Habit: spreading, rhizomatous perennial
Flowers: tall, graceful, plume-like; summer
Foliage: large, tropical-looking; heart-shaped
Hardiness: C–D
Warnings: prone to aphids; may be invasive in warmer climates (contain and deadhead to prevent spread)
Expert Advice: *Macleaya* makes a stately single feature in a garden or easily fills a large patch for a striking mass planting or temporary screen.

Growing Requirements

Light: sun to p.m. sun; tolerates more sun with good soil moisture
Soil: deep, fertile, moist, well-drained soil; tolerates sandy soil; tolerates periods of dryness
Location: mixed borders
Propagation: seed; division; root cuttings
Expert Advice: Seed outdoors in spring. Plants will bloom the following year.

Buying Considerations

Professionals
Popularity: relatively unknown as a foliage plant
Availability: generally available as bare root
Size to Sell: sells best in smaller sizes as it matures fast
On the Shelf: rapidly overgrows pot
Shrinkage: low; requires little maintenance

Collectors
Popularity: not generally of interest to collectors

Gardeners
Ease of Growth: very easy to grow
Start with: one plant for feature plant and several for mass plantings

What to Try First ...
Macleaya cordata, Macleaya microcarpa 'Kelway's Coral Plume'

On the Market

Macleaya
'Plum Tassel' • Smoky-plum plumes in summer • Large, blue-grey foliage • 1.5–2 m high, 90–100 cm wide

Macleaya cordata
Cream plumes in summer • Large, heart-shaped, blue-grey foliage • 1.5–2.5 m high, 90–100 cm wide

Macleaya microcarpa
Copper plumes in summer • Blue-grey foliage • 2–3 m high, 1+ m wide

'Kelway's Coral Plume' • Apricot plumes in summer • Blue-grey foliage • 1.5–2.5 m high, 1 m wide

'Spetchley Ruby' • Coral plumes in summer • Bronze foliage • 1.5–2.5 m high, 1 m wide

Malva

p. 420

Genus Information

Origin: Europe, Asia, tropical Africa, southern Africa and North America
Selected Common Names: hollyhock, mallow, musk mallow
Nomenclature: From the Latin *malva* and from the Greek *malache* or *malachos* (soothing), referring to its medicinal properties.
Notes: A genus of some 30 species of annuals, biennials or perennials.

General Features

Height: 20–150 cm high
Spread: 30–60 cm wide
Habit: upright, short-lived perennial
Flowers: bowl-shaped; showy; summer to fall; long blooming period
Foliage: rounded, heart or kidney-shaped; (some) aromatic
Hardiness: C–D
Warnings: prone to powdery mildew, aphids and rust
Expert Advice: Prefers cool summers. Many species will not overwinter in colder climates but they self-sow readily and bloom the 1st year. To help overwinter the plant, cut down the stems in late summer to force new growth.

Growing Requirements

Light: sun
Soil: fertile, moist, well-drained soil; tolerates poor soil
Location: mixed borders; wild gardens
Propagation: seed (self-sows readily); basal cuttings

M

Buying Considerations

Professionals

Popularity: garden standard; fast seller in bloom
Availability: readily available as finished product and bare root
Size to Sell: sells best in smaller sizes (when blooming) as it matures fast
On the Shelf: rapidly overgrows pot
Shrinkage: high; sensitive to overwatering

Collectors

Popularity: not generally of interest to collectors

Gardeners

Ease of Growth: mostly easy to grow
Start with: one small plant for feature plant

What to Try First ...

Malva alcea, Malva alcea var. *fastigiata, Malva moschata* f. *alba, Malva moschata rosea*

On the Market

Malva
  'Bibor Fehlo' • Wavy, magenta flowers with purple veins in summer • 90–100 cm high, 60 cm wide

Malva alcea
  Purplish-pink flowers in summer to fall • 90–100 cm high, 45–60 cm wide
  'Burgundy Wine' • Flowers in late summer to fall • 90–100 cm high, 45–60 cm wide

Malva alcea var. *fastigiata*
  Deep-pink flowers in summer to fall • 60–90 cm high, 45–60 cm wide

Malva moschata
  Deep-rose to white flowers in summer to fall • Aromatic foliage • 60–90 cm high, 45–60 cm wide

Malva moschata f. *alba*
  Hibiscus-like, white flowers in summer to fall • Aromatic foliage • 30–60 cm high, 45–60 cm wide

Malva moschata rosea
  Hibiscus-like, rose-mauve flowers in summer to fall • Aromatic foliage • 60–90 cm high, 45–60 cm wide

Malva sylvestris
  'Marina' (Dema) • Purple-pink flowers with magenta veins in summer • 90–100 cm high, 45–60 cm wide
  'Primley Blue' • Pale-blue flowers in summer • 20–30 cm high, 30–60 cm wide
  'Zebrina' • Pink or white flowers with purple stripes in summer • 60–l00 cm high, 45–60 cm wide

Malva sylvestris ssp. *mauritanica*
Rich-magenta flowers with veins in summer • 1–1.5 m high, 60–90 cm wide

Matteuccia　　　p. 420

Genus Information

Origin: Europe, East Asia and North America
Selected Common Names: ostrich fern
Nomenclature: Named for Carlo Matteucci, 1811–1868, an Italian physicist. The species name *struthiopteris* is from the Greek *struthokamelos* (ostrich) and *pteris* (fern), giving rise to the common name ostrich fern.

General Features

Height: 1–1.5 m high
Spread: 60–75 cm wide
Habit: upright, vase-shaped, spreading rhizomatous fern
Foliage: dark green; tall, arching, ostrich plume-like fronds
Hardiness: A
Warnings: not prone to insects or disease
Expert Advice: The hardiest fern for colder climates like the Prairies.

Growing Requirements

Light: shade to a.m. sun; tolerates more sun with good soil moisture
Soil: loamy, moist, acidic soil
Location: woodland gardens; pond edges; stream sides; shady mixed borders; foliage may burn and break in windy locations
Propagation: spores; division

Buying Considerations

Professionals

Popularity: popular, old-fashioned, garden standard, foliage plant
Availability: readily available as finished product and bare root
Size to Sell: sells best in smaller sizes as it matures fast
On the Shelf: high ornamental appeal; foliage breakage (display out of wind); do not allow to dry out
Shrinkage: low; sensitive to underwatering; requires little maintenance

Collectors

Popularity: not generally of interest to collectors

Gardeners

Ease of Growth: very easy to grow
Start with: one small plant for feature plant and several for mass plantings

What to Try First ...

Matteuccia struthiopteris

M

On the Market

Matteuccia struthiopteris
Arching, pale-green fronds • 1–1.5 m high,
60–75 cm wide

Meconopsis

p. 420 📷

Genus Information

Origin: Himalayas, Europe, Western China and
Eastern Europe
Selected Common Names: Himalayan poppy,
Himalayan blue poppy, Welsh poppy
Nomenclature: From the Greek *mekon* (poppy)
and *opsis* (appearance).
Notes: A genus of some 43 species including
annuals, biennials and perennials. Not true
poppies, although the flowers look similar.

General Features

Height: 20 cm–2.5 m high
Spread: 15–100 cm wide
Habit: clump-forming biennial or monocarpic
perennial
Flowers: elegant, poppy-like; spring to fall
Foliage: usually hairy or bristly; mid-green
Hardiness: C–D
Warnings: prone to powdery mildew and aphids
Expert Advice: Many of these species are reputed
to be monocarpic, which means the plant dies
after flowering. To ensure a longer life, do not
allow the plant to flower for the first 2 years.
Doing so will force the plant to develop
multiple crowns. Many hybrids available in
Europe have huge flowers (up to 20 cm across),
but they are very rare and extremely expensive.

Growing Requirements

Light: shade to a.m. sun
Soil: cool, moist, rich, acidic soil; do not let plants
dry out
Location: woodland; shade gardens; sheltered
locations; foliage may burn in windy locations
Propagation: seed; division; separate and replant
offshoots
Expert Advice: They are heavy feeders and benefit
from regular fertilizing. Mulch at the base of the
plants to keep the roots cool and moist. Seed is
notoriously difficult to germinate and takes a
long time to reach blooming size. Divide every
5 years.

Buying Considerations

Professionals

Popularity: popular; fast seller in bloom
Availability: generally available as finished
product from specialty growers
Size to Sell: sells best in smaller sizes (when
blooming)
Shrinkage: high; sensitive to overwatering or
underwatering

Collectors

Popularity: of interest to collectors—unique,
rare, challenge, exceptional beauty (some
variation in colour exists within species);
M. quintuplinervia is extremely rare

Gardeners

Ease of Growth: mostly difficult to grow as it
needs close attention to growing conditions
Start with: one small plant for feature plant or
several for mass plantings; best when mass
planted

What to Try First ...

*Meconopsis betonicifolia, Meconopsis grandis,
Meconopsis punicea, Meconopsis quintuplinervia,
Meconopsis* x *sheldonii*

On the Market

Meconopsis betonicifolia
Sky-blue flowers in early summer •
90–120 cm high, 45–60 cm wide
Meconopsis betonicifolia var. *alba*
White flowers in early summer • 90–120 cm
high, 45–60 cm wide
Meconopsis cambrica
Lemon-yellow flowers in spring to fall •
30–45 cm high, 20–30 cm wide
'Frances Perry' • Single, scarlet flowers in
spring to fall • 25–30 cm high, 15–20 cm
wide
'Muriel Brown' • Semi-double, red flowers
in spring to fall • 30 cm high, 15–25 cm
wide
Meconopsis cambrica var. *aurantiaca*
Orange flowers in spring to fall • 30–40 cm
high, 25–30 cm wide
Meconopsis cambrica flore-pleno
Semi-double, yellow flowers in spring to fall
• 30–45 cm high, 20–30 cm wide
Meconopsis delavayi
Deep-purple flowers in summer • 20–25 cm
high, 30–40 cm wide
Meconopsis dhwojii
Soft-yellow flowers in early summer •
Monocarpic evergreen • 60–100 cm high,
30–45 cm wide
Meconopsis grandis
Rich-blue flowers in early summer •
60–100 cm high, 60 cm wide
Meconopsis horridula
Dark-blue flowers in early summer •
Monocarpic • 25–90 cm high, 45 cm wide
'Alba' • White flowers in early summer •
Monocarpic • 25–90 cm high, 45 cm wide

M

Meconopsis integrifolia
Yellow flowers in early summer •
Monocarpic • 60–90 cm high, 45–60 cm
wide

Meconopsis napaulensis
Red, purple or blue flowers in summer •
Monocarpic evergreen • 1–2.5 m high,
60–90 cm wide
(Blue form) • Blue flowers in early summer
• Monocarpic evergreen • 60–75 cm high,
60–75 cm wide

Meconopsis paniculata
Pale-yellow flowers in early summer •
Monocarpic evergreen • 1–2 m high,
45–60 cm wide

Meconopsis punicea
Red flowers in spring to summer •
40–75 cm high, 30 cm wide

Meconopsis quintuplinervia
Pale mauve-blue flowers in summer •
30–45 cm high, 30 cm wide

Meconopsis regia
Yellow flowers in early summer •
Monocarpic evergreen • 60 cm–2 m high,
30–100 cm wide

Meconopsis x sheldonii
Blue flowers in early summer • 90–150 cm
high, 60 cm wide
'Lingholm' • Blue flowers in early summer •
90–150 cm high, 60 cm wide

Meconopsis superba
White flowers in summer • 60 cm–2 m
high, 60–100 cm wide

Meconopsis villosa
Yellow flowers in early summer • Evergreen
• 45–60 cm high, 45–60 cm wide

Mentha

p. 420

Genus Information

Origin: Eurasia and Africa
Selected Common Names: mint
Nomenclature: Named for Xaverjo Manetti,
1723–1785, a botanist and director of the
botanic garden in Florence, Italy.
Other Uses: *Mentha* has medicinal, culinary
and fragrance uses.

General Features

Height: 60–90 cm high
Spread: 45–60 cm wide
Habit: upright, spreading perennial
Flowers: summer; attractive to bees
Foliage: aromatic; used for teas

Hardiness: C
Warnings: prone to aphids; invasive (contain to
prevent spread)
Expert Advice: Shear in midsummer to keep plant
compact and encourage fresh growth.

Growing Requirements

Light: sun
Soil: fertile, moist soil; tolerant of wide range
of soils; drought tolerant
Location: herb gardens; mixed borders
Propagation: division; separate and replant
rhizomes

Buying Considerations

Professionals

Popularity: relatively unknown; sells well in
bloom
Availability: occasionally available from
specialty growers
Size to Sell: sells best in smaller sizes (when
blooming) as it matures fast
On the Shelf: keep stock rotated; rapidly
overgrows pot
Shrinkage: low; requires little maintenance

Collectors

Popularity: not generally of interest to
collectors (although of interest to herbalists)

Gardeners

Ease of Growth: very easy to grow
Start with: one small plant for feature plant

What to Try First ...

Mentha 'Purple Sensation'

On the Market

Mentha
'Purple Sensation' • Fragrant, purple flowers
in summer • Aromatic foliage • 60–90 cm
high, 45–60+ cm wide

Mentha x piperita
'Todd Mitchum' • Fragrant, spiked, lilac-
pink flowers in summer • Aromatic, red-
purple foliage • 30–90 cm high, 45–60+
cm wide

Mertensia

p. 420

Genus Information

Origin: Eastern Europe, Asia, North America and
Greenland
Selected Common Names: bluebells, oyster plant
Nomenclature: Named for Francis Mertens,
1764–1831, a professor of botany in Berlin.

General Features

Height: 10–60 cm
Spread: 20–90+ cm
Habit: spreading or clump-forming perennial
Flowers: bluebell-like; spring to summer; deadhead to extend blooming season; may rebloom in fall
Foliage: blue-green
Hardiness: B–C
Warnings: prone to powdery mildew

Growing Requirements

Light: shade to a.m. sun; filtered sun best
Soil: cool, moist, organic, well-drained soil
Location: woodland gardens
Propagation: seed; division

Buying Considerations

Professionals

Popularity: gaining popularity; fast seller in bloom
Availability: generally available as bare root from specialty growers
Size to Sell: sells best in smaller sizes (when blooming) as it matures fast
On the Shelf: keep stock rotated; rapidly overgrows pot
Shrinkage: low shrinkage; some species go dormant after blooming

Collectors

Popularity: not generally of interest to collectors

Gardeners

Ease of growth: mostly easy to grow but needs close attention to growing conditions
Start with: one small plant for feature plant

What to Try First ...

Mertensia maritima, Mertensia primuloides, Mertensia sibirica 'Blue Bells', *Mertensia sibirica* var. *yezoensis, Mertensia simplicissima, Mertensia virginica*

On the Market

Mertensia maritima
Blue bells in early summer • Blue-green foliage • 10 cm high, 60–90 cm+ wide

Mertensia primuloides
Deep blue flowers with white or yellow centres in spring • 10–15 cm high, 20 cm wide

Mertensia virginica
(syn. *M. pulmonarioides*)
Bell-like, light-blue flowers in spring • Bluish-green foliage • 30–60 cm high, 25 cm wide

---

Mertensia sibirica **(syn. *M. pterocarpa*)**
'**Blue Bells**' • Funnel-shaped, deep blue flowers in late spring to midsummer
• 45–60 cm high, 30–45 cm wide

Mertensia sibirica var. *yezoensis*
(syn. *M. pterocarpa* var. *yezoensis*)
Purple-blue flowers in spring to summer • Blue-green foliage • 20–30 cm high, 25 cm wide

Mertensia simplicissima
(syn. *M. maritima* ssp. *asiatica*)
Sky-blue flowers in spring to fall • Blue-green foliage • 10 cm high, 60–90+ cm wide

Minuartia

p. 420

Genus Information

Origin: temperate regions and colder regions of the Northern Hemisphere
Selected Common Names: sandwort
Nomenclature: Named for Juan Minuart, 1693–1768, an 18th century botanist.
Notes: A genus of some 100 species. *Minuartia* closely resembles *Arenaria*.

General Features

Height: 8–15 cm high
Spread: 20 cm wide
Habit: mat- or cushion-forming groundcover perennial
Flowers: tiny, white; long blooming period; spring to summer
Foliage: mid-green
Hardiness: A
Warnings: not prone to insects or disease
Expert Advice: This much underused perennial is tough, hardy and very forgiving of many growing conditions. It is an excellent, long-blooming perennial groundcover.

Growing Requirements

Light: sun
Soil: fertile, well-drained soil; tolerant of wide range of soils
Location: rock gardens; alpine gardens; trough; scree; between paving stones
Propagation: seed; division; cuttings

Buying Considerations

Professionals

Popularity: relatively unknown
Availability: occasionally available from specialty growers
Size to Sell: sells best in smaller sizes (when blooming) as it matures fast
On the Shelf: rapidly overgrows pot
Shrinkage: low; requires little maintenance

M

On the Market

Minuartia verna
White flowers in spring • 8–15 cm high, 20 cm wide

Miscanthus

p. 420

Genus Information

Origin: East Asia and Africa
Selected Common Names: Chinese silver grass, maiden grass, zebra grass
Nomenclature: From the Greek *mischos* (stalk) and *anthos* (flower), referring to the beautiful plumes.
Notes: A genus of some 20 species.

General Features

Height: 90 cm–3 m high
Spread: 60 cm–2 m wide
Habit: rhizomatous, warm-season grass
Flowers: silvery-white to coppery-red, feathery plumes; late summer to fall; good for cutflowers; good for drying; good for winter interest
Foliage: narrow, fine to wide, coarse blades; green to variegated (striped or banded)
Hardiness: D
Warnings: prone to aphids and rust
Expert Advice: A warm-season grower that requires long, hot summers to reach its full potential. It breaks dormancy late, but it grows rapidly in summer heat with good soil moisture. Most *Miscanthus* are not hardy in colder areas (with the exception of *M.* 'Purpurascens', *M. floridulus*, *M. sacchariflorus*, *M. sinensis* 'Huron Sunrise'and *M. sinensis* 'Huron Sunset') and are best used as annuals in containers. The hardy species and varieties are best grown in a sheltered location with good snow coverage in winter. Most will not plume in areas with short summers but still provide striking foliage.

Growing Requirements

Light: sun
Soil: deep, evenly moist, fertile, well-drained soil
Location: sheltered and hot mixed borders; next to buildings, fences; provide snow coverage
Propagation: seed; division; separate and replant rhizomes

On the Market

Miscanthus
'Giganteus' • Silvery plumes in fall • Wide, deep-green foliage with white midveins • 2.5–3+ m high, 1–1.5 m wide
'Purpurascens' • Vertical, silvery-white plumes in late summer • Purple foliage • Hardy variety • 1.5 m high, 90–120 cm wide

Miscanthus floridulus
Silvery plumes in summer • Grey-green foliage with silver midveins • Hardy variety • 2.5+ m high, 1–1.5 m wide

Miscanthus sacchariflorus
Silvery-white plumes in fall • Upright, arching foliage turning yellow in fall • Hardy variety • 1–2.4 m high, 1–1.4 m wide

Miscanthus sinensis
'Goldfeder' (Gold Feather) • Silvery seed heads in late summer • Gold-striped foliage • 1.5–2 m high, 90–120 cm wide
'Gracillimus' • Copper-red plumes in fall • Fine-textured foliage • 1.3–2 m high, 90–120 cm wide
'Graziella' • Silvery plumes in late summer • Green foliage turning red-orange in fall • 1–2 m high, 90–120 cm wide
'Huron Sunrise' • Silvery seed heads in midsummer • Hardy variety • 1–1.5 m high, 90–120 cm wide

M

'Huron Sunset' • Silvery seed heads in fall • Hardy variety • 1–1.5 m high, 90–120 cm wide

'Kirk Alexander' • Grey, purple-tinted spikelets in fall • Horizontal bands of yellow variegation on leaves • 1–2 m high, 90–120 cm wide

'Malepartus' • Copper seed heads open to silver in fall • 1–2 m high, 90–120 cm wide

'Morning Light' • Reddish seed heads in fall • Narrow, cream-variegated foliage • 1–1.5 m high, 90–120 cm wide

'November Sunset' • Reddish seed heads in fall • Narrow, silver-veined foliage • 1–2 m high, 90–120 cm wide

'Punktchen' (Little Dot) • Seed heads in midsummer • Horizontal bands of yellow variegation on leaves • 90–120 cm high, 60–90 cm wide

'Sarabande' • Bronze plumes in fall • Silvery, fine-textured foliage • 1–2 m high, 90–120 cm wide

'Silberfeder' (Silver Feather) • Silver plumes in fall • 1.5–2 m high, 90–120 cm wide

'Silberspinne' (Silver Spider) • Silver plumes with pink tints in fall • Narrow foliage • 1–2 m high, 90–100 cm wide

'Strictus' (Zebrinus Strictus) • Reddish seed heads in fall • Horizontal bands of yellow variegation on leaves • 1.5–2.5 m high, 90–120 cm wide

'Variegatus' • Red-tinted seed heads in fall • White-striped foliage • 1–2 m high, 90–120 cm wide

'Yaku-jima' • Silver seed heads in fall • Narrow-leaved • 90–100 cm high, 90 cm wide

'Zebrinus' • Copper-tinted seed heads in fall • Horizontal bands of yellow variegation on leaves • 1–2.4 m high, 90–120 cm wide

Miscanthus sinensis var. *condensatus*
'Cabaret' • Copper-purple seed heads in fall • Leaves with white centres and dark-green margins • 1–2.5 m high, 90–120 cm wide

(select) • Copper-red seed heads in fall • 1–2 m high, 90–120 cm wide

'Cosmopolitan' • Copper-red seed heads in fall • Leaves with dark-green centres and white margins • 1–3 m high, 90–120 cm wide

Molinia

p. 420

Genus Information

Origin: Eurasia
Selected Common Names: giant Moor grass, purple Moor grass, striped Moor grass
Nomenclature: Named for Juan Molina, 1740–1829, a writer of natural history in Chile.

General Features

Height: 45 cm–2.4 m high
Spread: 45–60 cm wide
Habit: upright, clump-forming, cool-season grass
Flowers: airy plumes
Foliage: solid green or variegated; strong, upright; good for winter interest
Hardiness: C
Warnings: prone to aphids and rust
Expert Advice: *Molinia* prefers damp, cool summers and will reliably produce plumes in colder areas. A very good, non-invasive, accent plant.

Growing Requirements

Light: p.m. sun
Soil: moist, organic, well-drained soil; tolerates poor, acidic soil
Location: mixed borders; woodland gardens
Propagation: seed; division

Buying Considerations

Professionals

Popularity: gaining popularity as a foliage plant
Availability: readily available as finished product and bare root
Size to Sell: sells best in smaller sizes as it matures fast
On the Shelf: high ornamental appeal; rapidly overgrows pot
Shrinkage: low; requires little maintenance

Collectors

Popularity: not generally of interest to collectors

Gardeners

Ease of Growth: very easy to grow
Start with: one small plant for feature plant

What to Try First ...

Molinia caerulea ssp. *arundinacea* 'Skyracer',
Molinia caerulea ssp. *caerulea* 'Strahlenquelle',
Molinia caerulea ssp. *caerulea* 'Variegata'

M

On the Market

Molinia caerulea ssp. *arundinacea*
(syn. *M. litoralis)*
'**Skyracer**' • Tan seed heads in summer •
1–2.4 m high, 45–60 cm wide

Molinia caerulea ssp. *caerulea*
'**Moorflamme**' • Seed heads in midsummer
• Orange-red fall foliage • 45–60 cm high,
45–60 cm wide

'**Strahlenquelle**' • Arching, purple seed
heads in midsummer • 45–60 cm high,
45–60 cm wide

'**Variegata**' • Purple seed heads in
midsummer • Cream-and-green-striped
foliage with purple stems • 45–60 cm high,
45–60 cm wide

Monarda

p. 420

Genus Information

Origin: North America
Selected Common Names: beebalm, Oswego tea,
wild bergamot
Nomenclature: Named for Nicholas Monardes,
1493–1588, a Spanish botanist and physician,
who was the author of the first medicinal flora
of North America.
Other Uses: At one time these plants were
collected and used to make tea, hence the
common names "Oswega tea" or "bergamot
tea."
Notes: *M. fistulosa*, our native species, is grown
commercially for its oil, which is extracted and
shipped to Europe, where it is in high demand.

General Features

Height: 15–120 cm high
Habit: rhizomatous, spreading perennial
Flowers: long blooming period; summer;
attractive to bees, butterflies and hummingbirds
Foliage: aromatic foliage
Hardiness: B–C
Warnings: prone to powdery mildew and aphids;
aggresive spreader (contain to prevent spread)
Expert Advice: Although this perennial is prone
to insects and disease, it is still well worth
growing. Space plants well for good air
circulation and plant mildew resistant varieties.

Growing Requirements

Light: sun
Soil: moderately fertile, moist, well-drained soil;
avoid winter wet; somewhat tolerant of dry
periods
Location: mixed borders
Propagation: seed; division; basal cuttings;
separate and replant stolons

On the Market

Monarda
'**Adam**' • Cherry-red flowers in summer •
Aromatic foliage • 60–90 cm high,
45–60 cm wide

'**Aquarius**' • Light-pink-purple flowers
in summer • Bronze-green, aromatic
foliage • Resistant to powdery mildew •
90–100 cm high, 60–90 cm wide

'**Baby Spice**' • Pink flowers in late spring
to early summer • Aromatic foliage •
20–30 cm high, 30–40 cm wide

'**Beauty of Cobham**' • Soft-pink flowers in
summer • Purple-tinted, aromatic foliage •
60–90 cm high, 45–60 cm wide

'**Blaustrumpf**' (**Blue Stocking**) • Blue-purple
flowers in summer • Aromatic foliage •
60–90 cm high, 45–60 cm wide

'**Cambridge Scarlet**' • Red flowers in
summer • Aromatic foliage • 60–90 cm
high, 45–60 cm wide

'**Colrain Red**' • Red flowers in summer •
Aromatic foliage • 60–90 cm high,
45–60 cm wide

'**Coral Reef**' • Large, deep-pink flowers in
summer • Shiny, aromatic foliage • 90 cm
high, 45–60 cm wide

'**Croftway Pink**' • Rose-pink flowers in
summer • Aromatic foliage • 60–90 cm
high, 45–60 cm wide

M

'Dr. Charm' • Red flowers in summer • Aromatic foliage • 60–90 cm high, 45–60 cm wide

'Fireball' • Large, red flowers in summer • Aromatic foliage • 30–40 cm high, 30–45 cm wide

'Gardenview Scarlet' • Bright-crimson-scarlet flowers in summer • Aromatic foliage • Resistant to powdery mildew • 60–90 cm high, 45–60 cm wide

'Jacob Cline' • Red flowers in summer • Aromatic foliage • 75–100 cm high, 60 cm wide

'Kardinal' • Red flowers in summer • Aromatic foliage • 90 cm high, 45–60 cm wide

'Keshia' • Large, magenta flowers in summer • Aromatic foliage • 60–90 cm high, 45–60 cm wide

'Mahogany' • Dark-red-brown flowers in summer • Aromatic foliage • 60–90 cm high, 45–60 cm wide

'Marshall's Delight' • Large, rose-pink flowers in summer • Shiny, aromatic foliage • Resistant to powdery mildew • 60–90 cm high, 45–60 cm wide

'On Parade' • Fuchsia-pink flowers in summer • Purple-tinted, aromatic foliage • 75–80 cm high, 45–60 cm wide

'Petite Delight' • Purple flowers in summer • Aromatic foliage • 20–30 cm high, 30–40 cm wide

'Petite Pink Supreme' • Large, cerise-pink flowers in summer • Aromatic foliage • 30–40 cm high, 30–45 cm wide

'Petite Wonder' • Rich-pink flowers in summer • Aromatic foliage • 30–40 cm high, 40–45 cm wide

'Pink Tourmaline' • Large, purple-pink flowers in summer • Aromatic foliage • 40–45 cm high, 45–60 cm wide

'Prarienacht' (Prairie Night) • Purple flowers in summer • Aromatic foliage • 90–120 cm high, 45–60 cm wide

'Purpurkrone' (Purple Crown) • Purple flowers in summer • Aromatic foliage • 60–90 cm high, 45–60 cm wide

'Raspberry Wine' • Wine-red flowers in summer • Dark-green, aromatic foliage • 60–90 cm high, 45–60 cm wide

'Schneewittchen' (Snow Maiden, Snow White) • White flowers in summer • Aromatic foliage • 90–100 cm high, 45–60 cm wide

'Scorpion' • Violet-red flowers in summer • Aromatic foliage • 90–100 cm high, 45–60 cm wide

'Stones Throw Pink' • Clear-pink flowers in summer • Aromatic foliage • 75–100 cm high, 45–60 cm wide

'Twins' • Dark-pink flowers in summer • Aromatic foliage • Resistant to powdery mildew • 60–75 cm high, 45–60 cm wide

'Violet Queen' • Dark-violet flowers in summer • Aromatic foliage • Resistant to powdery mildew • 75–90 cm high, 45–60 cm wide

Monarda austromontana
Pink-purple flowers in summer • Aromatic foliage • 15 cm high, 15 cm wide

Monarda fistulosa
Large, lilac-purple flowers in summer • Aromatic foliage • 90–120 cm high, 45–60 cm wide

Monarda fistulosa var. *menthaefolia*
Mauve flowers in summer • Aromatic foliage • 30–75 cm high, 30–45 cm wide

Monarda punctata
Purple-spotted, yellow or pink flowers in midsummer to fall • Aromatic foliage • 30–90 cm high, 25–45 cm wide

Monardella p. 420

Genus Information

Origin: western North America
Selected Common Names: coyote mint
Nomenclature: The name is a diminutive of *Monarda*, to which the plant is closely related.
Other Uses: Some species are used in medicinal teas.
Notes: A genus of some 20 species.

General Features

Height: 15–60 cm high
Spread: 30–90 cm wide
Habit: herbaceous perennial
Flowers: feathery; summer
Foliage: aromatic
Hardiness: D
Warnings: prone to aphids; not prone to diseases
Expert Advice: Shear in summer to keep plant compact and promote fresh growth.

Growing Requirements

Light: sun
Soil: poor, sharply drained, dry, sandy soil; avoid winter wet
Location: rock gardens
Propagation: seed; division; semi-ripe cuttings

M

Buying Considerations

Professionals
Popularity: relatively unknown;
Availability: occasionally available from specialty growers
Size to Sell: sells best in smaller sizes
On the Shelf: rapidly overgrows pot
Shrinkage: low; requires little maintenance

Collectors
Popularity: not generally of interest to collectors

Gardeners
Ease of Growth: mostly easy to grow
Start with: one small plant for feature plant

What to Try First ...
Monardella nana ssp. *tenuiflora, Monardella odoratissima* ssp. *glauca, Monardella villosa* ssp. *obispoensis*

On the Market

Monardella nana ssp. *tenuiflora*
Feathery, pale-yellow flowers in early summer • Aromatic foliage • 30 cm high, 30+ cm wide

Monardella odoratissima ssp. *glauca*
Feathery, rose-violet flowers in summer • Aromatic foliage • 15–35 cm high, 30+ cm wide

Monardella villosa ssp. *globosa*
Feathery, light-purple flowers in early summer • Dark slate-grey, aromatic foliage • 30–60 cm high, 60–90 cm wide

Monardella villosa ssp. *obispoensis*
Pale-lavender flowers in summer • Aromatic foliage • 20–30 cm high, 30+ cm wide

Myosotis p. 420

Genus Information
Origin: Europe, Asia, Australia, North America and South America
Selected Common Names: wild forget-me-not, woodland forget-me-not
Nomenclature: From the Greek *mys* (mouse) and *ous* (ear), referring to the foliage.
Notes: A genus of some 50 species, including annuals, biennials and perennials.

General Features
Height: 10–30 cm high
Spread: 15–30 cm wide
Habit: clump- or mat-forming, spreading or rhizomatous biennial or short-lived perennial
Flowers: dainty, clustered; blue, pink or white; spring
Foliage: tiny, mid-green
Hardiness: C–D
Warnings: prone to powdery mildew and aphids

Growing Requirements
Light: sun or shade
Soil: moist soil; *(M. alpestris)* lean soil
Location: woodland gardens; wild gardens; mixed borders; *M. scorpioides* can be used as a marginal aquatic
Propagation: seed (self-sows readily); division

Buying Considerations

Professionals
Popularity: popular, old-fashioned garden standard; fast seller in bloom
Availability: readily available as finished product
Size to Sell: sells best in smaller sizes (when blooming) as it matures fast
On the Shelf: keep stock rotated; rapidly overgrows pot; requires regular cleaning (older growth blackens)
Shrinkage: high; sensitive to overwatering or underwatering

Collectors
Popularity: not generally of interest to collectors

Gardeners
Ease of Growth: mostly easy to grow but needs close attention to growing conditions
Start with: one small plant for feature plant

What to Try First ...
Myosotis sylvatica, Myosotis sylvatica 'Victoria Blue', *Myosotis sylvatica* 'Victoria Rose', *Myosotis sylvatica* 'Victoria White'

On the Market
Myosotis alpestris
Yellow-eyed, rich-blue flowers in spring to early summer • 15 cm high, 15 cm wide

M

Myosotis scorpioides
Blue flowers with white, pink or yellow eye in early summer • 15–30 cm high, 15–30 cm wide

Myosotis sylvatica
Blue, rose or white flowers in spring to early summer • 15–25 cm high, 15–25 cm wide

'**Gold 'n' Sapphires**' • Dark-blue flowers in spring to early summer • Yellow foliage • 15–20 cm high, 15–20 cm wide

Victoria Series
'**Victoria Blue**' • Blue flowers in early spring to early summer • 10–15 cm high, 15–25 cm wide

'**Victoria Rose**' • Rose-pink flowers in early spring to early summer • 10–15 cm high, 15–25 cm wide

'**Victoria White**' • White flowers in early spring to early summer • 10–15 cm high, 15–25 cm wide

Myosotis sylvatica f. lactea
White flowers in early spring to early summer • 15–25 cm high, 15–25 cm wide

Nepeta

p. 420

Genus Information

Origin: Eurasia, North Africa and the mountains of tropical Africa
Selected Common Names: catmint
Nomenclature: From the name used by Pliny, likely after Nepi in Italy.
Notes: A genus of some 250 species.

General Features

Height: 15–90 cm high
Spread: 15–90 cm wide
Habit: clump-forming, spreading perennial; may require staking
Flowers: tubular-shaped blooms borne on spikes; summer to fall; deadhead to extend blooming season; attractive to bees
Foliage: aromatic (unpleasant to some)
Hardiness: C
Warnings: prone to aphids
Expert Advice: *N. racemosa* blooms from summer to fall, providing reliable colour in the mixed border. Cut back in midsummer to keep plants compact, promote new growth and new blooms.

Growing Requirements

Light: sun to p.m. sun
Soil: well-drained soil; drought tolerant
Location: mixed borders; rock gardens; alongside sidewalks; edging beds
Propagation: seed (self-sows); divisions, cuttings
Expert Advice: Seed indoors in February or March or outdoors in spring. Divide every 3 years. Take softwood cuttings in late spring or early summer.

Buying Considerations

Professionals

Popularity: popular, old-fashioned garden standard; fast seller in bloom
Availability: readily available as finished product and bare root
Size to Sell: sells best in smaller sizes (when blooming) as it matures fast
On the Shelf: keep stock rotated; rapidly overgrows pot; deadhead regularly
Shrinkage: low

Collectors

Popularity: not generally of interest to collectors

Gardeners

Ease of Growth: very easy to grow

Start with: one small plant for feature plant and several for mass plantings

What to Try First ...

Nepeta 'Six Hills Giant', *Nepeta* 'Walker's Low', *Nepeta* x *faassenii* 'Dropmore', *Nepeta nervosa*, *Nepeta racemosa*, *Nepeta subsessilis*, *Nepeta subsessilis* 'Sweet Dreams'

On the Market

Nepeta
  'Six Hills Giant' • Lavender-blue flowers in summer • Aromatic, light-grey foliage • 60–90 cm high, 60 cm wide

  'Walker's Low' • Lavender-blue flowers in summer to fall • 25–30 cm high, 30–40 cm wide

Nepeta x *faassenii*
  'Dropmore' • Lavender-blue flowers in summer • 30–60 cm high, 30–45 cm wide

Nepeta grandiflora
  'Dawn to Dusk' • Tubular, pink flowers in summer to fall • Aromatic foliage • 30–60 cm high, 45–60 cm wide

Nepeta nervosa
  Light-blue flowers in summer to fall • 45–60 cm high, 30 cm wide

Nepeta racemosa (syn. *N. mussinii*)
  Spiked, violet-blue flowers in summer to fall • Mint-scented foliage • 30 cm high, 30–45 cm wide

  'Blue Wonder' • Spiked, violet-blue flowers in summer to fall • Mint-scented foliage • 30–40 cm high, 30–45 cm wide

  'Little Titch' • Pale lavender-blue flowers in late spring to summer • 15–25 cm high, 15–25 cm wide

  'Snowflake' • Spiked, white flowers in summer • 30–40 cm high, 40–45 cm wide

Nepeta sibirica
  'Souvenir d'Andre Chaudron' (Blue Beauty) • Spiked, dark-lavender-blue flowers in summer • Aromatic foliage • 45–50 cm high, 30–45 cm wide

Nepeta subsessilis
  Blue-purple flowers in midsummer to fall • Aromatic foliage • Well-drained, moist, cool soil • 60–90 cm high, 30 cm wide

  'Sweet Dreams' • Bi-tone, soft pink flowers in midsummer to fall • Aromatic foliage • 45–55 cm high, 30 cm wide

Oenothera

p. 420 📷

Genus Information

Origin: North America
Selected Common Names: evening primrose, sundrops
Nomenclature: From the name used by Theophrastus, the Greek philosopher and scientist.
Other Uses: The seed-oil of *Oenothera* is particularly rich in gamma linolenic acid that has been used as an effective treatment for eczema and premenstrual syndrome. It may also prevent blood clotting and is reputed to cure chronic fatigue syndrome.
Notes: A genus of some 125 species.

General Features

Height: 10–90 cm high
Spread: 15–60 cm wide
Habit: tap-rooted, clump-forming perennial
Flowers: delicate, paper-like; late spring to late summer; some species only bloom at dusk, on cloudy days or in the evening—they are known as "evening primrose"; some species are day flowering
Foliage: mid-green; lance-shaped
Hardiness: C–D
Warnings: prone to aphids

Growing Requirements

Light: sun
Soil: moderately fertile, sandy, well-drained soil; tolerant of dry periods
Location: mixed borders; raised beds; rock gardens; wild gardens; slopes
Propagation: seed (self-sows); division; softwood cutting
Expert Advice: Heavy clay soil may cause root rot. Seed indoors in February (may take 2–3 weeks to germinate). Seed outdoors in early spring. Seed needs light to germinate (do not cover with soil mix).

Buying Considerations

Professionals

Popularity: popular; fast seller in bloom
Availability: readily available as finished product
Size to Sell: sells best in smaller sizes (when blooming) as it matures fast
On the Shelf: rapidly overgrows pot; cut back in pots
Shrinkage: low; sensitive to overwatering or underwatering

Collectors

Popularity: not generally of interest to collectors

Gardeners

Ease of Growth: mostly easy to grow but needs close attention to growing conditions
Start with: one small plant for feature plant and several for mass plantings; best mass planted

What to Try First ...

Oenothera acaulis 'Aurea', *Oenothera caespitosa*, *Oenothera fruticosa* 'Fyrverkeri', *Oenothera fruticosa* ssp. *glauca* 'Fruhlingsgold', *Oenothera fruticosa* ssp. *glauca* 'Youngii', *Oenothera macrocarpa*, *Oenothera speciosa* 'Rosea'

On the Market

Oenothera
'Lemon Sunset' • Yellow flowers in summer • 75–90 cm high, 45–60 cm wide

Oenothera acaulis
'Aurea' • Fragrant, white flowers in summer to fall • 15–20 cm high, 20–50 cm wide

Oenothera caespitosa
Fragrant, white flowers, aging to pink, in summer • 10–40 cm high, 15–30 cm wide

Oenothera fremontii
'Lemon Silver' • Yellow flowers in late summer to fall • 10 cm high, 20 cm wide

Oenothera fruticosa
Rich-yellow flowers in late spring to late summer • Red-tinged leaves • 45–60 cm high, 30–60 cm wide

'Fyrverkeri' (Fireworks) • Bright-yellow flowers in late spring to late summer • Red stems • 25–45 cm high, 45–60 cm wide

'Hoheslicht' (Highlight) • Clear-yellow flowers in late spring to late summer • 45–60 cm high, 30–45 cm wide

'Illumination' • Rich-yellow flowers in late spring to late summer • Red-tinged leaves • 45–60 cm high, 30–60 cm wide

'Silberblatt' • Yellow flowers in late spring to late summer • Silver and green foliage • 30–40 cm high, 40–45 cm wide

'Yellow River' • Large, canary-yellow flowers in late spring to late summer • Red stems • 45–60 cm high, 45–60 cm wide

Oenothera fruticosa ssp. *glauca* (syn. *O. tetragona*)
Clustered, light-yellow flowers in late spring to late summer • 45–60 cm high, 30–45 cm wide

'Fruhlingsgold' • Yellow flowers in late spring to late summer • Yellow and green foliage • 30–40 cm high, 40–45 cm wide

'Sonnenwende' (Summer Solstice) • Yellow flowers in late spring to late summer • Red-tinged foliage • 30–45 cm high, 45 cm wide

'Youngii' • Clustered, yellow flowers in summer • 45–60 cm high, 30–45 cm wide

Oenothera macrocarpa (syn. *O. missouriensis)*
Fragrant, large, bright-yellow flowers in summer • 15–30 cm high, 30–50 cm wide

'Commanche Campfire' • Yellow flowers in summer • Silvery foliage with pink stems • 15–30 cm high, 45–60 cm wide

Oenothera pallida
Fragrant white flowers aging pink in summer • 20–50 cm high, 20–30 cm wide

Oenothera rosea
Rose flowers in summer • 15–60 cm high, 30–40 cm wide

Oenothera speciosa
Fragrant, white to pink flowers in early summer to fall • 30–60 cm high, 30–45 cm wide

'Rosea' • Rose-pink flowers in early summer to fall • 30 cm high, 30–45 cm wide

'Siskiyou' • Pink flowers in early summer to fall • 30–60 cm high, 30–45+ cm wide

'Woodside White' • Creamy-white flowers in early summer to fall • 25–30 cm high, 30–45 cm wide

Omphalodes

p. 420

Genus Information

Origin: Asia, Europe, North Africa and Mexico
Selected Common Names: creeping forget-me-not, navelwort
Nomenclature: From the Greek *omphalos* (navel) and *oides* (like), referring to the nutlets, which are said to resemble a navel.

General Features
Height: 10–25 cm high
Spread: 30–60+ cm wide
Habit: clump-forming to spreading, groundcover biennial or perennial
Flowers: vibrant; spring to late spring; short blooming period; may rebloom in fall
Foliage: (some) evergreen
Hardiness: C–D
Warnings: prone to aphids

Growing Requirements
Light: shade to a.m. sun
Soil: moist, fertile, organic soil
Location: woodland gardens; cool locations
Propagation: seed; division
Expert Advice: Divide in spring. Division can be difficult as it resents being disturbed.

On the Market

Omphalodes cappadocica
'Lilac Mist' • Lilac flowers in late spring • Evergreen foliage• 10–15 cm high, 45–60+ cm wide

'Starry Eyes' • Blue flowers with white edges in spring • Evergreen foliage • 40 cm high, 45–60+ cm wide

Omphalodes verna
Bright-blue flowers in spring • 15 cm high, 30 cm wide

O

Onoclea

p. 421

Genus Information

Origin: East Asia and eastern North America
Selected Common Names: sensitive fern
Nomenclature: From the Greek *onos* (vessel) and *kleio* (to close), in reference to the closely rolled fertile fronds.

General Features
Height: 30–60 cm high
Spread: 45–60+ cm wide
Habit: colony-forming, rhizomatous groundcover fern
Flowers: fertile black fronds; late summer
Foliage: fronds open pinkish-bronze aging to green
Hardiness: C
Warnings: not prone to insects or disease
Expert Advice: When cut, the arching fronds of *Onoclea* tend to curl. Plant with *Hosta*, *Heuchera* and *Primula*.

Growing Requirements

Light: a.m sun
Soil: fertile, moist, organic soil
Location: bog gardens; ponds; woodland gardens; foliage may burn or break in windy locations
Propagation: spores; division

Buying Considerations

Professionals

Popularity: gaining popularity as a foliage plant
Availability: generally available as finished product and bare root
Size to Sell: sells best in smaller sizes
On the Shelf: high ornamental appeal; foliage breakage (display out of winds)
Shrinkage: low; requires little maintenance

Collectors

Popularity: of interest to collectors—novelty plant

Gardeners

Ease of Growth: mostly easy to grow but needs close attention to growing conditions
Start with: one small plant for feature plant and several for mass planting

What to Try First ...

Onoclea sensibilis

On the Market

Onoclea sensibilis
Pinkish-bronze fronds in spring • 30–60 cm high, 45–60+ cm wide

Onopordum

p. 421

Genus Information

Origin: Europe
Selected Common Names: Scotch cotton thistle, Scotch thistle
Nomenclature: From the Latinized form of a Greek name, *Onopordon*.
Notes: A genus of some 40 species.

General Features

Height: 90 cm–3 m high
Spread: 60–150 cm wide
Habit: large, clump-forming, tap-rooted biennial
Flowers: large, round, thistle-like; summer; attractive to bees and butterflies
Foliage: silvery-white; coarse, thistly
Hardiness: B–C
Warnings: prone to grubs; invasive in warmer climates (deadhead to prevent spread)
Expert Advice: *Onopordum* makes an excellent feature plant in a xeriscape landscape.

Growing Requirements

Light: sun
Soil: fertile, well-drained, alkaline soil; drought tolerant
Location: gravel gardens; mixed borders; wild gardens
Propagation: seed (self-sows readily)

Buying Considerations

Professionals

Popularity: relatively unknown foliage plant
Availability: occasionally available from specialty growers
Size to Sell: sells best in smaller sizes (when blooming) as it matures fast
On the Shelf: high ornamental appeal; rapidly overgrows pot
Shrinkage: high; sensitive to overwatering

Collectors

Popularity: not generally of interest to collectors

Gardeners

Ease of Growth: very easy to grow
Start with: one small plant for feature plant

What to Try First ...

Onopordum acanthium, Onopordum nervosum

On the Market

Onopordum acanthium
Purple flowers in summer • Cottony foliage • 90 cm–3 m high, 60–90 cm wide

Onopordum nervosum
Thistle-like, rose flowers in summer • 1.5–3 m high, 90–150 cm wide

Onosma

Genus Information

Origin: Mediterranean and East Asia
Selected Common Names: gold drop, lady's ear drops
Nomenclature: The name is from the Greek *onos* (ass) and *osme* (smell), referring to the plants being liked by asses.
Notes: A genus of some 150 species.

General Features

Height: 15–50 cm high
Spread: 25–45 cm wide
Habit: tuft-forming perennial
Flowers: nodding, tubular; short blooming period
Foliage: grey-green, fuzzy; (some) evergreen
Hardiness: C
Warnings: prone to powdery mildew and aphids; contact with foliage may irritate skin

Growing Requirements

Light: sun
Soil: well-drained, sandy soil; avoid excessive and winter wet; drought tolerant
Location: rock gardens; scree; wall crevices
Propagation: seed (self-sows); softwood cuttings
Expert Advice: The plant will not tolerate water consistently on the foliage. Resents being disturbed.

Buying Considerations

Professionals
Popularity: relatively unknown
Availability: occasionally available from specialty growers
Size to Sell: sells best in smaller sizes (when blooming) as it matures fast
On the Shelf: rapidly overgrows pot
Shrinkage: low; requires little maintenance

Collectors
Popularity: of interest to collectors—unique, rare

Gardeners
Ease of Growth: mostly easy to grow but needs close attention to growing conditions
Start with: one small plant for feature plant

What to Try First ...

Onosma alborosea, Onosma echioides, Onosma helvetica

On the Market

Onosma alborosea
Nodding, white flowers, aging to pink, then blue, in summer • Evergreen foliage • 15–25 cm high, 25–30 cm wide

Onosma echioides
Nodding, tubular, gold flowers in summer • 20–30 cm high, 30–40 cm wide

Onosma helvetica
Nodding, bell-shaped, pale-yellow flowers in summer • Grey-green, fuzzy foliage • 30–50 cm high, 30–45 cm wide

Opuntia

p. 421

Genus Information

Origin: western United States, Canada, Northern Mexico, South America
Selected Common Names: prickly pear cactus
Nomenclature: From a pre-Linnaean name for a kind of spiny plant associated with the ancient Greek town of Opus or the surrounding region known as Eastern or Opuntian Locris.

General Features

Height: 5–100 cm high
Spread: 30–100+ cm wide
Habit: low-growing to semi-upright, clump-forming cactus
Flowers: range of colours, paper-like; spring to summer
Foliage: barbed, spiny pads (some spineless)
Hardiness: B–D
Warnings: contact with barbed spines may irritate skin; spines can be difficult to see and remove
Warnings: prone to grubs; painful to handle
Expert Advice: An extremely hardy and easy-to-grow cactus that often does not flower in cultivation as it needs the stress of drought to promote flowering. Some are grown for their edible fruit. Selections will vary from coloured spines, spineless types, large and small growers. White, pink and red-flowered cultivars are becoming available but are difficult to obtain.

Growing Requirements

Light: sun
Soil: gritty, moderately fertile, sharply drained soil; avoid winter wet; severe drought tolerance
Location: hot, dry sites; rock gardens; scree; xeriscape gardens
Propagation: seed; separate and replant rooted stem segments

Buying Considerations

Professionals
Popularity: gaining popularity; interesting foliage plant; sells well in bloom
Availability: generally available as bare root from specialty growers
Size to Sell: sells best in smaller sizes (when blooming)
On the Shelf: high ornamental appeal
Shrinkage: low shrinkage; requires little maintenance

Collectors
Popularity: of interest to collectors—native cacti

Gardeners
Ease of Growth: mostly easy to grow but needs close attention to growing conditions
Start with: one small plant for feature plant

What to Try First ...

Opuntia (O. polyacantha x O. fragilis), Opuntia fragilis, Opuntia erinacea 'Erinacea', Opuntia imbricata, Opuntia polyacantha

On the Market

Opuntia (O. polyacantha x *O. fragilis)*
Yellow flowers in late spring to early summer • 10–20 cm high, 30–60+ cm wide

Opuntia erinacea
'Erinacea' • Pink flowers in early summer • Bluish-green stems with white spines • 15–30 cm high, 60–100+ cm wide

Opuntia fragilis
Soft-yellow flowers in early summer • Prickly, green pads • 5–10 cm high, 30–45 cm wide

Opuntia humifusa
'Lemon Spreader' • Large, yellow flowers in summer • Flattened, greyish-green stems • 10–30 cm high, 60–100+ cm wide

Opuntia imbricata
Pink-purple flowers in late spring to early summer • 50–100 cm high, 45–60 cm wide

Opuntia lindheimeri
'Linguiformis Maverick' • Pink flowers in spring • 60–100 cm high, 60–100+ cm wide

Opuntia phaeacantha
'Major' • Yellow-orange flowers in late spring to early summer • 30–100 cm high, 60–100 cm wide

Opuntia polyacantha
Yellow flowers in early summer • Prickly pads • 8–15 cm high, 30–60+ cm wide

'Apricot Splendor' • Yellow flowers in late spring to early summer • Yellow-brown spines • 20 cm high, 30–60+ cm wide

'Gold Spines' • Yellow flowers in late spring to early summer • Yellow-brown spines • 20 cm high, 30–60+ cm wide

'Juniperina' • Yellow flowers in early summer • 10–25 cm high, 30–60+ cm wide

'Minima' • Yellow flowers in late spring to early summer • Yellow-brown spines • 20 cm high, 30–60+ cm wide

'Red Spines' • Yellow flowers in late spring to early summer • Mahogany-red spines • 20 cm high, 30–60+ cm wide

'Schweriniana' • Yellow flowers in late spring to early summer • Yellow-brown spines • 20 cm high, 30–60+ cm wide

'Trichophora' • Yellow flowers in late spring to early summer • Yellow-brown spines • 20 cm high, 30–60+ cm wide

Orostachys
p. 421

Genus Information

Origin: central Asia, northern Asia and Europe
Selected Common Names: false houseleek
Nomenclature: From the Greek *oros* (mountain) and *stachys* (spike), in reference to the pyramidal flower spikes that are borne above the rosettes in the plant's 2nd year.
Notes: A genus of some 10 species, some hardier than others.

General Features

Height: 2–35 cm high
Spread: 5–20 cm wide
Habit: mat-forming, colony-forming, monocarpic perennial
Flowers: summer to fall
Foliage: succulent
Hardiness: C
Warnings: prone to aphids; not prone to diseases

Growing Requirements

Light: sun
Soil: dry, poor soil; avoid winter wet
Location: alpine gardens; raised beds; rock gardens; xeriscape gardens
Propagation: separate and replant offshoot rosettes
Expert Advice: After flowering, the rosettes die but are usually replaced by new offsets. To prevent the mother plant from dying, remove the flowering spikes when they appear.

Buying Considerations

Professionals

Popularity: relatively unknown foliage plant
Availability: occasionally available from specialty growers
Size to Sell: sells best in smaller sizes; matures quickly
On the Shelf: high ornamental appeal; rapidly overgrows pot
Shrinkage: low; requires little maintenance

Collectors

Popularity: of interest to collectors—unique, rare, novelty plant; *O. spinosa* (non-flowering form) is an oddity

Gardeners

Ease of Growth: mostly easy to grow but needs close attention to growing conditions
Start with: several small plants for instant visual effect

What to Try First ...

Orostachys aggregata, Orostachys fimbriata, Orostachys iwarenge, Orostachys spinosa, Orostachys spinosa (non-flowering form), *Orostachys spinosa* var. *minuta, Orostachys spinosa* var. *minuta* (non-flowering form)

On the Market

Orostachys aggregata
Pyramidal-spiked, white flowers in fall •
Monocarpic, dense rosettes of succulent
foliage • 5–10 cm high, 10–20 cm wide

Orostachys boehmeri
Pyramidal-spiked, white flowers in fall •
Monocarpic, succulent foliage • 5–10 cm
high, 10–20 cm wide

Orostachys eburnifolia
Pyramidal-spiked • Monocarpic, bronze-
green, succulent foliage • 5–10 cm high,
10–20 cm wide

Orostachys fimbriata
(syn. *Sedum limuloides*)
White flowers in late summer to fall •
Monocarpic rosettes of succulent foliage •
15 cm high, 10–20 cm wide

Orostachys furusei
Greenish-white flowers in late summer •
Monocarpic, succulent foliage • 2–5 cm
high, 10–20 cm wide

'Frosty Chicks' • Greenish-white flowers in
late summer • Monocarpic, frosty-blue
succulent foliage • 5–10 cm high,
10–20 cm wide

Orostachys iwarenge
Pyramidal-spiked, white flowers in summer
• Monocarpic, succulent foliage • 10–15 cm
high, 10–20 cm wide

Orostachys malacophylla
Greenish-white flowers in summer •
Monocarpic, soft-green rosettes of succulent
foliage • 5–7 cm high, 5–15 cm wide

Orostachys spinosa
Greenish-yellow flowers in summer •
Monocarpic, succulent foliage • 25–35 cm
high, 5–10 cm wide

(Non-flowering form) • Non-flowering •
Brownish-grey, succulent foliage •
8–10 cm high, 10–20 cm wide

Orostachys spinosa var. *minuta*
Yellow flowers in fall • Monocarpic
rosettes of succulent foliage • 2–5 cm high,
10–15 cm wide

(Non-flowering form) • Non-flowering •
Rosettes of succulent foliage • 2–5 cm
high, 10–20 cm wide

Osmunda
p. 421

Genus Information

Origin: worldwide, except for Australia
Selected Common Names: cinnamon fern,
interrupted fern, royal fern
Nomenclature: Named for the Nordic god, Thor,
who was also called Osmunder. The name is
also possibly from the Latin *os* (mouth) and
mundare (to clean).
Notes: A genus of some 12 species. *Osmunda*'s
fibrous rootstock is a source of osmunda fiber
used in orchid mixes.

General Features

Height: 60–120 cm high
Spread: 60 cm–2 m wide
Habit: colony-forming, terrestrial fern
Flowers: cinnamon-brown fertile fronds; summer
Foliage: bright-green; arching
Hardiness: B–C
Warnings: not prone to insects or disease
Expert Advice: Grow as a backdrop to *Hosta*,
Heuchera and other shade plants.

Growing Requirements

Light: shade; tolerates more sun with good
soil moisture
Soil: fertile, moist, organic, acidic soil
Location: shady mixed borders; waterside
plantings; woodland gardens; foliage burns
and breaks in windy sites
Propagation: spores
Expert Advice: Propagation by spores will
result in cultivars coming true to type.

Buying Considerations

Professionals
Popularity: popular foliage plant
Availability: readily available as finished
product and bare root
Size to Sell: sells best in smaller sizes as it
matures fast
On the Shelf: high ornamental appeal; foliage
breakage (display out of wind)
Shrinkage: low; requires little maintenance

Collectors
Popularity: not generally of interest to
collectors

Gardeners
Ease of Growth: mostly easy to grow but
needs close attention to growing conditions
Start with: one small plant for feature plant
and several for mass plantings

What to Try First ...
Osmunda cinnamomea, *Osmunda claytoniana*,
Osmunda regalis

On the Market

Osmunda cinnamomea
Cinnamon-brown, erect, fertile fronds in summer amid green fronds • 90–100 cm high, 60 cm wide

Osmunda claytoniana
Fertile fronds covered in black sporangia in summer amid green fronds • 60–120 cm high, 60 cm wide

Osmunda regalis
Green fronds • 60–100 cm high, 1–2 m wide

Oxalis
p. 421

Genus Information

Origin: Europe, Asia, Chile and southern Argentina
Selected Common Names: redwood sorrel, sorrel, wood sorrel
Nomenclature: From the Greek *oxis*, referring to the sour taste of the plant's leaves.
Notes: A genus of some 800 species of annuals and perennials. The family includes some troublesome weeds.

General Features
Height: 2–20 cm high
Spread: 5–30 cm wide
Habit: low-growing perennial
Flowers: white to pink; spring to summer; goes dormant after flowering; may rebloom in fall
Foliage: neatly pleated, clover-like foliage; closes at night and in shade
Hardiness: C–D
Warnings: prone to aphids; not prone to diseases
Expert Advice: Woodland species (*O. oregana*) are perfect for naturalizing. Seed pods can eject seeds a considerable distance when disturbed.

Growing Requirements
Light: sun to p.m. sun
Soil: fertile, organic, sandy, well-drained soil; woodland species; *O. oregana* prefers fertile, organic, moist, well-drained soil
Location: alpine gardens; raised beds; rock gardens; troughs; wall crevices; *O. oregana* in woodland gardens
Propagation: seed (self-sows); division

Buying Considerations

Professionals
Popularity: relatively unknown; fast seller in bloom
Availability: occasionally available from specialty growers
Size to Sell: sells best in mature sizes (when blooming) as it matures slowly
On the Shelf: keep stock rotated

Shrinkage: high; goes dormant in pot

Collectors
Popularity: of interest to collectors—unique, rare, exceptional beauty

Gardeners
Ease of Growth: mostly easy to grow but needs close attention to growing conditions
Start with: several mature plants for instant visual effect

What to Try First ...
Oxalis 'Ione Hecker', *Oxalis* 'Kathleen Fairbairn', *Oxalis adenophylla*, *Oxalis depressa*, *Oxalis oregana*

On the Market

Oxalis
'Ione Hecker' • Pink flowers with darker veins in summer • Grey-green foliage • 5–8 cm high, 15–20+ cm wide
'Kathleen Fairbairn' • Fragrant, purple flowers with dark markings in late spring to summer • Clover-like foliage • 5–10 cm high, 5–10 cm wide

Oxalis adenophylla
Lilac-pink flowers with dark veins in summer • Clover-like foliage • 5–10 cm high, 8–15 cm wide

Oxalis depressa (syn. O. inops)
Bright rose-pink flowers with yellow throat in summer • Clover-like foliage • 4–12 cm high, 15–20+ cm wide

Oxalis aff. depressa
Rose-pink flowers in summer • Grey-green foliage • 5–10 cm high, 15–20+ cm wide

Oxalis magellanica
'Nelson' (Flore Pleno) • Double, white to cream flowers in late spring to early summer • Bronze foliage • 2–5 cm high, 15–30 cm wide

Oxalis oregana
White or pink flowers, often with purple veins, in late spring to fall • Clover-like foliage • 6–20 cm high, 15–25+ cm wide

Oxytropis
p. 421

Genus Information

Origin: northern temperate regions
Selected Common Names: locoweed, Perry's vetch, point vetch
Nomenclature: From the Greek *oxys* (sharp) and *tropis* (keel), referring to the petal of the plant being toothed at the apex.

Notes: A genus of some 300 species. Some species are toxic to cattle, sheep and horses, which gave rise to the common name "locoweed." We generally recommend only alpine varieties, which are more ornamental.

General Features
Height: 2–60 cm high
Spread: 15–40 cm wide
Habit: tap-rooted, clump-forming perennial
Flowers: pea-like; spring to summer
Foliage: (some) downy
Hardiness: C
Warnings: prone to aphids; not prone to diseases
Expert Advice: Produces ornamental seed pods.

Growing Requirements
Light: sun
Soil: well-drained soil; drought tolerant; downy-foliage types should avoid winter wet
Location: raised beds; rock gardens; scree
Propagation: seed (self-sows readily); division
Expert Advice: Division is difficult as it resents being disturbed.

Buying Considerations

Professionals
Popularity: relatively unknown
Availability: occasionally available from specialty growers
Size to Sell: sells best in smaller sizes (when blooming) as it matures fast
On the Shelf: rapidly overgrows pot
Shrinkage: low; requires little maintenance

Collectors
Popularity: not generally of interest to collectors

Gardeners
Ease of Growth: mostly easy to grow but needs close attention to growing conditions
Start with: one small plant for feature plant

What to Try First …
Oxytropis campestris, Oxytropis deflexa, Oxytropis multiceps, Oxytropis podocarpa

On the Market

Oxytropis campestris
Pea-like, white to yellowish flowers in spring • 10–20 cm high, 20–30 cm wide

Oxytropis deflexa
Pea-like, pendulous, blue-purple flowers in summer • 8–45 cm high, 30–40 cm wide

Oxytropis gaudinii
Pea-like, blue-violet flowers in summer • 5 cm high, 15 cm wide

Oxytropis multiceps
Pea-like, pink to purple flowers in spring • Silky, silvery foliage • 2 cm high, 30–40 cm wide

Oxytropis parryi
Pea-like, pink-purple flowers in late summer • 10 cm high, 30 cm wide

Oxytropis podocarpa
Pea-like, lavender-purple flowers in spring • 5–8 cm high, 30–40 cm wide

O

Pachysandra p. 421

Genus Information

Origin: East Asia and the United States
Selected Common Names: Japanese spurge
Nomenclature: The name is from the Greek *pachys* (thick) and *aner* (man), referring to the stamen.

General Features

Height: 15–20 cm high
Spread: 60–90 cm wide
Habit: spreading groundcover perennial
Flowers: unisexual, petal-less; early summer
Foliage: glossy, evergreen to semi-evergreen; prone to desiccation in colder climates
Hardiness: C
Warnings: prone to aphids; not prone to diseases
Expert Advice: *Pachysandra* forms a dense carpet of foliage—it is a great groundcover for shady, damp areas with mature trees. Provide snow cover in winter in colder climates.

Growing Requirements

Light: shade to a.m. sun
Soil: fertile, well-drained, moist soil; tolerates acidic soil
Location: mixed borders; woodland gardens
Propagation: division; cuttings in summer

Buying Considerations

Professionals
Popularity: popular foliage plant
Availability: readily available as finished product
Size to Sell: sells best in smaller sizes; matures slowly
On the Shelf: keep stock rotated
Shrinkage: low; requires little maintenance

Collectors
Popularity: not generally of interest to collectors

Gardeners
Ease of Growth: mostly easy to grow but needs close attention to growing conditions
Start with: several small plants for mass plantings

What to Try First ...
Pachysandra terminalis, *Pachysandra terminalis* 'Variegata'

On the Market

Pachysandra terminalis
Spiked, white flowers in early summer • Glossy, evergreen foliage • 15–20 cm high, 60–90+ cm wide

'**Variegata**' • White flowers in early summer • White-and-green foliage • 15–20 cm high, 60–90+ cm wide

Paeonia p. 421

Genus Information

Origin: Europe, Eastern Asia and western North America
Selected Common Names: Japanese peony, peony, tree peony
Nomenclature: From the Greek *paionia*. Possibly from Paion, physician to the gods who used the plant medicinally.
Notes: Prized by gardeners, collectors and breeders alike for their stunning blooms in a range of colours. We divide peonies into 5 categories for growing information and display purposes: *Hybrid, Lactiflora, Itoh, Species* and *Tree.*
Expert Advice: A long-lived perennial that does not require dividing to maintain vigour.

Paeonia, Hybrid p. 421

General Features

Height: 35–95 cm high
Spread: 60–100 cm wide
Habit: long-lived, upright, clump-forming perennial
Flowers: single, semi-double or double; (some) fragrant; prominent stamens; spring to early summer
Foliage: glossy; dark to mid-green
Hardiness: B–D
Warnings: prone to Botrytis, ants and aphids
Expert Advice: Hybrid peonies are generally more compact than other peonies. They bloom earlier and have thicker stems, which hold up the flowers better in adverse weather (less-staking is required).

Growing Requirements

Light: sun to p.m. sun
Soil: moist, fertile, well-drained, acid-free soil
Location: mixed borders; cutting gardens
Propagation: seed (species only); division
Expert Advice: Plant with eyes 5 cm deep or less. Planting too deeply will result in foliage production only and possibly rot. Divide in early fall. Cut back in spring as old wood may survive the winter.

Buying Considerations

Professionals
Popularity: popular, old-fashioned garden standard; fast seller in bloom
Availability: readily available as finished product and bare root from specialty growers
Size to Sell: sells best in smaller sizes (when blooming) as it matures fast
On the Shelf: rapidly overgrows pot
Shrinkage: low; requires little maintenance

On the Market

Paeonia

'Ace of Hearts' • Single, cardinal-red flowers in spring • 60 cm high, 60–75 cm wide

'America' • Single, scarlet-red flowers in spring • 90 cm high, 75–100 cm wide

'Angel Cobb Freeborn' • Large, double, coral-red flowers in spring • 60–90 cm high, 75–100 cm wide

'Athena' • Single, ivory and rose flowers in spring • 60 cm high, 60–75 cm wide

'Avant Garde' • Single, pink flowers with red veins in spring • 1 m high, 75–100 cm wide

'Birthday' • Single, pink flowers in spring • 60–90 cm high, 75–100 cm wide

'Blaze' • Single, red flowers with gold centre in spring • 65–75 cm high, 60–90 cm wide

'Bravura' • Single, red flowers with yellow centre in spring • 80–90 cm high, 75–100 cm wide

'Carol' • Double, cardinal-red flowers in spring • 70 cm high, 60–90 cm wide

'Chocolate Soldier' • Single, dark reddish-brown flowers in spring • 70 cm high, 60–90 cm wide

'Claire de Lune' • Single, creamy-white flowers in spring • 90 cm high, 90 cm wide

'Colour Magnet' • Single, violet-pink flowers in spring • 80–90 cm high, 75–100 cm wide

'Command Performance' • Double, cardinal-red flowers in spring • 60 cm high, 60–75 cm wide

'Constance Spry' • Semi-double, cerise-rose flowers in spring • 60–90 cm high, 75–100 cm wide

'Coral 'n' Gold' • Single, coral-pink flowers in spring • 90 cm high, 75–100 cm wide

'Coral Charm' • Semi-double, coral-peach flowers in spring • 90 cm high, 75–100 cm wide

'Coral Fay' • Semi-double, rose-red flowers in spring • 95 cm high, 75–100 cm wide

'Crusader' • Semi-double, deep-red flowers in spring • 80 cm high, 60–90 cm wide

'Cytherea' • Semi-double, light-crimson flowers in spring • 60 cm high, 60–75 cm wide

'Dancing Butterflies' • Single, yellow-centred, pink flowers in spring • 70–80 cm high, 60–90 cm wide

'Dandy Dan' • Semi-double, dark-red flowers in spring • 60–70 cm high, 60–90 cm wide

'Early Scout' • Single, crimson-red flowers in early spring • Fine, cut-leaf foliage • 45–55 cm high, 60–75 cm wide

'Eliza Lundy' • Double, dark-maroon flowers in spring • 75 cm high, 60–90 cm wide

'Ellen Cowley' • Semi-double, cherry-red flowers in spring • 70 cm high, 60–90 cm wide

'Eventide' • Single, rose-red flowers with white stripes in spring • 85 cm high, 75–100 cm wide

'Fairy Princess' • Single, red flowers with gold centre in spring • 50–60 cm high, 60–75 cm wide

'Firelight' • Single, pale-pink flowers with red flares in spring • 65 cm high, 60–90 cm wide

'Flame' • Single, crimson flowers and gold stamens in spring • 80 cm high, 60–90 cm wide

'Green Lotus' • White flowers with lime and pink tones in spring • 65–75 cm high, 60–75 cm wide

'Henry Bockstoce' • Fully double, dark-red flowers in spring • 75 cm high, 60–90 cm wide

'Honor' • Single or semi-double, pink flowers in spring • 90 cm high, 75–100 cm wide

P

'Koningin Wilhelmina' • Semi-double, fuchsia-pink flowers in spring • 80 cm high, 60–90 cm wide

'Lorelei' • Fragrant, double, peach-pink flowers in spring • 60 cm high, 60–75 cm wide

'Mai Fleuri' • Single, white flowers, tinted pale-pink, in spring • 70 cm high, 60–90 cm wide

'Merry Mayshine' • Single, crimson flowers with yellow centre in spring • 60 cm high, 60–75 cm wide

'Paula Fay' • Fragrant, semi-double, vivid-pink flowers in spring • 80–90 cm high, 75–100 cm wide

'Peppermint Stick' • Cream flowers with red striping in spring • 70–80 cm high, 60–75 cm wide

'Peter Barr' • Single, red flowers in spring • 60 cm high, 60–75 cm wide

'Picotee' • Single, white flowers with pink edge in spring • 45 cm high, 60–75 cm wide

'Pink Firefly' • Light-pink flowers with streaks and gold centre in spring • 70–80 cm high, 60–90 cm wide

'Pink Luau' • Semi-double, pink flowers with raspberry streaks in spring • 80–85 cm high, 75–100 cm wide

'Polly Sharp' • Single, ruffled, pink flowers in spring • 60 cm high, 60–75 cm wide

'Raspberry Rumba' • White flowers with raspberry streaks in spring • 75–85 cm high, 60–90 cm wide

'Red Charm' • Double, crimson-red flowers in spring • 90 cm high, 75–100 cm wide

'Red Monarch' • Deep-red flowers in spring • 90 cm high, 75–100 cm wide

'Requiem' • Fragrant, single, white flowers with pink blush in spring • 70–95 cm high, 75–100 cm wide

'Rose Diamond' • Single, salmon-rose flowers in spring • 60 cm high, 60–75 cm wide

'Sorbet' • Double, pink and soft-yellow flowers in spring • 65–75 cm high, 60–90 cm wide

'Thumbellina' • Fragrant, single, rosy-pink flowers in spring • 35–40 cm high, 60–75 cm wide

'Walter Mains' • Japanese, red flowers with red or white centre in spring • 80 cm high, 60–90 cm wide

Paeonia, Lactiflora p. 421

General Features
Height: 55–120 cm high
Spread: 55–100 cm wide
Habit: long-lived, upright, clump-forming perennial
Flowers: single, semi-double or double; spring
Foliage: glossy; dark green
Hardiness: B–D
Warnings: prone to Botrytis and aphids
Expert Advice: Lactiflora peonies are prized for their massive blooms borne on stalks which may be too weak to support their weight. Staking is usually a necessity with double-flowered varieties. Available in single, double or Japanese flower forms.

Growing Requirements
Light: sun to p.m. sun
Soil: fertile, moist, well-drained, acid-free soil
Location: mixed borders
Propagation: seed; division
Expert Advice: Plant with eyes 5 cm deep or less. Planting too deeply will result in foliage production only and possibly rot. Divide in early fall.

Buying Considerations

Professionals
Popularity: popular, old-fashioned garden standard; fast seller in bloom; new varieties
Availability: readily available as finished product and bare root from specialty growers
Size to Sell: sells best in smaller sizes (when blooming) as it matures fast
On the Shelf: rapidly overgrows pot
Shrinkage: low; requires little maintenance

Collectors
Popularity: of interest to collectors—rare varieties, specific flower colours and forms

Gardeners
Ease of Growth: mostly easy to grow but needs close attention to growing conditions
Start with: one small plant for feature plant

What to Try First ...
Paeonia 'Armistice', *Paeonia* 'Barrington Belle', *Paeonia* 'Cherry Hill', *Paeonia* 'Cornelia Shaylor', *Paeonia* 'Fancy Nancy', *Paeonia* 'Gay Paree', *Paeonia* 'Karl Rosenfield', *Paeonia* 'Maestro', *Paeonia* 'Miss America'

P

On the Market

Paeonia

'A la Mode' • Single, white flowers with gold centre in spring • 85 cm high, 85–100 cm wide

'Abalone Pearl' • Single, coral-pink flowers with gold stamens in spring • 60–70 cm high, 60–80 cm wide

'Adolphe Rousseau' • Semi-double, black-red flowers in spring • 95 cm high, 95–100 cm wide

'Albert Crousse' • Fragrant, double, light-pink flowers in spring • 95 cm high, 90–100 cm wide

'Alice Roberts' • Japanese, pink flowers in spring • 75 cm high, 75–90 cm wide

'Angel Cheeks' • Double, pink flowers in late spring • 90 cm high, 90–100 cm wide

'Argentine' • Fragrant, double, creamy-white flowers in spring • 70 cm high, 70–90 cm wide

'Armistice' • Double, bright-rose-pink flowers in spring • 90 cm high, 90–100 cm wide

'Askashigata' • Japanese, rose-pink flowers in spring • 90 cm high, 90–100 cm wide

'Attar of Roses' • Double, pink flowers in spring • 60–90 cm high, 60–90 cm wide

'Auguste Dessert' • Semi-double, light-pink flowers in spring • 75 cm high, 75–90 cm wide

'Avalanche' (Albatre) • Fragrant, double, blush-white flowers in spring • 90 cm high, 90–100 cm wide

'Barrington Belle' • Japanese, rose-red flowers in spring • 85 cm high, 85–100 cm wide

'Belleville' • Japanese, light-purple flowers in spring • 90 cm high, 90–100 cm wide

'Best Man' • Double, deep rose-red flowers in spring • 75–90 cm high, 75–100 cm wide

'Better Times' • Double, rose flowers in spring • 90 cm high, 90–100 cm wide

'Betty Warner' • Japanese, rose-red flowers in spring • 90 cm high, 90–100 cm wide

'Big Ben' • Fragrant, double, deep-red flowers in spring • 75 cm high, 75–90 cm wide

'Bowl of Beauty' • Japanese, fuchsia-pink flowers in spring • 90 cm high, 90–100 cm wide

'Break o' Day' • Japanese, magenta flowers in spring • 85 cm high, 85–100 cm wide

'Buddha's Seat' (Fuo Zuo) • Japanese, pink flowers in spring • 90 cm high, 90–100 cm wide

'Butter Bowl' • Fragrant, Japanese, pale-pink flowers with yellow centre in spring • 90 cm high, 90–100 cm wide

'Cascade Gem' • Japanese, sparkling white flowers in spring • 75–90 cm high, 75–90 cm wide

'Charles Burgess' • Japanese, crimson flowers in spring • 90 cm high, 90–100 cm wide

'Charlie's White' • Double, pure white flowers in spring • 1.2 m high, 90–100 cm wide

'Charm' • Fragrant, Japanese, gold-centred, red flowers in late spring • 75–90 cm high, 75–90 cm wide

'Cheddar Gold' • Fragrant, Japanese, white flowers in spring • 75 cm high, 75–90 cm wide

'Cherry Hill' • Fragrant, semi-double, red flowers in spring • 85 cm high, 85–100 cm wide

'Cincinnati' • Double, deep-pink flowers in spring • 80 cm high, 80–100 cm wide

'Colours' • Japanese, fuchsia-pink flowers in spring • 90 cm high, 90–100 cm wide

'Cornelia Shaylor' • Double, soft-pink flowers in spring • 90 cm high, 90–100 cm wide

'Cream Puff' • Japanese, blush-pink flowers in spring • 75–90 cm high, 75–90 cm wide

'Dayton' • Double, pink flowers in spring • 90 cm high, 90–100 cm wide

'Detroit' • Double, red flowers in spring • 90 cm high, 90–100 cm wide

'Dinner Plate' • Double, shell-pink flowers in spring • 85 cm high, 85–100 cm wide

'Dixie' • Double, rich-red flowers in spring • 90 cm high, 90–100 cm wide

'Do Tell' • Japanese, rose-pink flowers in spring • 80 cm high, 80–100 cm wide

'Doreen' • Japanese, fuchsia-rose flowers in spring • 80 cm high, 80–100 cm wide

'Dr. Alexander Fleming' • Fragrant, double, deep-pink flowers in spring • 1.1 m high, 90–100 cm wide

'Dragon's Nest' • Japanese, rose-red flowers in spring • 95 cm high, 90–100 cm wide

'Duchesse d'Orleans' • Fragrant, double, pink flowers in spring • 90 cm high, 90–100 cm wide

P

'Edulis Superba' • Fragrant, double, bright-pink flowers in spring • 95 cm high, 90–100 cm wide

'Edward F. Flynn' • Double, crimson-red flowers in spring • 90 cm high, 90–100 cm wide

'Fairy's Petticoat' • Fragrant, double, blush-pink flowers in spring • 80 cm high, 80–100 cm wide

'Fancy Nancy' • Japanese, cerise-pink flowers in spring • 75 cm high, 75–90 cm wide

'Feather Top' • Japanese, magenta and buff flowers in spring • 90 cm high, 90–100 cm wide

'Felix Crousse' (Victor Hugo) • Fragrant, double, rose-red flowers in spring • 75 cm high, 75–90 cm wide

'Felix Supreme' • Double, rich ruby-red flowers in spring • 1 m high, 90–100 cm wide

'Festiva Maxima' • Fragrant, double, creamy-white flowers in spring • 1 m high, 90–100 cm wide

'Festiva Supreme' • Fragrant, fully double, white flowers in late spring • 1 m high, 90–100 cm wide

'Frosted Purple' • Japanese, purple-pink flowers in spring • 75–90 cm high, 75–90 cm wide

'Garden Lace' • Japanese, creamy-pink flowers in spring • 90 cm high, 90–100 cm wide

'Gay Paree' • Japanese, magenta flowers with creamy centre in spring • 1.1 m high, 90–100 cm wide

'Gilbert H. Wild' • Fragrant, double, rose flowers in spring • 75–90 cm high, 75–90 cm wide

'Glowing Candles' • Japanese, pale-pink flowers in spring • 75–90 cm high, 75–90 cm wide

'Gold Mine' • Double, golden-yellow flowers in spring • 85 cm high, 85–100 cm wide

'Hargrove Hudson' • Double, soft-pink flowers in spring • 90 cm high, 90–100 cm wide

'Harriet Olney' • Single, deep-rose flowers in spring • 90–100 cm high, 90–100 cm wide

'Harry L. Smith' • Double, red flowers in spring • 90 cm high, 90–100 cm wide

'Heidi' • Japanese, pink flowers in spring • 90 cm high, 90–100 cm wide

'High Fashion' • Double, pink flowers with lilac centre in spring • 90 cm high, 90–100 cm wide

'Highlight' • Double, velvety, dark-red flowers in spring • 90 cm high, 90–100 cm wide

'Honey Gold' • Fragrant, double, creamy-white flowers in spring • 90 cm high, 90–100 cm wide

'Jacorma' • Double, bright-pink flowers in spring • 90 cm high, 90–100 cm wide

'James R. Mann' • Double, rose-pink flowers in spring • 90 cm high, 90–100 cm wide

'Jappensha-Ikhu' • Japanese, rose flowers with yellow centre in spring • 90 cm high, 90–100 cm wide

'Jay Cee' • Double, rich-red flowers in spring • 80–90 cm high, 80–100 cm wide

'Jean Cooperman' • Double, soft crimson-red flowers in spring • 90 cm high, 90–100 cm wide

'Jean Ericksen' • Japanese, deep-red flowers in spring • 90 cm high, 90–100 cm wide

'Jinzanciyi' • Japanese, soft lavender flowers in spring • 90 cm high, 90–100 cm wide

'Kansas' • Double, carmine-red flowers in spring • 90 cm high, 90–100 cm wide

'Karen Gray' • Japanese, fuchsia flowers in spring • 65 cm high, 65–85 cm wide

'Karl Rosenfield' • Double, wine-red flowers in spring • 80 cm high, 80–100 cm wide

'Kelway's Glorious' • Fragrant, double, creamy-white flowers in spring • 1 m high, 90–100 cm wide

'Kukenu-Jishia' • Japanese, light-pink flowers in spring • 90 cm high, 90–100 cm wide

'La Belle' • Fragrant, double, pink flowers in spring • 60 cm high, 60–80 cm wide

'La Perle' • Fragrant, double, lavender flowers in spring • 80 cm high, 80–100 cm wide

'Largo' • Japanese, rose-pink flowers in spring • 90 cm high, 90–100 cm wide

'Leto' • Japanese, white flowers in spring • 75–90 cm high, 75–90 cm wide

'Lord Calvin' • Double, white flowers in spring • 90 cm high, 90–100 cm wide

'Louis Joliet' • Double, red flowers in spring • 80 cm high, 80–100 cm wide

'Louis van Houtte' • Double, cherry-red flowers in spring • 90–100 cm high, 90–100 cm wide

P

'Madame de Verneville' • Fragrant, double, white flowers in spring • 80 cm high, 80–100 cm wide

'Madame Emile Debatene' • Double, rose-pink flowers in spring • 75 cm high, 75–90 cm wide

'Mandarin's Coat' • Japanese, deep-rose flowers with gold edge in spring • 90 cm high, 90–100 cm wide

'Marshmallow Puff' • Double, pure white flowers in spring • 70 cm high, 70–90 cm wide

'Mary Eddy Jones' • Fragrant, double, light-pink flowers in spring • 90 cm high, 90–100 cm wide

'Matilda Lewis' • Double, deep garnet-red flowers in spring • 90 cm high, 90–100 cm wide

'Mikado' • Japanese, dark rose-crimson flowers in spring • 90 cm high, 90–100 cm wide

'Milton Jack' • Double, dark rose-red flowers in spring • 90 cm high, 90–100 cm wide

'Mischief' • Single, apple blossom–pink flowers in spring • 90–120 cm high, 90–100 cm wide

'Miss America' • Fragrant, semi-double, white flowers in spring • 90 cm high, 90–100 cm wide

'Missie's Blush' • Fragrant, double, blush flowers in spring • 90 cm high, 90–100 cm wide

'Mme. Emile Lemoine' • Double, white flowers with pink flecks in spring • 90 cm high, 90–100 cm wide

'Monsieur Jules Elie' • Fragrant, double, rose-pink flowers in spring • 90 cm high, 90–100 cm wide

'Monsieur Martin Cahuzac' • Double, deep black-red flowers in spring • 90 cm high, 90–100 cm wide

'Mother's Choice' • Fragrant, double, pure white flowers in spring • 90 cm high, 90–100 cm wide

'Mr. Ed' • Fragrant, double, pink and cream flowers in spring • 90 cm high, 90–100 cm wide

'Mr. G.F. Hemerick' • Japanese, magenta flowers with creamy centre in spring • 75 cm high, 75–90 cm wide

'Mrs. Edward Harding' • Frilled, double, pinkish-white flowers in spring • 60–70 cm high, 65–85 cm wide

'Music Man' • Double, red flowers in spring • 90 cm high, 90–100 cm wide

'My Love' • Double, white flowers in spring • 60–90 cm high, 60–90 cm wide

'My Pal Rudy' • Fragrant, double, rich-rose flowers in spring • 90–100 cm high, 90–100 cm wide

'Nice Gal' • Fragrant, semi-double, rose flowers in spring • 55 cm high, 55–75 cm wide

'Nick Shaylor' • Double, blush-pink flowers in spring • 85 cm high, 85–100 cm wide

'Nippon Beauty' • Japanese, deep-red flowers in spring • 90 cm high, 90–100 cm wide

'Nippon Gold' • Japanese, light-pink flowers in spring • 90 cm high, 90–100 cm wide

'Nymphe' • Fragrant, single, light-pink flowers in spring • 65 cm high, 65–80 cm wide

'Opal Hamilton' • Japanese, orchid-pink flowers in spring • 90 cm high, 90–100 cm wide

'Peppermint' • Double, pale-pink flowers with red flecks in spring • 90 cm high, 90–100 cm wide

'Petticoat Flounce' • Double, soft salmon-pink flowers in spring • 85 cm high, 85–100 cm wide

'Philippe Rivoire' • Fragrant, double, dark crimson-red flowers in spring • 75 cm high, 75–90 cm wide

'Phoenix Plume in Gold Plate' • Semi-double, yellow and pink flowers in spring • 80–90 cm high, 80–100 cm wide

'Pillow Talk' • Double, soft-pink flowers in spring • 80 cm high, 80–100 cm wide

'Pink Cameo' • Double, pink flowers with pink centres in spring • 90 cm high, 90–100 cm wide

'Pink Formal' • Double, pale mauve-pink flowers in spring • 90 cm high, 90–100 cm wide

'Pink Hawaiian Coral' • Fragrant, semi-double, coral-pink flowers in spring • 90 cm high, 90–100 cm wide

'Pink Parfait' • Double, pink flowers edged in silver in spring • 90–100 cm high, 90–100 cm wide

'Pride of Langport' • Japanese, soft peach-pink flowers in spring • 75–90 cm high, 75–90 cm wide

P

'Primevere' • Fragrant, Japanese, white flowers in spring • 90 cm high, 90–100 cm wide

'Prince of Darkness' • Double, dark-maroon flowers in spring • 90 cm high, 90–100 cm wide

'Raspberry Ice' • Double, purple-red flowers with twisted centre in spring • 90 cm high, 90–100 cm wide

'Raspberry Sundae' • Fragrant, double, white and red flowers in spring • 90 cm high, 90–100 cm wide

'Ray Payton' • Japanese, cranberry-red flowers in spring • 90 cm high, 90–100 cm wide

'Red Carpet' • Double, velvet-red flowers in spring • 90 cm high, 90–100 cm wide

'Reine Deluxe' • Double, apple blossom–pink flowers in spring • 75–90 cm high, 75–90 cm wide

'Reverend H.N. Traggitt' • Double, white flowers in spring • 90 cm high, 90–100 cm wide

'Royal Charter' • Double, velvet-red flowers in spring • 90 cm high, 90–100 cm wide

'Sam Donaldson' • Double, deep garnet-red flowers in spring • 90 cm high, 90–100 cm wide

'Santa Fe' • Single, fuchsia-pink with pink centres in spring • 90 cm high, 90 cm-1 m wide

'Sarah Bernhardt' • Fragrant, double, apple blossom–pink flowers in spring • 95 cm high, 90–100 cm wide

'Serene Pastel' • Double, pink-tinged, salmon flowers in spring • 70–80 cm high, 75–90 cm wide

'Shanhe Hong' • Japanese, red flowers in spring • 90 cm high, 90–100 cm wide

'Shawnee Chief' • Double, dark-red flowers in spring • 90 cm high, 90–100 cm wide

'Shirley Temple' • Double, creamy-white flowers in spring • 85–95 cm high, 85–100 cm wide

'Show Girl' • Japanese, pink flowers in spring • 90 cm high, 90–100 cm wide

'Solange' • Fragrant, double, cream flowers in spring • 85 cm high, 85–100 cm wide

'Spring Bouquet' • Double, white flowers with red marks in spring • 80 cm high, 80–100 cm wide

'Springfield' • Double, apple blossom–pink flowers in spring • 90 cm high, 90–100 cm wide

'Sword Dance' • Japanese, red flowers with gold centre in spring • 75–90 cm high, 75–90 cm wide

'Taff' • Fragrant, double, blush-rose flowers in spring • 70–75 cm high, 75–90 cm wide

'The Nathans' • Fragrant, double, pink flowers in spring • 60–90 cm high, 90–100 cm wide

'Therese' • Fragrant, double, magenta flowers with creamy centre in spring • 80 cm high, 80–100 cm wide

'Tom Cat' • Double, cream-centred, carmine-red flowers in spring • 65–70 cm high, 65–90 cm wide

'Top Brass' • Double, ivory flowers with yellow or pink centre in spring • 1 m high, 90–100 cm wide

'Unknown Soldier' • Fragrant, double, deep-red flowers in spring • 65 cm high, 65–80 cm wide

'Vogue' • Fragrant, double, rose-pink flowers in spring • 85 cm high, 85–100 cm wide

'Walter Faxon' • Double, shell-pink flowers in spring • 90 cm high, 90–100 cm wide

'Wilford Johnson' • Double, bright-pink flowers in spring • 75–90 cm high, 75–90 cm wide

'Wine Red' • Double, wine-crimson flowers in spring • 75–90 cm high, 75–90 cm wide

'Xishi Fen' • Japanese, coral-pink flowers in spring • 90 cm high, 90–100 cm wide

Paeonia, Itoh
p. 421

General Features
Height: 50–90 cm high
Spread: 60–100 cm wide
Habit: long-lived, clump-forming perennial
Flowers: extra large, single, semi-double or double; late spring; good for cutflowers
Foliage: fern-like to deeply lobed
Hardiness: C–D
Warnings: not prone to insects or disease
Expert Advice: A cross between herbaceous and tree peony, this category was difficult to achieve. The extension of yellow into the herbaceous peony family was a very exciting first. Generally expensive due to the fact that propagation is slow via division. Old wood may survive winter, so wait until spring to cut back.

Growing Requirements
Light: sun
Soil: moist, fertile, well-drained, acid-free soil
Location: mixed borders
Propagation: division

P

Buying Considerations

Professionals

Popularity: gaining popularity; fast seller in bloom; has new varieties
Availability: occasionally available from specialty growers
Size to Sell: sells best in smaller sizes (when blooming) as it matures fast
On the Shelf: rapidly overgrows pot
Shrinkage: low; requires little maintenance

Collectors

Popularity: of interest to collectors—unique, rare, exceptional beauty

Gardeners

Ease of Growth: mostly easy to grow but needs close attention to growing conditions
Start with: one larger plant for feature plant

What to Try First ...

Paeonia 'Bartzella', Paeonia 'Border Charm', Paeonia 'Cora Louise', Paeonia 'First Arrival', Paeonia 'Garden Treasure', Paeonia 'Morning Lilac', Paeonia 'Prairie Charm', Paeonia 'Rose Fantasy', Paeonia 'Yellow Crown'

On the Market

Paeonia

'Bartzella' • Fragrant, semi-double to double, sulphur-yellow flowers in late spring • 90 cm high, 90–100 cm wide

'Border Charm' • Single, yellow flowers with red flares in late spring • 60 cm high, 60–90 cm wide

'Cora Louise' • Semi-double, white flowers with lavender flares in late spring • 50–60 cm high, 60–90 cm wide

'First Arrival' • Semi-double, lavender-pink flowers in late spring • 60 cm high, 60–90 cm wide

'Garden Treasure' • Fragrant, semi-double, bright-yellow flowers in late spring • 75 cm high, 75–100 cm wide

'Hidden Treasure' • Single or semi-double, medium-yellow flowers in spring • 50 cm high, 60–90 cm wide

'Hillary' • Double, red flowers maturing to cream in spring • 75–85 cm high, 90 cm

'Lafayette Escadrille' • Single, dark-red flowers in spring • 50–60 cm high, 60–90 cm wide

'Lemon Dream' • Semi-double, yellow with varying amounts of pink in spring • 90 cm high, 90 cm wide

'Morning Lilac' • Semi-double, lavender flowers in late spring • 60 cm high, 60–90 cm wide

'Old Rose Dandy' • Single, yellow-beige flowers with rose tones in spring • 75 cm high, 75 cm wide

'Oriental Gold' • Semi-double to double, yellow flowers with red flares in spring • 90 cm high, 90 cm wide

'Pastel Splendor' • Single, white with pink and yellow tones in spring • 90 cm high, 90 cm wide

'Pherson's Yellow' • Semi-double, yellow flowers in spring • 90 cm high, 90 cm wide

'Prairie Charm' • Semi-double, pale-yellow flowers with purple flares in spring • 75 cm high, 75 cm wide

'Rose Fantasy' • Single, fuchsia-rose flowers edged in silver in spring • Arching foliage • 75–90 cm high, 75–90 cm wide

'Scarlet Heaven' • Single, scarlet-red flowers in spring • 65–75 cm high, 90 cm wide

'Viking Full Moon' • Single to semi-double, soft greenish-yellow flowers in spring • 75 cm high, 75–90 cm wide

'Yellow Crown' • Semi-double, yellow flowers with red flares in spring • 90 cm high, 90 cm wide

'Yellow Emperor' • Fragrant, semi-double, yellow flowers in spring • 90 cm high, 90 cm wide

'Yellow Heaven' • Fragrant, semi-double, yellow flowers with red flares in spring • 90 cm high, 90 cm wide

Paeonia, Species p. 421

General Features

Height: 25–100 cm high
Spread: 30–100 cm wide
Habit: long-lived, upright, clump-forming perennial
Flowers: (most) single; early spring
Foliage: glossy; dark-green to blue-green; (some) fern-like
Hardiness: B–D
Warnings: prone to Botrytis and aphids
Expert Advice: Species peonies are the first to bloom in spring. A few require staking. Some are quite rare, expensive and difficult to find.

Growing Requirements

Light: sun
Soil: fertile, moist, well-drained, acid-free soil
Location: mixed borders
Propagation: seed; division
Expert Advice: Plant with eyes 5 cm deep or less. Planting too deeply will result in foliage production only and possibly rot. Species peonies do not require division to maintain vigour but may be divided in early fall for propagation purposes.

P

Buying Considerations

Professionals

Popularity: gaining popularity; fast seller in bloom

Availability: occasionally available as finished product and bareroot from specialty growers

Size to Sell: sells best in smaller sizes (when blooming)

Shrinkage: low; requires little maintenance

Collectors

Popularity: of interest to collectors—rare varieties, specific flower colours and forms, expensive

Gardeners

Ease of Growth: mostly easy to grow

Start with: one larger plant for feature plant

What to Try First ...

Paeonia mascula, Paeonia mlokosewitschii, Paeonia obovata, Paeonia tenuifolia, Paeonia veitchii

On the Market

Paeonia anomala
Single, magenta-red flowers with yellow stamens in late spring • 50 cm high, 50–60 cm wide

Paeonia anomala var. *intermedia*
Single, bright-red flowers in spring • 50–60 cm high, 50–60 cm wide

Paeonia brownii
Single, nodding, maroon-bronze flowers in early summer • 25–45 cm high, 30–45 cm wide

Paeonia cambessedesii
Single, deep-rose flowers with yellow stamens in spring • Purple-veined, leathery foliage • 45–55 cm high, 45–55 cm wide

Paeonia franchettii
Single, iridescent, purple-bronze flowers in spring • 1 m high, 1 m wide

Paeonia x *handel-mazzetti*
Single, bronze-yellow flowers in spring • 90 cm high, 90 cm wide

Paeonia japonica
Single, white flowers with yellow stamens in late spring • 40–50 cm high, 45–60 cm wide

Paeonia lactiflora (P. albiflora)
Fragrant, single, white flowers in early summer • 50–70 cm high, 50–70 cm wide

Paeonia mairei
Single, rose-pink flowers in late spring • 60–100 cm high, 60–90 cm wide

Paeonia mascula
Single, purple-red flowers with yellow stamens in late spring • 60–100 cm high, 60–100 cm wide

Paeonia mascula ssp. *arietina*
Single, red-pink flowers with yellow stamens in late spring • 50–75 cm high, 50–75 cm wide

Paeonia mascula ssp. *mascula*
Single, magenta flowers in late spring • 60–90 cm high, 60–90 cm wide

Paeonia mlokosewitschii
Single, primrose-yellow flowers in late spring • 60–100 cm high, 60–90 cm wide

Paeonia obovata
Single, white to rosy-purple flowers in spring • 60 cm high, 60–90 cm wide

Paeonia obovata var. *willmottiae*
Single, white flowers with gold anthers in spring • Purple leaf stalks, stems and undersides • 55 cm high, 55–65 cm wide

Paeonia officinalis
'Alba Plena' • Double, white flowers, flushed pink, in spring • 70–80 cm high, 60–90 cm wide

'Anemoniflora Rosea' • Single, pinkish-red flowers with yellow stamens in spring • 60–70 cm high, 60–90 cm wide

'Mollis' • Single, pink-red flowers with yellow centre in late spring • Blue-green, deeply lobed foliage • 30–45 cm high, 60 cm wide

'Rosea Plena' • Double, bright-pink flowers in spring • 60–90 cm high, 75–100 cm wide

'Rosea Superba Plena' • Double, rose-pink flowers in spring • 60–70 cm high, 60–90 cm wide

'Rubra Plena' • Double, satiny, crimson-red flowers in spring • 70–80 cm high, 60–90 cm wide

Paeonia officinalis ssp. *microcarpa*
Single, red flowers in late spring • 30–40 cm high, 25–40 cm wide

Paeonia officinalis ssp. *villosa*
(syn. *P. mollis*)
Single, red or white flowers in late spring • Blue-green, deeply lobed foliage • 30–45 cm high, 60 cm wide

Paeonia peregrina
'Otto Froebel' (Sunshine) • Single, satiny, vermilion-red flowers in spring • 50–80 cm high, 75–90 cm wide

Paeonia tenuifolia
Single, red flowers in spring • Fern-like foliage • 45–60 cm high, 60 cm wide
'Plena' • Double, red flowers in spring • Fern-like foliage • 45–60 cm high, 60 cm wide
'Rosea' • Single, pink flowers in spring • Fern-like foliage • 40–50 cm high, 45–60 cm wide

Paeonia tenuifolia ssp. lithophila
Single, red flowers in spring • Fern-like foliage • 30–45 cm high, 45 cm wide

Paeonia veitchii
Single, pink or magenta flowers in late spring • 50–60 cm high, 45–60 cm wide

Paeonia veitchii var. woodwardii
Single, rose-red flowers in early summer • 30 cm high, 30–40 cm wide

Paeonia wittmanniana
Single, cream-yellow flowers in late spring • 90–100 cm high, 90 cm wide

Paeonia, Tree
p. 421

General Features
Height: 75–150 cm high
Spread: 90–150 cm wide
Habit: long-lived, upright, clump-forming perennial
Flowers: single, semi-double or double; spring
Foliage: glossy; dark green
Hardiness: C–D
Warnings: not prone to insects or disease
Expert Advice: Tree peonies perform well in warmer climates, but in colder areas may experience winter die-back. They bloom on old wood, so if die-back occurs to soil level, new growth will come up from the base, but no flowers will be produced that year. It may take 3–5 years before first blooms occur after planting. Plant in a sheltered area and mulch for winter.

Growing Requirements
Light: sun
Soil: fertile, moist, well-drained, acid-free soil
Location: mixed borders
Propagation: grafted; division; cuttings
Expert Advice: Tree peonies are grafted, so they are therefore generally planted deeper than other peonies, especially in colder climates. Plant 15 cm below graft and mulch base. If the section above the graft dies, the original herbaceous peony rootstock will come up instead.

Buying Considerations

Professionals
Popularity: popular perennial; sells well in bloom
Availability: readily available as finished product
Size to Sell: sells best in larger sizes (when blooming) as it matures slow
Shrinkage: low; requires little maintenance

Collectors
Popularity: of interest to collectors—rare varieties, specific flower colours and forms, (some) expensive

Gardeners
Ease of Growth: mostly easy to grow but requires close attention to growing conditions
Start with: one mature plant for feature plant

What to Try First ...
Paeonia rockii, Paeonia suffruticosa 'Black Pirate', *Paeonia suffruticosa* 'Hatsugarashu', *Paeonia suffruticosa* 'High Noon', *Paeonia suffruticosa* 'Kokuryu-nishiki', *Paeonia suffruticosa* 'Renown', *Paeonia suffruticosa* 'Shima Nishiki', *Paeonia suffruticosa* 'Shin-tenchi'

On the Market

Paeonia delavayi
Single, purple-red flowers in late spring • 1+ m high, 60 cm wide

Paeonia x lemoinei
'Souvenir de Maxime Cornu' (Kinkaku) • Fragrant, double, orange-yellow flowers in late spring • 90–100+ cm high, 90–100 cm wide

Paeonia lutea
'Yellow Queen' • Fragrant, nodding, yellow flowers in spring • 90–100+ cm high, 90+ cm wide

Paeonia lutea var. ludlowii
Fragrant, yellow flowers in late spring • 90–150+ cm high, 150+ cm wide

Paeonia rockii
Single, pure white flowers with dark-purple flares in spring • 1–2 m high, 1–2 m wide

Paeonia suffruticosa
Single flowers in late spring • 90–100+ cm high, 90 cm wide
'Black Pirate' • Semi-double, mahogany-red flowers in late spring • 1+ m high, 90 cm wide
'Chojuraku' • Semi-double, red flowers in late spring • 1+ m high, 1 m wide

P

'Fen-dang-bai' • Fragrant, single, pure white flowers in late spring • 90+ cm high, 90 cm wide

'Golden Isles' • Double, bright-yellow flowers in late spring • 1+ m high, 90 cm wide

'Golden Temple of Nara' • Double, orange-yellow flowers in late spring • 90+ cm high, 90 cm wide

'Hana-kisoi' • Semi-double, cherry blossom-pink flowers in late spring • 90–100+ cm high, 90 cm wide

'Hatsugarashu' • Single, maroon flowers in late spring • 90–100+ cm high, 60–90 cm wide

'High Noon' • Semi-double, lemon-yellow flowers in late spring • 90–100+ cm high, 90 cm wide

'Imamura Saki' • Semi-double, pink flowers in late spring • 1+ m high, 1 m wide

'Kamada-fuji' • Semi-double, lavender-blue flowers in late spring • 1+ m high, 1 m wide

'Kamata Tapestries' • Double, wisteria-blue flowers in late spring • 90+ cm high, 90 cm wide

'Kaow' • Semi-double, cardinal-red flowers in late spring • 1+ m high, 1 m wide

'Kokuryu-nishiki' • Double, black-purple flowers in late spring • 1+ m high, 1 m wide

'Luo Yang Hong' • Fragrant, double, magenta-red flowers in late spring • 90+ cm high, 90 cm wide

'Ohujinishiki' • Semi-double, purple flowers in late spring • 1+ m high, 1 m wide

'Reine Elizabeth' • Double, salmon-pink flowers in late spring • 1+ m high, 1 m wide

'Renown' • Single, copper-red flowers with gold in late spring • 1.1+ m high, 1 m wide

'Rimpo' • Fragrant, semi-double, maroon flowers in late spring • 1+ m high, 1 m wide

'Sahohime' (Princess Saho) • Double, white flowers in late spring • 1+ m high, 90 cm wide

'Shichifukujin' • Double, crimson flowers edged with pink in late spring • 75–100+ cm high, 90–100 cm wide

'Shima Nishiki' • Fragrant, red-and-white-striped flowers in late spring • 90–100+ cm high, 90 cm wide

'Shimadajin' • Semi-double, magenta flowers in late spring • 1+ m high, 1 m wide

'Shimino Fuji' • Semi-double, pink-purple flowers in late spring • 1+ m high, 1 m wide

'Shin-tenchi' • Semi-double, orchid-pink flowers in late spring • 90+ cm high, 90 cm wide

'Snow Mountain' • Fragrant, single, white flowers in late spring • 90+ cm high, 90 cm wide

'Suminoy Ichi' • Semi-double, black-red flowers in late spring • 90–100+ cm high, 90 cm wide

'Sweet Seventeen' • Double, bright-scarlet flowers in late spring • 90+ cm high, 90 cm wide

'The Yoshino River' • Bright-pink flowers in late spring • 90+ cm high, 90 cm wide

'Wu Long Peng Sheng' • Fragrant, double, magenta-red flowers in late spring • 90+ cm high, 90 cm wide

'Xiao Ye Zi Hong' • Fragrant, single, maroon flowers in late spring • 90+ cm high, 90 cm wide

'Yachiyo-tsubaki' • Semi-double, phlox-pink flowers in late spring • 1+ m high, 1 m wide

'Yagumo' • Single, purple-red flowers in late spring • 1+ m high, 90 cm wide

'Ying-luo-bao-zhu' • Fragrant, double, pink flowers in late spring • 90+ cm high, 90 cm wide

'Zhao Fen' • Fragrant, single or double, pink flowers in late spring • 90+ cm high, 90 cm wide

'Zhuang Yuan Hong' • Semi- to double, magenta-pink flowers in late spring • 1+ m high, 90 cm wide

Panicum

p. 421

Genus Information

Origin: tropical regions, Europe and temperate North America

Selected Common Names: blue switch grass, switch grass

Nomenclature: From the Latin for millet.

Notes: A genus of some 470 species, this genus was once a main component of the American tall-grass prairie and included annuals and perennials.

P

General Features

Height: 90 cm–2.4 m high
Spread: 60–75 cm wide
Habit: upright, clump-forming perennial grass
Flowers: plumes; late summer to fall; good for drying
Foliage: long, arching blades; good fall colour
Hardiness: B–C
Warnings: prone to aphids and rust
Expert Advice: An excellent grass for the mixed border, *Panicum* reliably plumes in colder climates and its foliage remains attractive through the winter into spring.

Growing Requirements

Light: sun
Soil: moderately fertile, moist, well-drained soil
Location: mixed borders
Propagation: division
Expert Advice: Divide every 3 years to keep vigorous and compact.

Buying Considerations

Professionals

Popularity: gaining popularity as a foliage plant
Availability: readily available as finished product and bare root from specialty growers
Size to Sell: sells best in smaller sizes as it matures fast
On the Shelf: high ornamental appeal; prone to rust in pots; rapidly overgrows pot
Shrinkage: low; requires little maintenance

Collectors

Popularity: of interest to collectors—native plant, exceptional beauty

Gardeners

Ease of Growth: mostly easy to grow
Start with: one small plant for feature plant and several for mass plantings

What to Try First ...

Panicum virgatum 'Heavy Metal', *Panicum virgatum* 'Prairie Sky', *Panicum virgatum* 'Rostrahlbusch', *Panicum virgatum* 'Warrior'

On the Market

Panicum virgatum
Seed heads in late summer to fall
• 90–120 cm high, 60–75 cm wide

'Heavy Metal' • Seed heads in late summer to fall • Grey-green foliage • 90–150 cm high, 60–75 cm wide

'Prairie Sky' • Seed heads in late summer to fall • Metallic-blue foliage • 90–120 cm high, 60–75 cm wide

'Rehbraun' • Seed heads in late summer • Red-brown foliage • 90–120 cm high, 60–75 cm wide

'Rostrahlbusch' • Dark red-burgundy fall colour • 90–120 cm high, 60–75 cm wide

'Warrior' • Seed heads in late summer to fall • Reddish fall colour • 90–120 cm high, 60–75 cm wide

Papaver p. 421

Genus Information

Origin: Europe, Asia, Australia, South Africa and western North America
Selected Common Names: Iceland poppy, oriental poppy, poppy
Nomenclature: From the Latin *pappa* (food or milk), referring to the plant's milky latex (sap).

General Features

Height: 10–110 cm high
Spread: 6–90 cm wide
Habit: tap-rooted, clump- to tuft-forming perennial
Flowers: papery, single; spring to fall; *P. orientale* has large, papery, single or double flowers in spring and goes dormant after flowering; some species produce large ornamental seed heads that can be used for drying
Foliage: mid-green; *P. orientale* has coarse, hairy, silver-grey foliage
Hardiness: A–C
Warnings: prone to aphids; not prone to diseases;
Expert Advice: Many species of poppies are short-lived (2–3 years at most). They readily self-sow but hybrids will not come true from seed. *P. orientale* is long-lived and self-sows, but not as readily as other poppies. Both types' blooms can be used as cutflowers. Immerse freshly cut stems in boiling water for 20–30 seconds to prevent the milky sap from blocking the stem.

Growing Requirements

Light: sun to p.m. sun
Soil: poor soil; tolerant of a wide range of soil conditions; drought tolerant; *P. orientale* prefers fertile, well-drained soil and tolerates periods of dryness
Location: mixed borders; rock gardens; alpine gardens
Propagation: seed (self-sows); division; cuttings
Expert Advice: Hybrid varieties may not come true from seed. *P. orientale* resents being disturbed and should only be divided when they loose vigour from overcrowding.
P. orientale may rebloom in late summer if cut down after flowering and fertilized.

P

Buying Considerations

Professionals

Popularity: popular, old-fashioned garden standard; fast seller in bloom; has new varieties
Availability: readily available as finished product and bare root
Size to Sell: sells best in smaller sizes (when blooming) as it matures fast
On the Shelf: rapidly overgrows pot; foliage and stem breakage common
Shrinkage: high; sensitive to overwatering; *P. orientale* goes dormant in pot after blooming

Collectors

Popularity: of interest to alpine collectors—rare species

Gardeners

Ease of Growth: very easy to grow
Start with: one small plant for feature plant and several for mass plantings

What to Try First ...

Papaver alboroseum, Papaver alpinum, Papaver degenii, Papaver nudicaule, Papaver nudicaule Champagne Bubbles Group, *Papaver nudicaule* Garden Gnome Group, *Papaver orientale* 'Brilliant', *Papaver orientale* 'Curlilocks', *Papaver orientale* 'Dwarf Allegro', *Papaver orientale* 'Garden Glory', *Papaver orientale* 'Patty's Plum', *Papaver orientale* 'Pink Ruffles', *Papaver orientale* 'Prinzessin Victoria Louise', *Papaver orientale* 'Queen Alexandra', *Papaver orientale* 'Royal Chocolate Distinction', *Papaver orientale* 'Turkenlouis', *Papaver orientale* 'Turkish Delight', *Papaver orientale* 'Watermelon'

On the Market

P

Papaver alboroseum
Paper-thin, white to pale-pink flowers with yellow centre in spring to fall • 10–15 cm high, 15–20 cm wide

Papaver alpinum
Peach-pink flowers in summer • Grey-green foliage • 10–15 cm high, 10–15 cm wide

Papaver degenii
Yellow flowers in late spring to late summer • 10–15 cm high, 6–10 cm wide

Papaver fauriei
Light-orange flowers in summer • 25–30 cm high, 25–30 cm wide

Papaver kerneri
Deep-yellow flowers in summer • 15 cm high, 15 cm wide

Papaver kluanense
Papery-thin, sulphur-yellow flowers in spring to fall • Grey-green, hairy foliage • 10 cm high, 8 cm wide

Papaver miyabeanum
Yellow flowers in summer • 5–10 cm high, 5–10 cm wide
'Pacino' • Chrome-yellow flowers in spring to fall • 10–15 cm high, 5–10 cm wide

Papaver nudicaule
Papery-thin flowers in spring to fall • 30–45 cm high, 15–30 cm wide
'Matador' • Large, papery-thin, scarlet flowers in spring to fall • 40–45 cm high, 30–40 cm wide
'Windsong' • Papery-thin, orange and yellow flowers in spring to fall • 20–40 cm high, 20–25 cm wide

Champagne Bubbles Group
Soft pastel, papery-thin flowers in spring to fall • 30–40 cm high, 15–30 cm wide

Garden Gnome Group
Papery-thin, red, pink, yellow, orange or white flowers in spring to fall • 25–30 cm high, 15–30 cm wide

Papaver nudicaule var. *croeceum* (syn. *P. croeceum*)
'Flamenco' • Orange to red flowers in summer • Toothed foliage • 20–25 cm high, 20–25 cm wide

Papaver orientale
'Allegro' • Orange-red flowers with black blotch in early summer • 60–70 cm high, 45–60 cm wide
'Beauty of Livermere' • Crimson-scarlet flowers with black blotch in early summer • 90–110 cm high, 45–60 cm wide
'Big Jim' • Deep raspberry-pink flowers in early summer • 85–95 cm high, 45–60 cm wide
'Black and White' • Single, white flowers with black blotch in early summer • 70–80 cm high, 45–60 cm wide
'Bolero' • Rose-pink flowers in early summer • 80 cm high, 45–60 cm wide
'Brilliant' • Scarlet-red flowers with black blotch in early summer • 75–90 cm high, 45–60 cm wide
'Brooklyn' • Dark rose-pink flowers with lighter edges in early summer • 70–80 cm high, 45–60 cm wide

'Carnival' • Orange-red flowers with black blotch in early summer • 75–85 cm high, 45–60 cm wide

'Carousel' • Bright-orange flowers with black blotch in early summer • 70–85 cm high, 45–60 cm wide

'Cedar Hill' • Salmon-pink flowers with black blotch in early summer • 45–50 cm high, 45–60 cm wide

'Central Park' • Large, wine-red flowers in late spring • 75–80 cm high, 30–40 cm wide

'China Boy' • White flowers with uneven orange margins in early summer • 75–90 cm high, 45–60 cm wide

'Curlilocks' • Fringed, orange-red flowers with black blotch in early summer • 70–80 cm high, 45–60 cm wide

'Domino' • White flowers with black centers in early summer • 40 cm high, 45–60 cm wide

'Doubloon' • Semi-double, orange-red flowers in early summer • 75–90 cm high, 45–60 cm wide

'Dwarf Allegro' • Vivid-scarlet flowers with black basal blotch in early summer • 40–50 cm high, 45–60 cm wide

'Fatima' • Ruffled, white flowers with pink edge in early summer • 60–75 cm high, 60 cm wide

'Feuerwerk' (Fireworks) • Bright-red flowers in early summer • 40–45 cm high, 45–60 cm wide

'Forncett Summer' • Fringed, semi-double, pink flowers in early summer • 75 cm high, 45–60 cm wide

'Garden Glory' • Orange-pink flowers with frilled edges in early summer • 75–90 cm high, 45–60 cm wide

'Glowing Rose' • Deep rose-pink flowers in early summer • 60–75 cm high, 45–60 cm wide

'Harvest Moon' • Semi-double, ruffled, orange flowers in early summer • 90–110 cm high, 45–60 cm wide

'Indian Chief' • Large, mahogany-red flowers in late spring • 60 cm high, 40 cm wide

'Juliane' • Pale-pink flowers in early summer • 70–85 cm high, 45–60 cm wide

'Karine' • Pink flowers with purple-red basal zone in early summer • 60–70 cm high, 45–60 cm wide

'Lady Moore' • Salmon-pink flowers with black blotch in early summer • 70–85 cm high, 45–60 cm wide

'Lighthouse' • Pale salmon-pink flowers in early summer • 80–95 cm high, 45–60 cm wide

'Little Candy Floss' • Pale-pink flowers with dark basal blotch in early summer • 30–35 cm high, 30–45 cm wide

'Little Dancing Girl' • Pale-pink flowers with dark basal blotch in early summer • 40–50 cm high, 45–60 cm wide

'Maiden's Blush' • Blush-pink flowers in early summer • 75–85 cm high, 45–60 cm wide

'Manhattan' • Fuchsia-pink flowers in early summer • 75–80 cm high, 45–60 cm wide

'Marcus Perry' • Satiny, orange-red flowers with dark blotch in early summer • 70–80 cm high, 45–60 cm wide

'Mrs Perry' • Salmon-pink flowers with purple blotch in early summer • 80–100 cm high, 45–60 cm wide

'Patty's Plum' • Rose-plum flowers with black basal blotch in early summer • 70–85 cm high, 45–60 cm wide

'Perry's White' • White flowers with purple basal blotch in early summer • 85–95 cm high, 45–60 cm wide

'Peter Pan' • Semi-double, orange-scarlet flowers in early summer • 65–75 cm high, 45–60 cm wide

'Petticoat' • Pleated, salmon-pink flowers in early summer • 70–80 cm high, 45–60 cm wide

'Picotee' • Salmon-orange flowers with white centre in early summer • 65–80 cm high, 45–60 cm wide

'Pink Ruffles' • Fringed, pink flowers in early summer • 50–60 cm high, 45–60 cm wide

'Pinnacle' • White flowers with salmon-orange edge in early summer • 65–80 cm high, 45–60 cm wide

'Prinzessin Victoria Louise' • Salmon-pink flowers with dark blotch in early summer • 70–90 cm high, 45–60 cm wide

'Queen Alexandra' • Salmon-scarlet flowers with dark blotch in early summer • 60–75 cm high, 45–60 cm wide

P

'Raspberry Queen' • Raspberry-pink flowers with dark streaks in early summer • 80 cm high, 45–60 cm wide

'Rembrandt' • Deep-red flowers in early summer • 75–85 cm high, 45–60 cm wide

'Royal Chocolate Distinction' • Chocolate-maroon flowers in early summer • 70–80 cm high, 45–60 cm wide

'Royal Wedding' • White flowers with black basal blotch in early summer • 75–85 cm high, 45–60 cm wide

'Salmon Glow' • Frilled, semi-double, salmon-orange flowers with silvery sheen in early summer • 85–95 cm high, 45–60 cm wide

'Showgirl' • Salmon-pink flowers with pale margins in early summer • 75–90 cm high, 45–90 cm wide

'Snow Queen' • Pure white flowers in early summer • 60–75 cm high, 45–60 cm wide

'Springtime' • Pale salmon-white flowers in early summer • 70–80 cm high, 45–60 cm wide

'Turkenlouis' • Fringed, scarlet-orange flowers in early summer • 70–80 cm high, 45–60 cm wide

'Turkish Delight' (Helen Elizabeth) • Single, salmon-pink flowers in early summer • 60–75 cm high, 45–60 cm wide

'Warlord' • Fiery-red flowers in early summer • 45 cm high, 45 cm wide

'Watermelon' • Watermelon-pink flowers with black blotch in early summer • 80–100 cm high, 45–60 cm wide

'Wunderkind' (Enchantress) • Raspberry-pink flowers with black blotch in early summer • 65–80 cm high, 45–60 cm wide

Papaver radicatum
Sulphur-yellow flowers in late spring • 20–30 cm high, 30 cm wide

Papaver rhaeticum
Yellow to orange flowers in summer • Grey-green foliage • 15–25 cm high, 15 cm wide

Papaver rupifragum
Brick-red flowers in late spring to fall • 15 cm high, 15 cm wide

Papaver sendtneri
White flowers in spring • 15 cm high, 15 cm wide

Papaver spicatum
Pale orange flowers in late spring to summer • 60–75 cm high, 30–45 cm wide

Paraquilegia   p. 421 📷

Genus Information

Origin: central Asia and the Himalayas
Selected Common Names: unknown
Nomenclature: From the Greek *para* (near) and the genus *Aquilegia* to which this plant is closely related.

General Features

Height: 5–10 cm high
Spread: 5–10 cm wide
Habit: clump-forming perennial
Flowers: columbine-like; spring
Foliage: columbine-like
Hardiness: C–D
Warnings: prone to aphids; not prone to diseases
Expert Advice: This is a collector's plant that is tricky in cultivation. It is slow to mature.

Growing Requirements

Light: shade to a.m. sun; shelter from hot p.m. sun
Soil: cool, alkaline, sharply-drained, lean soil; avoid winter wet
Location: rock gardens; scree; troughs; tufa
Propagation: seed; basal cuttings in summer

Buying Considerations

Professionals

Popularity: relatively unknown
Availability: occasionally available from specialty growers
Size to Sell: sells best in mature sizes (when blooming) as it matures slowly
Shrinkage: low; requires little maintenance

Collectors

Popularity: of interest to collectors—unique, exceptional beauty, rare, challenge, novelty

Gardeners

Ease of Growth: mostly difficult to grow as it needs close attention to growing conditions
Start with: several mature plants for instant visual effect

What to Try First ...

Paraquilegia anemonoides

On the Market

Paraquilegia anemonoides
(syn. *P. grandiflora*)
Lilac to violet-blue, sometimes white flowers in spring • Columbine-like foliage • 5–10 cm high, 5–10 cm wide

Paronychia

p. 422

Genus Information

Origin: temperate and tropical regions
Selected Common Names: nailwort
Nomenclature: From the Greek *para* (beside) and *onyx* (nail), referring to the use of the plant to treat whitlows under the finger- or toenails.

General Features

Height: 2–15 cm high
Spread: 10–45 cm wide
Habit: mat-forming, groundcover perennial
Flowers: papery bracts; spring to summer
Foliage: mid-green
Hardiness: D
Warnings: not prone to insects or disease

Growing Requirements

Light: sun
Soil: sharply drained, dry, lean soil; avoid winter wet
Location: between paving stones; raised beds; rock gardens
Propagation: seed; division; cuttings
Expert Advice: Divide in spring. Take stem cuttings in summer.

Buying Considerations

Professionals

Popularity: relatively unknown foliage plant
Availability: occasionally available from specialty growers
Size to Sell: sells best in smaller sizes as it matures fast
On the Shelf: high ornamental appeal; rapidly overgrows pot
Shrinkage: low; requires little maintenance

Collectors

Popularity: not generally of interest to collectors

Gardeners

Ease of Growth: mostly easy to grow but needs close attention to growing conditions
Start with: one small plant for feature plant and several for mass plantings

What to Try First ...

Paronychia cephalotes, Paronychia kapela, Paronychia pulvinata, Paronychia sessiliflora

On the Market

Paronychia cephalotes
Silver-white flower bracts in late spring to early summer • 5–10 cm high, 30–45 cm wide

Paronychia kapela
Silver-white flower bracts in summer • 5–15 cm high, 20–30 cm wide

Paronychia kapela ssp. serpyllifolia
Green-white flowers in silver-white paper bracts in summer • Silvery, blue-green foliage • 2–5 cm high, 10–20 cm wide

Paronychia pulvinata
Silver-white flowers in papery bracts in summer • 5–10 cm high, 15–30 cm wide

Paronychia sessiliflora
Brown-amber flowers in summer • Prickly, yellow-green foliage • 5–10 cm high, 15–30 cm wide

Pedicularis

p. 422

Genus Information

Origin: northern temperate regions and the Andes
Selected Common Names: elephant heads
Nomenclature: From the Latin for the plant *pediculus* (louse), referring to the belief that eating these plants caused lice infestations.
Notes: The genus includes annuals, biennials and perennials.

General Features

Height: 30–60 cm high
Spread: 30–40 cm wide
Habit: semi-parasitic biennial or perennial
Flowers: elephant-head shaped; summer
Foliage: exotic-looking; evergreen
Hardiness: A–C
Warnings: not prone to insects or disease
Expert Advice: Some species are parasitic and not easily cultivated. It is likely that grasses and perhaps other plants are the hosts; planting among these gives the best chance of success. This plant is for the collector.

Growing Requirements

Light: shade
Soil: rich, moist, organic soil
Location: alpine gardens; rock gardens; wild gardens
Propagation: seed; division

Buying Considerations

Professionals

Popularity: relatively unknown
Availability: occasionally available from specialty growers
Size to Sell: sells best in mature sizes (when blooming) as it matures slowly
Shrinkage: low; requires little maintenance

Collectors

Popularity: of interest to collectors—unique, exceptional beauty, rare, challenge

P

On the Market
Pedicularis groenlandica
Red to purple flowers that resemble an elephant's head in summer • Native to Alberta • 30–60 cm high, 30–40 cm wide

Pediocactus
p. 422

Genus Information
Origin: United States
Selected Common Names: snowball cactus
Nomenclature: From the Greek *pedion* (plain) and cactus, referring to the name of the Great Plains region where the species is native.
Notes: With the exception of *P. simpsonii,* plants are difficult to grow on their own root and are normally grafted.

General Features
Height: 10–15 cm high
Spread: 10–15 cm wide
Habit: clump-forming cactus
Flowers: range of colours; spring
Foliage: prickly, fine spines
Hardiness: B–C
Warnings: painful to handle; not prone to insects or disease
Expert Advice: An interesting and surprisingly hardy cactus.

Growing Requirements
Light: sun to p.m. sun
Soil: dry, moderately fertile, sharply drained soil; avoid winter wet
Location: alpine gardens
Propagation: seed
Expert Advice: Propagate seed at 19–24°C in spring. Soil should contain at least 50% grit. Grow extremely dry to promote flowering.

Buying Considerations
Professionals
Popularity: relatively unknown
Availability: occasionally available from specialty growers
Size to Sell: sells best in smaller sizes (when blooming)
Shrinkage: low; requires little maintenance
Collectors
Popularity: of interest to collectors—unique, rare

On the Market
Pediocactus simpsonii
Pink, white, magenta or yellowish flowers in spring • Round, mid-green stems with fine spines • 10–15 cm high, 10–15 cm wide

Pediocactus simpsonii var. *simpsonii*
Deep-pink to white flowers in spring • 10–15 cm high, 10–15 cm wide

Penstemon
p. 422

Genus Information
Origin: North America and Central America
Selected Common Names: cliff beardtongue, beardtongue
Nomenclature: From the Greek *pente* (5) and *stemon* (stamen), referring to the 5th sterile stamen.
Notes: A genus of some 250 species. Related to *Chelone*. It is one of the most widespread of American perennials.

General Features
Height: 1–120 cm high
Spread: 10–90 cm wide
Habit: upright, clump-forming or mat-forming biennial or subshrubby perennial
Flowers: colourful, tubular, foxglove-like; spring to summer; attracts hummingbirds
Foliage: deciduous or evergreen; dark-green (some grey-green)
Hardiness: C–D
Warnings: prone to aphids

Growing Requirements
Light: sun
Soil: Alpine/Rock Garden types prefer sharp to well-drained soil and tolerate dry soil; avoid winter wet; Tall/Garden types prefer fertile, well-drained soil and tolerate periods of dryness
Location: mixed borders; raised beds; rock gardens; wild gardens; woodland gardens
Propagation: seed; cuttings
Expert Advice: Seed in spring. Take softwood and semi-ripe cuttings from non-flowering shoots in summer. We divide *Penstemon* into 2 types for display and information purposes: *Alpine/ Rock Garden* and *Tall/Garden.*

Buying Considerations

Professionals

Popularity: gaining popularity; sells well in bloom

Availability: Tall/Garden types generally available as finished product and bare root; Alpine/Rock Garden types generally available as bare root from specialty growers

Size to Sell: sells best in smaller sizes (when blooming) as it matures fast

On the Shelf: keep stock rotated; rapidly overgrows pot

Shrinkage: low; sensitive to overwatering; requires little maintenance

Collectors

Popularity: of interest to collectors—unique, exceptional beauty, rare, challenge

Gardeners

Ease of Growth: mostly easy to grow but needs close attention to growing conditions

Start with: one small plant for feature plant; mat-forming types best in mass planting

What to Try First ...

Penstemon 'Pink Chablis', *Penstemon* 'Pink Holly', *Penstemon* 'Prairie Dusk', *Penstemon* 'Prairie Fire', *Penstemon caespitosus, Penstemon caespitosus* var. *desertipicti, Penstemon davidsonii* var. *davidsonii, Penstemon davidsonii* var. *menziesii, Penstemon digitalis* 'Husker Red', *Penstemon fruticosus, Penstemon fruticosus* 'Purple Haze', *Penstemon fruticosus* var. *fruticosus, Penstemon hirsutus* var. *pygmaeus, Penstemon newberryi, Penstemon pinifolius, Penstemon pinifolius* 'Mersea Yellow', *Penstemon procerus* var. *formosus, Penstemon procumbens* 'Claude Barr', *Penstemon rupicola*

On the Market

Penstemon, Alpine/Rock Garden

Penstemon

'Breitenbush Blue' • Blue-lilac flowers in summer • 8–10 cm high, 30+ cm wide

'Dragontail' • Violet-pink flowers in late spring to early summer • Blue-green foliage • 1–2 cm high, 10–15 cm wide

'Edithae' • Lavender flowers in late spring to early summer • 10–15 cm high, 20–30 cm wide

'Pink Dragon' • Salmon-pink flowers in late spring to early summer • 8–12 cm high, 10–20 cm wide

'Pink Holly' • Pink flowers in summer • Waxy, blue, holly-like foliage • 10–15 cm high, 20–30 cm wide

'Waxworks' • White flowers, flushed lavender, in summer • Dark, waxy foliage • 15–20 cm high, 30–45 cm wide

Penstemon acaulis var. *yampaensis* (syn. *P. yampaensis*)
Large, lilac-blue flowers in spring to early summer • 3–5 cm high, 20–30 cm wide

Penstemon angustifolius
Blue to pink flowers in spring to early summer • Well-drained, dry, sandy, neutral to alkaline soil • 10–40 cm high, 20–30 cm wide

Penstemon aridus
Blue to purple-blue flowers in early summer • Grey-green foliage • 10–15 cm high, 15–25 cm wide

Penstemon caespitosus
Blue-purple flowers in late spring to early summer • 2–3 cm high, 60–90 cm wide

'Albus' • White flowers in late spring to summer • 2–3 cm high, 30–60 cm wide

Penstemon caespitosus var. *desertipicti*
Clear-blue flowers in late spring to summer • Grey-green foliage • 2–3 cm high, 30–60 cm wide

Penstemon confertus
Cream-white flowers in late spring to summer • Moist, fertile soil • 20–40 cm high, 30–45 cm wide

Penstemon davidsonii
Lavender to purple-violet flowers in late spring to summer • 10–20 cm high, 30–45 cm wide

Penstemon davidsonii var. *davidsonii*
Lavender to purple-violet flowers in late spring to summer • 10–20 cm high, 30–45 cm wide

'Mt. Adam's Dwarf' • Lavender flowers in late spring to summer • 1–2 cm high, 30–45 cm wide

Penstemon davidsonii var. *menziesii*
Lavender to purple-violet flowers in late spring to summer • 10–15 cm high, 20–30 cm wide

'Broken Top Mountain' • Rich-purple flowers in late spring to summer • 8–12 cm high, 20–30 cm wide

'Microphyllus' • Lavender to purple-violet flowers in late spring to summer • 1–2 cm high, 20–30 cm wide

'Rampart White' • White flowers in late spring to summer • 10–15 cm high, 20–30 cm wide

P

Penstemon ellipticus
Large, tubular, lavender flowers in summer
• 5–15 cm high, 45–60 cm wide

Penstemon fruticosus
Purple to blue flowers in late spring to
early summer • Evergreen • 30–45 cm high,
45–60 cm wide

'Pink Rock' • Bright-pink flowers in late
spring to early summer • Evergreen •
30–45 cm high, 45–60 cm wide

'Purple Haze' • Mauve-purple flowers in
spring to early summer • Shiny, rich-green
evergreen foliage • 30–45 cm high, 45–60
cm wide

Penstemon fruticosus var. fruticosus
Blue-purple flowers in late spring to early
summer • Evergreen • 30–45 cm high,
45–60 cm wide

Penstemon fruticosus var. scouleri
Purple-blue flowers in late spring to early
summer • Evergreen • 30–45 cm high,
45–60 cm wide

Penstemon fruticosus var. serratus
Lavender-blue flowers in late spring to
early summer • Evergreen • 20–30 cm high,
45–60 cm wide

'Holly' • Bright-blue flowers in late spring
to early summer • Glossy, evergreen
foliage • 20–30 cm high, 45–60 cm wide

Penstemon hallii
Blue-violet flowers in summer • 10–20 cm
high, 20–30 cm wide

Penstemon hirsutus var. pygmaeus
Violet-purple flowers with white throat in
late spring to early summer • Purple-tinted
foliage • 5–10 cm high, 10–15 cm wide

Penstemon humilis
Azure to blue-violet, rarely white flowers
in late spring to summer • 10–30 cm high,
15–25 cm wide

Penstemon humilis var. brevifolius
Azure-blue flowers in late spring to early
summer • 10–15 cm high, 15–25 cm wide

Penstemon laricifolius ssp. laricifolius
Purple flowers in spring to early summer •
10–20 cm high, 15–20 cm wide

**Penstemon leiophyllus var. francisci-
pennellii**
Huge, blue-violet flowers in summer •
10–30 cm high, 10–15 cm wide

Penstemon linarioides
Blue to violet flowers, with darker streaks,
in summer • Semi-evergreen foliage
• 15–40 cm high, 15–25 cm wide

Penstemon linarioides ssp. coloradoensis
Lavender to violet flowers in summer •
15–40 cm high, 15–25 cm wide

Penstemon newberryi
Rose-red to rose-purple flowers in summer
• Evergreen foliage • Cool, well-drained,
gritty, neutral to acidic soil • 15–30 cm high,
20–30 cm wide

Penstemon newberryi ssp. newberryi
Rose-red to rose-purple flowers in summer
• Evergreen foliage • Cool, well-drained,
gritty, neutral to acidic soil • 15–30 cm high,
20–30 cm wide

Penstemon newberryi ssp. sonomensis
Dark rose-purple flowers in summer •
Evergreen foliage • Cool, well-drained,
gritty, neutral to acidic soil • 10–20 cm high,
15–25 cm wide

Penstemon nitidus
Turquoise flowers in early spring •
10–30 cm high, 10–20 cm wide

Penstemon palmeri
Fragrant, soft pink, white or lilac flowers in
summer • 50–120 cm high, 20–30 cm wide

Penstemon petiolatus
Rose-magenta flowers in spring • Sharply
drained, gritty, neutral to alkaline soil •
10–20 cm high, 30–50 cm wide

Penstemon pinifolius
Orange-red flowers in summer • Pine-
like, evergreen foliage • 15–40 cm high,
30–45 cm wide

'Compactum' • Tubular, orange-red flowers
in summer • Pine-like, evergreen foliage
• 10–15 cm high, 30–45 cm wide

'Fuzzy Buzz' • Tangerine-red flowers in
summer • Pine-like, evergreen foliage
• 15–40 cm high, 30–45 cm wide

'Iron Man' • Tangerine to yellow flowers
in summer • Pine-like, evergreen foliage
• 15–40 cm high, 30–45 cm wide

'Magdalena Sunshine' • Yellow flowers
with orange throat in summer • Pine-
like, evergreen foliage • 15–40 cm high,
30–45 cm wide

'Mersea Yellow' • Soft-yellow flowers in
summer • Pine-like, evergreen foliage •
15–40 cm high, 30–45 cm wide

Penstemon procerus
Blue or purple flowers in summer
• 5–15 cm high, 15–25 cm wide

Penstemon procerus var. formosus
Bright-blue or purple flowers in summer •
5–15 cm high, 15–25 cm wide

Penstemon procerus var. tolmiei
Bright-blue, sometimes cream flowers in
summer • 5–15 cm high, 15–25 cm wide
'Nisqually Cream' • Cream-white flowers in
summer • 5–15 cm high, 15–25 cm wide

Penstemon procumbens
Purple-blue flowers in spring to early
summer • 2–3 cm high, 60–90 cm wide
'Claude Barr' • Purple-blue flowers in late
spring to early summer • 2–3 cm high,
60–90 cm wide

Penstemon rupicola
Pink, red or rose-purple flowers in late
spring to early summer • 8–12 cm high,
30–45 cm wide
'Myrtle Herbert' • Dark-pink flowers in late
spring to early summer • 5–8 cm high,
20–30 cm wide

Penstemon teucrioides
Blue to purple-blue flowers in summer
• 5–12 cm high, 45–60 cm wide

Penstemon uintahensis
Sky-blue flowers in summer • 5–15 cm high,
20–30 cm wide

Penstemon virens
Light- to dark-blue or blue-violet flowers in
summer • 10–30 cm high, 25–40 cm wide

Penstemon, Tall/Garden   p. 422

Penstemon
Morden • Mixed-colour flowers in late
summer • 30–60 cm high, 20–40 cm wide
'Prairie Blizzard' • Large, white flowers in
late spring to late summer • 45–60 cm
high, 45–60 cm wide
'Prairie Dusk' • Tubular, red-violet flowers
in late spring to late summer • 45–60 cm
high, 45–60 cm wide
'Prairie Fire' • Scarlet flowers in late
spring to late summer • 45–60 cm high,
45–60 cm wide
'Prairie Splendor' • Deep-pink flowers in
late spring to late summer • 45–60 cm
high, 45–60 cm wide
Scharf Hybrid • Blood-red flowers in
summer • 30–45 cm high, 25–40 cm wide
'Skinner's Purple' • Deep purple flowers in
summer • 45–60 cm high, 30–45 cm wide

Saskatoon Hybrid 'Pink Chablis' • Compact,
bright pink flowers in summer • 20–50 cm
high, 30–45 cm wide

Penstemon barbatus
Red flowers, tinted pink to carmine, in
summer • 50–90 cm high, 30–45 cm wide
'Elfin Pink' • Tubular, clear-pink flowers in
summer • 20–30 cm high, 15–25 cm wide

Hyacinth Group
Mix of scarlet, rose, violet or dark-blue
flowers in summer • 30–60 cm high, 3
0–45 cm wide

Penstemon cardinalis
Red flowers with yellow throat in summer •
50–75 cm high, 30–45 cm wide

Penstemon deustus var. pedicellatus
White flowers in summer • 15–45 cm high,
15–30 cm wide

Penstemon digitalis
'Husker Red' • Cream-white flowers,
sometimes tinted purple, in summer •
Dark burgundy-bronze foliage and stems •
50–75 cm high, 20–30 cm wide

Penstemon glaber
Sky- to dark-blue flowers in summer •
50–75 cm high, 30–45 cm wide

**Penstemon glaber var. alpinus
(syn. P. alpinus)**
Sky-to dark-blue flowers in summer •
30–45 cm high, 20–30 cm wide

Penstemon gracilis
Lilac flowers in late spring to midsummer •
30–50 cm high, 20–30 cm wide

Penstemon grandiflorus
'Prairie Snow' • White flowers in spring •
45–60 cm high, 20–30 cm wide

Penstemon speciosus
Bright-blue flowers in spring to early
summer • 20–90 cm high, 20–40 cm wide

Penstemon strictus
Blue-purple flowers in summer • 45–60 cm
high, 45–60 cm wide
'Bandera' • Dark blue-purple flowers in
summer • 45–60 cm high, 45–60 cm wide

Penstemon whippleanus
Wine-red flowers, sometimes cream or
violet, in early summer • 45–60 cm high,
20–30 cm wide
'Blue Spire' • Violet-blue flowers in late
summer • Aromatic, grey foliage •
75–100 cm high, 60–90 cm wide

P

Perovskia

p. 422

Genus Information

Origin: Asia Minor and the Himalayas
Selected Common Names: Russian sage
Nomenclature: Named for Bohdan Perovskii, a Russian statesman in the 19th century.
Notes: This plant was the Perennial Plant of the Year for 1995 as chosen by PPA (Perennial Plant Association).

General Features

Height: 45–100 cm high
Spread: 45–90 cm wide
Habit: upright, subshrubby perennial; may require staking
Flowers: airy, lavender spires; summer to late summer; good for cutflowers; good for drying; attractive to bees and butterflies
Foliage: aromatic, grey foliage; remove dead stems in spring and cut back to 20 cm to promote branching
Hardiness: C–D
Warnings: prone to aphids; not prone to diseases

Growing Requirements

Light: sun
Soil: poor to moderately fertile, well-drained soil; tolerates alkaline soil; drought tolerant
Location: sunny, hot, dry areas; mixed borders
Propagation: cuttings
Expert Advice: Take softwood cuttings in late spring and lateral shoot cuttings in summer.

Buying Considerations

Professionals
Popularity: popular, fast-selling foliage plant
Availability: readily available as finished product and bare root
Size to Sell: sells best in smaller sizes (when blooming) as it matures slowly
On the Shelf: high ornamental appeal; rapidly overgrows pot
Shrinkage: low; requires little maintenance

Collectors
Popularity: not generally of interest to collectors

Gardeners
Ease of Growth: mostly easy to grow
Start with: one small plant for feature plant

What to Try First ...
Perovskia 'Blue Spire', *Perovskia* 'Filigran', *Perovskia atriplicifolia*, *Perovskia atriplicifolia* 'Little Spire', *Perovskia atriplicifolia* 'Longin'

On the Market

Perovskia
'Blue Spire' • Violet-blue flowers in late summer • Aromatic, grey foliage • 75–100 cm high, 60–90 cm wide
'Filigran' • Blue flowers in late summer • Aromatic, grey, finely cut foliage • 60–75 cm high, 50–75 cm wide

Perovskia atriplicifolia
Blue-mauve flowers in late summer • Aromatic, grey foliage • 75–100 cm high, 60–90 cm wide
'Little Spire' • Violet flowers in late summer • Aromatic, grey foliage • 45–60 cm high, 45–60 cm wide
'Longin' • Smoky-blue flowers in summer • Aromatic, grey foliage • 75–100 cm high, 50–75 cm wide

Persicaria

p. 422

Genus Information

Origin: Asia, Europe and North America
Selected Common Names: fleeceflower, Himalayan fleeceflower, knotweed
Nomenclature: From the Latin *persica* (Persia) or from *persica* (peach) and *aria* (resemblance), referring to the leaves of some species resembling peach leaves.
Notes: Members of this genus have endured a number of name changes in the last few years. They have been bounced around between *Persicaria, Reynoutria, Fallopia* and *Polygonum*.

General Features

Height: 8–150 cm high
Spread: 45–120 cm wide
Habit: rhizomatous or stoloniferous groundcover perennial
Flowers: colourful, long-blooming spikes; summer to fall; good for cutflowers; good for drying
Foliage: evergreen; good fall colour
Hardiness: C–D
Warnings: prone to aphids; not prone to diseases; contact with foliage may irritate skin; *P. capitata* and *P. virginiana* may be invasive (contain to prevent spread)
Expert Advice: An excellent, low-maintenance groundcover that provides blooms well into fall and interesting ornamental seed heads. Mulch tender species for winter and provide snow cover to prevent desiccation.

P

Growing Requirements

Light: sun or shade
Soil: fertile, moist soil; tolerant of poor soils; drought tolerant
Location: erosion control; slopes; banks; mixed borders; rock gardens; woodland gardens
Propagation: seed; division; cuttings
Expert Advice: Seeding is difficult as germination is slow and sporadic. Division is the easiest method of propagation. *Persicaria* does not require division to maintain vigour.

Buying Considerations

Professionals

Popularity: gaining popularity; fast seller in bloom
Availability: generally available as bare root from specialty growers
Size to Sell: sells best in smaller sizes (when blooming) as it matures fast
On the Shelf: high ornamental appeal; rapidly overgrows pot
Shrinkage: low; requires little maintenance

Collectors

Popularity: not generally of interest to collectors

Gardeners

Ease of Growth: very easy to grow
Start with: one small plant for feature plant and several for mass plantings

What to Try First ...

Persicaria affinis, *Persicaria affinis* 'Border Jewel', *Persicaria affinis* 'Darjeeling Red', *Persicaria polymorpha*

On the Market

Persicaria affinis
Pink flowers, aging to burnt-red, in midsummer to fall • Evergreen foliage • 15–25 cm high, 60–90+ cm wide

'Border Jewel' • Pink flowers in early summer to fall • Evergreen foliage • 15–25 cm high, 60–90+ cm wide

'Darjeeling Red' • Pink flowers, aging to burnt-red, in midsummer to fall • Evergreen foliage • 15–25 cm high, 60–90+ cm wide

'Donald Lowndes' • Soft-pink flowers, aging to dark-pink, in midsummer to fall • Evergreen foliage • 15–25 cm high, 60–90+ cm wide

'Kabouter' • Spiked, red flowers in midsummer to fall • Evergreen foliage • 15–25 cm high, 60–90+ cm wide

'Superba' (Dimity) • Soft-pink flowers, aging to pink-red, in midsummer to fall • Evergreen foliage • 8–10 cm high, 45–60+ cm wide

Persicaria amplexicaulis
'Firetail' • Bright-red flowers in midsummer to fall • Not reliably hardy on the Prairies (mulch for winter) • 90–120 cm high, 90–120 cm wide

'Taurus' (Blotau) • Rich rose-red flowers in midsummer to fall • Not reliably hardy on the Prairies (mulch for winter) • 60–75 cm high, 90–120 cm wide

Persicaria bistorta
'Superba' • Soft-pink flowers in summer to early summer • 75–90 cm high, 60–90+ cm wide

Persicaria campanulata
Fragrant, bell-shaped, pink or white flowers in summer • Not reliably hardy on the Prairies (mulch for winter) • 75–100 cm high, 75–100 cm wide

Persicaria campanulata var. *lichiangense*
Clustered, white flowers in summer • 75–100 cm high, 75–100 cm wide

Persicaria microcephala
'Red Dragon' • Small, white flowers in early summer • Burgundy foliage with silver marks • 30–60 cm high, 50–75+ cm wide

Persicaria polymorpha
Cream-white flowers in late spring to early summer • 1–1.5 m high, 75–100 cm wide

Persicaria vacciniifolia
Bright-pink flowers in late summer to fall • Not reliably hardy on the Prairies (mulch for winter) • 10–20 cm high, 45–60+ cm wide

Persicaria virginiana
'Painter's Palette' • Green flowers, turning red, in late summer • Green-and-white foliage with red-brown V-marks • Not reliably hardy on the Prairies (mulch for winter) • 60–100 cm high, 60–100 cm wide

Persicaria virginiana (syn. *P. filiformis*)
Compton's form • Spiked, green-white flowers in summer • Variegated foliage, aging to chocolate-brown-silver • Not reliably hardy on the Prairies (mulch for winter) • 75–90 cm high, 75–90 cm wide

P

Petasites

p. 422

Genus Information

Origin: northern temperate regions
Selected Common Names: butterbur, giant Japanese butterbur, Japanese butterbur
Nomenclature: From the Greek *petasos* (a broad rimmed hat), referring to the leaf shape.

General Features

Height: 75–100 cm
Spread: 90–150 cm
Habit: rapid-spreading, rhizomatous groundcover perennial
Flowers: fragrant; flowers before foliage appears; spring; attractive to bees
Foliage: very large, tropical-looking
Hardiness: C
Warnings: prone to slugs; not prone to diseases; can be an aggressive spreader
Expert Advice: A large, exotic-looking perennial that easily fills wet or moist areas with a single plant.

Growing Requirements

Light: shade
Soil: fertile, moist to wet, organic soil
Location: pond gardens; water edges; wild gardens; woodland gardens; waterside plantings
Propagation: seed; division

Buying Considerations

Professionals
Popularity: relatively unknown foliage plant
Availability: generally available as bare root
Size to Sell: sells best in smaller sizes (when blooming) as it matures fast
On the Shelf: high ornamental appeal; rapidly overgrows pot
Shrinkage: low shrinkage sensitive to underwatering

Collectors
Popularity: not generally of interest to collectors

Gardeners
Ease of Growth: mostly easy to grow but needs close attention to growing conditions
Start with: one small plant for feature plant

What to Try First ...
Petasites japonicus var. *giganteus*, *Petasites japonicus* var. *giganteus* 'Variegatus'

On the Market

Petasites japonicus
Fragrant, yellow-white flowers in early spring • Large, kidney-shaped foliage • 75–100 cm high, 90–150+ cm wide

Petasites japonicus var. *giganteus*
Fragrant, yellow-white flowers in early spring • Large, kidney-shaped foliage • 75–100 cm high, 90–150+ cm wide

'Variegatus' • Fragrant, yellow-white flowers in early spring • White-and-green foliage • 75–100 cm high, 90–150+ cm wide

Petasites japonicus var. *giganteus* f. *purpureus*
Fragrant, pink flowers in early spring • large, purple-green foliage • 75–100 cm high, 90–150+ cm wide

Petrocallis

p. 422

Genus Information

Origin: the mountains of southern Europe and Iran
Selected Common Names: rock beauty
Nomenclature: From the Greek *petra* (rock) and *kallis* (beauty), referring to the plant's location in the wild.

General Features

Height: 2–5 cm high
Spread: 10–15 cm wide
Habit: mat- to cushion-forming alpine perennial
Flowers: vanilla-scented; early summer
Hardiness: C
Warnings: not prone to insects or disease
Expert Advice: One of the first alpines to bloom each spring—beautiful and rare.

Growing Requirements

Light: sun
Soil: well-drained, alkaline soil
Location: wall crevices; raised beds; rock gardens; scree
Propagation: seed; cuttings

Buying Considerations

Professionals
Popularity: relatively unknown
Availability: occasionally available from specialty growers
Size to Sell: sells best in smaller sizes (when blooming)
Shrinkage: low; requires little maintenance

Collectors
Popularity: of interest to alpine collectors—unique, exceptional beauty, rare

Gardeners
Ease of Growth: very easy to grow
Start with: one mature plant for feature plant and several for instant visual effect

What to Try First ...
Petrocallis pyrenaica

On the Market

Petrocallis pyrenaica
Fragrant, white or pink flowers in early
spring • 2–5 cm high, 10–15 cm wide

On the Market

Petrocoptis pyrenaica ssp. *glaucifolia*
(syn. *P. lagascae*)
Pink-purple, sometimes white flowers in
summer • Blue-green foliage • 10–15 cm
high, 15–25 cm wide

Petrocoptis p. 422

Genus Information

Origin: the Pyrenees of Spain
Selected Common Names: none
Nomenclature: Named from the Greek *petra*
(rock) and *koptoto* (cut or break), this plant
is the equal in Greek of *Saxifrage*.
Notes: Related to *Lychnis* and *Silene,* but differing
in the seeds.

General Features

Height: 10–15 cm high
Spread: 15–25 cm wide
Habit: cushion- or tussock-forming mountainous
perennial
Flowers: tiny; summer
Foliage: blue-green
Hardiness: C–D
Warning: not prone to insects or disease

Growing Requirements

Light: sun
Soil: sharply drained, lean soil; avoid winter wet
Location: front of mixed borders; raised beds;
rock gardens; scree
Propagation: seed
Expert Advice: Often blooms the 1st year from
seed.

Buying Considerations

Professionals

Popularity: relatively unknown
Availability: occasionally available from
specialty growers
Size to Sell: sells best in smaller sizes (when
blooming) as it matures fast
Shrinkage: low; requires little maintenance

Collectors

Popularity: of interest to collectors—unique,
rare

Gardeners

Ease of Growth: mostly easy to grow but
needs close attention to growing conditions
Start with: one mature plant for feature plant

What to Try First ...

Petrocoptis pyrenaica ssp. *glaucifolia*

Petrorhagia p. 422

Genus Information

Origin: Eurasia
Selected Common Names: tunic flower
Nomenclature: From the Greek *petra* (rock)
and *rhagas* (fissure).
Notes: Related to *Dianthus* and *Gypsophila*
and is the intermediate between the 2.

General Features

Height: 10–20 cm high
Spread: 20–30 cm wide
Habit: sprawling to mat-forming perennial
Flowers: tiny masses; long blooming period
Foliage: grass-like
Hardiness: C
Warning: not prone to insects or disease

Growing Requirements

Light: sun
Soil: poor to moderately fertile, well-drained soil
Location: mixed borders; rock gardens; cascading
over walls
Propagation: seed (self-sows); cuttings
Expert Advice: Take stem cuttings in summer.

Buying Considerations

Professionals

Popularity: relatively unknown
Availability: occasionally available as finished
product from specialty growers
Size to Sell: sells best in smaller sizes (when
blooming) as it matures fast
On the Shelf: keep stock rotated; deadhead
regularly; rapidly overgrows pot
Shrinkage: low; requires little maintenance

Collectors

Popularity: not generally of interest to
collectors

Gardeners

Ease of Growth: very easy to grow
Start with: one small plant for feature plant
and several for mass plantings

What to Try First ...

Petrorhagia saxifraga, Petrorhagia saxifraga
'Rosette'

P

On the Market

Petrorhagia saxifraga (syn. *Tunica saxifraga*)
White or pink flowers with darker veins in summer • Grassy foliage • 10–20 cm high, 20–30 cm wide

'Pleniflora Rosea' • Double, pink flowers with darker veins in summer • Grass-like foliage • 10–20 cm high, 20–30 cm wide

'Rosette' • Double, dark-pink flowers with darker veins in summer • Grass-like foliage • 10–20 cm high, 20–30 cm wide

Phacelia

p. 422 📷

Genus Information

Origin: North America and South America
Selected Common Names: California bluebell
Nomenclature: From the Greek *phakelos* (a cluster), referring to the arrangement of the flowers.
Notes: Genus includes annuals, biennials and perennials.

General Features

Height: 10–50 cm high
Spread: 10–45 cm wide
Habit: clump-forming, biennial or short-lived mountainous perennial
Flowers: blue; nectar-rich; summer
Foliage: blue-green, campanula-like
Hardiness: C
Warning: not prone to insects or disease; contact with foliage may irritate skin
Expert Advice: A ruggedly hardy plant whose foliage contrasts well with flowers.

Growing Requirements

Light: sun
Soil: sharply drained, neutral to acidic, lean soil; avoid winter wet
Location: mixed borders; scree; wild gardens
Propagation: seed; division

Buying Considerations

Professionals

Popularity: relatively unknown; fast seller in bloom
Availability: occasionally available from specialty growers
Size to Sell: sells best in smaller sizes (when blooming)
On the Shelf: high ornamental appeal; keep stock rotated
Shrinkage: low; requires little maintenance

Collectors

Popularity: of interest to collectors—unique, exceptional beauty, rare

Gardeners

Ease of Growth: very easy to grow
Start with: one small plant for feature plant

What to Try First ...

Phacelia sericea

On the Market

Phacelia sericea
Blue-purple flowers in summer • Silvery, silky-hairy foliage • Native to Alberta Rockies • 10–45 cm high, 10–30 cm wide

Phalaris

p. 422 📷

Genus Information

Origin: northern temperate regions, California, South America and the Mediterranean
Selected Common Names: ribbon grass
Nomenclature: From the classical Greek name for grass.

General Features

Height: 30–90 cm high
Spread: 60–90+ cm wide
Habit: spreading, rhizomatous grass
Flowers: spikelets; midsummer; seed heads aging to tan in fall
Foliage: solid to variegated foliage
Hardiness: C
Warnings: prone to aphids and rust; may be invasive (contain and remove seed heads to prevent spread)
Expert Advice: Shear to keep plant compact and promote fresh growth. Its variegated colour is best in cool weather. Although this plant must be contained in a mixed border to prevent its spread, it does make a wonderful groundcover.

Growing Requirements

Light: sun to p.m. sun
Soil: moist, well-drained soil; tolerant of wide range of soils (including those with high salinity); drought tolerant
Location: alleyways; pond sides; stream sides; banks; early dormancy may occur in hot locations; use as groundcover
Propagation: seed; division

Buying Considerations

Professionals

Popularity: popular foliage plant
Availability: readily available as finished product and bare root
Size to Sell: sells best in smaller sizes as it matures fast
On the Shelf: high ornamental appeal; keep stock rotated; rapidly overgrows pot
Shrinkage: low; requires little maintenance

Collectors

Popularity: not generally of interest to collectors

Gardeners

Ease of Growth: very easy to grow
Start with: one small plant for feature plant

What to Try First ...

Phalaris arundinacea 'Dwarf Garters', *Phalaris arundinacea* 'Feesey', *Phalaris arundinacea* var. *picta*, *Phalaris arundinacea* var. *picta* 'Tricolor'

On the Market

Phalaris arundinacea
'Dwarf Garters' • Green spikelets, followed by creamy seed heads, in summer • White-striped foliage • 30–40 cm high, 60–90+ cm wide

'Feesey' (Strawberries and Cream) • Spikelets turn to pinkish seed heads in summer • Green-and-white-striped foliage • 60–90 cm high, 60–90+ cm wide

'Luteopicta' • Spikelets turn to creamy seed heads in summer • Soft gold-and-green-striped foliage • 60–90 cm high, 60–90+ cm wide

Phalaris arundinacea var. *picta*
Green spikelets, followed by creamy seed heads, in summer • White-striped foliage • 60–90 cm high, 60–90+ cm wide

'Tricolor' • Spikelets turn to pinkish seed heads in summer • Green-and-white-striped foliage • 60–90 cm high, 60–90 cm+ wide

Phlomis p. 422

Genus Information

Origin: Europe and Asia
Selected Common Names: Jerusalem sage
Nomenclature: From the Greek *phlomos* (mullein), referring to the woolly stems and leaves.

General Features

Height: 75–100 cm high
Spread: 60–90 cm wide
Habit: upright, clump-forming perennial
Flowers: showy, tubular blooms in whorls; summer
Foliage: woolly, arrow-shaped; mid-green; withstands wind well
Hardiness: C
Warnings: not prone to insects or disease

Growing Requirements

Light: sun
Soil: fertile, well-drained soil
Location: mixed borders
Propagation: seed; division; cuttings
Expert Advice: Divide frequently to keep vigorous. Take softwood or semi-hardwood cuttings in late spring or early summer.

Buying Considerations

Professionals

Popularity: relatively unknown
Availability: occasionally available from specialty growers
Size to Sell: sells best in smaller sizes (when blooming) as it matures fast
On the Shelf: rapidly overgrows pot
Shrinkage: low; requires little maintenance

Collectors

Popularity: not generally of interest to collectors (but is considered a novelty plant)

Gardeners

Ease of Growth: very easy to grow
Start with: one small plant for feature plant

What to Try First ...

Phlomis tuberosa

On the Market

Phlomis tuberosa
Lilac-purple flowers in summer • 75–100 cm high, 60–90 cm wide

Phlox p. 422

Genus Information

Origin: North America and Siberia
Selected Common Names: phlox
Nomenclature: Named from the Greek *phlox*, the name used for *Lychnis* by Theophrastes.
Notes: An important and popular genus.
Expert Advice: We divide *Phlox* into 3 categories for display and growing information: *Creeping/Moss, Tall Garden* and *Woodland*.

Phlox, Creeping/Moss p. 422

General Features

Height: 2–20 cm high
Spread: 5–45 cm wide
Habit: cushion-forming, low-growing perennial
Flowers: tiny; (some) fragrant; spring to early summer; may rebloom in early fall
Foliage: light- to mid-green; (some) evergreen
Hardiness: A–D
Warnings: prone to downy mildew (control by cutting out affected areas); not prone to insects

Growing Requirements

Light: sun to p.m. sun
Soil: sharply drained, lean, gritty soil; avoid winter wet
Location: alpine gardens; front of mixed borders; rock gardens; wall crevices
Propagation: seed; division
Expert Advice: Hybrid varieties may not come true from seed.

Buying Considerations

Professionals

Popularity: popular, old-fashioned garden standard; fast seller in bloom
Availability: readily available as finished product and bare root from specialty growers
Size to Sell: sells best in smaller sizes (when blooming) as it matures fast
On the Shelf: high ornamental appeal; keep stock rotated; rapidly overgrows pot
Shrinkage: low; sensitive to overwatering; requires little maintenance

Collectors

Popularity: of interest to collectors—unique, rare, exceptional beauty

Gardeners

Ease of Growth: mostly easy to grow but needs close attention to growing conditions
Start with: one small plant for feature plant in rock garden or several for mass plantings

What to Try First ...

Phlox 'Foxy Lady', *Phlox bifida* 'Betty Blake', *Phlox caespitosa*, *Phlox douglasii* 'Crackerjack', *Phlox douglasii* 'Ellie B', *Phlox douglasii* 'George Arends', *Phlox douglasii* 'Red Admiral'

On the Market

P

Phlox
'Boranovice' • Red flowers in spring • 3–5 cm high, 5–10 cm wide
'Foxy Lady' • Magenta-red flowers • 5–8 cm high, 10–20 cm wide
'Rubie's Choice' • Rose flowers in spring • 10–15 cm high, 30–45+ cm wide
'Tiny Bugles' • Bugle-like, pale-blue flowers in spring to early summer • Evergreen, needle-like foliage • 2–5 cm high, 10–15 cm wide

Phlox (P. adsurgens x *P. nivalis)*
'Sunrise' • Peach-pink flowers in late spring to summer • 20–30 cm high, 30–45 cm wide

Phlox alyssifolia
Fragrant, pink to purple, rarely white flowers in late spring to early summer • 5–10 cm high, 20–30 cm wide

Phlox amoena
Pink to purple flowers in late spring to early summer • 10–20 cm high, 20–30 cm wide

Phlox bifida
Fragrant, lavender to white flowers in spring to early summer • Evergreen foliage • 10–20 cm high, 10–20 cm wide
'Betty Blake' • Fragrant, lavender flowers in spring to early summer • Evergreen foliage • 10–20 cm high, 10–20 cm wide
'Colvin's White' • Fragrant, pure white flowers in spring to early summer • Evergreen foliage • 10–20 cm high, 10–20 cm wide
'Starbrite' • Fragrant, pink to white flowers in spring to early summer • Evergreen foliage • 10–20 cm high, 10–20 cm wide

Phlox caespitosa
Fragrant, white to lavender flowers in spring to early summer • 5–10 cm high, 15–25 cm wide

Phlox colubrina
Fragrant, white, rarely pink flowers in spring • 20–40 cm high, 30–50 cm wide

Phlox condensata
(syn. *P. caespitosa* ssp. *condensata*)
Fragrant, soft-pink to white flowers in spring to early summer • 2–4 cm high, 10–15 cm wide

Phlox diffusa
Pink, lilac or white flowers in spring to early summer • 5–15 cm high, 10–20 cm wide

Phlox diffusa ssp. *longistylus*
Lilac, pink or white flowers in spring to early summer • 5–15 cm high, 10–20 cm wide

Phlox douglasii
Red, pink, purple or white flowers in spring to early summer • 5–15 cm high, 30–45+ cm wide
'Boothman's Variety' • Lavender-blue flowers with dark eye in spring to early summer • 5–15 cm high, 30–45+ cm wide
'Crackerjack' • Magenta-red flowers in spring to early summer • Evergreen foliage • 5–15 cm high, 30–45+ cm wide
'Ellie B' • Pink flowers in spring to early summer • Evergreen foliage • 5–15 cm high, 30–45+ cm wide

'George Arends' • Lilac-pink flowers in spring to early summer • Evergreen foliage • 5–15 cm high, 30–45+ cm wide

'Pink Star' • Pink flowers in spring to early summer • Evergreen foliage • 5–15 cm high, 30–45+ cm wide

'Punnett's Pink' • Pink flowers in spring to early summer • Evergreen foliage • 5–15 cm high, 30–45+ cm wide

'Red Admiral' • Carmine-red flowers in spring to early summer • Evergreen foliage • 5–15 cm high, 30–45+ cm wide

'Rose Cushion' • Pale-pink flowers in spring • Evergreen foliage • 5–15 cm high, 30–45+ cm wide

'Rose Queen' • Rose-pink flowers in spring to early summer • Evergreen foliage • 5–15 cm high, 30–45+ cm wide

'Rosea' • Bright rose-pink flowers in spring to early summer • Evergreen foliage • 5–15 cm high, 30–45+ cm wide

'Salmon Jewel' • Salmon-pink flowers in spring to early summer • Evergreen foliage • 5–15 cm high, 30–45+ cm wide

'Tycoon' • Bright-pink flowers in spring to early summer • Evergreen foliage • 5–10 cm high, 30–45+ cm wide

'Waterloo' • Crimson-red flowers in spring to early summer • Evergreen foliage • 5–15 cm high, 30–45+ cm wide

Phlox grayi
Purple to pink, rarely white, flowers in spring • 8–15 cm high, 20–30+ cm wide

Phlox griseola (syn. *P. tumulosa*)
Fragrant, pale-purple or white flowers in spring • Grey-green foliage • 3–10 cm high, 10–15 cm wide

Phlox hendersonii
Pale-blue to white flowers in spring • 3–5 cm high, 10–30 cm wide

Phlox hoodii (syn. *P. canescens*)
Fragrant, lavender to white flowers in early spring • Evergreen, needle-like foliage • 3–6 cm high, 10–30 cm wide

Phlox hoodii var. *muscoides*
(syn. *P. muscoides and bryoides*)
Fragrant, white, pink or lavender flowers in early spring • 2–4 cm high, 10–30 cm wide

Phlox kelseyi
Fragrant, large, white, lilac or lavender flowers in late spring to summer • Needle-like foliage • 7–15 cm high, 10–20 cm wide

'Lemhi Midnight' • Deep violet-blue flowers in late spring to summer • 7–15 cm high, 10–20 cm wide

'Lemhi Purple' • Violet-purple flowers in late spring to summer • Needle-like foliage • 7–15 cm high, 10–20 cm wide

'Rosette' • Fragrant, pink flowers in late spring to summer • Needle-like foliage • 5–10 cm high, 10–20 cm wide

Phlox nana
'Arroya' • Carmine-rose flowers in late spring to summer • 10–25 cm high, 15–30 cm wide

'Tangelo' • Rusty-orange flowers with yellow eye in late spring to summer • 10–25 cm high, 15–30 cm wide

Phlox nana ssp. *ensifolia* (syn. *P. mesoleuca*)
'Santa Fe' • Fragrant, pink flowers in late spring to summer • Needle-like foliage • 10–25 cm high, 15–30 cm wide

Phlox nivalis
'Eco Flirtie Eyes' • Pink flowers with wine-coloured eye in white ring in spring • Evergreen foliage • 20–30 cm high, 30–45 cm wide

Phlox ovata
Purple, pink or rarely white flowers in late spring to summer • Evergreen foliage • 20–50 cm high, 45–60 cm wide

Phlox x *procumbens*
'Miller's Hybrid' • Lavender flowers in spring • 15–25 cm high, 20–30 cm wide

'Millstream' • Pink flowers with darker eye in spring • 15–25 cm high, 20–30 cm wide

'Variegata' **(Folio-variegata)** • Rose-pink flowers in spring • Variegated foliage • 15–25 cm high, 20–30 cm wide

Phlox pulvinata
(syn. *P. caespitosa* ssp. *pulvinata*)
Fragrant, white to lavender flowers in spring to early summer • 3–7 cm high, 10–20 cm wide

Phlox sibirica ssp. *borealis*
(syn. *Phlox borealis*)
Lavender, lilac or white flowers in spring to early summer • 5–10 cm high, 45–60+ cm wide

Phlox subulata
White, pink, red or lilac flowers in spring • Evergreen, needle-like foliage • 5–15 cm high, 30–45+ cm wide

'Apple Blossom' • Apple blossom–pink flowers with dark eye in spring • Evergreen, needle-like foliage • 5–15 cm high, 30–45+ cm wide

P

'Blue Hills' • Steel-blue flowers in spring • Evergreen, needle-like foliage • 5–15 cm high, 30–45+ cm wide

'Case's White' • White flowers in spring • Evergreen, needle-like foliage • 5–15 cm high, 30–45+ cm wide

'Coral Edge' • White flowers with coral edge in spring • Evergreen, needle-like foliage • 5–15 cm high, 30–45+ cm wide

'Coral Eye' • White-pink flowers with coral eye in spring • Evergreen, needle-like foliage • 5–15 cm high, 30–45+ cm wide

'Crimson Beauty' • Crimson-red flowers in spring • Evergreen, needle-like foliage • 5–15 cm high, 30–45+ cm wide

'Emerald Pink' • Soft-pink flowers in spring • Evergreen, needle-like foliage • 5–15 cm high, 30–45+ cm wide

'Firecracker' • Bright-red flowers in spring • Evergreen, needle-like foliage • 5–15 cm high, 30–45+ cm wide

'Laura' • Baby-pink flowers with dark eye in spring • Evergreen, needle-like foliage • 5–15 cm high, 30–45+ cm wide

'Laura Beth' • Rose-pink flowers in spring • Variegated, evergreen, needle-like foliage • 5–15 cm high, 30–45+ cm wide

'Lavender Blush' • Lavender-pink flowers in spring • Evergreen, needle-like foliage • 5–15 cm high, 30–45+ cm wide

'Little Shirley' • Bright mauve-pink flowers in spring • Evergreen, needle-like foliage • 5–15 cm high, 30–45+ cm wide

'Maischnee' (May Snow) • Large, pure white flowers in spring • Evergreen, needle-like foliage • 5–15 cm high, 30–45+ cm wide

'McDaniel's Cushion' (Daniel's Cushion) • Deep pink flowers in spring to early summer • Evergreen, needle-like foliage • 5–15 cm high, 30–45+ cm wide

'Millstream Jupiter' • Lilac flowers in spring • Evergreen, needle-like foliage • 5–15 cm high, 30–45+ cm wide

'Nettleton Variation' • Pink flowers in spring • Variegated, evergreen, needle-like foliage • 5–15 cm high, 30–45+ cm wide

'Oakington Blue Eyes' • Blue flowers in spring • Evergreen, needle-like foliage • 5–15 cm high, 30–45+ cm wide

'Ronsdofer Schone' (Beauty of Ronsdorf) • Dark-pink flowers in spring • Evergreen, needle-like foliage • 5–15 cm high, 30–45+ cm wide

'Schneewittchen' (Snow Maiden) • White flowers in spring • Evergreen, needle-like foliage • 5–15 cm high, 30–45+ cm wide

'Tamaongalei' (Candy Stripe, Tycoon) • Pink-and-white-striped flowers in spring • Evergreen, needle-like foliage • 5–15 cm high, 30–45+ cm wide

'Temiskaming' • Deep-magenta flowers in spring • Evergreen, needle-like foliage • 5–15 cm high, 30–45+ cm wide

'Whiteout' • White flowers in spring • Evergreen, needle-like foliage • 5–15 cm high, 30–45+ cm wide

'Winifred' (Winifred Bevington) • Magenta-pink flowers in spring • Evergreen, needle-like foliage • 5–15 cm high, 30–45+ cm wide

Phlox subulata ssp. *brittonii* (syn. *P. douglasii* 'Brittonia') Medium-pink flowers in spring to early summer • Evergreen foliage • 5–15 cm high, 30–45+ cm wide

Phlox subulata ssp. *brittonii* (syn. *P. douglasii* 'Brittonii Rosea') **'Rosea'** • Lacy, notched, lavender flowers in spring • Evergreen foliage • 5–15 cm high, 30–45+ cm wide

Phlox subulata silenefolia White flowers in spring • Evergreen, needle-like foliage • 5–15 cm high, 30–45+ cm wide

Phlox, Tall Garden   p. 422

General Features

Height: 30–150 cm high
Spread: 20–90 cm wide
Habit: upright, clump-forming perennial; may require staking
Flowers: large, showy blooms in clusters; fragrant; midsummer; good cutflower; deadhead to promote blooming
Foliage: light to mid-green
Hardiness: C–D
Warnings: prone to powdery mildew; not prone to insects
Expert Advice: Although some varieties have been bred for improved powdery mildew resistance, no varieties are completely resistant. To help prevent this problem keep soil evenly moist, do not water foliage or crowd plants and plant in an area with good air circulation.

Growing Requirements

Light: sun to p.m. sun
Soil: fertile, moist, well-drained soil; *P. glaberrima* prefers fertile, moist, well-drained, neutral to acidic soil
Location: mixed borders; cutting gardens
Propagation: seed; division

P

Expert Advice: Hybrid varieties may not come true from seed. *P. paniculata* requires frequent division, as the centres tend to die out.

Buying Considerations

Professionals

Popularity: popular, old-fashioned garden standard; fast seller in bloom
Availability: readily available as finished product and bare root
Size to Sell: sells best in smaller sizes (when blooming) as it matures fast
On the Shelf: keep stock rotated; deadhead regularly; rapidly overgrows pot
Shrinkage: low; sensitive to overwatering

Collectors

Popularity: of interest to collectors—unique, rare, exceptional beauty

Gardeners

Ease of Growth: mostly easy to grow but needs close attention to growing conditions
Start with: one small plant for feature plant and several for mass plantings

What to Try First ...

Phlox carolina 'Bill Baker', *Phlox carolina* 'Miss Lingard', *Phlox maculata* 'Natascha', *Phlox maculata* 'Rosalinde', *Phlox paniculata* 'Darwin's Joyce', *Phlox paniculata* 'David', *Phlox paniculata* 'Goldmine', *Phlox paniculata* 'Juliet', *Phlox paniculata* 'Laura', *Phlox paniculata* 'Miss Holland', *Phlox paniculata* 'Miss Pepper', *Phlox paniculata* 'Mount Fujii', *Phlox paniculata* 'Popeye', *Phlox paniculata* 'Prince of Orange', *Phlox paniculata* 'Red Riding Hood', *Phlox paniculata* 'Silvermine'

On the Market

Phlox x *arendsii*
  'Lilac Star' • Fragrant, lilac-purple flowers in summer • 35–45 cm high, 30–45 cm wide
  'Ping Pong' • Fragrant, rose flowers with dark-rose eye in summer • 35–45 cm high, 30–45 cm wide
  'Pink Attraction' • Fragrant, soft-pink flowers in summer • 30–40 cm high, 30–45 cm wide
  'Purple Star' • Fragrant, pink-purple flowers in summer • 35–45 cm high, 30–45 cm wide
  'Susanne' • White flowers with red eye in late spring to late summer • 40–60 cm high, 30–45 cm wide

Spring Pearl Series
  'Miss Jill' • Fragrant, cream flowers with tiny, pink eye in summer • 40–55 cm high, 30–45 cm wide
  'Miss Jo-Ellen' • Fragrant, white flowers with dark-pink eye in summer • 30–55 cm high, 30–45 cm wide
  'Miss Karen' • Fragrant, dark-rose flowers with red eye in summer • 40–55 cm high, 30–45 cm wide
  'Miss Margie' • Fragrant, lilac-blue flowers in summer • 30–55 cm high, 30–45 cm wide
  'Miss Mary' • Fragrant, red flowers in summer • 40–55 cm high, 30–45 cm wide
  'Miss Wilma' • Fragrant, lilac-blue flowers with white eye in summer • 45–50 cm high, 30–45 cm wide

Phlox carolina
  'Bill Baker' • Pink flowers with lighter eye in summer • Mildew resistant • 40–50 cm high, 20–30 cm wide
  'Magnificence' • Carmine-pink flowers in summer • 60–90 cm high, 30–45 cm wide
  'Miss Lingard' • Fragrant, white flowers in summer • Mildew resistant • 60–90 cm high, 30–45 cm wide

Phlox glaberrima
Purple to pink, rarely white, flowers in late spring to early summer • Fertile, moist, well-drained, neutral to acidic soil • 60–90 cm high, 25–45 cm wide
  'Interior' • Rose to red-purple flowers in late spring to early summer • Fertile, moist, well-drained, neutral to acidic soil • 30–45 cm high, 25–35 cm wide

Phlox maculata
  'Alpha' • Fragrant, lilac-pink flowers with dark eye in summer • 60–90 cm high, 45–60 cm wide
  'Delta' • Fragrant, lavender-pink flowers in summer • 60–90 cm high, 45–60 cm wide
  'Natascha' • Fragrant, white and pink, striped flowers in summer • Mildew resistant • 45–60 cm high, 30–45 cm wide
  'Omega' • Fragrant, white flowers with violet eye in summer • 60–90 cm high, 45–60 cm wide
  'Rosalinde' • Fragrant, deep rose-pink flowers in summer • Mildew resistant • 60–90 cm high, 45–60 cm wide

Phlox paniculata
Fragrant white to lilac flowers in midsummer • 60–90 cm high, 45–60 cm wide

P

'Ada Blackjack' • Fragrant, purple-mauve flowers in midsummer • 90–100 cm high, 60–75 cm wide

'Amethyst' • Fragrant, violet flowers in midsummer • 90–120 cm high, 45–60 cm wide

'Becky Towe' • Fragrant, salmon-carmine flowers with magenta eye in midsummer • Gold-edged, variegated foliage • 50–75 cm high, 45–60 cm wide

'Blue Boy' • Fragrant, mauve-blue flowers with white eye in midsummer • 75–100 cm high, 60 cm wide

'Blue Paradise' • Fragrant, violet-blue flowers with dark eye in midsummer • 75–100 cm high, 45–60 cm wide

'Brigadier' • Fragrant, salmon-orange flowers with red eye in midsummer • Deep-green foliage • 60–90 cm high, 60 cm wide

'Bright Eyes' • Fragrant, pale-pink flowers with red eye in midsummer • 60–75 cm high, 60 cm wide

'Caroline van den Berg' • Fragrant, lilac-blue flowers in midsummer • 75–100 cm high, 45–60 cm wide

'Cinderella' • Fragrant, pink flowers in midsummer • 60–75 cm high, 60 cm wide

'Creme de Menthe' • Fragrant, white flowers with pink centre in midsummer • Variegated foliage • 40–60 cm high, 60 cm wide

'Darwin's Joyce' • Fragrant, light-pink flowers with dark-pink eye in midsummer • Dark-green foliage with wide, creamy edges • Mildew resistant • 75–95 cm high, 45–60 cm wide

'David' • Fragrant, huge, pure white flowers in midsummer • Mildew resistant • 75–100 cm high, 45–60 cm wide

'Dodo Hanbury Forbes' • Fragrant, clear pink flowers with red eye in midsummer • 75–90 cm high, 60 cm wide

'Dusterlohe' (Dusky Flame, Nicky) • Fragrant, blue-violet flowers in midsummer • 60–70 cm high, 60 cm wide

'Eclaireur' • Fragrant, purple flowers with pink eye in midsummer • 60–75 cm high, 45–60 cm wide

'Eden's Crush' • Fragrant, pink flowers with dark eye in midsummer • 60–70 cm high, 45–60 cm wide

'Eva Cullum' • Fragrant, clear-pink flowers with red eye in midsummer • 60–75 cm high, 60 cm wide

'Eva Foerster' • Fragrant, salmon-pink flowers with white eye in midsummer • 60–75 cm high, 60 cm wide

'Fairest One' • Fragrant, soft-pink flowers in midsummer • 60 cm high, 60 cm wide

'Flamingo' • Fragrant, flamingo-pink flowers with red eye in midsummer • 60–90 cm high, 60 cm wide

'Franz Schubert' • Fragrant, lilac-pink flowers with darker eye in midsummer • 75–100 cm high, 45–60 cm wide

'Goldmine' • Fragrant, deep-pink flowers in summer • Gold-edged, green foliage • Mildew resistant • 50–75 cm high, 45–60 cm wide

'Harlequin' • Fragrant, reddish-purple flowers in midsummer • Variegated foliage • 50–75 cm high, 45–60 cm wide

'Ice Cap' • Fragrant, white flowers in midsummer • 60–90 cm high, 45–60 cm wide

'Jules Sandeau' • Fragrant, pure pink flowers in midsummer • 40–60 cm high, 40–50 cm wide

'Juliet' • Fragrant, pink flowers with white eye in midsummer • Mildew resistant • 60 cm high, 45–60 cm wide

'Kirmeslaendler' • Fragrant, white flowers with red eye in midsummer • 60–70 cm high, 60 cm wide

'Laura' • Fragrant, purple flowers with white eye in midsummer • Mildew resistant • 75–90 cm high, 45–60 cm wide

'Lichtspel' • Fragrant, rose-pink flowers in midsummer • 60 cm high, 60 cm wide

'Little Boy' • Fragrant, mauve-blue flowers with white eye in midsummer • 40–75 cm high, 30–60 cm wide

'Little Princess' • Fragrant, pink flowers with white eye in midsummer • 30–50 cm high, 30–45 cm wide

'Lizzy' • Fragrant, bright-pink flowers with white eye in midsummer • 40–50 cm high, 45–60 cm wide

'Miss Candy' • Fragrant, pink flowers with darker eye in midsummer • 75–90 cm high, 45–60 cm wide

'Miss Holland' • Fragrant, white flowers with red eye in midsummer • Mildew resistant • 60–75 cm high, 45–60 cm wide

P

'Miss Kelly' • Fragrant, lilac-pink flowers in midsummer • 90–120 cm high, 60 cm wide

'Miss Marple' • Fragrant, white flowers with pink-red eye in midsummer • 75–90 cm high, 45–60 cm wide

'Miss Pepper' • Fragrant, pale-pink flowers with dark eye in midsummer • Dark-green foliage • Mildew resistant • 75–90 cm high, 60 cm wide

'Miss Universe' • Fragrant, white flowers in midsummer • 75–100 cm high, 60 cm wide

'Miss Violet' • Fragrant, violet flowers in midsummer • 75–90 cm high, 45–60 cm wide

'Moosejaw' • Fragrant, mauve-pink flowers in midsummer • 75–90 cm high, 60 cm wide

'Morris Bero' • Fragrant, rose-pink flowers in midsummer • 40–45 cm high, 40–45 cm wide

'Mount Fuji' (Mount Fujiyama) • Fragrant, pure white flowers in midsummer • Mildew resistant • 60–75 cm high, 60 cm wide

'Natural Feelings' • Fragrant, pink and green rosebud-like bracts with virtually no petals in midsummer • 50–70 cm high, 45–60 cm wide

'Nicky' • Fragrant, purple flowers with pale centres in midsummer • 75–90 cm high, 45–60 cm wide

'Norah Leigh' • Fragrant, pale-lilac flowers in midsummer • Variegated foliage • 75–90 cm high, 45–60 cm wide

'Pax' • Fragrant, white flowers in midsummer • 60 cm high, 60 cm wide

'Pinafore Pink' • Fragrant, pink flowers with red eye in midsummer • 40–45 cm high, 60 cm wide

'Popeye' • Fragrant, pale-pink flowers with darker eye in midsummer • Mildew resistant • 75–90 cm high, 45–60 cm wide

'Prime Minister' • Fragrant, white flowers with red eye in midsummer • 75–100 cm high, 60 cm wide

'Prince of Orange' (Orange Perfection) • Fragrant, orange-scarlet flowers in midsummer • Mildew resistant • 75–100 cm high, 60 cm wide

'Red Eyes' • Fragrant, pink flowers with red eye in midsummer • 75–90 cm high, 45–60 cm wide

'Red Feelings' • Fragrant, ruby-red bracts in midsummer • 50–70 cm high, 45–60 cm wide

'Red Riding Hood' • Fragrant, cherry-red flowers in midsummer • Dark-green foliage • Mildew resistant • 45–75 cm high, 45–60 cm wide

'Rembrandt' • Fragrant, pure white flowers in midsummer • 60–75 cm high, 45–60 cm wide

'San Antonio' • Fragrant, purple-red flowers in midsummer • 60–80 cm high, 45–60 cm wide

'Silvermine' • Fragrant, white flowers in midsummer • Gold-edged, variegated foliage • Mildew resistant • 60–80 cm high, 45–60 cm wide

'Speed Limit 45' • Fragrant, soft-pink flowers with darker eye in midsummer • 80–90 cm high, 45–60 cm wide

'Starfire' • Fragrant, crimson-red flowers in midsummer • 75–90 cm high, 75–90 cm wide

'Tenor' • Fragrant, rose-red flowers in midsummer • 45–60 cm high, 45 cm wide

'The King' • Fragrant, blue-purple flowers in midsummer • 60–85 cm high, 60 cm wide

'Uspech' • Fragrant, blue-mauve flowers with white eye in midsummer • 45–60 cm high, 45 cm wide

'Village Joy' • Fragrant, bright-pink flowers in midsummer • 60 cm high, 60 cm wide

'Vintage Wine' • Fragrant, wine-red flowers in midsummer • 60–80 cm high, 60 cm wide

'Wilhelm Kesselring' • Fragrant, violet-red flowers with white eye in midsummer • 60–80 cm high, 60 cm wide

'Windsor' • Fragrant, reddish-pink flowers in midsummer • 60–75 cm high, 60 cm wide

Flame Series

'Lilac Flame' • Fragrant, lilac flowers in midsummer • 25–30 cm high, 30 cm wide

'Pink Flame' • Fragrant, pink flowers with white eye in midsummer • 25–30 cm high, 30 cm wide

'Purple Flame' • Fragrant, purple flowers in midsummer • 25–30 cm high, 30 cm wide

P

Phlox, Woodland p. 422

General Features
Height: 10–90 cm high
Spread: 20–60 cm wide
Habit: upright, clump-forming to creeping perennial
Flowers: (many) fragrant; spring to summer
Foliage: light- to mid-green; semi-evergreen to evergreen
Hardiness: B–C
Warnings: prone to powdery mildew; not prone to insects
Expert Advice: Woodland types of *Phlox* make excellent groundcovers and benefit from shearing after blooming to keep them from looking straggly and unkempt. They may rebloom in fall.

Growing Requirements
Light: shade to a.m. sun
Soil: fertile, moist, well-drained, neutral to acidic soil
Location: shady mixed borders; woodland gardens; under trees
Propagation: seed; division; layering
Expert Advice: Hybrid varieties may not come true from seed. Cutting out rooted sections is a simple method of increasing stock.

Buying Considerations

Professionals
Popularity: gaining popularity; fast seller in bloom; has new varieties
Availability: readily available as bare root from specialty growers
Size to Sell: sells best in smaller sizes (when blooming) as it matures fast
On the Shelf: deadhead regularly; rapidly overgrows pot
Shrinkage: low; sensitive to overwatering

Collectors
Popularity: not generally of interest to collectors

Gardeners
Ease of Growth: very easy to grow
Start with: several for mass plantings

What to Try First ...
Phlox divaricata 'Blue Perfume', *Phlox divaricata* 'Clouds of Perfume', *Phlox divaricata* 'Sweet Lilac', *Phlox stolonifera* 'Pink Ridge', *Phlox stolonifera* 'Sherwood Purple'

On the Market

Phlox divaricata
Fragrant, violet, lavender or white flowers in spring to early summer • Semi-evergreen foliage • 20–40 cm high, 30–45+ cm wide

'Blue Perfume' • Fragrant, blue-violet flowers in spring to early summer • Semi-evergreen foliage • 20–40 cm high, 30–45+ cm wide

'Clouds of Perfume' • Fragrant, lilac-blue flowers in spring to early summer • Semi-evergreen foliage • 20–40 cm high, 30–45+ cm wide

'Eco Texas Purple' • Fragrant, violet-purple flowers with red-violet eye in spring to early summer • Semi-evergreen foliage • 20–40 cm high, 30–45+ cm wide

'Fuller's White' • Fragrant, white flowers with yellow eye in spring to early summer • Semi-evergreen foliage • 15–30 cm high, 30–45+ cm wide

'London Grove' • Fragrant, deep-blue flowers in spring to early summer • Semi-evergreen foliage • 20–40 cm high, 30–45+ cm wide

'Louisiana Blue' • Fragrant, dark-blue flowers in spring to early summer • Semi-evergreen foliage • 20–40 cm high, 30–45+ cm wide

'Montrose Tricolor' • Fragrant, blue flowers in spring to early summer • White, green and pink foliage • 15–30 cm high, 30–45+ cm wide

'Nell' • Fragrant, blue flowers with white eye in spring to early summer • Semi-evergreen foliage • 20–40 cm high, 30–45+ cm wide

'Plum Perfect' • Fragrant, plum-purple flowers with darker eye in spring to early summer • Semi-evergreen foliage • 20–40 cm high, 30–45+ cm wide

'Sweet Lilac' • Fragrant, lilac flowers in spring to early summer • Semi-evergreen foliage • 20–40 cm high, 30–45+ cm wide

'White Perfume' • Fragrant, white flowers in spring to early summer • Semi-evergreen foliage • 20–40 cm high, 30–45+ cm wide

Phlox divaricata ssp. *laphamii*
Fragrant, lilac to violet-blue flowers in spring to early summer • Semi-evergreen foliage • 20–40 cm high, 30–45+ cm wide

'Chattahoochee' • Lavender-blue flowers with maroon eye in summer • Semi-evergreen foliage • 10–20 cm high, 30–45+ cm wide

P

Phlox stolonifera

Violet to lavender flowers in late spring to summer • Evergreen foliage • 15–20 cm high, 30–45+ cm wide

'Blue Ridge' • Blue flowers in late spring to summer • Evergreen foliage • 15–25 cm high, 30–45+ cm wide

'Bruce's White' • White flowers with yellow eye in late spring to summer • Evergreen foliage • 15–25 cm high, 30–45+ cm wide

'Home Fires' • Deep-pink flowers in late spring to summer • Evergreen foliage • 15–25 cm high, 30–45+ cm wide

'Pink Ridge' • Pink flowers in late spring to summer • Evergreen foliage • 15–25 cm high, 30–45+ cm wide

'Sherwood Purple' • Deep purple-blue flowers in late spring to summer • Evergreen foliage • 15–20 cm high, 30–45+ cm wide

variegated • Pink flowers in late spring to summer • Variegated foliage • 15–25 cm high, 30–45+ cm wide

Phragmites   p. 423

Genus Information

Origin: temperate and tropical regions
Selected Common Names: giant reed
Nomenclature: From the Greek *phragma* (fence or screen), in reference to the screening effect of many of these plants growing together.
Notes: A genus of some 4 species.

General Features

Height: 2–3 m high
Spread: 60+ cm wide
Habit: spreading, semi-aquatic perennial
Flowers: plumes; late summer; good for cutflowers; good for drying
Foliage: flat, linear foliage; good fall colour; slow to emerge in spring
Hardiness: B
Warnings: prone to rust; not prone to insects; aggressive spreader (keep contained to prevent spread)
Expert Advice: Grow in a large container submerged in water or ground to restrict spread.

Growing Requirements

Light: sun
Soil: deep, fertile, moist to wet soil
Location: pond gardens; water gardens; waterside plantings
Propagation: division

Buying Considerations

Professionals

Popularity: relatively unknown foliage plant
Availability: occasionally available as finished product and bare root from specialty growers
Size to Sell: sells best in smaller sizes as it matures fast
On the Shelf: high ornamental appeal; rapidly overgrows pot
Shrinkage: low; requires little maintenance

Collectors

Popularity: of interest to water gardening enthusiasts

Gardeners

Ease of Growth: mostly easy to grow
Start with: one small plant for feature plant

What to Try First ...

Phragmites australis 'Variegatus'

On the Market

Phragmites australis
'Variegatus' • Brownish-purple plumes in late summer to fall • Golden-yellow-striped foliage that fade almost to white • 2–3 m high, 60+ cm wide

Phuopsis   p. 423

Genus Information

Origin: Caucasus region of Russia
Selected Common Names: crosswort
Nomenclature: Unknown
Notes: One species in this genus; was formerly with *Crucianella*.

General Features

Height: 15–20 cm high
Spread: 30–45 cm wide
Habit: mat-forming, stem-rooting groundcover perennial
Flowers: mounds of tubular, funnel-shaped blooms; unpleasant smell; summer
Foliage: narrow; pale-green; scented when crushed
Hardiness: D
Warnings: prone to aphids; not prone to diseases
Expert Advice: Cut back after flowering to keep plant compact and encourage fresh growth.

Growing Requirements

Light: sun to p.m. sun
Soil: fertile, gritty, moist, well-drained soil
Location: front of border; banks; rock gardens
Propagation: seed; division; cuttings
Expert Advice: Taking stem-tip cuttings in spring to early summer is the easiest propagation method.

P

Buying Considerations

Professionals
Popularity: relatively unknown
Availability: occasionally available from specialty growers
Size to Sell: sells best in smaller sizes (when blooming) as it matures fast
On the Shelf: rapidly overgrows pot
Shrinkage: low; requires little maintenance

Collectors
Popularity: not generally of interest to collectors

Gardeners
Ease of Growth: very easy to grow
Start with: many for mass planting

What to Try First ...
Phuopsis stylosa

On the Market

Phuopsis stylosa
Pink flowers in summer • 15–20 cm high, 30–45+ cm wide

x *Phylliopsis*　　　p. 423 📷

Genus Information
Origin: man-made cross
Selected Common Names: unknown
Nomenclature: Hybrid of *Phyllodoce* and *Kalmiopsis*.
Notes: An intergeneric cross between *Phyllodoce* and *Kalmiopsis*.

General Features
Height: 20–30 cm high
Spread: 20–30 cm wide
Habit: dwarf, upright shrub
Flowers: pink; bell-shaped; borne in clusters; late spring and intermittently through summer
Foliage: glossy, needle-like; evergreen
Hardiness: C
Warnings: not prone to insects or disease
Expert Advice: An underused plant that tolerates warm, dry summers. A nice substitute for *Daphne*. Can be expensive.

Growing Requirements
Light: shade to a.m. sun
Soil: cool, fertile, moist, organic, acidic soil
Location: rock gardens
Propagation: cuttings
Expert Advice: Provide cuttings with gentle bottom heat.

Buying Considerations

Professionals
Popularity: relatively unknown; fast seller in bloom
Availability: occasionally available from specialty growers
Size to Sell: sells best in mature sizes (when blooming); matures slowly
On the Shelf: high ornamental appeal
Shrinkage: low; requires little maintenance

Collectors
Popularity: of interest to collectors—unique, exceptional beauty, rare

Gardeners
Ease of Growth: mostly easy to grow but needs close attention to growing conditions
Start with: one mature plant for feature plant and instant visual effect

What to Try First ...
x *Phylliopsis* 'Sugar Plum'

On the Market

x *Phylliopsis*
　'**Sugar Plum**' • Pink flowers in late spring • Dark, needle-like evergreen foliage • 20–30 cm high, 20–30 cm wide

x *Phylliopsis hillieri*
　'**Pinocchio**' • Red-purple flowers in spring • Dark, needle-like evergreen foliage • 20–30 cm high, 20–30 cm wide

Phyllodoce　　　p. 423 📷

Genus Information
Origin: arctic and alpine regions of the Northern Hemisphere
Selected Common Names: mountain heather
Nomenclature: Named for the sea nymph of Greek mythology who was one of Cyrene's attendants.
Notes: A genus of some 8 species.

General Features
Height: 10–30 cm high
Spread: 20–45 cm wide
Habit: spreading or upright, heather-like subshrub
Flowers: bell-, pitcher-or urn-shaped; borne in clusters or solitary; late spring to early summer
Foliage: narrow, linear; leathery; evergreen
Hardiness: B
Warnings: some species will not bloom at lower elevations (but still an attractive plant)
Expert Advice: *P. empetriformis* is native to the Rocky Mountains.

Growing Requirements

Light: shade to a.m. sun
Soil: cool, fertile, moist, organic, well-drained, acidic soil
Location: rock gardens
Propagation: seed; cuttings
Expert Advice: Germinate seeds at 6–12°C. Take softwood or semi-ripe cuttings in summer. Provide cuttings with gentle bottom heat. Use of a rooting hormone is advised.

Buying Considerations

Professionals

Popularity: relatively unknown
Availability: occasionally available from specialty growers
Size to Sell: sells best in mature sizes (when blooming); matures slowly
On the Shelf: high ornamental appeal
Shrinkage: low; requires little maintenance

Collectors

Popularity: of interest to alpine collectors— unique, exceptional beauty, variety

Gardeners

Ease of Growth: mostly easy to grow but requires close attention to growing conditions
Start with: one mature plant for feature plant

What to Try First ...

Phyllodoce aleutica ssp. *glanduliflora*, *Phyllodoce caerulea*, *Phyllodoce empetriformis*, *Phyllodoce* x *intermedia* 'Drummondii'

On the Market

***Phyllodoce aleutica* ssp. *glanduliflora* (syn. *P. glanduliflora*)**
Fragrant, cream flowers in late spring to early summer • Dark-green evergreen foliage • 10–30 cm high, 20–30 cm wide
'Flora Slack' • White flowers in late spring to early summer • Evergreen foliage • 10–30 cm high, 20–30 cm wide

Phyllodoce caerulea
Lilac to pink-purple flowers in late spring to early summer • Glossy, dark-green evergreen foliage • 15–30 cm high, 25–40 cm wide

Phyllodoce empetriformis
Pink to rose-purple flowers in late spring to early summer • Evergreen foliage • 15–40 cm high, 30–45 cm wide

Phyllodoce* x *intermedia
'Drummondii' • Red-purple flowers in late spring to early summer • Evergreen foliage • 15–25 cm high, 20–35 cm wide

Physalis   p. 423

Genus Information

Origin: temperate regions and the Americas
Selected Common Names: Chinese lantern
Nomenclature: From the Greek *physa* (bladder), referring to the blown-up calyx.
Notes: This plant is a member of the *Solanaceae* (tomato) family and is related to cape gooseberry and tomatillo.

General Features

Height: 60–75 cm high
Spread: 60–90 cm wide
Habit: vigorous, spreading, rhizomatous groundcover perennial
Flowers: nodding, bell-shaped blooms; summer; papery seed pods; good for drying
Foliage: triangular to diamond-shaped
Hardiness: B
Warnings: prone to aphids and spider mites; not prone to diseases; contact with foliage may irritate skin; invasive (keep contained to prevent spread and deadhead to prevent self-seeding)
Expert Advice: Grown for its unusual and striking orange seed pods which are used in dried flower arrangements. A useful plant for difficult areas where its rapidly spreading habit is contained.

Growing Requirements

Light: sun
Soil: poor to moderately fertile, dry soil
Location: difficult areas; alleyways; slopes; along driveways
Propagation: seed (self-sows readily); division

Buying Considerations

Professionals

Popularity: garden standard; fast seller in pod
Availability: readily available as finished product
Size to Sell: sells best in smaller sizes as it matures fast
On the Shelf: rapidly overgrows pot
Shrinkage: low; requires little maintenance

P

Collectors

Popularity: not generally of interest to collectors

Gardeners

Ease of Growth: very easy to grow
Start with: one small plant for feature plant

What to Try First ...

Physalis alkekengi var. *franchettii*

On the Market

Physalis alkekengi
Star-shaped, cream flowers in midsummer followed by green seed pods turning orange as they mature • 60–75 cm high, 60–90+ cm wide

Physalis alkekengi var. *franchettii*
Star-shaped, cream flowers in midsummer followed by orange berries • 60–75 cm high, 60–90+ cm wide

What to Try First ...
Physaria alpina, Physaria didymocarpa

On the Market

Physaria alpina
Yellow to orange flowers in spring • Silver-grey foliage • 10–15 cm high, 10–15 cm wide

Physaria didymocarpa
Yellow flowers in summer • Silver-grey foliage • 8–10 cm high, 10–15 cm wide

Physaria
p. 423

Genus Information

Origin: western North America
Selected Common Names: twin pod, bladder pod
Nomenclature: From the Greek *physa* (bladder), in reference to the fruits.
Notes: A genus of some 14 species.

General Features

Height: 8–15 cm high
Spread: 10–15 cm wide
Habit: short-lived, tap-rooted perennial
Flowers: borne on spikes; spring to summer
Foliage: compact, silvery; rosette-forming
Hardiness: C
Warnings: not prone to insects or disease
Expert Advice: Produces interesting bladder-like, inflated seed pods. A good rockery plant for dry areas.

Growing Requirements

Light: sun
Soil: sharply drained, lean soil; avoid winter wet
Location: raised beds; rock gardens; scree
Propagation: seed; division
Expert Advice: Divide in spring. Separate and replant rosettes.

Buying Considerations

Professionals

Popularity: relatively unknown
Availability: occasionally available from specialty growers
Size to Sell: sells best in smaller sizes as it matures fast
On the Shelf: high ornamental appeal when pods are on the plant; keep stock rotated; rapidly overgrows pot
Shrinkage: low; requires little maintenance

Collectors

Popularity: not generally of interest to collectors

Gardeners

Ease of Growth: very easy to grow
Start with: one small plant for feature plant

Physoplexis
p. 423

Genus Information

Origin: Europe
Selected Common Names: devil's claw
Nomenclature: From the Greek *physa* (bladder) and *plexis* (weaving), referring to the joining of the corolla.
Notes: Formerly in the genus *Phyteuma*.

General Features

Height: 5–10 cm high
Spread: 5–15 cm wide
Habit: tuft-forming, alpine perennial
Flowers: huge flowers for a small plant; large, unusual, pointed, claw-like; late summer; goes dormant after flowering
Foliage: basal tufts; heart-shaped, toothed
Hardiness: C–D
Warnings: not prone to insects or diseases
Expert Advice: It is extremely rare and best in an alpine garden.

Growing Requirements

Light: sun
Soil: sharply drained, lean, alkaline soil; avoid winter wet
Location: rock crevices; scree; tufa
Propagation: seed; division; cuttings
Expert Advice: Take basal cuttings in summer.

Buying Considerations

Professionals

Popularity: relatively unknown
Availability: occasionally available from specialty growers
Size to Sell: sells best in mature sizes (when blooming) as it matures slowly
Shrinkage: low; requires little maintenance

Collectors

Popularity: of interest to collectors—unique, exceptional beauty, rare

Gardeners

Ease of Growth: mostly easy to grow but needs close attention to growing conditions
Start with: one mature plant for feature plant

P

What to Try First ...
Physoplexis comosa

On the Market

Physoplexis comosa
Pink-lilac flowers with black-violet tips in late summer • 5–8 cm high, 5–10 cm wide

Physostegia

p. 423

Genus Information

Origin: North America
Selected Common Names: false dragonhead, false lion's heart, obedient plant
Nomenclature: From the Greek *physa* (bladder) and *stege* (a covering).
Notes: Obedient plant, the common name, is so-called because whatever direction the flowers are physically turned on the plant, they will stay that way.

General Features

Height: 45–100 cm high
Spread: 45–60 cm wide
Habit: upright, rhizomatous perennial
Flowers: tubular blooms borne on stalks; midsummer to fall; good for cutflowers
Foliage: mid-green; toothed
Hardiness: B–C
Warnings: prone to powdery mildew and aphids; may be invasive in warm climates (contain and deadhead to prevent spread); *P. viginiana* 'Miss Manners' not as aggressive
Expert Advice: The stiff stalks of this plant stand up well to wind and make a nice addition to a cutting garden.

Growing Requirements

Light: sun to p.m. sun; tolerates more sun with good soil moisture
Soil: fertile, moist soil; tolerates dry soil but restricts growth
Location: mixed borders; cutting gardens
Propagation: seed; division
Expert Advice: Divide frequently to keep vigorous.

Buying Considerations

Professionals
Popularity: garden standard; sells well in bloom
Availability: readily available as finished product and bare root
Size to Sell: sells best in smaller sizes (when blooming) as it matures fast
On the Shelf: rapidly overgrows pot
Shrinkage: low; requires little maintenance

Collectors
Popularity: not generally of interest to collectors

Gardeners
Ease of Growth: very easy to grow
Start with: one small plant for feature plant

What to Try First ...
Physostegia virginiana 'Miss Manners',
Physostegia virginiana 'Summer Snow',
Physostegia virginiana 'Vivid', *Physostegia virginiana* ssp. *speciosa* 'Bouquet Rose',
Physostegia virginiana ssp. *speciosa* 'Variegata'

On the Market

Physostegia virginiana
Lilac to purple-pink flowers in midsummer to fall • Dark-green, willowy foliage • 60–100 cm high, 45–60 cm wide

'Alba' • White flowers in midsummer to fall • Dark-green, willowy foliage • 60–90 cm high, 45–60 cm wide

'Crown of Snow' (Schneekrone) • Spiked, white flowers in midsummer to fall • 50–75 cm high, 45–60 cm wide

'Miss Manners' • White flowers in midsummer to fall • Less agressive than other *Physostegia* • 45–60 cm high, 45–60 cm wide

'Red Beauty' • Deep rose-red flowers in midsummer to fall • 60–90 cm high, 45–60 cm wide

'Rosea' • Pink flowers in midsummer to fall • Dark-green, willow foliage • 45–60 cm high, 45–60 cm wide

'Summer Snow' (Snow Queen) • White flowers in midsummer to fall • 60–90 cm high, 45–60 cm wide

'Vivid' • Deep pink-purple flowers in midsummer to fall • 45–60 cm high, 45–60 cm wide

Physostegia virginiana ssp. *speciosa*
'Bouquet Rose' • Bright-pink flowers in midsummer to fall • 60–75 cm high, 45–60 cm wide

'Variegata' • Magenta-pink flowers in midsummer to fall • White-edged, greyish foliage • 60–90 cm high, 45–60 cm wide

Phyteuma

p. 423

Genus Information

Origin: Europe and Asia
Selected Common Names: horned rampion, rampion, weakstem rampion
Nomenclature: From the name used by Dioscorides for an obscure plant, meaning "the plant."

P

General Features

Height: 10–45 cm high
Spread: 10–20 cm wide
Habit: tuft- or clump-forming perennial
Flowers: unusual, spiked blooms borne in rounded clusters on stalks; summer
Foliage: long, lance-shaped
Hardiness: C–D
Warnings: not prone to insects or disease; prone to slugs

Growing Requirements

Light: sun
Soil: fertile, well-drained, neutral to acidic soil; tolerates dry soil; avoid winter wet
Location: raised beds; rock gardens; scree
Propagation: seed; division
Expert Advice: Seed in fall and plant seedlings in their own pot right from the start. Division can be difficult as it resents being disturbed. Divide in spring.

Buying Considerations

Professionals
Popularity: relatively unknown
Availability: occasionally available from specialty growers
Size to Sell: sells best in smaller sizes (when blooming) as it matures fast
On the Shelf: rapidly overgrows pot
Shrinkage: low; requires little maintenance

Collectors
Popularity: not generally of interest to collectors

Gardeners
Ease of Growth: very easy to grow
Start with: one small plant for feature plant

What to Try First ...
Phyteuma humile, Phyteuma scheuchzeri

On the Market

Phyteuma hemisphaericum
Round, spiked, deep-blue flowers in summer • 5–15 cm high, 10–15 cm wide

Phyteuma humile
Round, spiked, violet-blue flowers in summer • 10–15 cm high, 10–15 cm wide

Phyteuma scheuchzeri
Round, spiked, deep-blue flowers in summer • 25–40 cm high, 10–20 cm wide

Pinguicula

p. 423

Genus Information

Origin: Newfoundland, the Northern Hemisphere and South America
Selected Common Names: butterwort
Nomenclature: From the Latin *pinguis* (fat), in reference to the greasy appearance of the foliage.
Notes: A genus of some 45 species.

General Features

Height: 8–20 cm high
Spread: 10–15 cm wide
Habit: carnivorous bog perennial
Flowers: summer
Foliage: rosette-forming; rounded to lance-shaped
Hardiness: B–C
Warnings: not prone to insects or disease
Expert Advice: Leaves secrete a sticky substance that traps insects. As the insect struggles to free itself, it stimulates the glands to secrete more sticky fluid and then an enzyme to slowly dissolve and digest the soft parts of the insect.

Growing Requirements

Light: sun
Soil: lean, moist to wet, organic, highly acidic soil
Location: bog gardens; waterside plantings
Propagation: seed (self-sows readily in wet conditions); division; cuttings
Expert Advice: Take leaf cuttings in spring.

Buying Considerations

Professionals
Popularity: relatively unknown
Availability: occasionally available from specialty growers
Size to Sell: sells best in mature sizes (when blooming) as it matures slowly
Shrinkage: low; requires little maintenance; sensitive to underwatering

Collectors
Popularity: of interest to bog and water garden enthusiasts—unique, exceptional beauty, rare, novelty

Gardeners
Ease of Growth: very easy to grow, refer to growing conditions
Start with: several mature plants for feature and instant visual effect

What to Try First ...
Pinguicula vulgaris

On the Market

Pinguicula vulgaris
Violet to purple flowers in summer •
Glandular, yellow-green to purplish leaves
• 8–20 cm high, 10–15 cm wide

Platycodon   p. 423

Genus Information

Origin: China, Manchuria and Japan
Selected Common Names: balloon flower, dwarf
balloon flower
Nomenclature: From the Greek *platys* (broad)
and *kodon* (bell), referring to the shape of the
flowers. The plant's flowers puff up like a
balloon until they are ready to open, which gave
rise to the common name "balloon flower."

General Features

Height: 10–60 cm high
Spread: 10–40 cm wide
Habit: clump-forming perennial
Flowers: large, bright, star-shaped; summer
Foliage: slow to emerge in spring
Hardiness: B–C
Warnings: prone to aphids; prone to crown
and root rot
Expert Advice: Be patient, this plant takes
2–3 seasons to look its best.

Growing Requirements

Light: sun
Soil: deep, fertile, well-drained soil; will rot in wet
soil; tolerant of dry periods
Location: mixed borders; rock gardens
Propagation: seed; separate and replant rooted
basal shoots
Expert Advice: Plants will flower in the second
year from seed. Hybridizes easily. May not
come true from seed. Established plants resent
being disturbed.

Buying Considerations

Professionals

Popularity: popular old-fashioned perennial;
fast seller in bloom
Availability: readily available as bare root
Size to Sell: sells best in larger sizes (when
blooming); matures slowly
Shrinkage: high; sensitive to overwatering

Collectors

Popularity: not generally of interest to
collectors

Gardeners

Ease of Growth: mostly easy to grow but
needs close attention to growing conditions
Start with: one mature plant for feature plant

What to Try First ...

Platycodon grandiflorus, Platycodon grandiflorus
'Astra Blue', *Platycodon grandiflorus* 'Astra
Double Blue', *Platycodon grandiflorus* 'Astra
Pink', *Platycodon grandiflorus* 'Perlmutterschale',
Platycodon grandiflorus 'Pink Gnome',
Platycodon grandiflorus 'Sentimental Blue',
Platycodon grandiflorus 'Tie Dye'

On the Market

Platycodon grandiflorus
'Albus' • Star-like, white flowers in summer
• 45–60 cm high, 30–40 cm wide
'Apoyama' • Star-like, deep-blue flowers in
summer • 10–20 cm high, 20–30 cm wide
'Freckles' • Star-like, white flowers with
blue flecks in summer • 45–60 cm high,
30–40 cm wide
'Fuji Blue' • Star-like, deep-blue flowers in
summer • 45–60 cm high, 30–40 cm wide
'Fuji Pink' • Star-like, shell-pink flowers in
summer • 45–60 cm high, 30–40 cm wide
'Fuji White' • Star-like, white flowers in
summer • 45–60 cm high, 30–40 cm wide
'Hakone Double Blue' • Double, star-like,
violet-blue flowers in summer • 45–60 cm
high, 30–40 cm wide
'Hakone White' • Double, star-like, white
flowers in summer • 45–60 cm high,
30–40 cm wide
'Komachi' • Purple-blue flowers retain
balloon shape in summer • 45–60 cm
high, 30–40 cm wide
'Mariesii' • Star-like, deep purple-blue
flowers in summer • 30–45 cm high,
20–30 cm wide
'Misato Purple' • Star-like, blue-purple
flowers in summer • 45–60 cm high,
30–40 cm wide
'Perlmutterschale' (Mother of Pearl) •
Star-like, pale-pink flowers in summer •
45–60 cm high, 30–40 cm wide
'Pink Gnome' • Star-like, pink flowers in
summer • 10–20 cm high, 20–30 cm wide
'Sentimental Blue' • Star-like, purple-blue
flowers in summer • 10–20 cm high,
20–30 cm wide
'Shell Pink' • Light-pink flowers in summer
• 45–60 cm high, 30–40 cm wide
'Tie Dye' • Star-like, blue flowers with white
streaks in summer • 45–60 cm high,
30–40 cm wide

P

Astra Series

'Astra Blue' • Star-like, blue flowers in summer • 10–20 cm high, 20–30 cm wide

'Astra Double Blue' • Double, blue flowers in summer • 20–25 cm high, 20–30 cm wide

'Astra Double Lavender' • Double, lavender flowers in summer • 20–25 cm high, 20–30 cm wide

'Astra Pink' • Star-like, pink flowers in summer • 10–20 cm high, 20–30 cm wide

Platycodon grandiflorus apoyama albus
'Fairy Snow' • Star-like, white flowers with blue veins in summer • 10–20 cm high, 20–30 cm wide

Platycodon grandiflorus roseus
Star-like, pink flowers in summer • 45–60 cm high, 30–40 cm wide

Podophyllum
p. 423

Genus Information

Origin: eastern North America, East Asia and the Himalayas
Selected Common Names: common Mayapple, Himalayan Mayapple
Nomenclature: From the Latin, referring to the stout, thick leaf (petiole).

General Features
Height: 20–45 cm high
Spread: 20–120 cm wide
Habit: rhizomatous woodland perennial
Flowers: white to pink; cup-shaped; spring; white to yellow fruits
Foliage: lobed; purplish-brown patched
Hardiness: C
Warnings: not prone to insects or disease; all plant parts are poisonous (except the fruit of some species)
Expert Advice: This plant produces large, brightly coloured fruit that is sometimes edible and often tasteless. The plants are pollinated by flies that are attracted by the slight carrion scent. It can take 3–4 years to form a nice patch in the garden (provided conditions are favourable).

Growing Requirements
Light: shade
Soil: deep, moist, organic soil
Location: mixed borders; woodland gardens
Propagation: seed; division

Buying Considerations

Professionals
Popularity: relatively unknown
Availability: occasionally available from specialty growers
Size to Sell: sells best in smaller sizes; matures slowly
On the Shelf: keep stock rotated; foliage breakage
Shrinkage: low; goes dormant in pot

Collectors
Popularity: not generally of interest to collectors

Gardeners
Ease of Growth: mostly easy to grow but needs close attention to growing conditions
Start with: one small plant for feature plant and several for instant visual effect

What to Try First ...
Podophyllum hexandrum, Podophyllum hexandrum 'Majus', Podophyllum peltatum

On the Market

Podophyllum hexandrum **(syn. *P. emodii*)**
Soft-pink to white flowers in spring followed by plum-like, red fruit • 25–45 cm high, 20–40 cm wide

'Majus' • White to pink flowers in spring followed by plum-like, red fruit • Reddish new foliage • 25–45 cm high, 20–40 cm wide

Podophyllum peltatum
White flowers in spring followed by red or yellowish plum like fruit • 20–45 cm high, 60–120 cm wide

Polemonium
p. 423

Genus Information

Origin: temperate regions, Arctic regions, the Northern Hemisphere, southern South America
Selected Common Names: charity, Greek valerian, Jacob's ladder
Nomenclature: Named for Polemon, a 2nd-century Greek philosopher.

General Features
Height: 5–90 cm
Spread: 10–60 cm
Habit: clump-forming or rhizomatous perennial
Flowers: fragrant, bright-blue, bell-like; late spring to summer
Foliage: interesting; opposite leaves borne ladder-like on stems; (some) variegated forms
Hardiness: B–C
Warnings: prone to powdery mildew; not prone to insects

Expert Advice: The taller species are a nice addition to the mixed border. The low-growing alpine species are lovely in a rockery. *Polemonium* self-sows readily, but is easily controlled by deadheading.

Growing Requirements

Light: sun to p.m. sun
Soil: fertile, moist, well-drained soil; tolerates periods of dryness
Location: cottage gardens; herb gardens; mixed borders; rock gardens
Propagation: seed (self-sows readily); division

Buying Considerations

Professionals

Popularity: popular, old-fashioned, fast-selling foliage plant
Availability: readily available as finished product and bare root
Size to Sell: sells best in smaller sizes (when blooming) as it matures fast
On the Shelf: high ornamental appeal; keep stock rotated; rapidly overgrows pot
Shrinkage: low shrinkage; requires little maintenance

Collectors

Popularity: not generally of interest to collectors

Gardeners

Ease of growth: very easy to grow
Start with: one small plant for feature plant

What to Try First ...

Polemonium caeruleum, *Polemonium caeruleum* 'Brise d'Anjou' , *Polemonium caeruleum* 'Snow and Sapphires', *Polemonium viscosum*, *Polemonium yezoense* 'Purple Rain'

On the Market

Polemonium caeruleum
Blue flowers in late spring to early summer • Fern-like foliage • 45–90 cm high, 30–45 cm wide

'Brise d'Anjou' (Blanjou) • Violet-blue flowers in late spring to early summer • Cream-edged foliage • 45–90 cm high, 30–45 cm wide

'Snow and Sapphires' • Fragrant, spiked, sky-blue flowers in late spring to early summer • White-edged, dark-green foliage • 45–90 cm high, 30–45 cm wide

Polemonium caeruleum ssp. *caeruleum* f. *album*
Spiked, white flowers in late spring to early summer • 45–90 cm high, 30–45 cm wide

Polemonium carneum
'Apricot Delight' • Spiked, yellow to peach flowers in late spring to early summer • 10–40 cm high, 20–30 cm wide

Polemonium chartaceum
Blue flowers in summer • 10–25 cm high, 10–20 cm wide

Polemonium eximium
Clear-blue flowers in summer • 10–30 cm high, 10–15 cm wide

Polemonium pauciflorum ssp. *pauciflorum* (syn. Silver-leaved)
Trumpet-shaped, yellow, often red-tinted flowers in summer • 15–50 cm high, 20–30 cm wide

Polemonium pulcherrimum
Blue flowers with yellow or white eye in late spring to early summer • 5–50 cm high, 20–30 cm wide

Polemonium pulcherrimum ssp. *delicatum*
Blue to violet, sometimes white flowers in late spring to early summer • 10–20 cm high, 20–30 cm wide

Polemonium reptans
'Stairway to Heaven' • Blue flowers in early to midsummer • Grey-green foliage with cream and pink margins • 30–60 cm high, 20–40 cm wide

'White Pearl' • White flowers in spring to early summer • 30–60 cm high, 20–40 cm wide

Polemonium viscosum
Blue flowers in late spring to early summer • 10–45 cm high, 10–20 cm wide

Polemonium yezoense
Blue to violet flowers in late spring to early summer • Purple-tinted foliage • 30–45 cm high, 20–30 cm wide

'Purple Rain' • Spiked, purple-blue flowers in late spring to early summer • Purple-tinted, fern-like foliage • 30–45 cm high, 20–30 cm wide

P

Polygala

p. 423

Genus Information

Origin: worldwide, except in New Zealand, Polynesia and the Arctic

Selected Common Names: milkwort, seneca snakeroot

Nomenclature: From the Greek *polys* (much) and *gala* (milk), referring to its reputation for the promotion of milk production. The name used by Dioscorides.

Notes: The genus includes annuals, evergreen perennials and shrubs.

General Features

Height: 5–20 cm high

Spread: 10–30 cm wide

Habit: clump-forming subshrub

Flowers: pea-like; late spring to early summer; long blooming period; may rebloom in fall

Foliage: leathery; evergreen

Hardiness: C–D

Warnings: not prone to insects or disease

Expert Advice: A nice plant for the alpine garden or rockery.

Growing Requirements

Light: sun

Soil: fertile, moist, well-drained, neutral to alkaline soil; avoid winter wet

Location: sheltered locations; raised beds; rock gardens; scree

Propagation: seed; division; cuttings

Expert Advice: Divide in spring. Take cuttings in summer. Provide cuttings with gentle bottom heat.

Buying Considerations

Professionals

Popularity: relatively unknown

Availability: occasionally available from specialty growers

Size to Sell: sells best in mature sizes (when blooming) as it matures slowly

Shrinkage: high; sensitive to overwatering

Collectors

Popularity: of interest to collectors—unique, exceptional beauty, rare, challenge

Gardeners

Ease of Growth: mostly difficult to grow as it needs close attention to growing

Start with: one mature plant for feature plant

What to Try First ...

Polygala amara, Polygala calcarea, Polygala chamaebuxus 'Kamniski', *Polygala vayredae*

On the Market

Polygala amara
Blue, violet, pink or white flowers in late spring to early summer • Evergreen • 10–20 cm high, 10–15 cm wide

Polygala calcarea
Gentian-blue, sometimes white flowers in late spring to early summer • Evergreen • 5–10 cm high, 10–20 cm wide

Polygala chamaebuxus
White and yellow flowers, aging purple, with keel in late spring to early summer • Evergreen • 5–15 cm high, 20–30 cm wide

'Kamniski' • Purple-and-yellow-bicoloured flowers in late spring to early summer • Evergreen • 5–15 cm high, 20–30 cm wide

Polygala chamaebuxus **var. *rhodoptera***
Purple-and-yellow-bicoloured flowers in late spring to early summer • Evergreen • 5–15 cm high, 20–30 cm wide

Polygala vayredae
Purple-pink-and-yellow-bicoloured flowers in late spring to early summer • Evergreen • 15–20 cm high, 20–30 cm wide

Polygonatum

p. 423

Genus Information

Origin: United States, Europe and Asia

Selected Common Names: Solomon's seal

Nomenclature: From the Greek *polys* (many) and *gonu* (joint), referring to the many-jointed rhizome.

General Features

Height: 20–120 cm high

Spread: 30–60 cm wide

Habit: upright, arching rhizomatous perennial

Flowers: fragrant; hanging, bell-like; good for cutflowers; spring

Foliage: opposite; borne on arching stems

Hardiness: B–C

Warnings: prone to slugs; not prone to diseases

Expert Advice: This plant produces red or black berries. Takes 3–4 years to form a nice clump on the Prairies. Plant with *Hosta, Heuchera, Primula* and other shade plants.

Growing Requirements

Light: shade

Soil: moist, organic, well-drained soil; tolerant of poor acidic soil; tolerates periods of dryness

Location: shady mixed borders; rock gardens; woodland gardens

Propagation: seed; division

Expert Advice: Seed in fall. Germination of seed can be slow. Seedlings take 3–5 years to reach blooming size. Division in the fall is the easiest method of propagation.

P

Buying Considerations

Professionals

Popularity: popular, old-fashioned foliage plant

Availability: readily available as finished product and bare root

Size to Sell: sells best in smaller sizes (when blooming); matures slowly

On the Shelf: high ornamental appeal; prone to foliage breakage

Shrinkage: low; requires little maintenance; goes dormant in pot later in season

Collectors

Popularity: not generally of interest to collectors

Gardeners

Ease of Growth: very easy to grow

Start with: one small plant for feature plant and several for mass plantings

What to Try First ...

Polygonatum biflorum, Polygonatum falcatum 'Variegatum', *Polygonatum* x *hybridum,* *Polygonatum* x *hybridum* 'Variegatum', *Polygonatum multiflorum, Polygonatum odoratum* var. *pluriflorum* 'Variegatum'

On the Market

Polygonatum biflorum
(syn. *P. canaliculatum*)
Green-white flowers in late spring followed by black fruit • 50–120 cm high, 45–60 cm wide

Polygonatum falcatum
'Variegatum' • White bell flowers in spring • White-and-green foliage • 45–80 cm high, 45–60 cm wide

Polygonatum humile
White flowers in spring • 20 cm high, 30–50+ cm wide

Polygonatum x *hybridum*
White flowers with green tips in spring followed by blue-black fruits • 50–100 cm high, 45–60 cm wide
'Variegatum' • White flowers with green tips in spring followed by blue-black fruits • Striped white foliage • 50–100 cm high, 45–60 cm wide

Polygonatum multiflorum
Fragrant, white flowers with green tips in spring followed by black fruits • 60–90 cm high, 45–60 cm wide

Polygonatum odoratum
Fragrant cream flowers with green tips in late spring followed by black fruits • 50–75 cm high, 45–60 cm wide

Polygonatum odoratum var. *pluriflorum*
'Variegatum' • Fragrant, cream flowers with green tips in late spring followed by black fruits • White-edged foliage • 50–75 cm high, 45–60 cm wide

Polygonatum sibiricum
Cream flowers with green tips in late spring • 1 m high, 45–60 cm wide

Polystichum
p. 423

Genus Information

Origin: worldwide

Selected Common Names: Christmas fern, soft shield fern, sword fern

Nomenclature: From the Greek *polys* (many) and *stix* (a row), referring to the regular rows of sori on many of the species.

General Features

Height: 30–90 cm high

Spread: 50–90 cm wide

Habit: clump-forming, rhizomatous fern

Foliage: lance-shaped, evergreen fronds

Hardiness: C

Warnings: not prone to insects or disease

Expert Advice: A good fern for the Prairies if grown in sheltered locations.

Growing Requirements

Light: shade; tolerates more sun with good soil moisture

Soil: well-drained, moist, neutral to alkaline soil; prefers soil pH of 6.5–7.5; will slowly decline in very acidic soil

Location: sheltered locations (foliage burns and breaks in windy locations); alpine gardens; mixed borders; woodland gardens

Propagation: spores; division

Expert Advice: Germinate spores at 15–16°C. Separate and replant bulbils.

Buying Considerations

Professionals

Popularity: popular foliage plant

Availability: readily available as finished product

Size to Sell: sells best in smaller sizes as it matures fast

On the Shelf: high ornamental appeal; prone to foliage breakage (display out of wind)

Shrinkage: low; requires little maintenance

Collectors

Popularity: not generally of interest to collectors

P

Gardeners

Ease of Growth: mostly easy to grow but needs close attention to growing conditions
Start with: one small plant for feature plant and several for mass plantings

What to Try First ...

Polystichum acrostichoides, Polystichum munitum, Polystichum setiferum 'Pulcherrimum Bevis'

On the Market

Polystichum Proliferum Group
Soft, feathery, evergreen fronds • 50–75 cm high, 60–75 cm wide

Polystichum acrostichoides
Evergreen foliage • 30–75 cm high, 60–90 cm wide

Polystichum munitum
Leathery, evergreen foliage • 60–90 cm high, 60–90 cm wide

Polystichum setiferum
Soft, feathery, lance-shaped, evergreen fronds • 60–90 cm high, 60–75 cm wide

'Herrenhausen' • Finely cut, lacy, evergreen fronds • 60–90 cm high, 60–90 cm wide

'Pulcherrimum Bevis' (Plumosum Bevis) • Pointed, lacy, evergreen fronds • 60–90 cm high, 60–90 cm wide

'Divisilobum' • Large, soft, evergreen fronds • 50–75 cm high, 50–75 cm wide

Potentilla   p. 424

Genus Information

Origin: worldwide
Selected Common Names: cinquefoil, potentilla
Nomenclature: From the Latin *potens* (powerful), in reference to the supposed medicinal properties.
Notes: A genus of some 500 species of annuals, biennials, perennials and shrubs.

General Features

Height: 2–45 cm high
Spread: 10–60 cm wide
Habit: clump or creeping, mat-forming groundcover perennial
Flowers: pretty, single, semi-double or double; spring to summer; long blooming period
Foliage: mid- to dark-green; strawberry-like
Hardiness: A–D
Warnings: prone to powdery mildew and aphids; (some) aggressive-spreaders (easily controlled by clipping back)

Expert Advice: Cut back to keep clump-forming types compact. Some make excellent groundcovers in difficult sites.

Growing Requirements

Light: sun to p.m. sun
Soil: lean to moderately fertile soil; tolerates poor, dry soil
Location: hot, dry, sunny areas; wall crevices; rock gardens; scree
Propagation: seed; division; cuttings
Expert Advice: Rich soil produces excessive growth at the expense of flowers. Divide in spring. Take rooted cuttings in early to midsummer.

Buying Considerations

Professionals

Popularity: popular, old-fashioned garden standard; fast seller in bloom
Availability: readily available as finished product and bare root
Size to Sell: sells best in smaller sizes (when blooming) as it matures fast
On the Shelf: keep stock rotated; rapidly overgrows pot
Shrinkage: low; requires little maintenance

Collectors

Popularity: of interest to alpine collectors; alpine varieties (especially *P. nitida* 'Alannah')—unique, exceptional beauty, rare

Gardeners

Ease of Growth: very easy to grow
Start with: one small plant for feature plant

What to Try First ...

Potentilla 'Arc-en-ciel', *Potentilla* 'Emilie', *Potentilla* 'Gibson's Scarlet', *Potentilla alba*, *Potentilla aurea*, *Potentilla megalantha*, *Potentilla nepalensis* 'Ron McBeath', *Potentilla neumanniana* 'Goldrausch', *Potentilla neumanniana* 'Orange Flame', *Potentilla nitida* 'Alannah', *Potentilla* x *tonguei*

On the Market

Potentilla
'Arc-en-ciel' • Deep-red flowers with darker eye and yellow centre in summer • 30–45 cm high, 30–45 cm wide

'Double French Red' • Double, rich-red flowers in summer • 30–45 cm high, 45–60 cm wide

'Emilie' • Double, red and yellow flowers in summer • 30–45 cm high, 45–60 cm wide

P

'Flamenco' • Pink flowers in summer •
30–45 cm high, 45–60 cm wide

'Gibson's Scarlet' • Single, scarlet-red
flowers in summer • 30–45 cm high,
45–60 cm wide

'Helen Jane' • Pale-pink flowers with dark
centres in summer • 30–45 cm high,
45–60 cm wide

'Herzblut' (Heart's Blood) • Semi-double,
blood-red flowers in summer • 30–45 cm
high, 45–60 cm wide

'Versicolor Plena' • Double, orange flowers
in summer • 30–45 cm high, 45–60 cm
wide

'William Rollison' • Semi-double, yellow to
orange-red flowers in summer • 30–45 cm
high, 45–60 cm wide

Potentilla alba
White flowers in late spring to early
summer • 5–10 cm high, 20–30 cm wide

Potentilla anatolica
White or pale-pink flowers in midsummer
• 30–45 cm high, 30–40 cm wide

Potentilla anserina
Yellow flowers in summer • Silver, ferny
foliage • 5–10 cm high, 60–75+ cm wide

Potentilla aurea
Yellow flowers, often with darker eye, in
summer • 10–30 cm high, 20–30 cm wide

Potentilla cinerea
Bright-yellow flowers in late spring to
summer • Grey-green foliage • 5–10 cm
high, 20–30 cm wide

Potentilla crantzii
Yellow flowers, often with orange eye, in
spring to early summer • 15–25 cm high,
30–45 cm wide

'Orange Glow' • Gold-yellow flowers in
spring to early summer • 5–10 cm high,
30–45 cm wide

Potentilla dickinsii nana
Yellow flowers in summer • Alpine •
5–10 cm high, 10–15 cm wide

Potentilla hippiana
Yellow flowers in summer • Well-drained,
poor to moderately fertile, alkaline soil •
30–60 cm high, 30–45 cm wide

Potentilla x hopwoodiana
Salmon-pink flowers with rose-red centres
and white edges in summer • Dark-green
foliage • 30–45 cm high, 30–40 cm wide

Potentilla hyparctica nana
Bright-yellow flowers in summer •
Silvery-grey, felted foliage • 5–10 cm
high, 15–30 cm wide

Potentilla megalantha
(syn. *P. fragariiformis*)
Yellow flowers in summer • 15–30 cm high,
15–30 cm wide

Potentilla nepalensis
'Miss Willmott' • Cherry-pink flowers with
darker-pink centre in summer • 30–45 cm
high, 45–60 cm wide

'Ron McBeath' • Carmine-red flowers in
summer • 30–45 cm high, 45–60 cm wide

Potentilla neumanniana
(syn. *P. verna* and *tabernaemontai*)
'Goldrausch' (Goldrush) • Yellow flowers
in spring to summer • 5–10 cm high,
30–45+ cm wide

'Orange Flame' • Yellow-orange flowers
in spring to summer • 5–10 cm high,
30–45+ cm wide

Potentilla nitida
Pink to rose-pink flowers, rarely white, in
summer • 5–10 cm high, 15–30 cm wide

'Alannah' • Soft-pink flowers with deep-
pink eye in summer • Silvery foliage
• 5–10 cm high, 15–30 cm wide

Potentilla nivea
Yellow flowers in summer • 15–20 cm high,
10–20 cm wide

Potentilla pamiroalaica
Gold-yellow flowers in summer • Silver-
grey foliage • 5–10 cm high, 15–20 cm wide

Potentilla reptans
'Pleniflora' • Yellow flowers in summer •
10–15 cm high, 50–75+ cm wide

Potentilla thurberi
Red-purple flowers in summer • 45–75 cm
high, 30–45 cm wide

'Monarch's Velvet' • Raspberry-red flowers
with velvet-red centres in summer •
30–40 cm high, 30–45 cm wide

Potentilla x tonguei
Apricot flowers with red eye in summer
to fall • 5–10 cm high, 20–30 cm wide

Potentilla uniflora
Yellow flowers in late spring to late summer
• Silvery foliage • 5–10 cm high, 15–30 cm
wide

P

Primula

p. 424 📷

Genus Information

Origin: Northern Hemisphere, tropical mountains and southern South America

Selected Common Names: primrose, cowslip primrose, oxlip primrose

Nomenclature: From the diminutive of the Latin *primus* (first). The name *Primula veris* means "first of spring."

Notes: In Europe the primrose is eagerly awaited as a sign of spring. It is a very important group of perennials found in gardens as far back as 1597. A genus of some 400 species.

Expert Advice: We divide *Primula* into 4 categories for growing information and display purposes: *Alpine, Auricula, Garden, Polyanthus* and *Woodland/Bog*.

Primula, Alpine

p. 424 📷

General Features

Height: 2–45 cm high
Spread: 10–30 cm wide
Habit: clump-forming perennial
Flowers: range of colours; early spring
Foliage: pale- to dark-green; (most) evergreen
Hardiness: A–D
Warnings: do not cut back evergreen types in fall; not prone to insects or diseases
Expert Advice: This category withstands the most sun of all the *Primulas*, provided they are kept moist and their roots cool. The Alpines are high altitude plants that remain very short.

Growing Requirements

Light: shade to a.m. sun; tolerates more sun with good soil moisture
Soil: cool, moist to wet, neutral to alkaline (some in acidic soil), sharply drained soil; avoid winter wet
Location: rock crevices; tufa; rock gardens
Propagation: seed; division
Expert Advice: Grow in lean soil for best performance.

Buying Considerations

Professionals

Popularity: relatively unknown; fast seller in bloom; new varieties available
Availability: occasionally available as finished product from specialty growers
Size to Sell: sells best in smaller sizes (when blooming) as it matures fast
Shrinkage: low; requires little maintenance

Collectors

Popularity: of interest to alpine collectors—unique species and varieties, rare, challenge

Gardeners

Ease of Growth: mostly easy to grow but needs close attention to growing conditions
Start with: one small plant for feature plant

What to Try First ...

Primula 'Aire Mist', *Primula* 'Peardrop', *Primula angustifolia*, *Primula marginata* 'Herb Dickson', *Primula modesta*, *Primula warshenewskiana*, *Primula wigramiana*

On the Market

Primula

'Aire Mist' • Stemless, white flowers in early spring • 5–10 cm high, 10–20 cm wide

'Broadwell Milkmaid' • Creamy-white flowers in early spring • 5–10 cm high, 10–20 cm wide

'Broadwell Pink' • Pink flowers in early spring • 5–8 cm high, 8–20 cm wide

'Clarence Elliot' • Mauve flowers with white eye in early spring • 5–10 cm high, 10–20 cm wide

'Ethel Barker' • Carmine-pink flowers with white eye in early spring • 5–12 cm high, 10–20 cm wide

'High Point' • Royal-purple flowers in early spring • Heavy coating of golden farina • 5–10 cm high, 10–20 cm wide

'Lismore Treasure' • Dark-violet-purple flowers in early spring • Evergreen • 5–10 cm high, 10–20 cm wide

'Lismore Yellow' • Cream flowers with dark eye in spring • 5–10 cm high, 10–20 cm wide

'Peardrop' • Red-pink, yellow-eyed flowers in early spring • 5–8 cm high, 8–20 cm wide

'Wharfedale Bluebell' • Silver-edged, blue flowers in early spring • 5–10 cm high, 10–20 cm wide

'Wharfedale Crusader' • Lilac-pink flowers in early spring • Evergreen • 5–10 cm high, 10–20 cm wide

'Wharfedale Ling' • Pink-edged, cream-white flowers in early spring • Evergreen • 5–10 cm high, 10–20 cm wide

'Wharfedale Superb' • Wavy-edged, white flowers with pink bands in early spring • Evergreen • 5–10 cm high, 10–20 cm wide

Primula (P. allionii x P. pubescens)

Purple flowers with white eye in early spring • Evergreen • 5–10 cm high, 10–20 cm wide

P

**Primula (P. marginata 'Holden Clough'
x P. allionii)**
Deep-pink flowers in early spring •
Evergreen • Well-drained, fertile, neutral
to alkaline, moist soil • 6–10 cm high,
10–20 cm wide

Primula (P. villosa x P. hirsuta)
Rose-red flowers in spring • Evergreen •
10–15 cm high, 10–15 cm wide

Primula algida
Violet to lilac flowers in spring • With farina
• 5–20 cm high, 10–15 cm wide

Primula allionii
Red-purple, pink or white flowers with
white eye in early spring • Evergreen •
5–10 cm high, 10–20 cm wide

'Austen' • Red-purple flowers in early spring
• 5–10 cm high, 10–20 cm wide

'Bill Martin' • Purple flowers in early spring
• 5–10 cm high, 10–20 cm wide

'Claude Flight' • Violet-edged, green-white
flowers in early spring • 5–10 cm high,
10–20 cm wide

'Crowsley Variety' • Crimson-purple flowers
in early spring • 5–10 cm high, 10–20 cm
wide

'Edinburgh' • Soft-pink flowers with
white eye in early spring • 5–10 cm high,
10–20 cm wide

'Eureka' • White flowers in early spring
• 5–10 cm high, 10–20 cm wide

'Gilderdale Glow' x 'Apple Blossom' •
White-eyed, rich-pink flowers in spring •
5–10 cm high, 10–20 cm wide

'Hemswell Blush' • Pink flowers with
yellow eye in early spring • 5–10 cm high,
10–20 cm wide

'Jenny' (JCA–4161-22) • Red-violet flowers
in early spring • Evergreen • 5–10 cm
high, 10–20 cm wide

'Kath Dryden' • Fragrant, pale-yellow
flowers in early spring • 5–10 cm high,
10–20 cm wide

'Marjorie Wooster' • Large, mauve-pink
flowers in early spring • 5–10 cm high,
10–20 cm wide

'Mars' • Magenta-pink flowers in early
spring • 5–10 cm high, 10–20 cm wide

'Mrs. Dyas' • Dark-pink flowers with
white eye in early spring • 5–10 cm high,
10–20 cm wide

'Neon' • Purple-red flowers in early spring •
5–10 cm high, 10–20 cm wide

'Perkie' • Red-purple flowers with white eye
in early spring • 5–10 cm high, 10–20 cm
wide

Primula allionii var. alba
White flowers in early spring • Evergreen •
5–10 cm high, 10–20 cm wide

Primula angustifolia
Purple-red to lilac flowers with yellow eye
in spring • 3–10 cm high, 15–20 cm wide

Primula aureata
Cream to yellow flowers with orange eye
in spring • Very heavy farina on foliage •
10–15 cm high, 10–20 cm wide

Primula clusiana
Rose to lilac flowers with white eye in
spring • Moist, organic, gritty, neutral to
alkaline soil • 5–15 cm high, 10–15 cm wide

Primula cusickiana ssp. domensis
Fragrant, rose to lavender flowers with
yellow eye in spring • 3–10 cm high,
15–20 cm wide

Primula darialica
Rose to carmine-red flowers with yellow
eye in spring • With farina • 3–10 cm high,
10–15 cm wide

Primula deorum
Fragrant, violet to crimson-purple flowers
in spring • Very moist, fertile, well-drained,
organic, neutral to acidic soil • 5–20 cm
high, 15–20 cm wide

Primula farinosa
Lilac-pink flowers with farina and yellow
eye in spring • 10–25 cm high, 10–25 cm
wide

'Alba' • White flowers with yellow eye in
spring • With farina • 10–25 cm high,
10–25 cm wide

Primula x floerkeana
Pink to purple flowers in spring • 2–8 cm
high, 10–20 cm wide

Primula forrestii
Fragrant, yellow flowers with orange eye in
early summer • Evergreen • 15–45 cm high,
20–30 cm wide

Primula x forsteri
Large, rose-purple to pink flowers in spring
• Evergreen • 5–8 cm high, 10–15 cm wide

'Bileckii' • Large, pink-red flowers with
white eye in spring • Evergreen • 5–8 cm
high, 10–15 cm wide

Primula frondosa
Pink to red-purple flowers with yellow eye
in spring • 10–15 cm high, 15–25 cm wide

P

Primula glaucescens
Pink-red to lilac flowers with white eye in spring • 3–15 cm high, 10–15 cm wide

Primula aff. x gobelii
Deep-purple flowers in spring • Grey foliage with heavy farina • 10 cm high, 15 cm wide

Primula hirsuta
Rose-pink flowers with white eye in spring • Evergreen • 8–10 cm high, 15–25 cm wide
'Alba' • White flowers in spring • Evergreen • 8–10 cm high, 15–25 cm wide

Primula iljinskyi
White to pink flowers with white eye in spring • 5–30 cm high, 10–20 cm wide

Primula integrifolia
Rose to purple flowers in late spring to early summer • Neutral to acidic, moist, well-drained, organic soil • 4–8 cm high, 5–10 cm wide

Primula x juribella
Rose-purple flowers in spring • 5–8 cm high, 10–20 cm wide

Primula x loiseleurii
'Aire Waves' • White flowers in early spring • Evergreen • 5–10 cm high, 10–20 cm wide

Primula marginata
Fragrant, lilac-blue flowers in spring • Evergreen • 10–15 cm high, 15–30 cm wide
'Alba' • Fragrant, white flowers in spring • 10–15 cm high, 15–30 cm wide
'Amethyst' • Fragrant, purple buds opening to amethyst flowers in spring • Evergreen • 10–15 cm high, 15–30 cm wide
'Doctor Jenkins' • Fragrant, light-lavender flowers in spring • 10–15 cm high, 15–30 cm wide
'Herb Dickson' • Fragrant, dark-blue flowers with white eye in spring • 10–15 cm high, 15–30 cm wide
'Kesselring's Variety' • Fragrant, rich-mauve flowers with white eye in spring • 10–15 cm high, 15–30 cm wide
'Pritchard's Variety' • Fragrant, mauve to lilac flowers in spring • 10–15 cm high, 15–30 cm wide
'Shark's Tooth' • Fragrant, lavender-blue flowers in spring • 10–15 cm high, 15–30 cm wide
'Teaser' • Fragrant, soft pink-purple flowers in spring • 10–15 cm high, 15–30 cm wide

Primula x meridiana
'Miniera' • Blue-purple flowers in early spring • Golden farina on foliage • 5–10 cm high, 10–20 cm wide

Primula minima
Large, rose to lilac flowers with white eye in spring • Moist, well-drained, organic, gritty, neutral to acidic soil • 5–8 cm high, 10–20 cm wide

Primula minima var. alba
Large, white flowers in spring • Evergreen • Moist, sharply drained, organic, gritty, neutral to acidic soil • 5–8 cm high, 10–20 cm wide

Primula modesta
Pink-purple flowers, sometimes white, with yellow eye in spring • 10–15 cm high, 15–20 cm wide

Primula modesta alba
White flowers with yellow eye in spring • 10–15 cm high, 15–20 cm wide

Primula modesta var. faurieae
Lavender flowers with yellow eye in spring • 5–10 cm high, 10–15 cm wide

Primula muscarioides
Fragrant, purple-blue flowers in early summer • Very moist, well-drained, organic soil • 20–40 cm high, 20–30 cm wide

Primula scotica
Fragrant, rose-red to purple flowers with yellow eye in spring • Heavy farina • 5–10 cm high, 10–15 cm wide

Primula specuicola
Lavender to violet flowers with yellow eye in spring • Do not water foliage • 10–15 cm high, 15–20 cm wide

Primula suffrutescens
Rose-pink to red-purple flowers with yellow eye in spring • Evergreen • 5–15 cm high, 10–15 cm wide

Primula x vochinensis (syn. P. x serrata)
Red-pink to red and purple-red flowers in spring • 5–10 cm high, 10–20 cm wide

Primula warshenewskiana
Pink flowers with white-ringed, yellow eye in spring • 5–8 cm high, 10–15 cm wide

Primula wigramiana
Fragrant, large, nodding, white flowers in summer • 15–25 cm high, 15–20 cm wide

Primula wulfeniana
Rose-purple to lilac flowers in spring • Evergreen • 5–10 cm high, 10–15 cm wide

Primula wulfeniana ssp. baumgarteniana (syn. P. baumgarteniana)
Soft-pink to lilac-pink flowers with whitish eye • 5–10 cm high, 10–15 cm wide

Primula, Auricula

p. 424

General Features

Height: 5–25 cm high
Spread: 10–30 cm wide
Habit: clump-forming perennial
Flowers: showy; spring; may rebloom in fall
Foliage: rosette-forming; (some) evergreen
Hardiness: A–D
Warnings: prone to aphids; not prone to diseases
Expert Advice: Auricula primroses are highly sought after collector's plants and have whole societies devoted to them. This category includes an array of colours and colour combinations including grey-, black- and green- hued blooms. Many of the auriculas have a fine meal on the flowers and foliage called farina.

Growing Requirements

Light: shade to a.m. sun; tolerates more sun with good soil moisture
Soil: organic, moist, well-drained soil; tolerates acidic soil
Location: shady mixed borders; rock gardens; rock crevices
Propagation: seed; division
Expert Advice: Although this group prefers evenly moist soil, the auriculas are more tolerant of drier sites and a little more sun than most other groups (except alpine primula). Divide auricula primroses every 3 years (after blooming) to maintain vigour.

Buying Considerations

Professionals

Popularity: popular, old-fashioned garden standard; fast seller in bloom
Availability: generally available as finished product from specialty growers
Size to Sell: sells best in smaller sizes (when blooming) as it matures fast
On the Shelf: rapidly overgrows pot
Shrinkage: high; sensitive to overwatering or underwatering

Collectors

Popularity: of interest to collectors—unique varieties, rare, exceptional beauty

Gardeners

Ease of Growth: easy to grow
Start with: one small plant for feature plant and several for mass plantings

What to Try First ...

Primula auricula 'Alice Haysom', *Primula auricula* 'Argus', *Primula auricula* 'Indian Love Call', *Primula auricula* 'Remus'

On the Market

Primula auricula
Fragrant, single, yellow flowers in spring • 15–25 cm high, 20–30 cm wide

'Alice Haysom' • Cardinal-red flowers with cream centre in spring • Heavy farina • 15–25 cm high, 20–30 cm wide

'Applecross' • Gold-centred, red flowers in spring • No farina • 15–25 cm high, 20–30 cm wide

'Arctic Fox' • Fragrant, double, lavender-purple flowers with creamy centres in spring • 15–25 cm high, 20–30 cm wide

'Argus' • Deep-plum to beetroot-coloured flowers with white eye in spring • No farina • 15–25 cm high, 20–30 cm wide

'Arrowhead Double Yellow' • Fragrant double, yellow-bronze flowers in spring • 15–25 cm high, 20–30 cm wide

'Arundell' • Fragrant, red-and-green-striped flowers in spring • With farina • 15–25 cm high, 20–30 cm wide

'Bob Lancashire' • Fragrant, green-edged flowers in spring • No farina on foliage • 15–25 cm high, 20–30 cm wide

'Bookham Firefly' • Maroon-edged, red flowers with gold centre in spring • No farina • 15–25 cm high, 20–30 cm wide

'Brazil' • Rich-yellow flowers in spring • With farina • 15–25 cm high, 20–30 cm wide

'Brownie' • Fragrant, double, purple-brown flowers in spring • 15–25 cm high, 20–30 cm wide

'Camelot' • Fragrant, double, purple flowers in spring • 15–25 cm high, 20–30 cm wide

'Chorister' • Bright-yellow flowers in spring • With farina • 15–25 cm high, 20–30 cm wide

'Cinnamon' • Fragrant, double, cinnamon flowers in spring • With farina • 15–25 cm high, 20–30 cm wide

'Clunie' • Fragrant, green-edged, red flowers in spring • No farina • 15–25 cm high, 20–30 cm wide

'Cortina' • Wine-red flowers with white centre and yellow eye in spring • Heavy farina • 15–25 cm high, 20–30 cm wide

'Devon Cream' • Fragrant, double, cream flowers with gold centre in spring • 15–25 cm high, 20–30 cm wide

P

'Donhead' • Fragrant, wine flowers with cream centre in spring • No farina • 15–25 cm high, 20–30 cm wide

'Doublet' • Fragrant, double, purple flowers in spring • 15–25 cm high, 20–30 cm wide

'Emily' • Fragrant, double, blush-pink flowers with green-yellow centre in spring • 15–25 cm high, 20–30 cm wide

'Fanny Meerbeck' • Dark-red flowers with white eye in spring • With farina • 15–25 cm high, 20–30 cm wide

'Frank Crosland' • Blue-purple flowers edged in ice-blue in spring • No farina • 15–25 cm high, 20–30 cm wide

'Gleam' • Yellow flowers in spring • With farina • 15–25 cm high, 20–30 cm wide

'Goldstrike' • Dusty-lilac flowers with yellow eye in spring • 15–25 cm high, 20–30 cm wide

'Gordon Douglas' • Soft- to violet-blue flowers with cream centre in spring • No farina • 15–25 cm high, 20–30 cm wide

'Green Parrot' • Green-edged, red flowers in spring • No farina • 15–25 cm high, 20–30 cm wide

'Greta' • Grey-edged, red flowers in spring • With farina • 15–25 cm high, 20–30 cm wide

'Grey Lag' • Grey-edged, black flowers in spring • With farina • 15–25 cm high, 20–30 cm wide

'Hetty Woolf' • Grey-edged flowers in spring • With farina • 15–25 cm high, 20–30 cm wide

'Indian Love Call' • Yellow flowers with gold centre in spring • No farina • 15–25 cm high, 20–30 cm wide

'Jenny' • Red flowers with gold centre in spring • 15–25 cm high, 20–30 cm wide

'Jolly Green Giant' • Green-edged flowers in spring • No farina • 15–25 cm high, 20–30 cm wide

'Karen Cordrey' • Fragrant, green-striped, red flowers in spring • With farina • 15–25 cm high, 20–30 cm wide

'Kim' • Black-red flowers with gold centre in spring • No farina • 10–15 cm high, 20–25 cm wide

'Lamplugh' • Fragrant, double, purple flowers in spring • 15–25 cm high, 20–30 cm wide

'Langley Park' • Light-pink centred flowers in spring • No farina • 15–25 cm high, 20–30 cm wide

'Lechistan' • Red flowers in spring • With farina • 15–25 cm high, 20–30 cm wide

'Lee Paul' • Brown-maroon flowers with bright-yellow centre in spring • No farina • 15–25 cm high, 20–30 cm wide

'Lovebird' • Grey-edged flowers in spring • With farina • 15–25 cm high, 20–30 cm wide

'Marie Crousse' • Fragrant, double, violet flowers in spring • 15–25 cm high, 20–30 cm wide

'Marmion' • Black flowers with grey edge in spring • With farina • 15–25 cm high, 20–30 cm wide

'Matthew Yates' • Fragrant, double, red-black flowers in spring • 15–25 cm high, 20–30 cm wide

'Midnight' • Deep-blue flowers in spring • With farina • 15–25 cm high, 20–30 cm wide

'Mink' • Reddish flowers with yellow eye in spring • No farina • 15–25 cm high, 20–30 cm wide

'Mr. A' • Dark-red flowers in spring • With farina • 15–25 cm high, 20–30 cm wide

'Nankenan' • Green and yellow flowers in spring • 15–25 cm high, 20–30 cm wide

'Osbourne Green' • Fragrant, green-edged, purple flowers with white centre in spring • 15–25 cm high, 20–30 cm wide

'Pinstripe' • Red and green-striped flowers in spring • 15–25 cm high, 20–30 cm wide

'Prague' • Green-edged flowers in spring • No farina • 15–25 cm high, 20–30 cm wide

'Queen Bee' • White-and-green-edged, red flowers in spring • With farina • 15–25 cm high, 20–30 cm wide

'Rajah' • Scarlet flowers with green edge in spring • Evergreen foliage with farina • 15–25 cm high, 20–30 cm wide

'Redstart' • Red flowers in spring • 15–25 cm high, 20–30 cm wide

'Remus' • Fragrant, blue flowers with white eye in spring • 15–25 cm high, 20–30 cm wide

'Rolts' • Green-edged, red flowers with white eye in spring • With farina • 15–25 cm high, 20–30 cm wide

'Rowena' • Mauve flowers with white centre in spring • No farina • 15–25 cm high, 20–30 cm wide

'Sandra' • Mauve-tinted flowers in spring • No farina • 15–25 cm high, 20–30 cm wide

'Sandwood Bay' • Bright-red flowers with gold centre in spring • No farina • 15–25 cm high, 20–30 cm wide

'Serenity' • Green-edged flowers with white eye in spring • No farina • 15–25 cm high, 20–30 cm wide

'Sirius' • Fragrant, maroon-yellow flowers with gold centre in spring • No farina • 15–25 cm high, 20–30 cm wide

'South Barrow' • Double, purple-red flowers in spring • 15–25 cm high, 20–30 cm wide

'Spring Meadows' • Green-edged, yellow flowers in spring • With farina • 15–25 cm high, 20–30 cm wide

'Standish' • Fragrant, double, cream to buff flowers in spring • 15–25 cm high, 20–30 cm wide

'Stubb's Tartan' • Large, grey and red flowers in spring • With farina • 15–25 cm high, 20–30 cm wide

'Susannah' • Double, lilac-pink flowers in spring • 15–25 cm high, 20–30 cm wide

'Sword' • Fragrant, double, green and red flowers in spring • 15–25 cm high, 20–30 cm wide

'The Baron' • Bright-yellow flowers in spring • With farina • 15–25 cm high, 20–30 cm wide

'The Snods' • Dark-red flowers with white eye in spring • With farina • 15–25 cm high, 20–30 cm wide

'Thetis' • Dark-blue flowers shaded to mid-blue in spring • No farina • 15–25 cm high, 20–30 cm wide

'Tinkerbell' • Green-edged, black flowers in spring • With farina • 15–25 cm high, 20–30 cm wide

'Tosca' • Green-edged flowers in spring • No farina on foliage • 15–25 cm high, 20–30 cm wide

'Trouble' • Fragrant, double, copper flowers in spring • 15–25 cm high, 20–30 cm wide

'Two Tone' • Fragrant, double, pale- and dark-mauve flowers in spring • 15–25 cm high, 20–30 cm wide

'Typhoon' • Brown-purple flowers with gold centre in spring • No farina • 15–25 cm high, 20–30 cm wide

'Walton Heath' • Fragrant, double, purple-blue flowers with violet tint, in spring • 15–25 cm high, 20–30 cm wide

'Winifrid' • Red flowers with gold centre in spring • No farina • 15–25 cm high, 20–30 cm wide

'Zambia' • Fragrant, double, red-black flowers in spring • 15–25 cm high, 20–30 cm wide

Primula auricula ssp. *bauhinii*
Fragrant, pale-yellow flowers with white eye in spring • With farina • 15–25 cm high, 20–30 cm wide

Primula x *berninae*
'Windrush' • Rose-purple flowers with white eye in spring • 5–10 cm high, 10–15 cm wide

Primula x *pubescens*
White, pink, red, purple or yellow flowers in spring • 8–15 cm high, 20–30 cm wide

'Bewerley White' • Cream-white flowers in spring • 8–15 cm high, 20–30 cm wide

'Biggie's Blue' • Dark purple-blue flowers in spring • 8–15 cm high, 20–30 cm wide

'Boothman's Variety' • Velvet-red flowers with white eye in spring • 8–15 cm high, 20–30 cm wide

'Christine' • Deep-rose flowers with white eye in spring • 8–15 cm high, 20–30 cm wide

'Cream Viscosa' • Pale-yellow flowers in spring • 8–15 cm high, 20–30 cm wide

'Exhibition Blue' • Blue flowers in spring • Evergreen • 8–15 cm high, 20–30 cm wide

'Exhibition Yellow' • Yellow flowers in spring• 8–15 cm high, 20–30 cm wide

'Freedom' (syn. *P. beluensis*) • Lilac flowers in spring • 8–15 cm high, 10–20 cm wide

Primula, Garden p. 424

General Features
Height: 10–50 cm high
Spread: 15–45 cm wide
Habit: clump-forming perennial
Flowers: range of colours; showy; spring to summer
Foliage: (some) rosette forming; (some) hairy
Hardiness: B–D
Warnings: prone to slugs; not prone to insects or diseases

Growing Requirements

Light: shade to a.m. sun; tolerates more sun with good soil moisture

Soil: cool, fertile, moist to wet, organic, well-drained soil; (some) gritty soil

Location: shady mixed borders; rock gardens; woodland gardens

Propagation: seed (can self-sow); division

Buying Considerations

Professionals

Popularity: gaining popularity

Availability: generally available as finished product from specialty growers

Size to Sell: sells best in smaller sizes (when blooming) as it matures fast

On the Shelf: rapidly overgrows pot

Shrinkage: high; sensitive to overwatering or underwatering; goes dormant in pot

Collectors

Popularity: of interest to collectors—unique, rare, exceptional beauty

Gardeners

Ease of Growth: mostly easy to grow but needs close attention to growing conditions

Start with: one small plant for feature plant and several for mass plantings

What to Try First ...

Primula denticulata, Primula parryi

On the Market

Primula auriculata
Lilac to red-purple flowers with paler eye in spring • 10–40 cm high, 15–45 cm wide

Primula denticulata
Ball-like, white, lilac, rose or purple flowers with yellow eye in spring • Flowers appear before foliage • 15–30 cm high, 30–45 cm wide

'Cashmeriana Rubin' • Ball-like, red-purple flowers in spring • 15–30 cm high, 30–45 cm wide

Dwarf form • Ball-like, white, lilac, rose or purple flowers with yellow eye in spring • 15–20 cm high, 10–30 cm wide

Primula denticulata var. *alba*
Ball-like, white flowers in spring • 15–30 cm high, 30–45 cm wide

Primula flaccida (syn. *P. nutans*)
Fragrant, lavender to violet-blue flowers in summer • With farina • 20–40 cm high, 20–30 cm wide

Primula halleri
Lilac flowers with yellow eye in spring • With farina • Moist, organic, well-drained, gritty, neutral to alkaline soil • 15–25 cm high, 10–25 cm wide

Primula heucherifolia
Mauve-pink to purple flowers in early spring • Hairy foliage • 15–30 cm high, 20–30 cm wide

Primula mollis
Rose to purple flowers with yellow eye in spring • 20–50 cm high, 30–45 cm wide

Primula munroi (syn. *P. involucrata*)
White, sometimes purple, flowers with yellow eye in spring • 10–30 cm high, 15–30 cm wide

Primula munroi ssp. *yargongensis* (syn. *P. involucrata* ssp. *yargongensis*)
Pink to purple flowers with yellow eye in spring • 10–30 cm high, 15–30 cm wide

Primula parryi
Fragrant, red-purple flowers with yellow eye in late spring to early summer • 15–40 cm high, 20–40 cm wide

Primula rosea
'Grandiflora' • Bright-rose flowers with yellow eye in spring • 10–20 cm high, 15–25 cm wide

Primula rusbyi
Rose-red to purple flowers with red-ringed, yellow eye in spring • 10–20 cm high, 20–35 cm wide

Primula x *venusta*
Crimson to purple flowers with white eye in spring • 15–25 cm high, 20–30 cm wide

Primula, Polyanthus

General Features

Height: 5–30 cm high

Spread: 10–40 cm wide

Habit: clump-forming perennial

Flowers: very showy; range of colours; spring; (some) with hose-in-hose (a double corolla)

Foliage: evergreen in warmer climates; (some) rosette forming

Hardiness: C–D

Warnings: prone to aphids, not prone to diseases

Growing Requirements

Light: shade to a.m. sun; tolerates more sun with good soil moisture

Soil: moist, organic, well-drained soil

Location: shady mixed borders; rock gardens; cottage gardens

Propagation: seed (can self-sow); division

Expert Advice: Divide every 3 years to maintain vigour.

P

Buying Considerations

Professionals

Popularity: old-fashioned garden standard; popular in bloom
Availability: generally available as finished product from specialty growers
Size to Sell: sells best in smaller sizes (when blooming) as it matures fast
On the Shelf: rapidly overgrows pot; needs cleaning on a regular basis
Shrinkage: low

Collectors

Popularity: some of interest to collectors—Gold-laced Group sought after

Gardeners

Ease of Growth: easy to grow
Start with: several for mass plantings

What to Try First …

Primula 'Alejandra', *Primula* 'Freckles', *Primula* Cowichan Group, *Primula* Gold-laced Group, *Primula* Wanda Group 'Wanda Hose-in-Hose'

On the Market

Primula

'Alan Robb' • Double, apricot-yellow flowers in spring • Rosette-forming • 15–20 cm high, 20–30 cm wide

'Alejandra' • Rich-red flowers in spring • 15–20 cm high, 20–30 cm wide

'Amanda Gabrielle' • Red-purple flowers in early spring • Golden farina on foliage • 5–10 cm high, 10–20 cm wide

'Assiniboine' • Salmon-apricot flowers in spring • 15–25 cm high, 30–40 cm wide

'Betty Green' • Velvet-red flowers with yellow eye in spring • 15–20 cm high, 20–30 cm wide

'Blue Riband' • Amethyst-blue flowers with yellow eye in spring • 15–20 cm high, 20–30 cm wide

'Blue Sapphire' • Double, vivid-blue flowers in spring • 15–20 cm high, 20–30 cm wide

'Bronwyn' • Powder-blue flowers in spring • Evergreen • 15–25 cm high, 20–30 cm wide

'Corporal Baxter' • Double, scarlet flowers in spring • 15–20 cm high, 20–30 cm wide

'Dorothy' • Fringed, cream to yellow flowers in spring • 15–20 cm high, 20–30 cm wide

'Francesca' • Single, fringed, green flowers in spring • Evergreen • 15–25 cm high, 20–30 cm wide

'Freckles' • Double, deep-red flowers with white spots in spring • 15–20 cm high, 20–30 cm wide

Gigantia mix • Mixed-colour flowers in spring • Evergreen • 15–25 cm high, 20–30 cm wide

'Granny Graham' • Double, blue-violet flowers in spring • 15–20 cm high, 20–30 cm wide

'Guinevere' • Pink flowers with yellow eye in spring • Bronze foliage • 15–20 cm high, 20–30 cm wide

'Jay Jay' • Magenta-red flowers in spring • 15–20 cm high, 20–30 cm wide

'Ken Dearman' • Orange, yellow and copper-shaded flowers in spring • 15–20 cm high, 20–30 cm wide

'Kinlough Beauty' • Salmon-pink flowers with cream stripe and yellow eye in spring • 15–20 cm high, 20–30 cm wide

'Lilian Harvey' • Double, cerise-pink flowers in spring • 15–20 cm high, 20–30 cm wide

'Lizzie Green' • Bright-red flowers in spring • 15–20 cm high, 20–30 cm wide

'Millicent' • Yellow flowers flushed pink in spring • 15–20 cm high, 20–30 cm wide

'Miss Indigo' • Double, deep rich-purple flowers with cream tips in spring • Evergreen • 15–20 cm high, 20–30 cm wide

'Mountain Purple' • Purple flowers in spring • 10–15 cm high, 20–30 cm wide

'Pacific Giant' • Mixed, bright-coloured, yellow-eyed flowers in spring • Evergreen • 15–25 cm high, 20–30 cm wide

'Perle von Bottrop' • Dark-purple flowers in spring • 15–20 cm high, 20–30 cm wide

'Purpurkissen' (Purple Cushion) • Purple flowers in spring • 15–20 cm high, 20–30 cm wide

'Red Velvet' • Double, bright-red flowers in spring • 15–20 cm high, 20–30 cm wide

'Rosetta Red' • Double, red flowers in spring • Evergreen • 15–25 cm high, 20–30 cm wide

'Schneekissen' (Snow Cushion) • White flowers in spring • 15–20 cm high, 20–30 cm wide

'Sue Jervis' • Double, pink flowers in spring • Evergreen • 15–20 cm high, 20–30 cm wide

P

'Tie Dye' • Purple, blue-streaked flowers in spring • Evergreen • 15–20 cm high, 20–30 cm wide

Bergfruhling Julianas Group
Purple flowers with yellow eye in spring • 15–20 cm high, 20–30 cm wide

Cowichan Group
'Cowichan Amethyst' • Amethyst flowers in spring • Evergreen • 15–25 cm high, 20–30 cm wide

'Cowichan Blue' • Rich-blue flowers in spring • Evergreen • 15–25 cm high, 20–30 cm wide

'Cowichan Garnet' • Garnet flowers in spring • Evergreen • 15–25 cm high, 20–30 cm wide

'Cowichan Ruby Red' • Dark ruby-red flowers in spring • Evergreen • 15–25 cm high, 20–30 cm wide

'Cowichan Velvet Moon' • Deep velvet-red flowers in spring • Evergreen • 15–25 cm high, 20–30 cm wide

'Cowichan Violet-Purple' • Violet-purple flowers in spring • Evergreen • 15–25 cm high, 20–30 cm wide

Gold-laced Group
Gold and brown flowers with gold lace on rim in spring • Evergreen • 15–25 cm high, 20–30 cm wide

'Barnhaven Gold' • Pale-yellow flowers in spring • Evergreen • 15–25 cm high, 20–30 cm wide

'Mahogany Sunrise' • Mahogany-red flowers with gold edge in spring • Evergreen • 15–25 cm high, 20–30 cm wide

'Yvonne' • Red-brown flowers with gold centre and gold edge in spring • Evergreen • 15–25 cm high, 20–30 cm wide

Wanda Group
'Wanda' • Purple-red flowers with yellow eye in spring • Glossy, burgundy-tinted foliage • 15–20 cm high, 20–30 cm wide

'Wanda Hose-in-Hose' • Purple-red flowers in spring • 15–20 cm high, 20–30 cm wide

Primula x *polyantha*
Mixed-coloured flowers in spring • Evergreen • 15–25 cm high, 20–30 cm wide

Primula x *tommasinii*
Fragrant, hose-in-hose, sulphur-yellow flowers in early spring • 30 cm high, 30 cm wide

You and Me Series
Fragrant, hose-in-hose, purple, red or rose flowers in spring • 30 cm high, 30 cm wide

Primula *veris*
Fragrant, nodding, gold-yellow flowers in spring • Evergreen • 15–30 cm high, 20–30 cm wide

'Aurea' • Rich-yellow flowers in spring • 15–30 cm high, 20–30 cm wide

'Sunset Shades' • Fragrant, mix of sunset-coloured flowers in spring • 15–30 cm high, 20–30 cm wide

Primula *veris* ssp. *macrocalyx*
Bright-yellow flowers in spring • Evergreen • 15–30 cm high, 20–30 cm wide

Primula *vulgaris*
Fragrant, pale-yellow flowers in spring • Evergreen • 15–25 cm high, 20–30 cm wide

Crayon Series
Mixed, bright-coloured flowers in spring • Evergreen • 15–25 cm high, 20–30 cm wide

'Lilacina Plena' (Quaker's Bonnet) • Double, soft-lilac flowers in spring • Evergreen • 15–25 cm high, 20–30 cm wide

'Mark Viette' • Fragrant, rose flowers in spring • Evergreen • 15–25 cm high, 20–30 cm wide

Northern Series
'Northern Pink' • Double, pink flowers in spring • Evergreen • 15–25 cm high, 20–30 cm wide

'Northern Red' • Double, red flowers in spring • Evergreen • 15–25 cm high, 20–30 cm wide

Primula *vulgaris* ssp. *sibthorpii*
Red, purple or pink, sometimes white, flowers in spring • Evergreen • 15–25 cm high, 20–30 cm wide

Primula, **Woodland/Bog**   p. 424

General Features
Height: 5–90 cm high
Spread: 10–60 cm wide
Habit: clump-forming, rhizomatous (colony-forming) perennial
Flowers: (many) very fragrant; (some) candelabra-shaped on stem; spring to late summer; (some) go dormant after flowering
Foliage: deciduous; (some) retain a small rosette at base
Hardiness: C–D
Warnings: prone to aphids, spider mites and slugs; not prone to diseases
Expert Advice: This group is best situated in moist to wet organic soil.

Growing Requirements

Light: shade to a.m. sun; tolerates more sun with good soil moisture
Soil: cool, fertile, moist to wet, organic, well-drained soil
Location: shady mixed borders; rock gardens; watersides; woodland gardens
Propagation: seed; division

Buying Considerations

Professionals

Popularity: gaining popularity; sells well in bloom
Availability: generally available as finished product
Size to Sell: sells best in smaller sizes (when blooming) as it matures fast
On the Shelf: rapidly overgrows pot
Shrinkage: high; sensitive to overwatering or underwatering; goes dormant in pot

Collectors

Popularity: of interest to collectors

Gardeners

Ease of Growth: mostly easy to grow but needs close attention to growing conditions
Start with: one small plant for feature plant

What to Try First ...

Primula alpicola var. *violacea*, *Primula chionantha* ssp. *chionantha*, *Primula chionantha* ssp. *sinopurpurea*, *Primula cortusoides*, *Primula elatior*, *Primula florindae*, *Primula sieboldii*

On the Market

Primula alpicola
Fragrant, white, yellow or violet flowers in late spring to early summer • 30–45 cm high, 20–30 cm wide

Primula alpicola var. *alba*
Fragrant, white flowers in late spring to early summer • 30–45 cm high, 20–30 cm wide

Primula alpicola var. *luna*
Fragrant, yellow flowers with farina in late spring to early summer • 30–45 cm high, 20–30 cm wide

Primula alpicola var. *violacea*
Fragrant, violet, sometimes pink to rose, flowers in late spring to early summer • 30–45 cm high, 20–30 cm wide

Primula beesiana
Candelabra-like, rose to red-purple flowers with yellow eye in summer • 45–60 cm high, 45–60 cm wide

Primula x *bulleesiana*
Orange-yellow to mauve flowers in summer • 30–60 cm high, 45–60 cm wide

Primula bulleyana
Candelabra-like, orange flowers in summer • 30–60 cm high, 30–60 cm wide

Primula burmanica
Candelabra-like, purple-red flowers with yellowish eye in spring • Very, moist, fertile, well-drained, organic soil • 45–60 cm high, 45–60 cm wide

Primula chionantha (syn. *P. nivalis*)
Violet to rose flowers in spring • Cool, very moist, well-drained, organic soil • 10–40 cm high, 20–30 cm wide

Primula chionantha ssp. *chionantha*
Fragrant, milk-white flowers in spring • Cool, very moist, well-drained, fertile, organic soil • 45–60 cm high, 30–45 cm wide

Primula chionantha var. *farinosa* (*P. nivalis* var. *farinosa*)
Dark-violet flowers in spring • White farina on foliage edge or underside • Cool, very moist, well-drained, gritty soil • 10–40 cm high, 20–30 cm wide

Primula chionantha ssp. *melanops* (syn. *P. melanops*)
Fragrant, purple flowers with black eye in summer • Cool, very moist, well-drained, organic, fertile soil • 20–35 cm high, 30–45 cm wide

Primula chionantha ssp. *sinoplantaginea* (syn. *P. sinoplantaginea*)
Fragrant, blue to purple flowers in summer • 10–20 cm high, 15–25 cm wide

Primula chionantha ssp. *sinopurpurea* (syn. *P. sinopurpurea*)
Violet to rose-purple flowers with white to grey eye in summer • Yellow farina on the underside of the foliage • 20–45 cm high, 30–45 cm wide

Primula capitata
Blue to dark-violet flowers in late summer • Rosette forming • 10–40 cm high, 20–40 cm wide

Primula capitata ssp. *mooreana*
Fragrant, deep-violet flowers in late summer • Rosette forming • 20–60 cm high, 30–45 cm wide

Primula cernua
Deep-violet flowers in summer • With farina • 15–40 cm high, 20–30 cm wide

Primula chungensis
Fragrant, yellow to orange flowers with red tubes in late spring to early summer • 50–75 cm high, 45–60 cm wide

P

Primula cockburniana
Candelabra-like, fiery-copper-orange flowers in summer • 15–30 cm high, 15–20 cm wide

Primula concholoba
Bell, soft-blue to purple flowers in late spring to early summer • With farina • 8–15 cm high, 10–15 cm wide

Primula cortusoides
Rose to purple-red flowers with yellow eye in early summer • 20–30 cm high, 20–30 cm wide

Primula elatior
Sulphur-yellow flowers in early spring • 15–20 cm high, 30 cm wide

Primula elatior ssp. meyeri (syn. *P. amoena*)
Purple to mauve flowers with yellow eye in spring • 10–30 cm high, 15–25 cm wide

Primula edelbergii
Gold-yellow flowers in spring • 10–20 cm high, 15–25 cm wide

Primula erthrocarpa
Soft-mauve flowers with yellow eye in spring • 15–30 cm high, 20–30 cm wide

Primula florindae
Fragrant, sulphur-yellow flowers in summer • The largest primrose • 60–90 cm high, 30–45 cm wide

Kellour hybrid • Fragrant, yellow to red flowers in summer • 60–90 cm high, 30–45 cm wide

Red form • Fragrant, orange-red flowers in summer • 60–90 cm high, 30–45 cm wide

Primula geraniifolia
Rose to purple flowers in summer • 15–30 cm high, 20–30 cm wide

Primula glomerata
Purple-blue flowers with darker eye in late summer • 10–30 cm high, 20–30 cm wide

Primula incana
Lavender-blue flowers with yellow eye in late spring • With farina • 20–45 cm high, 15–20 cm wide

Primula ioessa
Fragrant, funnel-shaped, lilac-blue to violet or white flowers in spring to early summer • 10–30 cm high, 15–30 cm wide

Primula irregularis
Pink flowers with yellow eye in spring • 10–15 cm high, 10–20 cm wide

Primula japonica
Purple, pink or white flowers in early summer • 30–45 cm high, 30–45 cm wide

'Alba' • White flowers in early summer • 30–45 cm high, 30–45 cm wide

'Atropurpurea' • White, purple or pink flowers in early summer • Dark foliage • 30–45 cm high, 30–45 cm wide

'Miller's Crimson' • Crimson flowers in early summer • 30–45 cm high, 30–45 cm wide

'Valley Red' • Deep-red flowers in early summer • 30–45 cm high, 30–45 cm wide

Primula x kewensis
Fragrant, yellow flowers in early spring • 20–40 cm high, 20–30 cm wide

Primula kisoana
Rose-violet or white flowers in spring • 10–20 cm high, 20–40 cm wide

Primula kisoana var. alba
White flowers in spring • 10–20 cm high, 20–40 cm wide

Primula latifolia (syn. *P. viscosa*)
Fragrant, red-violet to purple flowers in late spring to early summer • Moist, neutral to acidic, sharply drained, organic soil • 15–20 cm high, 20–30 cm wide

Primula laurentiana (syn. *P. mistassinica* var. *macropoda*)
Lilac-pink to purple flowers with yellow eye in spring to early summer • Moist, fertile, neutral to alkaline soil • 5–30 cm high, 10–15 cm wide

Primula macrophylla
Lilac, purple, or violet flowers with black or yellow eye in summer • 10–30 cm high, 20–30 cm wide

Primula poissonii
Purple-red flowers with gold eye in summer • Shiny, evergreen foliage • Organic, fertile, very moist soil • 30–45 cm high, 25–40 cm wide

Primula polyneura
Rose to purple, sometimes red, flowers with yellow eye in late spring to early summer • Hairy foliage • Moist, well-drained, organic, deep soil • 30–45 cm high, 30–45 cm wide

**Primula prolifera
(syn. *P. helodoxa and smithiana*)**
Fragrant, candelabra-like, gold-yellow, sometimes violet, flowers in spring • Evergreen • 50–75 cm high, 40–60 cm wide

Primula pulverulenta
Red-purple or red flowers with darker-red or purple eye in summer • 60–90 cm high, 45–60 cm wide

Primula reidii
Fragrant, large, white or soft-blue to mid-blue flowers in early summer • Sharply drained, organic, very moist, gritty soil • 5–15 cm high, 10–15 cm wide

Primula saxatilis
Mauve to pink-purple flowers in summer • 10–25 cm high, 20–30 cm wide

Primula secundiflora
Nodding, rose to red-purple flowers in late spring • Evergreen • 30–90 cm high, 45–60 cm wide

Primula spectabilis
Pink to lilac flowers, often with white eye, in spring to early summer • 5–15 cm high, 10–15 cm wide

Primula sieboldii
White, pink or magenta flowers in early summer • 15–30 cm high, 30–45 cm wide

'Akatonbo' • Lacy, dark cerise-red flowers in early summer • 15–30 cm high, 30–45 cm wide

'Benkeijo' • Purple-red flowers with white eye in early summer • 15–30 cm high, 30–45 cm wide

'Cherubim' • Pink flowers in early summer • 15–30 cm high, 30–45 cm wide

'Dawson's Southern Cross' • Large, silver-white flowers with mauve reverse sides in early summer • 15–30 cm high, 30–45 cm wide

'Fimbriated Red' • Cerise-red flowers in early summer • 15–30 cm high, 30–45 cm wide

'Geisha Girl' • Shocking-pink flowers with white frosting in early summer • 15–30 cm high, 30–45 cm wide

'Isotaka' • White flowers with purple reverse in early summer • 15–30 cm high, 30–45 cm wide

'Kuisakigami' • Notched, white flowers in early summer • 15–30 cm high, 30–45 cm wide

'Lilac Sunbonnet' • Soft-lilac flowers in early summer • 15–30 cm high, 30–45 cm wide

'Mikado' • Red-purple flowers in early summer • 15–30 cm high, 30–45 cm wide

'Mikunino-Homari' • Shell-pink flowers with white eye in early summer • 15–30 cm high, 30–45 cm wide

'Musashino' • Large, pale rose-pink flowers in early summer • 15–30 cm high, 30–45 cm wide

'Neon Lights' • Fuchsia, snowflake-shaped flowers with duller reverse sides in early summer • 15–30 cm high, 30–45 cm wide

'Sayogorama' • White and soft pink flowers in early summer • 15–30 cm high, 30–45 cm wide

'Shi-un' • Fringed, deep-lavender flowers in early summer • 15–30 cm high, 30–45 cm wide

'Snowflake' • Large, snow-white flowers in early summer • 15–30 cm high, 30–45 cm wide

'Sumina' • Large, wisteria-blue flowers in early summer • 15–30 cm high, 30–45 cm wide

'Yubisugata' • Jagged, white and lavender flowers with white eye in early summer • 15–30 cm high, 30–45 cm wide

Primula sieboldii var. *purpurea*
Small, vivid purple-red flowers in early summer • 15–30 cm high, 30–45 cm wide

Primula sikkimensis
Fragrant, cream to sulphur-yellow flowers in late spring to early summer • 60–90 cm high, 30–60 cm wide

Primula sikkimensis var. *pudibunda*
Soft-yellow flowers in late spring to early summer • 30–45 cm high, 30–45 cm wide

Primula vialii
Fragrant, blue-violet and red, poker flowers in early summer • 30–60 cm high, 20–30 cm wide

'Miracle' • Blue-violet and red poker flowers in early summer • 30–60 cm high, 20–30 cm wide

Primula waltonii
Fragrant, pink to wine-red flowers with red eye in late spring to early summer • 30–50 cm high, 20–30 cm wide

Primula wilsonii
Fragrant, red to black flowers with gold-green ring at base in summer • 30–60 cm high, 30–45 cm wide

Primula wilsonii var. *anisodora* (syn. *P. anisodora*)
Fragrant, purple to black flowers with green ring at base in summer • 30–60 cm high, 30–45 cm wide

Prunella

Genus Information

Origin: Europe and Asia
Selected Common Names: big flower selfheal
Nomenclature: From *Brunella*, but the derivation is obscure. The name may have come from the German *Die Breaume* (quinsy), which is the throat infection that this plant was reputed to cure.

General Features

Height: 15–30 cm high
Spread: 60–90 cm wide
Habit: upright, rapidly spreading perennial
Flowers: Tiny, tubular blooms borne on the end of stalk; summer; attracts bees and butterflies
Foliage: semi-evergreen
Hardiness: C
Warnings: prone to aphids and powdery mildew; vigorous spreader (contain to prevent spread and deadhead to prevent self-seeding)
Expert Advice: A very useful and underused perennial that has not been well-received commercially. Site it where it can spread without crowding out other plants.

Growing Requirements

Light: sun to p.m. sun
Soil: well-drained soil; drought tolerant
Location: banks; meadows; mixed borders; wild gardens; groundcover
Propagation: seed (self-sows readily); division
Expert Advice: Germinate seed at 6–12°C in spring. Divide in fall.

Buying Considerations

Professionals

Popularity: relatively unknown
Availability: occasionally available from specialty growers
Size to Sell: sells best in smaller sizes (when blooming) as it matures fast
Shrinkage: low; requires little maintenance

Collectors

Popularity: not generally of interest to collectors

Gardeners

Ease of Growth: very easy to grow
Start with: one small plant for feature plant

What to Try First ...

Prunella grandiflora

On the Market

Prunella grandiflora
Spiked, violet-purple flowers in summer •
15–30 cm high, 60–90+ cm wide

'Rotkappchen' (Little Red Riding Hood)
• Carmine-red flowers in summer
• 15–30 cm high, 60–90+ cm wide

Pulmonaria

p. 424

Genus Information

Origin: Europe and Asia
Selected Common Names: Bethlehem sage, lungwort, spotted dog
Nomenclature: From the Latin *pulmonarius* (having lung disease), in reference to the spotted leaves of *P. officinalis* that are said to resemble diseased lungs.

General Features

Height: 20–45 cm high
Spread: 30–60 cm wide
Habit: rhizomatous, creeping groundcover perennial
Flowers: pink, blue or pink, fading to blue; early spring
Foliage: coarse, hairy; green to spotted; long to oval-shaped; attractive all season
Hardiness: C
Warnings: prone to powdery mildew in drier locations, aphids and slugs; contact with foliage may irritate skin
Expert Advice: A valuable early source of nectar for bees. Plant to great effect with *Dicentra*, *Hosta* and *Primula*.

Growing Requirements

Light: shade to a.m sun; tolerates more sun with good soil moisture
Soil: fertile, organic, well-drained soil; tolerates acidic soil; tolerates some dryness once established
Location: mixed borders; wild gardens; woodland gardens
Propagation: seed; division; root cuttings
Expert Advice: Hybridizes easily. May not come true from seed. Divide in spring or fall, although *Pulmonaria* does not require dividing to maintain vigour.

Buying Considerations

Professionals

Popularity: popular; fast selling with interesting foliage; has new varieties
Availability: readily available as finished product from specialty growers
Size to Sell: sells best in smaller sizes (when blooming) as it matures fast
On the Shelf: high ornamental appeal; keep stock rotated; rapidly overgrows pot
Shrinkage: high; sensitive to overwatering or underwatering; keep evenly moist

Collectors

Popularity: not generally of interest to collectors

Gardeners

Ease of Growth: very easy to grow
Start with: one plant for feature plant and several for mass plantings

P

What to Try First ...

Pulmonaria 'Baby Blue', *Pulmonaria* 'Berries and Cream', *Pulmonaria* 'Blue Ensign', *Pulmonaria* 'Cotton Cool', *Pulmonaria* 'Little Star', *Pulmonaria* 'Pierre's Pure Pink', *Pulmonaria* 'Raspberry Splash', *Pulmonaria* 'Roy Davidson', *Pulmonaria* 'Victorian Brooch', *Pulmonaria longifolia* 'Bertram Anderson', *Pulmonaria longifolia cevennensis, Pulmonaria rubra, Pulmonaria rubra* 'Redstart', *Pulmonaria saccharata* 'Argentea', *Pulmonaria saccharata* 'Silverado'

On the Market

Pulmonaria

'Baby Blue' • Pink, fading to blue flowers in spring • Silver foliage • 20–25 cm high, 30 cm wide

'Berries and Cream' • Raspberry-red flowers in spring • Silver-white foliage with green edge • 20–30 cm high, 45–60 cm wide

'Blue Ensign' • Funnel-shaped, large, blue flowers in spring • 20–30 cm high, 45–60 cm wide

'British Sterling' • Magenta buds open to blue flowers in spring • Silver foliage with green edge • 20–30 cm high, 45–60 cm wide

'Bubble Gum' • Tubular, pink flowers in spring • Silver foliage • 20–30 cm high, 45–60 cm wide

'Cotton Cool' • Blue flowers in spring • Narrow, silvery foliage • 20–30 cm high, 45–60 cm wide

'De Vroomen's Pride' • Blue flowers, fading to pink, in spring • Silver-green foliage with green edge • 20–30 cm high, 45–60 cm wide

'Diana Clare' • Violet-blue flowers in spring • Silvery, apple-green foliage • 20–30 cm high, 45–60 cm wide

'Excalibur' • Violet-blue flowers, fading to pink, in spring • Silver foliage with green edge • 20–30 cm high, 45–60 cm wide

'Fiona' • Pink flowers with white edge in spring • Green foliage • 20–30 cm high, 45–60 cm wide

'Gaelic Magic' • Pink flowers in spring • Silver-spotted, green foliage • 30–40 cm high, 45–60 cm wide

'Gaelic Sunset' • Pink flowers in spring • Silver-splotched, light green foliage • 30–40 cm high, 45–60 cm wide

'Golden Haze' • Light blue flowers in early spring • Narrow, white-spotted foliage with gold edge • 20–30 cm high, 30–45 cm wide

'Irish Spring' • Pink to blue flowers in spring • Mint-green overlaid on darker foliage • 20–30 cm high, 45–60 cm wide

'Leopard' • Pink and red flowers in spring • Silver-spotted, green foliage • 20–30 cm high, 45–60 cm wide

'Little Star' • Cobalt-blue flowers in spring • Silver-white foliage • 20–30 cm high, 30–45 cm wide

'Majeste' • Blue flowers, fading to pink, in spring • Shiny, silver-green foliage • 20–30 cm high, 45–60 cm wide

'Margery Fish' • Coral-red flowers, fading to violet, in spring • White-spotted, green foliage • 20–30 cm high, 45–60 cm wide

'Mary Mottram' • Blue flowers in spring • Silver-white foliage with green edge • 20–30 cm high, 45–60 cm wide

'Milchstrasse' (Milky Way) • Red buds, opening to blue, in spring • Heavy, silver-white, spotted foliage • 20–30 cm high, 45–60 cm wide

'Mrs. Kittle' • Soft-blue flowers in spring • Silver-spotted foliage • 20–30 cm high, 45–60 cm wide

'Northern Lights' • Cranberry to blue-purple flowers in spring • Silver and green foliage • 20–30 cm high, 45–60 cm wide

'Opal' (Ocupol) • Soft-blue flowers in spring • Silver-spotted foliage • 20–30 cm high, 45–60 cm wide

'Pierre's Pure Pink' • Shell-pink flowers in spring • Silver-spotted, green foliage • 20–30 cm high, 45–60 cm wide

'Polar Splash' • Blue to pink flowers in spring • Silver-spotted foliage • 20–30 cm high, 45–60 cm wide

'Purple Haze' • Pink flowers, fading to purple, in spring • Silver-spotted foliage • 20–30 cm high, 45–60 cm wide

'Raspberry Ice' • Raspberry-pink flowers in spring • Cream-edged, mint-green foliage • 30–35 cm high, 45–60 cm wide

'Raspberry Splash' • Raspberry-red flowers in spring • Pointed, white-spotted, upright foliage • 20–30 cm high, 30–45 cm wide

'Regal Ruffles' • Purple-violet flowers in spring • Heavy, silver-spotted foliage • 20–30 cm high, 45–60 cm wide

P

'Roy Davidson' • Light blue to blue flowers in spring • White-spotted foliage • 20–30 cm high, 30–45 cm wide

'Samarai' • Blue flowers in spring • Shiny, silver-green foliage • 20–30 cm high, 45–60 cm wide

'Silver Shimmers' • Steel-blue flowers in spring • Narrow, wavy, silvery foliage • 20–25 cm high, 30–45 cm wide

'Silver Streamers' • Purple-blue flowers in spring • Ruffled-edged, silver foliage • 20–30 cm high, 30–45 cm wide

'Sissinghurst White' • Soft-pink flowers, opening to white, in spring • Silver-spotted, green foliage • 20–30 cm high, 45–60 cm wide

'Smoky Blue' • Pink flowers, fading to blue, in spring • Silver-spotted foliage • 20–30 cm high, 45–60 cm wide

'Spilled Milk' • Rose-pink flowers, fading to blue, in spring • Silver foliage • 20–30 cm high, 45–60 cm wide

'Victorian Brooch' • Outward-facing, magenta-coral flowers with ruby-red centre in early spring to early summer • Long, silver-spotted foliage • 20–30 cm high, 30–45 cm wide

Pulmonaria angustifolia
'Blaues Meer' (Blue Sea) • Gentian-blue flowers in spring • 20–30 cm high, 45–60 cm wide

Pulmonaria angustifolia ssp. *azurea*
Sky-blue flowers with red buds in spring • 20–30 cm high, 45–60 cm wide

Pulmonaria longifolia
'Bertram Anderson' • Deep violet-blue flowers in spring • Silver-spotted foliage • 20–30 cm high, 45–60 cm wide

Pulmonaria longifolia ssp. *cevennensis*
Blue flowers in spring • Long, narrow, white-spotted foliage • 20–30 cm high, 45–60 cm wide

Pulmonaria mollis
'Samobor' • Blue-purple flowers in spring • Soft foliage • 30–45 cm high, 45–60 cm wide

Pulmonaria officinalis
'Blue Mist' • Deep-blue flowers in spring • 20–30 cm high, 45–60 cm wide

Pulmonaria rubra
Salmon to red flowers in spring • 30–45 cm high, 45–60 cm wide

'Ann' • Soft-red flowers with lighter streaks in spring • 30–45 cm high, 45–60 cm wide

'Barfield Pink' • Pink flowers with white veins and edges in spring • 20–30 cm high, 45–60 cm wide

'David Ward' • Coral-red flowers in spring • Mint-green foliage with white edge • 30–45 cm high, 45–60 cm wide

'Redstart' • Coral-red flowers in early spring • 30–45 cm high, 45–60 cm wide

Pulmonaria saccharata
Rose-red, opening to blue flowers in spring • Spotted foliage • 20–30 cm high, 45–60 cm wide

'Argentea' • Red flowers, fading to blue, in spring • Heavy, silver-frosted foliage • 20–30 cm high, 45–60 cm wide

'Dora Bielefeld' • Non-fading, pink flowers in spring • Silver-spotted foliage • 20–30 cm high, 45–60 cm wide

'Mrs. Moon' • Red-tinted, lilac flowers in spring • 20–30 cm high, 45–60 cm wide

'Silverado' • Blue, pink and white flowers in spring • Silver foliage • 20–30 cm high, 45–60 cm wide

Pulsatilla
p. 424 📷

Genus Information

Origin: Europe, Asia and North America
Selected Common Names: Pasque flower, prairie crocus, windflower
Nomenclature: From the Latin, referring to how the plant pulsates in the wind.
Notes: Formerly in the genus *Anemone*. *Pulsatilla* is different from *Anemone* by the nectar-secreting staminodes and feather-like styles.

General Features

Height: 15–60 cm high
Spread: 10–30 cm wide
Habit: clump-forming perennial
Flowers: large; early spring; may rebloom in fall; produces fluffy seed heads; good for winter interest
Foliage: fern-like, hairy
Hardiness: A–C
Warnings: prone to aphids; not prone to diseases; contact with sap may irritate skin; ingesting flowers or foliage may cause stomach upset
Expert Advice: This plant is known as Pasque (or Easter) flower, which is about the time in blooms in some places. In northern gardens it blooms in early spring.

Growing Requirements

Light: sun to p.m. sun
Soil: fertile, moist, sharply drained soil
Location: rock gardens; edging borders; scree
Propagation: seed; root cuttings
Expert Advice: Germinate seed when ripe by planting outdoors in fall. Plants will bloom the 2nd year. Division is quite difficult as it resents being disturbed.

Buying Considerations

Professionals
Popularity: popular garden standard; fast seller in bloom
Availability: readily available as finished product
Size to Sell: sells best when blooming
On the Shelf: keep stock rotated
Shrinkage: low; requires little maintenance

Collectors
Popularity: not generally of interest to collectors

Gardeners
Ease of Growth: very easy to grow
Start with: one small plant for feature plant or many for mass plantings

What to Try First ...
Pulsatilla kostyczewii, Pulsatilla patens, Pulsatilla vulgaris, Pulsatilla vulgaris ssp. *grandis* 'Papageno', *Pulsatilla vulgaris* var. *rubra*

On the Market

Pulsatilla alpina ssp. *apiifolia*
Soft-yellow flowers in early spring • Fern-like foliage • 20–45 cm high, 20–30 cm wide

Pulsatilla halleri
Violet to lavender flowers in late spring • Fern-like foliage • 15–30 cm high, 20–30 cm wide

Pulsatilla kostyczewii
Large, rose-pink flowers in spring • Fern-like foliage • 15–30 cm high, 15–30 cm wide

Pulsatilla lutea
Yellow flowers in late spring • Fern-like foliage • 20–30 cm high, 15–30 cm wide

Pulsatilla occidentalis
Cream-white flowers, outsides often flushed purple, in spring • Tolerates dry soil • 15–60 cm high, 20–30 cm wide

Pulsatilla patens **(syn.** *Anemone patens***)**
Mauve-pink flowers, sometimes cream, in early spring • Fern-like foliage • 10–15 cm high, 10–20 cm wide

Pulsatilla turczaninovii
Deep purple-blue flowers in late spring • Fern-like foliage • 5–35 cm high, 20–30 cm wide

Pulsatilla vernalis
White flowers, outside flushed pink or violet, in spring • Fern-like foliage • 15–30 cm high, 15–30 cm wide

Pulsatilla vulgaris
Purple to burgundy flowers, sometimes white or deep red, in spring • Fern-like foliage • 15–45 cm high, 15–30 cm wide

'Alba' • White flowers in spring • Fern-like foliage • 15–45 cm high, 15–30 cm wide

'Elegans' • Rose-red flowers in spring • Fern-like foliage • 15–45 cm high, 15–30 cm wide

Heiler hybrids • Mix of colours that flower in spring • Fern-like foliage • 15–45 cm high, 15–30 cm wide

'Nigrum' • Red-black flowers in spring • Fern-like foliage • 15–45 cm high, 15–30 cm wide

'Rode Klokke' (Red Clock, Red Bells) • Red flowers in spring • Fern-like foliage • 15–45 cm high, 15–30 cm wide

Pulsatilla vulgaris ssp. *grandis*
'Papageno' • Single to semi-double, fringed, white, pink, red or purple flowers in spring • Fern-like foliage • 15–45 cm high, 15–30 cm wide

Pulsatilla vulgaris var. *rubra*
Deep-red flowers in spring • Fern-like foliage • 20–45 cm high, 15–30 cm wide

P

Ramonda

p. 424 📷

Genus Information

Origin: Europe
Selected Common Names: Pyrenean primrose
Nomenclature: Named for Louis Ramond, the Baron de Carbonniere, 1753–1827, who was a French botanist.
Notes: *Ramonda* is a member of the African violet family.

General Features

Height: 5–10 cm high
Spread: 6–20 cm wide
Habit: rosette-forming perennial
Flowers: short blooming period; spring to early summer
Foliage: hairy, crinkled; evergreen
Hardiness: C
Warnings: not prone to insects or disease

Growing Requirements

Light: shade to a.m. shade; shelter from hot p.m. sun
Soil: fertile, moist, sharply drained, alkaline soil; avoid winter wet
Location: rock gardens; tufa; wall crevices
Propagation: seed; division; leaf cuttings
Expert Advice: The plant dislikes having standing water on its foliage, so it grows particularly well in protected vertical wall crevices. Seedlings are very slow to grow.

Buying Considerations

Professionals

Popularity: relatively unknown
Availability: occasionally available from specialty growers
Size to Sell: sells best in mature sizes (when blooming); matures slowly
Shrinkage: low; sensitive to overwatering; requires little maintenance

Collectors

Popularity: of interest to collectors—unique, exceptional beauty, rare, challenge, novelty

Gardeners

Ease of Growth: mostly difficult to grow as it needs close attention to growing conditions
Start with: one mature plant for feature plant

What to Try First ...

Ramonda myconi, Ramonda myconi var. *alba*

On the Market

Ramonda myconi
Violet to pink flowers in spring to early summer • Crinkly, evergreen foliage • 5–10 cm high, 15–20 cm wide

Ramonda myconi var. *alba*
Pure white flowers in late spring to early summer • Crinkly, evergreen foliage • 5–10 cm high, 15–20 cm wide

Ramonda nathaliae
Lilac to violet flowers with orange eye in late spring • Evergreen foliage • 5–8 cm high, 6–12 cm wide

Ramonda serbica
Pink to violet flowers with yellow eye in early summer • Evergreen foliage • 5–10 cm high, 15–20 cm wide

Ranunculus

p. 424 📷

Genus Information

Origin: temperate and boreal regions and tropical mountains
Selected Common Names: buttercup
Nomenclature: From the Latin *rana* (a frog), referring to the wet habitats in which some species grow. A name used by Pliny.
Notes: Genus includes annual, biennial and perennial species.

General Features

Height: 5–100 cm high
Spread: 5–75 cm wide
Habit: spreading or clump-forming perennial
Flowers: yellow or white; cup-shaped; spring to summer; alpine types bloom intermittently through season
Foliage: mid- to dark-green; (some) semi-evergreen
Hardiness: B–C
Warnings: prone to powdery mildew and aphids; (some) may be invasive in warmer climates (contain and deadhead to prevent spread); contact with sap may irritate skin
Expert Advice: There are different types of *Ranunculus* suited for every garden type.

Growing Requirements

Light: sun to p.m. sun
Soil: fertile, moist, organic, sharply drained to well-drained soil
Location: cool alpine gardens; rock gardens; woodland gardens; mixed borders
Propagation: seed; division
Expert Advice: Alpine types have erratic germination from seed.

Buying Considerations

Professionals
Popularity: relatively unknown
Availability: generally available as bare root from specialty growers
Size to Sell: sells best in smaller sizes (when blooming) as it matures fast
On the Shelf: keep stock rotated; rapidly overgrows pot
Shrinkage: low; requires little maintenance

Collectors
Popularity: not generally of interest to collectors except for some of the alpines

Gardeners
Ease of Growth: very easy to grow
Start with: one small plant for feature plant

What to Try First ...
Ranunculus acris 'Flore Pleno', *Ranunculus crenatus*, *Ranunculus ficaria* 'Brazen Hussy', *Ranunculus gramineus*, *Ranunculus repens* 'Buttered Popcorn'

On the Market

Ranunculus aconitifolius
Single, white flowers in spring to early summer • Dark-green foliage • 45–75 cm high, 45–60 cm wide
'Flore Pleno' • Double, white flowers in spring to early summer • 45–75 cm high, 45–60 cm wide

Ranunculus acris
'Flore Pleno' • Sunny-yellow flowers in summer • 45–90 cm high, 20–30 cm wide

Ranunculus alpestris
Pure white flowers in late spring to midsummer • Semi-evergreen alpine (prefers gritty soil) • 5–10 cm high, 5–10 cm wide

Ranunculus crenatus
Large, white flowers with yellow eye in spring • Semi-evergreen alpine (prefers gritty soil) • 5–10 cm high, 10–15 cm wide

Ranunculus ficaria
'Brazen Hussy' • Sulphur-yellow flowers in spring • Heart-shaped, glossy, chocolate-brown foliage • Gritty soil • May be invasive • 5–10 cm high, 20–30+ cm wide

Ranunculus grahamii
Yellow flowers in spring • 5–10 cm high, 15–20 cm wide

Ranunculus gramineus
Gold flowers in spring • Narrow foliage • 25–50 cm high, 10–15 cm wide

Ranunculus lyallii
Large, white flowers in early summer • Leathery, dark-green foliage • 75–100 cm high, 40–75 cm wide

Ranunculus millefoliatus
Yellow flowers in spring to summer • Gritty, sharply drained, organic, neutral to alkaline soil • 10–20 cm high, 20–30 cm wide

Ranunculus montanus
Yellow flowers in late spring to summer • Glossy, deep-green foliage • May be invasive • 15–30 cm high, 20–30 cm wide

Ranunculus repens
'Buttered Popcorn' • Gold-yellow flowers in late spring to summer • Cream-and-gold-splashed foliage • May be invasive • 10–15 cm high, 60–75+ cm wide

Ranunculus repens var. *peniflorus*
Double, yellow flowers in late spring to summer • 30–60 cm high, 60–75+ cm wide

Ranunculus sartorianus
Yellow flowers in late spring to early summer • Gritty soil • 10–20 cm high, 10–15 cm wide

Ranunculus semiverticillatus
White or rarely pink flowers in spring • Grey-green foliage • Gritty soil • 8–12 cm high, 5–10 cm wide

Ranzania

Genus Information
Origin: Japan
Selected Common Names: unknown
Nomenclature: Named for Ono Ranzan, a Japanese naturalist.
Notes: A genus of one species closely related to *Podophyllum* and *Epimedium*.

General Features
Height: 15–40 cm high
Spread: 15–20 cm wide
Habit: creeping, rhizomatous woodland perennial
Flowers: mauve, bell-shaped; spring; flowers before foliage appears
Foliage: attractive, palmate
Hardiness: D
Warnings: not prone to insects or disease
Expert Advice: Relatively unknown. Grows well in moist climates. Takes several years to put on a good show.

Growing Requirements
Light: shade
Soil: humus-rich, moist, neutral to acidic soil
Location: mixed borders; rock gardens; woodland gardens
Propagation: seed; division
Expert Advice: Seed can take up to 18 months to germinate and 3–5 years to reach flowering size.

R

Buying Considerations

Professionals
Popularity: very unknown
Availability: occasionally available from specialty growers
Size to Sell: sells best in mature sizes (when blooming) as it matures slowly
Shrinkage: high; goes dormant in pot

Collectors
Popularity: of interest to collectors—unique, challenge, rare

Gardeners
Ease of Growth: mostly easy to grow but needs close attention to growing conditions
Start with: one mature plant for feature plant

What to Try First ...
Ranzania japonica

On the Market

Ranzania japonica (syn. *Podophyllum japonicum*)
Nodding, mauve flowers in spring • 15–40 cm high, 15–20 cm wide

Ratibida
p. 424

Genus Information
Origin: North America and Mexico
Selected Common Names: Mexican hat, prairie coneflower
Nomenclature: Named by Constantine Rafinesque-Schmaltz, a botanist who often gave plants unexplained names.

General Features
Height: 20–120 cm high
Spread: 20–45 cm wide
Habit: tap-rooted, upright, clump-forming biennial or perennial
Flowers: yellow, coneflower-like; summer to fall; good for cutflowers
Foliage: narrow; mid-green
Hardiness: B–C
Warnings: prone to powdery mildew and aphids

Growing Requirements
Light: sun
Soil: lean, well-drained, neutral to moderately alkaline soil; drought tolerant
Location: mixed borders; native plant borders; wild gardens
Propagation: seed
Expert Advice: Growing in rich soil produces open, floppy growth. Resents being disturbed.

Buying Considerations

Professionals
Popularity: relatively unknown
Availability: occasionally available from specialty growers
Size to Sell: sells best in smaller sizes (when blooming) as it matures fast
On the Shelf: prone to powdery mildew; rapidly overgrows pot
Shrinkage: high; sensitive to overwatering

Collectors
Popularity: not generally of interest to collectors

Gardeners
Ease of Growth: generally easy to grow
Start with: one small plant for feature plant

What to Try First ...
Ratibida columnifera, Ratibida columnifera f. *pulcherrima*

On the Market

Ratibida columnifera
Daisy-like, yellow flowers with green, cone-shaped centre in summer • 60–90 cm high, 30–45 cm wide

Ratibida columnifera f. *pulcherrima*
Daisy-like, mahogany-red flowers with brown, cone-shaped centre in summer • 20–30 cm high, 20–30 cm wide

Ratibida pinnata
Daisy-like, yellow flowers in summer to fall • 90–120 cm high, 30–45 cm wide

Rheum
p. 424

Genus Information
Origin: Asia and Europe
Selected Common Names: Chinese rhubarb, Himalayan rhubarb, Tibetan rhubarb
Nomenclature: From the Greek *rheon* (rhubarb).
Notes: A member of the buckwheat family. Related to *Persicaria* and *Fallopia*.

General Features
Height: 1–2.5 m high
Spread: 50–180 cm wide
Habit: large, rhizomatous, clump-forming perennial
Flowers: spires; summer
Foliage: large; colourful; deeply lobed, tropical-looking
Hardiness: B–C
Warnings: prone to aphids; leaves are poisonous; not prone to disease
Expert Advice: It is ornamental and not edible.

Growing Requirements

Light: sun to p.m. sun
Soil: deep, evenly moist, organic soil; early dormancy may occur in dry soil
Location: mixed borders; waterside plantings; woodland gardens
Propagation: seed; division
Expert Advice: Seed in fall. Hybridizes easily and may not come true from seed. Divide in spring.

Buying Considerations

Professionals

Popularity: gaining popularity as a foliage plant
Availability: generally available as bare root from specialty growers
Size to Sell: sells best in smaller sizes as it matures fast
On the Shelf: high ornamental appeal; keep stock rotated; rapidly overgrows pot
Shrinkage: low; requires little maintenance

Collectors

Popularity: of interest to collectors; *Rheum nobile* is unique, exceptional beauty

Gardeners

Ease of Growth: very easy to grow
Start with: one small plant for feature plant

What to Try First ...

Rheum alexandrae, Rheum nobile, Rheum palmatum 'Atrosanguineum', *Rheum palmatum* Red select, *Rheum palmatum rubrum*

On the Market

Rheum
'Ace of Hearts' (Ace of Spades) • Pink flowers in summer • Heart-shaped, dark-green foliage • 1–1.2 m high, 1–1.2 m wide

Rheum alexandrae
Greenish-yellow flowers covered in large cream bracts in early summer • Glossy, green foliage • 1–1.2 m high, 50–75 cm wide

Rheum australe
Cream or dark-red flowers in summer • Rounded foliage • 1.5–2 m high, 90–120 cm wide

Rheum nobile
Cream-green flowers covered with large cream bracts in early summer • Glossy, green foliage • 1.5–2 m high, 50–75 cm wide

Rheum palmatum
Cream or deep-red flowers in early summer • Deeply lobed, palmate foliage • 2–2.5 m high, 1.2–1.8 m wide

'Atrosanguineum' (Atropurpureum) • Crimson-red flower spikes in early summer • Lobed, palmate foliage, crimson-red when young • 2–2.5 m high, 1.2–1.8 m wide

Red select • Deep-red flower spikes in early summer • Red foliage • 1–1.5 m high, 90–150 cm wide

Rheum palmatum rubrum
Red flower spikes in early summer • Deep-red-flushed, lobed, palmate foliage • 2–2.5 m high, 1.2–1.8 m wide

Rheum palmatum var. *tanguticum*
White, pink or crimson flowers in summer • Deep-lobed, dark-purple foliage • 2–2.5 m high, 1.2–1.8 m wide

Rhodiola

p. 424

Genus Information

Origin: Europe, Asia and North America
Selected Common Names: king's crown, roseroot, rose crown
Nomenclature: Diminutive of the Latin *rhudon* (rose), referring to the rose-scented roots.
Notes: Formerly part of the genus *Sedum*.

General Features

Height: 5–40 cm high
Spread: 15–60 cm wide
Habit: rhizomatous, clump-forming perennial
Flowers: small, star-shaped; prominent stamens; unisexual or bisexual
Foliage: succulent, *Sedum*-like
Hardiness: A–C
Warnings: prone to aphids; not prone to disease
Expert Advice: A very hardy, very attractive and very easy-to-grow perennial that tolerates more sun than *Sedums*.

Growing Requirements

Light: sun to p.m. sun
Soil: moderate to poor soil; tolerant of poor soils and dry periods
Location: mixed borders; rock gardens
Propagation: seed; division; leaf cuttings

R

The Buyer's Guide for Professionals, Collectors & Gardeners **327**

Buying Considerations

Professionals

Popularity: relatively unknown

Availability: occasionally available from specialty growers

Size to Sell: sells best in smaller sizes (when blooming) as it matures fast

On the Shelf: rapidly overgrows pot

Shrinkage: low; requires little maintenance

Collectors

Popularity: not generally of interest to collectors

Gardeners

Ease of Growth: very easy to grow

Start with: one small plant for feature plant

What to Try First ...

Rhodiola integrifolia, Rhodiola rosea

On the Market

Rhodiola integrifolia (syn. *Sedum integrifolium*)
Red-purple, sometimes yellow flowers in summer • Succulent foliage • 5–30 cm high, 45–60 cm wide

Rhodiola pachyclados (syn. *Sedum pachyclados*)
White flowers in summer • Succulent foliage • Avoid winter wet • 5 cm high, 15+ cm wide

Rhodiola rosea (syn. *Sedum rosea*)
Yellow-orange flowers in late spring to early summer • Dome of succulent foliage • 10–30 cm high, 30–45 cm wide

Rhodiola sinuata (syn. *Sedum linearifolium*)
Yellow flowers in spring • Succulent foliage • 15 cm high, 20 cm wide

Rodgersia

R p. 424

Genus Information

Origin: Burma, China, Japan and Nepal.

Selected Common Names: featherleaf Rodger's flower, fingerleaf Rodger's flower, Rodger's flower

Nomenclature: Named for John Rodgers, 1812–1882, commander of an expedition on which *Rodgersia podophylla* was discovered.

General Features

Height: 90–150 cm high

Spread: 60–120 cm wide

Habit: large, rhizomatous, clump-forming perennial

Flowers: astilbe-like, fluffy; spring to summer

Foliage: large; deeply cut, tropical-looking; good fall colour; slow to emerge in spring

Hardiness: C

Warnings: prone to aphids; not prone to disease

Growing Requirements

Light: shade to a.m. sun

Soil: moist, organic soil; tolerates more dryness in shadier sites

Location: bog gardens; mixed borders; pond gardens; waterside plantings; woodland gardens; foliage may burn in windy locations

Propagation: seed; division

Expert Advice: Hybridizes easily and may not come true from seed. Divide in spring. Plant crowns 2–3 cm below ground level. Takes up to 3 years for a good show.

Buying Considerations

Professionals

Popularity: gaining popularity as an interesting foliage plant

Availability: generally available as finished product

Size to Sell: sells best in smaller size

On the Shelf: high ornamental appeal; keep stock rotated;

Shrinkage: low; requires little maintenance

Collectors

Popularity: of interest to collectors—unique

Gardeners

Ease of Growth: generally easy to grow but needs close attention to growing conditions

Start with: one mature plant for feature plant

What to Try First ...

Rodgersia aesculifolia, Rodgersia henrici (hybrid), *Rodgersia pinnata, Rodgersia podophylla*

On the Market

Rodgersia aesculifolia
Fragrant, cream to pink flowers in late spring to early summer • 90–150 cm high, 90–120 cm wide

Rodgersia henrici (hybrid)
Red-purple flowers in late spring to early summer • 90–150 cm high, 90–120 cm wide

Rodgersia pinnata
Red, pink, or white flowers in summer • 90–120 cm high, 90–120 cm wide

'Elegans' • Cream to pink-tinted flowers in summer • 90–120 cm high, 90–120 cm wide

'Superba' • Bright-pink flowers in summer • 90–120 cm high, 90–120 cm wide

Rodgersia podophylla
Cream flowers in late spring to early summer • Deeply lobed foliage • 90–120 cm high, 60–90 cm wide

Rudbeckia

p. 424

Genus Information
Origin: North America
Selected Common Names: black-eyed Susan, showy coneflower, rudbeckia
Nomenclature: Named for Olaus Rudbeck, 1660–1740, a Swedish botanist.
Notes: Genus includes annuals, biennials and perennials.

General Features
Height: 20 cm–3 m high
Spread: 20–90 cm wide
Habit: upright, clump-forming, rhizomatous, short-lived perennial
Flowers: large, bright, daisy-like; late summer to early fall; good for cutflowers
Foliage: prominently veined, toothed
Hardiness: C–D
Warnings: prone to powdery mildew and aphids; *R. laciniata* self-sows freely and spreads in rich soils (contain and deadhead to prevent unwanted spread)
Expert Advice: *Rudbeckia* blooms right up until hard frosts. Plant with *Perovskia* and *Echinacea*.

Growing Requirements
Light: sun
Soil: fertile, moist, well-drained soil; tolerant of dry periods and poor soil
Location: mixed borders; wild gardens
Propagation: seed; division; basal cuttings
Expert Advice: Germinate seed at 16–18°C.

Buying Considerations

Professionals
Popularity: popular, old-fashioned garden standard; fast seller in bloom
Availability: readily available as finished product and bare root
Size to Sell: sells best in smaller sizes (when blooming) as it matures fast
On the Shelf: keep stock rotated; rapidly overgrows pot
Shrinkage: low; requires little maintenance

Collectors
Popularity: not generally of interest to collectors

Gardeners
Ease of Growth: mostly easy to grow
Start with: one small plant for feature plant

What to Try First ...
Rudbeckia laciniata 'Goldquelle', *Rudbeckia laciniata* 'Herbstsonne', *Rudbeckia fulgida* var. *sullivantii* 'Goldsturm', *Rudbeckia laciniata*, *Rudbeckia occidentalis* 'Black Beauty'

On the Market
Rudbeckia
Large, maroon-red flowers in summer to fall • 45–60 cm high, 30–45 cm wide
Rudbeckia fulgida var. *speciosa*
'Viette's Little Suzy' (Blovi) • Deep-yellow flowers with black, cone-shaped centre in midsummer to fall • 25–35 cm high, 20–40 cm wide
Rudbeckia fulgida var. *sullivantii*
'Goldsturm' (Gold Storm) • Deep-yellow flowers in midsummer to fall • 45–60 cm high, 30–45 cm wide
Rudbeckia hirta
Golden-yellow flowers in summer to fall • 60–90 cm high, 30–45 cm wide
'Double Gold' • Double, gold flowers in summer to fall • 60–90 cm high, 30–45 cm wide
'Goldilocks' • Semi-double to double, golden-orange flowers in summer to fall • 45–60 cm high, 30–45 cm wide
'Irish Eyes' (Green Eyes) • Yellow flowers with green centre in summer to fall • 60–75 cm high, 30–45 cm wide
Rustic mix • Mix of gold, brown-red, bronze or orange flowers in summer to fall • 45–60 cm high, 30–45 cm wide
Becky Series
Mix of gold, lemon and red-brown flowers in summer to fall • 20–30 cm high, 30–45 cm wide
Rudbeckia laciniata
Golden-yellow flowers with green centre in midsummer to fall • 1.5–3 m high, 60–90 cm wide
'Goldquelle' (Gold Fountain) • Large, double, yellow flowers with green centre, turning yellow, in summer • 60–90 cm high, 45–60 cm wide
'Herbstsonne' (Autumn Sun) • Lemon-yellow flowers with green, cone-shaped centre in late summer to fall • 1.5–2.5 m high, 60–90 cm wide
'Hortensia' (Golden Glow) • Double, golden-yellow flowers in summer • 1.5–1.8 m high, 1–2 m wide

R

'Juligold' (July Gold) • Single, golden-yellow flowers in summer • 1.5–1.8 m high, 45–60 cm wide

Rudbeckia maxima
Yellow flowers with brown centre in late summer to fall • Blue-green foliage • 1.5–2 m high, 60–90 cm wide

Rudbeckia occidentalis
'Black Beauty' • Black, gold-ringed cones in summer • 90–120 cm high, 60–75 cm wide

'Green Wizard' • Green flowers in summer • 90–120 cm high, 60–75 cm wide

Rudbeckia subtomentosa
Yellow flowers with brown centres in summer to fall • Aromatic foliage • 90 cm–1.5 m high, 30–60 cm wide

Rudbeckia triloba
Yellow to orange flowers with black, cone-shaped centre in late summer to fall • 90–150 cm high, 45–60 cm wide

Sagina

p. 424

Genus Information

Origin: northern temperate regions and tropical mountains

Selected Common Names: Irish moss, Scotch moss

Nomenclature: From the Latin for fodder, this genus name was originally used for *Spergula arvensis*.

Other Uses: Formerly cultivated for fodder.

Notes: Plants in this genus have been bounced around recently between the *Arenaria*, *Sagina* and *Minuartia* genera. The family includes some troublesome weeds.

General Features

Height: 2–5 cm high

Spread: 25–40 cm wide

Habit: mat-forming perennial

Flowers: tiny, white; summer

Foliage: bright-green; mossy

Hardiness: C

Warnings: prone to downy mildew; not prone to insects

Expert Advice: Tends to die out over the years in patches that can be filled with new plants.

Growing Requirements

Light: sun; shelter from hot p.m. sun; prefers cool areas

Soil: moist, well-drained, neutral to acidic soil

Location: alpine gardens; between paving stones; rock gardens

Propagation: seed; division; cuttings

Expert Advice: Take cuttings in summer.

Buying Considerations

Professionals

Popularity: popular foliage plant

Availability: readily available as finished product

Size to Sell: sells best in smaller sizes as it matures fast

On the Shelf: high ornamental appeal; keep stock rotated; rapidly overgrows pot

Shrinkage: low; sensitive to overwatering; requires little maintenance

Collectors

Popularity: not generally of interest to collectors

Gardeners

Ease of Growth: generally easy to grow but needs close attention to growing conditions

Start with: several for mass plantings

What to Try First ...

Sagina subulata, *Sagina subulata* var. *glabrata* 'Aurea'

On the Market

Sagina subulata
  Tiny, white flowers in summer • Mossy foliage • 2–5 cm high, 25–40+ cm wide

Sagina subulata var. *glabrata*
  'Aurea' • Tiny, white flowers in summer • Lime-green, mossy foliage • 2–5 cm high, 25–40+ cm wide

Salvia

p. 424

Genus Information

Origin: worldwide

Selected Common Names: blue sage, sage

Nomenclature: From the name used by Pliny, which is from the Latin *salvare* (to save or heal), referring to the supposed medical properties of some species.

Notes: A genus of some 900 species of annuals, biennials and perennials.

General Features

Height: 10–150 cm high

Spread: 15–90 cm wide

Habit: upright, clump-forming biennial or perennial

Flowers: stalks; early summer to fall; long blooming period; attractive to bees and butterflies

Foliage: woolly; silvery-green; aromatic

Hardiness: B–D

Warnings: prone to powdery mildew and aphids

Expert Advice: *Salvia* x *sylvestris* 'May Night' may repel cats.

Growing Requirements

Light: sun

Soil: moist, organic, well-drained soil; tolerates poor soil; drought tolerant

Location: mixed borders; raised beds; rock gardens; wild gardens; *S. caespitosa* in alpine gardens; scree

Propagation: seed (self-sows readily); cuttings

Expert Advice: Take softwood or semi-ripe cuttings in summer.

Buying Considerations

Professionals

Popularity: popular garden standard; fast seller in bloom; many new varieties available

Availability: readily available as finished product and bare root

Size to Sell: sells best in smaller sizes (when blooming) as it matures fast

On the Shelf: keep stock rotated; rapidly overgrows pot

Shrinkage: low; requires little maintenance

S

Collectors
Popularity: not generally of interest to collectors

Gardeners
Ease of Growth: very easy to grow
Start with: one small plant for feature plant

What to Try First ...
Salvia nemorosa 'Marcus', *Salvia nemorosa* 'Ostfriesland', *Salvia nemorosa* 'Viola Klose', *Salvia* x *sylvestris* 'Blaukonigin', *Salvia* x *sylvestris* 'Caradonna', *Salvia* x *sylvestris* 'Mainacht', *Salvia* x *sylvestris* 'Rugen'

On the Market

Salvia
  'Miss Indigo' • Lavender flowers in early summer to fall • 45–60 cm high, 45–60 cm wide

Salvia argentea
  Pinkish-white to white flowers in midsummer • Soft, silver-woolly foliage • Moist, organic, sharply drained soil • 60–90 cm high, 45–60 cm wide

Salvia azurea ssp. *pitcheri*
  Large, azure-blue flowers in late summer to fall • 90–150 cm high, 60–90 cm wide

Salvia caespitosa
  Large, lilac-pink to violet-blue flowers in summer • Grey foliage • Alpine • 10–15 cm high, 45–60 cm wide

Salvia forsskaolii
  Spiked, violet-blue to pink-magenta flowers in summer • Grey-green foliage • 60–90 cm high, 60–90 cm wide

Salvia lyrata
  'Burgundy Bliss' • White, lavender-flushed flowers in summer • Burgundy foliage • 30–60 cm high, 20–30 cm wide

Salvia nemorosa
  'Amethyst' • Lilac-pink flowers in summer • Grey-green foliage • 60–75 cm high, 30–45 cm wide

  'Lubecca' • Violet-blue flowers in midsummer to fall • 30–45 cm high, 30–45 cm wide

  'Marcus' • Dark violet-purple flowers in summer to fall • 15–25 cm high, 15–30 cm wide

  'Negrito' • Deep-blue flowers in summer • 30–45 cm high, 30–45 cm wide

  'Ostfriesland' (East Friesland) • Violet-blue flowers in summer • 45–60 cm high, 45–60 cm wide

  'Pusztaflamme' (Plumosa) • Spiked, deep-lavender flowers in summer • 30–45 cm high, 30–45 cm wide

  'Senior' • Dark purple-blue flowers in summer • 45–60 cm high, 45–60 cm wide

  'Viola Klose' • Dark violet-blue flowers in late spring • 40–45 cm high, 30–45 cm wide

  'Wesuwe' • Violet-blue flowers in summer to fall • 30–45 cm high, 30–45 cm wide

Salvia x *superba*
  'Adrian' • Purple flowers in late spring to late summer • Aromatic foliage • 30–45 cm high, 30–45 cm wide

Salvia x *sylvestris*
  'Blauhugel' (Blue Hill) • Pure blue flowers in summer • 30–50 cm high, 30–45 cm wide

  'Blaukonigin' (Blue Queen) • Rich violet-blue flowers in summer • 45–60 cm high, 45–60 cm wide

  'Caradonna' • Violet-purple flowers with purple stems in summer • 60–75 cm high, 45–60 cm wide

  'Dear Anja' • Light-purple flowers in summer • 40–60 cm high, 45–60 cm wide

  'Lye End' • Lilac-blue flowers in summer • 45–60 cm high, 45–60 cm wide

  'Mainacht' (May Night) • Fragrant, blue-violet flowers in summer • 60–75 cm high, 45–60 cm wide

  'Rose Queen' • Rose flowers in summer to fall • 60–75 cm high, 45–60 cm wide

  'Rugen' • Deep-blue flowers in summer • 30–45 cm high, 30–45 cm wide

  'Schneehugel' (Snow Hill) • Pure white flowers in summer • 30–45 cm high, 45–60 cm wide

  'Tanzerin' • Purple-blue flowers in summer • 60–75 cm high, 45–60 cm wide

Salvia verticillata
  'Purple Rain' • Purple-grey flowers in summer • 40–60 cm high, 30–45 cm wide

Sanguinaria
p. 425 📷

Genus Information
Origin: eastern North America
Selected Common Names: bloodroot
Nomenclature: From the Latin *sanguis* (blood), referring to the orange-red sap that comes from the rhizomes. This feature also gives rise to the common name "bloodroot." Indigenous peoples used the sap as face paint.
Notes: A member of the poppy family.

General Features

Height: 15–25 cm high
Spread: 15–30 cm wide
Habit: rhizomatous, spreading woodland perennial
Flowers: very early spring; emerge from the leaves; short blooming period
Foliage: lobed; heart to kidney-shaped
Hardiness: C
Warnings: prone to slugs; not prone to disease; goes dormant in summer
Expert Advice: *S. canadensis* f. *multiplex* 'Plena' has blooms that are longer lasting than those of the species.

Growing Requirements

Light: shade; tolerates a.m. sun if kept reliably moist
Soil: fertile, moist, organic, well-drained soil
Location: mixed borders; woodland gardens
Propagation: seed; division
Expert Advice: Can be started from seed, but division is easier. The seed germinates erratically and the plants can take as long as 3 years to reach blooming size.

Buying Considerations

Professionals

Popularity: gaining popularity
Availability: occasionally available as finished product and bare root from specialty growers
Size to Sell: sells best in mature sizes (when blooming) as it matures slowly
Shrinkage: low; requires little maintenance; goes dormant in pot

Collectors

Popularity: of interest to collectors—novelty

Gardeners

Ease of Growth: mostly easy to grow
Start with: one mature plant for feature plant

What to Try First ...

Sanguinaria canadensis, Sanguinaria canadensis f. *multiplex* 'Plena'

On the Market

Sanguinaria canadensis
Single, pure white flowers in early spring • 15–25 cm high, 15–30 cm wide

Sanguinaria canadensis f. *multiplex*
'Plena' • Large, fully double, pure white flowers in early spring • 15–25 cm high, 15–30 cm wide

Sanguisorba

Genus Information

Origin: Northern Hemisphere
Selected Common Names: burnet
Nomenclature: From the Latin *sanguis* (blood) and *sorbeo* (to soak up), referring to the plant's former use as an infusion to prevent bleeding.
Other Uses: Some species are grown for the young leaves, which are added to soups, drinks and salads.
Notes: Genus includes perennials and shrubs.

General Features

Height: 60–90 cm high
Spread: 45–60 cm wide
Habit: rhizomatous, tall groundcover perennial; may require staking
Flowers: bottlebrush-like; spring to fall; good for cutflowers
Foliage: opposite; round
Hardiness: C–D
Warnings: prone to aphids; not prone to disease

Growing Requirements

Light: sun to p.m. sun
Soil: moist, well-drained, neutral to acidic soil
Location: kitchen gardens; mixed borders; wild gardens
Propagation: seed; division
Expert Advice: Divide in spring.

Buying Considerations

Professionals

Popularity: relatively unknown; not much commercial demand
Availability: occasionally available as bare root from specialty growers
Size to Sell: sells best in smaller sizes as it matures fast
Shrinkage: low; requires little maintenance

Collectors

Popularity: not generally of interest to collectors, but of interest to herbalists

Gardeners

Ease of Growth: very easy to grow
Start with: one small plant for feature plant

What to Try First ...

Sanguisorba menziesii, Sanguisorba obtusa

On the Market

Sanguisorba dodecandra
Bottlebrush-like, white to greenish flowers in summer • 60–90 cm high, 45–60 cm wide

Sanguisorba menziesii
Bottlebrush-like, maroon-red flowers in spring • 60–75 cm high, 45–60 cm wide

S

Sanguisorba obtusa
Bottlebrush-like, bright-pink-red flowers in summer to fall • 60–90 cm high, 45–60 cm wide

Santolina
p. 425 📷

Genus Information
Origin: Mediterranean
Selected Common Names: lavender cotton
Nomenclature: From the Latin *Sanctum linum* (holy flax), the old name for *S. virens*.
Notes: Genus includes perennials and shrubs.

General Features
Height: 20–30 cm high
Spread: 30–45 cm wide
Habit: clump-forming perennial
Flowers: tiny, yellow; summer
Foliage: evergreen; aromatic; finely cut; grey to silvery
Hardiness: D
Warnings: not prone to insects or disease
Expert Advice: Deadhead and cut back to keep plant compact and encourage fresh growth.

Growing Requirements
Light: sun
Soil: lean, sharply drained, neutral to alkaline soil; drought tolerant
Location: warm, dry locations; low hedges; mixed borders; rock gardens
Propagation: seed; cuttings
Expert Advice: Take semi-ripe cuttings in summer.

Buying Considerations

Professionals
Popularity: relatively unknown foliage plant
Availability: occasionally available from specialty growers
Size to Sell: sells best in smaller sizes; matures slowly
Shrinkage: low; requires little maintenance

Collectors
Popularity: of interest to collectors—unique, rare, novelty

Gardeners
Ease of Growth: very easy to grow
Start with: one small plant for feature plant

What to Try First ...
Santolina chamaecyparissus 'Small-Ness'

On the Market
Santolina chamaecyparissus
'Small-Ness' • Yellow flowers in summer • Aromatic, grey foliage • 20–30 cm high, 30–45 cm wide

Saponaria
p. 425 📷

Genus Information
Origin: Europe and southwestern Asia
Selected Common Names: bouncing bet, lady by the gate, soapwort
Nomenclature: From the Medieval Latin *sapo* (soap), the name used for *S. officinalis*, referring to the root sap of several species, which creates lather when mixed with water.
Notes: Supposedly, barmaids (nicknamed "bets") would wash out bottles with a bouncing motion, hence the common name "bouncing bet."

General Features
Height: 3–90 cm high
Spread: 10–90 cm wide
Habit: mat-forming to loose and upright, spreading groundcover perennial
Flowers: some are fragrant
Foliage: mid-green; (some) shiny
Hardiness: C
Warnings: not prone to insects or disease
Expert Advice: *S. officinalis* is an aggressive spreader (contain and deadhead to prevent spread). Deadhead to promote more blooms.

Growing Requirements
Light: sun to p.m. sun
Soil: mat-forming types prefer fertile, gritty, well-drained to sharply drained soil; tolerates dry soil; (most) neutral to alkaline soil; upright types prefer fertile, well-drained soil
Location: mat-forming types prefer dry walls, scree and rock gardens; upright types good for cottage gardens, mixed borders and rock gardens
Propagation: seed; division; softwood cuttings

Buying Considerations

Professionals
Popularity: popular; fast seller in bloom
Availability: generally available as finished product
Size to Sell: sells best in smaller sizes (when blooming) as it matures fast
On the Shelf: rapidly overgrows pot
Shrinkage: low; requires little maintenance

Collectors
Popularity: of interest to collectors—exceptional beauty, fragrance

On the Market

Saponaria
'Bressingham' • Bright-neon-pink flowers in spring • Loose, mat-forming • 6–10 cm high, 20–30 cm wide

Saponaria x boisseri
Clear-pink flowers in summer • Mat-forming • 5–10 cm high, 20–30 cm wide

Saponaria caespitosa
Rose-purple flowers in summer • Mat-forming • 10–15 cm high, 10–15 cm wide

Saponaria chlorifolia
Pink flowers in spring • Blue-grey foliage • Mat-forming • 15–20 cm high, 30–45 cm wide

Saponaria x lempergii
'Max Frei' • Soft-pink flowers in summer • Bushy, upright • 30–40 cm high, 30–45 cm wide

Saponaria ocymoides
Pink to soft-purple flowers in late spring to summer • Mat-forming • 10–15 cm high, 30–45 cm wide

'Alba' • White flowers in late spring to summer • 10–15 cm high, 30–45 cm wide

'Alba Compacta' • White flowers in late spring to summer • 8–12 cm high, 20–30 cm wide

'Rubra Compacta' • Rich-red flowers in late spring to summer • 8–12 cm high, 20–30 cm wide

'Snow Tip' • White flowers in late spring to summer • 10–15 cm high, 30–45 cm wide

Saponaria officinalis
Pink flowers in summer to fall • Upright • 60–90 cm high, 60–90 cm wide

'Rosea Plena' • Fragrant, double, rose-pink flowers in summer to fall • 60–90 cm high, 60–90 cm wide

'Rubra Plena' • Fragrant, double, rose-red flowers, fading to pink, in summer to fall • 60–90 cm high, 60–90 cm wide

Saponaria x olivana
Soft-pink flowers in summer • Shiny foliage • Mat-forming • 4–8 cm high, 10–20 cm wide

Saponaria pamphylica
Pink flowers in summer • Mat-forming • 15–30 cm high, 30–40 cm wide

Saponaria pulvinaris
Large, carmine-pink flowers in summer • Mat-forming • 3–6 cm high, 30–45 cm wide

Saponaria pumilio
Large, pink-purple flowers in summer • Mat-forming • Neutral to acidic soil • 3–6 cm high, 25–40 cm wide

Sarracenia

p. 425

Genus Information

Origin: eastern North America
Selected Common Names: purple pitcher plant
Nomenclature: Named for Dr. Michel Sarrazin de l'Etang (1659–1734), a physician in Quebec who sent plants to France.

General Features

Height: 15–45 cm high
Spread: 30–45 cm wide
Habit: carnivorous, clump-forming, rhizomatous native perennial
Flowers: purple-veined, purple or green pitchers; spring
Hardiness: A
Warnings: not prone to insects or disease
Expert Advice: Many wild and man-made hybrids exist that are hardy on the east coast of Canada, but *S. purpurea* is the only one we have had success with growing on the Prairies.

Growing Requirements

Light: sun or shade; tolerates more sun with good soil moisture
Soil: organic, wet, acidic soil; needs pure peat
Location: bog gardens
Propagation: seed; division
Expert Advice: Plants from seed take 3–4 years to flower. Do not fertilize.

Buying Considerations

S

Size to Sell: sells best in mature sizes as it
matures slowly
Shrinkage: low; sensitive to underwatering;
requires little maintenance

Collectors
Popularity: of interest to collectors—rare,
novelty

Gardeners
Ease of Growth: mostly difficult to grow
Start with: one mature plant for feature plant

What to Try First ...
Sarracenia purpurea

On the Market

Sarracenia purpurea
Dark-purple to red flowers in spring •
Purple-veined, purple or green pitchers •
15–45 cm high, 30–45 cm wide

Saxifraga   p. 425 [image]

Genus Information

Origin: Europe, Asia, North America and the
mountains of South America
Selected Common Names: encrusted saxifrage,
mossy saxifrage, saxifrage
Nomenclature: From the Latin *saxus* (rock) and
fragare (to break), referring to the plant's
supposed ability to break up kidney or bladder
stones.
Notes: A genus of some 450 species.
Expert Advice: We divide *Saxifraga* into 2 groups
for growing information and display purposes:
Kabschia/Encrusted and *Mossy*.

Saxifraga, Kabschia/
Encrusted   p. 425 [image]

General Features
Height: 1–70 cm high
Spread: 0.5–40 cm wide
Habit: clump-forming perennial
Flowers: tiny, pretty; very early spring to fall
Foliage: evergreen; limestone deposits may form
on foliage
Hardiness: A–D
Warnings: not prone to insects or disease
Expert Advice: Deadhead flowers, but do
not cut back foliage.

Growing Requirements
Light: shade to a.m. sun; shelter from hot p.m.
sun
Soil: lean, gritty soil; keep moist during active
growth; keep soil drier during dormancy
Location: north side of a rock; alpine gardens;
scree; troughs; wall crevices
Propagation: seed; division; cuttings of
non-flowering rosettes

Buying Considerations

Professionals
Popularity: gaining popularity; sells well in
bloom
Availability: occasionally available from
specialty growers
Size to Sell: sells best in mature sizes (when
blooming) as it matures slowly
On the Shelf: high ornamental appeal
Shrinkage: high; sensitive to overwatering

Collectors
Popularity: of interest to collectors—unique,
rare, challenge, exceptional beauty

Gardeners
Ease of Growth: mostly difficult to grow
Start with: one mature plant for feature plant

What to Try First ...
Saxifraga 'Hluboka', *Saxifraga* 'Peter Burrow',
Saxifraga 'Tumbling Waters', *Saxifraga* 'Tvuj
Den', *Saxifraga* 'Tvuj Usmev', *Saxifraga* 'Tvuj
Uspech'

On the Market

Saxifraga
'A.C.U. Berry' • Violet-purple flowers in
spring • Evergreen foliage • 2–5 cm high,
15–20 cm wide
'Apple Blossom' • Soft-pink flowers in
spring • Evergreen foliage • 8–15 cm high,
30 cm wide
'Bohemia' • Orange-red flowers, aging
to yellow, in spring • Evergreen foliage •
5–8 cm high, 10–15 cm wide
'Corrie Fee' • White flowers in spring •
Evergreen foliage • 2–5 cm high,
15–20 cm wide
'Dartington Double' • Double, red, pink or
white flowers in spring • Evergreen foliage
• 3–10 cm high, 10–15 cm wide
'Hluboka' • Pink flowers in spring •
Evergreen foliage • 2–8 cm high, 6–10 cm
wide
Kabschia and Engler hybrids • Various
colours of flowers in spring • Evergreen
foliage • 2–5 cm high, 10–15 cm wide
'Kath Dryden' • Lilac-pink, darker-eyed
flowers in spring • Evergreen foliage •
5–8 cm high, 15 cm wide
'Kbely' • Large, white flowers in spring •
Evergreen foliage • 8–10 cm high, 15 cm
wide

S

'Lusanna' • Deep lilac-pink flowers with lilac veins in spring • Evergreen foliage • 8 cm high, 10 cm wide

'Meteor' • Yellow flowers in spring • Evergreen foliage • 3–8 cm high

'Peach Blossom' • Creamy-pink flowers in spring • Evergreen foliage • 8 cm high, 15 cm wide

'Pearly King' • Pink flowers in spring • Evergreen foliage • 10–15 cm high

'Peter Burrow' • Rose-red flowers in spring • 2–5 cm high, 6–10 cm wide

'Sandpiper' • Yellow flowers in spring • Evergreen foliage • 4–6 cm high, 6–8 cm wide

'Snow Midget' • White flowers in spring • Evergreen foliage • 15 cm high

'Tumbling Waters' • Arching, clustered, white flowers in spring • Evergreen foliage • 30–40 cm high, 10–15 cm wide

'Tvuj Den' (Your Day) • Pink flowers in spring • Evergreen foliage • 2–5 cm high, 6–10 cm wide

'Tvuj Usmev' (Your Smile) • Pink flowers in spring • Evergreen foliage • 2–5 cm high, 6–10 cm wide

'Tvuj Uspech' (Your Success) • Red-pink flowers in spring • Evergreen foliage • 2–5 cm high, 6–10 cm wide

'Uladana' • White flowers in spring • Evergreen foliage • 2–5 cm high, 6–10 cm wide

'Winifred Bevington' • White flowers with red dots in spring • Evergreen foliage • 12–15 cm high

Saxifraga x *anglica*
Pink to red flowers in spring • Evergreen foliage • 2–8 cm high, 10–15 cm wide

'Beatrix Stanley' • Rich-red flowers in spring • Evergreen foliage • 5 cm high, 10–15 cm wide

'Clare' • Wine-red flowers in spring • Evergreen foliage • 2–4 cm high, 10–15 cm wide

'Cranbourne' • Rose-pink flowers in spring • Blue-grey, evergreen foliage • 2–5 cm high, 10–15 cm wide

'Myra Cambrica' • Cherry-red flowers in spring • Evergreen foliage • 2–5 cm high, 10–15 cm wide

'Pearl Rose' • Pink flowers in spring • Evergreen foliage • 3–5 cm high, 10–15 cm wide

'Valerie Keevil' • Deep-rose flowers in spring • Evergreen foliage • 2–8 cm high, 10–15 cm wide

Saxifraga x *apiculata*
Soft primrose-yellow flowers in spring • Evergreen foliage • 5–8 cm high, 25–40 cm wide

'Alba' • White flowers in spring • Evergreen foliage • 5–8 cm high, 25–40 cm wide

'Gregor Mendel' • Primrose-yellow flowers in spring • Evergreen foliage • 8 cm high, 45 cm wide

Saxifraga x *arco-valleyi*
'Hocker Edge' • Pale lilac-pink flowers in spring • Evergreen foliage • 2–5 cm high, 5–15 cm wide

'Labe' • Soft-pink flowers in spring • Evergreen foliage • 10–15 cm high, 10–15 cm wide

'Sara Sinclair' • Pink flowers in spring • Evergreen foliage • 2–5 cm high, 6–10 cm wide

Saxifraga asiatica
Stemless, large, pink flowers in spring • Evergreen foliage • 2–5 cm high, 2–5 cm wide

Saxifraga aspera
White to cream flowers in spring • Evergreen foliage • 8–15 cm high, 15–20 cm wide

Saxifraga x *bertolonii*
Purple flowers in spring • Evergreen foliage • 1–2 cm high, 5–10 cm wide

'Berenica' • Violet-purple flowers in spring • Evergreen foliage • 2–5 cm high, 6–10 cm wide

Saxifraga x *biasoletii*
Purple-red flowers in spring • Evergreen foliage • 5 cm high, 10 cm wide

'Chrystalie' • Purple-rose flowers in spring • Evergreen foliage • 10–20 cm high, 1.5–6 cm wide

Saxifraga x *boeckeleri*
Orange-red flowers in spring • Evergreen foliage • 8 cm high, 15 cm wide

Saxifraga x *borisii*
'Becky Foster' • Yellow flowers in spring • Evergreen foliage • 5–8 cm high, 10–15 cm wide

'Claudia' • Pale-yellow flowers in spring • Evergreen foliage • 5–8 cm high, 10–15 cm wide

S

'Faust' • Pale-yellow flowers in spring •
Evergreen foliage • 5–8 cm high,
10–15 cm wide

'Kyrilli' • Yellowish flowers in spring •
Evergreen foliage • 2–5 cm high,
10–15 cm wide

'Mariana' • Yellow flowers in spring • Grey-
green, evergreen foliage • 2–5 cm high,
10–15 cm wide

'Mona Lisa' • Yellow flowers in spring •
Evergreen foliage • 5–8 cm high,
10–15 cm wide

'Vincent van Gogh' • Primrose-yellow
flowers in spring • Grey, evergreen foliage
• 5–10 cm high, 20–25 cm wide

Saxifraga x *boydii*
Yellow flowers in early spring • Evergreen
foliage • 8 cm high, 15 cm wide

'Aretiastrum' • Yellow flowers in spring •
Evergreen foliage • 5 cm high, 15 cm wide

'Cherrytrees' • Rich-yellow flowers in spring
• Grey-green, evergreen foliage • 5–10 cm
high, 15–20 cm wide

'Cleo' • White flowers in spring • Grey-
green, evergreen foliage • 3–4 cm high,
6–10 cm wide

'Faldonside' • Intense yellow flowers in
spring • Grey, evergreen foliage • 2–5 cm
high, 10–15 cm wide

'Friar Tuck' • Yellow flowers in spring •
Evergreen foliage • 2–5 cm high, 6–10 cm
wide

'Hindhead Seedling' • Large, soft yellow
flowers in spring • Evergreen foliage •
5–8 cm high, 15–20 cm wide

'Luteola' • Warm yellow flowers in spring
• Evergreen foliage • 2–4 cm high,
10–15 cm wide

'William Boyd' • Yellow flowers in spring •
Evergreen foliage • 2 cm high, 20 cm wide

Saxifraga x *boydilacina*
'Moonbeam' • Creamy-yellow flowers with
brownish veins in spring • Evergreen
foliage • 4–6 cm high, 15–20 cm wide

'Penelope' • Amber flowers with rose veins
in spring • Evergreen foliage • 10 cm high,
15–20 cm wide

Saxifraga x *burisculata*
'King Lear' • White flowers in spring •
Evergreen foliage • 2–5 cm high,
14–20 cm wide

Saxifraga x *burnatii*
White flowers in late spring to early
summer • Evergreen foliage • 10–20 cm
high, 20–25 cm wide

Saxifraga burseriana
White flowers in early spring • Evergreen
foliage • 5–10 cm high, 15–20 cm wide

'Brookside' • White flowers in spring •
Evergreen foliage • 2–5 cm high,
6–10 cm wide

'Cordata' • White flowers in spring •
Evergreen foliage • 4–6 cm high,
6–10 cm wide

'G.M. Hopkins' • White flowers in spring •
Evergreen foliage • 2–5 cm high, 6–10 cm
wide

'Grandiflora' • Yellow to cream flowers in
spring • Evergreen foliage • 5–8 cm high,
10–15 cm wide

'John Tomlinson' • White flowers in spring •
Evergreen foliage • 4–6 cm high, 6–10 cm
wide

'Princess' • White flowers in spring •
Evergreen foliage • 4–6 cm high,
6–10 cm wide

Saxifraga callosa ssp. *callosa*
White flowers in spring • Silvery, evergreen
foliage • 2–30 cm high, 10–15 cm wide

Saxifraga callosa var. *lantoscana*
White flowers in spring • Evergreen foliage
• 8 cm high, 20 cm wide

Saxifraga caucasica
Gold-yellow flowers in spring • Bright-
green, spiny, evergreen foliage • 8 cm high,
10–15 cm wide

Saxifraga cotyledon
White flowers in late spring to early
summer • Evergreen foliage • 5–10 cm high,
15–20 cm wide

'Southside Seedling' • Red and white flowers
in spring • Evergreen foliage • 25–30 cm
high, 15–20 cm wide

Saxifraga cotyledon f. *pyramidalis*
White flowers in late spring to early
summer • Evergreen foliage • 5–60 cm high,
7–12 cm wide

Saxifraga x *edithae*
'Karel Stivin' • Dark-purple flowers in
spring • Evergreen foliage • 5–8 cm high,
10–15 cm wide

Saxifraga x *elizabethae*
'Boston Spa' • Primrose-yellow flowers in
spring • Evergreen foliage • 2–5 cm high,
6–10 cm wide

'Brno' • Yellow flowers in spring • Evergreen
foliage • 5–7 cm high, 20 cm wide

'Carmen' • Clear-yellow flowers in early
spring • Evergreen foliage • 8 cm high,
20 cm wide

'Foster's Gold' • Sulphur-yellow flowers in spring • Evergreen foliage • 10 cm high, 20–30 cm wide

'Icicle' • White flowers with greenish veins in spring • Evergreen foliage • 2–4 cm high, 6–10 cm wide

'L.C. Godseff' • Yellow flowers in spring • Evergreen foliage • 5–7 cm high, 20 cm wide

'Primrose Dame' • Yellow flowers in spring • Evergreen foliage • 2–4 cm high, 6–10 cm wide

Saxifraga x *eudoxiana*
'Gold Dust' • Golden-yellow flowers in spring • Evergreen foliage • 5–9 cm high, 20–30 cm wide

Saxifraga federici-augusti ssp.*grisebachii*
Pink flowers in spring • Grey-green rosettes • Gritty, sharply drained, alkaline soil • 15–25 cm high, 10–15 cm wide

Saxifraga ferdinandi-coburgi
Golden-yellow flowers in late spring to early summer • Grey-green rosettes • 5–12 cm high, 25–30 cm wide

'Drakula' • Golden-yellow flowers in spring • Grey-green, spiny rosettes • 5–12 cm high, 10–15 cm wide

Saxifraga ferdinandi-coburgi var. *rhodopea*
Bright-yellow flowers in spring • Evergreen foliage • 8 cm high, 15 cm wide

Saxifraga x *gloriana*
Lilac-pink flowers in spring • Evergreen foliage • 2–4 cm high, 15–20 cm wide

'Amitie' • Lilac-pink flowers in spring • Evergreen foliage • 2–4 cm high, 15–20 cm wide

'Godiva' • Rich-pink flowers in spring • Deep-green, evergreen foliage • 5 cm high, 15–20 cm wide

Saxifraga x *goringana*
'Nancye' • Cerise to pale lilac-pink flowers • 1–8 cm high, 1.5–15 cm wide

Saxifraga x *gratoides*
Deep-yellow flowers in spring • Evergreen foliage • 5 cm high, 15 cm wide

Saxifraga x *hofmanii*
'Volgeri' • Light-red flowers in spring • Evergreen foliage • 2–5 cm high, 6–10 cm wide

Saxifraga x *hornibrookii*
'Ariel' • Wine-red flowers in spring • Silvery, evergreen foliage • 5–8 cm high, 5–10 cm wide

'Delia' • Deep mauve-pink flowers in spring • Evergreen foliage • 5–8 cm high, 5–10 cm wide

'Riverslea' • Deep wine-red flowers in spring • Evergreen foliage • 2–5 cm high, 6–10 cm wide

Saxifraga hypnoides (syn. *Saxifraga kingii)*
'Kingii' • White flowers in spring • Rosette, evergreen foliage • 3 cm high, 20 cm wide

Saxifraga hypostoma
White flowers in spring • 1–2 cm high, 40 cm wide

Saxifraga x *ingwersenii*
'Simplicity' • Pastel-pink flowers in spring • Evergreen foliage • 8 cm high, 15 cm wide

Saxifraga x *irvingii*
'Harry Marshall' • Salmon-pink flowers with pink veins in spring • Evergreen foliage • 8–10 cm high, 10–15 cm wide

'His Majesty' • White, pink-tinged flowers in spring • Evergreen foliage • 2–5 cm high, 6–10 cm wide

'Jenkinsiae' • Blush-pink flowers in spring • Evergreen foliage • 5–8 cm high, 10–15 cm wide

'Mother of Pearl' • Pink flowers in spring • Silver-grey, evergreen foliage • 2–4 cm high, 6–10 cm wide

'Mother of Queen' • Deep rose-red flowers in spring • Evergreen foliage • 2–5 cm high, 6–10 cm wide

'R.V. Pritchard' • Pale-pink flowers in spring • Evergreen foliage • 2–8 cm high, 6–10 cm wide

Saxifraga juniperifolia
Fragrant, yellow flowers in spring • Evergreen foliage • 5–10 cm high, 30–40 cm wide

Saxifraga x *kayei*
'Buttercup' • Deep-yellow flowers in spring • Evergreen foliage • 3–6 cm high, 6–10 cm wide

Saxifraga x *kellereri*
'Johann Kellerer' • Pink-lilac flowers in spring • Evergreen foliage • 6–8 cm high, 10–15 cm wide

'Suendermannii' • Soft-pink flowers in early spring • Silver-grey, evergreen foliage • 15 cm high, 20 cm wide

'Suendermannii Major' • Salmon-pink flowers in early spring • Grey, evergreen foliage • 10–15 cm high, 15–20 cm wide

S

Saxifraga kinlayi
Flowers in spring • Red-tinted, evergreen
foliage • 2 cm high, 5–10 cm wide

Saxifraga x *kochii*
Red flowers in spring • Evergreen foliage •
2–5 cm high, 15–20 cm wide

Saxifraga x *laeviformis*
'Egmont' • Muddy-yellow flowers in spring
• Evergreen foliage • 4–10 cm high

Saxifraga x *landaueri*
'Schleicheri' • Large, rosy-pink flowers in
spring • Evergreen foliage • 8–10 cm high,
15 cm wide

Saxifraga x *lilacina*
'Opalescent' • Pale beige-pink flowers, aging
to yellow, in spring • Evergreen foliage •
2–5 cm high, 6–10 cm wide

Saxifraga longifolia
White flowers in spring • Evergreen foliage
• 70 cm high, 20 cm wide

Hybrids • White flowers in spring •
Evergreen foliage • 30–45 cm high,
20 cm wide

Saxifraga x *macnabiana*
White flowers with purple spots in summer
• 30–45 cm high, 25–40 cm wide

Saxifraga x *malbyana*
'Primulina' • Yellow flowers in spring •
Evergreen foliage • 3–6 cm high,
6–10 cm wide

Saxifraga marginata
'Intermedia' • Fragrant, white flowers in
spring • Evergreen foliage • Alkaline,
moist, well-drained, organic soil •
6–14 cm high, 10–15 cm wide

Saxifraga marginata var. *boryi*
White flowers in spring • Blue-grey,
evergreen foliage • 2 cm high, 8 cm wide

Saxifraga marginata var. *rochelina*
White flowers in spring • Evergreen foliage
• 5–10 cm high, 15–20 cm wide

Saxifraga media
Pink flowers in late spring • Evergreen
foliage • 1.5–12 cm high, 15–35 cm wide

Saxifraga x *megaseiflora*
'Grebovka' • White flowers in spring •
Evergreen foliage • 2–8 cm high, 6–10 cm
wide

'Jan Naruda' • Soft-pink flowers in spring •
Evergreen foliage • 2–8 cm high, 6–10 cm
wide

'Jupiter' • Orange-yellow flowers in
spring • Evergreen foliage • 5–10 cm
high, 10–20 cm wide

'Kampa' • Creamy-yellow flowers in
spring • Evergreen foliage • 2–5 cm
high, 6–10 cm wide

'Karel Capek' • Rose flowers in spring •
Evergreen foliage • 5 cm high, 10 cm wide

'Krasava' • Cup-shaped, pink flowers in
spring • Evergreen foliage • 5–10 cm high,
20 cm wide

'Robin Hood' • Rose-pink flowers in spring
• Evergreen foliage • 5 cm high, 10 cm
wide

'Troja' • Pink flowers with a yellowish tone
in spring • Evergreen foliage • 2–8 cm
high, 6–10 cm wide

'Vladimir' • Beige-yellow flowers in spring •
Evergreen foliage • 2–4 cm high, 5–10 cm
wide

Saxifraga x *millstreamiana*
'Luna' • Light-yellow flowers in spring •
Evergreen foliage • 2–7 cm high, 5–10 cm
wide

Saxifraga oppositifolia
Rose or purple flowers in spring • Evergreen
foliage • Native to Alberta Rockies • 5–8 cm
high, 15–20 cm wide

'Florrisa' • Lilac flowers in spring •
Evergreen foliage • 2–5 cm high,
15–20 cm wide

'Nancy Form' • Bright rose-purple flowers
in spring • Evergreen foliage • 2–5 cm
high, 15 cm wide

'Ruth Draper' • Large, rose-purple flowers
in spring • Green foliage with silver marks
• 2–5 cm high, 15 cm wide

'Splendens' • Rose-purple flowers in spring
• Evergreen foliage • 2–5 cm high

'Theoden' • Rose-purple flowers in
spring • Evergreen foliage • 2–5 cm
high, 15–20 cm wide

'Vaccarina' • Deep red-purple flowers in late
spring • Evergreen foliage • 5–8 cm high,
15–20 cm wide

'Wetterhorn' • Large, rose-red flowers in
spring • Evergreen foliage • 2–5 cm high,
15 cm wide

Saxifraga oppositifolia var. *alba*
White flowers in spring • Evergreen foliage
• 5–8 cm high, 15–20 cm wide

Saxifraga paniculata
White or cream flowers in spring •
Evergreen foliage • 8–15 cm high,
15–20 cm wide

S

'Correvoniana' • White flowers in spring • Evergreen foliage • 2 cm high, 2 cm wide

'Foster's Red' • Rich-red flowers in spring • Evergreen foliage • 20–30 cm high, 15–20 cm wide

'Lutea' • Yellow flowers in late spring to early summer • Evergreen foliage • 5 cm high, 5 cm wide

'Millstream' • Rich-red flowers in late spring to early summer • Evergreen foliage • 8 cm high, 25 cm wide

'Minutifolia' • White flowers in spring • Evergreen foliage • 2 cm high, 2 cm wide

'Norway' • White flowers in summer • Evergreen foliage • 10–20 cm high, 20–25 cm wide

'Rosea' • Rose-pink flowers with large rosettes in spring • Evergreen foliage • 8 cm high, 30 cm wide

Saxifraga paniculata var. *brevifolia*
Clustered, white flowers in summer • Evergreen foliage • 5–10 cm high, 15–20 cm wide

Saxifraga paniculata minutifolia
'Red Backed Spider' • Creamy-white flowers in spring • Evergreen foliage with red underside • 5 cm high, 15 cm wide

Saxifraga polodiae
White flowers in spring • Evergreen foliage • 3 cm high, 20 cm wide

Saxifraga porophylla
Rosy-purple flowers in spring • Evergreen foliage • 5 cm high, 15 cm wide

Saxifraga punctissima
White, pink-spotted flowers in spring • Evergreen foliage • 10–15 cm high, 15–20 cm wide

Saxifraga x rosinae
'Rosina Sundermann' • White flowers in spring • Evergreen foliage • 5 cm high, 15 cm wide

Saxifraga x salmonica
'Kestoniensis' • Yellow flowers in spring • Evergreen foliage • 5–8 cm high, 10–15 cm wide
'Melrose' • White flowers in spring • Evergreen foliage • 2–5 cm high, 10–15 cm wide
'Salmonii' • White flowers in spring • Evergreen foliage • 2–5 cm high, 10–15 cm wide

Saxifraga sancta
Yellow flowers in spring • Bright-green, needle-like, evergreen foliage • 5–15 cm high, 15–30 cm wide

Saxifraga sancta var. *pseudo-sancta*
Yellow flowers in spring • Evergreen foliage • 5–15 cm high, 15–30 cm wide

Saxifraga scardica
White-tinged, pink flowers in spring • Evergreen foliage • 10–15 cm high, 25 cm wide

Saxifraga scleropoda
Yellow flowers in late spring • Evergreen foliage • 2–4 cm high, 0.5–1 cm wide

Saxifraga sempervivum
Soft-purple flowers in spring • Spiny, grey-green, evergreen foliage • 8–15 cm high, 15–25 cm wide

Saxifraga spruneri
Pure white flowers in spring • Hairy, evergreen foliage • 8 cm high, 10–15 cm wide

Saxifraga stribrnyi
Red-purple flowers in spring • Silver-grey, evergreen foliage • 5–10 cm high, 10–15 cm wide

Saxifraga taygetea
White flowers with red eye in spring • Evergreen foliage • 5–15 cm high, 15–20 cm wide

Saxifraga x timballii
White flowers in spring • Evergreen foliage • 2–4 cm high, 10–15 cm wide

Saxifraga x tirolensis
White flowers in spring • Silvery, evergreen foliage • 10 cm high, 15–20 cm wide

Saxifraga trifurcata
White flowers in spring • 15 cm high, 30+ cm wide

Saxifraga versiculata
White flowers with yellow eye in spring • Silvery, evergreen foliage • 10 cm high, 30 cm wide

Saxifraga x webrii
'Pygmalion' • Light yellow flowers in spring • Evergreen foliage • 2–5 cm high, 6–10 cm wide

Saxifraga x wendelacina
'Wendy' • Lilac-pink flowers in spring • Evergreen foliage • 2–5 cm high, 10–15 cm wide

Saxifraga wendelboi
White flowers in spring • Evergreen foliage • 2–6 cm high, 10–15 cm wide

S

General Features
Height: 5–40 cm high
Spread: 10–30 cm wide
Habit: clump-forming perennial
Flowers: tiny; spring to summer
Foliage: leathery, glossy, evergreen; limestone deposits may form on foliage
Hardiness: B–D
Warnings: prone to aphids: not prone to disease
Expert Advice: Forms attractive clumps in 2–3 years.

Growing Requirements
Light: shade to a.m. sun; shelter from hot p.m. sun
Soil: moist, well-drained, organic soil; will not tolerate dryness
Location: rock gardens; border edges
Propagation: seed; division; cuttings of non-flowering rosettes

Buying Considerations

Professionals
Popularity: gaining popularity; fast seller in bloom
Availability: readily available as finished product
Size to Sell: sells best in smaller sizes (when blooming) as it matures fast
Shrinkage: high; sensitive to overwatering (turns black in centre); requires little maintenance

Collectors
Popularity: of interest to collectors—unique, rare, challenge, exceptional beauty

Gardeners
Ease of Growth: generally easy to grow
Start with: one plant for feature plant

What to Try First ...
Saxifraga x *arendsii*, *Saxifraga fortunei* 'Five Colour'

On the Market
Saxifraga
'Black Beauty' • Deep-red flowers in spring • Evergreen foliage • 5–8 cm high
'Blood Red' • Blood-red flowers in spring • Evergreen foliage • 5–8 cm high
'Bob Hawkins' • White flowers in spring • Silvery, variegated, evergreen foliage • 15 cm high

'Elf' • Carmine-red flowers in spring • Evergreen foliage • 5–8 cm high
'Gaiety' • Deep-pink flowers in spring • Evergreen foliage • 10 cm high
'Hi Ace' • White flowers in spring • White, variegated, evergreen foliage • 15 cm high
'Ingeborg' • Deep-red flowers in spring • Evergreen foliage • 15 cm high, 20–30 cm wide
'Leuchtkafer' • Red flowers in spring • Evergreen foliage • 15 cm high, 20–30 cm wide
'Peter Pan' • Bright-pink flowers from red buds in spring • Evergreen foliage • 10–15 cm high, 20–30 cm wide
'Pixie' • Pink flowers in spring • Evergreen foliage • 5 cm high, 20–30 cm wide
'Purple Robe' • Deep rose-maroon flowers in spring • Evergreen foliage • 10 cm high, 45 cm wide
'Purpurteppich' • Purple-carmine flowers in spring • 20 cm high, 30 cm wide
'Rosemarie' • Rose-pink flowers in spring • Evergreen foliage • 2–5 cm high, 10–15 cm wide
'Whitehill' • Cream flowers in spring • Metallic-blue, evergreen foliage • 15 cm high, 15 cm wide
Saxifraga x *andrewsii*
White, pink-tinged flowers in spring • Evergreen foliage • 15–25 cm high, 20–30 cm wide
Saxifraga x *arendsii*
Pink, red or white flowers in spring • Evergreen foliage • 15 cm high, 20–30 cm wide
'Fireworks' • Carmine-pink flowers in spring • Evergreen foliage • 15 cm high, 20–30 cm wide
'Flower Carpet' • Pink flowers in spring • Evergreen foliage • 15 cm high, 20–30 cm wide
'Luschtinez' • Bright-red flowers in spring • Evergreen foliage • 8–10 cm high, 20–30 cm wide
Saxifraga bronchialis
Soft-yellow flowers in spring • Evergreen foliage • 5–10 cm high, 15 cm wide
Saxifraga aff. *brunonis*
Yellow flowers in late spring to summer • Evergreen foliage • 2 cm high, 15 cm wide

S

Saxifraga cespitosa

'Atropurpurea' • Red flowers in spring • Evergreen foliage • 10 cm high, 20–30 cm wide

'Findling' • White flowers in spring • 10 cm high, 20–30 cm wide

'Ice Field Pass' • White flowers with red spots in spring • Evergreen foliage • 5–8 cm high, 15 cm wide

Saxifraga cochlearis

Large, white flowers • Silver-grey, evergreen foliage • 15–20 cm high, 15–20 cm wide

'Major' • White flowers in early spring • Evergreen foliage • 8–10 cm high, 30–40 cm wide

'Minor' • White flowers in early spring • Evergreen foliage • 10–15 cm high, 10–15 cm wide

Saxifraga exarata ssp. moschata

'Cloth of Gold' • White flowers in late spring to early summer • Golden-yellow, evergreen foliage • 5–10 cm high, 10–15 cm wide

Saxifraga flagellaris

Butter-yellow flowers in spring • Deciduous foliage • Moist, well-drained, organic, acidic, cool soil • 5–8 cm high, 30 cm wide

Saxifraga fortunei

'Five Colour' • White flowers in fall • Cream-and-pink variegated, evergreen foliage • Alkaline-free, organic, moist, cool, fertile soil • 40 cm high, 20–30 cm wide

Saxifraga stolonifera

White flowers in summer • Large, leafy spreader • 10–15 cm high, 30–45 cm wide

'Harvest Moon' • White flowers in summer • Gold-veined foliage • 10–15 cm high, 30–45 cm wide

Saxifraga umbrosa

White flowers with red spots in spring • Evergreen foliage • 30 cm high, 30–45 cm wide

'Elliot' • Pink flowers in spring • Evergreen foliage • 15 cm high, 30+ cm wide

Saxifraga x urbium

'London Pride' • White flowers with red spots in spring • Evergreen, leathery foliage • 5 cm high, 30 cm wide

'Variegata' • White flowers with red spots in spring • Gold-and-green, evergreen, leathery foliage • 30 cm high, 30 cm wide

Scabiosa
p. 425

Genus Information

Origin: Europe, Asia, Africa and the Mediterranean

Selected Common Names: pincushion flower, dove scabious

Nomenclature: From the Latin *scabies* (itch), which this plant is supposed to cure. The common name derived from the resemblance of the flowers to pincushions.

Notes: This genus includes annuals, biennials and perennials. The variety 'Butterfly Blue' was the Perennial Plant of the Year for 2000 as chosen by the PPA (Perennial Plant Association).

General Features

Height: 10–90 cm high

Spread: 20–60 cm wide

Habit: clump-forming to mounding perennial

Flowers: pincushion-like; summer to fall; long blooming period; floriferous; good for cutflowers; good for drying; deadhead to extend blooming season; attractive to bees and butterflies

Hardiness: C–D

Warnings: prone to powdery mildew and aphids

Growing Requirements

Light: sun

Soil: fertile, well-drained soil; tolerates dry soil; avoid winter wet

Location: cottage gardens; rock gardens; wild gardens; mixed borders

Propagation: seed; division; basal cuttings

Expert Advice: Divide frequently to keep vigorous.

Buying Considerations

Professionals

Popularity: popular; fast seller in bloom

Availability: readily available as finished product

Size to Sell: sells best in smaller sizes (when blooming) as it matures fast

On the Shelf: rapidly overgrows pot

Shrinkage: low; requires little maintenance

Collectors

Popularity: not generally of interest to collectors

Gardeners

Ease of Growth: generally easy to grow

Start with: one small plant for feature plant

What to Try First ...

Scabiosa 'Butterfly Blue', *Scabiosa* 'Pink Mist', *Scabiosa caucasica* 'Blue Perfection', *Scabiosa caucasica* 'Clive Greaves', *Scabiosa columbaria*

S

On the Market

Scabiosa

'Butterfly Blue' • Lavender-blue flowers in summer • Grey-green foliage • 25–40 cm high, 30–45 cm wide

'Pink Mist' • Lavender-pink flowers in summer • 25–40 cm high, 30–45 cm wide

Scabiosa caucasica

Blue, white or lavender flowers in summer • Fertile, well-drained, alkaline soil • 45–60 cm high, 45–60 cm wide

'Blue Perfection' • Lavender-blue flowers in summer • Fertile, well-drained, alkaline soil • 45–60 cm high, 45–60 cm wide

'Clive Greaves' • Lavender-blue flowers in summer • Fertile, well-drained, alkaline soil • 45–60 cm high, 45–60 cm wide

'Fama' • Sky-blue flowers in summer • Fertile, well-drained, alkaline soil • 45–60 cm high, 45–60 cm wide

'Kompliment' (Compliment) • Blue flowers in summer • Fertile, well-drained, alkaline soil • 45–60 cm high, 30–45 cm wide

'Miss Willmott' • Cream-white flowers in summer • Fertile, well-drained, alkaline soil • 75–90 cm high, 30–45 cm wide

Scabiosa caucasica **var.** *alba*

White flowers in summer • Fertile, well-drained, dry, alkaline soil • 45–60 cm high, 45–60 cm wide

Scabiosa columbaria

Lilac-blue flowers in summer to early fall • 45–60 cm high, 30–45 cm wide

'Blue Buttons' (Walminiblue) • Sky-blue flowers in summer to early fall • 30–45 cm high, 30–45 cm wide

'Misty Butterflies' • Large, soft-pink to mauve-blue flowers in summer to early fall • 20–25 cm high, 25–30 cm wide

'Pink Buttons' (Walminipink) • Rose-pink flowers in summer to early fall • 30–45 cm high, 30–45 cm wide

Scabiosa fischeri

Blue-purple flowers in late summer • 45–60 cm high, 30–45 cm wide

Scabiosa japonica **var.** *alpina*

Lavender flowers in summer • 10–20 cm high, 20–30 cm wide

Scabiosa lucida

Lilac flowers in summer • 15–30 cm high, 30–45 cm wide

Schivereckia p. 425

Genus Information

Origin: Russia, Asia Minor and southeastern Europe

Selected Common Names: unknown

Nomenclature: unknown

Notes: A genus of some 2–5 species of perennials. Closely related to *Draba* and *Alyssum*.

General Features

Height: 10–25 cm high

Spread: 15–30 cm wide

Habit: cushion-forming perennial

Flowers: white; early summer

Foliage: evergreen

Hardiness: C

Warnings: prone to aphids; not prone to disease

Growing Requirements

Light: sun

Soil: well-drained, neutral to alkaline soil; drought tolerant; avoid winter wet

Location: rock gardens; scree; tufa; troughs

Propagation: seed (self-sows readily); division; cuttings

Buying Considerations

Professionals

Popularity: relatively unknown

Availability: occasionally available from specialty growers

Size to Sell: sells best in smaller sizes as it matures fast

On the Shelf: rapidly overgrows pot

Shrinkage: low; requires little maintenance

Miscellaneous: little commercial appeal; generally unattractive

Collectors

Popularity: not generally of interest to collectors

Gardeners

Ease of Growth: very easy to grow

Start with: one small plant for feature plant

What to Try First ...

Schivereckia berteroides

On the Market

Schivereckia berteroides

White flowers in early summer • Grey-green, evergreen foliage • 20–25 cm high, 20–30 cm wide

Schivereckia podolica

White flowers in early summer • Evergreen • 10–25 cm high, 15–25 cm wide

Schizachyrium   p. 425

Genus Information

Origin: worldwide
Selected Common Names: little blue stem
Nomenclature: From the Latin name, referring to the split chaff.
Notes: A genus of some 100 species. Once covered much of the grassland regions of North America. Closely related to *Andropogon,* differing by having only 1 terminal raceme with oblique branches, a strong rachis and pedicels, as well as stalked spikelets.

General Features

Height: 60–120 cm high
Spread: 30–90 cm wide
Habit: upright, clump-forming perennial grass
Flowers: wispy spikelets; late summer; good for drying
Foliage: blue-green; good fall colour
Hardiness: C
Warnings: not prone to insects or disease
Expert Advice: May take 2–3 years to reach a sizeable clump but worth the wait.

Growing Requirements

Light: sun
Soil: fertile, sharply drained soil; tolerant of a wide range of soil
Location: meadow gardens; mixed borders; wild gardens
Propagation: seed; division
Expert Advice: Sow seed at 13–15°C in spring. Divide in spring.

Buying Considerations

Professionals
Popularity: relatively unknown foliage plant
Availability: generally available as finished product
Size to Sell: sells best in smaller sizes; matures slowly
On the Shelf: high ornamental appeal
Shrinkage: low; requires little maintenance

Collectors
Popularity: not generally of interest to collectors

Gardeners
Ease of Growth: very easy to grow
Start with: one small plant for feature plant and several for instant visual effect

What to Try First ...
Schizachyrium scoparium 'The Blues'

On the Market

Schizachyrium scoparium
Wispy, silver-purple spikelets in late summer • Foliage turns purple to orange-red in fall • 60–120 cm high, 30–60 cm wide
'The Blues' • Wispy, silver-purple spikelets in late summer • Foliage turns burgundy-red in fall • 60–90 cm high, 30–60 cm wide

Scutellaria   p. 425

Genus Information

Origin: temperate and mountainous tropical regions, except southern Africa
Selected Common Names: alpine skullcap, skullcap
Nomenclature: From the Latin *scutella* (shield or dish), referring to the crest or pouch on the upper calyx lip.
Other Uses: Reputed in North America as a cure for rabies and in Europe for treating epilepsy.
Notes: The genus includes annuals, perennials and subshrubs.

General Features

Height: 5–30 cm high
Spread: 10–45 cm wide
Habit: rhizomatous, clump-forming perennial; (some) upright
Flowers: hooded; summer; long blooming period; attracts bees and hummingbirds
Hardiness: C–D
Warnings: prone to aphids; not prone to disease

Growing Requirements

Light: sun
Soil: fertile, gritty, well-drained, neutral to alkaline soil; tolerant of a wide range of soils
Location: alleyways; banks
Propagation: seed (self-sows readily); division; cuttings
Expert Advice: Seed in spring. Take basal cuttings or softwood cuttings.

Buying Considerations

Professionals
Popularity: relatively unknown; sells best in bloom
Availability: occasionally available from specialty growers
Size to Sell: sells best in smaller sizes (when blooming) as it matures fast
On the Shelf: rapidly overgrows pot
Shrinkage: low; requires little maintenance

S

Collectors

Popularity: not generally of interest to collectors

Gardeners

Ease of Growth: very easy to grow

Start with: one small plant for feature plant and several for mass plantings

What to Try First ...

Scutellaria indica var. *parviflolia*, *Scutellaria orientalis*, *Scutellaria orientalis* ssp. *bicolor*

On the Market

Scutellaria alpina
Hooded, purple flowers with white lower lip in summer • 15–25 cm high, 30–45 cm wide

'Arcobaleno' (Rainbow) • Hooded, bicoloured flowers in summer • 10–15 cm high, 30–45 cm wide

Scutellaria guiliemi var. *parviflora*
'Alba' • Large hooded, white flowers in summer • 15–20 cm high, 30–45 cm wide

Scutellaria indica var. *parviflolia*
Hooded, purple-blue flowers in summer • 5–20 cm high, 10–20 cm wide

Scutellaria orientalis
Hooded, yellow flowers in summer • 20–30 cm high, 15–30 cm wide

Scutellaria orientalis ssp. *bicolor*
Hooded, yellow-and-purple-brown, bicoloured flowers in summer • 20–30 cm high, 15–30 cm wide

Scutellaria pontica
Hooded, purple-pink flowers in summer • 10–15 cm high, 10–20 cm wide

Scutellaria resinosa
Hooded, violet-blue flowers in summer • Blue-grey foliage • 15–25 cm high, 20–30 cm wide

S *Sedum* p. 425 📷

Genus Information

Origin: north temperate regions and tropical mountains

Selected Common Names: stonecrop

Nomenclature: From the Latin *sedere* (to sit), referring to the way in which some species attach themselves to rocks.

Notes: The largest genus in the *Crassulaceae* family, with over 300 species, mostly succulent, including annuals, biennials, perennials, shrubs and trees. In warmer climates, tree sedums grow to over 10 m in height.

General Features

Height: 2–60 cm high

Spread: 3–60 cm wide

Habit: creeping and spreading to upright, clump-forming, long-lived perennials

Flowers: late spring to fall; attractive to bees and butterflies

Foliage: succulent; grey-green to burgundy edged; good fall colour

Hardiness: B–D

Warnings: prone to aphids; not prone to disease; contact with sap may irritate skin

Expert Advice: Because this genus is so varied, retailers often divide perennial *Sedums* into two categories: creeping and upright. The growing requirements are the same, but they tend to be located in the garden based upon their height and habit. The creeping types make excellent groundcovers. The upright types provide late-season blooms.

Growing Requirements

Light: sun to p.m. sun

Soil: moderately fertile, well-drained soil; tolerant of wide range of soils; avoid winter wet; drought tolerant to tolerant of dry periods

Location: sunny, hot, dry areas; tolerant of a wide range of locations; creeping types in raised beds, rock gardens, scree; upright types in mixed borders, rock gardens; *S. villosum* prefers moist, boggy sites

Propagation: seed; division; cuttings; offsets

Expert Advice: Seed hardy species in fall and tender species in spring. Divide in spring and divide fast-spreading species frequently to keep vigorous. Take stem or leaf cuttings in early summer.

Buying Considerations

Professionals

Popularity: popular foliage plant; sells well in bloom and for foliage

Availability: readily available as finished product and bare root

Size to Sell: sells best in smaller sizes as it matures fast

On the Shelf: high ornamental appeal; keep stock rotated; rapidly overgrows pot; upright types subject to foliage breakage

Shrinkage: low; sensitive to overwatering; requires little maintenance

Collectors

Popularity: of interest to collectors—unique, rare

Gardeners

Ease of Growth: very easy to grow

Start with: one small plant for feature plant and several for mass plantings

On the Market

Sedum

'Abbeydore' • Red buds opening to pink flowers in summer • Blue-green, waxy foliage • 45 cm high, 45 cm wide

'Blue Ridge' • Blue, succulent foliage • 2 cm high, 45–60 cm wide

'Blue Spruce' • Yellow flowers in late spring to early summer • Blue, needle-like foliage • 10–15 cm high, 45 cm wide

'Button' • Pink-white flowers • Blue-grey, button-like, succulent foliage • 8–10 cm high, 20–30 cm wide

'Frosty Morn' • Soft-pink to white flowers in summer • White-edged, light-green, succulent foliage • 20–30 cm high, 25–40 cm wide

'Herbstfreude' (Autumn Joy) • Clustered, deep-pink flowers, fading to copper-red, in late summer to fall • 45–60 cm high, 45–60 cm wide

'Lynda Windsor' • Ruby-red flowers in summer to fall • Dark-purple, succulent foliage • 30–45 cm high, 25–40 cm wide

'Mr. Goodbud' • Light buds opening to dark-mauve flowers in late summer to fall • 40–45 cm high, 30–40 cm wide

'Pink Chablis' • Pink flowers in summer • Cream-edged, blue-green, succulent foliage • 10–15 cm high, 20–30 cm wide

'Postman's Pride' • Red flowers in summer to fall • Dark purple-black, succulent foliage • 45 cm high, 30 cm wide

'Purple Emperor' • Red flowers in summer to fall • Dark purple-black, succulent foliage • 40 cm high, 30 cm wide

'Samuel Oliphant' • Pink flowers in late summer to fall • Green-centred, cream foliage with a pink edge • 30–40 cm high, 30–40 cm wide

'Vera Jameson' • Pink flowers in late summer to fall • Deep-purple foliage and stems • 25 cm high, 30–60 cm wide

Sedum acre

Bright-yellow flowers in late spring to early summer • Evergreen, succulent foliage • 5–8 cm high, 40–45+ cm wide

Sedum album

'Bella d'Inverno' • Pale-pink to white flowers in late spring to late summer • Variegated foliage • 10–15 cm high, 30–45 cm wide

'Coral Carpet' • Pink flowers in late spring to late summer • Succulent foliage, reddish in cooler weather • 5 cm high, 30 cm wide

Sedum album ssp. teretifolium

'Murale' • White flowers in late spring to late summer • 20 cm high, 30–45 cm wide

Sedum anacampseros

Star-shaped, rose flowers in summer • Thick, reddish, succulent foliage • 5–10 cm high, 10–20 cm wide

Sedum anacampseros ssp. rufescens

Star-shaped, magenta-rose flowers in summer • Thick, reddish, succulent foliage • 5–10 cm high, 10–20 cm wide

Sedum anglicum

Star-like, pale-pink flowers in late spring • Green-tinged, red, succulent foliage • 2–5 cm high, 15+ cm wide

'Love's Triangle' • Star-like, pale-pink flowers in late spring • Blue-grey, succulent foliage • 2–5 cm high, 15+ cm wide

Sedum anglicum ssp. pyrenaicum

Star-like, pink flowers in late spring • Green-tinged, red, succulent foliage • 2–5 cm high, 15+ cm wide

Sedum brevifolium

White flowers with red veins in early summer • 2–5 cm high, 30–45 cm wide

Sedum cauticola (syn. Hylotelephium cauticolum)

Bright-purple flowers in fall • Succulent foliage, blue to purple in fall • 8–15 cm high, 30–40 cm wide

'Lidakense' • Pink-purple flowers in fall • Grey-purple, succulent foliage • 10–15 cm high, 30–40 cm wide

Sedum cyaneum

Lilac-purple flowers • Succulent, evergreen foliage • 8–10 cm high

Sedum dasyphyllum

Pink flowers in early summer • Succulent, evergreen foliage • 2–5 cm high, 30–45 cm wide

S

Sedum dasyphyllum ssp. *dasyphyllum* var. *glanduliferum*
Pink flowers in early summer • Sky-blue to mauve foliage • 2–5 cm high, 30–45 cm wide

Sedum divergens
Yellow flowers in summer • Succulent, evergreen foliage • 10 cm high, 30–45+ cm wide

Sedum erythrosticum f. *variegatum*
White and pink flowers in fall • Pale glaucous-green and yellow, succulent foliage • 30–60 cm high, 30–45 cm wide

Sedum ewersii
Rose-pink flowers in late spring to late summer • Succulent, evergreen foliage • 10–15 cm high, 45–60 cm wide

Sedum ewersii var. *homophyllum*
Pink flowers in late spring to late summer • Succulent foliage • 10–15 cm high, 45–60 cm wide

Sedum grisebachii
Gold-yellow flowers in summer • Bright-green, succulent foliage aging to red • 8–12 cm high, 10–15 cm wide

Sedum hispanicum
Pink flowers in early summer • 2–5 cm high, 40–60 cm wide

Sedum hispanicum var. *minus*
Purple flowers in summer • 2–5 cm high, 25–40 cm wide

'Aureum' • White flowers in summer • Lime-green, succulent foliage • 2–5 cm high, 30–45 cm wide

Pink form • Pale-pink flowers in summer • Pink-tipped, blue-grey, succulent foliage • 2–5 cm high, 40–60 cm wide

Sedum hybridum
'Immergrunchen' • Yellow flowers in spring to summer • 10 cm high, 30+ cm wide

Sedum kamtschaticum
Yellow flowers in summer • Succulent foliage • 20–25 cm high, 30+ cm wide

Sedum kamtschaticum var. *ellacombeanum* (syn. *S. ellacombeanum*)
Yellow flowers in summer • Succulent, evergreen foliage • 10–15 cm high, 45–60 cm wide

Sedum kamtschaticum var. *floriferum*
'Weihenstephaner Gold' • Flat, gold-yellow flowers in late spring to late summer • Succulent foliage • 15 cm high, 45–60 cm wide

Sedum kamtschaticum var. *kamtschaticum*
'Variegatum' • Yellow-gold flowers in summer • Cream-edged, succulent foliage • 20–25 cm high, 30 cm wide

Sedum lanceolatum
Yellow flowers in summer • 3 cm high, 3–5 cm wide

Sedum laxum ssp. *heckneri*
Pink or white flowers in early summer • 10–15 cm high, 5–10 cm wide

Sedum lydium
White flowers in summer • Reddish, succulent, evergreen foliage • 8–15 cm high

Sedum mentha-requenii
Non-conspicuous, green-cream flowers in late spring • Tiny foliage • 1–2 cm high, 20–30 cm wide

Sedum montanum
Yellow flowers in summer • Blue-green, succulent foliage • 10–20 cm high, 30–45+ cm wide

Sedum obtusatum
Pink flowers with red veins in summer • Pale foliage with red edge • 1–3 cm high, 10–40 cm wide

Sedum pachyclados (syn. *Rhodiola pachyclados*)
White flowers in summer • Flat, rosette foliage • 5 cm high, 15+ cm wide

Sedum pilosum (syn. *Hylotelephium pilosum*)
Rose-red flowers in late spring to early summer • Evergreen, succulent foliage • 10–15 cm high, 6–8 cm wide

Sedum pluricaule var. *ezawe*
Light-purple flowers in late summer • Purple, succulent foliage • 3–6 cm high, 20–30 cm wide

Sedum populifolium
White to pink flowers in early summer • 30 cm high, 30–45 cm wide

Sedum pruinatum
Straw-yellow flowers in summer • Blue-green, needle-like foliage • 5–8 cm high, 25 cm wide

Sedum pulchellum
Lilac-pink flowers, aging to cream, in summer • Evergreen, succulent foliage with bronze tones • 10–15 cm high, 6–8 cm wide

Sedum rhodantha (syn. *Rhodiola rhodanthum*)
Rose-pink flowers in summer • 20–40 cm high, 30–45 cm wide

'Bertram Anderson' • Dusty-pink flowers in summer • Purple, succulent foliage • 15 cm high, 30 cm wide

Sedum x rubrotinctum
Soft-pink flowers in spring to early summer • Evergreen foliage • 5–8 cm high, 40–45 cm wide

Sedum rupestre (syn. S. reflexum)
'Big Blue' • White flowers in summer • Evergreen, succulent foliage • 20–30 cm high, 30–45 cm wide

Sedum rupestre erectum
Bright-yellow flowers in early summer • 30 cm high, 30+ cm wide

Sedum selskianum
Yellow flowers in summer • Graceful, arching, reddish stems • 20–40 cm high, 20–40 cm wide

Sedum sempervivoides
Carmine-red flowers • Grey-mottled, purple, succulent, evergreen foliage • 15 cm high, 10 cm wide

Sedum sexangulare
Yellow flowers in late spring to early summer • Purple-bronze, succulent, evergreen foliage • 5–10 cm high, 30–45 cm wide

Sedum sieboldii
Star-shaped, bright-pink flowers in fall • Round, blue-grey, succulent foliage • 15–25 cm high, 20–30+ cm wide

'Mediovariegatum' • Purple-pink flowers in fall • Grey-blue, succulent foliage with red edges and cream marbling • 15–25 cm high, 25–40 cm wide

Sedum spathulifolium
'Cape Blanco' • Yellow flowers in late spring • Blue-grey, succulent, evergreen foliage • 8 cm high, 60 cm wide

'Carnea' • Yellow flowers in late spring to late summer • Crimson-tinged, succulent, evergreen foliage • 15 cm high, 30 cm wide

'Purpureum' • Yellow flowers in late spring to early summer • Purple, succulent, evergreen foliage • 5–10 cm high, 45 cm wide

'William Pascoe' • Yellow flowers in late spring • Blue-green, succulent, evergreen foliage • 5 cm high, 20 cm wide

Sedum spectabile
Pink flowers in late summer to fall • 30–45 cm high, 45–60 cm wide

'Brilliant' • Carmine-pink flowers in late summer to fall • 45 cm high, 30–45 cm wide

'Carmen' • Bright-pink flowers in late summer to fall • 40–45 cm high, 45–60 cm wide

'Hotstuff' • Bright-pink flowers in late summer to fall • 20–30 cm high, 35–40 cm wide

'Iceberg' • White flowers in late summer to fall • Succulent foliage • 30–35 cm high, 30 cm wide

'Indian Chief' • Coppery-red flowers in late summer to fall • 40–45 cm high, 45–60 cm wide

'Meteor' • Shell-pink flowers, aging to bronze-red, in late summer to fall • 30–40 cm high, 30–40 cm wide

'Neon' • Electric purple-pink flowers in late summer to fall • 40 cm high, 45–60 cm wide

'Stardust' • Clustered, white flowers in late summer to fall • 45–60 cm high, 60 cm wide

Sedum spurium
Pink, red or white flowers in summer • Evergreen, succulent foliage • 5–10 cm high, 45–60+ cm wide

'Blaze of Fulda' • Burgundy flowers in summer • Dark-maroon, succulent, evergreen foliage • 5–10 cm high, 45–60+ cm wide

'Red Carpet' • Red flowers in summer • Brilliant red, succulent, evergreen foliage • 5–10 cm high, 45–60+ cm wide

'Schorbuser Blut' (Dragon's Blood) • Wine-red to purple flowers in summer • Evergreen, succulent foliage • 5–10 cm high, 45–60+ cm wide

'Variegatum' (Tricolor) • Pink flowers in summer • Red, white and green, succulent, evergreen foliage • 5–10 cm high, 45–60+ cm wide

'Voodoo' • Bright-rose flowers in summer • Dark maroon-red, succulent, evergreen foliage • 5–10 cm high, 45–60 cm+ wide

Sedum tatarinowii
White to pink flowers in summer • Rosy-pink fall foliage • 20–30 cm high, 15–20 cm wide

Sedum telephium
Rose-pink flowers in late spring to fall • 20–30 cm high, 30–40 cm wide

S

'Hester' • Pink flowers in summer to fall • 45–60 cm high, 45 cm wide

'Matrona' • Orange-pink flowers in late summer to fall • Purple-grey, succulent foliage • 40–45 cm high, 30 cm wide

'Mohrchen' • Bright-red flowers in late summer to fall • Burgundy, succulent foliage • 60 cm high, 60 cm wide

'Munstead Red' • Dark purple-red flowers in late summer to fall • Succulent foliage with red stems • 30–40 cm high, 30 cm wide

'Rosy Glow' • Purple-red flowers in late summer to fall • Light-green, succulent foliage • 20–30 cm high, 30–40 cm wide

Sedum telephium ssp. *maximum*
'Atropurpureum' • Rose-pink flowers in late summer to fall • Purple, succulent foliage • 50 cm high, 30 cm wide

Sedum telephium ssp. *ruprechettii*
'Hab Gray' • Cream-yellow flowers in late summer • Pink-grey foliage • 30 cm high, 30–40 cm wide

Sedum ternatum
'Larinem Park' • Bluish-white flowers in late spring • 10 cm high, 30+ cm wide

Sedum villosum
Rose-lilac flowers in summer • Moist to boggy, organic soil • 5–10 cm high, 10–20 cm wide

Growing Requirements
Light: shade
Soil: humus-rich, moist, well-drained soil
Location: alpine gardens; rock gardens under rock outcroppings
Propagation: spores; division; layering

Buying Considerations
Professionals
Popularity: relatively unknown foliage plant
Availability: occasionally available from specialty growers
Size to Sell: sells best in mature sizes as it matures slowly
On the Shelf: high ornamental appeal
Shrinkage: low; requires little maintenance
Collectors
Popularity: Of interest to collectors—unique, rare
Gardeners
Ease of Growth: mostly easy to grow but needs close attention to growing conditions
Start with: one mature plant for feature plant or several for mass plantings

What to Try First ...
Selaginella sanguinolenta var. *compressa*

On the Market
Selaginella sanguinolenta var. *compressa*
Wiry, dark-green foliage with zigzag pattern • 5–10 cm high, 10–20 cm wide

Selaginella

Genus Information
Origin: tropical, subtropical and temperate regions
Selected Common Names: spike club moss
Nomenclature: A diminutive of *Selago*, the old name for another lycopod.
Notes: A genus with over 700 species grown for their foliage. Closely related to *Lycopodium*.

General Features
Height: 5–10 cm high
Spread: 10–20 cm wide
Habit: slow-growing, creeping, rhizomatous groundcover perennial
Foliage: tiny, wiry; evergreen
Hardiness: C
Warnings: not prone to insects or disease
Expert Advice: Very hardy but slow-growing, performing best under a rock outcrop or on the north side of a rock. Prefers high humidity.

Semiaquilegia p. 425

Genus Information
Origin: East Asia
Selected Common Names: false columbine
Nomenclature: From the Latin *semi* (half) and *Aquilegia*, to which is it closely related.
Notes: A small genus of perennials that differ from *Aquilegia* in that the flower petals resemble a columbine but without the spurs on the flowers.

General Features
Height: 20–40 cm high
Spread: 20–30 cm wide
Habit: short-lived, clump-forming perennial
Flowers: columbine-like; early summer
Foliage: columbine-like
Hardiness: C
Warnings: prone to powdery mildew, aphids and columbine worms

Growing Requirements
Light: sun
Soil: moist, rich, well-drained soil
Location: mixed borders; rock gardens; woodland gardens
Propagation: seed; division
Expert Advice: Seeding is the easiest method of propagation and is done in spring.

Buying Considerations
Professionals
Popularity: relatively unknown
Availability: occasionally available from specialty growers
Size to Sell: sells best in smaller sizes (when blooming) as it matures fast
On the Shelf: rapidly overgrows pot
Shrinkage: low; requires little maintenance
Collectors
Popularity: not generally of interest to collectors
Gardeners
Ease of Growth: very easy to grow
Start with: one small plant for feature plant
What to Try First ...
Semiaquilegia ecalcarata 'Flore Pleno'

On the Market
Semiaquilegia ecalcarata
Columbine-like, pink to purple flowers in early summer • 20–40 cm high, 20–30 cm wide
'Flore Pleno' • Double, columbine-like, pink to purple flowers in early summer • 20–40 cm high, 20–30 cm wide

Sempervivum   p. 425 📷
Genus Information
Origin: Europe, North Africa and West Asia
Selected Common Names: hen and chicks, houseleek
Nomenclature: From *semper* (forever) and *vivere* (to live).
Other Uses: In Europe, *Sempervivum tectorum* was grown on house roofs (attached with a mix of cow dung and soil) in the belief that it protected against storms, pestilence and fire. Foliage was used medicinally.
Notes: A genus of some 42 species, with many hundreds of cultivars in existence.

General Features
Height: 1–25 cm high
Spread: 4–30 cm wide
Habit: mat- to rosette-forming, monocarpic groundcover perennial
Flowers: interesting; summer
Foliage: succulent; colour changes with season
Hardiness: C
Warnings: prone to aphids; not prone to disease
Expert Advice: *Sempervivum*s are interesting and extremely easy-to-grow plants. They die after flowering but produce numerous offsets or "chicks" as they are commonly called. Many new cultivars are available.
Growing Requirements
Light: sun
Soil: gritty, poor to moderately fertile, sharply drained, neutral to alkaline soil; avoid winter wet; drought tolerant
Location: rock gardens; scree; wall crevices; edging paths; between stepping stones
Propagation: seed; offsets
Expert Advice: Flower stalks may be removed to keep plants tidy.

Buying Considerations
Professionals
Popularity: popular, old-fashioned, garden standard foliage plant
Availability: readily available as finished product from specialty growers
Size to Sell: sells best in smaller sizes
On the Shelf: high ornamental appeal; keep stock rotated
Shrinkage: low; sensitive to overwatering; requires little maintenance
Collectors
Popularity: of interest to collectors—rare, exceptional beauty
Gardeners
Ease of Growth: very easy to grow
Start with: one small plant for feature plant and several for mass plantings
What to Try First ...
Sempervivum 'Ashes of Roses', *Sempervivum* 'Black Mini', *Sempervivum* 'Cobweb Joy', *Sempervivum* 'Frosty', *Sempervivum* 'Fuzzy Wuzzy', *Sempervivum* 'Pacific Devil's Food', *Sempervivum arachnoideum* 'Pygmalion', *Sempervivum arachnoideum* 'Rubrum', *Sempervivum calcareum* 'Nigricans', *Sempervivum octopodes*

S

On the Market

Sempervivum

'Achalur' • Dark-green, red-tipped, evergreen, succulent rosettes of leaves • 7+ cm high, 15–30 cm wide

'Adelgonde' • Watermarked, green, rose-tipped, evergreen, succulent rosettes of leaves • 7+ cm high, 15–30 cm wide

'Aldo Moro' • Evergreen, succulent rosettes of leaves • 4–7 cm high, 15–30 cm wide

'Allison' • Evergreen, succulent rosettes of leaves • 4–7 cm high, 15–30 cm wide

'Andrenor' • Red-tipped, evergreen, succulent rosettes of leaves • 7+ cm high, 15–30 cm wide

'Ann-Christy' • Evergreen, succulent rosettes of leaves • 4–7 cm high, 15–30 cm wide

'Apache' • Evergreen, downy rosettes of leaves aging to deep-pink • 5–6 cm high, 15–30 cm wide

'Aross' • Evergreen, succulent rosettes of leaves • 4–7 cm high, 15–30 cm wide

'Ashes of Roses' • Grey-green, red-backed, evergreen, succulent rosettes of leaves with cilia • 5–6 cm high, 15–30 cm wide

'Atrorubens' • Evergreen, succulent rosettes of leaves • 4–7 cm high, 15–30 cm wide

'Atroviolaceum' • Plum, with blue-green heart, evergreen, succulent rosettes of leaves • 5–7+ cm high, 15–30 cm wide

'Aureum' • Grey-green, tipped and backed with rose-red, evergreen, succulent rosettes of leaves • 5–6 cm high, 15–30 cm wide

'Aymon Correvon' • Evergreen, succulent rosettes of leaves • 7+ cm high, 15–30 cm wide

'Banderiza' • Evergreen, succulent rosettes of leaves • 4–7 cm high, 15–30 cm wide

'Bernstein' • Bright-red, with apple-green heart, evergreen, succulent rosettes of leaves • 5–6 cm high, 15–30 cm wide

'Bibi' • Evergreen, succulent rosettes of leaves • 4–7 cm high, 15–30 cm wide

'Black Mini' • Purple-tipped, evergreen, succulent rosettes of leaves • 5–6 cm high, 15–30 cm wide

'Blue Boy' • Bluish-grey, evergreen, succulent rosettes of leaves • 1–4 cm high, 15–30 cm wide

'Blue Moon' • Evergreen, succulent rosettes of leaves • 4–7 cm high, 15–30 cm wide

'Bold Chick' • Evergreen, succulent rosettes of leaves • 7+ cm high, 15–30 cm wide

'Boule de Neige' (Snowball) • Grey-green and russet, evergreen, succulent rosettes of heavily ciliated leaves • 1–4 cm high, 15–30 cm wide

'Bronze Pastel' • Bronze-red, evergreen, succulent rosettes of leaves edged in silvery hairs • 1–4 cm high, 15–30 cm wide

'Brown Owl' • Evergreen, succulent rosettes of leaves with chocolate-brown tips and edges • 5–6 cm high, 15–30 cm wide

'Burnatii' • Evergreen, succulent rosettes of leaves • 5–6 cm high, 15–30 cm wide

'Butterfly' • Rich-red, green-edged, evergreen, succulent, heavily fringed leaves • 5–6 cm high, 15–30 cm wide

'C. William' • Long, pointed, rose-pink to grey-green, evergreen, succulent rosettes of leaves • 5–6 cm high, 15–30 cm wide

'Cafe' • Black-tipped, evergreen, succulent rosettes of leaves • 5–6 cm high, 15–30 cm wide

'Candy Floss' • Light-green, evergreen, succulent, cobweb-type rosettes of leaves with bright-red outer leaves • 1–4 cm high, 15–30 cm wide

'Chivalry' • Evergreen, succulent rosettes of leaves • 7+ cm high, 15–30 cm wide

'Clara Noyes' • Copper-rose, downy, evergreen, succulent rosettes of leaves • 5–6 cm high, 15–30 cm wide

'Claret' • Evergreen, succulent rosettes of leaves • 7+ cm high, 15–30 cm wide

'Cobweb Capers' • Evergreen, succulent rosettes of leaves with webbed tips • 1–4 cm high, 15–30 cm wide

'Cobweb Joy' • Olive-green, red-tipped, webbed, evergreen, succulent rosettes of leaves • 5–6 cm high, 15–30 cm wide

'Cold Fire' • Evergreen, succulent rosettes of leaves • 4–7 cm high, 15–30 cm wide

'Collage' • Gold-green, deep-rose-centred, evergreen, succulent rosettes of leaves • 5–6 cm high, 15–30 cm wide

'Collector Anchisi' • Small, emerald-green, red-tipped, evergreen, succulent rosettes of leaves • 1–4 cm high, 15–30 cm wide

'Comte de Congae' • Grey-green, sharply red-tipped, evergreen, succulent rosettes of leaves, with gold-toned offsets on red stolons • 7+ cm high, 15–30 cm wide

'Cornelia' • Evergreen, succulent rosettes of leaves • 4–7 cm high, 15–30 cm wide

S

'Corsair' • Soft-green, rose-centred, evergreen, succulent rosettes of fringed and tufted leaves • 5–6 cm high, 15–30 cm wide

'Cresta' • Evergreen, succulent rosettes of leaves • 4–7 cm high, 15–30 cm wide

'Crimson Velvet' • Narrow, downy, crimson, evergreen, succulent rosettes of leaves • 5–6 cm high, 15–30 cm wide

'Crispyn' • Grey-green, purple-flushed, woolly, evergreen, succulent rosettes of leaves • 5–6 cm high, 15–30 cm wide

'Cynthian' • Evergreen, succulent rosettes of leaves • 1–7 cm high, 15–30 cm wide

'Dallas' • Evergreen, succulent rosettes of leaves • 7+ cm high, 15–30 cm wide

'Dark Cloud' • Grey-green and dusky-purple, large, pointy, dark-tipped, evergreen, succulent rosettes of leaves • 7+ cm high, 15–30 cm wide

'Deep Fire' • Apple-green, red-tinged, evergreen, succulent rosettes of leaves with cilia • 5–6 cm high, 15–30 cm wide

'Director Jacobs' • Maroon, velvet, evergreen, succulent rosettes of leaves • 7+ cm high, 15–30 cm wide

'Dolo' • Red, apple-green-centred, evergreen, succulent rosettes of leaves • 7+ cm high, 15–30 cm wide

'Dream Catcher' • Evergreen, succulent rosettes of leaves • 4–7 cm high, 15–30 cm wide

'Dynamo' • Red, dark-tipped, evergreen, succulent rosettes of lightly fringed leaves • 7+ cm high, 15–30 cm wide

'El Toro' • Red-toned, evergreen, succulent, open rosettes of large, flat leaves • 7+ cm high, 15–30 cm wide

'Elvis' • Evergreen, succulent rosettes of leaves • 4–7 cm high, 15–30 cm wide

'Euphemia' • Grey-green, evergreen, succulent, tight rosettes of leaves with hairy tips • 5–6 cm high, 15–30 cm wide

'Fame' • Evergreen, succulent rosettes of leaves • 4–7 cm high, 15–30 cm wide

'Finerpointe' • Narrow, pointed, deep rose-red, evergreen, downy, fringed succulent leaves • 5–6 cm high, 15–30 cm wide

'Flamingo' • Evergreen, succulent rosettes of leaves with pink and red tones in cool seasons • 15 cm high, 30–45 cm wide

'Flander's Passion' • Purple-grey, evergreen, succulent rosettes of leaves • 7+ cm high, 15–30 cm wide

'Frodo' • Evergreen, succulent rosettes of leaves • 4–7 cm high, 15–30 cm wide

'Frosty' • Evergreen, succulent rosettes of leaves • 4–7 cm high, 15–30 cm wide

'Fuzz Globe' • Evergreen, succulent rosettes of leaves • 4–7 cm high, 15–30 cm wide

'Fuzzy Wuzzy' • Pink and green, fringed, tufted, evergreen, succulent rosettes of leaves • 5–6 cm high, 15–30 cm wide

'Galahad' • Rose-wine, satiny, evergreen, succulent rosettes of leaves • 5–6 cm high, 15–30 cm wide

'Glaucum Minor' • Evergreen, succulent rosettes of leaves • 4–7 cm high, 15–30 cm wide

'Granada' • Flowers in summer • Burgundy-grey, velvety, evergreen, succulent rosettes of leaves, with bright red offsets • 7+ cm high, 15–30 cm wide

'Grapetone' • Flowers in summer • Evergreen, succulent rosettes of leaves • 1–7 cm high, 15–30 cm wide

'Grey Dawn' • Flowers in summer • Evergreen, succulent rosettes of leaves • 4–7 cm high, 15–30 cm wide

'Gypsy' • Flowers in summer • Evergreen, succulent rosettes of leaves • 4–7 cm high, 15–30 cm wide

'Hester' • Flowers in summer • Dark-green, evergreen, succulent rosettes of leaves with purple backs and tips • 5–6 cm high, 15–30 cm wide

'Icicle' • Flowers in summer • Green, webbed, evergreen, succulent rosettes of leaves with cherry-red bases • 5–6 cm high, 15–30 cm wide

'Irazu' • Flowers in summer • Pale olive-green, pink-flushed, evergreen, succulent rosettes of leaves • 1–4 cm high, 15–30 cm wide

'IWO' • Flowers in summer • Satiny, light-green, evergreen, succulent rosettes of leaves with red tips and edges • 7+ cm high, 15–30 cm wide

'Jeramia' • Flowers in summer • Rich-plum, lightly fringed, evergreen, succulent rosettes of leaves • 5–6 cm high, 15–30 cm wide

'Jewel Case' • Flowers in summer • Gold-green, peachy-red-shaded, evergreen, succulent, flat rosettes of leaves with delicate cilia • 5–6 cm high, 15–30 cm wide

S

'Jungle Fires' • Flowers in summer • Green, sharply plum-tipped, evergreen, succulent rosettes of leaves • 7+ cm high, 15–30 cm wide

'Jurina' • Flowers in summer • Olive-green, evergreen, succulent rosettes of leaves with rose-purple backs • 7+ cm high, 15–30 cm wide

'Kalinda' • Flowers in summer • Evergreen, succulent rosettes of leaves • 4–7 cm high, 15–30 cm wide

'Kappa' • Flowers in summer • Deep-red, domed, evergreen, succulent rosettes of leaves with light webbing • 5–6 cm high, 15–30 cm wide

'Kermit' • Flowers in summer • Deep green, red-flushed, evergreen, succulent, compact rosettes of leaves • 5–6 cm high, 15–30 cm wide

'Kimono' • Flowers in summer • Emerald-green, purple-tipped, evergreen, succulent rosettes of leaves • 5–6 cm high, 15–30 cm wide

'Kramer Spinrad' • Flowers in summer • Evergreen, webbed, succulent, flat rosettes of leaves • 7+ cm high, 15–30 cm wide

'Launcelot' • Flowers in summer • Evergreen, succulent rosettes of leaves • 4–7 cm high, 15–30 cm wide

'Lavender and Old Lace' • Flowers in summer • Evergreen, succulent rosettes of leaves • 4–7 cm high, 15–30 cm wide

'Leneca' • Flowers in summer • Satiny, red, green-tipped, evergreen, succulent rosettes of leaves • 7+ cm high, 15–30 cm wide

'Lentezon' • Flowers in summer • Evergreen, succulent rosettes of leaves • 4–7 cm high, 15–30 cm wide

'Leucadia' • Flowers in summer • Green, copper-red-tipped, evergreen, succulent rosettes of leaves • 5–6 cm high, 15–30 cm wide

'Liliane' • Flowers in summer • Evergreen, succulent rosettes of leaves • 4–7 cm high, 15–30 cm wide

'Lynn's Choice' • Flowers in summer • Evergreen, succulent rosettes of leaves • 7+ cm high, 15–30 cm wide

'Magnificum' • Flowers in summer • Evergreen, succulent rosettes of leaves • 7+ cm high, 15–30 cm wide

'Majestic' • Flowers in summer • Evergreen, succulent rosettes of leaves • 7+ cm high, 15–30 cm wide

'Maria Laach' • Flowers in summer • Dark-green, evergreen, succulent rosettes of leaves with mahogany tips and backs • 5–6 cm high, 15–30 cm wide

'Maya' • Flowers in summer • Evergreen, succulent rosettes of leaves • 4–7 cm high, 15–30 cm wide

'Merlin' • Flowers in summer • Evergreen, succulent rosettes of leaves • 7+ cm high, 15–30 cm wide

'Mike' • Flowers in summer • Evergreen, succulent rosettes of leaves • 4–7 cm high, 15–30 cm wide

'Minaret' • Flowers in summer • Evergreen, succulent rosettes of leaves • 7+ cm high, 15–30 cm wide

'Missouri Rose' • Flowers in summer • Evergreen, succulent rosettes of leaves • 4–7 cm high, 15–30 cm wide

'Montgomery' • Flowers in summer • Evergreen, succulent rosettes of leaves • 1–7 cm high, 15–30 cm wide

'More Honey' • Flowers in summer • Orange-red, green-based, evergreen, succulent rosettes of leaves • 7+ cm high, 15–30 cm wide

'Neptune' • Flowers in summer • Evergreen, succulent rosettes of leaves • 7+ cm high, 15–30 cm wide

'Nightwood' • Flowers in summer • Evergreen, succulent rosettes of leaves • 4–7 cm high, 15–30 cm wide

'Nortoft's Beauty' • Flowers in summer • Evergreen, succulent rosettes of leaves • 4–7 cm high, 15–30 cm wide

'Oddity' • Flowers in summer • Evergreen, succulent rosettes of leaves • 7+ cm high, 15–30 cm wide

'Ohio Burgundy' • Flowers in summer • Deep-burgundy, velvety, evergreen, succulent rosettes of leaves • 7+ cm high, 15–30 cm wide

'Old Rose' • Flowers in summer • Velvety, rose-purple, broad feather-edged, evergreen, succulent rosettes of leaves • 5–6 cm high, 15–30 cm wide

'Olivette' • Flowers in summer • Olive-green, brown-edged, evergreen, succulent rosettes of leaves • 7+ cm high, 15–30 cm wide

'Pacific Charm' • Flowers in summer • Evergreen, succulent rosettes of leaves • 4–7 cm high, 15–30 cm wide

'Pacific Clydesdale' • Flowers in summer • Evergreen, succulent rosettes of leaves • 4–7 cm high, 15–30 cm wide

'Pacific Daemon' • Flowers in summer • Dusky-mulberry, pointed, evergreen, succulent rosettes of leaves • 5–6 cm high, 15–30 cm wide

'Pacific Day Dream' • Flowers in summer • Evergreen, succulent rosettes of leaves • 4–7 cm high, 15–30 cm wide

'Pacific Devil's Food' • Flowers in summer • Satiny, deep chocolate-red, evergreen, succulent rosettes of leaves • 5–6 cm high, 15–30 cm wide

'Pacific Feather Power' • Flowers in summer • Evergreen, succulent rosettes of leaves • 4–7 cm high, 15–30 cm wide

'Pacific Greensleeves' • Flowers in summer • Evergreen, succulent rosettes of leaves • 4–7 cm high, 15–30 cm wide

'Pacific Hairy Hep' • Flowers in summer • Apple-green, flushed and tipped rosy-red, cilia-edged, evergreen, succulent rosettes of leaves • 5–6 cm high, 15–30 cm wide

'Pacific Knight' • Flowers in summer • Evergreen, succulent rosettes of leaves • 4–7 cm high, 15–30 cm wide

'Pacific Majesty' • Flowers in summer • Evergreen, succulent rosettes of leaves • 4–7 cm high, 15–30 cm wide

'Pacific Phoenix Fire' • Flowers in summer • Evergreen, succulent rosettes of leaves • 4–7 cm high, 15–30 cm wide

'Pacific Rim' • Flowers in summer • Evergreen, succulent rosettes of leaves • 4–7 cm high, 15–30 cm wide

'Pacific Sexy' • Flowers in summer • Evergreen, succulent rosettes of leaves • 7+ cm high, 15–30 cm wide

'Pacific Shadows' • Flowers in summer • Satiny, rose-purple, evergreen, succulent rosettes of leaves • 5–6 cm high, 15–30 cm wide

'Pacific Sparkler' • Flowers in summer • Evergreen, succulent rosettes of leaves • 1–7 cm high, 15–30 cm wide

'Pacific Spring Frost' • Flowers in summer • Evergreen, succulent rosettes of leaves • 4–7 cm high, 15–30 cm wide

'Pacific Trails' • Flowers in summer • Evergreen, succulent rosettes of leaves • 1–7 cm high, 15–30 cm wide

'Pacific Velveteen' • Flowers in summer • Evergreen, succulent rosettes of leaves • 4–7 cm high, 15–30 cm wide

'Pastel' • Flowers in summer • Evergreen, succulent rosettes of leaves • 4–7 cm high, 15–30 cm wide

'Pekinese' • Flowers in summer • Evergreen, succulent rosettes of leaves • 4–7 cm high, 15–30 cm wide

'Peterson's Ornatum' • Flowers in summer • Rose-red, with grey-green heart, evergreen, succulent rosettes of leaves • 7+ cm high, 15–30 cm wide

'Pink Charm' • Flowers in summer • Evergreen, succulent rosettes of leaves • 4–7 cm high, 15–30 cm wide

'Pink Puff' • Flowers in summer • Grey-green, downy, evergreen, succulent rosettes of leaves with purple tips and backs • 5–6 cm high, 15–30 cm wide

'Pixie' • Flowers in summer • Evergreen, succulent rosettes of leaves • 1–7 cm high, 15–30 cm wide

'Plastic' • Flowers in summer • Evergreen, succulent rosettes of leaves • 1–7 cm high, 15–30 cm wide

'Pseudo-androsace' • Pink flowers in summer • Fuzzy, evergreen, succulent rosettes of leaves • 5 cm high, 15–20 cm wide

'Pseudo-draba' • Flowers in summer • Pointy, lime-green, evergreen, succulent rosettes of leaves • 7+ cm high, 15–30 cm wide

'Regal' • Flowers in summer • Evergreen, succulent rosettes of leaves • 1–7 cm high, 15–30 cm wide

'Rococo' • Flowers in summer • Evergreen, succulent rosettes of leaves • 1–7 cm high, 15–30 cm wide

'Ronny' • Flowers in summer • Evergreen, succulent rosettes of leaves • 1–7 cm high, 15–30 cm wide

'Rosealind' • Flowers in summer • Evergreen, succulent rosettes of leaves • 1–7 cm high, 15–30 cm wide

'Royal Opera' • Flowers in summer • Evergreen, succulent rosettes of leaves • 1–7 cm high, 15–30 cm wide

'Rubellum Mahogany' • Flowers in summer • Evergreen, succulent rosettes of leaves • 7+ cm high, 15–30 cm wide

S

'Rubra Ash' • Flowers in summer • Rosy-purple, softly furred, evergreen, succulent rosettes of leaves • 7+ cm high, 15–30 cm wide

'Serapis' • Flowers in summer • Evergreen, succulent rosettes of leaves • 1–7 cm high, 15–30 cm wide

'Sideshow' • Flowers in summer • Evergreen, succulent rosettes of leaves • 4–7 cm high, 15–30 cm wide

'Silber Kameol' • Flowers in summer • Evergreen, succulent rosettes of leaves • 1–7 cm high, 15–30 cm wide

'Silver Cup' • Flowers in summer • Grey-green, evergreen, succulent, tight rosettes of leaves with dark-red backs and light cilia • 1–4 cm high, 15–30 cm wide

'Silver Olympic' • Flowers in summer • Evergreen, succulent rosettes of leaves • 4–7 cm high, 15–30 cm wide

'Soft Line' • Flowers in summer • Evergreen, succulent rosettes of leaves • 1–7 cm high, 15–30 cm wide

'Sopa' • Flowers in summer • Evergreen, succulent rosettes of leaves • 5–6 cm high, 15–30 cm wide

'Spherette' • Flowers in summer • Evergreen, succulent rosettes of leaves • 4–7 cm high, 15–30 cm wide

'Spice' • Flowers in summer • Green, aging to maroon, velvety, evergreen, succulent rosettes of leaves • 7+ cm high, 15–30 cm wide

'Spinell' • Flowers in summer • Evergreen, succulent rosettes of leaves • 1–7 cm high, 15–30 cm wide

'Spode' • Flowers in summer • Evergreen, succulent rosettes of leaves • 1–7 cm high, 15–30 cm wide

'Susan' • Flowers in summer • Evergreen, succulent rosettes of leaves • 4–7 cm high, 15–30 cm wide

'Tamberlane' • Flowers in summer • Evergreen, succulent rosettes of leaves • 4–7 cm high, 15–30 cm wide

'Tederheid' • Flowers in summer • Evergreen, succulent rosettes of leaves • 4–7 cm high, 15–30 cm wide

'Temby' • Flowers in summer • Evergreen, succulent rosettes of leaves • 1–7 cm high, 15–30 cm wide

'The Flintstones' • Flowers in summer • Evergreen, succulent rosettes of leaves • 1–7 cm high, 15–30 cm wide

'Theoden' • Flowers in summer • Evergreen, succulent rosettes of leaves • 7+ cm high, 15–30 cm wide

'Thunder' • Flowers in summer • Evergreen, succulent rosettes of leaves • 4–7 cm high, 15–30 cm wide

'Tiara' • Flowers in summer • Evergreen, succulent rosettes of leaves • 4–7 cm high, 15–30 cm wide

'Tip Top' • Flowers in summer • Bright-green, red-tipped, evergreen, succulent, small rosettes of leaves • 1–4 cm high, 15–30 cm wide

'Titania' • Flowers in summer • Evergreen, succulent rosettes of leaves • 4–7 cm high, 15–30 cm wide

'Tourmalyi' • Flowers in summer • Evergreen, succulent rosettes of leaves • 1–7 cm high, 15–30 cm wide

'Tracy Sue' • Flowers in summer • Evergreen, succulent rosettes of leaves • 4–7 cm high, 15–30 cm wide

'Uranus' • Flowers in summer • Evergreen, succulent rosettes of leaves • 1–7 cm high, 15–30 cm wide

'Ursaline' • Flowers in summer • Evergreen, succulent rosettes of leaves • 1–7 cm high, 15–30 cm wide

'Velanovsky' • Flowers in summer • Evergreen, succulent rosettes of leaves • 4–7 cm high, 15–30 cm wide

'Virgil' • Flowers in summer • Evergreen, succulent rosettes of leaves • 4–7 cm high, 15–30 cm wide

'Virginius' • Flowers in summer • Evergreen, succulent rosettes of leaves • 1–7 cm high, 15–30 cm wide

'Webby Ola' • Flowers in summer • Evergreen, succulent rosettes of leaves • 4–7 cm high, 15–30 cm wide

'Weirdo' • Flowers in summer • Evergreen, succulent rosettes of leaves • 4–7 cm high, 15–30 cm wide

'Westerlin' • Flowers in summer • Evergreen, succulent rosettes of leaves • 7+ cm high, 15–30 cm wide

'Whitening' • Flowers in summer • Evergreen, succulent rosettes of leaves • 4–7 cm high, 15–30 cm wide

'Winter Beauty' • Flowers in summer • Evergreen, succulent rosettes of leaves • 1–7 cm high, 15–30 cm wide

S

'Zarubianum' • Flowers in summer • Evergreen, succulent rosettes of leaves • 1–7 cm high, 15–30 cm wide

'Zenobia' • Flowers in summer • Evergreen, succulent rosettes of leaves • 7+ cm high, 15–30 cm wide

Sempervivum
(S. arachnoideum x S. nevadense)
Red-pink flowers in summer • Red-flushed, evergreen, succulent rosettes of leaves with hairy edges and tips • 1–4 cm high, 15–30 cm wide

Sempervivum
(S. arachnoideum x S. pittonii)
Red-pink flowers in summer • Hairy, red-backed, evergreen, succulent, tight rosettes of leaves • 1–4 cm high, 15–30 cm wide

Sempervivum
(S. dolomiticum x S. montanum)
Pink flowers in summer • Green, narrow, pointed, downy, evergreen, succulent rosettes of leaves • 1–4 cm high, 15–30 cm wide

Sempervivum arachnoideum
Red-pink flowers in late spring • Webbed, evergreen, succulent rosettes of leaves • 4–12 cm high, 30–45 cm wide

'Gladys' • Red-pink flowers in summer • Grey-green, lightly webbed, evergreen, succulent rosettes of leaves • 1–4 cm high, 15–30 cm wide

'Linde' • Red-pink flowers in summer • Webbed, evergreen, succulent rosettes of leaves • 1–4 cm high, 15–30 cm wide

'Pygmalion' • Red-pink flowers in summer • Deep-red, webbed, evergreen, succulent rosettes of leaves • 1–4 cm high, 15–30 cm wide

'Rubrum' • Red-pink flowers in summer • Red-flushed, evergreen, succulent, small, webbed rosettes of leaves • 5–6 cm high, 15–30 cm wide

'Sparkle' • Red-pink flowers in late spring • Webbed, evergreen, succulent rosettes of leaves • 4–7 cm high, 30–45 cm wide

Sempervivum arachnoideum var. bryoides
Red-pink flowers in summer • Evergreen, succulent, heavily webbed, tiny rosettes of leaves • 1 cm high, 15–30 cm wide

Sempervivum arachnoideum minor
Red-pink flowers in late spring • Webbed, evergreen, succulent rosettes of leaves • 1–7 cm high, 30–45 cm wide

Sempervivum arachnoideum ssp. tomentosum
Red-pink flowers in summer • Purple, webbed, evergreen, succulent rosettes of leaves • 5–6 cm high, 15–30 cm wide

Sempervivum atropurpureum
(syn. 'Atropurpureum')
Pink-purple flowers in summer • Grey-green, blood-red-tipped, evergreen, succulent rosettes of leaves • 7+ cm high, 15–30 cm wide

Sempervivum ballsii
from **Smolikas** • Pink flowers in summer • Grey-green, blood-red-tipped, evergreen, succulent rosettes of leaves • 4–7 cm high, 15–30 cm wide

Sempervivum x barbulatum
(from **Valle Quarozzo**) • Flowers in summer • Grey-green, purple-tipped, evergreen, succulent rosettes of leaves • 1–4 cm high, 15–30 cm wide

Sempervivum x barbulatum rubrum
'Red Mountain' • Flowers in summer • Grey-green, purple-tipped, evergreen, succulent rosettes of leaves • 4–7 cm high, 15–30 cm wide

Sempervivum borissovae
Rose-red flowers in summer • Grey-green, blood-red-tipped, evergreen, succulent rosettes of leaves • 4–15 cm high, 15–30 cm wide

Sempervivum calcareum
from **Mont Ventoux** • Pink-purple flowers in summer • Grey-green, blood-red-tipped, evergreen, succulent rosettes of leaves • 5–6 cm high, 15–30 cm wide

'Greenii' • Pink-purple flowers in summer • Green, red-tipped, evergreen, succulent rosettes of leaves • 1–4 cm high, 15–30 cm wide

'Grigg's Surprise' (Monstrosum) • Pink-purple flowers in summer • Grey-green, blood-red-tipped, evergreen, succulent rosettes of leaves • 1–7 cm high, 15–30 cm wide

'Guiseppi' • Pink-purple flowers in summer • Grey-green, blood-red-tipped, evergreen, succulent rosettes of leaves • 4–7 cm high, 15–30 cm wide

'Nigricans' • Pink-purple flowers in summer • Grey-green, blood-red-tipped, evergreen, succulent rosettes of leaves • 4–7 cm high, 15–30 cm wide

S

'Pink Pearl' • Pink-purple flowers in summer • Grey-green, blood-red-tipped, evergreen, succulent rosettes of leaves • 7+ cm high, 15–30 cm wide

'Sir William Lawrence' • Pink-purple flowers in summer • Red-tipped, evergreen, succulent rosettes of leaves • 7+ cm high, 15–30 cm wide

Sempervivum cantabricum

from Lago de Enol • Red to white flowers in summer • Grey-green, blood-red-tipped, evergreen, succulent rosettes of leaves • 4–7 cm high, 15–30 cm wide

Sempervivum ciliosum

Lemon-yellow flowers in summer • Bright-green, red-tipped, evergreen, succulent, hairy rosettes of leaves • 5–8 cm high, 15–30 cm wide

from Mali Hat • Lemon-yellow flowers in summer • Purple-backed, evergreen, succulent, hairy rosettes of leaves • 1–4 cm high, 15–30 cm wide

from Romania • Lemon-yellow flowers in summer • Evergreen, succulent, hairy rosettes of leaves • 1–4 cm high, 15–30 cm wide

Sempervivum dolomiticum

Pink flowers in summer • Green, evergreen, succulent rosettes of leaves with deep-red backs • 1–4 cm high, 15–30 cm wide

Sempervivum erythraeum

Red-purple flowers in summer • Grey-green, blood-red-tipped, evergreen, succulent rosettes of leaves • 1–7 cm high, 15–30 cm wide

SM 1031 • Pink-purple flowers in summer • Grey-green, blood-red-tipped, evergreen, succulent rosettes of leaves • 1–7 cm high, 15–30 cm wide

Sempervivum x *fauconnettii*

Purple-pink flowers in summer • Green, red-backed, tufted, evergreen, succulent rosettes of leaves • 1–4 cm high, 15–30 cm wide

Sempervivum giuseppii

from Pena Esquiqueta • Rose-red, white-edged flowers in summer • Soft-green, red-backed, evergreen, succulent, tight rosettes of leaves • 5–8 cm high, 15–30 cm wide

Sempervivum hausmani

Flowers in summer • Pale-green, rosy-tinged, velvety, evergreen, succulent rosettes of leaves • 5–6 cm high, 15–30 cm wide

Sempervivum hispidium

Pink-purple flowers in summer • Grey-green, blood-red-tipped, evergreen, succulent rosettes of leaves • 4–7 cm high, 15–30 cm wide

Sempervivum kindingeri

Creamy-yellow flowers in summer • Grey-green, blood-red-tipped, evergreen, succulent rosettes of leaves • 1–7 cm high, 15–30 cm wide

Sempervivum leucanthum rubrum

Pale green-yellow flowers in summer • Grey-green, blood-red-tipped, evergreen, succulent rosettes of leaves • 4–7 cm high, 15–30 cm wide

Sempervivum marmoreum

'Brunneifolium' • Red, white-edged flowers in summer • Tan, pink-tinged, evergreen, succulent rosettes of leaves • 5–6 cm high, 15–30 cm wide

'Chocolate' • Red, white-edged flowers in summer • Dark-chocolate, evergreen, succulent rosettes of leaves • 5–6 cm high, 15–30 cm wide

Sempervivum octopodes

Yellow flowers in summer • Evergreen, purple, succulent rosettes of leaves • 2 cm high, 10 cm wide

Sempervivum octopodes var. *apetalum*

Yellow flowers in summer • Bright-green, evergreen, succulent, tight rosettes of leaves • 1–4 cm high, 15–30 cm wide

Sempervivum pumilum

from Armchi • Rose-purple flowers in summer • Evergreen, succulent, green rosettes that close up to balls of old-rose in winter • 1 cm high, 15–30 cm wide

Sempervivum reginae-amaliae

(from Vardusa) • Flowers in summer • Yellow-green and carmen-pink, evergreen, succulent rosettes of leaves • 1–4 cm high, 15–30 cm wide

Sempervivum tectorum

'Nigrum' • Flowers in summer • Evergreen, succulent rosettes of leaves • 4–7 cm high, 15–30 cm wide

Sempervivum wulfenii

Flowers in summer • Evergreen, succulent rosettes of leaves • Poor, to moderately fertile, sharply drained, gritty, acidic soil • 10–25 cm high, 4–8 cm wide

from Prague • Flowers in summer • Grey-green, purple-tipped, evergreen, succulent rosettes of leaves • 7+ cm high, 15–30 cm wide

Senecio

p. 425 📷

Genus Information

Origin: worldwide
Selected Common Names: groundsel
Nomenclature: From the Latin *senex* (an old man), referring to the white or grey pappus.
Notes: A genus of some 1000–1500 species. Includes annuals, biennials, perennials, shrubs and trees.

General Features

Height: 15–45 cm high
Spread: 15–25 cm wide
Habit: clump-forming, low or upright perennial
Flowers: daisy-like, spring to fall; short blooming period
Foliage: grey-green; (most) hairy; evergreen
Hardiness: C–D
Warnings: prone to aphids; not prone to disease; all plant parts cause severe discomfort if ingested

Growing Requirements

Light: sun
Soil: fertile, well-drained to dry soil
Location: front of mixed borders; rock gardens; wild gardens
Propagation: seed; division; cuttings
Expert Advice: Take softwood or semi-ripe cuttings in summer.

Buying Considerations

Professionals

Popularity: relatively unknown
Availability: occasionally available from specialty growers
Size to Sell: sells best in smaller sizes (when blooming) as it matures fast
Shrinkage: low; requires little maintenance

Collectors

Popularity: of interest to collectors—unique, rare

Gardeners

Ease of Growth: very easy to grow
Start with: one small plant for feature plant

What to Try First ...

Senecio abrotanifolius, Senecio speciosus

On the Market

Senecio abrotanifolius
Yellow to orange-scarlet flowers in midsummer to fall • Evergreen • 15–45 cm high, 15–30 cm wide

Senecio aucheri
Clear-yellow flowers in spring • 5–10 cm high, 30–45 cm wide

Senecio speciosus
Orange flowers in summer • 8–12 cm high, 10–15 cm wide

Shortia

p. 425 📷

Genus Information

Origin: North America and Asia
Selected Common Names: fringed galax, Nippon bells, Oconee bells
Nomenclature: Named for Charles Short, 1794–1863, a botanist from Kentucky.

General Features

Height: 8–20 cm high
Spread: 15–25 cm wide
Habit: slow-creeping or mat-forming perennial
Flowers: deeply fringed; early spring
Foliage: glossy; evergreen; good fall colour
Hardiness: C–D
Warnings: prone to slugs; not prone to insects or disease
Expert Advice: An excellent woodland or shady, moist garden plant that provides an attractive mat of glossy foliage. Performs best in areas with cool, damp summers.

Growing Requirements

Light: shade
Soil: cool, humus-rich, moist, acidic soil
Location: alpine houses; rock gardens; woodland gardens
Propagation: seed; separate and replant rooted runners; cuttings
Expert Advice: Seed must be sown fresh. Seedlings take several years to reach blooming size. Divisions are slow to establish and can be tricky. Take basal cuttings in early summer.

Buying Considerations

Professionals

Popularity: relatively unknown
Availability: occasionally available from specialty growers
Size to Sell: sells best in smaller sizes (when blooming); matures slowly
Shrinkage: low; requires little maintenance

Collectors

Popularity: of interest to collectors—unique, exceptional beauty, rare

Gardeners

Ease of Growth: mostly easy to grow but needs close attention to growing conditions
Start with: one mature plant for feature plant

What to Try First ...

Shortia galacifolia, Shortia soldanelloides, Shortia uniflora

S

On the Market

Shortia galacifolia
Cream, often pink-flushed, flowers in spring • Glossy foliage turns bronze-red in fall • 8–20 cm high, 15–25 cm wide

Shortia soldanelloides
Fringed, pink flowers in spring • Glossy foliage • 10–20 cm high, 15–25 cm wide

Shortia soldanelloides var. *ilicifolia*
White, rarely pink, flowers in spring • 10–20 cm high, 15–25 cm wide

Shortia soldanelloides var. *intercedens*
White flowers in spring • 10–20 cm high, 15–25 cm wide

Shortia uniflora
Fringed, pink flowers in spring • Glossy foliage • 10–20 cm high, 15–25 cm wide

Sidalcea
p. 425

Genus Information

Origin: western North America
Selected Common Names: checker mallow, foothill checker mallow, Oregon mallow
Nomenclature: From *Sida* and *Alcea*, two genera of the *Malvaceae* family.
Notes: Genus includes annuals and perennials. Related to *Malva* and *Sphaeralcea*.

General Features

Height: 45–120 cm high
Spread: 30–60 cm wide
Habit: rhizomatous or clump-forming, native groundcover perennial
Flowers: satiny; summer; long blooming period; good for cutflowers; deadhead to extend blooming season
Foliage: mid-green; rounded to kidney-shaped
Hardiness: C–D
Warnings: prone to powdery mildew, aphids and rust; (some) spread aggressively and self-sow (contain and deadhead to prevent spread)

Growing Requirements

Light: sun
Soil: deep, fertile, moist, organic, well-drained soil; tolerant of a wide range of soils
Location: mixed borders; woodland gardens; tolerates hot, dry locations
Propagation: seed; division
Expert Advice: Divide every 2–3 years to keep vigorous. Divide in spring.

Buying Considerations

Professionals

Popularity: gaining popularity; fast seller in bloom
Availability: readily available as finished product and bare root
Size to Sell: sells best in smaller sizes (when blooming) as it matures fast
On the Shelf: rapidly overgrows pot
Shrinkage: low; requires little maintenance

Collectors

Popularity: not generally of interest to collectors

Gardeners

Ease of Growth: very easy to grow
Start with: one small plant for feature plant

What to Try First ...

Sidalcea 'Elsie Heugh', *Sidalcea* 'Little Princess', *Sidalcea* 'Party Girl', *Sidalcea* 'Sussex Beauty', *Sidalcea candida*, *Sidalcea oregana* 'Brilliant'

On the Market

Sidalcea
'Elsie Heugh' • Pink flowers in summer • 60–75 cm high, 45–60 cm wide

'Little Princess' • Pink flowers in summer • 60–90 cm high, 45–60 cm wide

'Monarch' • Red flowers in summer • 45–60 cm high, 30–45 cm wide

'Mr Lindbergh' • Red-rose flowers in summer • 60–75 cm high, 45–60 cm wide

'Party Girl' • Pink flowers in summer • 60–75 cm high, 45–60 cm wide

'Purpetta' • Maroon flowers in summer • 75–90 cm high, 45–60 cm wide

'Rosy Gem' • Salmon flowers in summer • 60–90 cm high, 45–60 cm wide

'Sussex Beauty' • Pink flowers on stiff stalks in summer • 60–75 cm high, 45–60 cm wide

Sidalcea candida
White flowers in summer • 60–90 cm high, 45–60 cm wide

Sidalcea oregana
Pink to deep-pink flowers in summer • 60–120 cm high, 45–60 cm wide

'Brilliant' • Rose-red flowers in summer • 60–75 cm high, 45–60 cm wide

Silene

p. 426 📷

Genus Information

Origin: Northern Hemisphere from the Arctic to tropical mountains and in South Africa and South America

Selected Common Names: campion; moss campion

Nomenclature: A classical plant name of unknown origin.

Notes: A genus of some 500 species that includes annuals, biennials and perennials.

General Features

Height: 2–120 cm high

Spread: 8–45 cm wide

Habit: cushion-, mat- or clump-forming perennial

Flowers: 5-notched or split petals; summer

Foliage: deciduous or evergreen; (some) variegated

Hardiness: A–D

Expert Advice: *S. acaulis* is slow-growing, but ruggedly hardy (circumpolar), forming a carefree, mossy mat of evergreen foilage.

Growing Requirements

Light: sun to p.m. sun

Soil: gritty, lean, well-drained soil

Location: alpine gardens; scree; troughs; wild gardens; woodland gardens; *S. acaulis* between paving stones

Propagation: seed; self-sows; division; cuttings

Buying Considerations

Professionals

Popularity: gaining popularity; fast seller in bloom

Availability: generally available as finished product and bare root from specialty growers

Size to Sell: sells best in smaller sizes (when blooming) as some mature fast

On the Shelf: keep stock rotated; (some) rapidly overgrows pot

Shrinkage: low; requires little maintenance

Collectors

Popularity: of interest to collectors—rare, exceptional beauty

Gardeners

Ease of Growth: very easy to grow

Start with: one small plant for feature plant and several for mass plantings

What to Try First ...

Silene acaulis, *Silene acaulis* 'Alba', *Silene acaulis* 'Frances', *Silene acaulis* Grand Ridge form, *Silene acaulis* 'Tatoosh', *Silene dinarica*, *Silene hookeri*, *Silene keiskei*, *Silene schafta*, *Silene uniflora* 'Robin Whitebreast'

On the Market

Silene

'Longwood' • Single, bright-pink flowers in spring to early summer • 15–30 cm high, 30–40 cm wide

Silene acaulis

Pink flowers in late spring to summer • Mossy, evergreen foliage • 2–5 cm high, 20–40 cm wide

'Alba' • White flowers in late spring to summer • Mossy, evergreen foliage • 2–5 cm high, 20–40 cm wide

'Frances' • Pale-pink flowers in late spring to summer • Mossy, evergreen foliage • 2–5 cm high, 20–40 cm wide

Grand Ridge form • Bright-pink flowers in late spring to summer • Mossy, evergreen foliage • 2–5 cm high, 20–40 cm wide

'Heidi' • Bright-pink flowers in late spring to summer • Tight, lacy, evergreen foliage • 2–5 cm high, 20–40 cm wide

'Pink Pearl' • Large, shell-pink flowers in late spring to summer • Mossy, evergreen foliage • 2–5 cm high, 20–40 cm wide

'Plena' • Double, pink flowers in late spring to summer • Mossy, evergreen foliage • 2–5 cm high, 20–40 cm wide

'Tatoosh' • Large, pink flowers in late spring to summer • Mossy, evergreen foliage • 2–5 cm high, 20–40 cm wide

ex. Walawala Mts. • Scarlet flowers in late spring to summer • Mossy, evergreen foliage • 2–5 cm high, 20–40 cm wide

'White Rabbit' • White flowers in late spring to summer • Mossy, evergreen foliage • 2–5 cm high, 20–40 cm wide

Silene acaulis ssp. acaulis

Pale-pink flowers in late spring to summer • Mossy, evergreen foliage • 2–5 cm high, 20–40 cm wide

Silene acaulis minima

Rose-red flowers in late spring to summer • Mossy, evergreen foliage • 2–5 cm high, 20–40 cm wide

Silene argaea

Pink flowers in late spring to early summer • 5–8 cm high, 8–12 cm wide

Silene caroliniana

'Hot Pink' • Bright-pink flowers in late spring to midsummer • 10–20 cm high, 10–15 cm wide

S

Silene caryophylloides ssp. echinus
Large, rose-pink flowers in late summer •
Gritty, fertile, sharply drained, neutral to
alkaline soil • 8–12 cm high, 15–25 cm wide

Silene dinarica
Rich-pink flowers in summer • 5–10 cm
high, 10–15 cm wide

Silene dioica
'Jade Valley' • Rose-pink flowers in late
spring to midsummer • Cream-variegated
foliage • 30–45 cm high, 30–45 cm wide

Silene elisabethae
Red to purple flowers in summer • Semi-
evergreen foliage • Gritty, fertile, sharply
drained, alkaline soil • 10–20 cm high,
10–15 cm wide

Silene fortunei
Pink flowers in summer • 10–15 cm high,
15–20 cm wide

Silene hookeri
Pink, rarely purple or white flowers in
summer • Gritty, fertile, sharply drained,
neutral to acidic soil • 5–15 cm high,
10–20 cm wide

Silene hookeri (syn. S. ingramii)
Red flowers in summer • Gritty, fertile,
sharply drained, neutral to acidic soil
• 5–15 cm high, 10–20 cm wide

Silene keiskei
Rose-pink flowers in late summer •
Evergreen foliage • 10–20 cm high,
15–25 cm wide

Silene keiskei var. minor
Rose-pink flowers in late summer •
Evergreen foliage • 5–10 cm high,
10–20 cm wide

Silene petersonii
Rosy-purple to pink, dark-veined flowers in
summer • 10–15 cm high, 15–20 cm wide

Silene regia
Showy, bright-red flower spikes in summer
• 45–120 cm high, 30–45 cm wide

Silene saxifraga
Nocturnal, white, rarely greenish, flowers in
summer • Gritty, sharply drained, neutral to
alkaline soil • 10–20 cm high, 10–20 cm
wide

Silene schafta
Bright-pink to purplish flowers in
midsummer to fall • 15–25 cm high,
20–30 cm wide

**Silene uniflora (syn. S. vulgaris ssp.
maritima)**
Bladder pod, white flowers in summer •
15–25 cm high, 30–45 cm wide

'Druett's Variegated' • Bladder pod, white
flowers in summer • Creamy-edged foliage
• 15–25 cm high, 30–45 cm wide
'Robin Whitebreast' (Weisskehlchen) •
Carnation-like, white flowers with
green blush in summer • 10–20 cm
high, 30–45 cm wide
'Rosea' • Bladder pod, rose-pink flowers in
summer • 10–20 cm high, 30–45 cm wide

Sisyrinchium   p. 426

Genus Information
Origin: North America and South America
Selected Common Names: blue-eyed grass
Nomenclature: Named by Theophrastus for a
plant related to the iris. Member of the iris
family.
Notes: A genus of some 90 species.

General Features
Height: 10–50 cm high
Spread: 10–40 cm wide
Habit: clump-forming perennial
Flowers: blue, trumpet-shaped or iris-like, each
lasting one day; summer; allow to self-seed;
flowers close on cool, cloudy days
Foliage: linear, basal, grass-like; deciduous or
evergreen; fan-like
Hardiness: C–D
Warnings: prone to aphids; not prone to disease
Expert Advice: *S. montanum* is native to the
Prairies, where it is seen growing in ditches
and woodland edges.

Growing Requirements
Light: sun
Soil: well-drained, moist soil
Location: mixed borders; alpine gardens; rock
gardens
Propagation: seed (self-sows readily); division

Buying Considerations
Professionals
Popularity: gaining popularity; fast seller in
bloom
Availability: generally available as finished
product from specialty growers
Size to Sell: sells best in smaller sizes (when
blooming) as it matures fast
Shrinkage: low; requires little maintenance
Collectors
Popularity: not generally of interest to
collectors
Gardeners
Ease of Growth: very easy to grow
Start with: one small plant for feature plant

S

On the Market

Sisyrinchium

'E.K. Balls' • Star-shaped, mauve flowers in summer • Grass-like foliage • 15–25 cm high, 10–15 cm wide

'Quaint and Queer' • Apricot flowers with purple centres in summer • Grass-like foliage • 15–30 cm high, 20–30 cm wide

Sisyrinchium idahoense

Dark-blue, yellow-eyed flowers in summer • Grass-like foliage • 10–20 cm high, 10–15 cm wide

Sisyrinchium montanum

Violet-blue flowers in summer • Grass-like foliage • Native to the Prairies • 15–50 cm high, 15–25 cm wide

Smilacina   p. 426 📷

Genus Information

Origin: Asia, North America and Central America
Selected Common Names: false Solomon's seal, Solomon's feathers, Solomon's plumes
Nomenclature: Name is a diminutive of *Smilax*.
Notes: Member of the lily family.

General Features

Height: 25–90 cm high
Spread: 45–60 cm wide
Habit: creeping, rhizomatous, clump-forming perennial
Flowers: tiny, star-shaped panicles of blooms; fragrant; spring
Foliage: oval, stalkless; unbranched, arching stems; young shoots can be eaten
Hardiness: C
Warnings: prone to slugs; not prone to disease

Growing Requirements

Light: shade; tolerates more sun with good soil moisture
Soil: moist, organic, well-drained, neutral to acidic soil
Location: mixed borders; woodland gardens
Propagation: seed; division
Expert Advice: Use only fresh seed. Old seed may take a year to germinate and viability drops quickly.

Buying Considerations

Professionals

Popularity: relatively unknown foliage plant
Availability: generally available as bare root from specialty growers
Size to Sell: sells best in smaller sizes (when blooming) as it matures fast
On the Shelf: rapidly overgrows pot
Shrinkage: low; goes dormant in pot; requires little maintenance

Collectors

Popularity: not generally of interest to collectors

Gardeners

Ease of Growth: mostly easy to grow but needs close attention to growing conditions
Start with: one small *S. racemosa* for feature plant and several of other species for mass plantings

On the Market

Smilacina oleracea

Rose-purple, rarely white, flowers in late spring • 60–90 cm high, 45–60 cm wide

Smilacina purpurea

Purple, rarely white, flowers in late spring • 25–50 cm high, 45–60 cm wide

Smilacina racemosa

Fragrant, cream flowers in late spring • 60–90 cm high, 45–60 cm wide

Soldanella   p. 426 📷

Genus Information

Origin: mountains of Europe
Selected Common Names: alpenclock, greater alpenclock, little alpenclock, snowbell
Nomenclature: From the Italian *soldo* (a coin), referring to the leaf shape.
Notes: A genus of some 10 species.

General Features

Height: 2–30 cm high
Spread: 5–30 cm wide
Habit: colony-forming, stoloniferous or rhizomatous, rosette-forming perennial
Flowers: nodding, fringed; early spring; prone to cold damage
Foliage: round, leathery; evergreen; prone to desiccation

S

Hardiness: C

Warnings: prone to aphids and slugs; not prone to disease

Expert Advice: At higher elevations the flowers appear through the snow as soon as the sun is warm enough for the plants to grow.

Growing Requirements

Light: shade to a.m. sun; shelter from hot p.m. sun

Soil: fertile, moist, well-drained soil

Location: cool rock gardens; northside of rock; provide winter protection

Propagation: seed; division

Expert Advice: Mulch for winter to protect flower buds.

Buying Considerations

Professionals

Popularity: relatively unknown; fast seller in bloom

Availability: occasionally available from specialty growers

Size to Sell: sells best in mature sizes (when blooming) as it matures slowly

Shrinkage: low; requires little maintenance

Collectors

Popularity: of interest to collectors—unique, exceptional beauty, rare, challenge

Gardeners

Ease of Growth: mostly easy to grow, needs close attention to growing conditions

Start with: one mature plant for feature and several for instant visual effect

What to Try First ...

Soldanella (S. carpatica x *S. montana)*, *Soldanella alpina*, *Soldanella carpatica*, *Soldanella hungarica*, *Soldanella* x *lungoviensis*, *Soldanella montana*, *Soldanella pusilla*

On the Market

Soldanella (S. carpatica x *S. montana)*
Fringed, pale-blue flowers in early spring • Evergreen foliage • 15–20 cm high, 15 cm wide

Soldanella alpina
Fringed, blue-violet flowers in early spring • Evergreen foliage • 10–15 cm high, 15–20 cm wide

Soldanella austriaca
Fringed, blue-violet flowers in early spring • Evergreen foliage • Fertile, moist, sharply drained, neutral to alkaline soil • 5–10 cm high, 10–15 cm wide

Soldanella carpatica
Blue-violet flowers in early spring • Evergreen foliage • 10–15 cm high, 15–20 cm wide

'Alba' • Fringed, white flowers in early spring • Evergreen foliage • 10–15 cm high, 15–20 cm wide

Soldanella hungarica
Fringed, lilac to violet flowers in early spring • Evergreen foliage • 5–10 cm high, 10–15 cm wide

Soldanella hungarica **var. major**
Large, lilac to violet flowers in early spring • Evergreen foliage • 15–25 cm high, 15–30 cm wide

Soldanella x *lungoviensis*
Fringed, amethyst-blue flowers in early spring • Evergreen foliage • 10–15 cm high, 15–25 cm wide

Soldanella minima
White to lilac flowers in early spring • Evergreen foliage • Moist, organic, sharply drained, neutral to alkaline soil • 2–5 cm high, 5–10 cm wide

Soldanella montana
Large, fringed, lilac to blue flowers in early spring • Evergreen foliage • 15–25 cm high, 15–25 cm wide

Soldanella pusilla
Blue to soft-violet flowers in early spring • Evergreen foliage • 5–10 cm high, 10–15 cm wide

Soldanella villosa
Fringed, violet flowers in early spring • Evergreen foliage • Moist, fertile, sharply drained, neutral to alkaline soil • 10–30 cm high, 10–20 cm wide

Solidago p. 426

Genus Information

Origin: North America, South America and Eurasia

Selected Common Names: goldenrod

Nomenclature: From the Latin *solidus* (whole), referring to its traditional healing properties.

Other Uses: The flowers supposedly mark the spot where treasure is buried. Planting it by the front door ensures good fortune to a household. It can be used to locate water deep underground.

Notes: A genus of some 100 species. Reputed to cause sneezing or hay fever, but it does not because the pollen is too heavy.

General Features

Height: 5–75 cm high
Spread: 10–60 cm wide
Habit: rhizomatous, clump-forming, woody-based perennial; (some) upright
Flowers: bright-yellow; good for cutflowers; late summer to fall; attractive to butterflies
Foliage: mid-green; lance-shaped
Hardiness: A–C
Warnings: prone to powdery mildew and aphids; may be invasive (contain and deadhead to prevent spread)
Expert Advice: Named hybrids are more garden worthy, being less invasive, more colourful and having larger flowerheads. Plant with *Echinacea, Perovskia* and ornamental grasses.

Growing Requirements

Light: sun
Soil: poor, sandy, well-drained soil; drought tolerant
Location: meadows; mixed borders; rock gardens; wild gardens
Propagation: seed (self-sows readily); division
Expert Advice: May not come true from seed.

Buying Considerations

Professionals

Popularity: popular; fast seller
Availability: readily available as finished product and bare root
Size to Sell: sells best in smaller sizes (when blooming) as it matures fast
On the Shelf: low ornamental appeal; overgrows pot
Shrinkage: low; requires little maintenance

Collectors

Popularity: not generally of interest to collectors

Gardeners

Ease of Growth: very easy to grow
Start with: one small plant for feature plant

What to Try First ...

Solidago 'Crown of Rays', *Solidago* 'Goldenmosa', *Solidago* 'Goldkind'

On the Market

Solidago

'Crown of Rays' (Strahlenkrone) • Large, flat-headed, bright-yellow flowers in late summer to fall • 45–60 cm high, 30–45 cm wide

'Gold Spangles' • Yellow plumes in late summer to fall • Gold-spangled foliage • 45–60 cm high, 45–60 cm wide

'Golden Dwarf' (Goldzwerg) • Gold-yellow flowers in late summer to fall • 20–30 cm high, 30–45 cm wide

'Goldenmosa' • Rich-yellow plumes in midsummer to fall • 60–75 cm high, 30–45 cm wide

'Goldkind' • Gold-yellow flowers in late summer to fall • 45–60 cm high, 30–45 cm wide

'Leraft' • Arching, gold-yellow flowers in late summer to fall • 60–75 cm high, 30–50 cm wide

Solidago multiradiata var. *arctica*
Yellow flowers in summer • Short, reddish stems • 5–10 cm high, 10–20 cm wide

Solidago sphacelata
'Golden Fleece' • Gold-yellow flowers in late summer to fall • 30–45 cm high, 45–60 cm wide

Solidago virgaurea ssp. *alpestris* var. *minutissima*
Deep-yellow flowers in late summer to fall • 5–10 cm high, 10–20 cm wide

Solidaster   p. 426 📷

Genus Information

Origin: cross of *Solidago* and *Aster*
Selected Common Names: golden aster
Nomenclature: From *Solidago* and *Aster*.
Notes: A natural hybrid of *Aster ptarmicoides* and an unidentified *Solidago* (probably *S. canadensis*) that was found in a nursery in France in 1910.

General Features

Height: 15–90 cm high
Spread: 15–30 cm wide
Habit: clump-forming perennial
Flowers: tiny, soft yellow, aster-like; late summer to fall; floriferous; good for cutflowers; long blooming period
Foliage: lance-shaped
Hardiness: C
Warnings: prone to powdery mildew and aphids
Expert Advice: Less coarse than *Solidago*. Plant with *Echinacea, Perovskia* and ornamental grasses.

Growing Requirements

Light: sun
Soil: fertile, well-drained soil; tolerates dry soil
Location: mixed borders
Propagation: division; basal cuttings

S

Buying Considerations

Professionals
Popularity: relatively unknown; fast seller in bloom
Availability: occasionally available as bare root
Size to Sell: sells best in smaller sizes (when blooming) as it matures fast
On the Shelf: keep stock rotated; rapidly overgrows pot
Shrinkage: low; requires little maintenance

Collectors
Popularity: not generally of interest to collectors

Gardeners
Ease of Growth: very easy to grow
Start with: one small plant for feature plant

What to Try First ...
Solidaster luteus

On the Market

Solidaster
  'Tweety' • Yellow flowers in late summer to fall • 15–30 cm high, 15–30 cm wide

Solidaster luteus
  Yellow flowers in late summer to fall • 60–90 cm high, 20–30 cm wide

Sorghastrum
p. 426

Genus Information
Origin: Africa and the Americas
Selected Common Names: Indian grass
Nomenclature: From *Sorghum* and the Latin suffix *astrum* (a poor imitation), referring to its close resemblance to *Sorghum*.
Notes: A genus of some 15 species.

General Features
Height: 1.2–2 m high
Spread: 60–75 cm wide
Habit: warm-season, tuft- or clump-forming grass
Flowers: seed heads held above foliage; late summer to fall; good for drying; good for dyeing
Foliage: green; gold fall colour
Hardiness: B–D
Warnings: prone to aphids; not prone to disease

Growing Requirements
Light: sun
Soil: rich, evenly moist soil; tolerates dry soil; avoid winter wet
Location: meadows; wild gardens
Propagation: seed (self-sows readily); division

Buying Considerations

Professionals
Popularity: relatively unknown foliage plant
Availability: generally available as finished product
Size to Sell: sells best in smaller sizes as it matures fast
On the Shelf: high ornamental appeal; rapidly overgrows pot
Shrinkage: low; requires little maintenance

Collectors
Popularity: not generally of interest to collectors

Gardeners
Ease of Growth: very easy to grow
Start with: one small plant for feature plant

What to Try First ...
Sorghastrum nutans

On the Market

Sorghastrum nutans
  Copper spikelets, turning gold, in late summer to fall • 1.2–2 m high, 60–75 cm wide

Spartina
p. 426

Genus Information
Origin: Europe, Asia and the Americas in temperate and sub-tropical regions
Selected Common Names: prairie cord grass
Nomenclature: From the Latin *spartum*, a grass used for cordage.
Other Uses: Once cut in large quantities for hay, bedding and sometimes mulch.
Notes: A genus of some 15 species. Much of the organic matter in the western United States' soils is comprised of this grass in its decomposed state.

General Features
Height: 1–1.5 m high
Spread: 60–90 cm wide
Habit: loose, spreading and clump-forming, warm-season, rhizomatous grass; deeply rooted
Flowers: ornamental seed heads; good for drying
Foliage: graceful, strong, upright, arching; good fall colour
Hardiness: C
Warnings: may be invasive (contain and deadhead to prevent spread)
Expert Advice: Be careful when choosing where to introduce this tenacious grass. Its large rhizomes become deeply rooted and are excellent for stabilizing banks and slopes.

Growing Requirements

Light: sun
Soil: moist to wet soil; salt tolerant
Location: bog gardens; mixed borders; wild gardens
Propagation: seed (self-sows readily); separate and replant rooted sections of rhizomes

Buying Considerations

Professionals
Popularity: gaining popularity as a foliage plant
Availability: generally available as finished product and bare root
Size to Sell: sells best in smaller sizes as it matures fast
On the Shelf: high ornamental appeal; rapidly overgrows pot
Shrinkage: low; requires little maintenance

Collectors
Popularity: not generally of interest to collectors

Gardeners
Ease of Growth: very easy to grow
Start with: one small plant for feature plant

What to Try First ...
Spartina pectinata 'Aureomarginata'

On the Market

Spartina pectinata
'Aureomarginata' (Variegata) • Soft-green spikelets in late summer to fall • Yellow-edged foliage • 1–1.5 m high, 60–90+ cm wide

Spiranthes
p. 426

Genus Information

Origin: North America, the Pacific and Europe
Selected Common Names: lady's tresses
Nomenclature: From the Greek *speira* (spiral) and *anthos*, referring to the flower spike.
Notes: A genus of some 50 species.

General Features

Height: 30–60 cm high
Spread: 8–12 cm wide
Habit: clump-forming, terrestrial orchid
Flowers: white, vanilla-scented spikes; goes dormant after flowering
Hardiness: C
Warnings: prone to slugs; not prone to disease
Expert Advice: Genus is protected under CITES which means it is illegal to dig up from the wild. We sell only CITES certified stock.

Growing Requirements

Light: a.m. sun
Soil: organic, humus-rich, moist soil; avoid winter wet
Location: sheltered locations; woodland gardens
Propagation: seed; division
Expert Advice: Seed propagation is very difficult, taking years to establish a good-sized plant.

Buying Considerations

Professionals
Popularity: relatively unknown
Availability: occasionally available from specialty growers; purchase only CITES certified stock
Size to Sell: sells best in mature sizes (when blooming) as it matures slowly
Shrinkage: high; goes dormant in pot

Collectors
Popularity: of interest to collectors—unique, exceptional beauty, rare, challenge

Gardeners
Ease of Growth: mostly difficult to grow as it needs close attention to growing conditions
Start with: one mature plant for feature plant

What to Try First ...
Spiranthes cernua f. *odorata*

On the Market

Spiranthes cernua f. *odorata*
Fragrant, vanilla-scented, white flowers in late summer to fall • 30–60 cm high, 8–12 cm wide

Spodiopogon

Genus Information

Origin: temperate regions and subtropical Asia
Selected Common Names: frost grass
Nomenclature: From the Greek *spodios* (ashen) and *pogon* (beard), referring to the grey hairs that surround the flower spikes, giving them a greyish appearance.
Notes: A genus of some 9 species. Related to *Andropogon*.

General Features

Height: 1–1.5 m high
Spread: 45–60 cm wide
Habit: upright, clump-forming grass
Flowers: purple-tinted spiklets; late summer
Foliage: sturdy, erect; bamboo-like
Hardiness: B–C
Warnings: prone to aphids and rust
Expert Advice: An attractive, non-invasive specimen grass. Adds winter interest.

Growing Requirements

Light: sun to p.m. sun
Soil: moist, average soil; tolerant of a wide range of soils; drought tolerant
Location: mixed borders; specimen plant
Propagation: seed; division

Buying Considerations

Professionals

Popularity: relatively unknown foliage plant
Availability: occasionally available as finished product
Size to Sell: sells best in smaller sizes as it matures fast
On the Shelf: high ornamental appeal
Shrinkage: low; requires little maintenance

Collectors

Popularity: not generally of interest to collectors

Gardeners

Ease of Growth: mostly easy to grow
Start with: one small plant for feature plant

What to Try First ...

Spodiopogon sibiricus

On the Market

Spodiopogon sibiricus
Purple-tinted spikelets in summer • Bamboo-like foliage • 1–1.5 m high, 45–60 cm wide

Sporobolus   p. 426 📷

Genus Information

Origin: western North America
Selected Common Names: prairie dropseed
Nomenclature: From the Greek *sporos* (seed) and *bolos* (throwing), referring to the ease of which the ripe seed is released.
Notes: A genus of some 100 species of annuals and perennials.

General Features

Height: 75–100 cm high
Spread: 45–60 cm wide
Habit: slow-growing, long-lived, mound-forming, warm-season perennial grass
Flowers: scented, airy panicles; late summer to fall
Foliage: fine-textured; good fall colour
Hardiness: B–C
Warnings: not prone to insects or disease
Expert Advice: A very hardy, attractive, underused specimen grass. Adds winter interest and grows well in difficult areas.

Growing Requirements

Light: sun
Soil: well-drained soil; drought tolerant
Location: difficult locations; specimen plant
Propagation: seed; division
Expert Advice: Clumps are very dense and division may be difficult.

Buying Considerations

Professionals

Popularity: gaining popularity as a foliage plant
Availability: generally available as finished product
Size to Sell: sells best in smaller sizes as it matures fast
On the Shelf: high ornamental appeal; rapidly overgrows pot
Shrinkage: low; requires little maintenance

Collectors

Popularity: not generally of interest to collectors

Gardeners

Ease of Growth: very easy to grow
Start with: one small plant for feature plant

What to Try First ...

Sporobolus heterolepis

On the Market

Sporobolus heterolepis
Fragrant, pale-pink spikelets in late summer to fall • Foliage turns copper-orange in fall • 75–100 cm high, 45–60 cm wide

Stachys   p. 426 📷

Genus Information

Origin: northern temperate regions, subtropical regions, Australasia and tropical and subtropical mountains
Selected Common Names: betony, common betony, lamb's ears
Nomenclature: From the Greek word for "spike," referring to the flower spikes. The soft, furry leaves give rise to the common name "lamb's ears."
Other Uses: In ancient times, *Stachys* was thought to possess the ability to ward off evil spirits. It was reputed to cure over 40 ailments and was commonly grown in medicinal herb gardens.
Notes: A genus of some 200–300 species, including annuals, perennials and shrubs.

S

General Features

Height: 15–60 cm high
Spread: 20–45 cm wide
Habit: rhizomatous or stoloniferous groundcover perennial
Flowers: small, spikes; summer; attractive to bees and butterflies
Foliage: short-stalked or stalkless; soft, furry; evergreen; grown mainly for foliage
Hardiness: C–D
Warnings: not prone to insects or disease

Growing Requirements

Light: sun
Soil: fertile, well-drained soil; avoid winter wet; (*S. lavandulifolia*) drought tolerant
Location: sunny, hot, dry areas; herb gardens; mixed borders; rock gardens; wild gardens
Propagation: seed; division; cuttings

Buying Considerations

Professionals

Popularity: popular foliage plant
Availability: readily available as finished product and bare root
Size to Sell: sells best in smaller sizes (when blooming) as it matures fast
On the Shelf: high ornamental appeal; keep stock rotated; rapidly overgrows pot
Shrinkage: low; requires little maintenance

Collectors

Popularity: not generally of interest to collectors

Gardeners

Ease of Growth: very easy to grow
Start with: one small plant for feature plant and several for mass plantings

What to Try First ...

Stachys byzantina 'Cotton Boll', *Stachys byzantina* 'Primrose Heron', *Stachys byzantina* 'Silver Carpet', *Stachys lavandulifolia*, *Stachys macrantha* 'Rosea', *Stachys macrantha* 'Superba'

On the Market

Stachys byzantina
Purple flowers in summer to fall • Silver-grey, woolly foliage • 45–60 cm high, 45–60+ cm wide

'**Big Ears**' (**Countess Helen von Stein**) • Purple flowers in summer • Silver-grey, woolly foliage • 45–60 cm high, 45–60+ cm wide

'**Cotton Boll**' (**Sheila McQueen**) • Small, cottony flowers in summer • Silver-grey, woolly foliage • 45–60 cm high, 45–60+ cm wide

'**Primrose Heron**' • Purple flowers in summer • Yellow-green foliage in spring, turning grey-green in summer • 45–60 cm high, 45–60+ cm wide

'**Silver Carpet**' • Non-blooming variety • Soft, silver-green foliage • 15–30 cm high, 45–60+ cm wide

Stachys lavandulifolia
Mauve flowers in summer • Silver-grey, woolly foliage • 15–30 cm high, 20–30 cm wide

Stachys lavandulifolia ssp. *lavandulifolia*
Mauve flowers in summer • Silver-grey, woolly foliage • 15–30 cm high, 20–30 cm wide

Stachys macrantha (*S. grandiflora*)
'**Robusta**' • Rose-pink flowers in summer • Grey-green, woolly foliage • 30–60 cm high, 30–45 cm wide

'**Rosea**' • Rose-pink flowers in summer • Grey-green, woolly foliage • 30–60 cm high, 30–45 cm wide

'**Superba**' • Purple-violet flowers in summer • 30–60 cm high, 30–45 cm wide

Stachys monieri
'**Hummelo**' • Pink to purple flowers in early summer to late summer • Silver-grey, woolly foliage • 25–50 cm high, 20–40 cm wide

Stachys officinalis
Pink flowers on sturdy, stiff stems in early summer to late summer • 40–55 cm high, 30–45 cm wide

Stokesia

Genus Information

Origin: southeastern United States
Selected Common Names: Stoke's aster
Nomenclature: Named for Jonathon Stokes, 1755–1831, an English botanist.

General Features

Height: 30–60 cm high
Spread: 30–45 cm wide
Habit: clump-forming perennial
Flowers: blue, white or pink; cornflower- or aster-like; summer to fall; good for cutflowers; deadhead to extend blooming season
Foliage: evergreen in warmer zones; slow to appear in spring
Hardiness: D
Warnings: not prone to insects or disease
Expert Advice: Often late to flower and short-lived on the Prairies.

S

Growing Requirements

Light: sun
Soil: fertile, moist, well-drained, neutral to acidic soil; avoid winter wet
Propagation: seed (self-sows); division; cuttings
Expert Advice: Seed in fall. Divide in spring. Take root cuttings.

Buying Considerations

Professionals
Popularity: relatively unknown
Availability: occasionally available as finished product and bare root
Size to Sell: sells best in smaller sizes (when blooming) as it matures fast
On the Shelf: keep stock rotated; rapidly overgrows pot
Shrinkage: low; requires little maintenance

Collectors
Popularity: not generally of interest to collectors

Gardeners
Ease of Growth: mostly easy to grow but needs close attention to growing conditions
Start with: one small plant for feature plant

What to Try First ...
Stokesia laevis 'Blue Danube', *Stokesia laevis* 'Purple Parasols'

On the Market

Stokesia laevis
'Blue Danube' • Aster-like, lavender-blue flowers in summer to fall • Evergreen • 30–60 cm high, 30–45 cm wide
'Purple Parasols' • Aster-like, blue to magenta flowers in summer to fall • Evergreen • 30–60 cm high, 30–45 cm wide

Stylophorum p. 426 📷

Genus Information

Origin: North America and East Asia
Selected Common Names: celandine poppy
Nomenclature: From the Greek *stylos* (style) and *phero* (I bear), referring to the columnar style.
Notes: A genus of some 3 species, and a member of the poppy family.

General Features
Height: 30–45 cm high
Spread: 30–45 cm wide
Habit: clump-forming perennial
Flowers: yellow to orange, poppy-like; spring; short blooming period; goes dormant after flowering; may rebloom in fall

Foliage: deeply lobed
Hardiness: C
Warnings: prone to powdery mildew and slugs
Expert Advice: Very hardy on the Prairies.

Growing Requirements
Light: shade; foliage may burn in direct sunlight
Soil: fertile, moist, organic soil
Location: mixed borders; rock gardens; woodland gardens
Propagation: seed (self-sows readily); division

Buying Considerations

Professionals
Popularity: relatively unknown
Availability: occasionally available as bare root
Size to Sell: sells best in smaller sizes (when blooming) as it matures fast
On the Shelf: keep stock rotated; rapidly overgrows pot
Shrinkage: low; requires little maintenance

Collectors
Popularity: not generally of interest to collectors

Gardeners
Ease of Growth: very easy to grow
Start with: one small plant for feature plant

What to Try First ...
Stylophorum diphyllum

On the Market

Stylophorum diphyllum
Poppy-like, bright-gold-yellow flowers in late spring to early summer • 30–45 cm high, 30–45 cm wide

Symphyandra p. 426 📷

Genus Information

Origin: Alps of Eastern Europe and in central Asia
Selected Common Names: ring bellflower
Nomenclature: From the Greek *symphyo* (to grow together) and *amer* (anther), referring to the anthers being connate.
Notes: A genus of some 12 species, and a member of the *Campanulaceae* family.

General Features
Height: 20–60 cm high
Spread: 15–40 cm wide
Habit: short-lived or monocarpic perennial
Flowers: *Campanula*-like, white or blue, bell-shaped; summer; long blooming period
Hardiness: C–D
Warnings: prone to powdery mildew and aphids
Expert Advice: As it is monocarpic, allow to self seed.

S

Growing Requirements

Light: sun
Soil: fertile, well-drained soil
Location: mixed borders; rock gardens; specimen plant
Propagation: seed (self-sows readily); division

Buying Considerations

Professionals
Popularity: relatively unknown
Availability: occasionally available from specialty growers
Size to Sell: sells best in smaller sizes (when blooming) as it matures fast
On the Shelf: rapidly overgrows pot
Shrinkage: low; requires little maintenance

Collectors
Popularity: of interest to collectors—unique, rare

Gardeners
Ease of Growth: mostly easy to grow but needs close attention to growing conditions
Start with: one small plant for feature plant

What to Try First ...

Symphyandra hofmannii, Symphyandra wanneri, Symphyandra zangezura

On the Market

Symphyandra armena
White or blue-flushed flowers in summer • 30–50 cm high, 20–30 cm wide

Symphyandra hofmannii
Large, cream-white flowers in summer • 30–60 cm high, 20–40 cm wide

Symphyandra pendula
Bell-shaped, cream-white flowers in summer • 40–60 cm high, 20–30 cm wide

Symphyandra wanneri
Bell-shaped, violet flowers in summer • 20–40 cm high, 15–30 cm wide

Symphyandra zangezura
Violet-blue flowers in summer • 20–30 cm high, 20–30 cm wide

Symphytum   p. 426

Genus Information

Origin: Europe, North Africa and West Asia
Selected Common Names: comfrey
Nomenclature: From the Greek *syn* (together) and *phyton* (plant), referring to the supposed healing powers of the plant.

Other Uses: *S. officinale* was used for teas, creams and other herbal remedies.
Notes: A genus of some 25 or more species.

General Features

Height: 30–120 cm high
Spread: 30–150 cm wide
Habit: long-lived perennial herb
Flowers: spring to summer; best to remove flowers from variegated varieties to maintain good leaf colour
Foliage: large; coarse, hairy
Hardiness: C
Warnings: prone to powdery mildew and aphids; contact with foliage may irritate skin; may be invasive (contain and deadhead to prevent spread)
Expert Advice: A nice, medium-sized perennial for the garden but take care not to allow it to run rampant.

Growing Requirements

Light: sun to p.m. sun
Soil: fertile, moist soil
Location: mixed borders; woodland gardens
Propagation: seed; division; root cuttings

Buying Considerations

Professionals
Popularity: relatively unknown
Availability: occasionally available as bare root
Size to Sell: sells best in smaller sizes (when blooming) as it matures fast
On the Shelf: *Symphytum* 'Goldsmith' has high ornamental appeal; keep stock rotated; rapidly overgrows pot
Shrinkage: low; requires little maintenance

Collectors
Popularity: not generally of interest to collectors

Gardeners
Ease of Growth: very easy to grow
Start with: one small plant for feature plant

What to Try First ...

Symphytum 'Goldsmith', *Symphytum caucasicum, Symphytum officinale*

On the Market

Symphytum
'Goldsmith' (Jubilee) • Cream, pink and blue flowers in spring • Cream-edged foliage • 30–45 cm high, 30–45 cm wide

'Hidcote Blue' • Red buds opening to blue flowers in spring to early summer • 30–45 cm high, 45–60 cm wide

Symphytum caucasicum
Blue flowers in summer • 60–75 cm high, 45–60 cm wide

S

Symphytum ibericum
Red-tipped buds open to cream-yellow flowers in late spring to early summer • 30–45 cm high, 45–60 cm wide

Symphytum officinale
Violet, rose, or cream flowers in late spring to early summer • 75–120 cm high, 90–150 cm wide

Symphytum x uplandicum
'Variegatum' • Pink flowers, aging to purple, in spring to summer • Variegated foliage • 75–90 cm high, 60–75 cm wide

Synthyris

Genus Information
Origin: western to central North America
Selected Common Names: lousewort
Nomenclature: From the Greek *syn* (with) and *thyris* (a window), referring to the valves of the capsule.
Notes: A genus of some 14 species.

General Features
Height: 5–30 cm high
Spread: 10–30 cm wide
Habit: clump-forming, rhizomatous perennial
Flowers: spike-like racemes, bell-shaped; spring to summer
Foliage: evergreen
Hardiness: A–D
Warnings: prone to aphids; not prone to disease
Expert Advice: Lower-elevation species (*S. missurica* var. *stellata*) are easier to grow.

Growing Requirements
Light: sun or shade
Soil: cool, humus-rich, lean, neutral to alkaline soil; alpine types avoid fall and winter wet;
Location: moist, shady mixed borders; woodland; alpine types in rock or scree gardens
Propagation: seed; division

Buying Considerations

Professionals
Popularity: relatively unknown
Availability: occasionally available from specialty growers
Size to Sell: sells best in smaller sizes (when blooming)
Shrinkage: low; requires little maintenance

Collectors
Popularity: of interest to collectors—unique, rare, novelty plant

Gardeners
Ease of Growth: mostly easy to grow but needs close attention to growing conditions
Start with: one small plant for feature plant

What to Try First ...
Synthyris laciniata, Synthyris missurica var. *stellata, Synthyris pinnatifida*

On the Market

Synthyris laciniata
Spiked, deep purple-blue flowers in spring • Alpine • 5–10 cm high, 10–15 cm wide

Synthyris missurica var. stellata
Violet-blue flowers in spring to early summer • 15–30 cm high, 15–30 cm wide

Synthyris pinnatifida
Densely spiked, deep blue-purple flowers in spring • Alpine • 15–30 cm high, 10–20 cm wide

Synthyris pinnatifida var. canescens
Blue-purple flowers in early spring • Alpine • 10–15 cm high, 10–15 cm wide

S

Talinum

p. 426

Genus Information

Origin: tropics and subtropics of Africa, North America and Central America

Selected Common Names: fameflower, spiny fameflower

Nomenclature: From the native African name meaning "unknown."

Notes: A genus of some 50 species of annuals and perennials. Most hardy types are from North America. Resembles *Lewisia* and is related to it and to *Calandrinia*.

General Features

Height: 2–25 cm high
Spread: 10–20 cm wide
Habit: clump-forming perennial
Flowers: short-lived, showy; summer; long blooming period
Foliage: semi-evergreen with succulent stems
Hardiness: C–D
Warnings: not prone to insects or disease

Growing Requirements

Light: sun
Soil: very lean, sharply drained soil; avoid winter wet; drought tolerant
Location: alpine gardens; rock gardens; troughs
Propagation: seed; division
Expert Advice: Rich soil produces soft, tender growth; grow very lean for best performance. Keep soil drier during dormancy.

Buying Considerations

Professionals

Popularity: relatively unknown
Availability: occasionally available from specialty growers
Size to Sell: sells best in smaller sizes (when blooming)
Shrinkage: low; sensitive to overwatering, requires little maintenance

Collectors

Popularity: of interest to collectors—unique, exceptional beauty, rare

Gardeners

Ease of Growth: mostly easy to grow but needs close attention to growing conditions
Start with: one small plant for feature plant

What to Try First ...

Talinum okanoganense, Talinum rugospermum, Talinum sedoides, Talinum spinescens

On the Market

Talinum calycinum
Rose-pink flowers in summer • Semi-evergreen, with succulent stems • 10–20 cm high, 10–20 cm wide

Talinum okanoganense
Satin-white flowers in summer • Succulent stems • 2–5 cm high, 10–20 cm wide

Talinum rugospermum
Rose-pink flowers in summer • Semi-evergreen, with succulent stems • 15–25 cm high, 10–20 cm wide

Talinum sedoides
Red flowers in summer • Semi-evergreen, with succulent stems • 10–15 cm high, 10–20 cm wide

Talinum spinescens
Rose to red-purple flowers in summer • Semi-evergreen, with succulent stems • 10–20 cm high, 10–15 cm wide

Tanacetum

p. 426

Genus Information

Origin: northern temperate regions
Selected Common Names: painted daisy, pyrethrum daisy
Nomenclature: From the medieval Latin *tanazita*, which is from the Greek *athanasia* (immortality).
Other Uses: *Tanacetum* has been used in folk medicine for relieving headaches, uterus problems and general aches and pains.
Notes: A genus of some 70 species of annuals or perennials. Closely related to *Chrysanthemum*.

General Features

Height: 10–75 cm high
Spread: 20–45 cm wide
Habit: upright, clump-forming perennial; may require staking
Flowers: colourful, daisy-like; late spring to late summer; good for cutflowers
Foliage: (some) aromatic or downy foliage
Hardiness: C–D
Warnings: prone to powdery mildew and aphids
Expert Advice: Most of the genus is short-lived. Deadhead *T. coccineum* to extend blooming season and cut back after flowering to encourage bushy growth.

Growing Requirements

Light: sun
Soil: well-drained soil; (some) tolerate poor, dry soil; downy-leaf types avoid winter wet
Location: herb gardens; mixed borders; rock gardens
Propagation: seed (self-sows readily); division; basal cuttings

T

Buying Considerations

Professionals

Popularity: popular garden standard; fast seller in bloom
Availability: readily available as finished product
Size to Sell: sells best in smaller sizes (when blooming) as it matures fast
On the Shelf: keep stock rotated; rapidly overgrows pot
Shrinkage: low; requires little maintenance

Collectors

Popularity: not generally of interest to collectors

Gardeners

Ease of Growth: very easy to grow
Start with: one small plant for feature plant

What to Try First ...

Tanacetum coccineum, Tanacetum coccineum 'James Kelway', *Tanacetum coccineum* (Robinson's mix), *Tanacetum haradjanii, Tanacetum parthenium* 'White Stars'

On the Market

Tanacetum coccineum
  Single or double, daisy-like, white, pink or red flowers with yellow centre in early summer • 45–75 cm high, 30–45 cm wide

  'James Kelway' • Daisy-like, deep crimson-pink flowers with yellow centre in early summer • 45–60 cm high, 30–45 cm wide

  'Red Dwarf' • Daisy-like, magenta-red flowers with yellow centre in early summer • 30–40 cm high, 20–30 cm wide

  'Robinson's Crimson' • Daisy-like, deep-scarlet flowers with yellow centre in early summer • 45–60 cm high, 45 cm wide

  'Robinson's Pink' • Single, daisy-like, bright-pink flowers with yellow centre in late spring to early summer • 45–60 cm high, 45 cm wide

  'Robinson's Red' • Single, daisy-like, bright-red flowers with yellow centre in late spring to early summer • 45–60 cm high, 45 cm wide

  'Robinson's Roseum' • Daisy-like, bright rose-pink flowers with yellow centre in early summer • 45–60 cm high, 30–45 cm wide

Tanacetum densum
  Daisy-like, bright-yellow flowers in early summer • Feathery, silver foliage • 20 cm high, 20 cm wide

Tanacetum haradjanii
  Daisy-like, bright-yellow flowers in late summer • Evergreen • 10–15 cm high, 20 cm wide

Tanacetum parthenium
  Daisy-like, yellow or white flowers in summer • Aromatic foliage • 45–60 cm high, 30 cm wide

  'White Stars' • Daisy-like, white flowers in summer • Aromatic foliage • 20–25 cm high, 20–25 cm wide

Tanacetum niveum
  Daisy-like, yellow-eyed, white flowers in late spring to late summer • Well-drained, fertile soil • 30–45 cm high, 30–60 cm wide

Tellima

Genus Information

Origin: western North America
Selected Common Names: fringe cups
Nomenclature: An anagram of *Mitella*, to which it is closely related.

General Features

Height: 70 cm high
Spread: 25 cm wide
Habit: rosette-forming groundcover perennial
Flowers: tiny blooms on long stems; spring to summer
Foliage: heart-shaped; grown mainly for the foliage
Hardiness: C
Warnings: prone to slugs; not prone to disease
Expert Advice: Plant with *Bergenia* for an interesting combination.

Growing Requirements

Light: shade to a.m. sun
Soil: moist, organic soil; drought tolerant
Location: mixed borders; rock gardens; woodland gardens
Propagation: seed; division

Buying Considerations

Professionals

Popularity: relatively unknown
Availability: occasionally available as bare root; from specialty growers
Size to Sell: sells best in smaller sizes as it matures fast
On the Shelf: high ornamental appeal; keep stock rotated; rapidly overgrows pot
Shrinkage: low; requires little maintenance

Collectors

Popularity: not generally of interest to collectors

Gardeners

Ease of Growth: mostly easy to grow but needs close attention to growing conditions
Start with: one small plant for feature plant and several for mass plantings

What to Try First ...

Tellima grandiflora 'Forest Frost'

On the Market

Tellima grandiflora
'**Forest Frost**' • Chartreuse flowers in spring • Heart-shaped foliage • 70 cm high, 25 cm wide

Tetraneuris p. 427

Genus Information

Origin: western United States
Selected Common Names: alpine sunflower
Nomenclature: From the Greek *tetra* (four) and *neura* (sinew).

General Features

Height: 5–40 cm high
Spread: 10–45 cm wide
Habit: tap-rooted perennial
Flowers: large, sunflower-like; late spring to early summer; may rebloom in fall
Foliage: aromatic
Hardiness: C–D
Warnings: not prone to insects or disease
Expert Advice: Produces big flowers relative to plant size.

Growing Requirements

Light: sun
Soil: lean, gritty, sharply drained, alkaline soil; avoid winter wet; drought tolerant
Location: rock gardens, scree
Propagation: seed (self-sows)
Expert Advice: Sow seed when ripe.

Buying Considerations

Professionals

Popularity: relatively unknown
Availability: occasionally available from specialty growers
Size to Sell: sells best in smaller sizes (when blooming) as it matures fast
Shrinkage: low; requires little maintenance

Collectors

Popularity: of interest to alpine collectors—unique

Gardeners

Ease of Growth: very easy to grow
Start with: one small plant for feature plant

What to Try First ...

Tetraneuris acaulis, Tetraneuris grandiflora

On the Market

Tetraneuris acaulis
(syn. *Hymenoxys acaulis*)
Daisy-like, yellow flowers in late spring to early summer • Aromatic foliage • 25–40 cm high, 30–45 cm wide

Tetraneuris acaulis var. *caespitosa*
Large, yellow flowers in early summer • Aromatic foliage • 5 cm high, 10 cm wide

Tetraneuris grandiflora
(syn. *Hymenoxys grandiflora*)
Large, daisy-like, yellow flowers in late spring to early summer • Aromatic foliage • 15 cm high, 30 cm wide

Teucrium p. 427

Genus Information

Origin: worldwide and the Mediterranean
Selected Common Names: germander, wall germander
Nomenclature: From the Greek *teukrion*, perhaps in reference to the Trojan king Teucer, who supposedly used it medicinally.
Notes: Used by Dioscorides and Theophrastus. A genus of some 100 species of perennials, subshrubs and shrubs.

General Features

Height: 10–50 cm high
Spread: 20–60 cm wide
Habit: shrubby perennial
Flowers: late spring to fall
Foliage: deciduous or evergreen; aromatic; shear in spring
Hardiness: C–D
Warnings: not prone to insects or disease

Growing Requirements

Light: sun
Soil: lean, gritty, well-drained, sandy soil
Location: dry, rocky locations; scree
Propagation: seed; softwood cuttings
Expert Advice: Grow alpine types in very lean soil to maintain compactness. If grown in rich soil they tend to die out quickly.

Buying Considerations

Professionals

Popularity: relatively unknown
Availability: occasionally available from specialty growers
Size to Sell: sells best in smaller sizes (when blooming) as it matures fast
On the Shelf: rapidly overgrows pot
Shrinkage: low; requires little maintenance

T

On the Market

Teucrium chamaedrys
Rose-pink flowers in summer • 30–50 cm
high, 25–30 cm wide

Teucrium subspinosum
Purple-red flowers in summer • Grey-green
foliage • 10 cm high, 20–30 cm wide

Thalictrum
p. 427

Genus Information

Origin: Asia, Europe and parts of North America
Selected Common Names: meadow rue
Nomenclature: Name used by Dioscorides
for a plant with coriander-like leaves that
was possibly a member of this genus.
Notes: A genus of some 130 species.

General Features

Height: 8–150 cm high
Spread: 10–80 cm wide
Habit: tuberous, rhizomatous or clump-forming
perennial
Flowers: tiny clusters; delicate; spring to fall; good
for cutflowers; short blooming period (except
T. kiusianum)
Foliage: columbine-like, lacy; slow to emerge in
spring
Hardiness: C
Warnings: not prone to insects or disease
Expert Advice: *Thalictrums* range from being tall
and showy to short and dainty. The taller types
make wonderful background plants in a mixed
border.

Growing Requirements

Light: sun to p.m. sun; *T. kiusianum* prefers shade
to a.m. sun
Soil: cool, fertile, moist, organic, well-drained soil
Location: mixed borders; rock gardens; troughs;
woodland gardens
Propagation: seed; division
Expert Advice: Divide every 2–3 years to
maintain vigour.

Buying Considerations

On the Market

Thalictrum alpinum
Tiny green flowers in summer • Fern-like
foliage • 8–15 cm high, 30 cm wide

Thalictrum aquilegiifolium
Clustered, pale-purple flowers in early
summer • Blue-green, columbine-like
foliage • 60–90+ cm high, 45 cm wide

'Thundercloud' • Tiny, deep-purple flowers
in late spring to early summer •
Columbine-like foliage • 60–90+ cm high,
45 cm wide

Thalictrum aquilegiifolium var. *album*
Tiny, white flowers in late spring •
Columbine-like, grey foliage • 45–75 cm
high, 45 cm wide

Thalictrum delavayi
Tiny, mauve flowers in summer to fall
• 90–120 cm high, 60 cm wide

'Hewitt's Double' • Tiny, double, lavender
flowers in midsummer to fall • 90–120 cm
high, 60 cm wide

Thalictrum flavum ssp. *glaucum*
Tiny, sulphur-yellow flowers in summer •
Lacy, blue-green foliage • 90–100 cm high,
45–60 cm wide

Thalictrum ichangense (syn. *T. coreanum)*
Lilac flowers in summer • Blue-green foliage
• 10–20 cm high, 30 cm wide

Thalictrum isopyroides
Tiny, green-cream flowers in midsummer •
Fine, blue-green foliage • 45 cm high,
45 cm wide

Thalictrum kiusianum
Tiny, pink flowers in summer • Fern-like
foliage • 10–15 cm high, 30–45 cm wide

Thalictrum lucidum
Fragrant, soft-yellow flowers in summer •
40–90 cm high, 80 cm wide

Thalictrum minus ssp. *adiantifolium*
Tiny, yellow-green flowers in summer •
Lacy, fern-like foliage • 40–100 cm high,
45–60 cm wide

Thalictrum minus ssp. *olympicum*
Tiny, pale-green flowers in summer •
15–30 cm high, 45–60 cm wide

Thalictrum rochebruneanum
'Lavender Mist' • Tiny, deep-lavender
flowers in summer • Purple flower
stems with fern-like foliage • 1–1.5 m
high, 30–45 cm wide

Thlaspi

p. 427

Genus Information

Origin: Northern Hemisphere and South America
Selected Common Names: pennycress
Nomenclature: From the Greek *thlao* (flatten) and
aspis (shield), referring to the shape of the fruit.
Notes: A genus of some 60 species of annuals and
perennials. Family includes some troublesome
weeds.

General Features

Height: 2–15 cm high
Spread: 5–30 cm wide
Habit: mat- to tuft-forming, short-lived perennial
Flowers: early spring; (some) fragrant
Foliage: aromatic; evergreen
Hardiness: C–D
Warnings: prone to aphids and flea beetles;
not prone to disease

Growing Requirements

Light: sun; shelter from hot p.m. sun
Soil: gritty, lean, moist, organic, well-drained soil
Location: alpine gardens; rock gardens; scree;
troughs
Propagation: seed (self-sows readily); division;
cuttings

On the Market

Thlaspi alpinum
White flowers in late spring • 5–10 cm high,
20–30 cm wide

Thlaspi bellidifolium
Fragrant, lilac to deep-purple flowers in
spring • 2–5 cm high, 5–10 cm wide

Thlaspi bulbosum
Clustered, purple flowers in spring •
5–10 cm high, 5–20 cm wide

Thlaspi cepaeifolium ssp. *rotundifolium*
Fragrant, pink-purple flowers in spring •
5–10 cm high, 5–10 cm wide

Thlaspi crassum
Pale-lilac flowers with dark veins in spring •
1–5 cm high

Thlaspi montanum
Fragrant, white flowers in late spring •
Gritty, lean, moist, organic, well-drained,
alkaline soil • 10–15 cm high, 15–30 cm
wide

Thlaspi stylosum
Fragrant, mauve flowers in spring •
3–5 cm high, 5–10 cm wide

Thlaspi violascens
White-violet flowers in spring to early
summer • 2–5 cm high, 10 cm wide

T

Thymus

p. 427

Genus Information

Origin: Eurasia

Selected Common Names: thyme, creeping thyme, woolly thyme, mother of thyme, lemon thyme

Nomenclature: From the Greek *thyo* (to perfume), referring to the aromatic leaves.

Other Uses: Some species are used for culinary purposes, others are strictly ornamental. Oils contain antiseptic, disinfectant and deodorant properties.

Notes: A genus of some 350 species.

General Features

Height: 1–30 cm high

Spread: 10–60 cm wide

Habit: mat- or cushion-forming groundcover or shrubby perennial

Flowers: late spring to late summer; good for drying; deadhead to keep plant compact; attracts bees

Foliage: aromatic; evergreen; (some) used for culinary purposes

Hardiness: B–D

Warnings: prone to aphids; not prone to disease

Growing Requirements

Light: sun

Soil: well-drained, neutral to alkaline soil; tolerant of a wide range of soils; tolerates poor dry soil

Location: between paving stones (tolerates light treading); herb gardens; mixed borders; rock gardens

Propagation: seed; division; cuttings

Expert Advice: Hybridizes easily. May not come true from seed.

Buying Considerations

Professionals

Popularity: popular garden standard; fast selling, with interesting foliage

Availability: readily available as finished product from specialty growers

Size to Sell: sells best in smaller sizes (when blooming) as it matures fast

On the Shelf: high ornamental appeal; keep stock rotated; rapidly overgrows pot

Shrinkage: low; requires little maintenance

Collectors

Popularity: of interest to collectors—unique, rare

Gardeners

Ease of Growth: very easy to grow

Start with: one small plant for feature and several for mass plantings

What to Try First ...

Thymus 'Doone Valley', *Thymus* 'Hartington Silver', *Thymus* 'Reiter's Red', *Thymus* Coccineus Group, *Thymus caespititius* 'Tuffet', *Thymus cilicicus*, *Thymus comosus*, *Thymus doerfleri* 'Bressingham', *Thymus neiceffii*, *Thymus praecox*, *Thymus praecox* 'Albiflorus', *Thymus pseudolanuginosus*, *Thymus serpyllum* 'Elfin', *Thymus serpyllum* var. *albus*

On the Market

Thymus

'Doone Valley' • Lavender flowers in summer • Aromatic, gold-speckled foliage • 10–15 cm high, 20–35 cm wide

'Hartington Silver' (Highland Cream) • Pale-pink flowers • Green-and-gold, aromatic foliage • 8 cm high, 30+ cm wide

'Lemon Ice' • White flowers in summer • Lemon-scented foliage • 1 cm high, 20 cm wide

'Longwood' • Large, lavender flowers in late spring to late summer • Grey, woolly foliage • 5–8 cm high, 30–45 cm wide

'Reiter Thyme' • Rose-purple flowers in spring to fall • 15 cm high, 60 cm wide

'Reiter's Red' • Crimson-red flowers in late spring to late summer • Thick, fine-textured, green foliage • 2 cm high, 30–45 cm wide

'Rose Williams' • Soft-pink flowers in summer • 10–20 cm high, 20–30 cm wide

Coccineus Group
Deep magenta-red, pink, mauve or white flowers in early summer •Aromatic foliage • 2–5 cm high, 30–45 cm+ wide

Thymus (T. pannonicus x *T. herba-barona)*
'Sagran' • Pale-pink flowers in summer • Shiny green, caraway-scented foliage • 2 cm high, 20 cm wide

Thymus argaeus
White flowers in spring • 5–10 cm high, 30+ cm wide

Thymus brachychilus
Pink flowers • Blue-grey foliage • 10 cm high, 30+ cm wide

Thymus bucharicus
Pink flowers in summer • Dark-green foliage • 2–4 cm high, 20–25 cm wide

Thymus caespititius
Pale rose-pink, lilac or white flowers in late spring • Aromatic, grey-green foliage • 2–7 cm high, 30 cm wide

T

'**Tuffet**' • Rose-pink flowers in summer •
Aromatic, grey-green foliage • 5 cm high,
30 cm wide

Thymus cilicicus
Lilac or mauve flowers in early summer
• 8–15 cm high, 20 cm wide

Thymus x *citriodorus*
Pale-purple flowers in summer • Lemon-
scented, green-and-yellow-variegated
foliage • 10–30 cm high, 25–30 cm wide
'**Argenteus**' • Pink to lilac flowers in
summer • Aromatic, white-and-green-
variegated foliage • 10–30 cm high, 30 cm
wide
'**Spring Gold**' • Pale-mauve flowers in
summer • Lemon-scented, golden foliage •
8–10 cm high, 30 cm wide

Thymus comosus
Rich-pink flowers • Grey foliage • 2–5 cm
high, 15–30 cm wide

Thymus doerfleri
'**Bressingham**' (Bressingham Pink) • Clear-
pink flowers in summer • Grey-green
foliage • 2–10 cm high, 35–60 cm wide

Thymus hyemalis
'**Compactus**' • Pink-purple flowers in
summer • 20 cm high, 30+ cm wide

Thymus lanicaulis
Rose-pink flowers in late spring to early
summer • 5–8 cm high, 25–30 cm wide

Thymus leucotrichus
Purple to mauve flowers in spring •
Aromatic foliage • 5–15 cm high, 20 cm
wide

Thymus mastichina
Wispy, greenish-white flowers in summer •
20–30 cm high, 40 cm wide

Thymus neiceffii
Soft-pink flowers in late spring to late
summer • Aromatic foliage • 5–10 cm high,
15–30 cm wide

Thymus nitens
Pink-purple flowers in early summer
• 8 cm high, 15 cm wide

Thymus pallasianus
Round, purple flowers in summer •
10–15 cm high, 20–25 cm wide

Thymus praecox
White, red or purple flowers in late spring
to late summer • Aromatic foliage • 5–10
cm high, 30–60+ cm wide

'**Albiflorus**' • White flowers in late spring to
late summer • Aromatic foliage • 5–10 cm
high, 30–60+ cm wide

Thymus pseudolanuginosus
Deep-pink flowers in late spring to early
summer • Thick, woolly, grey-green foliage
• 1–2 cm high, 30–45+ cm wide

Thymus pulegioides
White, mauve or crimson flowers in late
spring • Aromatic foliage • 5–25 cm high,
30–45+ cm wide
'**Archer's Gold**' • Soft-lilac flowers in
summer • Lemon-scented, gold foliage •
10–15 cm high, 30–40 cm wide
'**Aureus**' • Purple flowers in summer •
Lemon-scented, yellow-and-green-
variegated foliage • 15 cm high, 30 cm
wide
'**Bertram Anderson**' • Fragrant, violet
flowers in summer to fall • Golden foliage
• 10–30 cm high, 30–45+ cm wide

Thymus quinquecostatus var. *ibukiensis*
Large, pink flowers in summer • 5–10 cm
high, 30+ cm wide

Thymus richardii ssp. *nitidus*
(syn. *T. nitidus*)
Lilac to pink flowers in summer • Aromatic
foliage • 5–10 cm high, 15–30 cm wide

Thymus serpyllum
Mauve or pink flowers in summer •
2–5 cm high, 10–25+ cm wide
'**Doretta Klaber**' • Lavender flowers in
summer • 5 cm high, 30 cm wide
'**Elfin**' • Pink flowers in summer • Aromatic
foliage • 5–8 cm high, 10–25+ cm wide
'**Magic Carpet**' • Carmine-pink flowers in
summer • Lemon-scented, slightly woolly
foliage • 2–5 cm high, 30–45 cm wide
'**Minor**' (Minus) • Pink flowers in summer •
2–5 cm high, 40–45 cm wide
'**Pink Chintz**' • Flesh-pink flowers in late
spring • 2 cm high, 30–45 cm wide
'**Rainbow Falls**' • Rose-purple flowers in
summer • Striking, red-and-gold foliage •
10–15 cm high, 30–45 cm wide

Thymus serpyllum var. *albus*
White flowers in spring to early summer •
Aromatic foliage • 10–15 cm high, 45 cm
wide

T

Tiarella p. 427 📷

Genus Information

Origin: East Asia and North America
Selected Common Names: foam flower
Nomenclature: From the diminutive of the Latin *tiara* (diadem), referring to the shape of the fruit.
Notes: A genus of some 7 species.

General Features

Height: 15–50 cm high
Spread: 15–55 cm wide
Habit: stoloniferous, rhizomatous or clump-forming groundcover perennial
Flowers: tiny, star-like flowers borne in plumes; long blooming period; spring to summer
Foliage: lobed; evergreen; good fall colour
Hardiness: C–D
Warnings: prone to powdery mildew and aphids
Expert Advice: Many new varieties being released by tissue culture labs in the U.S. are proving to be very hardy and useful on the Prairies. Many new forms have interesting leaves, both in colour and form. Very reliable.

Growing Requirements

Light: shade
Soil: cool, moist, organic, acidic soil; avoid winter wet
Location: under planting in mixed shrub borders; woodland gardens
Propagation: seed; division
Expert Advice: Division in spring.

Buying Considerations

Professionals

Popularity: gaining popularity as a foliage plant; has new varieties
Availability: generally available as finished product and bare root
Size to Sell: sells best in smaller sizes (when blooming) as it matures fast
On the Shelf: high ornamental appeal; keep stock rotated; rapidly overgrows pot

Collectors

Popularity: not generally of interest to collectors

Gardeners

Ease of Growth: very easy to grow
Start with: one small plant for feature plant and several for mass plantings

What to Try First ...

Tiarella 'Black Velvet', *Tiarella* 'Iron Butterfly', *Tiarella* 'Jeepers Creepers', *Tiarella* 'Mint Chocolate', *Tiarella* 'Pink Bouquet', *Tiarella* 'Pink Skyrocket', *Tiarella* 'Skeleton Key', *Tiarella* 'Spring Symphony', *Tiarella cordifolia*, *Tiarella wherryi* 'Heronswood Mist'

On the Market

Tiarella

'Black Snowflake' • Creamy-white flowers in summer • Black-centred, green foliage • 30–40 cm high, 30–45 cm wide

'Black Velvet' • Fragrant, white flowers in spring to summer • Black-centred, green foliage • 45–50 cm high, 30–40 cm wide

'Crow Feather' • Pink flowers in spring • Bright-green foliage • 20–30 cm high, 25–30 cm wide

'Inkblot' • Blush-pink flowers in spring • 20–30 cm high, 40–50 cm wide

'Iron Butterfly' • Soft-pink, fragrant flowers in spring • 20–40 cm high, 20–25 cm wide

'Jeepers Creepers' • Creamy-white flowers in summer • Black-centred, green foliage • 20–30 cm high, 30–45 cm wide

'Lacquer Leaf' • White flowers in early spring • 20–40 cm high, 30 cm wide

'Mint Chocolate' • Pink-tinted flowers in spring • Mint-green and chocolate foliage • 20–40 cm high, 30 cm wide

'Neon Lights' • Pink-tinged flowers in late spring • Black foliage with neon-green edge • 20–40 cm high, 55 cm wide

'Pink Bouquet' • Fragrant, pink flowers in early spring • 20–25 cm high, 20–25 cm wide

'Pink Skyrocket' • Fragrant, pink flowers in late spring to summer • Dark-veined foliage • 15–25 cm high, 25–30 cm wide

'Pinwheel' • Soft-pink flowers in spring • 30–40 cm high, 40–50 cm wide

'Skeleton Key' • Blush-pink flowers in early spring • Deeply cleft foliage • 20–30 cm high, 30–45 cm wide

'Spring Symphony' • Pink flowers in spring to late summer • Green foliage with black midrib • 20–25 cm high, 20–30 cm wide

'Tiger Stripe' • Pink flowers in early spring • Purple-and-green foliage • 20–35 cm high, 35–40 cm wide

Tiarella cordifolia

Fragrant, white flowers in spring • 20–30 cm high, 30–45 cm wide

'Slick Rock' • Fragrant, soft-pink flowers in spring • Maple-shaped foliage • 20–30 cm high, 30–45 cm wide

Tiarella wherryi

Fragrant, white flowers in late spring
to early summer • Maple-like leaves •
15–20 cm high, 15–30 cm wide

'Heronswood Mist' • Cream flowers in
spring • Foliage splashed with pink, cream
and green • 15–30 cm high, 20–25 cm
wide

Townsendia   p. 427

Genus Information

Origin: Canada and the United States
Selected Common Names: Easter daisy
Nomenclature: Named for David Townsend
(1787–1858), a Pennsylvanian botanist.
Notes: Genus includes annuals, biennials and
perennials.

General Features

Height: 2–30 cm
Spread: 10–20 cm
Habit: tap-rooted, rosette-forming biennial or
short-lived perennial
Flowers: large, stemless or near-stemless aster-
like; spring to summer (many flower
intermittently)
Foliage: neat; silvery-grey
Hardiness: C
Warnings: prone to aphids; not prone to diseases

Growing Requirements

Light: sun
Soil: organic, sandy, sharply-drained, neutral to
alkaline soil; avoid winter wet; keep soil drier
after flowering: drought tolerant
Location: rock gardens; troughs; scree
Propagation: seed (self-sows readily); cuttings
Expert Advice: Often monocarpic. Save seed. Use
fresh, ripe seed and transplant seedlings early to
minimize damage to tap root or sow in situ.
Resents being disturbed.

Buying Considerations

Professionals

Popularity: relatively unknown
Availability: occasionally available from
specialty growers
Size to Sell: sells best in smaller sizes
(when blooming)
On the Shelf: keep stock rotated
Shrinkage: low shrinkage; requires little
maintenance

Collectors

Popularity: of interest to alpine collectors

Gardeners

Ease of Growth: mostly easy to grow but
needs close attention to growing conditions
Start with: several small plants for instant
visual effect

What to Try First ...

*Townsendia alpigena, Townsendia condensata,
Townsendia exscapa, Townsendia hookeri,
Townsendia parryi, Townsendia rothrockii*

On the Market

***Townsendia alpigena* var. *alpigena*
(syn. *T. montana*)**
Daisy-like, purple flowers in summer •
Grey-green foliage • 5–8 cm high,
10–15 cm wide

Townsendia condensata
White, pink or lavender flowers in spring
to early summer • Spatulate, woolly leaves •
2–5 cm high, 10–15 cm wide

Townsendia eximia
Daisy-like, blue-purple flowers in spring •
10–30 cm high, 10–15 cm wide

***Townsendia exscapa* (syn. *T. wilcoxiana*)**
Daisy-like, white flowers flushed with
purple in spring to midsummer • 5 cm high,
10–15 cm wide

Townsendia formosa
Daisy-like, lavender flowers in spring to
midsummer • 12–30 cm high, 10–15 cm
wide

Townsendia hookeri
Daisy-like, white flowers in spring to
midsummer • 5–10 cm high, 15–20 cm wide

Townsendia incana
Daisy-like, white flowers in spring •
2–5 cm high, 5–10 cm wide

Townsendia leptotes
Pale-lavender to white flowers in spring •
Grey-green foliage • 5–8 cm high, 8–10 cm
wide

Townsendia minima
Daisy-like, white flowers in late spring to
summer • 5 cm high, 10 cm wide

Townsendia parryi
Daisy-like, mauve flowers in summer •
Native to the Prairies • 5–15 cm high,
10–15 cm wide

Townsendia rothrockii
Daisy-like, pale-lilac flowers in spring to
early summer • 2–5 cm high, 10 cm wide

Townsendia spathulata
Daisy-like, pink-lavender flowers in spring •
Silver-grey foliage • 2.5–5 cm high, 8 cm
wide

T

Tradescantia
p. 427 📷

Genus Information

Origin: North America, South America and Europe
Selected Common Names: spiderwort
Nomenclature: Named for John Tradescant, 1608–1662, a British gardener and naturalist.
Notes: A genus of some 65 species.

General Features

Height: 30–60 cm high
Spread: 30–60 cm wide
Habit: clump- or mat-forming perennial
Flowers: 3-petalled; each bloom lasts 1 day; long blooming period; deadhead to extend blooming season
Foliage: arching, grass-like
Hardiness: C
Warnings: prone to slugs; not prone to insects or disease; contact with foliage may irritate skin

Growing Requirements

Light: sun to p.m. sun
Soil: cool, fertile, moist soil
Location: mixed borders
Propagation: division

Buying Considerations

Professionals

Popularity: gaining popularity; fast seller in bloom
Availability: generally available as finished product and bare root
Size to Sell: sells best in smaller sizes (when blooming) as it matures fast
On the Shelf: rapidly overgrows pot
Shrinkage: low; requires little maintenance

Collectors

Popularity: not generally of interest to collectors

Gardeners

Ease of Growth: mostly easy to grow but needs close attention to growing conditions
Start with: one small plant for feature plant

What to Try First ...

Tradescantia 'Bilberry Ice', *Tradescantia* 'Blushing Bride', *Tradescantia* 'Concord Grape', *Tradescantia* 'Perinne's Pink', *Tradescantia* 'Valour', *Tradescantia* 'Zwanenburg Blue', *Tradescantia virginiana* 'Caerulea Plena'

On the Market

Andersoniana Group

'Bilberry Ice' • Lilac, white-edged flowers in summer • Grass-like foliage • 40–60 cm high, 45–60 cm wide

'Blue and Gold' • Gentian-blue flowers in summer • Golden, grass-like foliage • 50–55 cm high, 35 cm wide

'Blue Stone' • Clear-blue flowers in spring to fall • Grass-like foliage • 30–60 cm high, 45–60 cm wide

'Blushing Bride' • White flowers in summer • Green leaves with pink and white bases • 50 cm high, 45–60 cm wide

'Charlotte' • Clear-pink flowers in spring to fall • Grass-like foliage • 30–45 cm high, 30–40 cm wide

'Concord Grape' • Purple flowers in summer • Frosty-blue, grass-like foliage • 40–45 cm high, 30 cm wide

'In the Navy' • Light-blue flowers with darker eye in early summer • Grass-like foliage • 40–45 cm high, 30–45 cm wide

'Karminglut' (Carmine Glow) • Carmine-red flowers in summer • Grass-like foliage • 40–60 cm high, 45–60 cm wide

'Little Doll' • Lilac-blue flowers in early summer to fall • Grass-like foliage • 30–35 cm high, 30–45 cm wide

'Perinne's Pink' • Pink flowers in summer • Blue-green foliage • 50 cm high, 45–60 cm wide

'Red Cloud' • Rosy-red flowers in summer • Grass-like foliage • 30–50 cm high, 40–45 cm wide

'Rubra' • Carmine-red flowers in summer • Grass-like foliage • 30–60 cm high, 40–45 cm wide

'Valour' • Red flowers in summer • Frosty-blue, grass-like foliage • 40–45 cm high, 30 cm wide

'Zwanenburg Blue' • Violet-purple flowers • Grass-like foliage • 45–60 cm high, 45–60 cm wide

Tradescantia virginiana

'Caerulea Plena' • Double, dark-blue flowers in summer • Grass-like foliage • 35–50 cm high, 30–45 cm wide

T

Tricyrtis

p. 427

Genus Information

Origin: eastern Himalayas (Nepal and China), Japan, Taiwan and the Philippines
Selected Common Names: Japanese toad lily
Nomenclature: From the Greek *treis* (three) and *kyrtos* (convex), referring to the bag-like bases of the 3 outer petals.

General Features

Height: 30–90 cm high
Spread: 30–60 cm wide
Habit: clump-forming, rhizomatous or stoloniferous perennial
Flowers: softly coloured, orchid-like; late summer to fall
Foliage: (some) colourful
Hardiness: C–D; mulch for winter
Warnings: prone to slugs; not prone to insects or disease
Expert Advice: Takes 2–3 years to look its best. Tends to bloom late on the Prairies, depending on the fall weather.

Growing Requirements

Light: shade to a.m. sun; tolerates more sun with good soil moisture
Soil: lean, moist, organic, well-drained soil
Location: rock gardens; mixed borders; woodland gardens
Propagation: seed; division; separate and replant stolons
Expert Advice: Sow fresh seed or stratify. *T. hirta* self-sows.

Buying Considerations

Professionals
Popularity: relatively unknown
Availability: generally available as finished product and bare root
Size to Sell: sells best in smaller sizes (when blooming) as it matures fast
On the Shelf: keep stock rotated; rapidly overgrows pot
Shrinkage: low; requires little maintenance

Collectors
Popularity: of interest to collectors—novelty plant

Gardeners
Ease of Growth: mostly easy to grow but needs close attention to growing conditions
Start with: one small plant for feature plant

What to Try First ...

Tricyrtis 'Kohaku', *Tricyrtis* 'Lightning Strike', *Tricyrtis hirta*

On the Market

Tricyrtis
'Kohaku' • White flowers with purple spots in late summer to fall • 60–90 cm high, 30–40 cm wide

'Lightning Strike' • Lavender-orchid flowers in late summer • Golden-streaked foliage matures to gold centre with green edge • 60 cm high, 30 cm wide

'White Towers' • White flowers in late summer to fall • 45–60 cm high, 30–40 cm wide

Tricyrtis hirta
White flowers with purple spots in late summer to fall • 60–80 cm high, 40–60 cm wide

'Hatatogisa' • White flowers with spots in late summer to fall • 60–90 cm high, 60 cm wide

'White Flame' • White flowers in late summer to fall • Variegated foliage • 30–45 cm high, 45 cm wide

Trifolium

p. 427

Genus Information

Origin: temperate and subtropical regions, except Australasia
Selected Common Names: alpine clover, deer clover, ornamental clover, shamrock
Nomenclature: From the Latin *tres* (three) and *folius* (leaf).
Notes: A genus of some 300 species of annuals, biennials or perennials.

General Features

Height: 8–60 cm high
Spread: 20–60 cm wide
Habit: vigorously spreading groundcover perennial
Flowers: small, pea-like; spring to summer
Foliage: 3-part (sometimes 5 or 7), palmate; *Trifolium repens* has unusually coloured foliage
Hardiness: C
Warnings: not prone to insects or disease
Expert Advice: Grown for its foliage, many make attractive groundcovers. Mowing after flowering keeps plant compact and encourages fresh growth.

Growing Requirements

Light: sun
Soil: moist, organic, well-drained soil; tolerant of a wide range of soils; drought tolerant
Location: lawns; meadows; wildflower gardens; banks; slopes
Propagation: seed; division

T

Buying Considerations
Professionals
Popularity: gaining popularity
Availability: generally available as finished product and bare root
Size to Sell: sells best in smaller sizes as it matures fast
On the Shelf: rapidly overgrows pot
Shrinkage: low; sensitive to underwatering; requires little maintenance
Collectors
Popularity: not generally of interest to collectors
Gardeners
Ease of Growth: very easy to grow
Start with: one small plant for feature plant and several for mass plantings
What to Try First ...
Trifolium alpinum, Trifolium repens 'Dragon's Blood', *Trifolium repens* 'Purpurascens'

On the Market

Trifolium alpinum
Fragrant, rose-red flowers in late spring to late summer • 10–20 cm high, 30 cm wide

Trifolium nanum
Pea-like, rose-purple flowers in early summer • 10–15 cm high, 20 cm wide

Trifolium repens
'Dragon's Blood' • Pea-like, white flowers in spring to summer • Purple-stained, mint-green foliage • 8–15 cm high, 30–60+ cm wide

'Purpurascens' • Fragrant, pea-like, white flowers in late spring to early summer • Black-green foliage • 10–15 cm high, 45–60+ cm wide

'Quinquefolium' (Pentaphyllum) • Pea-like, white flowers in spring to summer • Green-edged purple foliage • 8–15 cm high, 30–60+ cm wide

Trifolium rubens
Bright-purple-red flowers in late spring • 45–60 cm high, 45–60 cm wide

Trillium p. 427

Genus Information
Origin: North America, the western Himalayas and northeastern Asia
Selected Common Names: Trinity flower, wood lily

Nomenclature: From the Greek *tris* (thrice), referring to the leaves and flower parts occurring in threes. One of the many common names is "wake robin," referring to the appearance of the first flowers with the spring arrival of the robin.
Notes: A genus of some 30 species. *Trillium grandiflorum* (great white trillium) is the provincial flower of Ontario.

General Features
Height: 15–60 cm high
Spread: 15–30 cm wide
Habit: rhizomatous, colony-forming perennial
Flowers: sessile (stalkless) or stalked (on a pedicel), upright, nodding or drooping; spring; goes dormant after flowering
Foliage: 3 leaves per stem; (some) mottled
Hardiness: C
Warnings: prone to slugs; not prone to insects or disease
Expert Advice: Challenging for the experienced gardener. Takes time to form nice colonies in cold climates. The over-enthusiastic collection of wild plants has led to their disappearance in many native habitats. Great worldwide interest and research into cultivation methods may help reduce the harvesting of wild plants.

Growing Requirements
Light: shade; *T. ovatum* and *T. sessile* tolerate more sun with good soil moisture
Soil: cool, moist, organic soil
Location: mixed borders; rock gardens; woodland gardens
Propagation: seed; division
Expert Advice: Divide after foliage dies down or from fresh seed sown 15 mm deep in a propagating mix with extra leaf mold. Plants from seed take 5–7 years before blooming and leaves will not appear until 2nd year.

Buying Considerations
Professionals
Popularity: gaining popularity; fast seller in bloom
Availability: occasionally available as bare root from specialty growers
Size to Sell: sells best in mature sizes (when blooming) as it matures slowly
On the Shelf: keep stock rotated
Shrinkage: high; goes dormant in pot
Collectors
Popularity: of interest to collectors—unique, exceptional beauty, variety, rare
Gardeners
Ease of Growth: mostly difficult to grow as it needs close attention to growing conditions
Start with: several mature plants for instant visual effect

What to Try First ...

Trillium cernuum, Trillium erectum, Trillium erectum f. *luteum, Trillium grandiflorum, Trillium luteum, Trillium ovatum, Trillium recurvatum, Trillium sessile, Trillium sulcatum, Trillium undulatum*

On the Market

Trillium (T. cernuum x T. erectum)
Nodding, red flowers in early spring •
25–30 cm high, 15–20 cm wide

Trillium (T. erectum x T. flexipes)
Tan flowers in spring • 20–25 cm high,
15–20 cm wide

Trillium (T. smallii x T. tschonoskii)
White flowers in spring • 20–30 cm high,
15–20 cm wide

Trillium albidum
White flowers in early spring • 20–45 cm
high, 15–20 cm wide

Trillium catesbaei
Nodding, white to rose flowers in spring •
Moist, organic, acidic soil in woodland
location • 20–45 cm high, 20 cm wide

Trillium cernuum
Nodding, white, maroon-centred flowers in
early spring • 10–40 cm high, 20–30 cm
wide

Trillium chloropetalum
Maroon flowers in spring • Brown-green
mottling on leaves • 20–65 cm high,
25–30 cm wide

Trillium cuneatum
Purple to bronze, green and yellow flowers
in spring • Strongly mottled leaves •
15–45 cm high, 15–30 cm wide

Trillium erectum
Large, red-purple flowers, rarely white,
in spring • Moist, organic, cool, acidic soil
in woodland location • 15–60 cm high,
15–30 cm wide

Trillium erectum f. luteum
Yellow flowers in early spring • Cool, moist,
organic, acidic soil in woodland location •
15–45 cm high, 15–30 cm wide

Trillium erectum var. album
White flowers in spring • 15–60 cm high,
15–30 cm wide

Trillium flexipes
White, heavily textured flowers in spring •
Moist, organic, alkaline soil in woodland
location • 20–50 cm high, 20–25 cm wide

Trillium grandiflorum
Large, white flowers, fading to a dull
pink-purple, in spring • 15–30 cm high,
20–30 cm wide

Trillium ludovicianum
Purple-green to purple flowers in spring •
Strongly marked leaves • 15–25 cm high,
15–20 cm wide

Trillium luteum
Yellow to greenish-yellow flowers in spring
• Mottled foliage • Moist, organic, alkaline
soil in woodland location • 15–40 cm high,
20–30 cm wide

Trillium nivale
Recurved, white flowers in early spring •
Moist, organic, alkaline, gritty soil •
3–5 cm high, 5–8 cm wide

Trillium ovatum
White flowers, fading to rose, in early spring
• 15–70 cm high, 15–20 cm wide

Trillium pusillum
White flowers, fading to pink, in early
spring • Organic, boggy soil • 8–20 cm high,
8–10 cm wide

Trillium recurvatum
Maroon-purple, rarely yellow, flowers
in early spring • Marbled leaves • Moist,
alkaline, fertile soil • 15–45 cm high,
20–30 cm wide

Trillium rugelii
Fragrant, strongly recurved, white
flowers, sometimes red or pink, in
spring • 15–40 cm high, 15–20 cm wide

Trillium sessile
Fragrant, maroon flowers in early spring •
Moist, organic, alkaline soil in woodland
location • 10–25 cm high, 10–15 cm wide

Trillium simile
Large, textured, creamy-white flowers in
early spring • 30–60 cm high, 20–30 cm
wide

Trillium sulcatum
Maroon-red flowers in spring • Moist,
organic, neutral to slightly acidic soil
in woodland location • 30–70 cm high,
20–30 cm wide

Trillium tschonoskii
White flowers in spring • 15–40 cm high,
20–30 cm wide

Trillium undulatum
White flowers with a central, purple,
inverted 'V' mark in spring • Cool, moist,
organic, acidic soil in woodland location •
20–50 cm high, 30 cm wide

T

Trillium vaseyi
Fragrant, large, nodding, magenta to crimson flowers in spring • 30–65 cm high, 25–40 cm wide

Trollius

p. 427

Genus Information
Origin: North America, Europe and Asia
Selected Common Names: globeflower, garden globeflower
Nomenclature: From the German *trollblume* (globeflower).
Notes: A genus of some 24 species.

General Features
Height: 10–90 cm high
Spread: 15–60 cm wide
Habit: clump-forming perennial
Flowers: buttercup-like, cup-shaped; spring to summer; may rebloom in fall
Foliage: deeply lobed
Hardiness: C
Warnings: not prone to insects or disease
Expert Advice: Cut back after flowering and mulch. It usually rewards with more blooms.

Growing Requirements
Light: shade to a.m. sun
Soil: fertile, constantly moist, well-drained soil
Location: damp meadows; watersides; woodland gardens
Propagation: seed; division
Expert Advice: Sow fresh seed. Seed may take 2 years to germinate. Divide every 3 years to maintain vigour.

Buying Considerations

Professionals
Popularity: popular, old-fashioned garden standard
Availability: readily available as finished product and bare root
Size to Sell: sells best in smaller sizes (when blooming) as it matures fast
On the Shelf: keep stock rotated; foliage breakage
Shrinkage: low; requires little maintenance

Collectors
Popularity: not generally of interest to collectors

Gardeners
Ease of Growth: very easy to grow
Start with: one small plant for feature plant

What to Try First ...
Trollius acaulis, *Trollius chinensis* 'Golden Queen', *Trollius* x *cultorum*, *Trollius* x *cultorum* 'Canary Bird', *Trollius* x *cultorum* 'Cheddar', *Trollius* x *cultorum* 'Earliest of All', *Trollius* x *cultorum* 'Lemon Queen', *Trollius* x *cultorum* 'Prichard's Giant', *Trollius europaeus* 'Superbus', *Trollius pumilus*

On the Market

Trollius
'Moon Glow' • Soft-yellow flowers in spring • 60 cm high, 45–60 cm wide
'Cressida' • Semi-double, butter-yellow flowers in early summer • 60–70 cm high, 45–60 cm wide

Trollius acaulis
Buttercup, golden-yellow flowers in early summer • 10–20 cm high, 20–30 cm wide

Trollius asiaticus
Golden-yellow to orange flowers in late spring to early summer • 20–80 cm high, 30–45 cm wide

Trollius chinensis
'Golden Queen' • Orange-yellow flowers in summer • 60–90 cm high, 45 cm wide

Trollius x *cultorum*
Globe-shaped, orange or yellow flowers in spring to midsummer • 60–90 cm high, 45 cm wide

'Alabaster' • Pale primrose-yellow flowers in spring • 45–60 cm high, 40–45 cm wide
'Byrne's Giant' • Lemon-yellow flowers in spring • 60–90 cm high, 45 cm wide
'Canary Bird' • Pale lemon-yellow flowers in spring • 45–60 cm high, 45 cm wide
'Cheddar' • Cream flowers in spring • 45–60 cm high, 45 cm wide
'Commander-in-chief' • Yellow flowers in late spring to early summer • 60 cm high, 45 cm wide
'Earliest of All' • Clear-yellow flowers in spring • 45–60 cm high, 45 cm wide
'Etna' • Orange-yellow flowers in spring • 60–75 cm high, 45 cm wide
'Feuertroll' (Fire Globe) • Fiery orange-red flowers in spring • 60–70 cm high, 40–45 cm wide
'Glory of Leiden' • Clear-yellow flowers in spring • 45–60 cm high, 30–45 cm wide

T

'Goldquelle' (Golden Fountain) • Lemon-yellow flowers in summer • 45–70 cm high, 30–45 cm wide

'Lemon Queen' • Pale-yellow flowers in late spring • 45–60 cm high, 45 cm wide

'Orange Globe' • Golden-orange flowers in late spring • 60–75 cm high, 45 cm wide

'Orange Princess' • Orange-yellow flowers in late spring • 75–90 cm high, 45–60 cm wide

'Prichard's Giant' • Large, orange-yellow flowers in late spring to early summer • 75–90 cm high, 45–60 cm wide

Trollius europaeus
Lemon-yellow flowers in spring to early summer • 60–80 cm high, 45 cm wide

'Superbus' • Sulphur-yellow flowers in late spring to early summer • 60 cm high, 45 cm wide

Trollius laxus
Green-yellow flowers in spring to summer • 20–50 cm high, 25–40 cm wide

Trollius pumilus
Golden-yellow flowers, tinged red on outside, in early summer • 20–30 cm high, 15–20 cm wide

Trollius stenopetalus
Single, yellow flowers in late spring to early summer • 75 cm high, 30–40 cm wide

T

Uvularia

p. 427 📷

Genus Information

Origin: eastern North America
Selected Common Names: big merrybells, little merrybells
Nomenclature: From the Latin *uvula* (the soft palate), referring to the drooping flowers.
Other Uses: Used by North American native peoples as a sedative and tonic to treat throat ailments. The young shoots were boiled and eaten like a vegetable.
Notes: A genus of some 5 species.

General Features

Height: 30–75 cm high
Spread: 20–30 cm wide
Habit: upright, rhizomatous perennial
Flowers: yellow, pendulous, bell-shaped; spring
Foliage: lance-shaped
Hardiness: C
Warnings: prone to slugs; not prone to insects or disease
Expert Advice: A slow-spreading perennial that colonizes nicely on the Prairies after 3–4 years. Looks great with ferns, *Hostas* and *Epimediums*.

Growing Requirements

Light: shade
Soil: fertile, moist, organic, well-drained, alkaline soil
Location: cool, shady mixed borders; rock gardens; woodland gardens
Propagation: seed; division

Buying Considerations

Professionals

Popularity: relatively unknown
Availability: occasionally available from specialty growers
Size to Sell: sells best in smaller sizes when blooming
Shrinkage: low; requires little maintenance

Collectors

Popularity: not generally of interest to collectors

Gardeners

Ease of Growth: mostly easy to grow but needs close attention to growing conditions
Start with: one small plant for feature plant

What to Try First ...

Uvularia grandiflora, Uvularia sessilifolia

On the Market

Uvularia grandiflora
Pendant, bell-shaped, yellow flowers in late spring • 30–75 cm high, 30 cm wide

Uvularia sessilifolia
Pendant, bell-shaped, straw-yellow flowers in late spring • 30–40 cm high, 20–30 cm wide

U

Valeriana

p. 427 📷

Genus Information

Origin: worldwide, except Australia
Selected Common Names: alpine valerian, common valerian
Nomenclature: Perhaps from the Latin *valere* (to be healthy), referring to the plant's strong medicinal properties.
Other Uses: Traditionally, *V. officinalis* was planted in herbal gardens and has been used in herbal and homeopathic medicine for many years. During the Second World War, shell and bombing "neurosis" was treated with valerian as a relaxant and sedative.
Notes: A genus of some 150–200 species.

General Features

Height: 8–120 cm high
Spread: 15–80 cm wide
Habit: clump-forming, spreading or rhizomatous perennial or shrublet; may require staking
Flowers: strongly scented; spring to summer
Foliage: aromatic
Hardiness: C
Warnings: prone to aphids; not prone to disease; invasive (contain and deadhead to prevent spread)
Expert Advice: The scent of the species *V. officinalis* drives cats into a euphoric frenzy. A distinctive and obnoxious smell arises when roots are dried.

Growing Requirements

Light: sun to p.m. sun; tolerates shade
Soil: moist, organic, well-drained, alkaline soil
Location: cottage gardens; alpine types in rock gardens
Propagation: seed (self-sows readily) division, basal cuttings
Expert Advice: Seed requires light to germinate.

Buying Considerations

Professionals
Popularity: gaining popularity
Availability: generally available as finished product and bare root
Size to Sell: sells best in smaller sizes as it matures fast
On the Shelf: keep stock rotated; rapidly overgrows pot
Shrinkage: low; requires little maintenance

Collectors
Popularity: not generally of interest to collectors (although grown by herbalists)

Gardeners
Ease of Growth: very easy to grow
Start with: one small plant for feature plant

What to Try First ...
Valeriana montana, Valeriana officinalis, Valeriana supina

On the Market

Valeriana arizonica
White or pale-pink flowers in spring • 10 cm high, 30–40 cm wide

Valeriana montana
White to light-pink flowers in spring • 10–50 cm high, 30–40 cm wide

Valeriana officinalis
White to pinkish flowers in summer • Aromatic foliage • 1–1.5 m high, 40–80 cm wide

Valeriana supina
Deep-pink flowers in summer • 8–12 cm high, 15–30 cm wide

Vancouveria

p. 427 📷

Genus Information

Origin: western North America, along the Pacific Coast from northern Washington to central California
Selected Common Names: American barrenwort, redwood ivy
Nomenclature: Named for George Vancouver, an 18th century British explorer.
Notes: A genus of some 3 species.

General Features

Height: 10–40 cm high
Spread: 30–40 cm wide
Habit: rhizomatous, creeping, woodland groundcover perennial
Flowers: late spring to summer
Foliage: slender, graceful; evergreen
Hardiness: C–D
Warnings: not prone to insects or diseases

Growing Requirements

Light: shade
Soil: fertile, moist, organic, well-drained soil
Location: mixed borders; rock gardens; underplanting in evergreen gardens; woodland gardens
Propagation: seed; division
Expert Advice: Propagate from ripe seed. Divide in spring.

Buying Considerations

Professionals
Popularity: relatively unknown, fast-selling foliage plant; has new varieties
Availability: occasionally available as bare root from specialty growers
Size to Sell: sells best in smaller sizes (when blooming) as it matures fast
On the Shelf: high ornamental appeal; rapidly overgrows pot
Shrinkage: low; requires little maintenance

V

On the Market

Vancouveria hexandra
Pendulous, white flowers in late spring •
10–40 cm high, 30–40 cm wide

Vancouveria planipetala **(syn. *Epimedium planipetala*)**
Pendulous, white flowers in summer •
20–35 cm high, 30–40 cm wide

Veratrum

Genus Information

Origin: the Northern Hemisphere
Selected Common Names: American false hellebore
Nomenclature: From the Latin *vere atrum* (truly black), referring to the black colour of the roots.
Other Uses: It has been recorded that North American native peoples used small amounts of the plant to control blood pressure.
Note: A genus of some 45 species.

General Features
Height: 60–120 cm high
Spread: 45–60 cm wide
Habit: clump-forming perennial
Flowers: shades of green, black or purple; plume-like; summer
Foliage: huge, dramatic, pleated; bright-green
Hardiness: C
Warnings: not prone to insects or disease; flowers and foliage are toxic; contact with foliage may irritate skin
Expert Advice: Can take up to 5 years to flower. For the collector. Grow with *Hostas* and ferns.

Growing Requirements
Light: shade; tolerates more sun with good soil moisture
Soil: fertile, moist, organic, well-drained, acidic soil
Location: mixed borders; woodland gardens; foliage may burn in windy locations
Propagation: seed, division
Expert Advice: Plants from seed can take up to 10 years to reach maturity. Germination is erratic. Best stratified for three months at 1.6–4.4°C followed by 20°C.

Buying Considerations

Professionals
Popularity: relatively unknown foliage plant
Availability: occasionally available from specialty growers
Size to Sell: sells best in mature sizes (when blooming) as it matures slowly
On the Shelf: high ornamental appeal
Shrinkage: low; requires little maintenance

Collectors
Popularity: of interest to collectors—unique, rare

Gardeners
Ease of Growth: mostly easy to grow
Start with: one mature plant for feature plant

What to Try First ...
Veratrum nigrum

On the Market

Veratrum nigrum
Plume-like, black-purple flowers in summer
• Strongly veined, pleated, light-green leaves
• 60–120 cm high, 45–60 cm wide

Verbascum p. 427

Genus Information

Origin: Europe, North America, North Africa and western and central Asia
Selected Common Names: mullein
Nomenclature: From the Latin name used by Pliny.
Other Uses: *Verbascum thapsus* has been used for many purposes in the past. Its stems were once dipped in tallow and used as candles. The flower spikes were used as torches. The Romans made hair dye from the plant. The Europeans used the woolly parts of the plant to line footwear. It was also used medicinally to treat bronchial congestions, earaches and migraines.
Notes: A genus of some 360 species.

General Features
Height: 20 cm–2 m high
Spread: 25–60 cm wide
Habit: clump-forming, mostly biennial; may require staking
Flowers: tall spikes; late spring to summer; long blooming period; deadhead to extend blooming season
Foliage: large; strap-like, furry, shiny or smooth; (some) evergreen
Hardiness: C–D
Warnings: prone to aphids; not prone to disease
Expert Advice: *V. thapsus* is native to the southern Prairies and arid areas of British Columbia.

Growing Requirements

Light: sun
Soil: dry, alkaline soil; tolerates poor soil; avoid winter wet; may require staking in fertile soil
Location: sunny, hot, dry areas; mixed borders; wild gardens; woodland gardens
Propagation: seed; division; cuttings
Expert Advice: Seeds are long-lived. Hybridizes easily, producing sterile offspring. Take root or semi-ripe cuttings of lateral shoots in late summer.

On the Market

Verbascum

'Cherry Helen' • Spiked, wine-red flowers in summer • 75–90 cm high, 45 cm wide

'Dark Eyes' • Yellow-cream flowers with a red eye in midsummer • Compact, silver-green foliage • 20–30 cm high, 30–45 cm wide

'Helen Johnson' • Spiked, buff-peach flowers in summer • 60–75 cm high, 45 cm wide

'Jackie' • Peach flowers with purple eye in summer • 20–60 cm high, 35 cm wide

'Letitia' • Spiked, bright-yellow flowers in summer • Evergreen, velvet-like foliage • 20–30 cm high, 25–30 cm wide

'Pink Petticoats' • Spiked, apricot-pink flowers in summer • 70–90 cm high, 45 cm wide

'Plum Smokey' • Plum-purple flowers in midsummer • 45 cm high, 30–45 cm wide

'Royal Pink' • Soft-pink flowers in summer • 30–40 cm high, 45 cm wide

'Silberkandelaber' (Silver Candelabra) • Spiked, yellow flowers in summer • Evergreen, silvery, woolly foliage • 1.5–2 m high, 60 cm wide

'Summer Sorbet' • Raspberry-peach flowers in midsummer • 45–60 cm high, 30–45 cm wide

Verbascum blattaria
Spiked, yellow flowers in midsummer • 1–1.5 m high, 60 cm wide

Verbascum blattaria f. *albiflorum*
Spiked, white flowers in summer • 1.5–2 m high, 60 cm wide

Verbascum bombyciferum
Sulphur-yellow flowers in summer • Evergreen foliage • 1–1.8 m high, 60 cm wide

'Polarsommer' (Arctic Summer) • Spiked, yellow flowers in summer • Evergreen, silver-white, felted foliage • 90–150 cm high, 45–60 cm wide

Verbascum chaixii
Pale-yellow flowers in midsummer • White, woolly stems • 60–90 cm high, 45 cm wide

'Album' • Spiked, white flowers with mauve eye in summer • 60–90 cm high, 45 cm wide

'Gainsborough' • Spiked, light-yellow flowers in summer • 90–120 cm high, 30–45 cm wide

'Pink Domino' • Rose-pink flowers with dark eye in summer • 1–1.2 m high, 30–45 cm wide

Verbascum nigrum
Spiked, yellow flowers in midsummer to fall • 90–100 cm high, 60 cm wide

Verbascum phoeniceum
White, pink or purple flower spikes in late spring • Evergreen foliage • 90–120 cm high, 45 cm wide

'Violetta' • Purple flower spikes in late-spring • Evergreen foliage • 90–120 cm high, 45 cm wide

Verbascum thapsus
Spiked, yellow flowers in summer • Densely woolly stems • 1.2–2 m high, 45 cm wide

V

Veronica

p. 428 📷

Genus Information

Origin: Asia, Europe, Turkey and north temperate regions
Selected Common Names: speedwell, creeping speedwell, spike speedwell
Nomenclature: Possibly named for St. Veronica. The common name "speedwell" (good bye), refers to the fact that the corolla falls off soon after flowers are picked.
Notes: A genus of some 250 species of annuals and perennials.

General Features

Height: 1–100 cm high
Spread: 5–60 cm wide
Habit: upright, clump-forming or creeping, mat-forming groundcover perennial
Flowers: delicate, mostly blue to purple shades, sometimes pink or white shades; spring to late summer; deadhead to extend blooming season
Foliage: mid-green to grey; (some) woolly, felted
Hardiness: A–D
Warnings: prone to aphids; not prone to disease
Expert Advice: Creeping, mat-forming veronicas make excellent groundcovers that continue to spread but are easily controlled by cutting back as roots are shallow. Upright veronicas are attractive in low-maintenance landscapes.

Growing Requirements

Light: sun
Soil: moist, organic, well-drained, alkaline soil; upright types tolerate dry, poor soil; creeping types are drought tolerant; woolly foliage types should avoid winter wet
Location: raised beds; rock gardens; scree; mixed borders
Propagation: seed; division; layered root cuttings
Expert Advice: Propagate by seed for species. Division is not difficult. Divide in spring or fall.

Buying Considerations

Professionals

Popularity: upright types are popular, old-fashioned garden standards and fast sellers in bloom; creeping types are gaining popularity and sell well in bloom
Availability: upright types readily available as finished product and bare root; creeping types occasionally available from specialty growers
Size to Sell: sells best in smaller sizes (when blooming) as it matures fast
On the Shelf: rapidly overgrows pot
Shrinkage: low; requires little maintenance

Collectors

Popularity: not generally of interest to collectors

On the Market

Veronica
'Blue Charm' • Spiked, lavender-blue flowers in summer • 75–90 cm high, 30–45 cm wide
'Evita' • Spiked, pink flowers in summer • 60–75 cm high, 30–45 cm wide
'Giles van Hees' • Spiked, rose-red flowers in summer • 15–20 cm high, 30–45 cm wide
'Goodness Grows' • Spiked, dark-blue flowers in summer • 25–30 cm high, 30–45 cm wide
'New Century' • Spiked, blue flowers • Deep-green foliage • 8 cm high, 30 cm wide
'Pink Damask' • Spiked, pink flowers in summer • 25–40 cm high, 30–40 cm wide
'Sunny Border Blue' • Spiked, violet-blue flowers in summer • 45–50 cm high, 30–45 cm wide
'Temptation' • Spiked, purple-rose flowers in early summer • 1 m high, 45–60 cm wide
'Waterperry Blue' • Large, sky-blue flowers in late spring to early summer • Shiny, green foliage • 10–15 cm high, 20–30 cm wide

Veronica allionii
Deep-blue flowers in summer • 5–15 cm high, 30–45 cm wide

Veronica alpina
'Alba' • White flowers in late spring to early summer • 5–15 cm high, 30–45 cm wide

Veronica aphylla
Deep-blue flowers with pink veins in late summer • 3–6 cm high, 20 cm wide

Veronica armena
Bright-blue flowers in summer • 5–15 cm high, 30 cm wide
'Rosea' • Rose flowers in summer • 5–15 cm high, 30 cm wide

Veronica austriaca ssp. *teucrium*
Spiked, deep-blue flowers in summer • 45–90 cm high, 45–60 cm wide

V

'Crater Lake Blue' • Spiked, gentian-blue flowers in summer • 25–30 cm high, 45–60 cm wide

'Royal Blue' • Spiked, deep-blue flowers in summer • 20–45 cm high, 30–45 cm wide

'Violet Surprise' • Deep-violet flowers in summer • 45–60 cm high, 30–45 cm wide

Veronica bellidioides
Dainty, spiked, blue flowers in summer • 5–20 cm high, 15–30 cm wide

Veronica bombycina
Ice-blue flowers in summer • White-felted foliage • 2–6 cm high, 5–15 cm wide

Veronica bombycina ssp. *bolkardaghensis*
Deep-blue flowers in summer • White-felted foliage • 2–6 cm high, 5–15 cm wide

Veronica caespitosa
Star-like, blue to violet flowers in summer • 5–7.5 cm high, 15–30 cm wide

'V.O.' • Star-like, blue flowers in early spring • 5–7.5 cm high, 15–30 cm wide

Veronica chamaedrys
'Miffy Brute' (Variegata) • Clear-blue flowers with white eye in late spring to summer • Yellow-variegated foliage • 10–20 cm high, 30–40+ cm wide

Veronica cinerea
Blue flowers with white eye in summer • Velvet, grey foliage • 6–20 cm high, 20–40 cm wide

Veronica corymbosa
Violet-blue flowers in early summer • 15–20 cm high, 20–25 cm wide

Veronica cuneifolia var. *cuneifolia*
Violet-blue flowers in summer • 7–8 cm high, 15–40 cm wide

Veronica cuneifolia ssp. *issaurica*
Blue or purple flowers in summer • 10–15 cm high, 20–40 cm wide

Veronica dichrus
(syn. *V. cuneifolia* var. *pilosa*)
Blue or purple flowers in summer • 7–10 cm high, 20–40 cm wide

Veronica filiformis
Pale lilac-blue flowers in late spring to early summer • 2–5 cm high, 45–60 cm wide

Veronica flexuosa
'Nana' • Rich-blue flowers in late spring to early summer • Shiny, green foliage • 5–10 cm high, 30–45 cm wide

Veronica fruticans (syn. *V. saxatilis*)
Deep-blue flowers with red eye in summer to fall • 5–15 cm high, 20 cm wide

Veronica fruticulosa
Pink flowers in summer • 5–15 cm high, 20 cm wide

Veronica gentianoides
Spiked, pale-violet flowers in early summer • 30–50 cm high, 45 cm wide

'Variegata' • Ice-blue flowers in early summer • Shiny, white-variegated foliage • 30–45 cm high, 45 cm wide

Veronica liwanensis
Sky-blue flowers in late spring to early summer • 3–10 cm high, 45 cm wide

Veronica longifolia
(syn. *Veronicastrum virginicum*)
'Blauriesin' (Foerster's Blue, Blue Giantess) • Spiked, blue flowers in summer • Lance-shaped foliage • 40–75 cm high, 30–45 cm wide

'Lilac Fantasy' • Spiked, lilac-blue flowers in summer • Lance-shaped foliage • 40–55 cm high, 30–45 cm wide

'Lila Karina' • Spiked, lavender-blue flowers in summer • 45–60 cm high, 30 cm wide

Veronica macrostachya
Azure-blue flowers in summer • 15–30 cm high, 10 cm wide

Veronica minuta var. *minuta*
Blue flowers in summer • 2 cm high, 15 cm wide

Veronica multifida
Blue flowers in early summer • 10–30 cm high, 20–30 cm wide

Veronica oltensis
Azure-blue flowers in late spring to summer • 5–8 cm high, 15–20 cm wide

Veronica onoei
Blue flowers in summer • Shiny, green foliage • 2 cm high, 60 cm wide

Veronica orientalis ssp. *orientalis*
Light-blue flowers in spring • 5–10 cm high, 30–45 cm wide

Veronica pectinata
Deep-blue flowers in spring to early summer • Toothed, comb-like, hairy foliage • 8–15 cm high, 25–30 cm wide

'Rosea' • Rose-pink flowers in spring to early summer • Evergreen foliage • 10 cm high, 25–30 cm wide

Veronica peduncularis
'Georgia Blue' • Deep-blue flowers with white eye in late spring to early summer • Bronze-tinged foliage • 10–15 cm high, 45–60 cm wide

V

Veronica petraea
Lilac-blue or pink flowers in late spring •
Purple foliage • 5–10 cm high, 25–30 cm
wide
'Madam Mercier' • Blue flowers in late
spring • 10 cm high, 25 cm wide
Veronica ponae
Blue flowers in late spring • 4–5 cm high,
20–30 cm wide
Veronica prostrata
Spiked, blue flowers in late spring to early
summer • 15–25 cm high, 30–45 cm wide
'Aztec Gold' • Spiked, lavender-blue flowers
in late spring to early summer • Gold
foliage • 8–15 cm high, 30–45 cm wide
'Blue Ice' • Spiked, blue flowers in late
spring to early summer • 10–15 cm high,
30–45 cm wide
'Buttercup' • Bavarian-blue flowers in late
spring to early summer • Brilliant gold
foliage • 10–15 cm high, 30–45 cm wide
'Dick's Wine' • Spiked, wine-red flowers in
late spring to early summer • 5–10 cm
high, 30–45 cm wide
'Heavenly Blue' • Spiked, gentian-blue
flowers in late spring to early summer •
8–10 cm high, 30–45 cm wide
'Mrs. Holt' • Spiked, pale-pink flowers in
late spring to early summer • 10–15 cm
high, 30–45 cm wide
'Trehane' • Spiked, deep-blue flowers in late
spring to early summer • Lime-green
foliage • 10–20 cm high, 30–45 cm wide
Veronica pseudoscinera
Deep-blue flowers in late spring • 5 cm
high, 10–20 cm wide
Veronica repens
Pale-blue flowers in late spring to early
summer • Shiny, green foliage • 5–10 cm
high, 20–30+ cm wide
'Alba' • White flowers in late spring to early
summer • 5 cm high, 20–30 cm wide
'Sunshine' • Spiked, bluish-purple flowers in
late spring to early summer • Gold foliage
• 2 cm high, 20–30 cm wide
Veronica saturejoides
Bright-blue flowers with reddish eye in early
summer • 5–10 cm high, 20–30 cm wide
Veronica schmidtiana
Light purple-blue flowers with dark veins in
summer • 10–25 cm high, 10–25 cm wide
'Nana' • Dark-blue flowers with white
splashes in summer • 5–10 cm high,
10–25 cm wide

Veronica schmidtiana f. lineariloba
Purple-blue flowers in summer
• 10–25 cm high, 10–25 cm wide
Veronica spicata
Blue, white or rose flowers in summer
• 30–60 cm high, 45 cm wide
'Barcarolle' • Spiked, rose flowers in
summer • 20–30 cm high, 30–40 cm wide
'Blaufuchs' (Blue Fox) • Spiked, lavender-
blue flowers in summer • 30–45 cm high,
30 cm wide
'Erika' • Spiked, pink flowers in summer •
25–30 cm high, 30–40 cm wide
'Glory' (Royal Candles) • Violet-blue
flowers in summer • 40–45 cm high,
45 cm wide
'Heidekind' • Spiked, rose-pink flowers in
summer • Silver-grey leaves • 20–30 cm
high, 30–40 cm wide
'Icicle' (White Icicle) • Spiked, white flowers
in summer • 45–60 cm high, 45–60 cm
wide
'Nana Blauteppich' (Dwarf Blue) •
Spiked, indigo-blue flowers in summer
• 10–20 cm high, 15–30 cm wide
'Noah Williams' • Spiked, white flowers in
summer • Lance-shaped, variegated
foliage • 40–60 cm high, 45 cm wide
'Romiley Purple' • Spiked, dark-violet
flowers in summer • 45–60 cm high,
45 cm wide
'Rotfuchs' (Red Fox) • Spiked, rose-red
flowers in summer • 30–45 cm high,
30 cm wide
'Sweet Sue' • Spiked, rich-pink flowers in
summer • 45–60 cm high, 40–45 cm wide
Veronica spicata ssp. **incana**
Spiked, purple-blue flowers in summer •
Silvery-grey, felted foliage • 30 cm high,
30 cm wide
Veronica surculosa
Deep-blue flowers with white edges in early
summer • 1–4 cm high, 30 cm wide
Siskiyou form • Spiked, white flowers with
blue eye in spring • Silver-grey foliage •
3–5 cm high, 30–45 cm wide
Veronica tauricola
Bright-blue flowers with white eye in
summer • Silvery-green foliage • 5–20 cm
high, 30–45 cm wide
Veronica thessalica
Cup-shaped, purple-blue flowers in summer
• 15 cm high, 30 cm wide

V

Veronica thymoides
Deep-blue to purple-blue flowers in early summer • Grey-green foliage • 2 cm high, 10–20 cm wide

Veronica thymoides ssp. *pseudocinerea*
Deep-blue flowers in early summer • Silver-grey foliage • 1–2 cm high, 15–20 cm wide

Veronica wormskjoldii
Blue to light-purple flowers in summer • 10–30 cm high, 30–45 cm wide

'Mann's Variety' • Intense blue flowers in summer • 8–10 cm high, 30–45 cm wide

Veronicastrum p. 428

Genus Information
Origin: North America and Siberia
Selected Common Names: Culver's root
Nomenclature: From *Veronica* and the Latin suffix *aster*, referring to its incomplete resemblance to *Veronica*.
Notes: A genus of only 2 species.

General Features
Height: 60–180 cm high
Spread: 45 cm wide
Habit: upright, clump-forming perennial
Flowers: *Veronica*-like spikes; summer
Foliage: dark-green; toothed
Hardiness: B–C
Warnings: not prone to insects or disease
Expert Advice: A much underused perennial that is attractive and quickly forms nice clumps.

Growing Requirements
Light: sun to p.m. sun
Soil: fertile, moist, organic soil; tolerates poor, dry soil; drought tolerant
Location: mixed borders
Propagation: seed; division

Buying Considerations

Professionals
Popularity: relatively unknown
Availability: generally available as bare root
Size to Sell: sells best in smaller sizes (when blooming) as it matures fast
On the Shelf: high ornamental appeal; keep stock rotated
Shrinkage: low; requires little maintenance

Collectors
Popularity: not generally of interest to collectors

Gardeners
Ease of Growth: very easy to grow
Start with: one small plant for feature plant

What to Try First ...
Veronicastrum virginicum, Veronicastrum virginicum 'Fascination', *Veronicastrum virginicum* 'Temptation'

On the Market

Veronicastrum virginicum
Spiked, white to pink or bluish-purple flowers in summer • 60–180 cm high, 45 cm wide

'Apollo' • Spiked, red-purple flowers in summer • Dark-green foliage • 90 cm high, 45 cm wide

'Fascination' • Spiked, light-pink flowers in summer • Reddish foliage • 1 m high, 45 cm wide

'Temptation' • Spiked, purple-rose flowers in early summer • 60–90 cm high, 45 cm wide

Veronicastrum virginicum var. *incarnatum* (syn. *V. virginicum* 'Roseum')
Spiked, soft-pink flowers in summer • 90–150 cm high, 45 cm wide

Vinca p. 428

Genus Information
Origin: Europe, North Africa and central Asia
Selected Common Names: creeping myrtle, periwinkle
Nomenclature: From the Latin *vinca, pervinca* or *vinciobind* (wind about), referring to its use in making wreaths, which was also the origin of the Middle English per wynke or periwinckle.
Notes: A genus of some 7 species.

General Features
Height: 5–20 cm high
Spread: 60+ cm wide
Habit: spreading groundcover perennial
Flowers: late spring to fall
Foliage: glossy; (most) evergreen; prone to desiccation
Hardiness: C
Warnings: not prone to insects or disease; may be invasive in warmer climates (contain to prevent spread); flowers and foliage are toxic
Expert Advice: Takes 2–3 years to form good coverage in northern gardens and may dessicate in spring winds. Seldom bears fruit in cultivation.

Growing Requirements
Light: sun to p.m. sun
Soil: moist soil; tolerant of wide range of soils (except dry)

V

Location: tolerant of wide range of locations, understory plantings, borders, woodland gardens, cascading over walls
Propagation: division, cuttings
Expert Advice: Take semi-ripe cuttings in spring.

Buying Considerations

Professionals
Popularity: popular, glossy foliage plant
Availability: readily available as finished product
Size to Sell: sells best in smaller sizes (when blooming) as it matures fast
On the Shelf: high ornamental appeal; keep stock rotated; rapidly overgrows pot
Shrinkage: low; requires little maintenance

Collectors
Popularity: not generally of interest to collectors

Gardeners
Ease of Growth: very easy to grow
Start with: several for mass plantings

What to Try First ...
Vinca minor, *Vinca minor* 'Atropurpurea', *Vinca minor* 'Gertrude Jekyll', *Vinca minor* 'La Grave', *Vinca minor* 'Sterling Silver'

On the Market

Vinca minor
Purple, blue or white flowers in late spring to fall • 10–20 cm high, 60+ cm wide

'Atropurpurea' (Purpurea) • Red-purple flowers in late spring to fall • 5–10 cm high, 60+ cm wide

'Azurea Flore Pleno' (Caerulea Plena) • Double, bright-blue flowers in late spring to fall • 15 cm high, 60+ cm wide

'Gertrude Jekyll' • White flowers in late spring to fall • Dark-green foliage • 10–20 cm high, 60 cm+ wide

'Illumination' • Lilac-blue flowers in late spring to fall • Bright-yellow foliage with dark-green edge • 8–15 cm high, 60+ cm wide

'La Grave' (Bowles' Blue) • Violet-blue flowers in late spring to fall • 5–10 cm high, 60+ cm wide

'Sterling Silver' • Blue flowers in late spring to fall • 10 cm high, 60+ cm wide

Vinca minor f. *alba*
White flowers in late spring to fall • Dark-green foliage • 10–20 cm high, 60+ cm wide

Viola
p. 428

Genus Information

Origin: north temperate and Andes regions
Selected Common Names: violet, viola
Nomenclature: Name used by Virgil and Pliny. A variation of the Greek *ion* and applied like that name to 3 groups of plants.
Other Uses: *Violas* have been cultivated for a long time. It has been recorded that the Greeks cultivated and sold violas for medicinal purposes back in 400BC. During the Victorian era, the viola became a favourite flower and was associated with romance. Today violas are still favoured and can be used in many ways, including adding them to your salad or as an edible garnish. Valued for fragrance, perfume and confectionary.
Notes: A genus of some 500 species of annuals, perennials and subshrubs.

General Features
Height: 2–30 cm high
Spread: 5–60 cm wide
Habit: clump-forming annual, biennial or perennial
Flowers: spring to summer
Foliage: evergreen, semi-evergreen or deciduous
Hardiness: A–D
Warnings: prone to powdery mildew and aphids; may be invasive (deadhead to prevent unwanted self-seeding)
Expert Advice: Situate carefully in a wild or woodland garden where they can naturalize freely.

Growing Requirements
Light: sun to p.m. sun
Soil: cool, gritty, moist, organic, well-drained soil; tolerant of wide range of soils; early dormancy may occur in dry soils
Location: front of mixed borders; rock gardens; scree; woodland gardens
Propagation: seed (self-sows readily); division; stem cuttings
Expert Advice: Seeds of alpine types often need stratification.

Buying Considerations

Professionals
Popularity: gaining popularity
Availability: generally available as finished product
Size to Sell: sells best in smaller sizes (when blooming) as it matures fast
On the Shelf: (some) rapidly overgrows pot
Shrinkage: low; requires little maintenance

Collectors
Popularity: not generally of interest to collectors

V

On the Market

Viola

Alaskan mix • Mauve flowers in spring to
summer • 10–15 cm high, 15–20 cm wide

'Black Magic' • Black-purple flowers in
spring to fall • 15 cm high, 20–30 cm wide

'Bowles' Black' • Black-purple flowers in
spring to fall • 15 cm high, 20–30 cm wide

'Dancing Geisha' • Fragrant, white flowers
in spring • Silvery, swirled, cut foliage •
15 cm high, 20 cm wide

'Duchesse de Parme' (Parma d'Ordinaire) •
Fragrant, double, lavender flowers in
spring • 7 cm high, 15 cm wide

'Eco Hybrid Silver Heart' • Violet flowers
in spring • Lobed foliage • 10–15 cm high,
15–25 cm wide

'Etain' • Lemon-yellow flowers with a
lavender edge in spring to summer •
20–25 cm high, 20–25 cm wide

'Mars' • Fragrant, purple flowers in spring •
Dark-green foliage with bright-purple
veins • 15–20 cm high, 20 cm wide

'Purple Showers' • Deep-purple flowers
in spring to early summer • 15 cm high,
45 cm wide

'Rebecca' • Fragrant, cream flowers with
violet spots in spring to fall • 20–25 cm
high, 20–30 cm wide

'Sylvia Hart' • Mauve flowers in spring •
Silvery foliage • 10–15 cm high, 15–20 cm
wide

Viola adunca

Fragrant, violet-lavender flowers with white
eye in spring • 8–10 cm high, 10–20 cm
wide

'Alba' • White flowers in spring • 5–8 cm
high, 10–15 cm wide

Viola adunca ssp. *bellidifolia*

Purple flowers in spring to late summer •
5 cm high, 5 cm wide

Viola aetolica

Yellow flowers in late spring to early
summer • Evergreen • 8–15 cm high,
15–30 cm wide

Viola altaica

Yellow flowers (sometimes purple) in late
spring to summer • 5–15 cm high, 15 cm
wide

Viola blanda

Fragrant, white flowers with purple veins
in spring • Evergreen • 2–10 cm high,
10–15 cm wide

Viola calcarata

Blue or yellow flowers in spring to summer
• 5–10 cm high, 25–30 cm wide

Viola canadensis

Fragrant, white flowers in spring to summer
• Evergreen • 20–30 cm high, 15–20 cm
wide

Viola corsica

Purple flowers in spring • 10–20 cm high,
10–20 cm wide

Viola dissecta

Fragrant, pale-rose flowers in spring •
Evergreen, dissected, dark-green foliage •
10 cm high, 10–15 cm wide

'Eco Rose' • Fragrant, pink flowers in spring
• Evergreen • 10–15 cm high, 10–15 cm
wide

Viola flettii

Violet-pink flowers with yellow eye in
summer • Kidney-shaped foliage • 10–15
cm high, 15–20 cm wide

Viola glabella

Yellow flowers with purple veins in late
spring • 5–30 cm high, 15–30 cm wide

Viola grisebachiana

Yellow or blue flowers in spring • 5–10 cm
high, 60 cm wide

Viola grypoceras var. *exilis* (syn. *V. koreana*)

White flowers in spring • Marbled foliage •
15–20 cm high, 15–20 cm wide

Viola hederacea

Violet flowers with white tips in summer •
5–10 cm high, 30 cm wide

'Baby Blue Eyes' • Blue-purple flowers in
early spring to early summer • 5–10 cm
high, 20–30 cm wide

Viola jooi

Fragrant, mauve flowers in spring to
summer • 7–10 cm high, 15–30 cm wide

Viola keiskei

Violet-blue flowers in spring • 5 cm high,
10–15 cm wide

V

Viola labradorica
Violet flowers in spring • 8–10 cm high,
30–45+ cm wide

Viola langsdorfii
Violet-blue or white flowers in spring •
15–20 cm high, 20–30 cm wide

Viola lutea
'Splendens' • Yellow, purple or bicoloured
flowers in spring to summer • 2–8 cm
high, 15 cm wide

Viola nephrophylla
Fragrant, violet-blue flowers with purple
veins in spring • Organic, boggy soil •
6–10 cm high, 15–20 cm wide

Viola odorata
'Royal Robe' • Fragrant, purple-violet
flowers in spring • 15–20 cm high, 30 cm
wide

'White Czar' • Fragrant, white, purple-
streaked flowers in late spring • 8–15 cm
high, 10–30 cm wide

Viola palmata
'Eco Harlequin' • Violet-purple flowers with
white spots in early spring • 10–15 cm
high, 15–30 cm wide

Viola pedata
Pale-violet flowers in spring to summer •
10–15 cm high, 10–15 cm wide

'Bicolor' • Dark-and-light-purple,
bicoloured flowers in spring • Well-
drained, organic, moist, acidic, gritty soil •
10–15 cm high, 10–15 cm wide

Viola pedatifida
Pea-like, violet flowers in spring to summer
• 10–15 cm high, 15–20 cm wide

'Alba' • Pea-like, white flowers with blue
veins in spring to summer • 8–10 cm high,
10–15 cm wide

Viola pubescens
Yellow flowers with purple veins in spring •
15–25 cm high, 15–40 cm wide

Viola pyrenaica
Blue flowers in spring • 10–15 cm high,
15–20 cm wide

Viola riviniana (syn. V. labradorica)
Violet flowers in spring • 8–10 cm high,
30–45+ cm wide

Viola sororia
Blue or white, purple-veined flowers in early
summer • 8–10 cm high, 15–20 cm wide

'Freckles' • White flowers flecked with blue
in spring to summer • 8–10 cm high, 15–
20 cm wide

Viola variegata
Light-purple flowers in spring • Variegated,
cyclamen-like foliage • 2–10 cm high, 10–20
cm wide

**Viola variegata var. nipponica (syn. V.
koreana)**
Soft-purple flowers in early spring • Silvery,
cyclamen-like foliage • 5–10 cm high, 10–
cm wide

Viola verecunda var. yakusimana
Tiny, white flowers with purple veins in
spring • 2 cm high, 5 cm wide

Vitaliana
p. 428

Genus Information
Origin: central and southern Europe
Selected Common Names: golden primrose
Nomenclature: Named for Donati Vitaliano,
1717–1762, a professor of botany at Turin, Italy.
Notes: A genus of only 1 species. Member of the
Primulacea family. Previously called *Androsace*
and *Douglasia*.

General Features
Height: 2–5 cm high
Spread: 10–20 cm wide
Habit: cushion- to mat-forming groundcover
perennial
Flowers: large, heavy, bright-yellow; spring
Foliage: evergreen
Hardiness: C
Warnings: not prone to insects or disease
Expert Advice: This perennial makes a great
groundcover that blooms so heavily that the
foliage is completely hidden. Wonderful in the
rock or alpine garden.

Growing Requirements
Light: sun
Soil: gritty, fertile, moist, sharply drained, lean
soil
Location: rock gardens; scree
Propagation: seed; root offsets

Buying Considerations
Professionals
Popularity: relatively unknown; fast seller in
bloom
Availability: occasionally available from
specialty growers
Size to Sell: sells best in mature sizes (when
blooming) as it matures slowly
On the Shelf: high ornamental appeal
Shrinkage: low; requires little maintenance
Collectors
Popularity: of interest to collectors—unique,
rare

V

Gardeners

What to Try First ...

Vitaliana primuliflora, Vitaliana primuliflora ssp. *cinerea, Vitaliana primuliflora* ssp. *praetutiana*

On the Market

Vitaliana primuliflora
(syn. *Douglasia vitaliana***)**
  Bright-yellow flowers in spring • Evergreen • 2–5 cm high, 20 cm wide

Vitaliana primuliflora ssp. *cinerea*
  Bright-yellow flowers in spring • Evergreen • 2–5 cm high, 10–15 cm wide

Vitaliana primuliflora ssp. *praetutiana*
  Bright-yellow flowers in spring • Grey-green, evergreen foliage • 2–5 cm high, 15+ cm wide

V

Waldsteinia

p. 428 📷

Genus Information

Origin: northern temperate regions
Selected Common Names: barren strawberry
Nomenclature: Named for Count Franz
Waldstein von Wartenburg (1759–1823),
an Austrian botanist.

General Features

Height: 15 cm high
Spread: 45–60 cm wide
Habit: creeping, stoloniferous or rhizomatous
perennial
Flowers: late spring to early summer
Foliage: semi-evergreen
Hardiness: C
Warnings: prone to powdery mildew and aphids;
may be invasive (contain to prevent spread)

Growing Requirements

Light: sun
Soil: dry, fertile soil; tolerates poor, dry soil
Location: sunny, hot, dry areas; front of mixed
borders; rock gardens; woodland gardens
Propagation: seed; runners
Expert Advice: Divide frequently to keep
vigorous.

Buying Considerations

Professionals

Popularity: relatively unknown
Availability: occasionally available
as finished product
Size to Sell: sells best in smaller sizes
(when blooming) as it matures fast
On the Shelf: keep stock rotated; rapidly
overgrows pot
Shrinkage: low; requires little maintenance

Collectors

Popularity: not generally of interest to
collectors

Gardeners

Ease of Growth: very easy to grow
Start with: one small plant for feature plant,
several for mass plantings

What to Try First ...

Waldsteinia ternata

On the Market

Waldsteinia ternata
Yellow flowers in late spring to early
summer • 15 cm high, 45–60 cm wide

Yucca

p. 428

Genus Information

Origin: North America, Central America and the West Indies

Selected Common Names: Adam's needle, desert candle, soapweed, soapwell, Spanish bayonet, yucca

Nomenclature: From the native name for *Manihot esculenta*. Named by Gerard, who mistook the genus for *Manihot*.

Notes: A genus of some 40 species.

General Features

Height: 30–75 cm high

Spread: 30–150 cm wide

Habit: upright, clump-forming perennial

Flowers: scented

Foliage: stiff, sword-like; evergreen; grown mainly for the foliage and its bold form

Hardiness: C–D

Warnings: not prone to insects or disease; do not cut back; foliage is sharp—handle carefully

Expert Advice: *Yuccas* will flower once they become established, which may take up to 7 years. Once mature they may not flower each year. Very striking plants.

Growing Requirements

Light: sun

Soil: well-drained, dry, sandy to gritty soil

Location: sheltered, sunny, hot, dry areas; foliage may burn in windy locations; mixed borders; raised beds; xeriscaping; Mediterranean gardens

Propagation: seed; root cuttings

Expert Advice: Pollinated by night moths. May need hand pollination to set seed. Shelter from drying winter winds.

Buying Considerations

Professionals

Popularity: popular foliage plant

Availability: generally available as finished product

Size to Sell: sells best in mature sizes as it matures slowly

On the Shelf: high ornamental appeal

Shrinkage: low; requires little maintenance

Collectors

Popularity: of interest to collectors; *Y. harrimaniae* is unique, rare

Gardeners

Ease of Growth: generally easy to grow but needs close attention to growing conditions

Start with: one mature plant for feature plant

What to Try First ...

Yucca angustissima, Yucca filamentosa, Yucca glauca, Yucca harrimaniae

On the Market

Yucca angustissima
Pale-green, purple-tinged flowers in summer • 40 cm high, 45 cm wide

Yucca baccata
Cream flowers in summer • Stiff, thick, dagger-like foliage • 60–75 cm high, 60–90 cm wide

Yucca filamentosa
White, yellow-tinged flowers in summer • Dark-green foliage edged with curly, white thread • 60–75 cm high, 60–100 cm wide

'Bright Edge' • White flowers in summer • Sword-like foliage edged with gold • 60 cm high, 60–100 cm wide

'Colour Guard' • White flowers in summer • Sword-like foliage with white and cream centre • 60–75 cm high, 60–100 cm wide

Yucca flaccida (syn. Y. filifera)
'Golden Sword' • White flowers in summer • Sword-like foliage with yellow centre • 55–75 cm high, 1–1.5 m wide

Yucca glauca
Waxy, white flowers in late summer • Sword-like foliage • 30–70 cm high, 60 cm wide

Yucca harrimaniae
White flowers in summer • Narrow leaves • 30–45 cm high, 30 cm wide

Y

Glossary

aff.: affinity to

f.: forma (form)

sp.: species

ssp.: subspecies

syn.: synonym

x: hybrid (cross)

var.: variety

A

alpine type: a plant that is usually, but not always, native to a mountainous region; typically thrives in rock gardens

anther: the pollen-bearing part of a flower, usually a small, yellow, round structure at the end of a thin filament

awn: a bristle-shaped appendage, typically found on a grass seed or grain

B

bare root: describes a plant that is sold in a dormant state with all the soil removed from the roots

basal cutting: a cutting taken from the base of a plant or stem

basal rosette: a tight arrangement of leaves that radiate out from the base of the stem

bee: a "furry" area on the inner surface of the lower petals of some tubular or trumpet-shaped flowers (as in *Delphinium*)

Botrytis: a fungus that causes blight or grey mould infections in plants

bracteole: a secondary bract, often found on a flower stalk

bract: a modified leaf found at the base of many flowers; usually green and usually smaller than the other leaves, but some bracts are large and showy, imitating a petal (as in *Poinsettia*)

bulb: an underground stem that functions as a food-storage organ (as in an onion); a plant that produces bulbs is perennial within its native zone

bulbil: a small bulb that forms on the stem of a plant (as in *Lilium*)

bulblet: a small bulb that forms at the base of a mature bulb (as in *Hyacinthus*)

bulbous: having the shape or character of a bulb

C

calyx: the part of a flower that is composed of the sepals; usually green, it occurs immediately below the petals

capitulum (pl. capitula): a dense, short, compact cluster of stalkless flowers (as in *Senecio*)

cilia: short, hair-like structures on foliage and flowers

CITES: Convention on International Trade in Endangered Species of Wild Flora and Fauna; an international agreement between governments that aims to ensure that international trade in specimens of wild animals and plants does not threaten their survival

clump-forming: a plant that reproduces vegetatively to form smaller clumps or crowns around the parent plant

colony forming: a plant that reproduces vegetatively to form an expanding assemblage of aboveground shoots that look like separate plants but are interconnected by a shared network of roots or rhizomes

connate: joined; especially used to describe structures that are joined from the start

corolla: the part of a flower composed of petals; usually the most conspicuous part of a flower

crown: the point on a plant where the root and stem meet; usually at the surface of the soil

cultivar: a contraction of the phrase "cultivated variety"; many varieties of plants, especially those used as food crops and in landscaping, were deliberately bred by a gardener, horticulturist or scientist

D

deciduous: describes a tree or shrub that loses its leaves once a year

deadhead: the process of removing dead or spent flowers to encourage more flowering, to improve the appearance of the plant and to prevent seed production; many perennials will continue to bloom throughout the growing season if they are deadheaded

deeply lobed: describes a leaf that has deep indentations along its edge

desiccate: to dry up

dioecious: describes a species in which the male and female flowers occur on separate plants

dormancy: a period when a plant rests and its growth slows or ceases

E

evergreen: describes a plant that keeps its leaves all year

F

farina: a powdery, mealy substance secreted by leaf glands

fleshy: succulent or juicy; typically used to describe leaves

floriferous: flower-bearing; blooming profusely

flower: the reproductive structure of a plant; it is usually composed of both male and female parts, and the petals are usually the most conspicuous element

foliage plant: a plant that is grown for the interesting colour or arrangement of its leaves, rather than its flowers

fringed: describes a leaf that has slender, hair-like structures along its edge

G

gibbous: swollen on one side

H

hairy: covered with short, hair-like structures

herbaceous: describes a plant with little or no woody tissue; usually dies back to the ground each year during winter

hose-in-hose: a flower that appears to have a double corolla, one within the other (as in some *Primula*)

hybrid: a crossbreed of two different species or varieties of plants; usually has some characteristics of each parent

I

in situ: in place

indusium: a thin, scale-like covering over an immature sorus

M

mixed border: a border planted with some combination of perennials, shrubs, ornamental grasses, annuals and bulbs

monocarpic: describes a plant that dies after flowering just once

monoecious: describes a plant in which the male and female reproduction structures occur in different flowers on the same plant

N

nodding: drooping

nutlet: a small nut

O

offset: a short side shoot arising from the base of a plant; also a small bulb arising from the base of the mother bulb.

ovate: describes a leaf that is egg-shaped, where the stem attaches to the broader end

P

palmate: describes a leaf that is divided into leaflets that radiate from a single point, like fingers radiating from the palm of a hand

palmately lobed: describes a leaf that is lobed from a single point, such that the lobes radiate like the fingers of a hand

pappus: a modified calyx, composed of scales, bristles or feather-like hairs

pedicel: the individual stalk to which a single flower is attached

peduncle: the primary stalk in a flower cluster, to which each pedicel attaches

pendant: hanging

petiole: the stalk that attaches a leaf to a stem

plume: a feather-like arrangement of flowers on a plant

R

raceme: a simple arrangement of flowers, each on its own stalk, along a central axis

rachis: the primary stem-like structure in a compound leaf to which the leaflets attach; also, the main stem of an inflorescence

recurved: curved downward or backward

reflexed: abruptly bent or turned downward

rhizomatous: having rhizomes

rhizome: a root-like, modified stem that grows horizontally under the soil (as in *Iris*); new roots, stems, leaves or flowers can grow from points along the rhizome

rock garden (or rockery): a usually dry and well-drained garden area that features extensive use of rocks or stones of different sizes along with plants native to rocky or alpine environments

rosette-forming: a small group of leaves that grow in a circular, overlapping arrangement

S

saccate: shaped liked a sac

scaling: a method of propagation in which a single scale is taken from a plant bulb to start a new bulb

semi-evergreen: trees or plants that keep some green foliage into winter

semi-ripe cuttings: cuttings taken in midsummer to fall to propagate woody plants

sepal: a leaf that is part of the calyx, which occurs at the base of the flower and functions as protection for the petals during the bud stage

sessile: a leaf or flower that attaches directly to a stem without a stalk

shrublet: a dwarf woody plant

sorus (pl. sori): a cluster of sporangia borne of the underside of a fern frond

spathe: a large bract or pair of bracts surrounding a flower cluster

spatulate: shaped like a spoon: round with a narrow base

species: a group of related plants sharing similar features and capable of interbreeding

species plant: a plant that is unaltered from its natural state and has not been cultivated

spike: a simple type of flower cluster with stalkless flowers along a central axis

spikelet: a small or secondary spike, typically part of the flower cluster of a grass

sporangium (pl. sporangia): a spore case; the structure in which spores are produced

spurred: describes a flower with tubular projections from the corolla or calyx

stamen: the male reproductive parts of a flower, consisting of the anther and its stalk-like filament

staminode: a sterile stamen

stolon: a horizontally growing stem that runs along the surface of the ground and produces roots and shoots at its nodes

stoloniferous: having stolons

stratification: a practice of stimulating seeds to germinate by placing alternate layers of moist growing medium and seed to simulate the conditions the seed "expects" from its native environment

symbiotic: describes an interaction between two organisms living together in a more or less intimate association, which may or may not be to their mutual benefit

T

tap root: the main root of a plant, typically growing straight down into the soil

terrestrial: growing on land

toothed: describes a leaf with its edge divided into small, tooth-like segments

tuber: an underground stem that is modified for food storage

tuberous: having the characteristics of or resembling a tuber

turkscap: a flower with strongly recurved petals

X

xeriscape: landscaping with drought-tolerant plants to reduce or eliminate the need for watering during dry conditions

The Genus Picture Key

There are over 370 genera in this book—each one potentially contains hundreds of different species and varieties. It was a daunting task to find and print an image of each of the plants listed (for some of the genera it was simply impossible to find an adequate picture) and would have resulted in an unwieldy volume. We've done our best to supply representative pictures of each genus that give an idea of the general look of the plant or flower. For some perennials, this will potentially help aid in identification while for others, taking into account the vagaries of nature, it may only be misleading.

Use this key as a helpful and colorful reference to the genus, but always remember there is a great deal of variation in flower, form and habit.

Acaena, p. 2 *Acantholimon*, p. 2 *Achillea*, p. 3 *Acinos*, p. 5

Aconitum, p. 5 *Acorus*, p. 6 *Actaea*, Baneberry, p. 7 *Actaea*, Bugbane, Snakeroot, p. 7

Adenophora, p. 8

Adiantum, p. 9

Adonis, p. 9

Aegopodium, p. 10

Aethionema, p. 11

Agastache, p. 12

Ajuga, p. 12

Alcea, p. 13

Alchemilla, p. 14

Allium, p. 15

Alyssum, p. 16

Ampelopsis, p. 17

Amsonia, p. 17

Anchusa, p. 18

Andropogon, p. 19

Androsace, p. 20

Anemone, Early Spring/Late
Summer Blooming, p. 22

Anemone, Late Summer/
Fall Blooming, p. 23

Anemonella, p. 24

Angelica, p. 24

Antennaria, p. 25

Anthemis, p. 25

Aquilegia, p. 27

Arabis, p. 29

Arctanthemum, p. 30

Arctostaphylos, p. 31

Arenaria, p. 31

Arisaema, p. 32

Aristolochia, p. 34

Armeria, p. 35

Armoracia, p. 35

Arnica, p. 36

Arrhenatherum, p. 36

Artemisia, p. 37

Aruncus, p. 38

Asarum, p. 39

Asclepias, p. 40

Asparagus, p. 40

Asperula, p. 41

Asplenium, p. 42

Aster, Fall Blooming, p. 43

Aster, Spring/Summer Blooming, p. 43

Astilbe, p. 44

Astragalus, p. 46

Astrantia, p. 47

Asyneuma, p. 48

Athyrium, p. 48

Aubrieta, p. 49

Aurinia, p. 50

Azorella, p. 51

Baptisia, p. 52

Bellis, p. 52

Bergenia, p. 53

Blechnum, p. 54

Bolax, p. 55

Boltonia, p. 55

Bromus, p. 57

Bruckenthalia, p. 57

Brunnera, p. 58

Buphthalmum, p. 59

Calamagrostis, p. 60

Callianthemum, p. 60

Callirhoe, p. 61

Calluna, p. 61

Caltha, p. 62

Calypso, p. 63

Calyptridium, p. 64

Calystegia, p. 64

Camassia, p. 65

Campanula, Alpine/ Rockery, p. 65

Campanula, Tall Growing, p. 69

Campanula, Biennial, p. 70

Campsis, p. 71

Carex, p. 72

Carlina, p. 73

Cassiope, p. 73

Castilleja, p. 74

Celastrus, p. 74

Centaurea, p. 75

Centranthus, p. 76

Cerastium, p. 76

Chelone, p. 77

Chrysanthemum, p. 77

Cirsium, p. 79

Claytonia, p. 80

Clematis, Large Flowered Hybrids, p. 80

Clematis, Hardy Herbaceous, p. 83

Clematis, Non-Vining, p. 84

Codonopsis, p. 85

Convallaria, p. 86

Coreopsis, p. 86

Cornus, p. 87

Coronilla, p. 88

Cortusa, p. 88

Corydalis, p. 89

Coryphantha, p. 90

Cotoneaster, p. 91

Cryptogramma, p. 92

Cyananthus, p. 92

Cyclamen, p. 93

Cypripedium, p. 93

Dactylorhiza, p. 96

Darmera, p. 97

Degenia, p. 97

Delosperma, p. 98

Delphinium, p. 98

Dennstaedtia, p. 100

Deschampsia, p. 101

Dianthus,
Alpine/Species, p. 102

Dianthus,
Garden Pinks, p. 104

Dianthus,
Maiden Pinks, p. 106

Dianthus, Sweet William/
Carnations, p. 106

Dicentra, p. 107

Dictamnus, p. 108

Digitalis, p. 109

Disporopsis, p. 110

Dodecatheon, p. 111

Doronicum, p. 112

Draba, p. 113

Dracocephalum, p. 114

Dryas, p. 115

Dryopteris, p. 116

Duchesnea, p. 117

Echinacea, p. 118

Echinocereus, p. 119

Echinops, p. 120

Edraianthus, p. 120

Elymus, p. 121

Epimedium, p. 122

Epipactis, p. 123

Eragrostis, p. 123

Eremurus, p. 124

Erigeron, p. 125

Erinus, p. 126

Eriogonum, p. 127

Eriophyllum, p. 128

Eritrichium, p. 129

Erodium, p. 129

Eryngium, p. 130

Erysimum, p. 131

Erythronium, p. 132

Eupatorium, p. 133

Euphorbia, p. 134

Fallopia, p. 136

Festuca, p. 136

Filipendula, p. 137

Fragaria, p. 138

Gaillardia, p. 140

Galium, p. 141

Gentiana, p. 142

Geranium, p. 145

Geum, p. 149

Gillenia, p. 149

Glaucidium, p. 150

Glechoma, p. 150

Globularia, p. 151

Glyceria, p. 152

Goniolimon, p. 152

Gypsophila, p. 153

Haberlea, p. 155

Hakonechloa, p. 155

Hedera, p. 156

Hedysarum, p. 156

Helenium, p. 157

Helianthemum, p. 158

Helianthus, p. 158

Helictotrichon, p. 159

Heliopsis, p. 160

Helleborus, p. 161

Hemerocallis, p. 162

Hepatica, p. 171

Hernieria, p. 172

Hesperis, p. 172

Heuchera, p. 173

Heucherella, p. 176

Hibiscus, p. 177

Hierochloe, p. 178

Holcus, p. 178

Hosta, p. 179

Houstonia, p. 185

Humulus, p. 186

Hypericum, p. 187

Hypsela, p. 188

Hyssopus, p. 188

Iberis, p. 189

Imperata, p. 189

Inula, p. 191

Iris, Bearded, p. 192

Iris, Species, p. 198

Iris, Water/Siberian, p. 200

Jeffersonia, p. 205

Jovibarba, p. 205

Juncus, p. 207

Junellia, p. 208

Kelseya, p. 209

Kirengeshoma, p. 209

Knautia, p. 210

Koeleria, p. 210

Lamium, p. 211

Lathyrus, p. 212

Lavandula, p. 212

Lavatera, p. 213

Leontopodium, p. 214

Lesquerella, p. 215

Leucanthemopsis, p. 216

Leucanthemum, p. 216

Lewisia, p. 217

Leymus, p. 219

Liatris, p. 219

Ligularia, p. 220

Lilium, Asiatic, L.A. Hybrid, p. 222

Lilium, Martagon, p. 227

Lilium, Oriental, p. 228

Lilium, Species, p. 230

Limonium, p. 232

Linanthus, p. 233

Linaria, p. 233

Linnaea, p. 234

Linum, p. 234

Lobelia, p. 235

Lonicera, p. 236

Lotus, p. 237

Lupinus, p. 237

Lychnis, p. 239

Lysimachia, p. 240

Macleaya, p. 242

Malva, p. 242

Matteuccia, p. 243

Meconopsis, p. 244

Mentha, p. 245

Mertensia, p. 245

Minuartia, p. 246

Miscanthus, p. 247

Molinia, p. 248

Monarda, p. 249

Monardella, p. 250

Myosotis, p. 251

Nepeta, p. 253

Oenothera, p. 254

Omphalodes, p. 255

Onoclea, p. 255

Onopordum, p. 256

Opuntia, p. 257

Orostachys, p. 258

Osmunda, p. 259

Oxalis, p. 260

Oxytropis, p. 260

Pachysandra, p. 262

Paeonia, Hybrid, p. 262

Paeonia, Lactiflora, p. 264

Paeonia, Itoh, p. 268

Paeonia, Species, p. 269

Paeonia, Tree, p. 271

Panicum, p. 272

Papaver, p. 273

Paraquilegia, p. 276

Paronychia, p. 277

Pedicularis, p. 277

Pediocactus, p. 278

Penstemon, Tall/Garden, p. 278

Perovskia, p. 282

Persicaria, p. 282

Petasites, p. 284

Petrocallis, p. 284

Petrocoptis, p. 285

Petrohagia, p. 285

Phacelia, p. 286

Phalaris, p. 286

Phlomis, p. 287

Phlox, Creeping /Moss, p. 287

Phlox, Tall Garden, p. 290

Phlox, Woodland, p. 294

Phragmites, p. 295   *Phuopsis*, p. 295   x *Phylliopsis*, p. 296   *Phyllodoce*, p. 296

Physalis, p. 297   *Physaria*, p. 298   *Physoplexis*, p. 298   *Physostegia*, p. 299

Phyteuma, p. 299   *Pinguicula*, p. 300   *Platycodon*, p. 301   *Podophyllum*, p. 302

Polemonium, p. 302   *Polygala*, p. 304   *Polygonatum*, p. 304   *Polystichum*, p. 305

Potentilla, p. 306

Primula, Alpine, p. 308

Primula, Auricula, p. 311

Primula, Garden, p. 313

Primula, Woodland/Bog, p. 316

Pulmonaria, p. 320

Pulsatilla, p. 322

Ramonda, p. 324

Ranunculus, p. 324

Ratibida, p. 326

Rheum, p. 326

Rhodiola, p. 327

Rodgersia, p. 328

Rudbeckia, p. 329

Sagina, p. 331

Salvia, p. 331

Sanguinaria, p. 332

Santolina, p. 334

Saponaria, p. 334

Sarracenia, p. 335

Saxifraga, Kabschia/
Encrusted, p. 336

Saxifraga, Mossy, p. 342

Scabiosa, p. 343

Schivereckia, p. 344

Schizachyrium, p. 345

Scutellaria, p. 345

Sedum, p. 346

Semiaquilegia, p. 350

Sempervivum, p. 351

Senecio, p. 359

Shortia, p. 359

Sidalcea, p. 360

Silene, p. 361

Sisyrinchium, p. 362

Smilacina, p. 363

Soldanella, p. 363

Solidago, p. 364

Solidaster, p. 365

Sorghastrum, p. 366

Spartina, p. 366

Spiranthes, p. 367

Sporobolus, p. 368

Stachys, p. 368

Stylophorum, p. 370

Symphyandra, p. 370

Symphytum, p. 371

Talinum, p. 373

Tanacetum, p. 373

Tetraneuris, p. 375

Teucrium, p. 375

Thalictrum, p. 376

Thlaspi, p. 377

Thymus, p. 378

Tiarella, p. 380

Townsendia, p. 381

Tradescantia, p. 382

Tricyrtis, p. 383

Trifolium, p. 383

Trillium, p. 384

Trollius, p. 386

Uvularia, p. 388

Valeriana, p. 389

Vancouveria, p. 389

Verbascum, p. 390

Veronica, p. 392   *Veronicastrum*, p. 395   *Vinca*, p. 395   *Viola*, p. 396

Vitaliana, p. 398   *Waldsteinia*, p. 400   *Yucca*, p. 401

Bibliography

Bailey, Liberty Hyde. *Hortus Third: A Concise Dictionary of Plants Cultivated in the United States and Canada*. Vols. VI, VIII, XVXV, XVII, XVIII, XXIV. New York: Macmillan, 1976.

Bath, Trevor and Joy Jones. *The Gardener's Guide to Growing Hardy Geraniums*. Newton Abbot, Devon: David & Charles, 1994.

Beckett, Kenneth, ed. *Alpine Garden Society Encyclopaedia of Alpines*. Pershore, Worcestershire: AGS Publications Ltd, 1993.

Bennett, Masha. *Pulmonarias and the Borage Family*. London: B.T. Batsford Ltd., 2003.

Brickell, Christopher, ed. *Reader's Digest A–Z Encyclopedia of Garden Plants*. Montreal: The Reader's Digest Association (Canada) Ltd., 1997.

Case, Frederick W., Jr., and Roberta B. Case. *Trilliums*. Portland, Oregon: Timber Press, 1997.

Cash, Catherine. *The Slipper Orchids*. Portland, Oregon: Timber Press, 1991.

Cobb, James L.S. *Meconopsis*. Bromley, Kent: Christopher Helm Ltd., 1989

Cribb, Phillip and Christopher Bailes. *Hardy Orchids: Orchids for the Garden and Frost-Free Greenhouse*. Portland, Oregon: Timber Press, 1989.

Cribb, Phillip. *The Genus Cypripedium*. Portland, Oregon: Timber Press, 1997.

Darke, Rick, ed. *The Royal Horticultural Society Manual of Grasses*. Portland, Oregon: Timber Press, 1994.

Davies, Dilys. *Alliums: The Ornamental Onions*. London: B.T. Batsford Ltd., 1992.

Greenlee, John. *The Encyclopedia of Ornamental Grasses*. New York: Michael Friedman Publishing Group, 2000.

Grey-Wilson, Christopher. *Clematis the Genus: A Comprehensive Guide for Gardeners Horticulturalists and Botanists*. Portland, Oregon: Timber Press, 2000.

—————. *Poppies*. Portland, Oregon: Timber Press, 2000.

Haw, Stephen G. *The Lilies of China*. London: B.T. Batsford Ltd., 1986.

Hinkley, Daniel J. *The Explorer's Garden: Rare and Unusual Perennials*. Portland, Oregon: Timber Press, 1999.

Hogan, Sean. *Flora: A Gardener's Encyclopedia*. Portland, Oregon: Timber Press, 2003.

Howells, John. *Trouble Free Clematis: The Viticellas*. Woodbridge, Suffolk: Garden Art Press, 1998.

Huxley, Anthony, ed. *The New Royal Horticultural Society Dictionary of Gardening*. London: Macmillan Reference Ltd. 1992.

Jelitto, Leo and Wilhelm Schacht. *Hardy Herbaceous Perennials*. 3rd Edition. Portland, Oregon: Timber Press, 1985.

Jermyn, Jim. *The Himalayan Garden: Growing Plants from the Roof of the World*. Portland, Oregon: Timber Press, 2001.

Kohlein, Fritz et al. *Gentians*. Jim Jermyn, ed. David Winstanley, trans. Portland, Oregon: Timber Press, 1991.

Lewis, Peter and Margaret Lynch. *Campanulas: A Gardener's Guide*. Portland, Oregon: Timber Press, 1998.

Liden, Magnus and Henrik Zetterlund. *Corydalis: A Gardener's Guide and a Monograph of the Tuberous Species*. Pershore, Worcestershire: AGS Publications Ltd., 1997.

Lord, Tony, ed. *The Royal Horticultural Society Plant Finder 2004–2005*. London: Dorling Kindersley, 2004.

Mathew, Brian. *The Genus Lewisia*. Portland, Oregon: Timber Press, 1989.

McGary, Jane, ed. *Bulbs of North America: A North American Rock Garden Society Publication*. Portland, Oregon: Timber Press, 2001.

McRae, Edward Austin. *Lilies: A Guide for Growers and Collectors*. Portland, Oregon: Timber Press, 1998.

Nold, Robert. *Columbines: Aquilegia, Paraquilegia, and Semiaquilegia*. Portland, Oregon: Timber Press, 2003.

—————. *Penstemons*. Portland, Oregon: Timber Press, 1999.

Pradhan, Udai C. *Himalayan Cobra-Lilies (Ariasaema): Their Botany and Culture*. Primulaceae Books, 1990.

Rice, Graham and Elizabeth Strangman. *The Gardener's Guide to Growing Hellebores*. Portland, Oregon: Timber Press, 1993.

Richards, John. *Primula*. Portland, Oregon: Timber Press, 1993.

Robinson, Mary A. *Primulas: The Complete Guide*. Swindon, Wiltshire: The Crowood Press, 1990.

Rogers, Allan. *Peonies*. Portland, Oregon: Timber Press, 1995.

Schacht, Wilhelm, ed. *Hardy Herbaceous Perennials*. Revised edition. Portland, Oregon: Timber Press, 1985.

Schmid, W. George. *The Genus Hosta*. Portland, Oregon: Timber Press, 1991.

Smith, George and Duncan Lowe. *The Genus Androsace: A Monograph for Gardeners and Botanists*. Pershore, Worcestershire: AGS Publications Ltd., 1997.

Smith, G.F. et al. *Primulas of Europe and America: An Alpine Garden Society Guide*. Woking, Surrey: The Alpine Garden Society, 1987.

Stearn, William. *The Genus Epimedium and Other Herbaceous Berberidaceae Including the Genus Podophyllum*. Portland, Oregon: Timber Press, 2002.

Stephenson, Ray. *Sedum: Cultivated Stonecrops*. Portland, Oregon: Timber Press, 1994.

Taylor, Sir George. *An Account of the Genus Meconopsis*. London: Waterstone & Co. Ltd., 1985 (1934).

Toomey, Mary and Everett Leeds. *An Illustrated Encyclopedia of Clematis*. Portland, Oregon: Timber Press, 2001.

Turner, Roger. *Euphorbias*. Portland, Oregon: Timber Press, 1995.

Ward, Peter. *Primroses & Polyanthus: A Guide to the Genuses*. London: B.T. Batsford Ltd., 1997.

Wyman, Donald. *Wyman's Gardening Encyclopedia*. New York: Scribner, 1986.

Yeo, Peter F. *Hardy Geraniums*. Beaverton, Oregon: Timber Press, 1985.

Zheng-yi, Wu, ed. *Flora of China*. St. Louis, Missouri: Missouri Botanical Garden Press, 1994–2002.

Index of Common Names

A

acanthus leaved thistle ᴧ *Carlina*, 73
Adam's needle ᴧ *Yucca*, 401
alpenclock ᴧ *Soldanella*, 363
alpine alyssum ᴧ *Alyssum*, 16
alpine balsam ᴧ *Erinus*, 126
alpine campion ᴧ *Lychnis*, 239
alpine clover ᴧ *Trifolium*, 383
alpine daisy ᴧ *Leucanthemopsis*, 216
alpine forget-me-not
    ᴧ *Eritrichium*, 129
alpine Marguerite ᴧ *Anthemis*, 25
alpine moon daisy ᴧ
    Leucanthemopsis, 216
alpine pink ᴧ *Dianthus*, 101
alpine rockcress ᴧ *Arabis*, 29
alpine rockcress ᴧ *Aubrieta*, 49
alpine sandwort ᴧ *Arenaria*, 31
alpine sea holly ᴧ *Eryngium*, 130
alpine skullcap ᴧ *Scutellaria*, 345
alpine snapdragon ᴧ *Linaria*, 233
alpine sunflower ᴧ *Tetraneuris*, 375
alpine thrift ᴧ *Armeria*, 35
alpine valerian ᴧ *Valeriana*, 389
alpine woodruff ᴧ *Asperula*, 41
alumroot ᴧ *Heuchera*, 173
alyssum ᴧ *Aurinia*, 50
American alumroot ᴧ *Heuchera*, 173
American barrenwort
    ᴧ *Vancouveria*, 389
American bittersweet ᴧ *Celastrus*, 74
American false hellebore
    ᴧ *Veratrum*, 390
American twinleaf ᴧ *Jeffersonia*, 205
anemone ᴧ *Anemone*, 22
Asian twinleaf ᴧ *Jeffersonia*, 205
asparagus ᴧ *Asparagus*, 40
aster ᴧ *Aster*, 42
astilbe ᴧ *Astilbe*, 44
avens ᴧ *Geum*, 149

B

baby's breath ᴧ *Gypsophila*, 153
balloon flower ᴧ *Platycodon*, 301
Baltic ivy ᴧ *Hedera*, 156
baneberry ᴧ *Actaea*, 7
barren strawberry
    ᴧ *Waldsteinia*, 400
barrenwort ᴧ *Epimedium*, 122
basket of gold ᴧ *Alyssum*, 16
basket of gold ᴧ *Aurinia*, 50
bear berry ᴧ *Arctostaphylos*, 31
bear hops ᴧ *Humulus*, 186
bear's ear ᴧ *Cortusa*, 88
bearded iris ᴧ *Iris*, 191
beardtongue ᴧ *Penstemon*, 278
bedstraw ᴧ *Galium*, 141
beebalm ᴧ *Monarda*, 249
bellflower ᴧ *Campanula*, 65
bergenia ᴧ *Bergenia*, 53
Bethlehem sage ᴧ *Pulmonaria*, 320
betony ᴧ *Stachys*, 368

big bluestem ᴧ *Andropogon*, 19
big flower selfheal ᴧ *Prunella*, 320
big leaf rayflower ᴧ *Ligularia*, 220
big merrybells ᴧ *Uvularia*, 388
bird's foot trefoil ᴧ *Lotus*, 237
bishop's hat ᴧ *Epimedium*, 122
bishop's weed ᴧ *Aegopodium*, 10
bitterroot ᴧ *Lewisia*, 217
black-eyed Susan ᴧ *Rudbeckia*, 329
black cohosh ᴧ *Cimicifuga*, 7
bladder pod ᴧ *Lesquerella*, 215
bladder pod ᴧ *Physaria*, 298
blanket flower ᴧ *Gaillardia*, 140
blazing star ᴧ *Liatris*, 219
bleeding heart ᴧ *Dicentra*, 107
bloodroot ᴧ *Sanguinaria*, 332
blue fescue ᴧ *Festuca*, 136
blue flax ᴧ *Linum*, 234
blue fumitory ᴧ *Corydalis*, 89
blue grama grass ᴧ *Bouteloua*, 56
blue grass ᴧ *Festuca*, 136
blue hair grass ᴧ *Koeleria*, 210
blue love grass ᴧ *Eragrostis*, 123
blue oat grass ᴧ *Helictotrichon*, 159
blue sage ᴧ *Salvia*, 331
blue star creeper ᴧ *Isotoma*, 203
blue switch grass ᴧ *Panicum*, 272
blue wild rye ᴧ *Elymus*, 121
bluebells ᴧ *Mertensia*, 245
blue-eyed grass ᴧ *Sisyrinchium*, 362
bog orchid ᴧ *Epipactis*, 123
boneset ᴧ *Eupatorium*, 133
bonnet bellflower ᴧ *Codonopsis*, 85
bouncing bet ᴧ *Saponaria*, 334
bowman's root ᴧ *Gillenia*, 149
boykinia ᴧ *Boykinia*, 56
brome grass ᴧ *Bromus*, 57
bugbane ᴧ *Actaea*, 7
bugloss ᴧ *Anchusa*, 18
bunchberry ᴧ *Cornus*, 87
burnet ᴧ *Sanguisorba*, 333
burning bush ᴧ *Dictamnus*, 108
bushy aster ᴧ *Aster*, 42
butterbur ᴧ *Petasites*, 284
buttercup ᴧ *Ranunculus*, 324
butterfly flower ᴧ *Asclepias*, 40
butterwort ᴧ *Pinguicula*, 300
button snakeroot ᴧ *Liatris*, 219

C

California bluebell ᴧ *Phacelia*, 286
calypso orchid ᴧ *Calypso*, 63
camas ᴧ *Camassia*, 65
campion ᴧ *Silene*, 361
canary clover ᴧ *Lotus*, 237
candle larkspur ᴧ *Delphinium*, 98
candytuft ᴧ *Iberis*, 189
Canterbury bells ᴧ *Campanula*, 65
cardinal flower ᴧ *Lobelia*, 235
carnation ᴧ *Dianthus*, 101
Carolina spring beauty
    ᴧ *Claytonia*, 80
Carpathian bellflower
    ᴧ *Campanula*, 65
Carpathian harebell
    ᴧ *Campanula*, 65
carpet bugle ᴧ *Ajuga*, 12
caspia ᴧ *Limonium*, 232
catchfly ᴧ *Lychnis*, 239

catmint ᴧ *Nepeta*, 253
celandine poppy ᴧ *Stylophorum*, 370
chalk plant ᴧ *Gypsophila*, 153
charity ᴧ *Polemonium*, 302
chatterbox orchid ᴧ *Epipactis*, 123
checker mallow ᴧ *Sidalcea*, 360
Chinese lantern ᴧ *Physalis*, 297
Chinese rhubarb ᴧ *Rheum*, 326
Chinese silver grass
    ᴧ *Miscanthus*, 247
chives ᴧ *Allium*, 15
Christmas fern ᴧ *Polystichum*, 305
Christmas rose ᴧ *Helleborus*, 161
chrysanthemum
    ᴧ *Arctanthemum*, 30
cinnamon fern ᴧ *Osmunda*, 259
cinquefoil ᴧ *Potentilla*, 306
circle flower ᴧ *Lysimachia*, 240
clematis ᴧ *Clematis*, 80
cliff beardtongue ᴧ *Penstemon*, 278
climbing asparagus ᴧ *Asparagus*, 40
climbing honeysuckle
    ᴧ *Lonicera*, 236
climbing monkshood ᴧ *Aconitum*, 5
clustered bellflower
    ᴧ *Campanula*, 65
cobra lily ᴧ *Arisaema*, 32
columbine ᴧ *Aquilegia*, 27
comfrey ᴧ *Symphytum*, 371
common betony ᴧ *Stachys*, 368
common hops ᴧ *Humulus*, 186
common Mayapple
    ᴧ *Podophyllum*, 302
common motherwort
    ᴧ *Leonurus*, 214
common rose mallow
    ᴧ *Hibiscus*, 177
common rupturewort
    ᴧ *Hernieria*, 172
common teasel ᴧ *Dipsacus*, 110
common valerian ᴧ *Valeriana*, 389
common yarrow ᴧ *Achillea*, 3
coneflower ᴧ *Echinacea*, 118
coralbells ᴧ *Heuchera*, 173
coreopsis ᴧ *Coreopsis*, 86
cornflower ᴧ *Centaurea*, 75
Corsican woodruff ᴧ *Asperula*, 41
cotoneaster ᴧ *Cotoneaster*, 91
cotton grass ᴧ *Eriophorum*, 128
cowslip primrose ᴧ *Primula*, 308
coyote mint ᴧ *Monardella*, 250
cranesbill ᴧ *Geranium*, 145
creeping Charlie ᴧ *Glechoma*, 150
creeping forget-me-not ᴧ
    Omphalodes, 255
creeping globeflower
    ᴧ *Globularia*, 151
creeping Jenny ᴧ *Lysimachia*, 240
creeping myrtle ᴧ *Vinca*, 395
creeping soft grass ᴧ *Holcus*, 178
creeping speedwell ᴧ *Veronica*, 392
creeping thyme ᴧ *Thymus*, 378
crimson scabious ᴧ *Knautia*, 210
crosswort ᴧ *Phuopsis*, 295
crown vetch ᴧ *Coronilla*, 88
Culver's root ᴧ *Veronicastrum*, 395
cushion spurge ᴧ *Euphorbia*, 134
cyclamen ᴧ *Cyclamen*, 93
Cypress spurge ᴧ *Euphorbia*, 134

D

daisy fleabane ↷ *Erigeron*, 125
dame's rocket ↷ *Hesperis*, 172
dark-eyed sunflower
    ↷ *Helianthus*, 158
daylily ↷ *Hemerocallis*, 162
deadnettle ↷ *Lamium*, 211
deer clover ↷ *Trifolium*, 383
deer fern ↷ *Blechnum*, 54
delphinium ↷ *Delphinium*, 98
desert candle ↷ *Eremurus*, 124
desert candle ↷ *Yucca*, 401
desert trumpet ↷ *Linanthus*, 233
devil's claw ↷ *Physoplexis*, 298
dittany ↷ *Dictamnus*, 108
dogtooth violet ↷ *Erythronium*, 132
double queen of the meadow
    ↷ *Filipendula*, 137
dove scabious ↷ *Scabiosa*, 343
dragon's head
    ↷ *Dracocephalum*, 114
dragon's mouth ↷ *Horminum*, 179
dragonroot jack-in-the-pulpit
    ↷ *Arisaema*, 32
Dutchman's pipe ↷ *Aristolochia*, 34
dwarf balloon flower
    ↷ *Platycodon*, 301
dwarf statice ↷ *Goniolimon*, 152
dwarf statice ↷ *Limonium*, 232

E

Easter daisy ↷ *Townsendia*, 381
edelweiss ↷ *Leontopodium*, 214
elephant ears ↷ *Bergenia*, 53
elephant ears ↷ *Ligularia*, 220
elephant heads ↷ *Pedicularis*, 277
encrusted saxifrage ↷ *Saxifraga*, 336
English daisy ↷ *Bellis*, 52
English ivy ↷ *Hedera*, 156
European dune grass ↷ *Leymus*, 219
evening primrose ↷ *Oenothera*, 254
evergreen candytuft ↷ *Iberis*, 189
everlasting ↷ *Anaphalis*, 18

F

fairy bells ↷ *Disporum*, 111
fairy thimble ↷ *Campanula*, 65
fall mum ↷ *Chrysanthemum*, 77
false columbine
    ↷ *Semiaquilegia*, 350
false dragonhead ↷ *Physostegia*, 299
false goatsbeard ↷ *Astilbe*, 44
false houseleek ↷ *Orostachys*, 258
false indigo ↷ *Baptisia*, 52
false lion's heart ↷ *Physostegia*, 299
false rockcress ↷ *Aubrieta*, 49
false Solomon's seal
    ↷ *Smilacina*, 363
false spirea ↷ *Astilbe*, 44
false sunflower ↷ *Heliopsis*, 160
fameflower ↷ *Talinum*, 373
feather reed grass
    ↷ *Calamagrostis*, 60
Featherleaf Rodger's flower
    ↷ *Rodgersia*, 328
fernleaf bleeding heart
    ↷ *Dicentra*, 107
fernleaf yarrow ↷ *Achillea*, 3

fescue ↷ *Festuca*, 136
feverweed ↷ *Eupatorium*, 133
fingerleaf Rodger's flower
    ↷ *Rodgersia*, 328
flat sea holly ↷ *Eryngium*, 130
fleabane ↷ *Erigeron*, 125
fleeceflower ↷ *Persicaria*, 282
fleur-de-lis ↷ *Iris*, 191
foam flower ↷ *Tiarella*, 380
foamy bells ↷ *Heucherella*, 176
foothill checker mallow
    ↷ *Sidalcea*, 360
foxglove ↷ *Digitalis*, 109
foxtail lily ↷ *Eremurus*, 124
fringe cups ↷ *Tellima*, 374
fringed galax ↷ *Shortia*, 359
frost grass ↷ *Spodiopogon*, 367
fumitory ↷ *Corydalis*, 89
funkia ↷ *Hosta*, 179

G

garden globeflower ↷ *Trollius*, 386
garden gloxinia ↷ *Incarvillea*, 190
gas plant ↷ *Dictamnus*, 108
Geneva bugle ↷ *Ajuga*, 12
geranium ↷ *Geranium*, 145
German iris ↷ *Iris*, 191
German statice ↷ *Goniolimon*, 152
germander ↷ *Teucrium*, 375
giant Japanese butterbur
    ↷ *Petasites*, 284
giant Moor grass ↷ *Molinia*, 248
giant reed ↷ *Phragmites*, 295
giant rockfoil ↷ *Bergenia*, 53
globe thistle ↷ *Echinops*, 120
globeflower ↷ *Globularia*, 151
globeflower ↷ *Trollius*, 386
goat's beard ↷ *Aruncus*, 38
goat's foot ↷ *Aegopodium*, 10
gold drop ↷ *Onosma*, 256
gold dust ↷ *Alyssum*, 16
golden aster ↷ *Solidaster*, 365
golden flax ↷ *Linum*, 234
golden foxtail lily
    ↷ *Eremurus*, 124
golden Hakone grass
    ↷ *Hakonechloa*, 155
golden primrose ↷ *Vitaliana*, 398
goldenray ↷ *Ligularia*, 220
golden star ↷ *Helenium*, 157
golden statice ↷ *Limonium*, 232
golden yarrow ↷ *Eriophyllum*, 128
goldenrod ↷ *Solidago*, 364
goldenstar ↷ *Chrysogonum*, 78
goose-neck loosestrife
    ↷ *Lysimachia*, 240
goutweed ↷ *Aegopodium*, 10
grass pink orchid ↷ *Calopogon*, 62
grassy bells ↷ *Edraianthus*, 120
great blue lobelia ↷ *Lobelia*, 235
great masterwort ↷ *Astrantia*, 47
greater alpenclock ↷ *Soldanella*, 363
Greek valerian ↷ *Polemonium*, 302
ground ivy ↷ *Glechoma*, 150
groundsel ↷ *Senecio*, 359

H

Hakone grass ↷ *Hakonechloa*, 155
hard rush ↷ *Juncus*, 207

harebell ↷ *Asyneuma*, 48
hay scented fern
    ↷ *Dennstaedtia*, 100
heart-leaf bergenia ↷ *Bergenia*, 53
heartleaf forget-me-not
    ↷ *Brunnera*, 58
heartleaf globeflower
    ↷ *Globularia*, 151
hedgehog cactus
    ↷ *Echinocereus*, 119
Helen's flower ↷ *Helenium*, 157
hellebore ↷ *Helleborus*, 161
helmut flower ↷ *Aconitum*, 5
hemp agrimony ↷ *Eupatorium*, 133
hen and chicks
    ↷ *Sempervivum*, 351
heron's bill ↷ *Erodium*, 129
hibiscus ↷ *Hibiscus*, 177
Himalayan blue poppy
    ↷ *Meconopsis*, 244
Himalayan desert candle
    ↷ *Eremurus*, 124
Himalayan fleeceflower
    ↷ *Persicaria*, 282
Himalayan Mayapple
    ↷ *Podophyllum*, 302
Himalayan poppy
    ↷ *Meconopsis*, 244
Himalayan rhubarb ↷ *Rheum*, 326
hollyhock ↷ *Alcea*, 13
hollyhock ↷ *Malva*, 242
hop vine ↷ *Humulus*, 186
horned rampion ↷ *Phyteuma*, 299
horseradish ↷ *Armoracia*, 35
hosta ↷ *Hosta*, 179
houseleek ↷ *Sempervivum*, 351
hummingbird vine ↷ *Campsis*, 71
hyssop ↷ *Agastache*, 12
hyssop ↷ *Hyssopus*, 188

I

ice plant ↷ *Delosperma*, 98
Iceland poppy ↷ *Papaver*, 273
Indian grass ↷ *Sorghastrum*, 366
Indian paintbrush ↷ *Castilleja*, 74
indigo ↷ *Indigofera*, 190
interrupted fern ↷ *Osmunda*, 259
Irish moss ↷ *Sagina*, 331
Italian aster ↷ *Aster*, 42
Italian bugloss ↷ *Anchusa*, 18

J

Jacob's ladder ↷ *Polemonium*, 302
Japanese blood grass
    ↷ *Imperata*, 189
Japanese butterbur ↷ *Petasites*, 284
Japanese fleeceflower ↷ *Fallopia*, 136
Japanese painted fern
    ↷ *Athyrium*, 48
Japanese peony ↷ *Paeonia*, 262
Japanese spurge ↷ *Pachysandra*, 262
Japanese thistle ↷ *Cirsium*, 79
Japanese toad lily ↷ *Tricyrtis*, 383
Japanese waxbells
    ↷ *Kirengeshoma*, 209
Jerusalem sage ↷ *Phlomis*, 287
juniper thrift ↷ *Armeria*, 35
Jupiter's beard ↷ *Centranthus*, 76
Jupiter's beard ↷ *Jovibarba*, 205

K

Kansas gayfeather ⁓ *Liatris*, 219
keeled garlic ⁓ *Allium*, 15
king's crown ⁓ *Rhodiola*, 327
kinnikinnik ⁓ *Arctostaphylos*, 31
knotweed ⁓ *Persicaria*, 282
Korean waxbells
⁓ *Kirengeshoma*, 209

L

lady by the gate ⁓ *Saponaria*, 334
lady fern ⁓ *Athyrium*, 48
lady's bedstraw ⁓ *Galium*, 141
lady's ear drops ⁓ *Onosma*, 256
lady's fingers ⁓ *Anthyllis*, 26
lady's mantle ⁓ *Alchemilla*, 14
lady's slipper ⁓ *Cypripedium*, 93
lady's tresses ⁓ *Spiranthes*, 367
ladybell ⁓ *Adenophora*, 8
lamb's ears ⁓ *Stachys*, 368
lavender cotton ⁓ *Santolina*, 334
leather leaf spring beauty
⁓ *Claytonia*, 80
leather-leaf ⁓ *Bergenia*, 53
lemon thyme ⁓ *Thymus*, 378
Lenten rose ⁓ *Helleborus*, 161
leopard plant ⁓ *Ligularia*, 220
leopard's bane ⁓ *Doronicum*, 112
lily ⁓ *Lilium*, 221
lily-of-the-valley ⁓ *Convallaria*, 86
little alpenclock ⁓ *Soldanella*, 363
little blue stem
⁓ *Schizachyrium*, 345
little merrybells ⁓ *Uvularia*, 388
liver balsam ⁓ *Erinus*, 126
locoweed ⁓ *Oxytropis*, 260
lousewort ⁓ *Synthyris*, 372
low Japanese fleeceflower
⁓ *Fallopia*, 136
lungwort ⁓ *Pulmonaria*, 320
lupine ⁓ *Lupinus*, 237

M

Magellan wheatgrass ⁓ *Elymus*, 121
maiden grass ⁓ *Miscanthus*, 247
maiden pink ⁓ *Dianthus*, 101
maidenhair fern ⁓ *Adiantum*, 9
mallow ⁓ *Althaea*, 15
mallow ⁓ *Malva*, 242
Maltese cross ⁓ *Lychnis*, 239
manna grass ⁓ *Glyceria*, 152
Marguerite daisy ⁓ *Anthemis*, 25
maroon scabious ⁓ *Knautia*, 210
marsh marigold ⁓ *Caltha*, 62
marsh orchid ⁓ *Dactylorhiza*, 96
masterwort ⁓ *Astrantia*, 47
matted sea lavender
⁓ *Limonium*, 232
meadow rue ⁓ *Thalictrum*, 376
Mexican hat ⁓ *Ratibida*, 326
milk vetch ⁓ *Astragalus*, 46
milkwort ⁓ *Polygala*, 304
mint ⁓ *Mentha*, 245
mistflower ⁓ *Eupatorium*, 133
mock strawberry ⁓ *Duchesnea*, 117
moneywort ⁓ *Lysimachia*, 240
monkshood ⁓ *Aconitum*, 5

Morden mum
⁓ *Chrysanthemum*, 77
morning glory ⁓ *Calystegia*, 64
mosquito grass ⁓ *Bouteloua*, 56
moss campion ⁓ *Silene*, 361
mossy saxifrage ⁓ *Saxifraga*, 336
mother of thyme ⁓ *Thymus*, 378
mountain avens ⁓ *Dryas*, 115
mountain bluet ⁓ *Centaurea*, 75
mountain bluet ⁓ *Houstonia*, 185
mountain heather ⁓ *Cassiope*, 73
mountain heather ⁓ *Phyllodoce*, 296
mountain sandwort ⁓ *Arenaria*, 31
mouse tail ⁓ *Ivesia*, 203
mullein ⁓ *Verbascum*, 390
musk mallow ⁓ *Malva*, 242

N

nailwort ⁓ *Paronychia*, 277
native pincushion cactus
⁓ *Coryphantha*, 90
navelwort ⁓ *Omphalodes*, 255
New England aster ⁓ *Aster*, 42
New York aster ⁓ *Aster*, 42
nipple cactus ⁓ *Coryphantha*, 90
Nippon bells ⁓ *Shortia*, 359
noble liverleaf ⁓ *Hepatica*, 171
northern bedstraw ⁓ *Galium*, 141
Nuttall's desert trumpet
⁓ *Linanthus*, 233

O

oak fern ⁓ *Gymnocarpium*, 153
obedient plant ⁓ *Physostegia*, 299
Oconee bells ⁓ *Shortia*, 359
old man ⁓ *Artemisia*, 37
Oregon fleabane ⁓ *Erigeron*, 125
Oregon mallow ⁓ *Sidalcea*, 360
oriental poppy ⁓ *Papaver*, 273
ornamental clover ⁓ *Trifolium*, 383
ornamental onion ⁓ *Allium*, 15
ostrich fern ⁓ *Matteuccia*, 243
Oswego tea ⁓ *Monarda*, 249
ox eye ⁓ *Heliopsis*, 160
oxeye daisy ⁓ *Buphthalmum*, 59
oxlip primrose ⁓ *Primula*, 308
oyster plant ⁓ *Mertensia*, 245

P

pacific bleeding heart
⁓ *Dicentra*, 107
painted daisy ⁓ *Tanacetum*, 373
parsley fern ⁓ *Cryptogramma*, 92
Pasque flower ⁓ *Pulsatilla*, 322
peachleaf bellflower
⁓ *Campanula*, 65
pennycress ⁓ *Thlaspi*, 377
peony ⁓ *Paeonia*, 262
pepperwort ⁓ *Lepidium*, 215
perennial bachelor's button ⁓
Centaurea, 75
perennial dusty miller ⁓ *Artemisia*,
37
perennial flax ⁓ *Linum*, 234
perennial morning glory
⁓ *Calystegia*, 64
perennial statice ⁓ *Limonium*, 232

perennial sweet pea ⁓ *Lathyrus*, 212
periwinkle ⁓ *Vinca*, 395
Perry's vetch ⁓ *Oxytropis*, 260
Persian bellflower ⁓ *Campanula*, 65
Persian onion ⁓ *Allium*, 15
pheasant's eye ⁓ *Adonis*, 9
phlox ⁓ *Phlox*, 287
pincushion flower ⁓ *Scabiosa*, 343
pincushion plant ⁓ *Knautia*, 210
pink ⁓ *Dianthus*, 101
pink turtlehead ⁓ *Chelone*, 77
plantain lily ⁓ *Hosta*, 179
plastic plant ⁓ *Bolax*, 55
plume poppy ⁓ *Macleaya*, 242
plume thistle ⁓ *Cirsium*, 79
point vetch ⁓ *Oxytropis*, 260
poor man's orchid ⁓ *Iris*, 191
poppy ⁓ *Papaver*, 273
poppy mallow ⁓ *Callirhoe*, 61
porcelain vine ⁓ *Ampelopsis*, 17
potentilla ⁓ *Potentilla*, 306
prairie coneflower ⁓ *Ratibida*, 326
prairie cord grass ⁓ *Spartina*, 366
prairie crocus ⁓ *Pulsatilla*, 322
prairie dropseed ⁓ *Sporobolus*, 368
prairie sandwort ⁓ *Arenaria*, 31
prairie smoke ⁓ *Geum*, 149
prickly pear cactus ⁓ *Opuntia*, 257
prickly thrift ⁓ *Acantholimon*, 2
primrose ⁓ *Primula*, 308
purple coneflower ⁓ *Echinacea*, 118
purple gas plant ⁓ *Dictamnus*, 108
purple Moor grass ⁓ *Molinia*, 248
purple pitcher plant
⁓ *Sarracenia*, 335
purple-leaf milkweed
⁓ *Euphorbia*, 134
pussy paws ⁓ *Calyptridium*, 64
pussy toes ⁓ *Antennaria*, 25
Pyrenean primrose ⁓ *Ramonda*, 324
pyrethrum daisy ⁓ *Tanacetum*, 373

Q

Quamash ⁓ *Camassia*, 65
queen of the meadow
⁓ *Filipendula*, 137
queen of the prairie
⁓ *Filipendula*, 137

R

rampion ⁓ *Phyteuma*, 299
rayflower ⁓ *Ligularia*, 220
red barrenwort ⁓ *Epimedium*, 122
red caesar ⁓ *Dianthus*, 101
redwood ivy ⁓ *Vancouveria*, 389
redwood sorrel ⁓ *Oxalis*, 260
ribbon grass ⁓ *Phalaris*, 286
ring bellflower ⁓ *Symphyandra*, 370
rock beauty ⁓ *Petrocallis*, 284
rock jasmine ⁓ *Androsace*, 20
rock rose ⁓ *Helianthemum*, 158
rock thyme ⁓ *Acinos*, 5
rockcress ⁓ *Arabis*, 29
rockcress ⁓ *Aubrieta*, 49
rockfoil ⁓ *Bergenia*, 53
Rodger's flower ⁓ *Rodgersia*, 328

Hole's

The success of this book is due entirely to the knowledge, experience and hard work of the staff here at Hole's and in particular the great crew of the Hole's Perennial Department, past and present.

General Editor	Jim Hole
Editors	Jan Goodall
	Stephen Raven
	Bob Stadnyk
Publication Management	Bruce Timothy Keith
	Christina McDonald
Editorial Staff	Linda Affolder
	Lee Craig
	Roland Lines
	Christina McDonald
	Betty Sampson
Contributing Writers	Lee Craig
	Roland Lines
	Christina McDonald
	Earl J. Woods
Photo Research	Betty Sampson
Additional Research & Development	Arlene Hancock
	Linda Haswell
	Mark Hughes
	Christina McDonald
	Maggie Nielsen
Cover Image	Akemi Matsubuchi
Book & Cover Design	Gregory Brown
Production	Gregory Brown
	Bruce Timothy Keith